Form and Substance

The Modern Essay

Joseph J. Comprone / *University of Cincinnati*

Form and Substance

The Modern Essay

WILLIAM C. BROWN PUBLISHING COMPANY

Dubuque, Iowa

Cover art is Oscar Bluemner's Morning Light. *Used by permission of the Hirshhorn Museum and Sculpture Garden, Smithsonian Institution, Washington, D.C.*

Library of Congress
Catalog Card Number: 75–21423

Printed in the United States of America

ISBN 0–697–03714–2

Acknowledgments

James Agee, "Work: Cotton," reprinted by permission of Houghton Mifflin Company from *Let Us Now Praise Famous Men* by James Agee and Walker Evans. Copyright © 1960 by Walker Evans. Copyright © Renewed 1969 by Mia Fritsch Agee.

James Baldwin, "Notes of a Native Son," reprinted by permission of Beacon Press from *Notes of a Native Son* by James Baldwin. Copyright © 1955 by James Baldwin.

Warren Bennis, "Everything You Always Wanted To Know About Change (but were afraid to ask)," reprinted by permission of *Environment/Planning and Design*. Copyright © 1971 by Herman Miller, Inc. Reprinted in *Today, Tomorrow . . . and the Day After*.

Bruno Bettelheim, "Joey: A 'Mechanical Boy,'" reprinted with permission of *Scientific American* (March 1959). Copyright © 1959 by Scientific American, Inc. All rights reserved.

Art Buchwald, "Fathers for Moral America," reprinted by permission of G. P. Putnam's Sons from *And I Told the President* by Art Buchwald. Copyright © 1964, 1965 by Art Buchwald.

William F. Buckley, Jr., "How I Came To Rock," reprinted by permission of G. P. Putnam's Sons from *The Governor Listeth* by William F. Buckley, Jr. Copyright © 1970 by William F. Buckley, Jr.

Rachel Carson, "The Other Road," reprinted by permission of Houghton Mifflin Company from *Silent Spring* by Rachel Carson. Copyright © 1962 by Rachel L. Carson.

Joan Didion, "Goodbye to All That," reprinted with the permission of Farrar, Straus & Giroux, Inc. from *Slouching Towards Bethlehem* by Joan Didion. Copyright © 1961, 1964, 1965, 1966, 1967, 1968 by Joan Didion.

Loren Eiseley, "One Night's Dying," is reprinted by permission of Charles Scribner's Sons from *The Night Country* by Loren Eiseley. Copyright © 1971 Loren Eiseley.

Craig R. Eisendrath and Thomas J. Cottle, "University Discontent and Reform," reprinted by permission of Schenkman Publishing Company, Cambridge, Mass., from *Out of Discontent* by Eisendrath, Cottle, and Fink. Copyright © 1972 by Schenkman Publishing Company.

William Faulkner, "Speech of Acceptance Upon the Award of the Nobel Prize for Literature," delivered in Stockholm, Sweden, 1954.

Betty Friedan, "The Problem That Has No Name," reprinted from *The Feminine Mystique* by Betty Friedan by permission of W. W. Norton & Company, Inc. Copyright © 1963, 1974 by Betty Friedan.

R. Buckminster Fuller, "Technology and Education," reprinted by permission of R. Buckminster Fuller from *Education Automation* by R. Buckminster Fuller. Copyright © 1962 by R. Buckminster Fuller. Originally published by Southern Illinois University Press.

Paul Goodman, "Memorandum to the Office of Education," reprinted by permission of Random House, Inc. from *People or Personnel and Like a Conquered Province* by Paul Goodman. Copyright © 1963, 1964, 1965 by Paul Goodman.

Robert Graves, "Real Women," reprinted by permission of Collins-Knowlton-Wing, Inc., from *Mammon and the Black Goddess* by Robert Graves. Copyright © 1963 by Robert Graves.

Mary Frances Greene and Orletta Ryan, "What It's Like To Go to School," reprinted by permission of Pantheon Books, a Division of Random House, Inc., from *The Schoolchildren,* by Mary Frances Greene and Orletta Ryan. Copyright © 1964, 1965, 1966 by Mary Frances Greene and Orletta Ryan.

Cecelia Holland, "I Don't Trust Anyone Under Thirty," reprinted with permission from *The Saturday Evening Post* (August 10, 1968). Copyright © 1968 The Curtis Publishing Company.

George Jackson, "A Letter to Angela Davis," reprinted from *Soledad Brother: The Prison Letters of George Jackson* by permission of Bantam Books. Copyright © 1970 by World Entertainers Limited. Published by Coward, McCann & Geoghegan, Inc., and Bantam Books, Inc.

Roger Kahn, "The Hardhat Who Sued Baseball," in *The Boys of Summer* by Roger Kahn, reprinted by permission of Harper & Row, Publishers, Inc. Copyright © 1971, 1972 by Roger Kahn.

John Fitzgerald Kennedy, "Inaugural Address," delivered at the Capitol, Washington, D.C., January 20, 1961.

Martin Luther King, Jr., "Letter From Birmingham Jail—April 16, 1963," from *Why We Can't Wait* by Martin Luther King, Jr., reprinted by permission of Harper & Row, Publishers, Inc. Copyright © 1963 by Martin Luther King, Jr.

Jonathan Kozol, "Free School as a Term Meaning Too Many Different Things: What Other People Mean: What I Mean: What I Don't Mean," reprinted by permission of Houghton Mifflin Company from *Free Schools* by Jonathan Kozol. Copyright © 1972 by Jonathan Kozol.

Keith Laumer, "The Lawgiver," reprinted by permission of Doubleday & Co., Inc., from *The Year 2000*, edited by Harry Harrison. Copyright © 1970 by Harry Harrison.

Robert Jay Lifton, "Beyond Atrocity," reprinted by permission of Random House, Inc. from *Crimes of War,* edited by Richard Falk, Gabriel Kolko, and Robert Jay Lifton. Copyright © 1971 by Education-Action Conference on American Crimes of War in Vietnam. First published in *The Saturday Review,* March 6, 1971.

Melvin Maddocks, "In Praise of Reticence," reprinted by permission from *Time,* The Weekly News Magazine (November 23, 1970). Copyright © Time, Inc.

Norman Mailer, "A Busload of Slogans," from *The Armies of the Night* by Norman Mailer, reprinted by arrangement with The New American Library, Inc., New York, N.Y. Copyright © 1968 by Norman Mailer.

W. S. Merwin, "The Death-defying Tortonis," reprinted by permission of Atheneum Publishers from *The Miner's Pale Children* by W. S. Merwin. Copyright © 1970 by W. S. Merwin. Originally appeared in *The New Yorker.*

Kate Millet, "Sexual Politics: A Manifesto for Revolution," reprinted by permission of Doubleday & Co., Inc. from *Sexual Politics* by Kate Millet. Copyright © 1969, 1970 by Kate Millet.

Jim Murray, "New Leaf for Woody," reprinted by permission of the *Los Angeles Times* (December 30, 1973). Copyright © 1973, *Los Angeles Times.*

Joyce Carol Oates, "By the River," reprinted by permission of the author and her agent, Blanche C. Gregory, Inc. Copyright © 1968 by Joyce Carol Oates. Originally published in *December* Magazine.

Flannery O'Connor, "A Good Man Is Hard To Find," reprinted from *A Good Man Is Hard To Find and Other Stories* by Flannery O'Connor, by permission of Harcourt Brace Jovanovich, Inc. Copyright © 1953, by Flannery O'Connor.

George Orwell, "Shooting an Elephant," reprinted by permission of Harcourt Brace Jovanovich, Inc., from *Shooting an Elephant and Other Essays* by George Orwell. Copyright © 1945, 1946, 1949, 1950, by Sonia Brownell Orwell.

Charles Reich, "The Limits of Duty," reprinted by permission from *The New Yorker* (June 19, 1971). Copyright © 1971 The New Yorker Magazine, Inc.

Lenore Romney, "Men, Women—and Politics," reprinted by permission of the Cowles Syndicate from *Look* Magazine. (April 16, 1971). Copyright © 1971 by Lenore Romney.

Arthur Schlesinger, Jr., "The Crisis in American Masculinity," reprinted by permission of Houghton Mifflin Company from *The Politics of Hope* by Arthur Schlesinger, Jr. Copyright © 1962 by Arthur M. Schlesinger, Jr. Originally published in *Esquire* magazine (1958).

Gay Talese, "Floyd Patterson," reprinted by permission of Harper & Row, Publishers, Inc., from *The Overreachers* by Gay Talese. Copyright © 1964 by Gay Talese.

Studs Terkel, "Earning One's Bread," reprinted by permission of Publishers-Hall Syndicate, 401 North Wabash Avenue, Chicago, Illinois (60611). Copyright © by Studs Terkel.

James Thurber, "The Catbird Seat," reprinted by permission of Mrs. James Thurber from *The Thurber Carnival,* published by Harper & Row, Publishers, Inc. Copyright © 1945 by James Thurber; copyright © 1973 by Helen W. Thurber and Rosemary Thurber Sauers. Originally printed in *The New Yorker.*

Barbara W. Tuchman, "Standing Up," "The People," and "The Countryside," reprinted with permission of Macmillan Publishing Co., Inc. from *Notes From China* by Barbara W. Tuchman. Copyright © 1972 by Barbara W. Tuchman. Copyright © 1972 by The Associated Press.

John Updike, "A & P," reprinted from *Pigeon Feathers and Other Stories,* by John Updike, by permission of Alfred A. Knopf, Inc. Copyright © 1959, 1960, 1961, 1962 by John Updike. Originally appeared in *The New Yorker.*

Kurt Vonnegut, Jr. "The Euphio Question," reprinted from the book, *Welcome to the Monkey House,* by Kurt Vonnegut, Jr. with permission of Delacorte Press/Seymour Lawrence. Copyright © 1951 by Kurt Vonnegut, Jr. Originally appeared in *Collier's.*

Tom Wolfe, "Porno-Violence," reprinted with permission of Tom Wolfe, c/o Marvin Josephson Associates, Inc. Copyright © 1967 Esquire, Inc. Originally published in *Esquire* magazine, July 1967, under the title: "(Intermission) Pause, Now, and Consider Some Tentative Conclusions About the Meaning of This Mad Perversion Called Porno-Violence: What It Is and Where It Comes From and Who Put the Hair on the Walls."

Virginia Woolf, "The Death of the Moth," reprinted by permission of Harcourt Brace Jovanovich, Inc., from *The Death of the Moth and Other Essays* by Virginia Woolf. Copyright © 1942 by Harcourt Brace Jovanovich, Inc.; copyright © 1970 by Marjorie T. Parsons, Executrix.

To my mother and father

Contents

3

4

Preface

Essay anthologies fill the shelves of most writing teachers. This anthology makes its claim for space on that shelf through several central qualities.

Form and Substance begins with a careful blending of modern and contemporary readings. Different voices speak out on a variety of subjects. Each reading has been selected because it projects a distinctive voice on a worthwhile and interesting subject, because its form follows an overall pattern of development without becoming dull or repetitive and, perhaps most importantly, because each essay provides a different perspective on a common theme. As a result, *Form and Substance* provides content for basic courses in reading and writing without demanding the usual and often deadly separation of form from content. Form interrelates with and supports content; rhetorical analyses coalesce naturally with discussions of general meaning and theme.

Form and Substance includes considerable rhetorical and thematic instruction. The book is, however, arranged in a format that will allow a teacher to *control* the student's access to this instruction. Brief thematic essays, for example, introduce each section and are interspersed throughout. Long rhetorical introductions to the formal principles underlying each section are placed at the *end* of the section, so that teachers who wish to introduce rhetoric themselves as their students read can either avoid or delay their students' reading of the essays on rhetorical form until they have finished the primary readings in a section. On the other hand, teachers who wish to teach by introducing rhetorical principles and then having students look for their application in the essays they read can present these discussions of rhetorical principles *before* students read the essays.

The readings in each section are arranged developmentally, beginning with shorter and less difficult essays and moving toward more abstract, longer, and more complex essays. A literary selection closes each section, providing a contrasting imaginative perspective on the themes and rhetorical principles developed there.

Formal organization

Form and Substance, as its title suggests, is organized around the four traditional modes of writing: *description, narration, exposition,* and *argument.* Description and narration are treated in the two opening parts. Neither the descriptive nor the narrative mode is presented as an end in itself, but to show the writer how to turn his or her experience—whether taken from reading, from everyday life, or from imagination—into the specific substance of essays. Description and narration, in other words, show the writer how to shape and develop his or her ideas through the selection and arrangement of details and examples. These first two parts show students how they can provide substance for the expository forms they will read and apply later.

Exposition is the basis for the lengthy third part of *Form and Substance.* Because college writers use exposition more than any other mode, this part is divided into four subcategories, according to four common methods of development: *definition, comparison and contrast, classification,* and *cause and effect.* Each subcategory includes its own collection of model essays as well as its own rhetorical introduction. This section as a whole shows the writer how to use the specific experiences of description and narration to support ideas and opinions, to convince a reader to share in a perspective or attitude.

Argument provides the substance of the fourth part, in which serious, humorous, and satiric means of persuasion are combined and contrasted. Part Four should help writers sharpen their persuasive skills through the study of contrasting logical, ethical, and satiric manipulations of style.

Parts One (description), Two (narration), and Four (argument) include from four to eight pieces each, all of which illustrate the specific rhetorical process described in the section's essay on form. Part Three includes nineteen expository essays, subdivided under the four categories of exposition. One short story on the section theme follows each group of essays.

Each section sharpens a particular skill while it moves naturally toward the more general, integrative skills required of an expository writer.

Substantive organization

Form and Substance provides unity of content as well as form. The readings in each major section and subsection are organized around a central theme. This theme is identified in a thematic introduction to each section and carried through by brief thematic commentaries interspersed among the readings. Thinking questions, on both form and substance, follow each essay; each section (or, in Part Three, subdivision) closes with an extended writing exercise related to both the form and the theme dealt with in the section.

Part One, for example, begins with a brief introduction to the theme of the section ("Man and His Work"), follows with a collection of four essays and additional interspersed thematic commentary, includes thinking questions on both form and substance after each essay, and concludes with a brief essay on the rhetorical mode (description) on which the section focuses, along with an extended writing exercise.

The readings in each section are organized around general topics—work, political rule, sex roles, the future—rather than on specific opinions or themes. Each essay then provides an individual perspective on this topic. This form of topical arrangement should allow teachers and students the general flexibility they need to develop their own opinions and reactions, without subjecting a class to unnecessary chaos and frustration in the process.

Developmental organization

Writers usually want to follow a clear method; they also want to read essays with a common theme. *Form and Substance* is primarily a writer's reader; it is organized on a simple developmental plan. Essays are arranged so that they progress from simpler, shorter pieces to longer, more complex treatments. Readings are also arranged to progress from discussion of specific experience and evidence—for example, the Studs Terkel and George Orwell essays that open Parts One and Two—to analyses of more theoretical and complex issues—for example, the Robert Graves and Arthur Schlesinger essays that close the subsection on definition.

Each section also directs students toward a particular writing goal, one that they should be able to master before going on to the goal or objective of the next part. The writing exercises that conclude the sections work from the concrete to the abstract, from the description and narration of a personal experience to the expository and argumentative development of an idea or thesis through references to personal experience, reading, and research.

Comments on the readings

Most readings are modern or contemporary, in idioms and styles that students will enjoy and comprehend. Yet none of the readings is too simple—or *simplistic.* They represent serious minds working on different problems and themes. Most sections also include a few traditional essays, such as those by Orwell and Woolf, that students and teachers should find familiar and instructive.

The readings in each section should interact naturally, providing useful comparisons and contrasts between themes and principles of writing. Comparisons between formal and substantive concerns are clarified in the introductions and thinking questions. *Form and Substance,* then, should provide at least a partial solution to the most persistent problem in writing courses: how to assimilate form and content, how to integrate finding something to say with finding a method or means of saying it.

* * *

Form and Substance, even with its emphasis on structure, does provide flexibility. Each part includes a variety of styles and approaches, while the rhetorical elements are arranged so that teachers and students can move among them freely, skipping some, rereading and emphasizing others. The thematic concerns are large enough to invite the reading of related essays from other sources, yet they are treated fully enough in each section to ensure a sound general understanding of the subject. Although the larger sections are carefully and developmentally organized, they are inclusive and varied enough to encourage flexibility.

Form and Substance/1

Form:

DESCRIPTION

Substance:

By the Sweat of Our Brows: MAN AND HIS WORK

/1 *Substance and Theme:*

MAN AND HIS WORK

The flashiest and toughest writers merely offend their readers when they set off fireworks with nothing to celebrate. Each section of this book provides a sequence of professional essays that develop a common theme and simultaneously provide models of a particular writing technique. The essays present discussions of activities and behaviors with which we are involved every day—for example, the theme of *work* developed in this section. They should help you understand the broader significance of everyday work, as it affects you and those around you. And they should help you clarify how the work that people do can affect all their relationships, both with their immediate friends and with the larger political and social aspects of their culture.

The selections in this section by Loren Eiseley, Gay Talese, and W. S. Merwin describe individuals working. All are engaged in very different kinds of work: a writer spending a productive but sleepless night, a boxer training for a championship fight, a tightrope walker performing his routine. Some work more with their bodies; others work more with their minds. Consider these questions.

1. *Why* do these people work? (For money? To feel important? Because they have nothing else to do? Because society says they should? Because their background has given them the drive to compete, to be more productive, to "beat" the other guy?)

2. Is their work the occasion of pleasure, pain, or both? (Exactly what kinds of feelings do they have as they work? Do they seem conscious and proud of how their work helps society, or are they doing "slave" labor,

without the dignity and respect associated with work that is highly valued by society?)

3. How does their work contribute to society? (Do they produce tangible "products"? Do they identify with the products their work provides? Are they providing some form of intangible pleasure or entertainment?)

4. How does the work define the workers themselves? (What do they seem to think of themselves as they work? What degree of importance is attached to the work by their society? Do these people "eat to work or work to eat"?)

Studs Terkel's opening essay, "Earning One's Bread," describes why most people work and argues that people in modern America seldom work for personal satisfaction, but for goals or objectives that are handed down to them by the larger society. Terkel's subjects rebel against their work. James Agee, on the other hand, gives us an exacting physical description of tenant farmers who, despite all kinds of physical and social hardships, are able to retain pride and dignity as they work. As you read the four essays and the short story in this section, keep in mind these tentative questions.

1. Must *everyone* work?
2. *Why* must everyone work?
3. Is it always possible for work to be socially productive?
4. Can work provide personal satisfaction *and* social gain?
5. How many different general classifications of work do you find represented in this section?

Earning One's Bread

STUDS TERKEL

1 Why do people work?

2 To make money, of course. To survive the day. The razor of necessity cuts close. The job is often a chore, rarely a delight. To earn one's bread by the sweat of one's brow is the lot of mankind. So The Scripture tells us. So the President echoes. So echo answers echo with a righteous and resounding Amen. No matter how demanding the task, no matter how it dulls the senses and breaks the spirit, one *must* work—or else.

3 Lately, though, there has been a questioning of this "work ethic," especially by the young. Strangely enough, it has touched off profound grievances in others, hitherto silent and anonymous.

4 Unexpected precincts are being heard from in a show of discontent by blue collar and white. Communiques are alarming concerning absenteeism in auto plants. On the evening bus, the tense, pinched faces of young file clerks and elderly secretaries tell us more than we care to know. On the expressways, middle-management men pose without grace behind their wheels, as they flee city and job.

5 In all, there is more than a slight ache. And there dangles the impertinent question: Ought there not be another increment, earned though not yet received, to one's daily work—an acknowledgement of a man's *being?*

6 Steve Hamilton is a professional baseball player. At 37, he is near the end of his career as a pitcher for the San Francisco Giants. "A lot of us are popular heroes. People recognize you on the street. I've never been a big star, I've done about as good as I can with the equipment I have. I played with Mickey Mantle and now I'm playing with Willie Mays. People always recognize them. But for someone to recognize me, it really made me feel good. I think everybody gets a kick out of feeling special."

7 Mike Fitzgerald was born the same year as Hamilton. He is a laborer in a steel mill. "I feel like the guys who built the Pyramids. Somebody built 'em. Somebody built the Empire State Building, too. There's hard work behind it. I would like to see a building, say the Empire State, with a foot-wide strip from top to bottom, and the name of every bricklayer on it, the name of every electrician. So when a guy walked by, he could take his son and say: 'See, that's me over there on the 45th floor. I put that steel beam in.' Picasso can point to a painting. I think I've done harder work than Picasso and what can I point to? Everybody should have something to point to.

8 "It's the nonrecognition by other people that gets you. Everybody says for a housewife to be called *just* a housewife is degrading. It is also degrading to be called *just* a laborer. The difference is that a man goes out and maybe gets smashed. I work so damn hard, I just want to come home and sit down and lay around. It isn't that the workingman is dumb. He's just tired, that's all.

9 "If my kid ever goes to college, I want him to have a little respect for those 'dumb somebodies,' to realize that his dad is one of those 'dumb somebodies.' This is why I work. Every time I see a young guy walk by with a shirt and tie and dressed up real sharp, I'm looking at my kid. That's it."

10 Sharon Atkins is a good twenty years older than Mike's kid. She's 24. She's been to college and acridly observes: "The first myth that blew up in my face is that a college education will get you a worthwhile job."

11 For the past two years, she's been a receptionist at an advertising agency. "I didn't look at myself as 'just a dumb broad' at the front desk, who took phone calls and messages. I thought I was something else. The office taught me differently." She was having a fairly intelligent discussion with some clients, until they discovered the nature of her job. "Two of them just stopped the conversation and turned around to find other people with name tags. I wasn't worth bothering with, I wasn't rejected because of what I had to say or the way I talked, but simply because of my function.

12 "I was being treated as just a piece of equipment, like the telephone. So I made up another name for my job—'communications control.'

13 "Just to fill in time at this boring job, I write letters to myself and to other people and never mail them. I call it the land of no-phone, where there is no machine telling me where I have to be every minute. This crummy little machine with buttons on it . . . You're just a little machine yourself. A monkey can do what I do.

14 "Until recently, I'd cry in the morning. I didn't want to get up. You tremble when you hear the first ring. After that, nothing. Unless there is somebody on the phone who is either very kind or very nasty. The rest are just non. They don't exist, they're just voices."

15 She experiences a single moment of triumph each day: at one minute to five. She turns off the machine.

16 Among her contemporaries, there is no such rejection: job and status have no meaning. Blue collar or white, teacher or cabbie, her friends judge her and themselves by their *beingness*. Nora Watson, a young journalist, recounts a party game: Who Are You? Older people respond with their job titles: I'm a copywriter. I'm an accountant. The young say: I'm me, my name is so-and-so. Frank Donner, a middle-aged journalist, observes: Older people *always* define themselves by their jobs, young people don't.

17 Harry Stallings, 27, is a spot welder in the assembly line at an auto plant. "They'll give better care to that machine than they will to you. You somehow get the feeling that that machine is better than you. You really begin to wonder. Look at the price they put on that machine. If it breaks down, there's somebody out there to fix it right away. If I break down, I'm just pushed over to the other side till another man takes my place. The only thing the company has in mind is to keep that line running. A man would be more eager to do a better job if he were given proper respect and the time to do it."

18 A farm equipment worker in Moline complains that the careless worker who turns out more that is bad is better regarded than the careful craftsman who turns out less that is good. The first is an ally of the Gross National Product. The other is a threat to the GNP, a kook—and the sooner he is penalized, the better.

19 Stallings keeps his own counsel. "I've been working three years for the company and have only 27 years to go until my pension." His laughter is without mirth. "I could maybe find a better place to work, but let's face it, where could I make the money I'm making? And this recession . . . Many young guys won't accept the stuff the old guys take. I can't blame the old guys. How would you feel if you had only two years to go till your pension?"

20 You would think that Ralph Grayson, a 25-year-old black, has it made. He supervises 20 people in the audit department of a large bank. Yet he is singularly discontented. He describes his job as watching other people. "You're like a foreman on an assembly line. Or like a technician sitting in a computer room watching the machinery. It's good for a person who enjoys that kind of job, who can dominate somebody else's life. I'm not too wrapped up in seeing a woman, 50 years old—white, incidentally—get thrown off her job because she can't cut it like the younger ones.

21 "I told my management she was a kind and gentle person. They said, 'We're not interested in your personal feelings. Document it up.' They look over my appraisal and say, 'We'll give her about five months to shape up or ship out.' People aren't treated as good as an IBM machine around here. I promised I'd never get myself an ulcer, so I'm looking around for something else."

22 It's too late for Geraldine Merton to look around for something else. Middle-aged, ailing, she works in a luggage factory. Though she is the union steward and quite militant in the matter of women's rights, she has been grievously hurt by members of her own sex.

23 "I attended a Governors' Conference on the status of women. Most of the others were teachers, social workers and nurses. When they found out what my job was, they were ice cold. I felt like I was a little piece of scum."

24 A bitter laugh erupts suddenly. "Don't they know how important I am? How could we employ teachers if it wasn't for the factory workers who manufacture the books they use—or the briefcases I make?"

25 The hunger persists, obstinately, for pride in a man's work. Conditions may be horrendous, tensions high and humiliations frequent, yet Paul Dietch finds his small triumphs. He drives his own truck, interstate, as a steel hauler. "Every load is a challenge. When I'm going to Hotpoint in Milwaukee, and I off-load, I have a feeling of having done a vital piece of work. It's not like putting a rivet in some machine, the end of which I'll never see. They're going to turn my steel into 10,000 washing machines, a hundred farm implements. I have problems in the morning with heartburn. I can't eat. Once I off-load, the pressure is gone. Then I can eat anything. I accomplished something."

26 Al Preston, a veteran car hiker, chuckles quietly. "The Cadillac owner will go around the car and I go around with him, lookin' for that scratch. It hurts my pride but I won't give him the satisfaction of showing it.

27 "I can drive any car like a baby, like a woman changes her baby's diapers. I could handle a car with one hand. Lot of customers would say: 'How you do this?' I'd say: 'Just the way you bake a cake, miss.' Oh, I'll admit it, the thrill is gone now. When I was younger, I could swing with that car. With one hand, I could back it all the way and whip it into that hole, with two inches to spare. They call me Lovin' Al, the Wizard. Now I'm older and tired and drive normal like everybody else."

28 Yolanda Leif graphically describes the trials of a waitress in a quality restaurant. They are compounded by her refusal to be demeaned. Yet pride in her skills helps her through the night.

29 "When I put the plate down, you don't hear a sound. When I pick up a glass, I want it to be just right. When someone says, 'How come you're just a waitress?' I say, 'Don't you think you deserve being served by me?' I feel like a ballerina when I move between the tables. I do it with an air. If I drop a fork, there's a certain way I pick it up, my way. I do it delicately. I spilled my tray once, with steaks for seven on it, a gigantic T-bone. When the tray fell, I moved with it, never made a sound. I like to have my station looking nice. I believe in pride and beauty."

30 Peggy Terry has her own sense of pride and beauty. Her jobs have varied with geography, climate and the ever-felt pinch of circumstance. "What I hated worst was being a waitress, the way you're treated. One guy said, 'You don't have to smile. I'm gonna give you a tip anyway.' I said, 'Keep it, I wasn't smiling for a tip.' Tipping should be done away with. It's like throwing a dog a bone. It makes you feel small."

31 Ballplayer. Laborer. Receptionist. Assembly line worker. Truck driver. Bank official. Car hiker. Waitress. What with the computer and all manner of automation, add scores of hundreds of new occupations and, thus, new heroes and anti-heroes to Walt Whitman's old anthem. The sound, though, is no longer melodious. The desperation is unquiet.

32 Perhaps Nora Watson has put her finger on it. She reflects on her father's work. He was a fundamentalist preacher, with whom she had been profoundly at odds.

33 "Whatever he was, he was. It was his calling, his vocation. He saw himself as a core resource of the community. He liked his work even though his family barely survived, because that was what he was supposed to be doing. His work was his life. He himself was not separate and apart from his calling. I think this is what all of us are looking for, a calling, not just a job. Most of us, like the assembly line worker, have jobs that are too small for our spirit. Jobs are just not big enough for people."

34 The most impertinent of all questions is asked *sotto voce*. More and more it surfaces in individual lives, as an acquaintance suffers a breakdown, as another quits his "career" in middle age, as most quietly dissolve and are suddenly old. There is the fixed smile of "retired" as against the fixed scowl of the man at work.

35 The common end appears to be a question mark.

What is there to show?

Does my job have any real meaning?

36 With technology, whether it be a wild horse or tamed, the questions transcend youth and age.

Thinking Questions: ***Form***

1. Write your own thesis for Terkel's essay. Your thesis should answer his opening question: "Why do people work?" Show how several of the sample reactions of individual workers support your interpretation of Terkel's thesis statement.

2. Terkel's descriptions are much less detailed than those of the essayists whose selections follow. Why? Do you think his specific examples of workers ought to be supplemented with broader statistics?

3. Describe, in detail, someone you know who does demonstrate pride in his or her work. Observe and take notes. Then begin with a general statement explaining why this worker demonstrates pride; to illustrate your thesis, give two or three concrete descriptions of your subject as he or she works.

4. Analyze Studs Terkel's personality. Is he tough, concerned, factual, stuffy, overly emotional? What elements in the language of the essay create Terkel's personality? Look closely at sentence structure, vocabulary, paragraph length, and overall style.

Thinking Questions: *Substance*

1. This essay offers a very opinionated description of why Americans work and how their attitudes toward work have shifted greatly in recent years. Terkel suggests that people recently have been asking that their work provide more than physical comfort and security; it should provide a sense of "being" (see paragraph 5) as well. Look closely at the examples Terkel uses to define that term, and apply it to the jobs that are described in the three essays that follow. Do the workers described in those essays retain a sense of *being* as they work?

2. Do you and your classmates respond to questions such as "Who are you?" with the answer "students"? Or do you have more complete and individualistic responses to such questions? Try questions out in class (see paragraph 16 of Terkel's essay for an example).

3. Write an essay in response to Harry Stallings's complaint against his work in paragraph 17. How would you suggest assuring that individuals keep their "being," even in modern technological jobs?

4. Choose one of the essays that follow and explain whether the worker or workers described in it have "pride in their work"? What gives a person pride in his or her work? Be specific.

* * *

FURTHER OBSERVATIONS ON INDIVIDUALS WORKING

Many of the social groups that came to prominence in the past three decades—the beatniks of the fifties, the hippies of the sixties, the Jesus freaks of the early seventies, and the feminists throughout this entire period—have illustrated in their ideals a desire to escape the routines of house and work, to escape the old-fashioned idea that a person is defined only by what he or she produces, through labor, for the larger society. Various means of personal discovery, such as jazz, drugs, rock music, new art forms, and, lately, a return to personalized, emotional religious beliefs and expressions, have come to replace the traditional function of work for many Americans. These people no longer define themselves by professional title or occupation or by society's description of a particular social function; rather they define themselves by the personal growth and satisfaction in their work. These social groups have tried to redefine *work* to avoid the unhappiness and dissatisfaction that Studs Terkel points out in "Earning One's Bread."

We must examine what many social critics and psychologists have pointed out about jobs in modern America: the contemporary individual's loss of respect for the inherent value of work. The automobile mechanic who took great pride in listening to a finely tuned engine has been replaced in many service centers with electronic tuning devices; teachers, more frequently than ever before, use electronic media to reach larger numbers of students, many of whom they know less well because they seldom see or talk with them; workers in the automobile industry do ever more specialized jobs and often do not understand how their particular "job" fits into the entire manufacturing process; large department stores have computerized their relations with customers so that individualized service is often difficult to obtain. And the credit card now has control over much of our lives, over our spending and living habits, and ultimately, over our attitudes toward work and production. Many of us are not finding immediate satisfaction through work; we are, instead, becoming increasingly satisfied only by the *ends* provided by work—by money and material comfort.

As you read through the remainder of Part One, consider these current criticisms of our attitudes toward work:

1. Work should not define and control the entire life of an individual.
2. Work should provide personal satisfaction as well as material gain.
3. Work should bring together, not separate, those who work. Work should encourage the sharing of efforts and talents rather than competition.
4. A man or woman should understand his or her function in any work situation, even when the job is a small part of a large process.

Then also consider the dangers to social cohesion that might evolve if every individual worker were to seek out *only* work that was personally satisfying as well as socially productive. Could we, if such were the case, survive as a mass society? Would all the jobs necessary to our survival get done?

*   *   *

In the next essay, James Agee describes the hard, physical work of tenant farmers in Alabama shortly after the Great Depression. Agee describes his subject with a painful, almost agonizing, sense of precision and detail, using concrete images to appeal to our senses, working our sensory grasp of the farmers' agonizing work into an effective identification with the farmers—we *feel* as if we are inside the skins of these struggling, barely surviving families. Whereas Studs Terkel gives us general summaries of men and women and their attitudes toward their jobs, James Agee gives us the physical environment and inner sensations of his subjects as they work, and we are left limp with the labor of picking cotton.

An interesting story lies behind the publishing of *Let Us Now Praise Famous Men,* the book from which this essay is taken.[1] In 1936, James Agee and photographer Walker Evans traveled to Alabama with the idea of recording in words and photographs the lives of sharecroppers and tenant farmers. For six weeks they lived with three tenant-farming families, took photographs and notes, recorded almost entire conversations and incidents in writing, slept, ate, and worked with their subjects. Agee had planned to write an objective, journalistic description of the lives of the tenant farmers. But his interest and love for the families soon replaced his desire to record what he saw objectively with a deeper, more subjective desire to capture the essence, the timelessness and essential courage of his subjects' lives. What began as a relatively simple and factual magazine article ended as a massive 500-page study.

In the process of observing and composing, Agee discovered that the tenant farmers, despite their extreme poverty and low status, were proud and dignified people, knowing the worth of their work even when others exploited or looked down on them. As you read, you may want to compare the meticulous care with which the Woods, Ricketts, and Gudger families carry out their labors with the feelings of despair and uselessness that are harbored by the contemporary laborers interviewed by Studs Terkel. Why were these poor and uneducated farm families able (at least as Agee saw them) to maintain a sense of dignity that production-line workers, with better pay, higher social status, and infinitely better working conditions, are not able to maintain?

---

1. Published originally by the Houghton-Mifflin Company in 1941, *Let Us Now Praise Famous Men* is now available in a Ballantine Books paperback edition. The introductory material in *Let Us Now Praise Famous Men* provides more detail on the composition of the book and the experience Agee and Evans shared as they gathered material for the book.

Work: Cotton

JAMES AGEE

1 Cotton is only one among several crops and among many labors: and all these other crops and labors mean life itself. Cotton means nothing of the sort. It demands more work of a tenant family and yields less reward than all the rest. It is the reason the tenant has the means to do the rest, and to have the rest, and to live, as a tenant, at all. Aside from a few negligibilities of minor sale and barter and of out-of-season work, it is his one possible source of money, and through this fact, though his living depends far less on money than on the manipulations of immediate nature, it has a certain royalty. It is also that by which he has all else besides money. But it is also his chief contracted obligation, for which he must neglect all else as need be; and is the central leverage and symbol of his privation and of his wasted life. It is the one crop and labor which is in no possible way useful as it stands to the tenant's living; it is among all these the one which must and can be turned into money; it is among all these the one in which the landowner is most interested; and it is among all these the one of which the tenant can hope for least, and can be surest that he is being cheated, and is always to be cheated. All other tasks are incidental to it; and it is constantly on everyone's mind; yet of all of them it is the work in which the tenant has least hope and least interest, and to which he must devote the most energy. Any less involved and self-contradictory attempt to understand what cotton and cotton work 'means' to a tenant would, it seems to me, be false to it. It has the doubleness that all jobs have by which one stays alive and in which one's life is made a cheated ruin, and the same sprained and twilight effect on those who must work at it: but because it is only one among the many jobs by which a tenant family must stay alive, and deflects all these others, and receives still other light from their more personal need, reward, and value, its meanings are much more complex than those of most jobs: it is a strong stale magnet among many others more weak and more yielding of life and hope. In the mind of one in whom all these magnetisms are daily and habituated from his birth, these meanings are one somber mull: yet all their several forces are pulling at once, and by them the brain is quietly drawn and quartered. It seems to me it is only through such a complex of meanings that a tenant can feel, toward that crop, toward each plant in it, toward all that work, what he and all grown women too appear to feel, a particular automatism, a quiet,

apathetic, and inarticulate yet deeply vindictive hatred, and at the same time utter hopelessness, and the deepest of their anxieties and of their hopes: as if the plant stood enormous in the unsteady sky fastened above them in all they do like the eyes of an overseer. To do all of the hardest work of your life in service of these drawings-apart of ambiguities; and to have all other tasks and all one's consciousness stained and drawn apart in it: I can conceive of little else which could be so inevitably destructive of the appetite for living, of the spirit, of the being, or by whatever name the centers of individuals are to be called: and this very literally: for just as there are deep chemical or electric changes in all the body under anger, or love, or fear, so there must certainly be at the center of these meanings and their directed emotions; perhaps most essentially, an incalculably somber and heavy weight and dark knotted iron of subnausea at the peak of the diaphragm, darkening and weakening the whole body and being, the literal feeling by which the words a broken heart are no longer poetic, but are merely the most accurate possible description.

2 Yet these things as themselves are withdrawn almost beyond visibility, and the true focus and right telling of it would be in the exact textures of each immediate task.

3 Of cotton farming I know almost nothing with my own eyes; the rest I have of Bud Woods. I asked enough of other people to realize that every tenant differs a little in his methods, so nothing of this can be set down as 'standard' or 'correct'; but the dissonances are of small detail rather than of the frame and series in the year. I respect dialects too deeply, when they are used by those who have a right to them, not to be hesitant in using them, but I have decided to use some of Woods' language here. I have decided, too, to try to use my imagination a little, as carefully as I can. I must warn you that the result is sure to be somewhat inaccurate: but it is accurate anyhow to my ignorance, which I would not wish to disguise.

4 From the end of the season and on through the winter the cotton and the corn stand stripped and destroyed, the cotton black and brown, the corn gray and brown and rotted gold, much more shattered, the banks of woodland bare, drenched and black, the clay dirt sombered wet or hard with a shine of iron, peaceful and exhausted; the look of trees in a once full-blown country where such a burning of war has gone there is no food left even for birds and insects, all now brought utterly quiet, and the bare homes dark with dampness, under the soft and mourning midwinter suns of autumnal days, when all glows gold yet lifeless, and under constrictions of those bitter freezings when the clay is shafted and sprilled with ice, and the aching thinly drifted snows which give the land its shape, and, above all, the long, cold, silent, inexhaustible, and dark winter rains:

5 In the late fall or middle February this tenant, which of the three or of the millions I do not care—a man, dressed against the wet coldness, may be seen small and dark in his prostrated fields, taking down these sometimes brittle, sometimes rotted forests of last year's crops with a club or with a cutter, putting death to bed, cleaning the land: and late in February, in fulfillment of an obligation to his landlord, he borrows a second mule and, with a two-horse plow, runs up the levees,[1] that is, the terraces, which shall preserve his land; this in a softening mild brightness and odoriferousness of presaging spring, and a rustling shearing apart of the heavy land, his mules moving in slow scarce-wakened method as of work before dawn, knowing the real year's work to be not started yet, only made ready for. It is when this is done, at about the first of March, that the actual work begins, with what is planted where, and with what grade and amount of fertilizer, determined by the landlord, who will also, if he wishes, criticize, advise, and govern at all stages of planting and cultivation. But the physical work, and for that matter the knowledge by which he works, is the tenant's, and this is his tenth or his fortieth year's beginning of it, and it is of the tenant I want to tell.

6 How you break the land in the first place depends on whether you have one or two mules or can double up with another tenant for two mules. It is much better to broadcast if you can. With two mules you can count on doing it all in that most thorough way. But if you have only one mule you break what you have time for, more shallowly, and, for the rest, you bed, that is, start the land.

7 To broadcast, to break the land broadcast: take a twister, which is about the same as a turning plow, and, heading the mule in concentrics the shape of the field, lay open as broad and deep a ribbon of the stiff dirt as the strength of the mule and of your own guidance can manage: eight wide by six deep with a single-horse plow, and twice that with a double, is doing well: the operation has the staggering and reeling yet steady quality of a small sailboat clambering a storm.

8 Where you have broadcast the land, you then lay out the furrows three and a half feet apart with a shovel plow; and put down fertilizer; and by four furrows with a turning plow, twist the dirt back over the fertilized furrow. But if, lacking mule power, you have still land which is not broken, and it is near time to plant, you bed the rest. There are two beddings. The first is hard bedding: breaking the hard pan between the rows.

9 Hard bedding: set the plow parallel to the line of (last year's) stalks and along their right, follow each row to its end and up the far side.

1. These farms are the width of a state and still more from the river. Is *levee* originally a land or a river word? It must be a river word, for terracing against erosion is recent in America. So the Mississippi has such power that men who have never seen it use its language in their work.

The dirt lays open always to the right. Then set the plow close in against the stalks and go around again. The stubble is cleaned out this second time round and between each two rows is a bed of soft dirt: that is to say, the hard pan is all broken. That is the first bedding.

10 Then drop guano along the line where the stalks were, by machine or by horn. Few tenants use the machine; most of them either buy a horn, or make it, as Woods does. It is a long tin cone, small and low, with a wood handle, and a hole in the low end. It is held in the left hand, pointed low to the furrow, and is fed in fistfuls, in a steady rhythm, from the fertilizer sack, the incipient frock, slung heavy along the right side.

11 After you have strowed the gyewanner you turn the dirt back over with two plowings just as before: and that is the second bedding. Pitch the bed shallow, or you won't be able to work it right.

12 If you have done all this right you haven't got a blemish in all your land that is not broke: and you are ready to plant.

13 But just roughly, only as a matter of suggestion, compute the work that has been done so far, in ten acres of land, remembering that this is not counting in ten more acres of corn and a few minor crops: how many times has this land been retraced in the rolling-gaited guidance and tensions and whippings and orderings of plowing, and with the steadily held horn, the steady arc of the right arm and right hand fisting and opening like a heart, the heavy weight of the sack at the right side?

14 Broadcasting, the whole unbroken plaque slivered open in rectilinear concenters, eight inches apart and six deep if with one mule, sixteen apart and twelve deep if with two: remember how much length of line is coiled in one reel or within one phonograph record: and then each furrow, each three and a half feet, scooped open with a shovel plow: and in each row the fertilizer laid: and each row folded cleanly back in four transits of its complete length: or bedding, the first bedding in four transits of each length; and then the fertilizer: and four more transits of each length: every one of the many rows of the whole of the field gone eight times over with a plow and a ninth by hand; and only now is it ready for planting.

Planting

15 There are three harrs you might use but the spring-toothed harr is best. The long-toothed section harrow tears your bed to pieces; the short-toothed is better, but catches on snags and is more likely to pack the bed than loosen it. The springtooth moves lightly but incisively with a sort of knee-action sensitiveness to the modulations of the ground, and it jumps snags. You harrow just one row at a time

and right behind the harrow comes the planter. The planter is rather like a tennis-court marker: a seed bin set between light wheels, with a little plow protruded from beneath it like a foot from under a hoop-skirt. The little beak of the plow slits open the dirt; just at its lifted heel the seed thrills out in a spindling stream; a flat wheel flats the dirt over: a light-traveling, tender, iron sexual act entirely worthy of setting beside the die-log and the swept broad-handed arm.[2]

16 Depending on the moisture and the soil, it will be five days to two weeks before the cotton will show.

17 Cultivating begins as soon as it shows an inch.

Cultivation

18 Barring off: the sweepings: chopping: laying by:

19 The first job is barring off.

20 Set a five- to six-inch twister, the smallest one you have, as close in against the stalks as you can get it and not damage them, as close as the breadth of a finger if you are good at it, and throw the dirt to the middle. Alongside this plow is a wide tin defender, which doesn't allow a blemish to fall on the young plants.

21 Then comes the first of the four sweepings. The sweeps are blunt stocks shaped a good deal like stingrays. Over their dull foreheads and broad shoulders they neither twist nor roll the dirt, but shake it from the middle to the beds on either side. For the first sweeping you still use the defender. Use a little stock, but the biggest you dare to; probably the eighteen-inch.

22 Next after that comes the chopping, and with this the whole family helps down through the children of eight or seven, and by helps, I mean that the family works full time at it. Chopping is a simple and hard job, and a hot one, for by now the sun, though still damp, is very strong, hot with a kind of itchy intensity that is seldom known in northern springs. The work is, simply, thinning the cotton to a stand; hills a foot to sixteen inches apart, two to four stalks to the hill. It is done with an eight to ten-inch hoe-blade. You cut the cotton flush off at the ground, bent just a little above it, with a short sharp blow of the blade of which each stroke is light enough work; but multiplied into the many hundreds in each continuously added hour, it aches

2. I am unsure of this planting machine; I did not see one there; but what Woods described to me seemed to tally with something I had seen, and not remembered with perfect clearness, from my childhood. The die-log is still used, Woods says, by some of the older-fashioned farmers and by some Negroes. I'm not very clear about it either, but I am interested because according to Woods its use goes a *way* on back. My 'impression' is that it's simple enough: a hollow homemade cylinder of wood with a hole in it to regulate and direct the falling stream of seed as would be more difficult by hand.

first the forearms, which so harden they seem to become one bone, and in time the whole spine.

23 The second sweeping is done with the twenty to twenty-two-inch stock you will use from now on; then comes hoeing, another job for the whole family; then you run the middles; that is, you put down soda by hand or horn or machine; soda makes the weed, guano puts on the fruit; then comes the third sweeping; and then another hoeing. The first and second sweepings you have gone pretty deep. The stuff is small and you want to give loose ground to your feed roots. The third sweeping is shallow, for the feed roots have extended themselves within danger of injury.

24 The fourth sweeping is so light a scraping that it is scarcely more than a ritual, like a barber's last delicate moments with his muse before he holds the mirror up to the dark side of your skull. The cotton has to be treated very carefully. By this last sweeping it is making. Break roots, or lack rain, and it is stopped dead as a hammer.

25 This fourth sweeping is the operation more properly known as laying by. From now on until picking time, there is nothing more a farmer can do. Everything is up to the sky, the dirt, and the cotton itself; and in six weeks now, and while the farmer is fending off such of its enemies as he can touch, and, lacking rations money to live on, is desperately seeking and conceivably finding work, or with his family is hung as if on a hook on his front porch in the terrible leisure, the cotton is making, and his year's fate is being quietly fought out between agencies over which he has no control. And in this white midsummer, while he is thus waiting however he can, and defending what little he can, these are his enemies, and this is what the cotton is doing with its time:

26 Each square points up. That is to say: on twig-ends, certain of the fringed leaves point themselves into the sharp form of an infant prepuce; each square points up: and opens a flat white flower which turns pink next day, purple the next, and on the next day shrivels and falls, forced off by the growth, at the base of the bloom, of the boll. The development from square to boll consumes three weeks in the early summer, ten days in the later, longer and more intense heat. The plants are well fringed with pointed squares, and young cold bolls, by the time the crop is laid by; and the blooming keeps on all summer. The development of each boll from the size of a pea to that point where, at the size of a big walnut, it darkens and dries and its white contents silently explode it, takes five to eight weeks and is by no means ended when the picking season has begun.

27 And meanwhile the enemies: bitterweed, ragweed, Johnson grass; the weevil, the army worm; the slippery chances of the sky. Bitterweed is easily killed out and won't come up again. Ragweed will, with another prong every time. That weed can suck your crop to death.

Johnson grass, it takes hell and scissors to control. You can't control it in the drill with your plowing. If you just cut it off with the hoe, it is high as your thumb by the next morning. The best you can do is dig up the root with the corner of your hoe, and that doesn't hold it back any too well.

28 There is a lot less trouble from the weevils[3] than there used to be, but not the army worms. Army worms are devils. The biggest of them get to be the size of your little finger. They eat leaves and squares and young bolls. You get only a light crop of them at first. They web up in the leaves and turn into flies, the flies lay eggs, the eggs turn into army worms by the millions and if they have got this good a start of you you can hear the sound of them eating in the whole field and it sounds like a brushfire. They are a bad menace but they are not as hard to control as the weevil. You mix arsenic poison with a sorry grade of flour and dust the plants late of an evening (afternoon) as soon of a morning (pre-morning); and the dew makes a paste of it that won't blow off.

29 It is only in a very unusual year that you do well with both of the most important crops, the two life mainly depends on, because they need rain and sun in such different amounts. Cotton needs a great deal less rain than corn; it is really a sun flower. If it is going to get a superflux of rain, that will best come before it is blooming; and if it has got to rain during that part of the summer when a fairsized field is blooming a bale a day, it had best rain late in the evening when the blooms are shutting or at night, not in the morning or the mid day: for then the bloom is blared out flat; rain gets in it easy and hangs on it; it shuts wet, sours, and sticks to the boll; next morning it turns red and falls. Often the boll comes off with it. But the boll that stays on is sour and rotted and good for nothing. Or to put it the other way around, it can take just one rain at the wrong time of day at the wrong time of summer to wreck you out of a whole bale.

30 It is therefore not surprising that they are constant readers of the sky; that it holds not an ounce of 'beauty' to them (though I know of no more magnificent skies than those of Alabama); that it is the lodestone of their deepest pieties; and that they have, also, the deep stormfear which is apparently common to all primitive peoples. Wind is as terrifying to them as cloud and lightning and thunder: and I remember how, sitting with the Woods, in an afternoon when George was away at work, and a storm was building, Mrs. Gudger and her children came hurrying three quarters of a mile beneath the blackening air to shelter among company. Gudger says: 'You can never tell what's in a cloud.'

---

3. If I remember rightly, people never learned any successful method against him, and it is some insect, whose name and kind I forget, who holds him in check.

Picking season

31 Late in August the fields begin to whiten more rarely with late bloom and more frequently with cotton and then still thicker with cotton, a sparkling ground starlight of it, steadily bursting into more and more millions of points, all the leaves seeming shrunken smaller; quite as at night the whole frontage of the universe is more and more thoroughly printed in the increasing darkness; and the wide cloudless and tremendous light holds the earth clamped and trained as beneath a vacuum bell and burningglass; in such a brilliance that half and two thirds of the sky is painful to look into; and in this white maturing oven the enlarged bolls are streaked a rusty green, then bronze, and are split and splayed open each in a loose vomit of cotton. These split bolls are now *burrs,* hard and edged as chiseled wood, pointed nearly as thorns, spread open in three and four and five gores or cells. It is slow at first, just a few dozen scattered here and there and then a few tens of dozens, and then there is a space of two or three days in which a whole field seems to be crackling open at once, and at this time it seems natural that it must be gone into and picked, but all the more temperate and experienced tenants wait a few days longer until it will be fully worth the effort: and during this bursting of bolls and this waiting, there is a kind of quickening, as if deep under the ground, of all existence, toward a climax which cannot be delayed much longer, but which is held in the tensions of this reluctance, tightening, and delay: and this can be seen equally in long, sweeping drivings of a car between these spangling fields, and in any one of the small towns or the county seats, and in the changed eyes of any one family, a kind of tightening as of an undertow, the whole world and year lifted nearly upon its crest, and soon beginning the long chute down to winter: children, and once in a while a very young or a very old woman or man, whose work is scarcely entered upon or whose last task and climax this may be, are deeply taken with an excitement and a restlessness to begin picking, and in the towns, where it is going to mean money, the towns whose existence is for it and depends on it, and which in most times of year are sunken in sleep as at the bottom of a sea: these towns are sharpening awake; even the white hot streets of a large city are subtly changed in this season: but Gudger and his wife and Ricketts and Woods, and most of the heads of the million and a quarter families who have made this and are to do the working of taking it for their own harm and another's use, they are only a little more quiet than usual, as they might be if they were waiting for a train to come in, and keep looking at the fields, and judging them; and at length one morning (the Ricketts women are already three days advanced in ragged work), Gudger says, Well:

32 Well; I reckon tomorrow we'd better start to picking:

33 And the next morning very early, with their broad hats and great sacks and the hickory baskets, they are out, silent, their bodies all slanted, on the hill: and in every field in hundreds of miles, black and white, it is the same: and such as it is, it is a joy which scarcely touches any tenant; and is worn thin and through in half a morning, and is gone for a year.

34 It is simple and terrible work. Skill will help you; all the endurance you can draw up against it from the roots of your existence will be thoroughly used as fuel to it: but neither skill nor endurance can make it any easier.

35 Over the right shoulder you have slung a long white sack whose half length trails the ground behind. You work with both hands as fast and steadily as you can. The trick is to get the cotton between your fingertips at its very roots in the burr in all three or four or five gores at once so that it is brought out clean in one pluck. It is easy enough with one burr in perhaps ten, where the cotton is ready to fall; with the rest, the fibers are more tight and tricky. So another trick is, to learn these several different shapes of burr and resistance as nearly as possible by instinct, so there will be no second trying and delay, and none left wasted in the burr; and, too, as quickly to judge what may be too rotted and dirtied to use, and what is not yet quite ready to take: there are a lot suspended between these small uncertainties, and there should be no delay, no need to use the mind's judgement, and few mistakes. Still another trick is, between these strong pulls of efficiency, proper judgement, and maximum speed, not to hurt your fingers on the burrs any worse than you can help. You would have to try hard, to break your flesh on any one burr, whether on its sharp points or its edges; and a single raindrop is only scarcely instrumental in ironing a mountain flat; but in each plucking of the hand the fingers are searched deep in along these several sharp, hard edges. In two hours' picking the hands are just well limbered up. At the end of a week you are favoring your fingers, still in the obligation of speed. The later of the three to five times over the field, the last long weeks of the season, you might be happy if it were possible to exchange them for boils. With each of these hundreds of thousands of insertions of the hands, moreover, the fingers are brought to a small point, in an action upon every joint and tendon in the hand. I suggest that if you will try, three hundred times in success, the following exercise: touch all five fingertips as closely as possible into one point, trying meanwhile to hold loose cotton in the palm of the hand: you will see that this can very quickly tire, cramp and deteriorate the whole instrument, and will understand how easily rheumatism can take up its strictures in just this place.

36 Meanwhile, too, you are working in a land of sunlight and heat

which are special to just such country at just that time of year: sunlight that stands and stacks itself upon you with the serene weight of deep sea water, and heat that makes the joined and muscled and fine-structured body glow like one indiscriminate oil; and this brilliant weight of heat is piled upon you more and more heavily in hour after hour so that it can seem you are a diving bell whose strained seams must at any moment burst, and the eyes are marked in stinging sweat, and the head, if your health is a little unstable, is gently roaring, like a private blow-torch, and less gently beating with aching blood: also the bag, which can hold a hundred pounds, is filling as it is dragged from plant to plant, four to nine burrs to a plant to be rifled swiftly, and the load shrugged along another foot or two and the white row stretched ahead to a blur and innumerably manifolded in other white rows which have not yet been touched, and younger bolls in the cleaned row behind already breaking like slow popcorn in the heat, and the sack still heavier and heavier, so that it pulls you back as a beast might rather than a mere dead weight: but it is not only this: cotton plants are low, so that in this heat and burden of the immanent sun and of the heavying sack you are dragging, you are continuously somewhat stooped over even if you are a child, and are bent very deep if you are a man or a woman. A strong back is a godsend, but not even the strongest back was built for that treatment, and there combine at the kidneys, and rill down the thighs and up the spine and athwart the shoulders the ticklish weakness of gruel or water, and an aching that is increased in geometric progressions, and at length, in the small of the spine, a literal and persistent sensation of yielding, buckling, splintering, and breakage: and all of this, even though the mercy of nature has hardened your flesh and has anesthetized your nerves and your powers of reflection and of imagination, yet reaches in time the brain and the more mirror-like nerves, and thereby is redoubled upon itself much more powerfully than before: and this is all compounded upon you during each successive hour of the day and during each successive day in a force which rest and food and sleep only partly and superficially refresh: and though, later in the season, you are relieved of the worst of the heat, it is in exchange at the last for a coolness which many pickers like even less well, since it so slows and chills the lubricant garment of sweat they work in, and seriously slows and stiffens the fingers which by then at best afford an excruciation in every touch.

37 The tenants' idiom has been used ad nauseam by the more unspeakable of the northern journalists but it happens to be accurate: that picking goes on each day from can to can't: sometimes, if there is a feeling of rush, the Ricketts continue it by moonlight. In the blasting heat of the first of the season, unless there is a rush to beat a rain or to make up an almost completed wagonload, it is customary

to quit work an hour and a half or even two hours in the worst part of the day and to sit or lie in the shade and possible draft of the hallway or porch asleep or dozing after dinner. This time narrows off as the weeks go by and a sense of rush and of the wish to be done with it grows on the pickers and is tightened through from the landlord. I have heard of tenants and pickers who have no rest-period and no midday meal,[4] but those I am acquainted with have it. It is of course no parallel in heartiness and variety to the proud and enormous meals which farm wives of the wheat country prepare for harvest hands, and which are so very zestfully regarded by some belated virgilians as common to what they like to call the American Scene. It is in fact that ordinary every day food, with perhaps a little less variety than in the earlier summer, hastily thrown together and heated by a woman who has hurried in exhausted from the field as few jumps as possible ahead of her family, and served in the dishes she hurriedly rinsed before she hurried out on the early morning as few jumps as possible behind them. When they are all done, she hurries through the dish washing and puts on her straw hat or her sun-bonnet and goes on back into the field, and they are all at it in a strung-out little bunch, the sun a bitter white on their deeply bent backs, and the sacks trailing, a slow breeze idling in the tops of the pines and hickories along the far side but the leaves of the low cotton scarcely touched in it, and the whole land, under hours of heat still to go, yet listed subtly forward toward the late end of the day. They seem very small in the field and very lonely, and the motions of their industry are so small, in range, their bodies so slowly moving, that it seems less that they are so hard at work than that they are bowed over so deeply into some fascination or grief, or are as those pilgrims of Quebec who take the great flights of stairs upon their knees, slowly, a prayer spoken in each step. Ellen lies in the white load of the cotton-basket in the shade asleep; Squinchy picks the front of his dress full and takes it to his mother; Clair Bell fills a hat time after time in great speed and with an expression of delight rushes up behind her mother and dumps the cotton on all of her she can reach and goes crazy with laughter, and her mother and the girls stop a minute and she is hugged, but they talk more among themselves than the other families, they are much more quiet than is usual to them, and Mrs.

4. On the big plantations, where a good deal of the picking is done by day labor and is watched over by riding bosses, all the equations of speed and unresting steadiness are of course intensified; the whole nature of the work, in the men and women and their children, is somewhat altered. Yet not so much as might at first seem. A man and his family working alone are drawn narrowly together in these weeds even within themselves, and know they are being watched: from the very first, in town, their landlords are observant of which tenants bring their cotton first to gin and of who is slow and late; also, there is nearly always, in the tenant's family, the exceedingly sharp need of cottonseed money.

Ricketts only pauses a minute, cleaning the cotton from her skirts and her hair and putting it in her sack, and then she is bowed over deeply at work again. Woods is badly slowed by weakness and by the pain in his shoulder; he welcomes any possible excuse to stop and sometimes has to pause whether there is any excuse or not, but his wife and her mother are both strong and good pickers, so he is able to get by without a hired hand. Thomas is not old enough yet to be any use. Burt too is very young for it and works only by fits and starts; little is expected of children so small, but it is no harm what little they do; you can't learn them too young. Junior is not very quick with it at best. He will work for a while furiously hard, in jealousy of Louise, and then slacken up with sore hands and begin to bully Burt. Katy is very quick. Last summer, when she was only eight, she picked a hundred and ten pounds in a day in a race with Flora Merry Lee. This summer she has had runarounds and is losing two fingernails but she is picking steadily. Pearl Woods is big for her age and is very steadily useful. Louise is an extraordinarily steady and quick worker for her age; she can pick a hundred and fifty pounds in a day. The two Ricketts boys are all right when their papa is on hand to keep them at their work; as it is, with Ricketts at the sawmills they clown a good deal, and tease their sisters. Mrs. Gudger picks about the average for a woman, a hundred and fifty to two hundred pounds a day. She is fast with her fingers until the work exhausts her; 'last half of the day I just don't see how I can keep on with it.' George Gudger is a very poor picker. When he was a child he fell in the fireplace and burnt the flesh off the flat of both hands to the bone, so that his fingers are stiff and slow and the best he has ever done in a day is a hundred and fifty pounds. The average for a man is nearer two hundred and fifty. His back hurts him badly too, so he usually picks on his knees, the way the others pick only when they are resting. Mrs. Ricketts used to pick three hundred and three hundred and fifty pounds in a day but sickness has slowed her to less than two hundred now. Mrs. Ricketts is more often than not a fantast, quite without realizing, and in all these figures they gave me there may be inaccuracy—according to general talk surrounding the Rust machine a hundred pounds a day is good picking—but these are their own estimates of their own abilities, on a matter in which tenants have some pride, and that seems to me more to the point than their accuracy. There are sometimes shifts into gayety in the picking, or a brief excitement, a race between two of the children, or a snake killed; or two who sit a few moments in their sweat in the shaded clay when they have taken some water, but they say very little to each other, for there is little to say, and are soon back to it, and mainly, in hour upon hour, it is speechless, silent, serious, ceaseless and lonely work along the great silence of the unshaded land, ending each day in a vast blaze of dust on the west, every leaf sharpened in long knives of shadow, the day drawn down through red to purple, and the leaves losing color, and the wild blind eyes of the cotton staring in twilight, in those odors of work done and of nature lost once more to night whose sweetness is a torture, and in the slow, loaded walking home, whose stiff and gentle motions are those of creatures just awakened.

38 The cotton is ordinarily stored in a small structure out in the land, the cotton house; but none of these three families has one. The Gudgers store it in one of the chambers of their barn, the Woods on their front porch, raising planks around it, the Ricketts in their spare room. The Ricketts children love to play in it, tumbling and diving and burying each other; sometimes, it is a sort of treat, they are allowed to sleep in it. Rats like it too, to make nest-es[5] in, and that draws ratsnakes. It is not around, though, for very long at a time. Each family has a set of archaic iron beam scales, and when these scales have weighed out fourteen hundred pounds of cotton it is loaded, if possible during the first of the morning, onto the narrow and high-boarded wagon, and is taken into Cookstown to gin.

39 It is a long tall deep narrow load shored in with weathered wagon-sides and bulged up in a high puff above these sides, and the mule, held far over to the right of the highway to let the cars go by, steps more steadily and even more slowly than ordinary, with a look almost of pomp, dragging the hearse-shaped wagon: its iron wheels on the left grince in the slags of the highway, those on the right in clay: and high upon the load, the father at the reins, the whole of the family is sitting, if it is a small family, or if it is a large, those children whose turn it is, and perhaps the mother too. The husband is dressed in the better of his work clothes; the wife, and the children, in such as they might wear to town on Saturday, or even, some of them, to church, and the children are happy and excited, high on the soft load, and even a woman is taken with it a little, much more soberly, and even the man who is driving, has in the tightness of his jaws, and in his eyes, which meet those of any stranger with the curious challenging and protective, fearful and fierce pride a poor mother shows when her child, dressed in its best, is being curiously looked at; even he who knows best of any of them, is taken with something of the same: and there is in fact about the whole of it some raw, festal quality, some air also of solemn grandeur, this member in the inconceivably huge and slow parade of mule-drawn,

5. Mrs. Gudger's word. Her saying of it was, 'rats likes it to make nest-es in.' It is a common pluralization in the south. There is no Cuteness in it, of speaking by diminutives,and I wonder whether this is not Scottish dialect, and whether they, too, are not innocent of the 'itsybitsying' which the middle-class literacy assumes of them. *Later.* On the proof-sheets is the following note, which I use with thanks: 'Isn't it the Middle-English plural? Chaucer used it for this same word and as a usual plural ending.'

crawling wagons, creaking under the weight of the year's blood-sweated and prayed-over work, on all the roads drawn in, from the utmost runners and ramifications of the slender red roads of all the south and into the southern highways, a wagon every few hundred yards, crested this with a white and this with a black family, all drawn toward those little trembling lodes which are the gins, and all and in each private and silent heart toward that climax of one more year's work which yields so little at best, and nothing so often, and worse to so many hundreds of thousands:

The gin itself, too, the wagons drawn up in line, the people waiting on each wagon, the suspendered white-shirted men on the platform, the emblematic sweep of the grand-shouldered iron beam scales cradling gently on the dark doorway their design of justice, the landlords in their shirt-sleeves at the gin or relaxed in swivels beside the decorated safes in their little offices, the heavy-muscled and bloodfaced young men in baseball caps who tumble the bales with short sharp hooks, the loafers drawn into this place to have their batteries recharged in the violence that is in process here in the bare and weedy outskirts of this bare and brutal town; all this also in its hard, slack, nearly speechless, sullen-eyed way, is dance-like and triumphal: the big blank surfaces of corrugated metal, bright and sick as gas in the sunlight, square their darkness round a shuddering racket that subsumes all easy speaking: the tenant gets his ticket and his bale number, and waits his turn in the long quiet line; the wagon ahead is emptied and moves forward lightly as the mule is cut; he cuts his own load heavily under as the gin head is hoisted; he reaches up for the suction pipe and they let it down to him; he swings and cradles its voracity down through the crest of and round and round his stack of cotton, until the last lint has leapt up from the wagon bed; and all the while the gin is working in the deafening appetites of its metals, only it is his work the gin is digesting now, and standing so close in next its flank, he is intimate with this noise of great energy, cost and mystery; and out at the rear, the tin and ghostly interior of the seed shed, against whose roof and rafters a pipe extends a steady sleet of seed and upon all whose interior surfaces and all the air a dry nightmare fleece like the false snows of Christmas movies hangs shuddering as it might in horror of its just accomplished parturition: and out in front, the last of the cotton snowlike relaxing in pulses down a slide of dark iron into the compress its pure whiteness; and a few moments merely of pressure under the floor level, the air of an off-stage strangling; and the bale is lifted like a theater organ, the presses unlatched, the numbered brass tag attached, the metal ties made fast: it hangs in the light breathing of the scales, his bale, the one he has made, and a little is slivered from it, and its weight and staple length are recorded on his ginning slip, and it is caught with the hooks and tumbled out of the way, his bale of cotton, depersonalized forever now, identical with all others, which shall be melted indistinguishably into an oblivion of fabrics, wounds, bleedings, and wars; he takes his ginning slip to his landlord, and gets his cottonseed money, and does a little buying; and gathers his family together; and leaves town. The exodus from town is even more formal than the parade in was. It has taken almost exactly eighteen minutes to gin each bale, once the waiting was over, and each tenant has done almost exactly the same amount of business afterward, and the empty, light grinding wagons are distributed along the roads in a likewise exact collaboration of time and space apart, that is, the time consumed by ginning plus business, and the space apart which, in that time, a mule traverses at his classic noctambular pace. It is as if those who were drawn in full by the sun and their own effort and sucked dry at a metal heart were restored, were sown once more at large upon the slow breadths of their country, in the precisions of some mechanic and superhuman hand.

41 That is repeated as many times as you have picked a bale. Your field is combed over three, four or five times. The height of the ginning season in that part of the country is early October, and in that time the loaded wagons are on the road before the least crack of daylight, the waiting is endless hours, and the gin is still pulsing and beating after dark. After that comes hog-killing, and the gristing of the corn and milling of the sorghum that were planted late to come ready late; and more urgent and specific meditation of whether or not to move to another man, and of whether you are to be kept; and settlement time; and the sky descends, the air becomes like dark glass, the ground stiffens, the clay honeycombs with frost, the corn and the cotton stand stripped to the naked bone and the trees are black, the odors of pork and woodsmoke sharpen all over the country, the long dark silent sleeping rains stream down in such grieving as nothing shall ever stop, and the houses are cold, fragile drums, and the animals tremble, and the clay is one shapeless sea, and winter has shut.

Thinking Questions: *Form*

1. As he describes the tenant farmers' work, Agee uses quite a few technical terms—"barring," "harrs," "twister," "defender," "broadcast." Can you define the terms from memory now that you have finished the essay? What devices does Agee use to describe the actions represented by these technical terms?

2. Since Agee wants us to *share* the experiences of the farmers, he must relate objective description (concrete images, graphic descriptions of machinery and actions) to the specific emotions and sensations of the farmers. Analyze this passage, (paragraph 22).

> Next after that comes the chopping, and with this the whole family helps down through the children of eight or seven, and by helps, I mean that the family works full time at it. Chopping is a simple and hard job, and a hot one, for by now the sun, though still damp, is very strong, hot with a kind of itchy intensity that is seldom known in northern springs. The work is, simply, thinning the cotton to a stand; hills a foot to sixteen inches apart, two to four stalks to the hill. It is done with an eight to ten-inch hoe-blade. You cut the cotton flush off at the ground, bent just a little above it, with a short sharp blow of the blade of which each stroke is light enough work; but multiplied into the many hundreds in each continuously added hour, it aches first the forearms, which so harden they seem to become one bone, and in time the whole spine.

How well does Agee bring together concrete description—the "ten-inch hoe-blade," "hills a foot to sixteen inches apart"—to create the impression that you are sharing the work of the farmers? How well are the workers' sensations—their *inner feelings* as they thin the cotton strands—supported, explained, and clarified by specific detail, for example, by the detailed description of how cotton is cut off at the ground by a "sharp blow of the blade" which "aches first the forearms . . . and in time the whole spine"?

3. What effect does Agee's use of "you," the second-person pronoun, have on you as you read? Does it make you feel more a part of the action? Do you find it a pushy form of address, an awkward attempt to assure that the reader shares the experiences of the farmers?

4. In the essay "Writing the Descriptive Essay," which concludes this section, we will discuss *subjectivity* and *objectivity*. An objective describer sticks to concrete facts, avoiding opinion and personal impression. Certainly Agee includes a great deal of hard fact and exact, even scientific, description. Yet his overall purpose is just as certainly to create empathy, a sense of sharing and identification, between the reader and the tenant farmers. Is Agee objective or subjective? Does his intention (to create empathy with the farmers) make even his concrete descriptions subjective?

5. Compare one of Agee's descriptive paragraphs with one of Studs Terkel's. How are they different? Which includes more detail? Who writes the longer paragraphs? Which writer uses a simple general-to-specific strategy of organization within most of his paragraphs? Which writer is more concerned with the general thesis behind his description; which is more concerned with the experience itself?

Thinking Questions: *Substance*

1. Agee begins by explaining how he thinks the tenant farmers must feel about their work. Summarize that described feeling in a sentence. What common image does Agee refer to in order to clarify the tenant farmers' feelings about cotton picking?

2. The work Agee describes here is extremely repetitive, year after year, season upon season, task upon task, actions and routines everlastingly repeated. What effects do you think these physical repetitions have on the bodies and minds of the workers?

3. Almost every writer who wishes to describe people as they carry out a specific action or function uses a technique called *objective correlative*. In other words, the writer tells the readers what is going on *inside* the characters by showing them how a particular character sees and experiences the outside world. The objects in a character's environment then come to signify or represent what he or she is thinking and feeling inside. Analyze several paragraphs, such as 36, in which specific pieces of objective description—concrete images, actions, or entire miniature descriptions—are used to demonstrate how the cotton pickers *feel* as they work?

4. In almost every essay, you will need to link together your generalizations (statements that describe or define an entire class or group of ideas or objects) and your specifics (either concrete objects or supporting ideas and evidence). Look at paragraph 34, which is very brief, and show how it draws from the specific evidence and concrete information Agee provides in surrounding paragraphs. Would you find Agee's generalization ("It is simple and terrible work") at all convincing without the extensive concrete description in surrounding paragraphs?

* * *

In the following selections, two essays and a story, Loren Eiseley, Gay Talese, and W. S. Merwin describe working individuals engaged in unique kinds of work. The subjects of each piece, however, are similar in that they all look for two human qualities in their work: the sense of respect and dignity their work creates for them in the eyes of others and the sense of inner worth, of self-fulfilling satisfaction and esteem their work provides them as individuals. Loren Eiseley's late-night reveries and writings provide him, despite or *because of* the sufferings that accompany them, opportunities both for personal growth and understanding and for social status as a writer and intellectual. Floyd Patterson's work provides physical satisfaction and a degree of wealth; it does not, however, provide the inner stability that we, as readers, come to realize has been Patterson's most sought-after and elusive goal. Finally, the Tartoni family, skilled high-wire performers, seem to capture in their work the ideal blend of inner satisfaction and social respect. As you read, work out your own attitudes toward the work of these three individuals. Imagine other jobs that might provide similar combinations of suffering, struggle, and esteem.

One Night's Dying

LOREN EISELEY

1 There is always a soft radiance beyond the bedroom door from a night-light behind my chair. I have lived this way for many years now. I sleep or I do not sleep, and the light makes no difference except if I wake. Then, as I awaken, the dim forms of objects sustain my grip on reality. The familiar chair, the walls of the book-lined study reassert my own existence.

2 I do not lie and toss with doubt any longer, as I did in earlier years. I get up and write, as I am writing now, or I read in the old chair that is as worn as I am. I read philosophy, metaphysics, difficult works that sometime, soon or late, draw a veil over my eyes so that I drowse in my chair.

3 It is not that I fail to learn from these midnight examinations of the world. It is merely that I choose that examination to remain as remote and abstruse as possible. Even so, I cannot always prophesy the result. An obscure line may whirl me into a wide-awake, ferocious concentration in which ideas like animals leap at me out of the dark, in which sudden odd trains of thought drive me inexorably to my desk and paper. I am, in short, a victim of insomnia—sporadic, wearing, violent, and melancholic. In the words of Shakespeare, for me the world "does murder sleep." It has been so since my twentieth year.

4 In that year my father died—a man well loved, the mainstay of our small afflicted family. He died slowly in severe bodily torture. My mother was stone-deaf. I, his son, saw and heard him die. We lived in a place and time not free with the pain-alleviating drugs of later decades. When the episode of many weeks' duration was over, a curious thing happened: I could no longer bear the ticking of the alarm clock in my own bedroom.

5 At first I smothered it with an extra blanket in a box beside my cot, but the ticking persisted as though it came from my own head. I used to lie for hours staring into the dark of the sleeping house, feeling the loneliness that only the sleepless know when the queer feeling comes that it is the sleeping who are alive and those awake are disembodied ghosts. Finally, in desperation, I gave up the attempt to sleep and turned to reading, though it was difficult to concentrate.

6 It was then that human help appeared. My grandmother saw the light burning through the curtains of my door and came to sit with me. A few years later, when I touched her hair in farewell at the beginning of a journey from which I would not return to see her alive, I

knew she had saved my sanity. Into that lonely room at midnight she had come, abandoning her own sleep, in order to sit with one in trouble. We had not talked much, but we had sat together by the lamp, reasserting our common humanity before the great empty dark that is the universe.

7 Grandmother knew nothing of psychiatry. She had not reestablished my sleep patterns, but she had done something more important. She had brought me out of a dark room and retied my thread of life to the living world. Henceforward, by night or day, though I have been subject to the moods of depression or gaiety which are a part of the lives of all of us, I have been able not merely to endure but to make the best of what many regard as an unbearable affliction.

8 It is true that as an educational administrator I can occasionally be caught nodding in lengthy committee meetings, but so, I have observed, can men who come from sound nights on their pillows. Strangely, I, who frequently grow round-eyed and alert as an owl at the stroke of midnight, find it pleasant to nap in daylight among friends. I can roll up on a couch and sleep peacefully while my wife and chatting friends who know my peculiarities keep the daytime universe safely under control. Or so it seems. For, deep-seated in my subconscious, is perhaps the idea that the black bedroom door is the gateway to the tomb.

9 I try in that bedroom to sleep high on two pillows, to have ears and eyes alert. Something shadowy has to be held in place and controlled. At night one has to sustain reality without help. One has to hear lest hearing be lost, see lest sight not return to follow moonbeams across the floor, touch lest the sense of objects vanish. Oh, sleeping, soundlessly sleeping ones, do you ever think who knits your universe together safely from one day's memory to the next? It is the insomniac, not the night policeman on his beat.

10 Many will challenge this point of view. They will say that electric power does the trick, that many a roisterer stumbles down the long street at dawn, after having served his purpose of holding the links of the mad world together. There are parts of the nighttime world, men say to me, that it is just as well I do not know. Go home and sleep, man. Others will keep your giddy world together. Let the thief pass quickly in the shadow, he is awake. Let the juvenile gangs which sidle like bands of evil crabs up from the dark waters of poverty into prosperous streets pass without finding you at midnight.

11 The advice is good, but in the city or the country small things important to our lives have no reporter except as he who does not sleep may observe them. And that man must be disencumbered of reality. He must have no commitments to the dark, as do the murderer and thief. Only he must see, though what he sees may come from the night side of the planet that no man knows well. For even in the early

dawn, while men lie unstirring in their sleep or stumble sleepy-eyed to work, some single episode may turn the whole world for a moment into the place of marvel that it is but that we grow too day-worn to accept.

12 For example, I call the place where I am writing now the bay of broken things. In the February storms, spume wraiths climb the hundred-foot cliff to fight and fall like bitter rain in the moonlight upon the cabin roof. The earth shakes from the drum roll of the surf. I lie awake and watch through the window beyond my bed. This is no ticking in my brain; this is the elemental night of chaos. This is the sea chewing its million-year way into the heart of the continent.

13 The caves beneath the cliff resound with thunder. Again those warring wraiths shoot high over the house. Impelled as though I were a part of all those leaping ghosts, I dress in the dark and come forth. With my back against the door, like an ancient necromancer, I hurl my mind into the white spray and try to summon back, among those leaping forms, the faces and features of the dead I know. The shapes rise endlessly, but they pass inland before the wind, indifferent to my mortal voice.

14 I walk a half mile to a pathway that descends upon a little beach. Below me is a stretch of white sand. No shell is ever found unbroken, even on quiet days, upon that shore. Everything comes over the rocks to seaward. Wood is riven into splinters; the bones of seamen and of sea lions are pounded equally into white and shining sand. Throughout the night the long black rollers, like lines of frothing cavalry, form ranks, drum towering forward, and fall, fall till the mind is dizzy with the spume that fills it. I wait in the shelter of a rock for daybreak. At last the sea eases a trifle. The tide is going out.

15 I stroll shivering along the shore, and there, exposed in inescapable nakedness, I see the elemental cruelty of the natural world. A broken-winged gull, hurled by the wind against the cliff, runs before me wearily along the beach. It will starve or, mercifully, the dogs will find it. I try not to hurry it, and walk on. A little later in a quieter bend of the shore, I see ahead of me a bleeding, bedraggled blot on the edge of the white surf. As I approach, it starts warily to its feet. We look at each other. It is a wild duck, also with a shattered wing. It does not run ahead of me like the longer-limbed gull. Before I can cut off its retreat it waddles painfully from its brief refuge into the water.

16 The sea continues to fall heavily. The duck dives awkwardly, but with long knowledge and instinctive skill, under the fall of the first two inshore waves. I see its head working seaward. A long green roller, far taller than my head, rises and crashes forward. The black head of the waterlogged duck disappears. This is the way wild things die, without question, without knowledge of mercy in the universe, knowing only themselves and their own pathway to the end. I wonder,

walking farther up the beach, if the man who shot that bird will die as well.

17 This is the chaos before man came, before sages imbued with pity walked the earth. Indeed it is true, and in my faraway study my hands have often touched with affection the backs of the volumes which line my shelves. Nevertheless, I have endured the nights and mornings of the city. I have seen old homeless men who have slept for hours sitting upright on ledges along the outer hallway of one of the great Eastern stations straighten stiffly in the dawn and limp away with feigned businesslike aloofness before the approach of the policeman on his rounds. I know that on these cold winter mornings sometimes a man, like the pigeons I have seen roosting as closely as possible over warm hotel air vents, will fall stiffly and not awaken. It is true that there are shelters for the homeless, but some men, like their ice-age forebears, prefer their independence to the end.

18 The loneliness of the city was brought home to me one early sleepless morning, not by men like me tossing in lonely rooms, not by poverty and degradation, not by old men trying with desperate futility to be out among others in the great roaring hive, but by a single one of those same pigeons which I had seen from my hotel window, looking down at midnight upon the smoking air vents and chimneys.

19 The pigeon, *Columba livia,* is the city bird *par excellence*. He is a descendant of the rock pigeon that in the Old World lived among the cliffs and crevices above the caves that early man inhabited. He has been with us since our beginning and has adapted as readily as ourselves to the artificial cliffs of man's first cities. He has known the Roman palaces and the cities of Byzantium. His little flat feet, suited to high and precarious walking, have sauntered in the temples of vanished gods as readily as in New York's old Pennsylvania Station. In my dim morning strolls, waiting for the restaurants to open, I have seen him march quickly into the back end of a delivery truck while the driver was inside a store engaged in his orders with the proprietor. Yet for all its apparent tolerance of these highly adapted and often comic birds, New York also has a beach of broken things more merciless than the reefs and rollers of the ocean shore.

20 One morning, strolling sleepless as usual toward early breakfast time in Manhattan, I saw a sick pigeon huddled at an uncomfortable slant against a building wall on the street corner. I felt sorry for the bird, but I had no box, no instrument of help, and I had learned long ago that pursuing wounded birds on city streets is a hopeless, dangerous activity. Pigeons, like men, die in scores every day in New York. As I hesitantly walked on, however, I wondered why the doomed bird was assuming such a desperately contorted position under the cornice that projected slightly over it.

21 At this moment I grew aware of something I had heard more loudly

in European streets as the factory whistles blew, but never in such intensity as here, even though American shoes are built of softer materials. All around me the march of people was intensifying. It was New York on the way to work. Space was shrinking before my eyes. The tread of innumerable feet passed from an echo to the steady murmuring of a stream, then to a drumming. A dreadful robot rhythm began to rack my head, a sound like the boots of Nazis in their heyday of power. I was carried along in an irresistible surge of bodies.

22 A block away, jamming myself between a waste-disposal basket and a lightpost, I managed to look back. No one hesitated at that corner. The human tide pressed on, jostling and pushing. My bird had vanished under that crunching, multifooted current as remorselessly as the wounded duck under the indifferent combers of the sea. I watched this human ocean, of which I was an unwilling droplet, rolling past, its individual faces like whitecaps passing on a night of a storm, fixed, merciless, indifferent; man in the mass marching like the machinery of which he is already a replaceable part, toward desks, computers, missiles, and machines, marching like the waves toward his own death with a conscious ruthlessess no watery shore could ever duplicate. I have never returned to search in that particular street for the face of humanity. I prefer the endlessly rolling pebbles of the tide, the moonstones polished by the pulling moon.

23 And yet, plunged as I am in dire memories and midnight reading, I have said that it is the sufferer from insomnia who knits the torn edges of men's dreams together in the hour before dawn. It is he who from his hidden, winter vantage point sees the desperate high-hearted bird fly through the doorway of the grand hotel while the sleepy doorman nods, a deed equivalent in human terms to that of some starving wretch evading Peter at heaven's gate, and an act, I think, very likely to be forgiven.

24 It is a night more mystical, however, that haunts my memory. Around me I see again the parchment of old books and remember how, on one rare evening, I sat in the shadows while a firefly flew from volume to volume lighting its small flame, as if in literate curiosity. Choosing the last title it had illuminated, I came immediately upon these words from St. Paul: "Beareth all things, believeth all things, hopeth all things, endureth all things." In this final episode I shall ask you to bear with me and also to believe.

25 I sat, once more in the late hours of darkness, in the airport of a foreign city. I was tired as only both the sufferer from insomnia and the traveler can be tired. I had missed a plane and had almost a whole night's wait before me. I could not sleep. The long corridor was deserted. Even the cleaning women had passed by.

26 In that white efficient glare I grew ever more depressed and weary. I was tired of the endless comings and goings of my profession; I was

tired of customs officers and police. I was lonely for home. My eyes hurt. I was, unconsciously perhaps, looking for that warm stone, that hawthorn leaf, where, in the words of the poet, man trades in at last his wife and friend. I had an ocean to cross; the effort seemed unbearable. I rested my aching head upon my hand.

27 Later, beginning at the far end of that desolate corridor, I saw a man moving slowly toward me. In a small corner of my eye I merely noted him. He limped, painfully and grotesquely, upon a heavy cane. He was far away, and it was no matter to me. I shifted the unpleasant mote out of my eye.

28 But, after a time, I could still feel him approaching, and in one of those white moments of penetration which are so dreadful, my eyes were drawn back to him as he came on. With an anatomist's eye I saw this amazing conglomeration of sticks and broken, misshapen pulleys which make up the body of man. Here was an apt subject, and I flew to a raging mental dissection. How could anyone, I contended, trapped in this mechanical thing of joints and sliding wires expect the acts it performed to go other than awry?

29 The man limped on, relentlessly.

30 How, oh God, I entreated, did we become trapped within this substance out of which we stare so hopelessly upon our own eventual dissolution? How for a single minute could we dream or imagine that thought would save us, children deliver us, from the body of this death? Not in time, my mind rang with my despair; not in mortal time, not in this place, not anywhere in the world would blood be stanched, or the dark wrong be forever righted, or the parted be rejoined. Not in this time, not mortal time. The substance was too gross, our utopias bought with too much pain.

31 The man was almost upon me, breathing heavily, lunging and shuffling upon his cane. Though an odor emanated from him, I did not draw back. I had lived with death too many years. And then this strange thing happened, which I do not mean physically and cannot explain. The man entered me. From that moment I saw him no more. For a moment I was contorted within his shape, and then out of his body—our bodies, rather—there arose some inexplicable sweetness of union, some understanding between spirit and body which I had never before experienced. Was it I, the joints and pulleys only, who desired this peace so much?

32 I limped with growing age as I gathered up my luggage. Something of that terrible passer lingered in my bones, yet I was released, the very room had dilated. As I went toward my plane the words the firefly had found for me came automatically to my lips. "Beareth all things," believe, believe. It is thus that one day and the next are welded together, that one night's dying becomes tomorrow's birth. I, who do not sleep, can tell you this.

Thinking Questions: *Form*

1. Notice how this essay is divided into clusters or blocks of paragraphs that are organized around specific descriptions of experiences in the writer's past life. Select one paragraph cluster (for example, the climactic final cluster, paragraphs 25 through 32) and define its significance in relation to the purpose of the entire essay. What does it say about human beings in general, about the necessity of thinking, about the relationship between work and survival?

2. Reread one of Eiseley's descriptive paragraph clusters and write out a short statement of purpose for that cluster. What generality, either in the essay itself or in your mind as you read it, serves to unify and clarify the purpose of the cluster? (See, for instance, the cluster including paragraphs 12 to 16, in which Eiseley describes his seaside walks to emphasize the relentless, lonely quality of the lives of all living things.)

3. Is this essay primarily subjective or objective, or a combination of both? Support your answer by referring to passages that either show or tell or do both. Analyze the vocabulary of the essay. Does the vocabulary suggest an attitude toward humanity in general, the function of the human mind and imagination? Writing *shows* when the writer shares the details of an experience as it impressed itself on his senses; writing *tells* when it emphasizes the general ideas that resulted from the experience rather than the experience itself.

4. Argue either for or against this resolution:

> Some men should work by the sweat of their brows; others should think about the results of other men's sweat.

In Communist China many intellectuals are forced to spend at least some time doing manual labor to ensure their comprehension of the social necessity and skill of physical labor. Should work always entail both physical and mental effort? Should a society, at the least, encourage mutual respect between those who work with their hands and with their minds? Go back through your own experience and find and describe personal illustrations to defend your position, much as Eiseley does in his essay. Notice the transitional sentences, pronouns, and repetitions that are used to provide coherence in Eiseley's essay. See especially the transitions between paragraphs 11 and 12 and the use of repeated structure in the opening sentences of paragraphs 14 and 15—all for coherence. Coherence is the art of clarifying connections and relationships in writing. Apply a few of Eiseley's transitional devices as you link your own experiences together to support a thesis.

Thinking Questions: *Substance*

1. Write a short essay in which you define *work*. Use a definition that draws from Eiseley's essay, as illustration and example. Is Eiseley *working* by traditional, nine-to-five, time-clock standards? After reading the essay,

do you have any suggestions as to what causes the author's insomnia? Is it his father's death? The ticking alarm clock? The author's desire to produce something before all time runs out?

2. Eiseley has learned "not merely to endure but to make the best of what many regard as an unbearable affliction." His insomnia, in other words, provides time for work, for thinking, for deep speculation and thought. Why is it that Eiseley finds it easier to sleep when others work and to work while others sleep (see paragraph 8)?

3. Compare hard physical labor with the hard mental work described by Eiseley. Which is the most difficult, and why? How many jobs combine physical and mental exertion? After you have read Gay Talese's essay on Floyd Patterson, compare Patterson's work in preparation for prize fighting with Eiseley's struggles with insomnia and his writing.

4. It is the thinker's work to weld together the disparate, disjointed happenings of the world. Thinkers do not produce a tangible product; they produce order, connection, coherence—they *make sense* out of a chaos of experience. Do you think people ought to be paid for the kind of thinking that has little or nothing to do with producing a tangible commodity? Is that terribly impractical? What type of work—thinking, doing, or a combination of the two—would you prefer? How does literature—usually the product of reflection and imagination—fit in with American ideals of work and production? How does the average person view the artist or intellectual in America?

Floyd Patterson

GAY TALESE

1 At the foot of a mountain in upstate New York, about sixty miles from Manhattan, there is an abandoned country clubhouse with a dusty dance floor, upturned barstools, and an untuned piano; and the only sounds heard around the place at night come from the big white house behind it—the clanging sounds of garbage cans being toppled by raccoons, skunks, and stray cats making their nocturnal raids down from the mountain.

2 The white house seems deserted, too; but occasionally, when the animals become too clamorous, a light will flash on, a window will open, and a Coke bottle will come flying through the darkness and smash against the cans. But mostly the animals are undisturbed until daybreak, when the rear door of the white house swings open and a

broad-shouldered Negro appears in gray sweat clothes with a white towel around his neck.

3 He runs down the steps, quickly passes the garbage cans and proceeds at a trot down the dirt road beyond the country club toward the highway. Sometimes he stops along the road and throws a flurry of punches at imaginary foes, each jab punctuated by hard gasps of his breathing—"hegh-hegh-hegh-hegh"—and then, reaching the highway, he turns and soon disappears up the mountain.

4 At this time of morning farm trucks are on the road, and the drivers wave at the runner. And later in the morning other motorists see him, and a few stop suddenly at the curb and ask: "Say, aren't *you* Floyd Patterson?"

5 "No," says Floyd Patterson. "I'm his brother, Raymond."

The motorists move on, but recently a man on foot, a disheveled man who seemed to have spent the night outdoors, staggered behind the runner along the road and yelled, "Hey, Floyd Patterson!"

"No, I'm his brother, Raymond."

"Don't tell *me* you're not Floyd Patterson. I know what Floyd Patterson looks like."

"Okay," Patterson said, shrugging, "if you want me to be Floyd Patterson, I'll be Floyd Patterson."

"So let me have your autograph," said the man, handing him a rumpled piece of paper and a pencil.

He signed it—"Raymond Patterson."

6 One hour later Floyd Patterson was jogging his way back down the dirt path toward the white house, the towel over his head absorbing the sweat from his brow. He lives alone in a two-room apartment in the rear of the house, and has remained there in almost complete seclusion since getting knocked out a second time by Sonny Liston.

7 In the smaller room is a large bed he makes up himself, several record albums he rarely plays, a telephone that seldom rings. The larger room has a kitchen on one side and on the other, adjacent to a sofa, is a fireplace from which are hung boxing trunks and T-shirts to dry, and a photograph of him when he was the champion, and also a television set. The set is usually on except when Patterson is sleeping, or when he is sparring across the road inside the clubhouse (the ring is rigged over what was once the dance floor), or when, in a rare moment of painful honesty, he reveals to a visitor what it is like to be the loser.

8 "Oh, I would give up anything to just be able to work with Liston, to box with him somewhere where nobody would see us, and to see if I could get past three minutes with him," Patterson was saying, wiping his face with the towel, pacing slowly around the room near the sofa. "I *know* I can do better. . . . Oh, I'm not talking about a rematch. Who would pay a nickel for another Patterson-Liston match?

I know *I* wouldn't. . . . But all I want to do is get past the first round."

9 Then he said, "You have no idea how it is in the first round. You're out there with all those people around you, and those cameras, and the whole world looking in, and all that movement, that excitement, and 'The Star-Spangled Banner,' and the whole nation hoping you'll win, including President Kennedy. And do you know what this all does? It blinds you, just blinds you. And then the bell rings, and you go at Liston and he's coming at you, and you're not even aware that there's a referee in the ring with you.

10 ". . . Then you can't remember much of the rest, because you don't want to. . . . All you recall is, all of a sudden, you're getting up, and the referee is saying, 'You all right?' and you say, 'Of *course* I'm all right,' and he says, 'What's your name?' and you say 'Patterson.'

11 "And then, suddenly, with all this screaming around you, you're down again, and know you have to get up, but you're extremely groggy, and the referee is pushing you back, and your trainer is in there with a towel, and people are all standing up, and your eyes focus directly at no one person—you're sort of floating.

12 "It's not a *bad* feeling when you're knocked out," he said. "It's a *good* feeling, actually. It's not painful, just a sharp grogginess. You don't see angels or stars; you're on a pleasant cloud. After Liston hit me in Nevada, I felt, for about four or five seconds, that everybody in the arena was actually in the ring with me, circled around me like a family, and you feel warmth toward all the people in the arena after you're knocked out. You feel lovable to all the people. And you want to reach out and kiss everybody—men and women—and after the Liston fight somebody told me I actually blew a kiss to the crowd from the ring. I don't remember that. But I guess it's true because that's the way you feel during the four or five seconds after a knock-out. . . .

13 "But then," Patterson went on, still pacing, "this good feeling leaves you. You realize where you are, and what you're doing there, and what has just happened to you. And what follows is a hurt, a confused hurt—not a physical hurt—it's a hurt combined with anger; it's a what-will-people-think hurt; it's an ashamed-of-my-own-ability hurt . . . and all you want then is a hatch door in the middle of the ring—a hatch door that will open and let you fall through and land in your dressing room instead of having to get out of the ring and face those people. The worst thing about losing is having to walk out of the ring and face those people. . . ."

14 Then Patterson walked over to the stove and put on a kettle for tea. He remained silent for a few moments. Through the walls could be heard the footsteps and voices of the sparring partners and the trainer, who live in the front of the house. Soon they would be in the country club getting things ready should Patterson wish to spar.

15 Patterson wants to continue as a prizefighter but his wife, whom he rarely sees any more, and most of his friends think he should quit. They point out that he does not need the money. Even he admits that from investments alone on his $8,000,000 gross earnings he should have an annual income of about $35,000 for the next twenty-five years. But Patterson, who is only twenty-eight years old and barely scratched, cannot believe that he is finished. He cannot help but think that it was something more than Liston that destroyed him—a strange, psychological force was also involved—and unless he can fully understand what it was, and learn to deal with it in the boxing ring, he may never be able to live peacefully anywhere but under this mountain. Nor will he ever be able to discard the false whiskers and mustache that, ever since Johansson beat him in 1959, he has carried with him in a small attaché case into each fight so he can slip out of the stadium unrecognized should he lose.

16 "I often wonder what other fighters feel, and what goes through their minds when they lose," Patterson said, placing the cups of tea on the table. "I've wanted so much to talk to another fighter about all this, to compare thoughts, to see if he feels some of the same things I've felt. But who can you talk to? Most fighters don't talk much anyway. And I can't even look another fighter in the eye at a weigh-in, for some reason.

17 "At the Liston weigh-in, the sportswriters noticed this, and said it showed I was afraid. But that's not it. I can never look *any* fighter in the eye because . . . well, because we're going to fight, which isn't a nice thing, and because . . . well, once I actually did look a fighter in the eye. It was a long, long time ago. I must have been in the amateurs then. . . . And when I looked at this fighter, I saw he had such a nice face. . . . And then he looked at *me* . . . and *smiled* at me . . . and *I* smiled back! . . . It was strange, very strange. When a guy can look at another guy and smile like that, I don't think they have any business fighting.

18 "I don't remember what happened in that fight, and I don't remember what the guy's name was. I only remember that, ever since, I have never looked another fighter in the eye. . . ."

19 The telephone rang in the bedroom. Patterson got up to answer it. It was his wife, Sandra. So he excused himself, shutting the bedroom door behind him.

20 Sandra Patterson and their four children live in a $100,000 home in an upper-middle-class white neighborhood in Scarsdale, New York. Floyd Patterson feels uncomfortable in this home surrounded by a manicured lawn and stuffed with soft furniture, and, since losing his title to Liston, he has preferred living full time at his camp, which his children have come to know as "Daddy's house." The children, the eldest of whom is a six-year-old daughter named Jeannie, do not

know exactly what their father does for a living. But Jeannie, who watched the last Liston-Patterson fight on closed-circuit television, accepted the explanation that her father performs in a kind of game where the men take turns pushing one another down; he had his turn pushing them down, and now it is their turn.

21 The bedroom door opened again, and Floyd Patterson, shaking his head was very angry and nervous.

22 "I'm not going to work out today," he said. "I'm going to fly down to Scarsdale. Those boys are picking on Jeannie again. She's the only Negro in this school, and the older kids give her a rough time, and some of the older boys tease her and lift up her dress all the time. Yesterday she went home crying, and so today I'm going down there and plan to wait outside the school for those boys to come out, and . . ."

"How old are they?" he was asked.

"Teenagers," he said. "Old enough for a left hook."

23 Patterson telephoned his pilot friend, Ted Hanson, who stays at the camp and does public relations work for him, and has helped teach Patterson to fly. Five minutes later Hanson, a lean white man with a crewcut and glasses, was knocking on the door; and ten minutes later both were in the car that Patterson was driving almost recklessly over the narrow, winding country roads toward the airport, about six miles from the camp.

24 "Sandra is afraid I'll cause trouble; she's worried about what I'll do to those boys; she doesn't want trouble!" Patterson snapped, swerving around a hill and giving his car more gas. "She's just not firm enough! She's afraid. . . . She was afraid to tell me about that grocery man who's been making passes at her. It took her a long time before she told me about that dishwasher repairman who comes over and calls her *'baby.'* They all know I'm away so much. And that dishwasher repairman's been to my home about four, five times this month already. That machine breaks down every week. I guess he fixes it so it breaks down every week. Last time, I laid a trap. I waited forty-five minutes for him to come, but then he didn't show up. I was going to grab him and say, 'How would you like it if I called *your* wife *"baby"?* You'd feel like punching me in the nose, wouldn't you? Well, that's what I'm going to do—if you ever call her *"baby"* again. You call her Mrs. Patterson; or Sandra, if you know her. But you don't know her, so call her Mrs. Patterson.' . . . And then I told Sandra that these men, this type of white man, he just wants to have some fun with colored women. He'll never marry a colored woman, just wants to have some fun. . . ."

25 Now he was driving into the airport's parking lot. Directly ahead, roped to the grass air strip, was the single-engine, green Cessna that Patterson bought and learned to fly in Denver before the second

Liston fight. Flying was a thing Patterson had always feared—a fear shared by, maybe inherited from, his manager, Cus D'Amato, who still will not fly.

26 D'Amato, who began training Patterson when the fighter was fourteen years old and exerted a tremendous influence over his psyche, is a strange but fascinating man of fifty-six who is addicted to spartanism and self-denial and is possessed by suspicion and fear: he avoids subways because he fears someone might push him onto the tracks; never has married because he believes a wife might be duped by his enemies; never reveals his home address because he suspects snipers.

27 "I must keep my enemies confused," D'Amato once explained. "When they are confused, then I can do a job for my fighters. What I do not want in life, however, is a sense of security; the moment a person knows security, his senses are dulled—and he begins to die. I also do not want many pleasures in life; I believe the more pleasures you get out of living, the more fear you have of dying."

28 Until a few years ago, D'Amato did most of Patterson's talking, and ran things like an Italian *padrone*. But later Patterson, the maturing son, rebelled against the Father Image. After losing to Sonny Liston the first time—a fight D'Amato had urged Patterson to resist—Patterson took flying lessons. And before the second Liston fight Patterson had conquered his fear of height, was master at the controls, was filled with renewed confidence—and knew, too, that even if he lost he at least possessed a vehicle that could get him out of town, fast.

29 But it didn't. After the fight, the little Cessna, weighed down by too much luggage, became overheated ninety miles outside of Las Vegas. Patterson and his pilot companion, having no choice but to turn back, radioed the airfield and arranged for the rental of a larger plane. When they landed, the Vegas air terminal was filled with people leaving town after the fight. Patterson hid in the shadows behind a hangar. His beard was packed in the trunk. But nobody saw him.

30 Later the pilot flew Patterson's Cessna back to New York alone. And Patterson flew in the larger, rented plane. He was accompanied on this flight by Ted Hanson, a friendly forty-two-year-old, thrice-divorced Californian, who once was a crop duster, a bartender, and a cabaret hoofer; later he became a pilot instructor in Las Vegas, and it was there that he met Patterson. The two became good friends. And, when Patterson asked Hanson to help fly the rented plane back to New York, Hanson did not hesitate, even though he had a slight hangover that night—partly due to being depressed by Liston's victory, partly to being slugged in a bar by a drunk after objecting to some unflattering things the drunk had said about the fight.

31 Once in the airplane, however, Ted Hanson became very alert. He had to be because, after the plane had cruised awhile at ten thousand

feet, Floyd Patterson's mind seemed to wander back to the ring, and the plane would drift off course, and Hanson would say, "Floyd, Floyd, how's about getting back on course?" and then Patterson's head would snap up and his eyes would flash toward the dials. And everything would be all right for a while. But then he was back in the arena, reliving the fight, hardly believing that it had really happened. . . .

32 ". . . And I kept thinking, as I flew out of Vegas that night, of all those months of training before the fight, all the roadwork, all the sparring, all the months away from Sandra . . . thinking of the time in camp when I wanted to stay up until 11:15 p.m. to watch a certain movie on the Late Show, but I didn't because I had roadwork the next morning. . . .

33 "And I was thinking about how good I'd felt before the fight, as I lay on the table in the dressing room. . . . I remember thinking, 'You're in excellent physical condition, you're in good mental condition—but are you vicious?' But you tell yourself, 'Viciousness is not important now, don't think about it now; a championship fight's at stake, and that's important enough and, who knows? maybe you'll get vicious once the bell rings.'

34 "And so you lay there trying to get a little sleep . . . but you're only in a twilight zone, half-asleep, and you're interrupted every once in a while by voices out in the hall, some guy's yelling, 'Hey, Jack,' or 'Hey, Al,' or, 'Hey, get those four-rounders into the ring.' And when you hear that you think, 'They're not ready for you yet.' So you lay there . . . and wonder, 'Where will I be tomorrow?' 'Where will I be three hours from now?' . . . Oh, you think all kinds of thoughts, some thoughts completely unrelated to the fight . . . you wonder whether you ever paid your mother-in-law back for all those stamps she bought a year ago . . . and you remember that time at 2 a.m. when Sandra tripped on the steps while bringing a bottle up to the baby . . . and then you get mad and ask: *'What am I thinking about these things for?'* . . . and you try to sleep . . . but then the door opens and somebody says to somebody else, 'Hey, is somebody gonna go to Liston's dressing room to watch 'em bandage up?'

35 "And so then you know it's about time to get ready. . . . You open your eyes. You get off the table. You glove up, you loosen up. Then Liston's trainer walks in. He looks at you, he smiles. He feels the bandages and later he says, 'Good luck, Floyd,' and you think, 'He didn't have to say that; he must be a nice guy.'

36 "And then you go out, and it's the long walk, always a long walk, and you think, 'What am I gonna be when I come back this way?' Then you climb into the ring. You notice Billy Eckstine at ringside leaning over to talk to somebody, and you see the reporters—some you like, some you don't like—and then it's 'The Star-Spangled Banner,' and the cameras are rolling, and the bell rings. . . .

37 "How could the same thing happen twice? How? That's all I kept thinking after the knockout. . . . Was I fooling these people all these years? . . . Was I ever the champion? . . . And then they lead you out of the ring . . . and up the aisle you go, past those people, and all you want is to get to your dressing room, fast . . . but the trouble was in Las Vegas they made a wrong turn along the aisle, and when we got to the end, there was no dressing room there . . . and we had to walk all the way back down the aisle, past the same people, and they must have been thinking, 'Patterson's not only knocked out, but he can't even find his dressing room.' . . .

38 "In the dressing room I had a headache. Liston didn't hurt me physically—a few days later I only felt a twitching nerve in my teeth—it was nothing like some fights I've had: like that Dick Wagner fight in '54 when he beat my body so bad I was urinating blood for days. . . . After the Liston fight, I just went into the bathroom, shut the door behind me, and looked at myself in the mirror. I just looked at myself, and asked, 'What happened?' and then they started pounding on the door, and saying, 'C'm'on out, Floyd, c'm'on out; the press is here, Cus is here, c'm'on out, Floyd.' . . .

39 "And so I went out, and they asked questions, but what can you say? . . . What you're thinking about is all those months of training, all the conditioning, all the depriving; and you think, 'I didn't have to run that extra mile, didn't have to spar that day, *I could have stayed up that night in camp and watched the Late Show. . . . I could have fought this fight tonight in no condition.' . . .*"

40 "Floyd, Floyd," Hanson had said, "let's get back on course. . . ."

41 Again Patterson would snap out of his reverie, and refocus on the Omnirange, and get his flying under control. After landing in New Mexico, and then in Ohio, Floyd Patterson and Ted Hanson brought the little plane into the New York air strip near the fight camp. The green Cessna that had been flown back by the other pilot was already there, roped to the grass at precisely the same spot it was on this day five months later, on this day when Floyd Patterson was planning to fly it toward perhaps another fight—a fight with some schoolboys in Scarsdale who had been lifting up his six-year-old daughter's dress.

42 Patterson and Ted Hanson untied the plane, and Patterson got a rag and wiped from the windshield the splotches of insects. Then he walked around behind the plane, inspected the tail, checked under the fuselage, then peered down between the wing and the flaps to make sure all the screws were tight. He seemed suspicious of something. D'Amato would have been pleased.

43 "If a guy wants to get rid of you," Patterson explained, "all he has to do is remove these little screws here. Then, when you try to come in for a landing, the flaps fall off, and you crash."

44 Then Patterson got into the cockpit and started the engine. A few moments later, with Hanson beside him, Patterson was racing the little plane over the grassy field, then soaring over the weeds, then flying high above the gentle hills and trees. It was a nice take-off.

45 Since it was only a forty-minute flight to the Westchester airport, where Sandra Patterson would be waiting with a car, Floyd Patterson did all the flying. The trip was uneventful until, suddenly behind a cloud, he flew into heavy smoke that hovered above a forest fire. His visibility gone, he was forced to the instruments. And at this precise moment a fly that had been buzzing in the back of the cockpit flew up front and landed on the instrument panel in front of Patterson. He glared at the fly, watched it crawl slowly up the windshield, then shot a quick smash with his palm against the glass. He missed. The fly buzzed safely past Patterson's ear, bounced off the back of the cockpit, circled around.

46 "This smoke won't keep up," Hanson assured. "You can level off."

Patterson leveled off.

47 He flew easily for a few moments. Then the fly buzzed to the front again, zigzagging before Patterson's face, then landed and proceeded to crawl across the panel. Patterson watched it, squinted. Then he slammed down at it with a quick right hand. Missed.

48 Ten minutes later, his nerves still on edge, Patterson began the descent. He picked up the radio microphone—"Westchester tower . . . Cessna 2729 uniform . . . three miles northwest . . . land in one-six on final. . . ." And then, after an easy landing, he climbed quickly out of the cockpit and strode toward his wife's station wagon outside the terminal.

49 But along the way a small man smoking a cigar turned toward Patterson, waved at him, and said, "Say, excuse me, but aren't you . . . aren't you . . . Sonny Liston?"

50 Patterson stopped. He glared at the man, bewildered. He wasn't sure whether it was a joke or an insult, and he really did not know what to do.

51 "Aren't you Sonny Liston?" the man repeated, quite serious.

"No," Patterson said, quickly passing by the man, "I'm his brother."

52 When he reached Mrs. Patterson's car, he asked, "How much time till school lets out?"

53 "About fifteen minutes," she said, starting up the engine. Then she said, "Oh, Floyd, I just should have told Sister, I shouldn't have . . ."

54 "*You* tell Sister; *I'll* tell the boys. . . ."

55 Mrs. Patterson drove as quickly as she could into Scarsdale, with Patterson shaking his head and telling Ted Hanson in the back, "Really can't understand these school kids. This is a religious school, and they want $20,000 for a glass window—and yet, some of them

carry these racial prejudices, and it's mostly the Jews who are shoulder-to-shoulder with us, and . . ."

56 "Oh, Floyd," cried his wife, "Floyd, *I* have to get along here. *You're* not here, *you* don't live here, *I* . . ."

57 She arrived at the school just as the bell began to ring.

It was a modern building at the top of the hill, and on the lawn was the statue of a saint and, behind it, a large white cross.

58 "There's Jeannie," said Mrs. Patterson.

"Hurry, call her over here," Patterson said.

"Jeannie! Come over here, honey."

59 The little girl, wearing a blue school uniform and cap, and clasping books in front of her, came running down the path toward the station wagon.

60 "Jeannie," Floyd Patterson said, rolling down his window, "point out the boys who lifted your dress."

61 Jeannie turned and watched as several students came down the path; then she pointed to a tall, thin curly-haired boy walking with four other boys, all about twelve to fourteen years of age.

62 "Hey," Patterson called to him, "can I see you for a minute?"

63 All five boys came to the side of the car. They looked Patterson directly in the eye. They seemed not at all intimidated by him.

64 "You the one that's been lifting up my daughter's dress?" Patterson asked the boy who had been singled out.

65 "Nope," the boy said, casually.

"Nope?" Patterson said, caught off guard by the reply.

"Wasn't him, Mister," said another boy. "Probably was his little brother, Dennis."

66 Patterson looked at Jeannie. But she was speechless, uncertain. The five boys remained there, waiting for Patterson to do something.

67 "Well, er, where's Dennis?" Patterson asked.

"Hey, Dennis!" one of the boys yelled. "Dennis come over here."

68 Dennis walked toward them. He resembled his older brother; he had freckles on his small, upturned nose, had blue eyes, dark curly hair and, as he approached the station wagon, he seemed equally unintimidated by Patterson.

69 "You been lifting up my daughter's dress?"

"Nope," said Dennis.

"Nope!" Patterson repeated, frustrated.

"Nope, I wasn't lifting it," Dennis said. "I was just touching it a little . . ."

70 The other boys stood around the car looking down at Patterson, and other students crowded behind them, and nearby Patterson saw several white parents standing next to their parked cars; he became self-conscious, began to tap nervously with his fingers against the dashboard. He could not raise his voice without creating an un-

pleasant scene, yet could not retreat gracefully; so his voice went soft, and he said finally, "Look, Dennis, I want you to stop it. I won't tell your mother—that might get you in trouble—but don't do it again, okay?"

71 "Okay."

The boys calmly turned and walked, in a group, up the street.

72 Sandra Patterson said nothing. Jeannie opened the door, sat in the front seat next to her father, and took out a small blue piece of paper that a nun had given her and handed it across to Mrs. Patterson. But Floyd Patterson snatched it. He read it. Then he paused, put the paper down, and quietly announced, dragging out the words, *"She didn't do her religion."*

73 Patterson now wanted to get out of Scarsdale. He wanted to return to camp.

74 After stopping at the Patterson home in Scarsdale and picking up Floyd Patterson, Jr., who is three, Mrs. Patterson drove them all back to the airport. Jeannie and Floyd, Jr., were seated in the back of the plane, and then Mrs. Patterson drove the station wagon alone up to camp, planning to return to Scarsdale that evening with the children.

75 It was 4 p.m. when Floyd Patterson got back to the camp, and the shadows were falling on the country club, and on the tennis court routed by weeds, and on the big white house in front of which not a single automobile was parked. All was deserted and quiet; it was a loser's camp.

76 The children ran to play inside the country club; Patterson walked slowly toward his apartment to dress for the workout.

77 "What could I do with those schoolboys?" he asked. "What can you do to kids of that age?"

78 It still seemed to bother him, the effrontery of the boys, the realization that he had somehow failed, the probability that, had those same boys heckled someone in Liston's family, the school yard would have been littered with limbs.

79 While Patterson and Liston both are products of the slum, and while both began as thieves, Patterson had been tamed in a special school with help from a gentle spinster; later he became a Catholic convert, and learned not to hate. Still later he bought a dictionary, adding to his vocabulary such words as "vicissitude" and "enigma." And when he regained his championship from Johansson, he became the great black hope of the Urban League.

80 He proved that it is not only possible to rise out of a Negro slum and succeed as a sportsman, but also to develop into an intelligent, sensitive, law-abiding citizen. In proving this, however, and in taking pride in it, Patterson seemed to lose part of himself. He lost part of his hunger, his anger—and as he walked up the steps into his apart-

ment, he was saying, "I became the good guy. . . . After Liston won the title, I kept hoping that he would change into a good guy, too. That would have relieved me of the responsibility, and maybe I could have been more of the bad guy. But he didn't. . . . It's okay to be the good guy when you're winning. But when you're losing, it is no good being the good guy. . . ."

81 Patterson took off his shirt and trousers and, moving some books on the bureau to one side, put down his watch, his cufflinks and a clip of bills.

82 "Do you do much reading?" he was asked.

83 "No," he said. "In fact, you know I've never finished reading a book in my whole life? I don't know why. I just feel that no writer today has anything for me; I mean, none of them has felt more deeply than I have, and I have nothing to learn from them. Although Baldwin to me seems different from the rest. What's Baldwin doing these days?"

84 "He's writing a play. Anthony Quinn is supposed to have a part in it."

"Quinn?" Patterson asked.

"Yes."

"Quinn doesn't like me."

"Why?"

85 "I read or heard it somewhere; Quinn had been quoted as saying that my fight was disgraceful against Liston, and Quinn said something to the effect that he could have done better. People often say that—*they* could have done better! Well, I think if *they* had to fight, *they* couldn't even go through the experience of waiting for the fight to begin. They'd be up the whole night before, and would be drinking, or taking drugs. They'd probably get a heart attack. I'm sure that if I was in the ring with Anthony Quinn I could wear him out without even touching him. I would do nothing but pressure him, I'd stalk him, I'd stand close to him. I wouldn't touch him, but I'd wear him out and he'd collapse. But Anthony Quinn's an old man, isn't he?"

"In his forties."

86 "Well, anyway," Patterson said, "getting back to Baldwin, he seems like a wonderful guy. I've seen him on television and, before the Liston fight in Chicago, he came by my camp. You meet Baldwin on the street and you say, 'Who's this poor slob?'—he seems just like another guy; and this is the same impression *I* give people when they don't know me. But I think Baldwin and me, we have much in common, and someday I'd just like to sit somewhere for a long time and talk to him. . . ."

87 Patterson, his trunks and sweat pants on, bent over to tie his shoelaces, and then, from a bureau drawer, took out a T-shirt across which was printed *The Deauville*. He has several T-shirts bearing the

same name. He takes good care of them. They are souvenirs from the high point of his life. They are from the Deauville Hotel in Miami Beach, which is where he trained for the third Ingemar Johansson match in March of 1961.

88 Never was Floyd Patterson more popular, more admired than during that winter. He had visited President Kennedy; he had been given a $25,000 jeweled crown by his manager; his greatness was conceded by sportswriters—and nobody had any idea that Patterson, secretly, was in possession of a false mustache and dark glasses that he intended to wear out of Miami Beach should he lose the third fight to Johansson.

89 It was after being knocked out by Johansson in their first fight that Patterson, deep in depression, hiding in humiliation for months in a remote Connecticut lodge, decided he could not face the public again if he lost. So he bought false whiskers and a mustache, and planned to wear them out of his dressing room after a defeat. He had also planned, in leaving his dressing room, to linger momentarily within the crowd and perhaps complain out loud about the fight. Then he would slip undiscovered through the night and into a waiting automobile.

90 Although there proved to be no need to bring the disguise into the second or third Johansson fights, or into a subsequent bout in Toronto against an obscure heavyweight named Tom McNeeley, Patterson brought it anyway; and, after the first Liston fight, he not only wore it during his forty-eight-hour automobile ride from Chicago to New York, but he also wore it while in an airliner bound for Spain.

91 "As I got onto this plane, you'd never have recognized me," he said. "I had on this beard, mustache, glasses, and hat—and I also limped, to make myself look older. I was alone. I didn't care what plane I boarded; I just looked up and saw this sign at the terminal reading 'Madrid,' and so I got on that flight after buying a ticket.

92 "When I got to Madrid I registered at a hotel under the name 'Aaron Watson.' I stayed in Madrid about four or five days. In the daytime I wandered around to the poorer sections of the city, limping, looking at the people, and the people stared back at me and must have thought I was crazy because I was moving so slow and looked the way I did. I ate food in my hotel room. Although once I went to a restaurant and ordered soup. I hate soup. But I thought it was what old people would order. So I ate it. And, after a week of this, I began to actually think I was somebody else. I began to believe it. . . . And it is nice, every once in a while, being somebody else. . . ."

93 Patterson would not elaborate on how he managed to register under a name that did not correspond to his passport; he merely explained, "With money, you can do anything."

94 Now, walking slowly around the room, his black silk robe over his sweat clothes, Patterson said, "You must wonder what makes a man do things like this. Well, I wonder too. And the answer is, I don't know . . . but I think that within me, within every human being, there is a certain weakness. It is a weakness that exposes itself more when you're alone. And I have figured out that part of the reason I do the things I do, and cannot seem to conquer that one word—*myself*—is because . . . is because . . . I am a coward. . . ."

95 He stopped. He stood very still in the middle of the room, thinking about what he had just said, probably wondering whether he should have said it.

96 "I am a coward," he then repeated, softly. "My fighting has little to do with that fact, too. I mean you can be a fighter—and a *winning* fighter—and still be a coward. I was probably a coward on the night I won the championship back from Ingemar. And I remember another night, long ago, back when I was in the amateurs, fighting this big, tremendous man named Julius Griffin. I was only 153 pounds. I was petrified. It was all I could do to cross the ring. And then he came at me, and moved close to me . . . and from then on I don't know anything. I have no idea what happened. Only thing I know is, I saw him on the floor. And later somebody said, 'Man, I never saw anything like it. You just jumped up in the air, and threw thirty different punches.' . . ."

97 "When did you first think you were a coward?" he was asked.

"It was after the first Ingemar fight."

"How does one see this cowardice you speak of?"

98 "You see it when a fighter loses. Ingemar, for instance, is not a coward. When he lost the third fight in Miami, he was at a party later at the Fontainebleau. Had I lost, I couldn't have gone to that party. And I don't see how he did. . . ."

99 "Have you no hate left?"

100 "I have hated only one fighter," Patterson said. "And that was Ingemar in the second fight. I had been hating him for a whole year before that—not because he beat me in the first fight, but because of what he did after. It was all that boasting in public, and his showing off his right-hand punch on television, his thundering right, his 'toonder and lightning.' And I'd be home watching him on television, and *hating* him. It is a miserable feeling, hate. When a man hates, he can't have any peace of mind. And for one solid year I hated him because, after he took everything away from me, deprived me of everything I was, he *rubbed it in*. On the night of the second fight, in the dressing room, I couldn't wait until I got into the ring. When he was a little late getting into the ring, I thought, "He's holding me up; he's trying to unsettle me—well, I'll get him!' "

101 "Why couldn't you hate Liston in the second match?"

102 Patterson thought for a moment, then said, "Look, if Sonny Liston walked into this room now and slapped me in the face, then you'd see a fight. You'd see the fight of your life because, then, a principle would be involved. I'd forget he was a human being. I'd forget I was a human being. And I'd fight accordingly."

103 "Could it be, Floyd, that you made a mistake in becoming a prize fighter?"

"What do you mean?"

104 "Well, you say you're a coward; you say you have little capacity for hate; and you seemed to lose your nerve against those schoolboys in Scarsdale this afternoon. Don't you think you might have been better suited for some other kind of work? Perhaps a social worker, or . . ."

105 "Are you asking why I continue to fight?"

"Yes."

106 "Well," he said, not irritated by the question, "first of all, I love boxing. Boxing has been good to me. And I might just as well ask you the question: 'Why do you write?' Or, 'Do you retire from writing every time you write a bad story?' . . . And as to whether I should have become a fighter in the first place, well, let's see how I can explain it. . . . Look, let's say you're a man who has been in an empty room for days and days without food . . . and then they take you out of that room and put you into another room where there's food hanging all over the place . . . and the first thing you reach for, you eat. When you're hungry, you're not choosy, and so I chose the thing that was closest to me. That was boxing. One day I just wandered into a gymnasium and boxed a boy. And I beat him. Then I boxed another boy. I beat him, too. Then I kept boxing. And winning. And I said, 'Here, finally, is something I can do!'

107 "Now I wasn't a sadist," he quickly added. "But I liked beating people because it was the only thing I could do. And whether boxing was a sport or not, I wanted to make it a sport because it was a thing I could succeed at. And what were the requirements? Sacrifice. That's all. To anybody who comes from Bedford-Stuyvesant in Brooklyn, sacrifice comes easy. And so I kept fighting, and one day I became heavyweight champion, and I got to know people like you. And you wonder how I can sacrifice, how I can deprive myself so much. You just don't realize where I've come from. You don't understand where I was when it began for me.

108 "In those days, when I was about eight years old, everything I got I stole. I stole to survive, and I did survive, but I seemed to hate myself. Even when I was younger, my mother told me I used to point to a photograph of myself hanging in the bedroom and would say, 'I don't like that boy!' One day my mother found three large X's scratched with a nail or something over that photograph of me. I

don't remember doing it. But I do remember feeling like a parasite at home. I remember how awful I used to feel at night when my father, a longshoreman, would come home so tired that, as my mother fixed food for him, he would fall asleep at the table because he was that tired. I would always take his shoes off and clean his feet. That was my job. And I felt so bad because here I was, not going to school, doing nothing, just watching my father come home; and on Friday nights it was even worse. He would come home with his pay, and he'd put every nickel of it on the table so my mother could buy food for all the children. I never wanted to be around to see that. I'd run and hide. And then I decided to leave home and start stealing—and I did. And I would never come home unless I brought something that I had stolen. Once I remember I broke into a dress store and stole a whole mound of dresses, at 2 a.m., and here I was, this little kid, carrying all those dresses over the wall, thinking they were all the same size, my mother's size, and thinking the cops would never notice me walking down the street with all those dresses piled over my head. They did, of course. . . . I went to the Youth House. . . ."

109 Floyd Patterson's children, who had been playing outside all this time around the country club, now became restless and began to call him, and Jeannie started to pound on his door. So Patterson picked up his leather bag, which contained his gloves, his mouthpiece, and adhesive tape, and walked with the children across the path toward the club.

110 He flicked on the light switches behind the stage near the piano. Beams of amber streaked through the dimly-lit room and flashed onto the ring. Then he walked to one side of the room, outside the ring. He took off his robe, shuffled his feet in the rosin, skipped rope, and then began to shadowbox in front of a spit-stained mirror, throwing out quick combinations of lefts, rights, lefts, rights, each jab followed by a *"hegh-hegh-hegh-hegh."* Then, his gloves on, he moved to the punching bag in the far corner, and soon the room reverberated to his rhythmic beat against the bobbling bag—rat-tat-tat-*tetteta,* rat-tat-tat-*tetteta,* rat-tat-tat-*tetteta,* rat-tat-tat-*tetteta!*

111 The children, sitting on pink leather chairs, moved from the bar to the fringe of the ring, watched him in awe, sometimes flinching at the force of his pounding against the leather bag.

112 And this is how they would probably remember him years from now: a dark, solitary, glistening figure punching in the corner of a forlorn spot at the bottom of a mountain where people once came to have fun—until the country club became unfashionable, the paint began to peel, and Negroes were allowed in.

113 As Floyd Patterson continued to bang away with lefts and rights, his gloves a brown blur against the bag, his daughter slipped quietly off her chair and wandered past the ring into the other room. There,

on the other side of the bar and beyond a dozen round tables, was the stage. She climbed onto the stage and stood behind a microphone, long dead, and cried out, imitating a ring announcer, "*Ladieeees and gentlemen* . . . tonight we present . . ."

114 She looked around, puzzled. Then, seeing that her little brother had followed her, she waved him up to the stage and began again: "*Ladiees and gentlemen* . . . tonight we present . . . *Floydie Patterson* . . ."

115 Suddenly, the pounding against the bag in the other room stopped. There was silence for a moment. Then Jeannie, still behind the microphone and looking down at her brother, said, "Floydie, come up here!"

116 "No," he said.

"Oh, come up here!"

"NO," he cried.

117 Then Floyd Patterson's voice, from the other room, called: "Cut it out. . . . I'll take you for a walk in a minute."

118 He resumed punching—rat-tat-tat-*tetteta*—and they returned to his side. But Jeannie interrupted, asking, "Daddy, how come you sweating?"

119 "Water fell on me," he said, still pounding.

"Daddy," asked Floyd, Jr., "how come you spit water on the floor before?"

120 "To get it out of my mouth."

121 He was about to move over to the heavier punching bag—but just then the sound of Mrs. Patterson's station wagon could be heard moving up the road.

122 Soon she was in Patterson's apartment cleaning up a bit, patting the pillows, washing the teacups that had been left in the sink. One hour later the family was having dinner together. They were together for two more hours; then, at 10 p.m., Mrs. Patterson washed and dried all the dishes, and put the garbage out in the can—where it would remain until the raccoons and skunks got to it.

123 And then, after helping the children with their coats and walking out to the station wagon and kissing her husband good-bye, Mrs. Patterson began the drive down the dirt road toward the highway. Patterson waved once, and stood for a moment watching the tail lights go, and then he turned and walked slowly back toward the house.

Thinking Questions: *Form*

1. In paragraphs 90 to 94 Floyd Patterson tells how he went to Madrid, Spain, in disguise after losing his title to Sonny Liston. In essence, this little scene helps provide an illustration of the problems Patterson has confronted his entire life, and an explanation for his constant wondering whether he is a coward (as pointed out directly in paragraph 94). Can you point to other personal anecdotes that Talese uses to develop his interpretation of Patterson's insecurity, his psychological problems?

2. This essay mixes objective description with a few scattered sentences and paragraphs in which Talese summarizes his interpretations of Patterson's character. Find one or two examples of summary sentences and show how they are developed from the concrete, objective descriptions of Floyd Patterson that lead up to them.

3. Define Talese's thesis: what he wants to say about Patterson, how he explains Patterson's insecurity and fear. Is Floyd Patterson a coward, according to Talese? How do you know? Then point out evidence of Talese's subjective purpose in the essay. Does he arrange his description so that it causes you to interpret Patterson's actions and speech in certain ways? Does he use vocabulary in describing Patterson's surroundings and actions that seems to indicate his own opinions of the man?

4. How would you describe Talese's personality as he writes? Does he try to appear objective? Is he distant from his subject? Would you say he is a friend or admirer of Patterson or an objective reporter? What specific devices of style and language—sentence structure, word choice, use of contractions, direct-interview format—can you cite to explain your description of Talese's personality?

Thinking Questions: *Substance*

1. Here is another concrete example showing a man as he works. As you read the essay, notice how Floyd Patterson relies on his work to define himself, to give himself an identity. Can you point to specific examples where Talese describes an incident, some of Patterson's dialogue, his surroundings at his training camp, in order to help you understand how Patterson defines his entire self by his profession?

2. "The worst thing about losing is having to face those people. . . ." What do statements like that tell you about Floyd Patterson? Does he fight because he loves to fight or because he gains others' respect when he fights? Cite other specific examples of his insecurity, his dependency on others, and show how his work helps him confront and deal with that basic insecurity.

3. Paragraphs 25 to 31 describe Patterson's relations with his fight manager, Cus D'Amato, and his experiences as he learned to fly. Examine these paragraphs as a cluster and explain how they contribute to the overall purpose of the essay. How do they contribute to Talese's overall interpretation of Patterson?

4. Take a close look at paragraph 79 in which Talese begins to develop explicitly his thesis on Floyd Patterson. Can you condense a thesis from it that will fit the entire essay and help explain Patterson's reasons for fighting? How is Patterson "the great black hope of the Urban League"? (The Urban League is a group of liberal, nonviolent city blacks who hope to foster black upward mobility through socially acceptable means.) What effect, according to Talese, has this "hope" had on Patterson as a workingman? Are other people in our society, white and black, working for reasons similar to Patterson's? Are they fulfilling someone else's "hope," rather than their own?

The Death-defying Tartonis

W. S. MERWIN

1 I go out first now. It is a position that I am not used to in some hair-thin secret chamber on the inside of the calves of my legs, and there perhaps I will never be used to it. Perhaps no one capable of assuming the position and surviving would ever grow used to it in every part of himself. Still, I have hopes. But given the assumptions on which I base the rest of my life, including its defiance, as they say, of death, it behooves me to conceal this truth—of my not yet being wholly accustomed to my position—from the others. To whom in any event it could never be completely and continuously (because of course it is alive) and luminously communicated, so that it would not, could not, contribute to their enlightenment but merely to their disturbance. I would do as well, in fact, to conceal it even from myself if I had not, during the past months and years, learned to control this stubborn refusal to be accustomed, this irreducible reluctance to regard my naked position as the first rider, as though it were a part of nature. Is it, in fact? But does nature defy death? I would do as well also not to ask such questions during the performance. The mind never despairs of escaping its own controls even if the escape can take no form except death itself.

2 I go out first now. It has been two and a half, nearly three years. Four years since I began to rehearse the position. I roll the front wheel onto the wire eighty feet above the ground, with nothing below it except dark air. Dark in our eyes despite the floodlights. I feel on my shoulders the feet in their tights. I feel the muscles in the arches of the feet contract a little. This helps me. More of my mind returns from somewhere to lend its shoulder, to hold us up. I go out only a

foot or two. We go out, for they have all assembled behind me. Behind me and above me—but at this point I must not think of them as being above me. I am not sure why. It would not help. We go out only a foot or two, very slowly, as though the front wheel were groping its way along the wire to make sure it continued. At about the point where my foot on the pedal would be clearing the platform (I imagine, for obviously I do not look to see) and there is nothing under the pedal but that darkness of which the rubber of the pedal is in truth a reflection, I stop. Even more slowly we go back to the platform. They help, from behind me. And for most of two minutes we appear to be adjusting something, arranging something which, if we had not happened to notice it, would have meant certain death for all of us. We make a great display of maintaining outward calm, of showing nothing to the audience, of not betraying that anything is wrong. Those above do not even climb down but stand there the whole time with their poles, staring straight ahead, which has been found most fitting. An assistant appears to be busying himself about us. We make use of this—in fact, very difficult—moment to breathe, deliberately but not in time, blinking our eyes at the top of each inhalation, at the bottom of each exhalation, until the moment when we must forget our breathing again and give ourselves solely to what we are doing. By then the announcer far below us is announcing our act for the second time, his voice appearing to show a touch of concern, as though our false start were not a part of the act but something unforeseen, unprecedented, and incalculable in its results. He is announcing us again but of course we do not hear it, for by then we are far advanced in our act, its silence, its echoes. Again I move forward, the feet gripping my shoulders, gripping tighter as the wheel, too, leaves the platform and the whole bicycle is out on the wire, the front wheel laying itself down inch by inch like a snail.

3 The wire. We call it a wire out of tradition rather than regard for accuracy. To be exact, it is a metal cable of about the diameter of an ordinary candle, enveloped over its whole length by a layer of soft rubber between an eighth and a quarter of an inch in thickness. The rubber layer has been specially applied by hand, for it is important that the bond between it and the cable should be perfect and should remain perfect. It must not slip. The outside of the rubber contains not a coating but an admixture of sharp sand of different degrees of coarseness, which must have been made into an integral part of the rubber layer for as long as the wire fills its present role. It would be better to have no sand at all than sand that might work loose and roll out. Or even just work loose. This is one of the things for which the wire is examined, inch by inch, after each performance. If a single grain of sand shows signs of independent movement, though it may be nothing more definable than the first movements

of a child's tooth, the whole wire is set aside—at least for repair. Naturally, when it is set up the wire is anchored to keep it from swaying.

4 And the bicycles. It seems hardly necessary to point out that they are not ordinary bicycles either, although everything (except that they are entirely covered with chrome, apart from the handgrips, pedals, and seats) has been arranged to make them suggest the most commonplace of contemporary wheels—the low balloon-tired sort that used to be won by selling magazine subscriptions door to door. But ours are almost as light as imported racing models. Even the girls carry theirs into the arena themselves, before the front wheels are hooked to a rope and one after the other the bicycles fly alone, straight up to the platform. (It may be their favorite moment in the whole act.) There they lean against their handlers and wait. Speed would be meaningless to these constructions. But the conveyance of power from the pedal to the rear wheel is far more sensitive than it is in ordinary bicycles, for one thing. For another, the tires are not completely round but are molded with a very slight longitudinal concavity, barely noticeable when the wheels are suspended or when the bicycle is standing by itself. At such moments this conformation appears as nothing more than a flatness in the crown of the tire, scored with secondary grooves, also running lengthwise, and a tertiary hatchwork in a triangular scale pattern reminiscent of a sharkskin. A recurrent pattern—but the shark, after all, is a professional survivor. It is only when the bicycle wheel is placed on the wire, on the platform, and the weight of the rider and then the additional weight of the others press the tire down onto the sanded envelope of the cable that the tire yields at the crown sufficiently to produce a groove, which runs the full length of the contact. A shallow grip. Of course each bicycle is very slightly different from the others, the result of endless adjustments, some of them conceived in the small hours of the night.

5 So I go out first, and the image of the front wheel laying itself down like a snail did not come to me by chance. We are used to leaving nothing to chance, insofar as possible—or so we have to believe, though of course chance, chance itself, is probably not even limited by our efforts. But in any case how often that snail has appeared to me in dreams. Since I was a child. Since the days of my first slow wheel. I watched him ("him," of course, hence the intimacy of my reservations, the ready and yet awed identification) set out calmly, as though I did not exist, as though my decisions, all the rest of me and what became of all the rest of me, were eventualities too remote for him to believe in. I have called to him in dreams and said, "Look, it's me!" But nothing. No response. Thank heaven. For I believe now that if there had been anything of the kind he would have lost some

innate certainty, or I would have come to doubt it, and we would all have plunged, long since, into the abyss that awaits us everywhere.

6 I have allowed my mind to run at times (but never during a performance; never when I was touching the bicycle) on his ability to proceed equally well along the side of a wire, or underneath it, for that matter. I have dwelt with satisfaction on the image of him climbing smooth walls, crossing ceilings, negotiating intricate joints in rafters, or elaborate knots, at a great height. I have had dreams in which he disappeared—yes, disappeared, and in the course of crossing the wire in the usual way. I was the shell, or rather the bicycle and I together were the shell, or rather the bicycle and I and all the rest of us were the shell and we were suddenly filled with a weightlessness that bore no relation to anything we had practiced. There we hung, a case enclosing a coil of nothing, balancing as well as we could now that we were deprived of movement and had nothing at our center, until a tiny upward breath swept us off into the void. Naturally I have remained silent about any such images of my own. As my fellow-performers have done with theirs, if they have any, as no doubt they do.

7 So I go out first but it has not always been so. I am not the oldest; no, I am really one of the younger members of what is known, for reasons of remote pathos, as the family. Behind me the front wheel of Claudio's bicycle follows the rear wheel of mine with only a few inches between them and nothing maintaining the distance except Claudio's foot on his pedal. Claudio is eight years older than I am and wears a dark reddish toupee for the act. Tartoni is his real name. And yet he has confided to me that if he had not been put to the act so young—as we all were—he might never have chosen it. He cannot be certain, but he might never have chosen it. It was one of those confidences probably forgotten almost immediately by the person who makes them, and I am sure that the thought has seldom if ever recurred to him. Claudio says very little and buys magazines about animals and nature when we have any time in a city. He is heavier than I am, heavier than any of us, but his tights always fit with wrinkles. For years, ever since I began to practice going out first, I have tried not to listen to his breathing.

8 It was once suggested that Claudio should go out first, but the thought troubled him and the idea was dropped.

9 Behind Claudio's bicycle comes the carefully braked front wheel of his younger brother, Rafael. Rafael married Marisa two years ago, after living with her for nearly three. He is much slighter than Claudio, blond, quicker but more nervous. He worries about money. He worries about the future of the act. He reads all the papers and discourses upon them to the rest of us, usually without anyone else entering a comment. Rafael needs an abdominal operation, but we

hope it will wait until the end of the season, because the formation as we practice it now allows of no alternatives.

10 Behind Rafael's bicycle comes his cousin Marcantonio's. Marcantonio's mother was born a Tartoni but tried to escape the whole world of the wire by marrying outside it. Perhaps because she had never known anyone except those who performed on the wire, she chose unfortunately. The marriage was brief and wretched; she herself returned, with her child, to the familiar circumstances. Not as a performer (she had never had the temperament) but as a dresser, old before her time, controlling her pessimism with an uncertainty that led us all to keep our distance from her. Yet allowing her son to be brought up as a cyclist—her own attempt to escape the wire had exhausted her belief in such a possibility. And Marcantonio avoided her more studiously than anyone, going so far as to have his tights made and repaired by someone else. And though the differences between our performances are almost immeasurable, it is my opinion that Marcantonio is the most reliable and sturdy of us all.

11 Last comes Cesare, gaunt, sinewy, and no more their brother than I am. He is the son of a trapeze artist who was killed when Cesare was very small. There was no one to train him in his father's act, but Carla Tartoni, the mother of the cyclists behind me, who died last year, brought him up as a matter of course and he was put to the wire at the same age as the rest of us. His passion is dancing and he is in love with a girl who has nothing to do with any act at all, which in itself has always been thought rather unlucky. She has never seen him perform and refuses to read the reviews of our act in the newspapers.

12 The feet on my shoulders belong to Augusta, one of the younger daughters. Younger than I am, and pretty. We grew up together. For a brief time in our early adolescence we slept together, until the full gravity of what we were doing dawned on us at the same time. Then we stopped without a word and without the least ill will. Now, years later, it is good that it happened. Neither she nor I has married. Again, one does not think of such things during the performance.

13 On Claudio's shoulders the feet are Alfredo's. He is not a member of the family either, but a tumbler whom they enlisted seven or eight years ago. He is the oldest of us, married, with children whom he never sees; he is almost the same age as Claudio's own father. He reads one boxful of books over and over.

14 On Rafael's shoulders are Emilia's feet. Emilia lives with Claudio. She is the daughter of another wire artist, who performs alone.

15 On Marcantonio's shoulders, Giorgio's feet. Giorgio is the youngest of the Tartonis, slight, small, homosexual, who wanted to be a clown.

16 On Cesare's shoulders, Anna's feet. She is the prettiest of the Tartoni girls, gentle, studious, and a singer.

17 The seats of the bicycles and the heights of the first row of balancers have been carefully adjusted so that their shoulders are all at the same height. This is important because when the balancers are in position a ladder is handed up to them, through which they all slip their heads. They lower it to their shoulders, which are padded to receive it, and the ladder provides a platform, running from Augusta in front to Anna in the rear. The balancing poles are then handed up, and the second row of balancers can start to climb, to stand on the ladder.

18 Mimi first, who was a classical dancer but required something more dangerous. She is jealous of Marisa and everyone pretends not to know.

19 Then Teodoro, who is little and dark like a jockey, and was a street urchin who used to play with us when we were first starting to learn, and picked up the act that way, and came with us. He is married and has five children who live with the troupe, but he is never around unless it is for some reason to do with work. He and Giorgio do not get along, but everyone is careful not to pay any attention.

20 Then Maria, Cesare's sister, adopted at the same time he was. She is in love with Marcantonio, and it would be a good thing, but that is no concern of the front tire's.

21 Finally, Ernesto Tartoni, short, neat, equable, the eldest of the sons, married without children, an impassioned and skillful devotee of the stock market, at which he has been moderately successful over the years, considering that he started with nothing.

22 On the shoulders of these four, a second ladder. On which a chair is placed. Into which Graziella climbs, wearing a long gown, mock-royal, with fluffy trim and spangles. And a rhinestone tiara. Graziella was also picked up on the street—an acquaintance of Teodoro's. She grew up with us. We first let her practice the act with us after watching her walk up a hawser onto a ship, on a dare, when she was a little girl. I suppose it would be said that Graziella and I are engaged. Yes, that at least.

23 When we are halfway across, we stop. The cyclists, one after the other, take their hands off the grips and hold them out like wings. Then each of the bottom row of balancers raises an arm. Last of all, Graziella rises, climbs the chair, and unfurls a flag. We remain there, not hearing the rolled drums or the applause, for a moment, and then continue.

24 Everyone's role, as may be imagined, is difficult. But for the cyclists it is more difficult than for anyone, and our training began almost as soon as we could walk. Even before, if you will, with toy bicycles. We came early to regard these two-wheeled fabrications as though the world itself revolved around them. We thought of them day and night. Everything we learned led back to them at once or seemed pointless.

At last we could ride. The fervor increased. We cared for nothing else. We learned to ride more and more slowly. We learned to ride backward. By pure force of concentration we learned to stop, to remain upright in one place. Then came the moment when an old wire was laid on the ground and we set the wheels on it and started. When that became practicable, the first of the drops—an old tent canvas, painted—was spread out under the wire. It represents an arena. At the edges are the first tiers of seats, with spectators painted sitting there, life-size. We soon ceased to notice them. In due course the wire was raised a few inches, just enough to clear the ground. Same canvas.

25 When we were used to the raised practice wire another canvas was spread under it. The arena was smaller. More tiers of spectators showed. They were smaller. As we grew more proficient the canvases depicted the arena and the audience farther and farther below us, until the arena looked the size of a dinner plate and the spectators the size of hatpins. Then a black canvas, which was hardest of all to get used to. Then we were ready to start learning the act itself.

26 But after all that, and even with luck, will we grow much older in the act?

27 The audiences are not what they were only a few years ago; our expenses are rising all the time; none of the young seem to feel that there is a future in following our exacting profession. Fewer and fewer people seem to believe in us, to say nothing of understanding our art.

28 But Grandfather Tartoni says that the decline of interest has nothing to do with the world but only with ourselves. He says we are no longer of interest because in truth we are not defying anything real at all. According to him we know too much, and it is all a game. Even if we were killed we would be killed in a game. That is what they mean when they say they don't believe we're really doing what we seem to be doing. The old man declares that in contrast to us he admired his son Tommaso, Claudio's father, just once, when he combined risk and wit and performed on the wire, at the age of eighteen, on a unicycle, on his head. And the old man is thinking (though he is too proud to mention it) of the day when he himself drove a bicycle with a huge front wheel—an ordinary high-seated penny-farthing without special tires or anything—across a city square, a hundred feet up, without rehearsal, simply because, as he once said, it got into him that he could. He watches us seldom, and with scorn, and he says we should turn to something we know nothing about if we are going to talk about defying death. The whole matter, he says, is far simpler than we have made it. It consists of nothing but being able to look straight ahead and see that there could not possibly be any other way.

Thinking Questions: *Form*

1. Describe the narrator's attitude toward his work. Look for details to support what you say. How does his body look? Is he muscle-bound, thin, with a long neck? What makes you think so? Where do you see signs of his own attitude toward his work? Is his attitude different from Grandfather Tartoni's, as described in paragraph 28? Would you say this first-person "I" narrator is objective in describing his work? How do you know? Are his words objective?

2. Why does the narrator make so much of the "snail" comparison—to help the reader visualize the act himself? Or can you think of other ideas the narrator represents through this comparison?

3. Notice the various points of view established in this essay (point of view is the writer's perspective on the subject, both his *physical* perspective as he describes or goes through an action or idea and his *rhetorical* perspective as he decides whether to remain objective or to become involved in what he describes). Paragraphs 1 through 5 are objective descriptions in which the narrator focuses on concrete objects. In paragraph 6 he begins to describe more subjectively, revealing some of his feelings and providing background information. Go through the rest of the essay and analyze how blocks or clusters of paragraphs develop different points of view. How do these points of view help the narrator achieve his overall purpose? What *is* his overall purpose?

4. Paragraphs 7 through 23 describe each member of the "family." Notice how the narrator mixes opinion with fact as he describes each performer. Could you write a longer, more detailed, character sketch of one of these performers, using the narrator's brief description as a factual base on which to construct a longer, fictional description?

Thinking Questions: *Substance*

1. Here we find a personal account by a man who works on a high wire in a circus. As in the Eiseley essay, we find descriptions of inner sensations—"some hair-thin secret chamber on the inside of the calves of my legs"—through concrete reference to objective terms. Are these people working only for money? Why *do* they work at such a high-risk job? What inner needs are gratified by the narrator's work?

2. Compare the physical labor of Floyd Patterson in Talese's essay with the high-wire performer's physical labor. How are they different?

3. Floyd Patterson, in the previous essay, feels constantly harassed, bothered, and tense because of his intense desire to succeed at his work. Yet Patterson's work, however challenging, does not present the immediate death risk that the work of the high-wire performer does. Could you, however, apply Tartoni's remark, ". . . we would all have plunged, long since, into the abyss that waits us everywhere," to Floyd Patterson's work as well? What kind of "abyss" is Patterson threatened with? How is his "abyss" different from the real physical threat to the high-wire performers?

4. How do you know, as you read this story, that teamwork is extremely important? Why do the performers never think very much about domestic struggles, personal differences, love affairs, or personalities when they are performing? In essence, this story shows us teamwork in detail, through many specific illustrations of the interdependence of the artists. Does this mutual dependence make their work more or less meaningful? Would Studs Terkel find this work more or less worthwhile than the work of those he interviewed in "Earning One's Bread"?

Writing Exercise I

DESCRIPTION

Organize your thoughts on the five pieces included in this section. Then write an essay in which you describe, in as much detail as possible, what you will be doing ten years from now. Compose an *ideal* description. Tell your readers *exactly* what your everyday activities will be, appeal to their eyes and ears, their overall idea of what work should be.

As you write your ideal description, remember that it should serve at least two purposes. First, it should give your readers concrete descriptive information. Second, while giving that information, it should also *imply* a definition of what meaningful work is. You should ask yourself as you write, without addressing the question directly in your essay, how the work you describe yourself doing will supply a sense of respect and pride, how it will produce necessary products or ideas for others, how you will retain a sense of "being" in this job.

Consult the essay on form that follows to help as you plan the form of your essay.

WRITING THE DESCRIPTIVE ESSAY

The ability to describe is essential to every kind of writing. The essay writer often must find words to describe what he or she sees and understands to provide evidence and support for opinions and interpretations.

The newswriter describes objectively; he or she gives readers a vision and understanding of events they have not themselves experienced. Novelists describe setting, the physical appearance and gestures of characters; they often must show what characters are thinking inside by describing them objectively from the outside. Even technical and business writers must use description, often with the difficult recognition that their words must not get in the way of their content. Some writers, in other words, want to describe *with style;* they want to entertain as they instruct. Other writers want to do a job, to get information across, to communicate an opinion or general idea. But the greater majority of writers want some of both; they want to describe accurately *and* pleasurably.

Description involves a threefold process: (1) observing; (2) perceiving and organizing; (3) writing (arranging, revising, and editing).

Observing

Nothing is more exasperating than sitting down to write and finding that you have forgotten most of what you wanted to describe. Try some of these observation exercises.

1. Find a newspaper photograph and study it. Then describe it in writing as accurately as you can from memory. How much did you forget? Why did you remember certain details and forget others? Was there a natural basis of selection apparent in what you wrote?
2. Look closely at a person around you, in class or in a restaurant, at home or in your dormitory. Observe him or her carefully, make a generalization about that person, and then write a few paragraphs from memory in an attempt to explain and support that generalization.
3. Think hard about some local place, somewhere that arouses a particular opinion or impression in you. Quickly jot down a summary of that impression and write a brief essay describing the place in a way that supports your summary impression. Be specific; remember details, colors, shapes, how you felt while you were there. Then go back to the scene, take notes, watch your impression grow and change, try to see new details, take new perspectives, and let your senses go. Now go back and revise that summary impression and the supporting essay.

Exercises like these ought to convince you that you cannot describe what you have not observed.

Perceiving and organizing

Careful and imaginative observation is only the beginning. You will need to follow your careful observation by recognizing and using perception—the process by which we begin to formulate, to make order of, our experience as a means of transferring to paper what we receive through our senses. Generally, this second stage includes four related steps:

1. Selection of detail and evidence
2. Formulation of generalities

3. Formulation of a general organizing plan
4. Decisions about how *you* want to fit into what you describe

Get used to taking notes on what you see. Follow notetaking by jotting down general impressions; one of these initial general impression sentences might become a thesis for an entire essay. And the rest, with some juggling and reworking, might become guiding sentences for paragraph groupings or clusters or for individual paragraphs.

After you have taken complete and accurate notes, you can go back and select a general impression sentence to head your essay. Then go back and whittle away at your detailed notes. Begin by deciding what details you will use. Then decide on their order of importance, how much space you will give to each detail or detail-cluster, where each described detail ought to fit into the finished essay.

Finally, you should ask yourself some questions about your own voice, the way you want to sound on paper as you write this description. Does the subject—for example, an observation of a building that ought to be condemned in a downtown area—warrant your intrusion? Should you jump in and interpret for your readers; should you tell them what you think or subtly imply what you think by describing in a way that suggests certain attitudes? Will a colloquial style suit your purpose? Or does your subject and audience demand some degree of formality? Such questions should help you choose words and sentences that will create the right distance between you and your readers.

Apply these four stages in the descriptive process to some common object. Suppose, for example, that you want to examine and describe Grant Wood's popular painting, *American Gothic.* You begin by studying the painting carefully, taking notes on facial expressions, clothing, the farmhouse background, the particular objects surrounding the two figures. Then, without consulting your detailed notes, you write a brief paragraph summarizing your general impression of the painting.

Spend the next block of time organizing. Relate your perceived details to your summary paragraph. Be ruthless: cut the details you do not need; expand those you choose to retain in as much concrete detail as possible; look for concrete adjectives, nouns, and verbs to describe what you see. Above all, decide on a plan or pattern of development. Will you work from the general to the specific or from the specific to the general? Where do you want your purpose to be clarified—as you begin, after a brief descriptive introduction, or at the end for conclusive emphasis?

Finally, ask yourself questions about your voice and style. Does this painting make you want to develop a serious or a comic message or impression? Should you take an informal or colloquial tone with your readers? And what decisions will you need to make as you choose words and form sentences to help shape the voice and tone you want?

A writer's voice is his or her characteristic manner of speaking; the writer uses language and structure to recreate in writing that manner of speaking. Voice can freshen up the conventional; it can also lend support to an idea by making the reader feel that he or she knows the writer better.

Tone, on the other hand, describes the way a writer treats the readers, how he or she uses words and sentence structure to relate to a particular audience. Martin Luther King, in an essay, "Letter from the Birmingham Jail" (included in Part Four of this book), maintains a highly serious and deeply moral tone as he pleads for civil justice. His sentences are formal, balanced, often parallel; his diction is also formal. King's style, especially his voice and tone, are fitted to the seriousness of his subject, to his plea for civil justice for all.

In Studs Terkel's essay that began this section, however, we find a more colloquial tone: the writer speaks to the reader in everyday language, without giving attention to formal diction or phrasing. As his title indicates, Terkel wants to provide a fundamental description of people's problems with their work; to have maintained a serious, moral tone, with the highly formal speaking voice of Martin Luther King, would, for Terkel's purposes, have been out of place.

You as writer create the context of an essay. By controlling voice and tone, you can present your subject to your readers in a way that effectively shapes a frame of mind, a mental context that supports the idea you want to communicate.

Writing, arranging, revising, and editing

All the initial steps will need reworking in this final writing stage. To do the job right you will need to consider at least four basic qualities of descriptive writing:

1. Subjectivity and objectivity
2. Generalizations and supporting evidence
3. Abstract and concrete; general and particular
4. Making and using analogies

Subjectivity and Objectivity. As you read the essays in this section, you are examining a variety of essay types. Most are *both* subjective and objective. A subjective essay demonstrates two qualities: its style is personal, the writer lets the choice of words and sentence structure show what he or she feels or thinks; the essay's purpose is explicitly presented and defended by the writer; a thesis is evolved and defended.

Suppose you wish to point out how pollution affects a local street corner. Your purpose is not to show that street corner exactly as it is, but to emphasize how it is affected by litter, garbage, vandals, and exhaust fumes. You, then, decide to write in a direct, tough, tell-it-like-it-is style; you occasionally use slang and colloquial language; you decide to address your readers directly with the pronoun "you"; you also decide to use words with emotional connotations. These are elements of style; they inject your personality and attitudes into your description. You begin to suggest what you think by the way you present yourself in words or sentences.

Of course you can also make your descriptions subjective by explicitly putting your opinions toward your subject into your essay. Begin some of your paragraphs by directly stating your opinions and then move naturally into specific descriptions of the sidewalk at the end of the day, at its dirtiest. Or refer to government statistics on the effects pollution has had on the environment in order to make this particular street corner representative of a much larger problem.

Subjective description works from thesis and purpose back through descriptions of supporting experience. It leads the reader by the hand.

You can, however, also establish an attitude through indirect description. In such description, you keep your language and style relatively neutral. And you do not beat your readers over the head with heavy-handed arguments or theses. But you do select supporting details carefully and place them in emphatic positions in the essay. You bring your readers directly up against the specifics through concrete wording and careful arrangement. Perhaps you begin by focusing in on a mud puddle in which an old shoe slowly rots. You show the shoe's color, the holes in its sides, the dark brown clots of mud (perhaps "clots" suggests the gruesome and bloody?), then you move to a description of several old dirty newspapers as they flutter weakly against the jagged bricks of an old building. These are all concrete bits of *objective* information; yet properly placed and specifically controlled they will develop attitude—perhaps more effectively because they provide the material evidence and encourage the reader to draw his or her own conclusions.

As we have already suggested, objective description focuses on the object itself. You strive to keep yourself out of your language by avoiding emotionally tinged words, by keeping your style as free of personality as you can. And, of course, you allow your description to speak for itself; you adhere to concrete detail and avoid making direct statements of personal opinion or attitude.

Effective essays are usually a balanced combination of subjectivity and objectivity. The purely objective essay is sometimes dull, unless it fits a very clear purpose. You may occasionally, for example, wish to record the objective process of dissecting an insect to be sure that you have seen all there is to see, to be sure that you know the parts of that insect before you go on to discover how it functions as an organism. Occasionally you will want to make totally subjective responses to highly emotional issues. But in most writing situations, we want a combination of subjective and objective description that will move and convince a reader. Without some sense of a writer's opinions and personality, the reader quickly loses interest; without at least a few important facts or details, your readers will doubt your credibility.

Generalizations and Supporting Evidence. Almost every essay includes some summary and abstraction. For example:

> My reading has convinced me that the 55-miles-an-hour speed limit, enacted during the 1974 energy crisis, ought to be retained.

You give the reader your opinion or impression, directly, in a way that combines your reaction to all that you have experienced or read.

Providing support usually involves taking the reader by the hand and bringing him through the reasons behind your generalizations.

> Fewer people are killed on highways when the speed limit is 55, and we conserve more energy. But, above all, we cut down tension by slowing, however slightly, the pace of our lives.

Such facts show a reader where the writer's generalization came from. But you can add even more appeal to your supporting material by including concrete, specific description of examples and illustrations. Suppose our hypothetical writer were to add this descriptive paragraph to the more factual methods of support.

> Just a few days ago I watched my neighbor scramble through breakfast, throw on his new pin-striped suit, and run down the sidewalk to the car. He jumped into the driver's seat, cursed the seatbelt when it wouldn't buckle, pounded the steering wheel with his fist when the car didn't start immediately, and swore at every stop sign until he had reached the throughway. But when he finally reached the throughway and the traffic had slowed to a fairly steady 55, he relaxed, talked and smoked, and told an occasional joke to pass the extra time.

That paragraph nicely illustrates the opinion that concludes the previous paragraph: "But, above all, we cut down tension by slowing, however slightly, the pace of our lives."

Support and generalizations should work together; then they provide substance *and* purpose to whatever you write. The integration of general ideas and specific support will help you effectively combine your specific observations and your general ideas.

Abstract and Concrete/General and Particular. As you write, revise, and edit, consider word choice in relation to your overall purpose. Concrete language will lend specific, sensory appeal to your description. Look at the difference between these two paragraphs, both describing the same situation.

> He was a big man and wore a dirty worksuit. He walked around the gas pump with his hands in his pockets. I was afraid that he would lean on my car while I ordered gas and ruin its new shine.

> He stood about *six inches* above the gas pump and *drummed* his *grimy* hands on the *gasoline hose.* As he walked *slowly* around the pump, his

> *light-green* eyes shifted from side to side as he dropped his hands into the *gray pockets* of a *stained worksuit.* I had just polished the car—about eight hours work. My work was about to be undone by his *grease-stained elbow.*

The writer of the second paragraph uses concrete language, both adjectives and nouns and occasionally a verb *(drummed),* to bring the scene more vividly before the reader's eyes. Concrete words represent objects we can experience through our senses. They give readers clear images to go along with abstract ideas. Be especially careful to avoid using too many abstract verbs and adjectives. Abstract words tell more about how you, as writer, feel than they do about your subject. Compare these two responses to a movie.

> It was great, fantastic. I felt wonderful all the way through, even when the hero died. Because I knew he was dying for a noble cause, I thought it was all worth it.

It is hard to find out anything about the movie itself there, although we find out a good deal about the writer. Most readers require more concrete evidence; they want to share the experience itself as well as the writer's reaction to it. Too many abstract verbs and modifiers produce essays without sensory appeal. Concrete modifiers, nouns, and verbs, however, help you share the experience behind your feelings and opinions.

> The movie was fantastic. All the way through I knew the young hero was bent on destruction. He seemed eager to destroy himself; every time he had the chance he drove a fast car, flew glider planes, climbed mountains, and eluded police in a chase. Finally, he drove his car into a concrete roadblock while trying to escape the police in a cross-country chase. Police sirens blared in the background, the red flashing lights seeming to signal the success of his frantic search for fiery destruction.

The terms *general* and *particular* refer to another set of elements of composition, different from *abstract* and *concrete,* but related. *Concrete* refers to objects and qualities that appeal directly to the senses; *particular* refers to a specific example or item that, in writing an essay, usually supports or clarifies a generalization. Suppose, for example, you overhear someone arguing that the American presidency has undergone a great deal of instability in the past decade and a half. You enter the conversation and ask what the arguer means. He immediately refers to John Kennedy's assassination, Lyndon Johnson's decision *not* to run for a second term because of the Vietnam War, and to Richard Nixon's resignation because of Watergate.

Such a line of argument progresses from the general to the specific. The examples in this case do not necessarily appeal to the reader's senses or present a physical image; they are not, in other words, *concrete* examples. Rather they are *particular* historical instances used as examples to prove a general assertion.

In writing descriptive essays, we often use *concrete* support for our generalizations; in writing informative or argumentative essays, we usually support general ideas by referring to *particular* examples.

Notice how the second paragraph about the movie uses both concrete and particular support for the general assertions—"The movie was fantastic. All the way through I knew the young hero was bent on destruction." The sentences that follow these assertions cite particular examples of what the hero did to give the writer this impression. The final sentence in the paragraph uses concrete diction—*police sirens, blared, red flashing lights, fiery destruction*—to make one of the particular examples more vivid for the reader. The particular fact that the hero drove his car into a concrete roadblock comes alive more powerfully because of the sensory appeal in this final sentence.

Remember these definitions as you revise and edit your descriptions:

Concrete words describe specific physical images, colors, shapes, objects, or people. They bring sensory experience into an essay. A writer, for example, tells what he or she thinks by describing what he or she saw.

Abstract words describe ideas or classes of objects, that is, objects, people, or words that represent an entire class: for example, the word *chair* as distinct from the green chair along the wall, the rocking chair, the sway-back chair, or any other particular kind of chair. Words such as *beautiful, wonderful, great,* and *outstanding* should be used sparingly and they should always refer to some concrete object—the beautiful young stallion, the wonderful flying-machine, a great game between the Giants and Dodgers, an outstanding award. And, even then, the words carry very little sensory appeal.

Particular words refer to examples that support a generality or logical inference, or to one item in a general class. They do not necessarily refer to objects perceived through the senses.

General words and sentences refer to ideas, opinions, or theses that a writer has composed after thinking over personal experience, reading, or the results of research. Generalities can be supported by either concrete appeal to the senses or by specific, particular examples and instances.

You might consider these three elements of description—subjectivity and objectivity, showing and telling, abstract and concrete words—after you have produced a rough draft, as you revise and edit. Read your draft; decide on your purpose as you consider your subject and readers and then go back and change wording, include more detail, select and arrange details carefully, and develop the right blend of subjectivity and objectivity.

Making and Using Analogies. Analogy is one of several types of comparison a writer can use to develop an idea. The general techniques of comparison as they apply to writing the informative or expository essay are covered fully in Part Three; there the general techniques of using the similarities and differences that exist within, between, or among one, two, or more general subjects are carefully outlined. In this section, we should explain a simpler and more basic method of comparison.

Generally, we can divide comparison as a rhetorical device into the following three types.

Figure of speech is a very specific sort of comparison in which *one* quality that is shared by two otherwise different things is emphasized, usually in order to add emphasis and intensity to the reader's comprehension of the writer's subject. A writer discussing the poor quality of waste collection in his city might, for example, say: "On the Tuesday afternoons following waste collection, our city becomes London shortly after a Nazi air raid." Here the writer emphasizes the similar messiness of both cities to emphasize the point. The many differences between his city and London after the air raids are purposely ignored. When a writer uses *like* or *as* to make the comparison obvious, it is *simile*. When the comparison is implied, as in our example sentence, the writer is using *metaphor*.

General comparisons occur when the entire essay compares and contrasts in order to develop the writer's purpose. In general comparisons, the two things or ideas compared are alike and unlike in many ways. The writer uses both similarities and differences to define the subject and develop the thesis. This general method of developing an entire essay will be thoroughly explained in Part Three.

Analogy falls between these two extremes of comparison. Like the figure of speech, the analogy is *not* a part of the writer's general subject; rather, it is used to illustrate and emphasize some part of the writer's main subject by comparing that part to a familiar and otherwise different thing.

Yet, like the general comparison, the analogy may be similar to the writer's subject in more than one way. *Analogy* is often an expression of relationship between two different things that have more than one point of likeness.

Analogies have one major function: they should explain the unfamiliar by comparing it to something that is familiar. They should, in other words, help *clarify* the point the writer is making. Many basic anatomy textbooks, for example, make analogies between the human heart and water pumps. Such a comparison is not a figure of speech because the two items compared are similar in many ways: both have a pumping function in which valves force a liquid through an intricate system of pipes. Yet most writers would use this comparison in a limited way, to clarify only a part of the general subject. After using the heart–water pump analogy, the writer would most likely go on to a particular explanation of the heart's functions and its relationship to the general circulatory system.

Notice how the figures of speech and analogies in these passages, all of which are taken from the essays and stories in this section, help clarify the writer's purpose while they also convince us of the writer's originality, his ability to perceive connections where they might otherwise not have been noticed.

> "I can drive any car like a baby, like a woman changes her baby's diapers. I could handle a car with one hand. Lots of customers would say: 'How you do this?' I'd say: 'Just the way you bake a cake, miss.'" (Paragraph 27, Studs Terkel, "Earning One's Bread")

> An obscure line may whirl me into a wide-awake, ferocious concentration in which ideas like animals leap at me out of the dark, in which sudden odd trains of thought drive me inexorably to my desk and paper. I am, in short, a victim of insomnia—sporadic, wearing, violent, and melancholic. (Paragraph 3, Loren Eiseley, "One Night's Dying")

> "Are you asking why I continue to fight?"
>
> "Yes"
>
> "Well," he said, not irritated by the question, "first of all, I love boxing. Boxing has been good to me. And I might just as well ask you the question: 'Why do you write?' Or, 'Do you retire from writing every time you write a bad story?' . . . And as to whether I should have become a fighter in the first place, well, let's see how I can explain it. . . . Look, let's say you're a man who has been in an empty room for days and days without food . . . and then they take you out of that room and put you into another room where there's food hanging all over the place . . . and the first thing you reach for, you eat. When you're hungry you're not choosy, and so I chose the thing that was closest to me. That was boxing. One day I just wandered into a gymnasium and boxed a boy. And I beat him. Then I boxed another boy. I beat him, too. Then I kept boxing. And winning. And I said, 'Here, finally, is something I can do!' (Paragraphs 105 and 106, Gay Talese, "Floyd Patterson")

Compare and contrast these figures of speech and analogies with paragraphs 5 and 6 in "The Death-defying Tartonis," where the narrator compares different aspects of tightrope walking with the movement of a snail. Some of these comparisons are extended beyond a sentence or two to clarify a major part of the writer's subject. As you study these different types of comparison, notice how each writer avoids the following errors.

1. *Do not confuse analogies and literal comparisons.* An analogy is more original and striking than the mere observation that one house looks much like another because they are both Victorian in style. A writer would use analogy if he or she said: "That house reminds me of the labyrinthine mind of an old man, filled with odd nooks and crannies, surrounded with gables, arches, and minute wood sculpturing, like the secret passages and dark and detailed decorations of the mind."

2. *Don't use false analogies.* Make sure there *is* a similarity between the two items you are comparing. Some readers might find Tartoni's snail–tightrope walker analogy difficult to visualize, despite its originality. Someone who argues that Coca-Cola rots the teeth because mechanics use

Coke to remove stuck kingpins on automobiles has forgotten that human teeth are not automobile kingpins.

3. *Remember that analogies should clarify your subject.* Figures of speech often confuse because of their originality; they are fine for poetry and for writing in which deeper insights and shared perceptions are important. Often, however, especially in exposition, a writer merely wants to make a difficult point clearer by comparing the subject with something familiar. Be sure the object of comparison *is* familiar. Someone who compares an atom with its nucleus and electrons to the inner workings of an atomic bomb had better be sure that the knowledge of his or her readers includes the inner workings of atomic bombs.

4. *Do not expect an analogy to win your argument.* They can help, but analogies depend too much on extraneous circumstances to be conclusive. The politician, for example, who tells us that his opponent, when told that he had spent too much money on his campaign, reacted like the child caught with his hand in the cookie jar, will not *convince* us of his opponent's guilt. There are far too many differences between the compared items to convince; this analogy might, however, make an effective, humorous opening to a longer speech. Use logic along with your analogies, especially when the seriousness of your argument or explanation demands both.

Form and Substance/2

Form:

NARRATION

Substance:

The Rulers and the Ruled:

POLITICS, PROTEST, AND ESTABLISHED GOVERNMENT

/2 *Substance and Theme:*

POLITICS, PROTESTS, AND ESTABLISHED GOVERNMENT

Most governments are set up to maintain order, always somewhat at the expense of individual freedom. Primitive cultures are often extremely authoritarian; they establish governing structures and simple laws to enforce them, and they often dispense severe and quick retribution to any who break those laws or taboos.

As civilization advances, however, governments, rulers, and laws are themselves judged by the individuals for whom they provide order. A civilized society usually tries to replace strictly arbitrary rules with rules that can be adapted to particular places and times. In ancient Greece the idea of democracy—rule by the majority for the good of a majority of individuals—established the general idea of *responsible* government. The individual good would be considered along with the collective good; the educated citizen deserved "rights" so long as he or she observed collective laws and customs and rules of common decency. As societies grow more sophisticated, they usually provide for increasingly complex systems of government and law, supposedly allowing individuals greater freedom within the law without threatening the intricate system of social checks and balances that holds a culture together.

Societies grow larger and more complex; simple truths and decencies, which at first were apprehended by common sense and mutual consideration, are then gradually replaced by the letter of the law, by ever more precise and legalistic verbal regulations and customs. As this growing body of governing material gains even more authority, tensions begin to develop, sometimes because a society grows too large to be controlled by individually apprehended ideas of "common decency," sometimes because individuals themselves no longer believe they have a clear, unbiased view of the Right Way. Conservatives demand strict application and adherence to law to ensure that people will not revert to savagery. Liberals, on the other hand, usually support the arguments of individuals who have been forced to relinquish some rights to the larger society.

There is, of course, nothing intrinsically wrong with power vested in a central government. The wrong, rather, resides in those individuals who, upon vesting governing powers in a central government, decide to rest easy, to obey the law without question, to sacrifice the rights of individual dissent out of laziness or lack of interest. The bank clerk, too busy making her way in the bank, would rather not consider political corruption, electronic eavesdropping, or energy crisis legislation. Truckdrivers hauling loads across country worry about their paychecks, federal highway taxes, and state gasoline taxes; they often tend to ignore other governing problems. The same is true of almost every group or individual. In the process, Big Government begins to work by expediency, to lose sight of the moral and legal principles often so eloquently espoused in the Constitution and by platforming politicians.

Once a country or nation becomes very large and its individual citizens begin to lose interest in matters of government not related to their immediate concerns, the government itself often begins to replace rule by reason with rule by power. The *efficient* takes precedence over the *right*.

George Orwell shows us that when a government rests on an unnatural basis, those who rule by power are, in turn, ruled by their need to assert and establish that power again and again. The rulers, in essence, are dominated by the ruled. Orwell writes as a British imperialist attempting to rule by distant authority; his pathetic need to maintain the show of power in the face of millions of uncomprehending and hostile Indians drives him to kill an elephant he does not want to kill, just to satisfy the power expectations of those he must rule. Above all, he must *save face* before those he rules. Without the trappings, the show, the rituals of authority, his power disintegrates. His subjects, the people supposedly under his control, in turn, respond only to his official title and power; they have no sense of justice, tradition, or individuality. Orwell turns a story about the public shooting of an elephant into a tract against rule by power, imperialism, and dependence on an arbitrary class system in government.

Charles Reich in "The Limits of Duty" points out that when customs and laws are questioned in a mass society, "Evil . . . comes about not necessarily when people violate what they understand to be their duty but, more and more often, when they are conscientiously doing what is expected of them." Civil disobedience asks the bystander or nearby worker to do or not do his expected job. People who in the 1950s protested the lack of civil rights for blacks in the South by lying down in front of segregated buses were, according to Reich, projecting a moral choice onto individuals—including bus drivers and all common citizens: "Get the job done, even at the expense of injuring or killing the protestors, or admit that something is wrong with law and custom." Reich's account of the sentiment during protest marches in the late sixties and early seventies brings us once again to the central question in this section:

> If an individual, after rational analysis and broad consideration, believes a civil law is unjust or immoral, how should he or she express that belief?

Reich argues that doing one's duty in a collective, technological, specialized society can often mean the sacrifice of ethical and moral principles. The technician who helps develop napalm, as Reich points out, may not believe in the random maiming and killing of people.[1] Yet the victims are far away and another man will use another machine, the airplane, to do the job. And, in most cases, the enemies would do the same if they had the power and knowledge. Should the technician refuse his part in the entire process and risk losing his job? Or, perhaps more importantly, should the governing system ask its citizens to do such jobs and to make such decisions? Political expediency says *yes;* absolute morality says *no.*

---

1. Napalm is a chemical jelly used in war, especially in jungle wars such as in Vietnam. The jelly is dispersed by plane over fertile countryside in order to *defoliate,* or destroy vegetation. It severely burns human beings upon contact. Napalm is also used in flamethrowers and incendiary bombs. It is an aluminum soap of various fatty acids that makes a firm jelly when mixed with gasoline.

Shooting an Elephant

GEORGE ORWELL

1 In Moulmein, in lower Burma, I was hated by large numbers of people—the only time in my life that I have been important enough for this to happen to me. I was sub-divisional police officer of the town, and in an aimless, petty kind of way anti-European feeling was very bitter. No one had the guts to raise a riot, but if a European woman went through the bazaars alone somebody would probably spit betel juice over her dress. As a police officer I was an obvious target and was baited whenever it seemed safe to do so. When a nimble Burman tripped me up on the football field and the referee (another Burman) looked the other way, the crowd yelled with hideous laughter. This happened more than once. In the end the sneering yellow faces of young men that met me everywhere, the insults hooted after me when I was at a safe distance, got badly on my nerves. The young Buddhist priests were the worst of all. There were several thousands of them in the town and none of them seemed to have anything to do except stand on street corners and jeer at Europeans.

2 All this was perplexing and upsetting. For at that time I had already made up my mind that imperialism was an evil thing and the sooner I chucked up my job and got out of it the better. Theoretically—and secretly, of course—I was all for the Burmese and all against their oppressors, the British. As for the job I was doing, I hated it more bitterly than I can perhaps make clear. In a job like that you see the dirty work of Empire at close quarters. The wretched prisoners huddling in the stinking cages of the lock-ups, the grey, cowed faces of the long-term convicts, the scarred buttocks of the men who had been flogged with bamboos—all these oppressed me with an intolerable sense of guilt. But I could get nothing into perspective. I was young and ill-educated and I had had to think out my problems in the utter silence that is imposed on every Englishman in the East. I did not even know that the British Empire is dying, still less did I know that it is a great deal better than the younger empires that are going to supplant it. All I knew was that I was stuck between my hatred of the empire I served and my rage against the evil-spirited little beasts who tried to make my job impossible. With one part of my mind I thought of the British Raj as an unbreakable tyranny, as something clamped down, in *saecula saeculorum,* upon the will of prostrate peoples; with another part I thought that the greatest joy in

the world would be to drive a bayonet into a Buddhist priest's guts. Feelings like these are the normal by-products of imperialism; ask any Anglo-Indian official, if you can catch him off duty.

3 One day something happened which in a roundabout way was enlightening. It was a tiny incident in itself, but it gave me a better glimpse than I had had before of the real nature of imperialism—the real motives for which despotic governments act. Early one morning the sub-inspector at a police station the other end of the town rang me up on the 'phone and said that an elephant was ravaging the bazaar. Would I please come and do something about it? I did not know what I could do, but I wanted to see what was happening and I got on to a pony and started out. I took my rifle, an old .44 Winchester and much too small to kill an elephant, but I thought the noise might be useful *in terrorem.* Various Burmans stopped me on the way and told me about the elephant's doings. It was not, of course, a wild elephant, but a tame one which had gone "must." It had been chained up, as tame elephants always are when their attack of "must" is due, but on the previous night it had broken its chain and escaped. Its mahout, the only person who could manage it when it was in that state, had set out in pursuit, but had taken the wrong direction and was now twelve hours' journey away, and in the morning the elephant had suddenly reappeared in the town. The Burmese population had no weapons and were quite helpless against it. It had already destroyed somebody's bamboo hut, killed a cow and raided some fruit-stalls and devoured the stock; also it had met the municipal rubbish van and, when the driver jumped out and took to his heels, had turned the van over and inflicted violences upon it.

4 The Burmese sub-inspector and some Indian constables were waiting for me in the quarter where the elephant had been seen. It was a very poor quarter, a labyrinth of squalid bamboo huts, thatched with palm-leaf, winding all over a steep hillside. I remember that it was a cloudy, stuffy morning at the beginning of the rains. We began questioning the people as to where the elephant had gone and, as usual, failed to get any definite information. That is invariably the case in the East; a story always sounds clear enough at a distance, but the nearer you get to the scene of events the vaguer it becomes. Some of the people said that the elephant had gone in one direction, some said that he had gone in another, some professed not even to have heard of any elephant. I had almost made up my mind that the whole story was a pack of lies, when we heard yells a little distance away. There was a loud, scandalized cry of "Go away, child! Go away this instant!" and an old woman with a switch in her hand came round the corner of a hut, violently shooing away a crowd of naked children. Some more women followed, clicking their tongues and exclaiming; evidently there was something that the children

ought not to have seen. I rounded the hut and saw a man's dead body sprawling in the mud. He was an Indian, a black Dravidian coolie, almost naked, and he could not have been dead many minutes. The people said that the elephant had come suddenly upon him round the corner of the hut, caught him with its trunk, put its foot on his back and ground him into the earth. This was the rainy season and the ground was soft, and his face had scored a trench a foot deep and a couple of yards long. He was lying on his belly with arms crucified and head sharply twisted to one side. His face was coated with mud, the eyes wide open, the teeth bared and grinning with an expression of unendurable agony. (Never tell me, by the way, that the dead look peaceful. Most of the corpses I have seen looked devilish.) The friction of the great beast's foot had stripped the skin from his back as neatly as one skins a rabbit. As soon as I saw the dead man I sent an orderly to a friend's house nearby to borrow an elephant rifle. I had already sent back the pony, not wanting it to go mad with fright and throw me if it smelt the elephant.

5 The orderly came back in a few minutes with a rifle and five cartridges, and meanwhile some Burmans had arrived and told us that the elephant was in the paddy fields below, only a few hundred yards away. As I started forward practically the whole population of the quarter flocked out of the houses and followed me. They had seen the rifle and were all shouting excitedly that I was going to shoot the elephant. They had not shown much interest in the elephant when he was merely ravaging their homes, but it was different now that he was going to be shot. It was a bit of fun to them, as it would be to an English crowd; besides they wanted the meat. It made me vaguely uneasy. I had no intention of shooting the elephant—I had merely sent for the rifle to defend myself if necessary—and it is always unnerving to have a crowd following you. I marched down the hill, looking and feeling a fool, with the rifle over my shoulder and an ever-growing army of people jostling at my heels. At the bottom, when you got away from the huts, there was a metalled road and beyond that a miry waste of paddy fields a thousand yards across, not yet ploughed but soggy from the first rains and dotted with coarse grass. The elephant was standing eight yards from the road, his left side towards us. He took not the slightest notice of the crowd's approach. He was tearing up bunches of grass, beating them against his knees to clean them and stuffing them into his mouth.

6 I had halted on the road. As soon as I saw the elephant I knew with perfect certainty that I ought not to shoot him. It is a serious matter to shoot a working elephant—it is comparable to destroying a huge and costly piece of machinery—and obviously one ought not to do it if it can possibly be avoided. And at that distance, peacefully

eating, the elephant looked no more dangerous than a cow. I thought then and I think now that his attack of "must" was already passing off; in which case he would merely wander harmlessly about until the mahout came back and caught him. Moreover, I did not in the least want to shoot him. I decided that I would watch him for a little while to make sure that he did not turn savage again, and then go home.

7 But at that moment I glanced round at the crowd that had followed me. It was an immense crowd, two thousand at the least and growing every minute. It blocked the road for a long distance on either side. I looked at the sea of yellow faces above the garish clothes—faces all happy and excited over this bit of fun, all certain that the elephant was going to be shot. They were watching me as they would watch a conjurer about to perform a trick. They did not like me, but with the magical rifle in my hands I was momentarily worth watching. And suddenly I realized that I should have to shoot the elephant after all. The people expected it of me and I had got to do it; I could feel their two thousand wills pressing me forward, irresistibly. And it was at this moment, as I stood there with the rifle in my hands, that I first grasped the hollowness, the futility of the white man's dominion in the East. Here was I, the white man with his gun, standing in front of the unarmed native crowd—seemingly the leading actor of the piece; but in reality I was only an absurd puppet pushed to and fro by the will of those yellow faces behind. I perceived in this moment that when the white man turns tyrant it is his own freedom that he destroys. He becomes a sort of hollow, posing dummy, the conventionalized figure of a sahib. For it is the condition of his rule that he shall spend his life in trying to impress the "natives," and so in every crisis he has got to do what the "natives" expect of him. He wears a mask, and his face grows to fit it. I had got to shoot the elephant. I had committed myself to doing it when I sent for the rifle. A sahib has got to act like a sahib; he has got to appear resolute, to know his own mind and do definite things. To come all that way, rifle in hand, with two thousand people marching at my heels, and then to trail feebly away, having done nothing—no, that was impossible. The crowd would laugh at me. And my whole life, every white man's life in the East, was one long struggle not to be laughed it.

8 But I did not want to shoot the elephant. I watched him beating his bunch of grass against his knees, with that preoccupied grandmotherly air that elephants have. It seemed to me that it would be murder to shoot him. At that age I was not squeamish about killing animals, but I had never shot an elephant and never wanted to. (Somehow it always seems worse to kill a *large* animal.) Besides, there was the beast's owner to be considered. Alive, the elephant was

worth at least a hundred pounds; dead, he would only be worth the value of his tusks, five pounds, possibly. But I had got to act quickly. I turned to some experienced-looking Burmans who had been there when we arrived, and asked them how the elephant had been behaving. They all said the same thing: he took no notice of you if you left him alone, but he might charge if you went too close to him.

9 It was perfectly clear to me what I ought to do. I ought to walk up to within, say, twenty-five yards of the elephant and test his behavior. If he charged, I could shoot; if he took no notice of me, it would be safe to leave him until the mahout came back. But also I knew that I was going to do no such thing. I was a poor shot with a rifle and the ground was soft mud into which one would sink at every step. If the elephant charged and I missed him, I should have about as much chance as a toad under a steam-roller. But even then I was not thinking particularly of my own skin, only of the watchful yellow faces behind. For at that moment, with the crowd watching me, I was not afraid in the ordinary sense, as I would have been if I had been alone. A white man mustn't be frightened in front of "natives"; and so, in general, he isn't frightened. The sole thought in my mind was that if anything went wrong those two thousand Burmans would see me pursued, caught, trampled on and reduced to a grinning corpse like that Indian up the hill. And if that happened it was quite probable that some of them would laugh. That would never do. There was only one alternative. I shoved the cartridges into the magazine and lay down on the road to get a better aim.

10 The crowd grew very still, and a deep, low, happy sigh, as of people who see the theatre curtain go up at last, breathed from innumerable throats. They were going to have their bit of fun after all. The rifle was a beautiful German thing with cross-hair sights. I did not then know that in shooting an elephant one would shoot to cut an imaginary bar running from ear-hole to ear-hole. I ought, therefore, as the elephant was sideways on, to have aimed straight at his ear-hole; actually I aimed several inches in front of this, thinking the brain would be further forward.

11 When I pulled the trigger I did not hear the bang or feel the kick—one never does when a shot goes home—but I heard the devilish roar of glee that went up from the crowd. In that instant, in too short a time, one would have thought, even for the bullet to get there, a mysterious, terrible change had come over the elephant. He neither stirred nor fell, but every line of his body had altered. He looked suddenly stricken, shrunken, immensely old, as though the frightful impact of the bullet had paralysed him without knocking him down. At last, after what seemed a long time—it might have been five seconds, I dare say—he sagged flabbily to his knees. His mouth slobbered. An enormous senility seemed to have settled upon him.

One could have imagined him thousands of years old. I fired again into the same spot. At the second shot he did not collapse but climbed with desperate slowness to his feet and stood weakly upright, with legs sagging and head drooping. I fired a third time. That was the shot that did for him. You could see the agony of it jolt his whole body and knock the last remnant of strength from his legs. But in falling he seemed for a moment to rise, for as his hind legs collapsed beneath him he seemed to tower upward like a huge rock toppling, his trunk reaching skywards like a tree. He trumpeted, for the first and only time. And then down he came, his belly towards me, with a crash that seemed to shake the ground even where I lay.

12 I got up. The Burmans were already racing past me across the mud. It was obvious that the elephant would never rise again, but he was not dead. He was breathing very rhythmically with long rattling gasps, his great mound of a side painfully rising and falling. His mouth was wide open—I could see far down into caverns of pale pink throat. I waited a long time for him to die, but his breathing did not weaken. Finally I fired my two remaining shots into the spot where I thought his heart must be. The thick blood welled out of him like red velvet, but still he did not die. His body did not even jerk when the shots hit him, the tortured breathing continued without a pause. He was dying, very slowly and in great agony, but in some world remote from me where not even a bullet could damage him further. I felt that I had got to put an end to that dreadful noise. It seemed dreadful to see the great beast lying there, powerless to move and yet powerless to die, and not even to be able to finish him. I sent back for my small rifle and poured shot after shot into his heart and down his throat. They seemed to make no impression. The tortured gasps continued as steadily as the ticking of a clock.

13 In the end I could not stand it any longer and went away. I heard later that it took him half an hour to die. Burmans were bringing dahs and baskets even before I left, and I was told they had stripped his body almost to the bones by the afternoon.

14 Afterwards, of course, there were endless discussions about the shooting of the elephant. The owner was furious, but he was only an Indian and could do nothing. Besides, legally I had done the right thing, for a mad elephant has to be killed, like a mad dog, if its owner fails to control it. Among the Europeans opinion was divided. The older men said I was right, the younger men said it was a damn shame to shoot an elephant for killing a coolie, because an elephant was worth more than any damn Coringhee coolie. And afterwards I was very glad that the coolie had been killed; it put me legally in the right and it gave me a sufficient pretext for shooting the elephant. I often wondered whether any of the others grasped that I had done it solely to avoid looking a fool.

Thinking Questions: *Form*

1. Analyze one of the narrative paragraphs in "Shooting an Elephant" (see paragraphs 3 through 13). Explain how the paragraph combines general and specific sentences. Are the general ideas clearly related to the specific experiences?

2. Look over the vocabulary in paragraphs 3 through 6. Would you say the words are primarily concrete or primarily abstract? Give examples.

3. Define the logical appeal in this essay. Can you divide Orwell's argument into sequential parts, working from his general thesis down through subtheses and support? After reading this essay, would you say that a writer who depends on personal experience to support an opinion can still develop a logical appeal? Support your answer by referring to specific paragraphs in the essay.

4. Describe the narrator's character. What kind of a person is he? How do you know? Is he formal, independent, tough, cowardly, or introspective? Is his vocabulary sophisticated ("perplexing," "jeer," "ravaging," "prostrate," *saecula saeculorum,*" "tyranny," "supplant") or informal and colloquial ("chucked up," "got out of it better," "the sea of yellow faces," "That would never do")? What about the sentences? Do they give you the feel of a careful, serious man or of an unhappy joker? Are they varied or of a consistent pattern? What do you think the narrator looks like?

5. Select one of Orwell's longer sentences. How are the parts of the sentence, the base clause with main subject and verb, and the supporting sentence modifiers, clauses, and phrases, made coherent? Examine this sentence, which opens paragraph 10: "The crowd grew very still, and a deep, low, happy sigh, as of people who see the theatre curtain go up at last, breathed from innumerable throats."

Thinking Questions: *Substance*

1. Can you put the thesis of this essay into a simple sentence? What sentence in the essay comes closest to functioning as a thesis sentence?

2. Why does Orwell not give his readers the opportunity to draw their own conclusions from his experience? Do you think he *should* have let his readers draw their own conclusions?

3. Can you think of a personal experience in which an individual who was supposed to rule as Orwell was *supposed* to rule ended up being led or controlled by the people he was supposedly ruling? Describe the experience specifically. Why was the "leader" not leading? Why were the "followers" not following? Was the problem in the rules or in the individuals involved?

4. Why does Orwell shoot this "grandmotherly" elephant? He seems to feel sorry for it, to respect its patience and calm. Yet he *does* shoot it. And why is the elephant-shooting incident seen as a "bit of fun" (paragraph 7) by the multitudes of Burmese onlookers?

5. Explain the significance of this passage, which occurs immediately before Orwell actually shoots the elephant.

> A white man mustn't be frightened in front of "natives"; and so, in general, he isn't frightened. The sole thought in my mind was that if anything went wrong those two thousand Burmans would see me pursued, caught, trampled on and reduced to a grinning corpse like that Indian up the hill. And if that happened it was quite probable that some of them would laugh. That would never do. There was only one alternative. I shoved the cartridges into the magazine and lay down on the road to get a better aim. (paragraph 9)

Why does Orwell put quotation marks around "natives"? Is he afraid of being injured by the elephant or by the natives? Or is he afraid of something worse?

The Limits of Duty

CHARLES REICH

1 In Washington, D.C., during the May [1971] anti-war protests, police in automobiles and on scooters aimed their vehicles directly at demonstrators and drove toward them at high speeds in order to herd them off the streets. If one of the protesters had been hit and killed, the police officer driving the vehicle would have been guilty of murder. Not accidental killing or manslaughter but murder. Thus, every one of these officers was potentially guilty of a crime similar to that for which Lieutenant Calley was tried and convicted.[1]

2 The applicable principle is deeply embedded in our common law. A leading early example is Halloway's Case (King's Bench, 1628). Halloway was the woodward of woods belonging to the Earl of Denbigh. He discovered a boy named Payne in a tree, attempting to steal wood. Payne had a rope tied around his middle, probably to aid him in climbing trees. Halloway ordered the boy down from the tree, and when he descended struck him two blows on his back with a cudgel. Then Halloway tied the other end of the rope to the tail of his horse. The frightened horse dragged Payne three furlongs, killing him. The question was whether this was manslaughter or murder, and the court held it to be murder, for Halloway knew, or should have known, the reckless and wanton risk he was taking with the boy's life. In such

1. Lieutenant William Calley was convicted of manslaughter for his role in the My Lai atrocity in Vietnam, in which women and children were slaughtered by American soldiers during a military raid. President Nixon attempted to influence the verdict but failed. Since his conviction, however, Calley has been paroled by the Army after serving less than a year of his sentence.

a case, the specific intention to kill is not required. The deliberate taking of the risk is enough. Halloway was hanged.

5 Students at Yale, where I teach in the law school, tell me that District of Columbia bus drivers also aimed their buses toward protesters at high speed and drove ahead without slowing down. How strange that those long-suffering civil servants the bus drivers are now guilty of reckless driving and assault, and, but for the agility of their potential victims, would be guilty of murder. Yet this is not an aberration. It is a pattern that is crucial to understanding what has gone wrong with America. Evil now comes about not necessarily when people violate what they understand to be their duty but, more and more often, when they are conscientiously doing what is expected of them. And for this evil the question of individual blame seems almost irrelevant.

4 Two oil tankers collide on a foggy morning in San Francisco Bay. The bay and ocean are contaminated, beaches are coated, wildlife is exterminated, a fragile beauty is destroyed for millions of people. Yet the tanker captains were doing their duty to move the oil on time, and behind them were company officials concerned with the maintenance of production schedules. No investigation, no technical fixing of blame would be likely to disclose what we have normally imagined to be the root of crime—a guilty mind or a malign heart. And what is true of the San Francisco oil spill is true of the other major evils that we see around us. From wiretapping to the prosecution of the Vietnam war, our crimes have been started and carried out by men zealously attempting to serve as they have been taught to serve.

5 It is this altered problem of evil that rightly troubles us in the Calley case. I believe that Calley was properly convicted of murdering Vietnamese civilians, even though the same result produced by different means is officially held to be wholly legal. Yet we must all believe that Calley, in his own wrong and frightened way, was seeking to perform his duty—to do what was expected of him. The enterprise upon which he was engaged is not condemned, only the means he chose to carry it out. Hence the profound disquiet among so many Americans, taught to serve employer or country, who cannot understand why the law apparently no longer cares about goals but only about a nicety of method. Plainly, our long-accepted criminal-law concepts do not fit the crimes of today.

6 The central reality is that evil today is the product of our system of organization and our technology, and that it occurs because personal responsibility and personal awareness have been obliterated by a system deliberately designed to do just that—eliminate or minimize the human element and insure the supremacy of the system. The whole purpose of this system is to reduce the human component; that is why we have organization charts, a hierarchy of supervision,

divided responsibilities, specialization. In the main, it is this rational organization of human effort that has brought us to our present stage of civilization, but we should realize that inherent in the very design of the system is the disappearance of individual blame, and hence the obsolescence of our concepts of individual criminal responsibility.

7 Let us follow the process of creating an evil more closely. A scientist who is doing his specialized duty to further research and knowledge develops the substance known as napalm. Another specialist makes policy in the field of our nation's foreign affairs. A third is concerned with maintaining the strength of our armed forces with the most modern weaponry. A fourth manufactures what the defense authorities require. A fifth drops napalm from an airplane where he is told to do so. The ultimate evil is the result of carefully segmented acts; the structure itself guarantees an evasion by everyone of responsibility for the full moral act. Indeed, the system, especially when it is combined with advanced technology, makes it unlikely that those who participate in the process will have any real awareness of the ultimate consequences. Neither the scientist nor the man in the State Department nor even the pilot actually sees the horrors of burning napalm on human flesh. The basic result of our system of doing things is to destroy awareness, alienate all of us from the consequences of our actions, and prevent the formation of that very responsibility which has been at the center of our idea of criminal justice.

8 Our traditional criminal law is based on a standard of conduct that assumes each individual to be a morally responsible human being. A man who runs a speedboat carelessly and kills someone is guilty of manslaughter if his actions fall below the standard. A man who allows his passions or desires to direct his actions so that he harms another person is guilty of assault or murder if, according to the standard, he should have controlled himself. The standard represents an ideal. Sometimes it is a cruel and unreasonable ideal, because the individual defendant lacks the capacity for measuring up to it. But the ideal does have a vital function. It establishes a large, even exalted, concept of man.

9 In the famous case of The Queen v. Dudley and Stephens, decided in 1884, four English seamen were cast away in an open boat on the high seas sixteen hundred miles from the Cape of Good Hope. After eighteen days, they were reduced to the utmost state of desperation, with neither food nor water. Dudley and Stephens then said that if no hope of rescue appeared one of the four should be sacrificed, so that the others might live. A third man refused to consent to the plan. The fourth, a boy of seventeen or eighteen, was not consulted; he was then in a helpless and weakened state. Dudley and Stephens

spoke of their having families, indicating that the boy should be chosen. On the twentieth day, no help appearing, the defendants, after praying for forgiveness, killed the boy, and the three men fed upon his blood and body for four days, after which they were rescued. Dudley and Stephens were brought to England and tried for murder. It was acknowledged that if the boy had not been killed all four would probably have perished before rescue, and the boy would probably have died first. Yet the two men were found guilty.

10 The opinion of the Queen's Bench was delivered by Lord Coleridge, the Lord Chief Justice of England. Acknowledging that the temptation had been great and the suffering awful, he declared, "We are often compelled to set up standards which we cannot reach ourselves, and to lay down rules which we could not ourselves satisfy." And he went on:

> Though law and morality are not the same, and many things may be immoral which are not necessarily illegal, yet the absolute divorce of law from morality would be of fatal consequence. . . .

11 Rather than kill the boy, said Lord Coleridge, the men should have been willing to lose their own lives:

> To preserve one's life is generally speaking a duty, but it may be the plainest and the highest duty to sacrifice it. War is full of instances in which it is a man's duty not to live, but to die. The duty, in the case of shipwreck, of a captain to his crew, of the crew to the passengers, of soldiers to women and children, as in the noble case of the *Birkenhead;* these duties impose on men the moral necessity, not of the preservation, but of the sacrifice of their lives for others, from which in no country, least of all, it is to be hoped, in England, will men ever shrink, as indeed, they have not shrunk. . . .

12 Although the circumstances make this case unique, the basic ideal is found throughout the Anglo-American common law. Commonwealth v. Pierce (1884), a classic American case, written by Mr. Justice Holmes, then a member of the Supreme Judicial Court of Massachusetts, dealt with the problem of a physician whose patient died after he had treated her by keeping her wrapped in flannel saturated with kerosene for three days. Admitting that the physician's intentions were good, Holmes said that if the treatment was morally reckless, judged by the standards of a reasonably prudent man, then the defendant must answer for consequences that he neither intended nor foresaw. If the treatment was dangerous according to common experience, "we cannot recognize a privilege to do acts manifestly endangering human life, on the ground of good intentions alone." Holmes also wrote:

> The very meaning of the fiction of implied malice in such cases at common law was, that a man might have to answer with his life for consequences which he neither intended nor foresaw . . . his failure or inability to predict them was immaterial if, under the circumstances known to him, the court or jury, as the case might be, thought them obvious.

13 Recently, I was watching the C.B.S. evening news when a few minutes were devoted to films of one of the favorite antipersonnel weapons used by Americans in Vietnam. It consists of a rocket tightly packed with many ordinary nails. The rocket is fired from a helicopter. The nails scatter widely, propelled with such force that they will go right through the body of anyone in their path. One of the advantages of the weapon, it was explained, is that the gunner doesn't need to see the target at all. The consequences can only be imagined, but what can they be except the reckless maiming of all human beings, old or young, innocent or guilty, who happen to be in the way? Lieutenant Calley is guilty, we are told, but the men who designed these instruments, the men who built them, the men who ordered them to be used, and the men who actually used them were all simply doing their duty. What a diminished view of man this purported version of the law gives us! It tells us that we are all "universal soldiers," in the phrase from one of Donovan Leitch's recordings, morally oblivious of the consequences of our actions. Lord Chief Justice Coleridge completed his argument for full moral responsibility by saying, "It is enough in a Christian country to remind ourselves of the Great Example whom we profess to follow." What has happened when the hard-working, God-fearing people of America are expected to be moral robots, making and firing the nails for mass killings?

14 Obviously, our thinking has been strained to adapt itself to the realities of technology and organization. That is why all those fixtures of the old criminal law, the guilty mind, the malign heart, actual or presumed malice, the common experience of prudent men, seem so out of place—indeed, ironic—in the Calley case. We all understand that such standards of responsibility are not expected of any of us. Nor would we feel more comfortable about the prosecution of high-ranking generals or political leaders under the Nuremberg theory. They, too, would be found to have been doing their duty.

15 The Calley case represents a momentary, vestigial reminder of the old law of responsibility. It was unfair to single out one man for such a revival of the old law, to be sure. Still, the reminder sent a shudder of awareness through all of us universal soldiers back home. It was not surprising that President Nixon hastily intervened. What led to his intervention was not just his seeming unconcern for legal processes, or his desire, as the *New Republic* put it, to coddle this particular criminal. The President insists, in every speech he makes, that we should do our small, segmented duties while he—or those in authority—assumes responsibility. The President's intervention was no surprise, because the Calley case confronts us with standards of responsibility that do not fit what the President and others insist are our duties and the limits of our duties. We are all supposed to be

motorists on a highway where the maximum speed is sixty and the minimum speed is fifty-nine.

16 Perhaps the best way to understand those who have resisted the draft—by seeking conscientious-objector status, by going to jail, by fleeing to Canada—is to acknowledge that they are demanding to live and to be judged by the old standards as fully responsible moral beings. They are seeking law, not evading it. Finding no acceptable standard of conduct available in today's organizational society, they have gone to standards that are not their own personal fiat but the old, traditional standards of religion, ethics, and common law. They are saying that they refuse to act in a way that common experience tells them will produce evil—evil that we know about or should know about. Theirs is a revolt for a larger view of man. And for all of us it poses a necessary question: Given that we must all live and work within large organizations, that we must all take only a small part in a large enterprise, how can we restore the awareness, the responsibility, and the law that are the moral essence of free men?

17 An organization is a hybrid form of machine—one part a tool or system, the other part human. We have made too little use of the human part. We have thought of the humanness as something to be suppressed for efficiency's sake, not something to be valued because it might supply a quality that would otherwise be lacking. All of us who work in organizations should begin to assume a responsibility that is larger than the particular job we do, and this responsibility should ultimately be recognized, protected, and enforced by law. It might take many forms. Perhaps there should be a right—analogous to the long-recognized right to strike for economic objectives—to refuse, on a selective moral basis, to do certain work and perform certain duties. Perhaps this right should be guaranteed to individuals as well as to organized groups. Perhaps the organization should be answerable, on a democratic basis to those who work within it, for its policies and their probable consequences. Surely the present rigid hierarchy of authority must give way to a concept that in an organization all the members have a share of authority.

18 A corollary to this is that law should be based on the assumption that institutions, far more than individuals, are likely to go astray. Perhaps the primary regulatory work of law should be shifted from that of managing people to that of managing organizations while safeguarding the individuality of the people within them. Because organizations are the most characteristic element of our civilization, the scope of action by the members, employees, or consumers must be widened, and the scope of action by systems and machines must be narrowed and must be supervised by law. In the deepest sense, the purpose of such changes is nothing less than a restoration of one of our richest and most neglected resources—the human potentiality

of the great mass of our people. Government by a managerial élite deprives us of the humanity of the many. Policy is made by a few, and the rest are coerced into following by laws that speak in the name of duty. The assumption is made that those who get to the top are naturally qualified to manage and plan for the rest of us, that we must accept what they require of us without allowing our moral knowledge to intervene. Such a neglect of our moral resources is as great a loss as our now well-known neglect of our environmental resources. We need the full participation of each individual. We can no longer afford to be a people who unthinkingly serve.

19 This brings us back to what happened in Washington. The procedures used against demonstrators who tried to block traffic were flagrantly un-Constitutional. There were arrests without cause—mass roundups, which often included any young person, however innocent, who happened to be visible to the police. Prisoners were not subject to normal arrest procedure. Many were kept at detention centers without being afforded the basic rights of arrested persons. All this, like the murderous driving, was not the product of officers gone berserk but was part of coldly rational plans sanctioned, and later praised, by high authorities. Indeed, the same high authorities have recommended that similar tactics be used again. Can the policemen and bus drivers in question say they are doing all they can to respect the fundamental law of the land if they simply follow orders? Can the civil servants who drove to work that morning, maybe sympathetic to the peace movement but afraid of a demerit, call themselves law-abiding? I am suggesting that following orders is no longer good enough for any of us—not if we want our Constitution preserved. Each of us has a permanent and personal duty to the supreme law of the land. I do not mean the "law" that the Nixon Administration speaks of—something that I would call "force," or "state power." I think the Nixon Administration is deeply contemptuous of law. We cannot count on Attorney General Mitchell to preserve the law, nor, I fear, can we count on the courts. And, from a certain point of view, that is as it should be. It is our Constitution, not theirs.

Thinking Questions: *Form*

1. Reich mixes many brief illustrations with the exposition of his thesis. Select several paragraphs and show how the brief narrations are used to illustrate a general idea. Does he always make the relationships between examples and ideas clear? *How* does he make them clear—with repetitions of his main ideas, with transitional sentences that tell a reader how an example will illustrate an idea?

2. What do you think of Reich's use of the first person ("I") in this essay? Does it make the essay too personal and informal in tone (the relationship between the reader and writer)? Why or why not?

3. How would you describe the tone of this essay? Is Reich preachy, concerned, too pushy, not pushy enough? Point to elements of form—word choice, sentence structure, use of pronouns, his selection and arrangement of examples—as you answer.

4. Is this essay directed to a special or a general audience? How can you tell? Reich is a lawyer; does he discuss legal problems in a way that only lawyers would understand?

5. Many contemporary essayists use a technique similar to Reich's. They develop a central problem and thesis and string together carefully described brief narrative examples to support it. Then they use rhetorical questions (questions the writer really already has answered implicitly in the essay, although the explicit answer of the question is left to the reader) to suggest the larger implications of the thesis. Notice Reich's use of rhetorical questions in his final paragraph: "Can the policemen and bus drivers . . . say they are doing all they can to respect the fundamental law of the land if they simply follow orders? Can the civil servants who drove to work that morning, maybe sympathetic to the peace movement but afraid of a demerit, call themselves law-abiding?" You answer these questions, using Reich's essay. Do you agree with the answers the essay would encourage?

Thinking Questions: *Substance*

1. Have two or three students in your class research the background of the William Calley case. These students should explain exactly how the major issues in the Calley trial and conviction apply to Reich's central thesis: that individuals must *not* let their sense of duty control their moral and ethical decisions. What was the public response to Calley's part in the My Lai atrocity? What was the general public reaction to his military conviction? Why?

2. Define the "altered problem of evil" (see paragraph 5) which Reich uses as a basic assumption in this essay. How does the collision of two oil tankers (described in paragraph 4) illustrate the "altered problem of evil"? Can basically *good* men do evil deeds, especially when they are following orders or a sense of duty?

3. Do you agree with Reich that modern societies have lost their trust in "ideals" (see paragraph 8)? Look over paragraphs 9 through 11 carefully; they provide Reich's illustrative example for this assertion. The case of the British seamen described in these paragraphs points out a central paradox in an individual's responsibility to law in any complex society: how and when does an individual decide that one law is *higher*, or more important and universal, than another? The British seamen who ate their fellow crew member had decided that the law of self-preservation was higher than the law against killing other humans. Likewise, the protesters who blocked roads and highways in reaction against what they

thought were unjust laws or acts of government—the Vietnam War or segregation laws, for example—were arguing that moral law was higher than civil law or government policy. Do people still act on higher "principles"?

4. Which of the following decisions is expedient; which is idealistic?

> George Orwell's decision to kill the elephant rather than lose face in front of those he was supposed to rule (in "Shooting an Elephant," the essay that opens this section). The federal judge's decision to sentence William Calley to prison because of his part in the My Lai massacre.

Use these examples to define *expediency*.

5. Answer, in your own words, the essential question in Reich's essay: "Given that we must all live and work within large organizations, that we must all take only a small part in a large enterprise, how can we restore the awareness, the responsibility, and the law that are the moral essence of free men?" Before you begin, decide whether you agree with the assumptions implicit in the question. *Is* there a "moral essence" that you believe is essential to free people? Can you define it? If there isn't, then what?

* * *

"A Busload of Slogans," Norman Mailer's essay on the antiwar march to the Pentagon in the late 1960s, illustrates another personal reaction to large government and bureaucratic law. He describes a group of students who join together to oppose specific policies of their government: its carrying on of what they believe is an unjust and undeclared war; its insensitivity to the individuals who fight that war; its ignorance of what they believe are essential moral and ethical principles. Their government, the protesters argue, acts expediently when it should act ethically and morally. In essence, these protesting individuals try to create a moral force to counteract the power of Big Government, represented in Mailer's essay by the impersonal and bureaucratic Pentagon, a conglomerate of sterile white hallways, offices, and well-trimmed courtyards.

One of the ironies of the peace movement in the late 1960s, however, was that the individuals involved, although many were motivated by sincere moral outrage, often came to use the tactics they claimed to abhor. Once they had joined together to oppose a large, impersonal, powerful bureaucracy, the protest groups began to argue, "Fight fire with fire, expediency with expediency." They shouted slogans at military police:

> "Hey, hey, LBJ! How many kids did you slay today?"
>
> "Hell, no, we won't go."
>
> "Bring the troops home now."

The slogan became a political weapon even in the mouths of those who claimed to be protesting against an immoral and corrupt war, perpetrated by a country they felt had come to be governed by expediency; slogans were also used *against* people, to separate them, rather than as a device to create respect, political unity, or moral understanding. As you read Mailer's essay, notice how a moral principle becomes a blunt instrument, a weapon for war rather than a tool to fashion understanding.

Barbara Tuchman, a noted contemporary historian and expert on China, offers us notes derived from a recent visit to the People's Republic of China. Tuchman's observations provide a sharp contrast to Mailer's. China seems serene, totally without the chaotic sense of struggle and disagreement that we find in Mailer's observations of the march on the Pentagon. In China everyone seems reconciled to their role in the larger society. Farmers plow and plant without question, using whatever tools and expertise are available. Production of food and industrial goods has greatly improved; although Communist China still lags behind some Western production standards, Tuchman gives us the idea that they are making strong and consistent progress.

Throughout her notes, however, Barbara Tuchman seems to imply some reservations about China's peacefulness, its growing productivity, its seeming total efficiency. As you read, ask yourself what might be the cause of those reservations? Perhaps at least some expressions of discontent and concern from the Chinese people she interviewed would have made the seeming peace, tranquility, and total unity more credible? Perhaps an American historian, used to the outspoken messiness of democracy, would find such total lack of disagreement and upheaval incredible, even distasteful?

Both Norman Mailer and Barbara Tuchman, in their very *different* essays on very different subjects, imply that governments, however much they strive to keep order, must allow for individual dissent. Their attitudes are implied by the way they describe and narrate what they have seen and experienced. Tuchman carries with her to China the historian's probing eye for details as they fit a developing cultural pattern. She compares what she sees and hears with what she can imagine she does *not* see and hear. And she writes essays in which her observations and reflections combine to capture the good and the bad of Communist Chinese life.

A Busload of Slogans

NORMAN MAILER

1 In fact, the bus is getting ready to leave the Pentagon. A driver has gotten on—to many cheers—and a wire gate is closed across the front to protect the chauffeur from attack by any prisoners while he is driving. There are also bars across each window. (Obviously Mailer has had the fantasy of bending the bars and making his escape, and has decided not to—it would certainly make him famous for too little.) The sun has been beating on the bus and it is as uncomfortably warm as a small Southern bus depot on an Indian summer afternoon, which is what the faces outside might suggest, if not for the Pentagon walls. And a battle has been taking place, even if no sign of it seems to be reaching here—except, gloomy thought, the battle cannot be going too well, for there is not the remotest sign of panic in this rear area. Except there also seems less air of self-congratulation. It is frustrating not to know.

2 The motor started. They backed up, turned around, pulled away. Now, their hands were out the window with their fingers extended in the V for Victory sign. They passed MPs standing at attention on the open end of the loading area, looking not unlike buoys in a channel as you pull out to sea. To a man, the prisoners in the bus began to yell, "Hell, no, we won't go; hell, no, we won't go!" and at the subtle shift of expression in each MPs face, other slogans were quickly fed: "End the war in Vietnam. Bring the boys home! End the war in Vietnam. Bring the boys home." There was a rollicking solidarity now on the bus, somewhere between young coal miners under arrest for a strike, and a high school team riding back from a successful game. In fact, the MPs had the look of substitutes on a high school football bench when the team is behind or the game is worrisome, they stood erectly at the highest pitch of attention—tweak them and they would have twanged like a bow—their chins jammed up under their upper jaws, jaws under their head, head in helmet, line of vision cut off six feet from the ground—that classic military attention which says: It don't matter how bad I am, when I stand like this, sir, I am being good.

3 "Hey, hey, LBJ! How many kids did you slay today?" shouted the prisoners in the bus to the MPs and waved their fingers in V for Victory. It felt like a victory, one hardly knew over what, perhaps over the lack of imagination (and so the secret consternation) of

those young MPs, same age as so many of the prisoners, but utterly uncomprehending of why anyone their age would wish for this purpose to get arrested.

4 They sang much of the way. Shouting their slogans to high school adolescents at the few intersections where they stopped for traffic lights in the small suburban shopping streets on their route, the kids looking surprisingly like high school kids in Hollywood and TV, the long pants, sweaters, sneakers; the girls in variations on middie blouses and mini-skirts, saddle shoes. A part of him had always tried to believe that the America he saw in family television dramas did not exist, had no power—as of course he knew it did—to direct the styles and the manners and therefore the ideas of America (for in a country where everyone lived so close to their senses, then style, precisely, and manner, precisely, carved ideas into the senses) ideas like conformity, cleanliness, America-is-always-right. They did not have to know too much about the endless reverberations of chic, no, clean American kids could end up giving lollipops (shaped like Grandma's half-dollar) to their favorite Vietnamese cripple—"Hey, Hank, was this little girl burned by VC or us?"

5 Now the kids on the street looked at them with blank faces. They had no idea of what the V for Victory sign meant, nor even the slogans, "Hey, hey LBJ." There was that dim look which must come toward teachers from the bigger boys in the rear row—by the use of cajolery and some sizable intimidation, not to mention soul-suffocating uses of repetition, yes, a passing grade of seventy lurks in those dim eyes. So these high school kids watching them pass had that same dim look. "Yes, Sally, yes, there's something I heard was going on at the Pentagon." No, if their bus made all the noise of a high school bus after winning a game, the game had taken place on Mars, Mars where all the bright kids went. Which is maybe why they made so much noise now. Because they had never traveled on a high school victory bus.

6 It offered its wry perspective. All the dull kids, too stupid to study, ovulating turgid fantasies in the back row, all liveliness sunk in premature sapience of burgeoning young meats, and up front, the bright middle-class children, little intellectual drills, their mental voracity driving them to further, better, higher critiques of the public material before them until—Vietnam! Would America have to end by taking all its bright children and packing them off in buses to the Muzak Run? (For they might offer music in the gas chambers in the new totalitarianism.) He still could not believe such a day would come, but it was sometimes harder to keep this faith intact at night. Recall him to: "That long dark night of the soul when it is always three o'clock in the morning."

7 Ah, yes, thought Mailer, as the shopping street flickered past the

bus window at a rate not faster than a good horse's trot, yes, bless Fitzgerald for his clear line—and why that long dark night, yes, why, when all was said? and Wolfe dead too early and Hemingway a suicide—how much guilt lay on the back of a good writer—it grew worse and worse. As the power of communication grew larger, so the responsibility to educate a nation lapped at the feet, new tide of a new responsibility, and one had become a writer after all to find a warm place where one was safe—responsibility was for the pompous, and the public servants; writers were born to discover wine. It was an old argument and he was worn with it—he had written a good essay once about the failure of any major American novelist to write a major novel which would reach out past the best-seller lists to a major part of that American audience brainwashed by Hollywood, TV, and *Time*. Yes, how much of Fitzgerald's long dark night may have come from that fine winnowing sense in the very fine hair of his nose that the two halves of America were not coming together, and when they failed to touch, all of history might be lost in the divide. Yes, there was a dark night if you had the illusion you could do something about it, and the conviction that not enough had been done. Or was it simply impossible—had the two worlds of America drifted irretrievably apart? Marooned on these unhappy and somewhat fruitless questions, he nonetheless enjoyed the ride through the late afternoon sunlight on these streets in Virginia (was there any other state with so sweet a name?) eddying through a melancholy which was not without its private flavor, for he felt remarkably disembodied from all proceedings—yes, he had a glint of the emotion; doubtless, he felt shriven. Did religious sentiments arrive thus often to men with as much meat on their bones as himself, wondered Mailer?

8 So it went. Lots of song, all the slogans. "Hell, no, we won't go." "Bring the troops home now." "Hey, hey, LBJ." He yelled with the rest. That was the advantage of being shriven—you could join the Communist Sing. And this fine young clergyman from Yale for companion.[1]

9 Then his thoughts began to meander again—down a long broad slow river of thought. He turned a bend—he had it. Delight. He had made the grand connection between Egyptian architecture and the Pentagon. Yes. The Egyptian forms, slab-like, excremental, thick walls, secret caverns, had come from the mud of the Nile, mud was the medium out of which the Egyptians built their civilization, abstract ubiquitous mud equaled in modern times only by abstract

1. This line refers to Yale chaplain William Sloan Coffin, who became a leader of the anti-Vietnam protest movement during the march on the Pentagon. Coffin remains active in liberal social causes today.

ubiquitous money, filthy lucre (thoughts of Norman O. Brown).[2] And American Civilization had moved from the existential sanction of the frontier to the abstract ubiquitous sanction of the dollar bill. Nowhere had so much of the dollar bill collected as at the Pentagon, giant mudpie on the banks of America's Nile, our Potomac! Well, decided Mailer, now much cheered, the secret in prison was to have a view out the window—but thoughts of Jack Ruby growing cancer in a windowless air-conditiond cell came to depress him.

Now they reached their prison. It was the U. S. Post Office in Alexandria. A square stolid red-brick building of that pale lusterless (abstract ubiquitous) brick (as opposed to the old wine-red, clay-red brick of the Smithsonian) was there on a street off the main shopping street to receive them.

2. Norman O. Brown, in a popular book entitled *Life Against Death,* equated man's desire to horde money with his psychological desire to retain his own waste, thus the term *filthy lucre. Life Against Death* is a neo-Freudian, psychoanalytical reading of Western Civilization.

Thinking Questions: ***Form***

1. Norman Mailer is a controversial and well-known writer. Ask friends or teachers their opinions of his personality, ideas, and work. Take notes and pull the opinions you hear into some kind of general impression before you continue. Then describe Mailer as he appears in this brief essay. Is he a traditional moralist defending a moral position? Look at his style, the way he chooses words and shapes sentences to create a speaking personality and uses it to define his character. Is he an intellectual? What makes you think so? What do you think of a writer who speaks of himself in the third person ("Ah, yes, thought Mailer, as the shopping street flickered past the bus window . . ."), as if he were another person or a character in his own novel?

2. Choose a single paragraph in this essay. Analyze the verb forms in the paragraph. Are they specific action verbs (see paragraph 2)? Are they varied? Do they help you feel a part of the action described, rather than a distant observer? Compare Mailer's verbs with the verbs in one of your own descriptive or narrative paragraphs.

3. Choose another paragraph and analyze the sentences. Are they varied or similar in length. Count the words. Do they usually follow a normal English word order (subject, verb, object or complement)? How about a sentence like this (in paragraph 2)? "There was a rollicking solidarity now on the bus, somewhere between young coal miners under arrest for a strike, and a high school team riding back from a successful game." Is this a typical sentence in this essay? Why or why not?

4. How are most of Mailer's paragraphs organized? Chronologically?

By a subjective sequence remembered by a character? By a subjective sequence as recalled by the narrator? All three?

5. Look over the concrete imagery (those images that appeal directly to your senses) in several of Mailer's paragraphs. Do you find that he selects and arranges in order to establish a particular impression? How would you summarize that impression? And how does the specific impression contribute to Mailer's development of a thesis, or at least an implied thesis, in his essay?

Thinking Questions: *Substance*

1. Throughout this essay, Mailer wants his readers to share in his experience. Can you point to several essential contrasts in the essay and point out how they contribute to the meaning of the entire essay? For example, how do the visual contrasts between the Pentagon and the "prison" in the U.S. Post Office in Alexandria, Virginia (paragraphs 9 and 10) help Mailer develop his thesis? Also, how do the environment that surrounds the protesters (the bus carrying them to jail, as described in paragraphs 1 and 2; the shouting and singing and general atmosphere within the bus, in paragraph 4) and the action that occurs on the streets outside the bus (paragraphs 5 and 7) contrast with the quiet, official serenity of the Pentagon? Can you find other examples of dramatic opposition between places and people that serve to develop Mailer's ideas?

2. Just what is Mailer saying about America through this narrative? Is he *for* the protesters completely? How can you tell? Does he claim to understand why the division symbolized by the march on the Pentagon has occurred in American society?

3. Compare Mailer's ideas on protest and its causes with Charles Reich's in "The Limits of Duty." Reich argues that men who work and live in a technological, specialist society—in which each person's sense of duty is defined by the limits of his or her job, which is in turn defined by employers or rulers—must individually expand his or her sense of duty beyond that defined by job or social function. Would Mailer agree? How do you know? Are the protesters in Mailer's essay successfully expanding their sense of duty beyond what would normally be included in their everyday jobs? Should, for example, the laborer on the automobile assembly line worry about government policies on foreign affairs? Should these workers expect to have some control over how the corporation sells the automobiles they make?

4. Why does Mailer describe the occasion of the march on the Pentagon by using F. S. Fitzgerald's quotation: "That long dark night of the soul when it is always three o'clock in the morning"? Does Mailer indicate that he believes a dawn will follow this nightmare of protest and confusion? What evidence does he provide for and against a positive conclusion to social upheaval and protest? Do you feel that Mailer's essay supports the belief that political expediency (the "ubiquitous sanction of the dollar bill") will inevitably compete with political idealism, and that such an opposition is behind the battle between the protesters and the establishment?

5. Much of the vocal, active political outrage and protest of the late 1960s and early 1970s has subsided. Find examples of protest movements today. Look in newspapers, magazines, cartoons—any popular medium. Are there as many active issues as there were when Vietnam, race, and pollution caused mass meetings and demonstrations? If there are, what are the differences between the ways current issues are debated, supported, or expressed and the ways they were expressed in the late 1960s and early 1970s? Is there more moderation? More apathy? Why, and are the differences good or bad? Consider writing an essay that contrasts the ecology movements of 1969 and 1974. Use personal experience *and* outside reading as source material. In the process, define the essential differences between the way people expressed support for ecological reform in 1969 and the way such support is expressed in 1974.

Notes from China

BARBARA TUCHMAN

Standing Up

1 In a country where misery and want were the foundation of the social structure, famine was periodic, death from starvation common, disease pervasive, thievery normal, and graft and corruption taken for granted, the elimination of these conditions in Communist China is so striking that negative aspects of the new rule fade in relative importance. The dominant fact is that for China's working class, which is to say over 80 percent of the world's most populous country, the lid of exploitation has been lifted. While visible betterment varies widely between the major cities and the provinces, it is probably true to say of all areas that the working class, in whose interest China is now governed, have found a sense of purpose, self-confidence, and dignity in the knowledge that they are the object of the state's concern, not, as in the past, society's victims.

2 The most obvious negative in the process is the mental monotone imposed upon the country. All thought, all ideas past, present, and future, not to mention the historic record, are twisted, manipulated, rolled out, and flattened into one, expressed in half a dozen slogans dinned incessantly and insistently into the heads of the public. As far as the life of the mind in China is concerned, its scope has rigid limits and its sound is a blaring, endlessly repeated single note, with effect (at least upon a Westerner) like the drip, drip, drip on the

victim's head of the ancient Chinese water torture—if it had made a loud noise. The message is that "the People" are the motive force; that Marxism-Leninism is universal truth, and that propelled by its principles and Chairman Mao's thought, China's working class can ultimately build Socialism, meaning well-being for everyone. The goal lies ahead and can only be reached by keeping the Revolution green, that is by continually renewed contact with the masses.

3 Domestically it seems to work. I say "seems" throughout these notes cautiously and advisedly because ignorance of the language is a barrier equal to being deaf. A six-week visitor under this handicap can offer conclusions as impressions only.

4 Perhaps too the transfer to collectivism has been made easier because China's life was in some ways collective to begin with. Consider the *kang,* the built-in wall-to-wall bed of north China on which, in the poorer homes, the whole family sleeps. With that in their background, collective adjustment is natural, not to say imperative.

5 In any event, from what we could see through eleven cities (Peking, Taiyuan, Yenan, Sian, Loyang, Chengchow, Wuhan, Nanking, Suchow, Shanghai, and Canton) and a variety of rural settlements, collective effort has made up China's oldest lack—enough food. Our reception at an agricultural commune in central Shansi included three or four heaping platters each of sliced tomatoes, fresh peaches, and sweetened stuffed dumplings made of glutinous rice (a substance to make a Western stomach quail) in far greater abundance than was required by the company. Admittedly this was laid on to impress the visitors (as was everything else we met in China), but the availability of such abundance to agricultural workers and their un-hungry attitude toward it were simply not possible in the past when, as one member of the commune said, "The lower peasants could not even have the chaff of the rice to eat."

6 Increased production, materially speaking, is what China's revolution is all about. It refutes all the firm statements of economists and agronomists in the past that China's arable land could not be augmented, nor the yield per unit of land be raised sufficiently to feed the expanding population. Both have been done, not by magic but because the people have been mobilized and motivated to do it—by expropriation and redistribution of land permitting communal farming in large tracts instead of fractional plots, and by the knowledge that everything they do to make improvements will now benefit themselves not the landlord.

7 I will cite no statistics on increased yield because I cannot judge their reliability, but in this summer's drought in north China with day after relentless day of no rain and of temperatures over 100, when one sees fresh water being pumped in life-giving gushes from irrigation channels, and sees surrounding fields green, vegetables ripen-

ing, and seedling crops sprouting instead of withering, one needs no statistics. In the old days this year's drought would have been lethal. The great Miyun Dam and Reservoir northeast of Peking, the pumping stations and sedimentation plants along the Yellow River that have at last harnessed "China's Sorrow," and similar projects constructed elsewhere under the new regime, besides providing hydroelectric power, have brought drought, flood, and famine under control. The result provides the agricultural surplus which, paid in kind to the state as a form of tax, supplies the capital for expansion of industry—the other of the two legs on which the new China walks.

8 In human terms the process has produced a new person—the worker from the ranks who can become manager of the enterprise. It is true that such people do not bear sole responsibility. They function in committee in a three-in-one arrangement of workers, technicians, and "cadres" or representatives of the Government. Even so, in their straight-forward look-you-in-the-eye greeting, their poise and self-respect, they are impressive, none more so than the woman Vice-Chairman of the Revolutionary Committee of the Szu Tzi Ching (Evergreen) Commune outside Peking.

9 Quiet, composed, and supremely assured, with bobbed hair, neat overblouse, loose trousers, and a big silver wristwatch, she knew every aspect of the operation: the crop rotation, marketing, fertilizing, spraying, trucking, livestock, the schools, clinics, and family lives of a commune of 6,000 acres and 41,000 people, formerly scattered in hopeless division in 138 villages. Born in a family in the "poor peasant" category, that is, hired or tenant farmers without land of their own, she was now playing a competent role where formerly she had no stake. Her colleague in charge of the orchards, a rough peasant with stubble of beard and sweat towel around his neck, had the same assured air, as did the girl supervisor of the pig sties. Both shook hands with confident equality and exhibited their domains with pride (each ripening peach on the trees was individually bagged and each pig had its own pen).

10 Their counterparts in industry—like the shop foreman whose intense pride is almost tangible as he watches a finished tractor leave the assembly plant—are equally forthright and precise, in notable contrast to civil servants who, being more vulnerable to the swings and switchbacks of official policy, try to be utterly orthodox and noncommittal to the point of speechlessness.

11 Obviously the commune and tractor plant were selected showplaces, but the fact that they exist at all and are managed in part by their workers is a piece of one of the greatest bootstrap operations in history. There have been harsh costs and there are negative aspects, but in these worker-managers China has visibly, to quote who else but the Chairman, "stood up."

The People

12 Who are "the People," the subject and object of every political slogan in China? According to Chairman Mao's definition, "the People" are all who support the Revolution (dutifully said to be 90 to 95 percent). The remainder, consisting of "class enemies," "bad elements," and counter-revolutionaries, are merely Citizens. This strikes me as a murky Thought, not one of the Chairman's best, or else a poor translation, but since it is the official translation, it will have to stand. Theoretically and ideally, then, the People are a mystic whole (leaving aside the bad elements), but in practice class origin is determining.

13 Workers, peasants, and soldiers are automatically People (although sometimes they are exhorted to "learn from the People," which is confusing) as is anyone of "poor and lower middle peasant" or other working-class family. Those who come from landlord, rich peasant, merchant-capitalist, or bourgeois origin are automatically out, or at least not full members of society until they have proved by deed and attitude that they have repudiated their class values and wholeheartedly adopted Chairman Mao's "correct revolutionary line" of service to the People. What this requires in outward conformity for those with inner reservations can only be conjectured.

14 The masses (and for China the word is appropriate in a descriptive, not necessarily Marxist, sense), pedaling unhurriedly to work on their millions of bicycles through the city streets, filling the now public parks of the Imperial City and Summer Palace, crowding a department store or a museum exhibit of People's Art, queueing at cooked food shops for a meal in a bowl, appear quite at ease. The economic security of food, paid work, and oldage pension is a great relaxer of tension, and this appears in faces and manner. China has never been in a hurry, and the pace, even in factory work, is still easy-going. There is no sense of pressure or tension in the air.

15 A foreigner feels safe (though not comfortable) walking alone anywhere at any time—if he can put up with attracting crowds of intense starers. In the countryside and provincial cities he also attracts smiles and spontaneous handclapping and almost never a scowl, for these Chinese are an agreeable and normally friendly people. Mrs. Chang Si-lan, a tiny spry lady in black whose two-room home (for a family of eight) we visited in a factory compound, welcomed us with such genuine delight that we fell into instant communication. It appeared that she and I were the same age: I pointed to my gray hair while hers was still black; she pointed to her absent teeth while I still had mine. She pressed us to sit beside her on the *kang,* passed cigarettes, and compared grandchildren. On Mrs. Chang's level the Chinese do not insist on talking in ritual fatuities.

16 Decorum is the word for the masses in the capital. Even more notable, in comparison to former times, is their remarkable appearance of health and well-being, though more so in Peking than in the provinces. The running nose of children, that endemic companion of poverty, has vanished, at least in the main cities. There are no cripples, no beggars, no open sores or disease, although hawking and spitting (outside Peking) are as bad as ever. Even Mao Tse-tung Thought has found no formula to prevail over that.

17 Opium-smoking, prostitution, and venereal disease have proved easier to eradicate, and according to claims have been wiped out. I cannot vouch for the claim but I can say that any overt interest in sex is simply nonexistent. When the subject came up in conversation with one female interpreter, it produced a grimace of disgust as if we had mentioned a cockroach, and the same expression contorted the face of a doctor of mental health when he was asked about perversions and homosexuality. "We don't have this in China," he replied succinctly.

18 At a military barracks we visited outside Nanking I noticed no provision for families. The state pays for an officer's home leave or for visits by his family to the post, I was told, but apart from that he does without a wife's companionship. After an officer has served fifteen years and "has a good record," he may apply to have his family live with him. To make sure I had this piece of startling information right, it was repeated for me and confirmed as true for the Army as a whole (although I suspect regional commands vary). When I ventured the comment that this must be a very monastic life, the officer replied, "We consider it a very happy life to live and work with our friends and comrades of the great proletarian People's Liberation Army." That is the way they really talk. (It should be added that the PLA has played a genuinely constructive role in the state which, considering the past role of soldiery in Chinese society, is a revolution in itself; but that is another matter.)

19 At a May 7th Cadre School deep in the country where bureaucrats and professionals come for a six-month term to be re-educated through manual labor, the experience was also celibate. Although they dislike any reference to the question, the Committee was willing to say that their members were too busy with field labor, brick-making, and building (which in fact was hard real work, not leaf-raking) to worry about their sex life. Sex was sublimated in the "struggle for production" and for renewed "revolutionary consciousness." It was the stock answer to be expected, but it is quite possible it may also be true. Whatever the truth, it is evident that in the new society the sex impulse has been pushed deep below the visible surface.

20 The effect on the family life of the "cadre" class is cooling. (This ubiquitous and absurd word, pronounced "cadder" by Chinese-

speaking English—*gan bou* in Chinese—is as basic in Communist usage as "peasant." Originally adopted to mean a government or party bureaucrat, it now loosely covers anyone in an administrative, professional, intellectual, or white-collar job, in short, everyone who is not worker, peasant, or soldier. There is a sharp distinction between lower-echelon cadres called "staff members" and the upper-echelon "leading cadre" who is a person in a position of authority: a minister, bureau chief, manager, director, or head of any organization, except that in the theory no one is head because everything is run by committee. The "leading cadre" in each case is Vice-Chairman of the relevant Revolutionary Committee. Perhaps in deference to Number One, a chairman is either non-existent or never appears.)

21 As regards family life, many of the cadre class are now confining themselves to one child or two and appear to maintain a rather detached marital relationship. Two of the various escorts who accompanied us at different places and who had working wives or husbands, sent their four-year-old children to boarding kindergarten from which the child comes home only for the one-day weekend. The first of these parents explained airily that "a child at home can be a nuisance, you know." A third had a more surprising solution: her four-year-old son was cared for at home by what she first described as a "roommate," and only at my evident bewilderment reluctantly confessed was a housemaid! I felt myself dangerously in the presence of Revisionism.

22 This attitude has not yet spread downward, for in the life of the streets, which is the life of the masses, babies and small children are cared for and carried around by brothers and sisters, parents and grandparents (in particular the grandfather); not in the backpack arrangement with head nodding used by the Japanese but cradled in a front-carry which is certainly less efficient but more affectionate.

23 Among the cadre class, however, homemaking, like child care, is de-emphasized. To eliminate the trouble of cooking, a working couple may often take their meals, including the evening meal, at the office cafeteria, the wife at her office and the husband at his.

24 The job unit governs the cadre's life, assigns housing, and determines political reliability and periods of May 7th "re-education" if required. More often than not, one is told, the subject volunteers for this experience, perhaps because he considers it the advisable thing to do or because he sincerely wants to renew his Marxist fervor (believed to atrophy in office jobs) through realistic manual labor, as well as to obey the Chairman's order to "combine theory with practice." At one May 7th labor camp for "leading cadres" in the Shensi hills not far from Yenan, the mood seemed positive and the members genuinely and vigorously engaged in outdoor labor under the blazing sun. But the sad, subdued look and remote eyes of a

gray-haired surgeon from the leading hospital of the provincial capital suggest that the process does not always work.

25 In contrast is the provincial political boss, generally designated Vice-Chairman of the Provincial Revolutionary Committee, who may or may not combine in his person the all-powerful office of Party Secretary for the municipality or region. These are hard, beefy men, something between Mike Quill and Khrushchev, whom we came to call the Commissars. From what answers we could elicit, they came mostly from the PLA or had an Army background, and no doubt represented the Army men sent in by Mao to regain control of provincial government after the frenzy of the Cultural Revolution of 1966-69.

26 We made the acquaintance of five or six of these comrades, more or less involuntarily on both sides, at dinners which the Association for Friendship with Foreign Countries, our sponsoring escorts, insisted on giving in each city to welcome visiting "foreign friends" (the new official designation for all foreigners). In the presence of the local commissar as presiding host, subordinates hardly venture a word; conversational attempts are left to the guests through an interpreter. The commissar, genial but bored, confines himself to the toast-drinking routine and suavely avoids any conversation above the level of "How long have you been in China?" and "How long will you stay?" These men, at least those we met, do not convey an impression of quality above the union-boss level. They may be dedicated Maoists under the surface, or they may represent the inevitable formation of a new power group to replace the old, the very thing Mao is trying to avoid. As always the foreigner feels inadequate to penetrate the reality.

The Countryside

27 The farmer is the eternal China. In the Sian Provincial Museum one can see a tomb carving of a Han Dynasty man driving a single-furrow iron plough pulled by a team of bullocks—and just outside town see the same arrangement functioning unchanged after two thousand years. In the fields groups of figures working together bend over the never-ending, back-breaking task of cultivation: transplanting rice seedlings, weeding the young corn, hoeing the vegetables, scything the ripe wheat or rice, and beginning over the plowing and harrowing of the field for the second crop.

28 In the north, plowing is by mule or bullock and occasionally, on the lands of a fortunate commune, by tractor. In the south and in the Yangtse Valley, the gray water buffalo with flat head and crescent horns that has not taken a hurried step for twenty centuries, provides the power. Here too, occasionally, a motored plough with a man

walking between the handles can be seen lurching axle-deep through the mud of a wet paddy field, looking awkward and incongruous. Whatever the place and whatever the power, the bending human figures under straw hats are never absent from the scene. Bent backs and straw hats are as integral to China as the gas station to America.

29 To the eye rural China is beautiful. Terraced slopes braced by strips of stone walls rise like earth ripples on the hills. The valleys below hold orchards and tile-roofed farmhouses and fields of wheat or corn or *kaoliang,* which looks like corn except that its grain is borne in a feathery cluster at the top. In the wide bed of a shallow river women and children scrub clothes against the rocks. Farther south, thatched roofs appear and yellow-flowered squash vines climb over them and over everything else, hiding the debris of farmyards. Fields of vegetables and rows of string-bean vines on neatly tied tripods make patterns against the flat rich green of rice paddies where the gleam of water shows through. Haystacks, some long, some conical, some with hat-brim tops looking peculiarly Chinese, fill the right places in the landscape as if an artist had placed them. Where there are canals, old wooden scows with dark sails move between the fields. In the distance mountains are never far away.

30 China has no landscape without figures. Through a lake of broad-leaved pink-flowering lotus, black-clad women with streaming hair wade waist-deep in water to pick the edible roots, making a picture so strange and poetic that they seem to belong to some ancient legend. On a village threshing floor chaff is shaken from the grain in shallow baskets; nearby a mule attached to a pole turns the mill-stone on his ceaseless round. A fishermen by a stream, looking exactly as he might in a Tang painting, tends a round-bottomed net hung from a bamboo frame. Where the stream flows by a village, three wizened old men retired from field work sit on a board turning a water wheel with their feet.

31 In the rice regions the early crop, already harvested, is spread out in neat golden bundles to dry. Alongside, after the soil has been turned and meticulously hoed and harrowed and the water pumped back, the thin, pale seedlings of the late crop, transplanted by hand, begin the cycle over again. Weeding, spraying, and fertilizing are still to come. No crop takes so much labor as the rice of Asia, but the yield per unit of land feeds the most mouths. The Chinese call wheat "the lazy man's crop."

32 The policy of dispersing industry to the countryside has already invaded the beauty. From the train window crossing the area between the Yellow River and the Yangtse, power line grids and the tall smoke-stacks and sharp outlines of factories suddenly appear here and there.

33 Old and new exist together. High on a hill in Shensi the fans of a radar station are visible. On the roadside below, a large grass-covered mound with a smoking chimney on top signifies a village brick-making kiln. Boys and women with buckets dangling from shoulder poles carry night soil from a pit to spill on the fields, and elsewhere a group moves among the corn in a cloud of chemical spray. Insecticide is so important in today's China that in one ballet we saw in Peking the girl dancers appeared with handsprayers as part of their costume. Except for locusts, insects seem extraordinarily absent, and birds too in consequence. For the sake of agricultural yield, China has taken a long step toward silent spring. Chemical fertilizer is spread by hand from baskets, and in one beanfield we passed, by women doling it from wash basins with measuring spoons.

34 The rural reality is of course less idyllic than the view. The soft clay soil is dust in dry weather and clinging mud impossible to escape after a rain. In one small farm village near the Yellow River of perhaps twenty or thirty houses encircled by a crumbling clay wall, pigs, ducks, chickens, mules, donkeys, and people merged in the mud, and bullocks lay in it comfortably sleeping. What farm life must be like in the sodden snow of winter with temperatures below freezing is imaginable. Communes are slowly improving the housing but the backlog is vast: the rural population living in communities under 2,000 is estimated at 500,000,000 or approximately 100,000,000 households. Not all have been communalized. Some still cultivate tiny front-yard plots of corn or vegetables no more than ten or twelve feet square, although their land, we were told, is state-owned. A privy here was simply a hole in the ground with two flat stones placed on top in the form of a V.

35 Though painful in the making, communalized farming is by now the rule and the law. At a meeting of a Production Brigade (one unit of a commune) in Shensi, the team leaders, each representing some twenty to twenty-five households, were brown and wrinkled traditional peasants in work-soiled clothes, many of them older men, each with a towel turban wrapped around his head. Three of the team leaders were women. The Vice-Chairman of the Brigade's Revolutionary Committee was the type of village elder one would not have expected could read, but he spoke from notes written down in a pocket notebook. Each member in turn reported his team's progress in the second round of weeding, the second application of fertilizer, and the threshing of already harvested wheat. No. 5 Team was short of manpower and had to call on the old women and children for this task. Throughout the talk the importance given to chemical fertilizer was notable. More than Maoist thought, this is what has raised yield in China. The best time for the third application of insecticide, new to this village, was debated. Following the team leaders, an "edu-

cated youth" of about sixteen or seventeen, sent to the Brigade after graduation from Middle School for his three-year term of manual labor, spoke up to urge greater use of the "scientific" knowledge of the young. He was earnestly supported by the local schoolteacher.

36 The only obvious Government or Party man present, a gray-haired individual in glasses with a sophisticated face, was the Commune representative. Remaining silent throughout the discussion, he spoke only at the end to remind members to repair storehouse roofs against heavy rainfall, and to report a new method of shooting rockets in the air to disperse hail. Except for a glancing reference by the schoolteacher, not a single Maoist slogan or exhortation about the "struggle for production" or "in agriculture learn from Dachai," or "repudiate the Revisionists and capitalist-roaders" was mentioned, although doubless this would not have been true of a younger group. It was the first, and except for a brilliant performance of traditional acrobats, magicians, and jugglers in Sian, the only such relief during the whole of our visit to China.

37 Mechanization of agriculture to replace the water buffaloes, the shoulder-pole baskets, and the bent human backs is the great goal. One could almost indulge in the dream that the Chinese might close themselves off from advancing history, as the last emperors tried vainly to do, and have got rid of the oppression of landlords and taxes and the cruelty of real want, might remain, despite the hard life, an agricultural people, both for the world's sake and their own. It somehow suits them.

Thinking Questions: *Form*

1. Contrast the forms of the three major parts—"Standing Up," "The People," and "The Countryside"—of Tuchman's notes. Which of the three is primarily general and abstract, introducing the thesis? What methods are used in each section to relate general observations and reflections to specifically described scenes and examples?

2. Notice how, in "Standing Up," Tuchman organizes each paragraph around a general idea about China and a specifically described example to illustrate that generality (see paragraphs 4 and 5, where the idea of collectivism is illustrated through the author's descriptions of the *kang*, a "built-in wall-to-wall bed of north China," and the food the author ate at an agricultural commune—"four heaping platters each of sliced tomatoes, fresh peaches, and sweetened stuffed dumplings. . ."). Show how illustration by example works in other paragraphs in this first section of the essay. Can you find a series of paragraphs in which one paragraph explains a general idea that is then exemplified in the paragraphs that follow?

3. Describe the differences between paragraph 15, where Tuchman narrates a scene in which she meets and converses with Mrs. Chang Silan, and paragraphs 16 and 17, where Tuchman uses simple enumeration of examples rather than narration to make her point. What would happen to the entire essay if *every* paragraph were to follow one or the other method of development?

4. Explain the function of these two specific analogies.

> "I cannot vouch for the claim but I can say that any overt interest in sex is simply nonexistent. When the subject came up in conversation with one female interpreter, it producd a grimace of *disgust as if we had mentioned a cockroach. . . .*" (Paragraph 17)

> "The result provides the agricultural surplus which, paid in kind to the state as a form of tax, supplies the capital for expansion of industry—*the other of the two legs* on which the new China *walks.*" (Paragraph 7)

How does the point made with the analogy contribute to Tuchman's general thesis on Communist China? What attitude toward the convention or behavior being described is conveyed by the analogy? How, in other words, does Tuchman use the analogy to inject her own reaction to what she is recording in her essay?

5. How would you rate these notes on a scale ranging from completely objective to completely subjective? To support your rating, provide specific references to Tuchman's word choice, her use of evidence, and her ability to relate examples to general opinions and attitudes. Could these notes be used to support a chapter on Communist China in a current World History textbook?

Thinking Questions: *Substance*

1. Paragraph 26 closes with the sentence, "As always the foreigner feels inadequate to penetrate the reality." Do you read this sentence as an indictment of the hypocrisy of Communist Chinese government officials or as a passing comment on the problems a historian confronts when he or she visits any country in which language and customs are strange and foreign? When you have finished the entire piece, are you convinced that Tuchman *is* positive or negative in her attitude toward Communist China? Does her surface appreciation of industrial and agricultural success and increased productivity apply also to the social well-being and inner freedom of the Chinese people?

2. Norman Mailer and Charles Reich argue for the right to dissent from government policy for every citizen. Barbara Tuchman appreciates the increased efficiency, production, and order she sees in China, especially when she contrasts current government with past regimes in which millions starved or lived in abject poverty. After you have finished the entire piece, do you believe that the increased order and efficiency is indeed worth the "mental monotone" Tuchman describes in this passage?

> The most obvious negative in the process is the mental monotone imposed upon the country. All thought, all ideas past, present, and future,

not to mention the historic record, are twisted, manipulated, rolled out, and flattened into one, expressed in a half a dozen slogans dinned incessantly and insistently into the heads of the public. (Paragraph 2)

3. In the second section of her notes, Barbara Tuchman describes the new class system in China. Industrial workers, farmers, soldiers, and "cadres" (anyone who works in an administrative, professional, intellectual, or white-collar job) are the four major classes. Given Tuchman's description of life in Communist China, what class would you select for yourself if you had the choice, and why? What particular benefits—physical, spiritual, or intellectual—would the class you have chosen afford?

4. Paragraphs 17 through 20 describe the sexual prudery and "decorum" of the Chinese. How does this restraint where sex is concerned fit in with the other customs and values of Communist China? Why would sexual restraint and control be important in a state in which discipline, order, efficiency, increased production, and The People are paramount values? Why, for example, would keeping soldiers from their wives and families except on special occasions increase their dedication to the People's Liberation Army?

5. Throughout her notes Barbara Tuchman works with ambivalent pairs of ideas. Here are two such pairs.

a. The pastoral beauty of the Chinese countryside as seen from a passing train (described in detail in paragraphs 29 and 30) is almost simultaneously contrasted with the "rural reality," which consists of small, overcrowded, mud-filled villages—"twenty or thirty houses encircled by a crumbling clay wall, pigs, ducks, chickens, mules, donkeys, and people merged in the mud . . ." (paragraph 34).

b. The essentially agricultural simplicity of the Chinese—endless rice-paddies filled with straw-hatted peasants manually working the land—is constantly compared with the production advantages of an industrialized and mechanized economy, as phrased in the next-to-last sentence: "One could almost indulge in the dream that the Chinese might close themselves off from advancing history, as the last emperors tried vainly to do, and having got rid of the oppression of landlords and taxes and the cruelty of real want, might remain, despite the hard life, an agricultural people . . ." (paragraph 37).

With these central ambivalences in mind, explain in your own words why Barbara Tuchman wrote these notes. What was she trying to say to Americans about China? What in Communist China might be emulated by Americans? What might be avoided? What might the Chinese try to avoid in America's advanced capitalism?

* * *

SUMMARY QUESTIONS: POLITICS, PROTEST, AND ESTABLISHED GOVERNMENT

1. What *is* expediency in government? Do you believe people should leave the big decisions—military and fiscal policy for example—to elected representatives? Can you give an example from the recent past of a justifiably expedient act by a well-known politician? Can you give an example of an unjustifiable act of political expediency? Be specific.

2. Can you think of a moral principle that you would argue justifies unlawful political obstruction? How would you bring the principle to the attention of fellow citizens? Give specific examples.

3. Can you think of any moral principle that people apply in an absolute way? War, for example, is an exception to the Fifth Commandment; any violent act done in self-defense is also an exception to our laws against violence.

4. If you find it difficult to find any absolute laws, does that mean you believe all governments should be expedient? What are the limits of expediency? Should, for example, one man be excused for murder because he comes from an impoverished and violent background while another man, raised in wealth and ease, must suffer for the same crime? Think up your own examples of moral or political expediency and use them as you develop a general definition.

* * *

MORE ON POLITICS AND PROTEST

James Baldwin's essay shifts the emphasis of this section from public to private concerns. Baldwin discusses his past: growing up in Harlem, his experiences with family, school, and religion, and primarily his relationship with his father. These experiences and relationships illustrate how one man learns to reconcile his desires, needs, and values with the demands and needs of those around him. Baldwin's past becomes our present; as we read, we should learn as well how much an individual must sacrifice and struggle to find a place in society, especially when he or she differs in color and background from the majority.

Baldwin's essay ends in a paradox: people must learn to accept life as it is while they continually struggle against its injustices. Learn to accept *and* fight back, Baldwin suggests. Perhaps his paradox is everyman's paradox—how to "get along" while remaining ourselves? And perhaps this paradox applies equally well to an individual's relations with a government.

"The Lawgiver," a science fiction story by Keith Laumer, picks up where the earlier essays by Charles Reich and Norman Mailer leave off. Just where does one draw the line between abstract principle and the demands of a particular situation? Even when faced with an undeniable world crisis, when severe overpopulation and crowding threaten life as we know it, individuals in this story only reluctantly sacrifice traditional emotions and ideas. A United States senator must decide whether or not to go against all that he has fought for, against a recent law outlawing the birth of babies except under special conditions, in order to save the life of an embryo fathered by his son. In the end, the senator makes a decision that we may agree with in principle but find distasteful, even horrifying, in practice. Ask yourself who is acting justly and consistently in this story—the common people who break the laws and oppose the senator, or the senator who lives by the law of his own making but not by the laws most people would consider more humane?

Notes of a Native Son

JAMES BALDWIN

1 On the 29th of July, in 1943, my father died. On the same day, a few hours later, his last child was born. Over a month before this, while all our energies were concentrated in waiting for these events, there had been, in Detroit, one of the bloodiest race riots of the century. A few hours after my father's funeral, while he lay in state in the undertaker's chapel, a race riot broke out in Harlem. On the morning of the 3rd of August, we drove my father to the graveyard through a wilderness of smashed plate glass.

2 The day of my father's funeral had also been my nineteenth birthday. As we drove him to the graveyard, the spoils of injustice, anarchy, discontent, and hatred were all around us. It seemed to me that God himself had devised, to mark my father's end, the most sustained and brutally dissonant of codas. And it seemed to me, too, that the violence which rose all about us as my father left the world had been devised as a corrective for the pride of his eldest son. I had declined to believe in that apocalypse which had been central to my father's vision; very well, life seemed to be saying, here is something that will certainly pass for an apocalypse until the real thing comes along. I had inclined to be contemptuous of my father for the conditions of his life, for the conditions of our lives. When his life had ended

I began to wonder about that life and also, in a new way, to be apprehensive about my own.

3 I had not known my father very well. We had got on badly, partly because we shared, in our different fashions, the vice of stubborn pride. When he was dead I realized that I had hardly ever spoken to him. When he had been dead a long time I began to wish I had. It seems to be typical of life in America, where opportunities, real and fancied, are thicker than anywhere else on the globe, that the second generation has no time to talk to the first. No one, including my father, seems to have known exactly how old he was, but his mother had been born during slavery. He was of the first generation of free men. He, along with thousands of other Negroes, came North after 1919 and I was part of that generation which had never seen the landscape of what Negroes sometimes call the Old Country.

4 He had been born in New Orleans and had been a quite young man there during the time that Louis Armstrong, a boy, was running errands for the dives and honky-tonks of what was always presented to me as one of the most wicked of cities—to this day, whenever I think of New Orleans, I also helplessly think of Sodom and Gomorrah. My father never mentioned Louis Armstrong, except to forbid us to play his records; but there was a picture of him on our wall for a long time. One of my father's strong-willed female relatives had placed it there and forbade my father to take it down. He never did, but he eventually maneuvered her out of the house and when, some years later, she was in trouble and near death, he refused to do anything to help her.

5 He was, I think, very handsome. I gather this from photographs and from my own memories of him, dressed in his Sunday best and on his way to preach a sermon somewhere, when I was little. Handsome, proud, and ingrown, "like a toe-nail," somebody said. But he looked to me, as I grew older, like pictures I had seen of African tribal chieftains: he really should have been naked, with war-paint on and barbaric mementos, standing among spears. He could be chilling in the pulpit and indescribably cruel in his personal life and he was certainly the most bitter man I have ever met; yet it must be said there was something else in him, buried in him, which lent him his tremendous power and, even, a rather crushing charm. It had something to do with his blackness, I think—he was very black—with his blackness and his beauty, and with the fact that he knew that he was black but did not know that he was beautiful. He claimed to be proud of his blackness but it had also been the cause of much humiliation and it had fixed bleak boundaries to his life. He was not a young man when we were growing up and he had already suffered many kinds of ruin; in his outrageously demanding and protective way he loved his children, who were black like him and menaced, like him;

and all these things sometimes showed in his face when he tried, never to my knowledge with any success, to establish contact with any of us. When he took one of his children on his knee to play, the child always became fretful and began to cry; when he tried to help one of us with our homework the absolutely unabating tension which emanated from him caused our minds and our tongues to become paralyzed, so that he, scarcely knowing why, flew into a rage and the child, not knowing why, was punished. If it ever entered his head to bring a surprise home for his children, it was, almost unfailingly, the wrong surprise and even the big watermelons he often brought home on his back in the summertime led to the most appalling scenes. I do not remember, in all those years, that one of his children was ever glad to see him come home. From what I was able to gather of his early life, it seemed that this inability to establish contact with other people had always marked him and had been one of the things which had driven him out of New Orleans. There was something in him, therefore, groping and tentative, which was never expressed and which was buried with him. One saw it most clearly when he was facing new people and hoping to impress them. But he never did, not for long. We went from church to smaller and more improbable church, he found himself in less and less demand as a minister, and by the time he died none of his friends had come to see him for a long time. He had lived and died in an intolerable bitterness of spirit and it frightened me, as we drove him to the graveyard through those unquiet, ruined streets, to see how powerful and overflowing this bitterness could be and to realize that this bitterness now was mine.

6 When he died I had been away from home for a little over a year. In that year I had had time to become aware of the meaning of all my father's bitter warnings, had discovered the secret of his proudly pursed lips and rigid carriage: I had discovered the weight of white people in the world. I saw that this had been for my ancestors and now would be for me an awful thing to live with and that the bitterness which had helped to kill my father could also kill me.

7 He had been ill a long time—in the mind, as we now realized, reliving instances of his fantastic intransigence in the new light of his affliction and endeavoring to feel a sorrow for him which never, quite, came true. We had not known that he was being eaten up by paranoia, and the discovery that his cruelty, to our bodies and our minds, had been one of the symptoms of his illness was not, then, enough to enable us to forgive him. The younger children felt, quite simply, relief that he would not be coming home anymore. My mother's observation that it was he, after all, who had kept them alive all these years meant nothing because the problems of keeping children alive are not real for children. The older children felt, with my father gone, that they could invite their friends to the house without fear that their

friends would be insulted or, as had sometimes happened with me, being told that their friends were in league with the devil and intended to rob our family of everything we owned. (I didn't fail to wonder, and it made me hate him, what on earth we owned that anybody else would want.)

8 His illness was beyond all hope of healing before anyone realized that he was ill. He had always been so strange and had lived, like a prophet, in such unimaginably close communion with the Lord that his long silences which were punctuated by moans and hallelujahs and snatches of old songs while he sat at the living-room window never seemed odd to us. It was not until he refused to eat because, he said, his family was trying to poison him that my mother was forced to accept as a fact what had, until then, been only an unwilling suspicion. When he was committed, it was discovered that he had tuberculosis and, as it turned out, the disease of his mind allowed the disease of his body to destroy him. For the doctors could not force him to eat, either, and, though he was fed intravenously, it was clear from the beginning that there was no hope for him.

9 In my mind's eye I could see him, sitting at the window, locked up in his terrors; hating and fearing every living soul including his children who had betrayed him, too, by reaching towards the world which had despised him. There were nine of us. I began to wonder what it could have felt like for such a man to have had nine children whom he could barely feed. He used to make little jokes about our poverty, which never, of course, seemed very funny to us; they could not have seemed very funny to him, either, or else our all too feeble response to them would never have caused such rages. He spent great energy and achieved, to our chagrin, no small amount of success in keeping us away from the people who surrounded us, people who had all-night rent parties to which we listened when we should have been sleeping, people who cursed and drank and flashed razor blades on Lenox Avenue. He could not understand why, if they had so much energy to spare, they could not use it to make their lives better. He treated almost everybody on our block with a most uncharitable asperity and neither they, nor, of course, their children were slow to reciprocate.

10 The only white people who came to our house were welfare workers and bill collectors. It was almost always my mother who dealt with them, for my father's temper, which was at the mercy of his pride, was never to be trusted. It was clear that he felt their very presence in his home to be a violation: this was conveyed by his carriage, almost ludicrously stiff, and by his voice, harsh and vindictively polite. When I was around nine or ten I wrote a play which was directed by a young, white schoolteacher, a woman, who then took an interest

in me, and gave me books to read and, in order to corroborate my theatrical bent, decided to take me to see what she somewhat tactlessly referred to as "real" plays. Theater-going was forbidden in our house, but, with the really cruel intuitiveness of a child, I suspected that the color of this woman's skin would carry the day for me. When, at school, she suggested taking me to the theater, I did not, as I might have done if she had been a Negro, find a way of discouraging her, but agreed that she should pick me up at my house one evening. I then, very cleverly, left all the rest to my mother, who suggested to my father, as I knew she would, that it would not be very nice to let such a kind woman make the trip for nothing. Also, since it was a schoolteacher, I imagine that my mother countered the idea of sin with the idea of "education," which word, even with my father, carried a kind of bitter weight.

11 Before the teacher came my father took me aside to ask *why* she was coming, what *interest* she could possibly have in our house, in a boy like me. I said I didn't know but I, too, suggested that it had something to do with education. And I understood that my father was waiting for me to say something—I didn't quite know what; perhaps that I wanted his protection against this teacher and her "education." I said none of these things and the teacher came and we went out. It was clear, during the brief interview in our living room, that my father was agreeing very much against his will and that he would have refused permission if he had dared. The fact that he did not dare caused me to despise him: I had no way of knowing that he was facing in that living room a wholly unprecedented and frightening situation.

12 Later, when my father had been laid off from his job, this woman became very important to us. She was really a very sweet and generous woman and went to a great deal of trouble to be of help to us, particularly during one awful winter. My mother called her by the highest name she knew: she said she was a "christian." My father could scarcely disagree but during the four or five years of our relatively close association he never trusted her and was always trying to surprise in her open, Midwestern face the genuine, cunningly hidden, and hideous motivation. In later years, particularly when it began to be clear that this "education" of mine was going to lead me to perdition, he became more explicit and warned me that my white friends in high school were not really my friends and that I would see, when I was older, how white people would do anything to keep a Negro down. Some of them could be nice, he admitted, but none of them were to be trusted and most of them were not even nice. The best thing was to have as little to do with them as possible. I did not feel this way and I was certain, in my innocence, that I never would.

13 But the year which preceded my father's death had made a great

change in my life. I had been living in New Jersey, working in defense plants, working and living among southerners, white and black. I knew about the south, of course, and about how southerners treated Negroes and how they expected them to behave, but it had never entered my mind that anyone would look at me and expect *me* to behave that way. I learned in New Jersey that to be a Negro meant, precisely, that one was never looked at but was simply at the mercy of the reflexes the color of one's skin caused in other people. I acted in New Jersey as I had always acted, that is as though I thought a great deal of myself—I had to *act* that way—with results that were, simply, unbelievable. I had scarcely arrived before I had earned the enmity, which was extraordinarily ingenious, of all my superiors and nearly all my co-workers. In the beginning, to make matters worse, I simply did not know what was happening. I did not know what I had done, and I shortly began to wonder what *anyone* could possibly do, to bring about such unanimous, active, and unbearably vocal hostility. I knew about jim-crow but I had never experienced it. I went to the same self-service restaurant three times and stood with all the Princeton boys before the counter, waiting for a hamburger and coffee; it was always an extraordinarily long time before anything was set before me; but it was not until the fourth visit that I learned that, in fact, nothing had ever been set before me: I had simply picked something up. Negroes were not served there, I was told, and they had been waiting for me to realize that I was always the only Negro present. Once I was told this, I determined to go there all the time. But now they were ready for me and, though some dreadful scenes were subsequently enacted in that restaurant, I never ate there again.

14 It was the same story all over New Jersey, in bars, bowling alleys, diners, places to live. I was always being forced to leave, silently, or with mutual imprecations. I very shortly became notorious and children giggled behind me when I passed and their elders whispered or shouted—they really believed that I was mad. And it did begin to work on my mind, of course; I began to be afraid to go anywhere and to compensate for this I went places to which I really should not have gone and where, God knows, I had no desire to be. My reputation in town naturally enhanced my reputation at work and my working day became one long series of acrobatics designed to keep me out of trouble. I cannot say that these acrobatics succeeded. It began to seem that the machinery of the organization I worked for was turning over, day and night, with but one aim: to eject me. I was fired once, and contrived, with the aid of a friend from New York, to get back on the payroll; was fired again, and bounced back again. It took a while to fire me for the third time, but the third time took. There were no loopholes anywhere. There was not even any way of getting back inside the gates.

15 That year in New Jersey lives in my mind as though it were the year during which, having an unsuspected predilection for it, I first contracted some dread, chronic disease, the unfailing symptom of which is a kind of blind fever, a pounding in the skull and fire in the bowels. Once this disease is contracted, one can never be really carefree again, for the fever, without an instant's warning, can recur at any moment. It can wreck more important things than race relations. There is not a Negro alive who does not have this rage in his blood—one has the choice, merely, of living with it consciously or surrendering to it. As for me, this fever has recurred in me, and does, and will until the day I die.

16 My last night in New Jersey, a white friend from New York took me to the nearest big town, Trenton, to go to the movies and have a few drinks. As it turned out, he also saved me from, at the very least, a violent whipping. Almost every detail of that night stands out very clearly in my memory. I even remember the name of the movie we saw because its title impressed me as being so patly ironical. It was a movie about the German occupation of France, starring Maureen O'Hara and Charles Laughton and called *This Land Is Mine*. I remember the name of the diner we walked into when the movie ended: it was the "American Diner." When we walked in the counterman asked what we wanted and I remember answering with the casual sharpness which had become my habit: "We want a hamburger and cup of coffee, what do you think we want?" I do not know why, after a year of such rebuffs, I so completely failed to anticipate his answer, which was, of course, "We don't serve Negroes here." This reply failed to discompose me, at least for the moment. I made some sardonic comment about the name of the diner and we walked out into the streets.

17 This was the time of what was called the "brownout," when the lights in all American cities were very dim. When we re-entered the streets something happened to me which had the force of an optical illusion, or a nightmare. The streets were very crowded and I was facing north. People were moving in every direction but it seemed to me, in that instant, that all of the people I could see, and many more than that, were moving toward me, against me, and that everyone was white. I remember how their faces gleamed. And I felt, like a physical sensation, a *click* at the nape of my neck as though some interior string connecting my head to my body had been cut. I began to walk. I heard my friend call after me, but I ignored him. Heaven only knows what was going on in his mind, but he had the good sense not to touch me—I don't know what would have happened if he had—and to keep me in sight. I don't know what was going on in my mind, either; I certainly had no conscious plan. I wanted to do something to crush these white faces, which were crushing me. I walked for perhaps a

block or two until I came to an enormous, glittering, and fashionable restaurant in which I knew not even the intercession of the Virgin would cause me to be served. I pushed through the doors and took the first vacant seat I saw, at a table for two, and waited.

18 I do not know how long I waited and I rather wonder, until today, what I could possibly have looked like. Whatever I looked like, I frightened the waitress who shortly appeared, and the moment she appeared all of my fury flowed towards her. I hated her for her white face, and for her great, astounded, frightened eyes. I felt that if she found a black man so frightening I would make her fright worth-while.

19 She did not ask me what I wanted, but repeated, as though she had learned it somewhere, "We don't serve Negroes here." She did not say it with the blunt, derisive hostility to which I had grown so accustomed, but, rather, with a note of apology in her voice, and fear. This made me colder and more murderous than ever. I felt I had to do something with my hands. I wanted her to come close enough for me to get her neck between my hands.

20 So I pretended not to have understood her, hoping to draw her closer. And she did step a very short step closer, with her pencil poised incongruously over her pad, and repeated the formula: ". . . don't serve Negroes here."

21 Somehow, with the repetition of that phrase, which was already ringing in my head like a thousand bells of a nightmare, I realized that she would never come any closer and that I would have to strike from a distance. There was nothing on the table but an ordinary watermug half full of water, and I picked this up and hurled it with all my strength at her. She ducked and it missed her and shattered against the mirror behind the bar. And, with that sound, my frozen blood abruptly thawed, I returned from wherever I had been, I *saw,* for the first time, the restaurant, the people with their mouths open, already, as it seemed to me, rising as one man, and I realized what I had done, and where I was, and I was frightened. I rose and began running for the door. A round, potbellied man grabbed me by the nape of the neck just as I reached the doors and began to beat me about the face. I kicked him and got loose and ran into the streets. My friend whispered, *"Run!"* and I ran.

22 My friend stayed outside the restaurant long enough to misdirect my pursuers and the police, who arrived, he told me, at once. I do not know what I said to him when he came to my room that night. I could not have said much. I felt, in the oddest, most awful way, that I had somehow betrayed him. I lived it over and over and over again, the way one relives an automobile accident after it has happened and one finds oneself alone and safe. I could not get over two facts, both equally difficult for the imagination to grasp, and one was that I could have been murdered. But the other was that I had been ready

to commit murder. I saw nothing very clearly but I did see this: that my life, my *real* life, was in danger, and not from anything other people might do but from the hatred I carried in my own heart.

II

23 I had returned home around the second week in June—in great haste because it seemed that my father's death and my mother's confinement were both but a matter of hours. In the case of my mother, it soon became clear that she had simply made a miscalculation. This had always been her tendency and I don't believe that a single one of us arrived in the world, or has since arrived anywhere else, on time. But none of us dawdled so intolerably about the business of being born as did my baby sister. We sometimes amused ourselves, during those endless, stifling weeks, by picturing the baby sitting within the safe, warm dark, bitterly regretting the necessity of becoming a part of our chaos and stubbornly putting it off as long as possible. I understood her perfectly and congratulated her on showing such good sense so soon. Death, however, sat as purposefully at my father's bedside as life stirred within my mother's womb and it was harder to understand why he so lingered in that long shadow. It seemed that he had bent, and for a long time, too, all of his energies towards dying. Now death was ready for him but my father held back.

24 All of Harlem, indeed, seemed to be infected by waiting. I had never before known it to be so violently still. Racial tensions throughout this country were exacerbated during the early years of the war, partly because the labor market brought together hundreds of thousands of ill-prepared people and partly because Negro soldiers, regardless of where they were born, received their military training in the south. What happened in defense plants and army camps had repercussions, naturally, in every Negro ghetto. The situation in Harlem had grown bad enough for clergymen, policemen, educators, politicians, and social workers to assert in one breath that there was no "crime wave" and to offer, in the very next breath, suggestions as to how to combat it. These suggestions always seemed to involve playgrounds, despite the fact that racial skirmishes were occurring in the playgrounds, too. Playground or not, crime wave or not, the Harlem police force had been augmented in March, and the unrest grew—perhaps, in fact, partly as a result of the ghetto's instinctive hatred of policemen. Perhaps the most revealing news item, out of the steady parade of reports of muggings, stabbings, shootings, assaults, gang wars, and accusations of police brutality, is the item concerning six Negro girls who set upon a white girl in the subway because, as they all too accurately put it, she was stepping on their toes. Indeed she was, all over the nation.

25 I had never before been so aware of policemen, on foot, on horseback, on corners, everywhere, always two by two. Nor had I ever been so aware of small knots of people. They were on stoops and on corners and in doorways, and what was striking about them, I think, was that they did not seem to be talking. Never, when I passed these groups, did the usual sound of a curse or a laugh ring out and neither did there seem to be any hum of gossip. There was certainly, on the other hand, occurring between them communication extraordinarily intense. Another thing that was striking was the unexpected diversity of the people who made up these groups. Usually, for example, one would see a group of sharpies standing on the street corner, jiving the passing chicks; or a group of older men, usually, for some reason, in the vicinity of a barber shop, discussing baseball scores, or the numbers, or making rather chilling observations about women they had known. Women, in a general way, tended to be seen less often together—unless they were church women, or very young girls, or prostitutes met together for an unprofessional instant. But that summer I saw the strangest combinations: large, respectable, churchly matrons standing on the stoops or the corners with their hair tied up, together with a girl in sleazy satin whose face bore the marks of gin and the razor, or heavy-set, abrupt, no-nonsense older men, in company with the most disreputable and fanatical "race" men, or these same "race" men with the sharpies, or these sharpies with the churchly women. Seventh Day Adventists and Methodists and Spiritualists seemed to be hobnobbing with Holy-rollers and they were all, alike, entangled with the most flagrant disbelievers; something heavy in their stance seemed to indicate that they had all, incredibly, seen a common vision, and on each face there seemed to be the same strange, bitter shadow.

26 The churchly women and the matter-of-fact, no-nonsense men had children in the Army. The sleazy girls they talked to had lovers there, the sharpies and the "race" men had friends and brothers there. It would have demanded an unquestioning patriotism, happily as uncommon in this country as it is undesirable, for these people not to have been disturbed by the bitter letters they received, by the newspaper stories they read, not to have been enraged by the posters, then to be found all over New York, which described the Japanese as "yellow-bellied Japs." It was only the "race" men, to be sure, who spoke ceaselessly of being revenged—how this vengeance was to be exacted was not clear—for the indignities and dangers suffered by Negro boys in uniform; but everybody felt a directionless, hopeless bitterness, as well as that panic which can scarcely be suppressed when one knows that a human being one loves is beyond one's reach, and in danger. This helplessness and this gnawing uneasiness does something, at length, to even the toughest mind. Perhaps the

best way to sum all this up is to say that the people I knew felt, mainly, a peculiar kind of relief when they knew that their boys were being shipped out of the south, to do battle overseas. It was, perhaps, like feeling that the most dangerous part of a dangerous journey had been passed and that now, even if death should come, it would come with honor and without the complicity of their countrymen. Such a death would be, in short, a fact with which one could hope to live.

27 It was on the 28th of July, which I believe was a Wednesday, that I visited my father for the first time during his illness and for the last time in his life. The moment I saw him I knew why I had put off this visit so long. I had told my mother that I did not want to see him because I hated him. But this was not true. It was only that I *had* hated him and I wanted to hold on to this hatred. I did not want to look on him as a ruin: it was not a ruin I had hated. I imagine that one of the reasons people cling to their hates so stubbornly is because they sense, once hate is gone, that they will be forced to deal with pain.

28 We traveled out to him, his older sister and myself, to what seemed to be the very end of a very Long Island. It was hot and dusty and we wrangled, my aunt and I, all the way out, over the fact that I had recently begun to smoke and, as she said, to give myself airs. But I knew that she wrangled with me because she could not bear to face the fact of her brother's dying. Neither could I endure the reality of her despair, her unstated bafflement as to what had happened to her brother's life, and her own. So we wrangled and I smoked and from time to time she fell into a heavy reverie. Covertly, I watched her face, which was the face of an old woman; it had fallen in, the eyes were sunken and lightless; soon she would be dying, too.

29 In my childhood—it had not been so long ago—I had thought her beautiful. She had been quick-witted and quick-moving and very generous with all the children and each of her visits had been an event. At one time one of my brothers and myself had thought of running away to live with her. Now she could no longer produce out of her handbag some unexpected and yet familiar delight. She made me feel pity and revulsion and fear. It was awful to realize that she no longer caused me to feel affection. The closer we came to the hospital, the more querulous she became and, at the same time, naturally, she grew more dependent on me. Between pity and guilt and fear I began to feel that there was another me trapped in my skull like a jack-in-the-box who might escape my control at any moment and fill the air with screaming.

30 She began to cry the moment we entered the room and she saw him lying there, all shriveled and still, like a little black monkey. The great, gleaming apparatus which fed him and would have compelled him to be still even if he had been able to move brought to mind, not

beneficence, but torture; the tubes entering his arm made me think of pictures I had seen when a child, of Gulliver, tied down by the pygmies on that island. My aunt wept and wept, there was a whistling sound in my father's throat; nothing was said; he could not speak. I wanted to take his hand, to say something. But I do not know what I could have said, even if he could have heard me. He was not really in that room with us, he had at last really embarked on his journey; and though my aunt told me that he said he was going to meet Jesus, I did not hear anything except that whistling in his throat. The doctor came back and we left, into that unbearable train again, and home. In the morning came the telegram saying that he was dead. Then the house was suddenly full of relatives, friends, hysteria, and confusion and I quickly left my mother and the children to the care of those impressive women, who, in Negro communities at least, automatically appear at times of bereavement armed with lotions, proverbs, and patience, and an ability to cook. I went downtown. By the time I returned, later the same day, my mother had been carried to the hospital and the baby had been born.

III

31 For my father's funeral I had nothing black to wear and this posed a nagging problem all day long. It was one of those problems, simple, or impossible of solution, to which the mind insanely clings in order to avoid the mind's real trouble. I spent most of that day at the downtown apartment of a girl I knew, celebrating my birthday with whiskey and wondering what to wear that night. When planning a birthday celebration one naturally does not expect that it will be up against competition from a funeral and this girl had anticipated taking me out that night, for a big dinner and a night club afterwards. Sometime during the course of that long day we decided that we would go out anyway, when my father's funeral service was over. I imagine *I* decided it, since, as the funeral hour approached, it became clearer and clearer to me that I would not know what to do with myself when it was over. The girl, stifling her very lively concern as to the possible effects of the whiskey on one of my father's chief mourners, concentrated on being conciliatory and practically helpful. She found a black shirt for me somewhere and ironed it and, dressed in the darkest pants and jacket I owned, and slightly drunk, I made my way to my father's funeral.

32 The chapel was full, but not packed, and very quiet. There were, mainly, my father's relatives, and his children, and here and there I saw faces I had not seen since childhood, the faces of my father's one-time friends. They were very dark and solemn now, seeming somehow to suggest that they had known all along that something

like this would happen. Chief among the mourners was my aunt, who had quarreled with my father all his life; by which I do not mean to suggest that her mourning was insincere or that she had not loved him. I suppose that she was one of the few people in the world who had, and their incessant quarreling proved precisely the strength of the tie that bound them. The only other person in the world, as far as I knew, whose relationship to my father rivaled my aunt's in depth was my mother, who was not there.

33 It seemed to me, of course, that it was a very long funeral. But it was, if anything, a rather shorter funeral than most, nor, since there were no overwhelming, uncontrollable expressions of grief, could it be called—if I dare to use the word—successful. The minister who preached my father's funeral sermon was one of the few my father had still been seeing as he neared his end. He presented to us in his sermon a man whom none of us had ever seen—a man thoughtful, patient, and forbearing, a Christian inspiration to all who knew him, and a model for his children. And no doubt the children, in their disturbed and guilty state, were almost ready to believe this; he had been remote enough to be anything and, anyway, the shock of the incontrovertible, that it was really our father lying up there in that casket, prepared the mind for anything. His sister moaned and this grief-stricken moaning was taken as corroboration. The other faces held a dark, non-committal thoughtfulness. This was not the man they had known, but they had scarcely expected to be confronted with *him;* this was, in a sense deeper than questions of fact, the man they had not known, and the man they had not known may have been the real one. The real man, whoever he had been, had suffered and now he was dead: this was all that was sure and all that mattered now. Every man in the chapel hoped that when his hour came he, too, would be eulogized, which is to say forgiven, and that all of his lapses, greeds, errors, and strayings from the truth would be invested with coherence and looked upon with charity. This was perhaps the last thing human beings could give each other and it was what they demanded, after all, of the Lord. Only the Lord saw the midnight tears, only He was present when one of His children, moaning and wringing hands, paced up and down the room. When one slapped one's child in anger the recoil in the heart reverberated through heaven and became part of the pain of the universe. And when the children were hungry and sullen and distrustful and one watched them, daily growing wilder, and further away, and running headlong into danger, it was the Lord who knew what the charged heart endured as the strap was laid to the backside; the Lord alone who knew what one *would* have said if one had had, like the Lord, the gift of the living word. It was the Lord who knew of the impossibility every parent in that room faced: how to prepare the child for the day when the child

would be despised and how to *create* in the child—by what means?—a stronger antidote to this poison than one had found for oneself. The avenues, side streets, bars, billiard halls, hospitals, police stations, and even the playgrounds of Harlem—not to mention the houses of correction, the jails, and the morgue—testified to the potency of the poison while remaining silent as to the efficacy of whatever antidote, irresistibly raising the question of whether or not such an antidote existed; raising, which was worse, the question of whether or not an antidote was desirable; perhaps poison should be fought with poison. With these several schisms in the mind and with more terrors in the heart than could be named, it was better not to judge the man who had gone down under an impossible burden. It was better to remember: *Thou knowest this man's fall; but thou knowest not his wrassling.*

34 While the preacher talked and I watched the children—years of changing their diapers, scrubbing them, slapping them, taking them to school, and scolding them had had the perhaps inevitable result of making me love them, though I am not sure I knew this then—my mind was busily breaking out with a rash of disconnected impressions. Snatches of popular songs, indecent jokes, bits of books I had read, movie sequences, faces, voices, political issues—I thought I was going mad; all these impressions suspended, as it were, in the solution of the faint nausea produced in me by the heat and liquor. For a moment I had the impression that my alcoholic breath, inefficiently disguised with chewing gum, filled the entire chapel. Then someone began singing one of my father's favorite songs and, abruptly, I was with him, sitting on his knee, in the hot, enormous, crowded church which was the first church we attended. It was the Abyssinia Baptist Church on 138th Street. We had not gone there long. With this image, a host of others came. I had forgotten, in the rage of my growing up, how proud my father had been of me when I was little. Apparently, I had had a voice and my father had liked to show me off before the members of the church. I had forgotten what he had looked like when he was pleased but now I remembered that he had always been grinning with pleasure when my solos ended. I even remembered certain expressions on his face when he teased my mother—had he loved her? I would never know. And when had it all begun to change? For now it seemed that he had not always been cruel. I remembered being taken for a haircut and scraping my knee on the footrest of the barber's chair and I remembered my father's face as he soothed my crying and applied the stinging iodine. Then I remembered our fights, fights which had been of the worst possible kind because my technique had been silence.

35 I remembered the one time in all our life together when we had really spoken to each other.

36 It was on a Sunday and it must have been shortly before I left home. We were walking, just the two of us, in our usual silence, to or from church. I was in high school and had been doing a lot of writing and I was, at about this time, the editor of the high school magazine. But I had also been a Young Minister and had been preaching from the pulpit. Lately, I had been taking fewer engagements and preached as rarely as possible. It was said in the church, quite truthfully, that I was "cooling off."

37 My father asked me abruptly, "You'd rather write than preach, wouldn't you?"

38 I was astonished at his question—because it was a real question. I answered, "Yes."

39 That was all we said. It was awful to remember that that was all we had *ever* said.

40 The casket now was opened and the mourners were being led up the aisle to look for the last time on the deceased. The assumption was that the family was too overcome with grief to be allowed to make this journey alone and I watched while my aunt was led to the casket and, muffled in black, and shaking, led back to her seat. I disapproved of forcing the children to look on their dead father, considering that the shock of his death, or, more truthfully, the shock of death as a reality, was already a little more than a child could bear, but my judgment in this matter had been overruled and there they were, bewildered and frightened and very small, being led, one by one, to the casket. But there is also something very gallant about children at such moments. It has something to do with their silence and gravity and with the fact that one cannot help them. Their legs, somehow, seem *exposed*, so that it is at once incredible and terribly clear that their legs are all they have to hold them up.

41 I had not wanted to go to the casket myself and I certainly had not wished to be led there, but there was no way of avoiding either of these forms. One of the deacons led me up and I looked on my father's face. I cannot say that it looked like him at all. His blackness had been equivocated by powder and there was no suggestion in that casket of what his power had or could have been. He was simply an old man dead, and it was hard to believe that he had ever given anyone either joy or pain. Yet, his life filled that room. Further up the avenue his wife was holding his newborn child. Life and death so close together, and love and hatred, and right and wrong, said something to me which I did not want to hear concerning man, concerning the life of man.

42 After the funeral, while I was downtown desperately celebrating my birthday, a Negro soldier, in the lobby of the Hotel Braddock, got into a fight with a white policeman over a Negro girl. Negro girls, white policemen, in or out of uniform, and Negro males—in or out of uni-

form—were part of the furniture of the lobby of the Hotel Braddock and this was certainly not the first time such an incident had occurred. It was destined, however, to receive an unprecedented publicity, for the fight between the policeman and the soldier ended with the shooting of the soldier. Rumor, flowing immediately to the streets outside, stated that the soldier had been shot in the back, an instantaneous and revealing invention, and that the soldier had died protecting a Negro woman. The facts were somewhat different—for example, the soldier had not been shot in the back, and was not dead, and the girl seems to have been as dubious a symbol of womanhood as her white counterpart in Georgia usually is, but no one was interested in the facts. They preferred the invention because this invention expressed and corroborated their hates and fears so perfectly. It is just as well to remember that people are always doing this. Perhaps many of those legends, including Christianity, to which the world clings began their conquest of the world with just some such concerted surrender to distortion. The effect, in Harlem, of this particular legend was like the effect of a lit match in a tin of gasoline. The mob gathered before the doors of the Hotel Braddock simply began to swell and to spread in every direction, and Harlem exploded.

43 The mob did not cross the ghetto lines. It would have been easy, for example, to have gone over Morningside Park on the west side or to have crossed the Grand Central railroad tracks at 125th Street on the east side, to wreak havoc in white neighborhoods. The mob seems to have been mainly interested in something more potent and real than the white face, that is, in white power, and the principal damage done during the riot of the summer of 1943 was to white business establishments in Harlem. It might have been a far bloodier story, of course, if, at the hour the riot began, these establishments had still been open. From the Hotel Braddock the mob fanned out, east and west along 125th Street, and for the entire length of Lenox, Seventh, and Eighth avenues. Along each of these avenues, and along each major side street—116th, 125th, 135th, and so on—bars, stores, pawnshops, restaurants, even little luncheonettes had been smashed open and entered and looted—looted, it might be added, with more haste than efficiency. The shelves really looked as though a bomb had struck them. Cans of beans and soup and dog food, along with toilet paper, corn flakes, sardines and milk tumbled every which way, and abandoned cash registers and cases of beer leaned crazily out of the splintered windows and were strewn along the avenues. Sheets, blankets, and clothing of every description formed a kind of path, as though people had dropped them while running. I truly had not realized that Harlem *had* so many stores until I saw them all smashed open; the first time the word *wealth* ever entered my mind in relation to Harlem was when I saw it scattered in the streets. But one's first,

incongruous impression of plenty was countered immediately by an impression of waste. None of this was doing anybody any good. It would have been better to have left the plate glass as it had been and the goods lying in the stores.

44 It would have been better, but it would also have been intolerable, for Harlem had needed something to smash. To smash something is the ghetto's chronic need. Most of the time it is the members of the ghetto who smash each other, and themselves. But as long as the ghetto walls are standing there will always come a moment when these outlets do not work. That summer, for example, it was not enough to get into a fight on Lenox Avenue, or curse out one's cronies in the barber shops. If ever, indeed, the violence which fills Harlem's churches, pool halls, and bars erupts outward in a more direct fashion, Harlem and its citizens are likely to vanish in an apocalyptic flood. That this is not likely to happen is due to a great many reasons, most hidden and powerful among them the Negro's real relation to the white American. This relation prohibits, simply, anything as uncomplicated and satisfactory as pure hatred. In order really to hate white people, one has to blot so much out of the mind—and the heart—that this hatred itself becomes an exhausting and self-destructive pose. But this does not mean, on the other hand, that love comes easily: the white world is too powerful, too complacent, too ready with gratuitous humiliation, and, above all, too ignorant and too innocent for that. One is absolutely forced to make perpetual qualifications and one's own reactions are always canceling each other out. It is this, really, which has driven so many people mad, both white and black. One is always in the position of having to decide between amputation and gangrene. Amputation is swift but time may prove that the amputation was not necessary—or one may delay the amputation too long. Gangrene is slow, but it is impossible to be sure that one is reading one's symptoms right. The idea of going through life as a cripple is more than one can bear, and equally unbearable is the risk of swelling up slowly, in agony, with poison. And the trouble, finally, is that the risks are real even if the choices do not exist.

45 "But as for me and my house," my father had said, "we will serve the Lord." I wondered, as we drove him to his resting place, what this line had meant for him. I had heard him preach it many times. I had preached it once myself, proudly giving it an interpretation different from my father's. Now the whole thing came back to me, as though my father and I were on our way to Sunday school and I were memorizing the golden text: *And if it seem evil unto you to serve the Lord, choose you this day whom you will serve; whether the gods which your fathers served that were on the other side of the flood, or the gods of the Amorites, in whose land ye dwell: but for me and*

my house, we will serve the Lord. I suspected in these familiar lines a meaning which had never been there for me before. All of my father's texts and songs, which I had decided were meaningless, were arranged before me at his death like empty bottles, waiting to hold the meaning which life would give them for me. This was his legacy: nothing is ever escaped. That bleakly memorable morning I hated the unbelievable streets and the Negroes and whites who had, equally, made them that way. But I knew that it was folly, as my father would have said, this bitterness was folly. It was necessary to hold on to the things that mattered. The dead man mattered, the new life mattered; blackness and whiteness did not matter; to believe that they did was to acquiesce in one's own destruction. Hatred, which could destroy so much, never failed to destroy the man who hated and this was an immutable law.

46 It began to seem that one would have to hold in the mind forever two ideas which seemed to be in opposition. The first idea was acceptance, the acceptance, totally without rancor, of life as it is, and men as they are: in the light of this idea, it goes without saying that injustice is a commonplace. But this did not mean that one could be complacent, for the second idea was of equal power: that one must never, in one's own life, accept these injustices as commonplace but must fight them with all one's strength. This fight begins, however, in the heart and it now had been laid to my charge to keep my own heart free of hatred and despair. This intimation made my heart heavy and, now that my father was irrecoverable, I wished that he had been beside me so that I could have searched his face for the answers which only the future would give me now.

Thinking Questions: *Form*

1. Examine point of view in this essay. Is the use of the first-person narrator effective? How effective is Baldwin's rhetorical perspective in the essay? Does he seem to analyze subjectively or objectively? Can a first-person narrator achieve objectivity? How? When Baldwin's narrator describes a distant experience, do you feel you are going through the experience with him? Or do you feel distant and analytical, as if you were engaged in a long and rambling talk about a person's past? Or are you between those extremes?

2. Describe the structure of "Notes of a Native Son." Why this particular title rather than, for example, "Message from a Native Son"? Is this essay chronologically organized? Why or why not? Or are the events arranged subjectively, as they would be recalled by a narrator or character?

3. Point out some dramatic frictions or tensions in Baldwin's narrative. Show where particular scenes or events have been purposely contrasted

to make a point. Why, for example, does Baldwin put his own birthday party celebration, his father's funeral, his sister's birth, and the Harlem race riot in immediate opposition? How do these dramatic contrasts coordinate the main ideas in the essay?

4. How would you describe Baldwin's narrator? Is he an intellectual, a wildly radical civil rights leader, a generally pessimistic social commentator, a New Yorker? How do you imagine he would dress and act at a party? Provide at least some support for your description by referring to the language of the essay.

5. Go through a particular section of Baldwin's essay and find an important generality or concept. In paragraph 44, for example, Baldwin gives us one of his opinions directly: "To smash something is the ghetto's chronic need." How does Baldwin support and clarify that idea? How does what happened during the Harlem riots contribute to his opinion?

Thinking Questions: *Substance*

1. Read this essay over and point out what you believe is its most important described experience. Single out a complete scene, an event that symbolizes Baldwin's general purpose, an extended piece of dialogue. Is the experience repeated or referred to at several points in the essay? Why?

2. Why does Baldwin begin with the comparison between his father's death and his youngest sister's birthday? Is that comparison *ironic?* There are generally two types of irony: *verbal irony,* in which a writer means something other than what he or she actually says, and *dramatic irony,* in which the writer and reader share knowledge that the person being discussed does not share. Both these types of irony should not be confused with simple *sarcasm,* where a speaker or writer says the opposite of what he or she really means. For example, a person who has just come out of a storm dripping wet might say to someone who asked about the weather: "Oh, it's great." (For a more complete discussion of irony, see Part Four.) How and why does this comparison seem ironic, especially after you have read and analyzed the entire essay? How does the irony help to develop Baldwin's thesis?

3. Which of the following statements best approximates Baldwin's thesis? Support your choice by referring specifically to the essay.

> Every individual, however seemingly evil on the surface, can be understood and appreciated were we to know him completely.
>
> *"Thou knowest this man's fall; but thou knowest not his wrassling."*
>
> Every man must learn how to be hated while he retains his ability to love.
>
> Life as it is must be accepted, in all its rancor, hatred and suffering; after acceptance comes understanding.

4. Can you explain why Baldwin understands his father only after his death? What does Baldwin understand after his father's death that he could not have appreciated before his death? Why does love, as Baldwin

defines it, include cruelty and pain more than it does pleasure and courtesy?

5. James Baldwin and Charles Reich *seem* to write about totally different subjects. Yet both deal intensely with questions of moral duty. Both seem to argue that individuals must avoid reducing human experience to a few simple moral truths. Simultaneously, both argue that we must keep a few moral principles firmly in mind if we intend to live sensitive, human, and compassionate lives. Compare Reich's ideas of higher laws with Baldwin's. What does, for example, the William Calley case signify in the way of universal moral principles for Charles Reich? What general moral principle does James Baldwin draw from his long and complex relationship with his father?

The Lawgiver

KEITH LAUMER

1 "You're no better than a murderer," the woman said. "A cold-blooded killer." Her plump face looked out of the screen at him hot-eyed, tight-mouthed. She looked like someone's aunt getting tough with the butcher.

2 "Madame, the provisions of the Population Control Act—" he started.

3 "That's right, give it a fancy name," she cut in. "Try and make it sound respectable. But that don't change it. It's plain murder. Innocent little babies that never done anybody harm—"

4 "We are not killing babies! A fetus at ninety days is less than one inch long—"

5 "Don't matter how long they are, they got as much right to live as anybody!"

6 He drew a calming breath. "In five years we'd be faced with famine. What would you have us do?"

7 "If you big men in Washington would go to work and provide for people, for the voters, instead of killing babies, there'd be plenty for everybody."

8 "As easy as that, eh? Does it occur to you, madame, that the land can't support the people if they're swarming over it like ants?"

9 "See? People are no more to you than ants!"

10 "People are a great deal more to me than ants! That's precisely why I've sponsored legislation designed to ensure that they don't live like insects, crowded in hives, dying of starvation after they've laid the countryside bare!"

11 "Look at you," she said, "taking up that whole fancy apartment. You got room there for any number o' homeless children."

12 "There are too many homeless children, that's the problem!"

"It says right in the Good Book, be fruitful and multiply."

"And where does it end? When they're stacked like cordwood in every available square inch of space?"

13 "Is that what you do? Heap up all them little bodies and set 'em afire?"

14 "There are no bodies affected by the law, only fertilized ova!"

"Every one's a human soul!"

"Madame, each time a male ejaculates, several million germ cells are lost. Do you feel we should preserve every one, mature it *in vitro*—"

15 "Well! You got your nerve, talking that way to a respectable lady! You! A divorced man—and that son of yours—"

16 "Thank you for calling, madame," he said, and thumbed the blanking control.

17 "I'm no madame. . . ." the voice died in a squeal. He went to the small bar at the side of the room, dispensed a stiff shot of over-proof SGA, took it down at a gulp. Back at the desk, he buzzed the switchboard.

18 "Jerry, no more calls tonight."

"Sorry about that last one, Senator. I thought—"

"It's all right. But no more. Not tonight. Not until I've had some sleep."

19 "Big day, eh, Senator, ramrodding the enabling act through like you did. Uh, by the way, Senator, I just had a flash from Bernie, on the desk. He says there's a party asking for you, says they claim they have to see you—"

20 "Not tonight, Jerry."

"They mentioned your son Ron, Senator. . . ."

"Yes? What about him?"

"Well, I couldn't say, Senator. But Bernie says they say it's pretty important. But like you said, "I'll tell him to tell them not tonight."

21 "Wait a minute, Jerry. Put this party on."

"Sure, Senator."

22 The face that appeared was that of a young man with a shaven skull, no eyebrows or lashes. He gazed out of the screen with a bored expression.

23 "Yes, what is it you want?"

The youth tipped his head sideways, pointing. "We've got somebody with us you ought to talk to," he said. "In person."

24 "I understand you mentioned my son's name."

25 "We'd better come up."

"If you have something of interest to me, I suggest you tell me what it is."

26 "You wouldn't like that. Neither would Ron."

"Where is Ron?"

The boy made a vague gesture. "Spy, zek. We tried. It's your rax from here on—"

27 "Kindly speak standard English. I don't understand you."

The youth turned to someone out of sight; his mouth moved, but the words were inaudible. He turned back.

28 "You want us to bring Rink up or no?"

"Who is Rink?"

"Rink will tell you all that."

"Very well. Take my car, number 763."

29 He went to the bar, dispensed another stiff drink, then poured it down the drain. He went to the window, deopaqued it. A thousand feet below a layer of mist, glowing softly from the city lights beneath it, stretched all the way to the horizon fifty miles distant.

30 When the buzzer sounded he turned, called "come in." The door slid back. The boy he had talked to and another came through, supporting between them a plump woman with a pale face. The men were dressed in mismatched vest-suits, many times reused. The woman was wrapped in a long cloak. Her hair was disarranged, so that a long black curl bobbed over the right side of her face. Her visible eye held an expression that might have been fear, or defiance. The men helped her to the low couch. She sank down on it heavily, closed her eyes.

31 "Well? What's this about Ron?" the senator asked.

The two men moved toward the door. "Ask Rink," one of them said.

"Just a minute! You're not leaving this woman here . . . ?"

"Better get a medic in, Senator," the shaved lad said.

32 He looked at her. "Is she ill?" She opened her eyes and pushed her hair out of her face. She was pale, and there were distinct dark hollows under her eyes.

33 "I'm pregnant," she said in a husky voice. "Awful damn pregnant. And Ron's the father."

34 He walked slowly across to stand before her. "Have you any proof of that remarkable statement?"

35 She threw the cloak open. Her body looked swollen enough to contain quadruplets.

36 "I'm not referring to the obvious fact of your condition," he said.

"He's the father, all right."

He turned abruptly, went to the desk put his finger on the vidscreen key.

37 "I'm not lying," she said. "The paternity's easy to check. Why would I try to lie?" She was sitting up now; her white fingers dug into the plum-colored cushions.

38 "I assume you make no claim of a legal marriage contract?"

"Would I be here?"

"You're aware of the laws governing childbirth—"

"Sure. I'm aware of the laws of nature, too."

"Why didn't you report to a PC station as soon as you were aware of your condition?"

39 "I didn't want to."

"What do you expect me to do?"

"Fix it so I can have the baby—and keep him."

"That's impossible, of course."

40 "It's your own grandson you're killing!" the woman said quickly. "You can talk about how one of your compulsory abortions is no worse than lancing a boil—but this"—she put her hands against her belly—"this is a baby, Senator. He's alive. I can feel him kicking."

41 His eyes narrowed momentarily. "Where is Ron?"

"I haven't seen him in six months. Not since I told him."

"Does he know you came here?"

"How would he know?"

He shook his head. "What in God's name do you expect of me, girl?"

42 "I told you! I want my son—alive!"

He moved away from the desk, noting as he did that the two men had left silently. He started to run his fingers through his hair, jerked his hands down, rammed them in the pockets of his lounging jacket. He turned suddenly to face the girl.

43 "You did this deliberately—"

"Not without help, I didn't."

"Why? With free anti-pregnancy medication and abort service available at any one of a thousand stations in the city, why?"

44 "Not just free, Senator—compulsory. Maybe I think the government—a bunch of politicians and bureaucrats—has no right to say who can have a child. Or maybe the pills didn't work. Or maybe I just didn't give a damn. What does it matter now?"

45 "You're not living naked in the woods now. You're part of a society; and that society has the right to regulate itself."

46 "And I have a right to have a baby! You didn't give me—or anybody—the right to live! You can't take it away!"

47 He took a turn up and down the room, stopped before her. "Even if I wanted to help you, what is it you imagine I could do?"

"Get me a birth permit."

"Nonsense. You don't even have a contract; and the qualifications—"

48 "You can fix it."

"I believe this whole thing is no more than a plot to embarrass me!"

49 The woman laughed. She threw back her head and screamed

laughter. "Ron was right! You're a fool! A cold-blooded old fool! Your own grandson—and you think he's something that was just thought up to annoy you!"

50 "Stop talking as though this were a living child instead of an illegal embryo!"

51 Her laughter died away in a half titter, half sob. "It's a funny world we've made for ourselves. In the old days before we got so goddamned smart a man would have been proud and happy to know he had a grandson. He'd look forward to all the things he'd teach him, all the things they'd do together. He'd be a little part of the future that he could see growing, living on after he was dead—"

52 "That's enough!" He drew a controlled breath and let it out. "Do you realize what you're asking of me?"

53 "Sure. Save my baby's life. Ron's baby."

His hands opened and closed. "You want me to attempt to deliberately circumvent the laws I've devoted my life to creating!"

54 "Don't put words to it. Just remember it's a baby's life."

"If I knew where Ron was . . ."

"Yes?"

55 "We could execute a marriage contract, predate it. I could manage that. As for a birth permit—" He broke off as the girl's face contorted in an expression like a silent scream.

56 "Better hurry up," she gasped. "They're coming faster now. . . ."

"Good God, girl! Why did you wait until now to bring this to me?"

"I kept hoping Ron would come back."

"I'll have to call a doctor. You know what that means."

"No! Not yet! Find Ron!"

57 "None of this will help if you're both dead." He keyed the screen, gave terse instructions. "Handle this quietly, Jerry. Very quietly," he finished.

58 "Damn you! I was a fool to come to you!"

"Never mind the hysterics. Just tell me where to start looking for Ron."

59 "I . . . I don't have any idea."

"Those friends of yours: what about them? Would they know?"

"I promised Limmy and Dan I wouldn't get them mixed up in anything."

60 He snorted. "And you're asking me to break my oath to the people of this country."

61 The girl gave him an address. "Don't put them in the middle, Senator. They were pretty decent, bringing me here."

62 "The obstetrician will be here in a few minutes. Just lie there quietly and try to relax."

63 "What if you can't find him?"

64 "I suppose you know the answer to that as well as I do."

"Senator—do they really—kill the babies?"

"The embryo never draws a breath. Under the legal definition it's not a baby."

65 "Oh, Senator—for God's sake, find him!"

He closed the door, shutting off his view of her frightened face.

66 Red light leaked out through the air baffles about the bright-plated plastic door. At the third ring—he could hear the buzzer through the panel—it opened on a shrill of voices, the rattle and boom of music. Acrid, stale-smelling air puffed in his face. A tall man with an oddly-trimmed beard looked at him through mirror-lens contacts. A tendril of reddish smoke curled from the room past his head.

67 "Uh?"

"I'd like to have a word with Mr. Limberg, please."

"Who?"

"Mr. Limberg. Limmy."

68 "Uh." The bearded man turned away. Beyond him, strangely costumed figures were dimly visible in the thick crimson fog, standing, sitting, lying on the floor. Some were naked, their shaved bodies decorated with painted patterns. A boy and girl dressed in striped tunics and hose undulated past arm in arm, looking curiously alike. The youth with the shaved head appeared, his mouth drawn down at the corners.

69 "I need to find Ron in a hurry. Can you tell me where he might be?"

"Rink had to blow her tonsils, uh?"

"This is important, Limmy. I have to find him. Seconds may be vital."

70 The boy pushed his lips in and out. Others had gathered, listening.

"Hey, who's the zek?" someone called.

"It's Eubank. . . ."

The youth stepped out, pulled the door shut behind him. "Look, I want no part, follow?"

71 "All I want is to find Ron. I'm not here to get anyone in trouble. I appreciate what you did for the girl."

72 "Ron's a pile, as far as I'm concerned. When I saw Rink meant to go through with it, I sent word to Ron. I didn't know if it reached him or not. But he screened me about half an hour ago. He's on his way here now from Phil."

73 "On the shuttle, I suppose. Good. I can contact him en route—"

"With what for fare? I heard you kept him broke."

"His allowance—never mind. If he's not riding the shuttle, how is he getting here?"

74 "Car."

"You must be mistaken. His license was lifted last year."

"Yeah. I remember when—and why. . . ."

"Are you saying . . . suggesting . . ."

75 "I'm not saying anything. Just that Ron said he'd be at your place as quick as he could get there."

76 "I see." He half turned away, turned back to thank the boy. But the door had already closed.

77 "Please try to understand, Lieutenant," Senator Eubank said to the hard, expressionless face on the screen. "I have reason to believe that the boy is operating a borrowed manually controlled vehicle on the Canado autopike, northbound from Philadelphia, ETD forty minutes ago. He's just received some very shocking news, and he's probably driving at a very high speed. He'll be in an agitated condition, and—"

78 "You have a description of this vehicle, Senator?"

"No. But surely you have means for identifying a car that's not locked into the system."

79 "That's correct—but it sometimes takes a few minutes. There are a lot of vehicles on the 'pike, Senator."

80 "You understand he's under great stress. The circumstances—"

"We'll take him off as gently as we can."

"And you'll keep me informed? I must see him at the first possible instant, you understand?"

81 "We'll keep you advised—" The police officer turned his head as if looking at someone off-screen.

82 "This may be something, Senator," he said. "I have a report on a four-seater Supercad at Exit 2983. He took the ramp too fast—he was going a little over two hundred. He went air-borne and crashed." He paused, listening, then nodded. "Looks like paydirt, Senator. The ID checks on the hot-list out of Philly. And it was on manual control."

83 The officer used his screamlight to clear a path through the crowd to the spot where the heavy car lay on its side under the arches of the overpass. Two men with cutting torches were crouched on top of it, sending up showers of molten droplets.

84 "He's alive in there?" Senator Eubank asked.

The lieutenant nodded. "The boys will have him out in a couple of minutes. The crash copter is standing by."

85 The torches stopped sputtering. The two men lifted the door, tossed it down behind the car. A white-suited medic with a bundle under his arm climbed up and dropped inside. Half a minute later the crane arm at the back of the big police cruiser hoisted the shock-seat clear of the wreck. From the distance of fifty feet, the driver's face was clay-white under the polyarcs.

86 "It's Ron."

The medic climbed down, bent over the victim as the Senator and his escort hurried up.

87 "How does it look?" the lieutenant asked.

88 "Not too good. Internals. Skull looks OK. If he's some rich man's pup, he may walk again—with a new set of innards—" The man broke off as he glanced up and saw the civilian beside the officer. "But I wouldn't waste any time taking him to the hospital," he finished.

89 The duty medtech shook his head. "I'm sorry, sir. He's on the table right at this moment. There's no way in the world for you to see him until he comes out. He's in very serious condition, Senator."

90 "I understand." As the tech turned away he called after him: "Is there a private screen I could use?"

"In the office, sir."

91 Alone, he punched his apartment code. The operator's face appeared on the screen. "I'm sorry, no—Oh, it's you, Senator. I didn't know you'd gone out—"

"Buzz my flat, Jerry."

92 The screen winked and cleared. After fifteen seconds' wait, the image of a small, sharp-eyed man appeared, rubbing at his elbows with a towel.

93 "About time you called in, John," he said. "First time in thirty years I've let myself be hauled out of my home in the midst of dinner."

"How is she?"

94 The elderly man wagged his head. "I'm sorry, John. She slipped away from me."

"You mean—she's dead?"

95 "What do you expect? A post-terminal pregnancy—she'd been taking drugs for a week to delay the birth. She'd had no medical attention whatever. And your living room rug doesn't make the best possible delivery table! There was massive hemorrhaging; it might have been different if I'd been working in a fully equipped labor room—but under the circumstances, that was out of the question, of course, even if there'd been time."

96 "You know . . . ?"

"The woman told me something of the circumstances."

"What about the child?"

"Child?" The little man frowned. "I suppose you refer to the fetus. It wasn't born."

97 "You're going to leave it inside the corpse?"

"What would you have me do?" The doctor lowered his voice. "John—is what she said true? About Ron being the father?"

"Yes—I think so."

98 The little man's mouth tightened. "Her heart stopped three and a half minutes ago. There's still time for a Caesarian—if that's what you want."

99 "I . . . I don't know, Walter."

"John, you devoted thirty years of your life to the amendment and the enabling act. It passed by a very thin cat's whisker. And the opposition hasn't given up, not by a damn sight. The repeal movement is already underway, and it has plenty of support." The doctor paused, peering at the senator. "I can bring the child out—but John—a lot of this is already in the record. There'd be no way of keeping it out of the hands of the other side: *your* law—violated by you, the first week it was in force. It would finish you, John—and Population Control, too, for a generation."

100 "There's no hope of resuscitating the mother?"

"None at all. Even today people sometimes die, John."

"I see. Thank you, Walter. You did your best."

"About the child . . . ?"

"There is no child. Just an illegal pregnancy."

101 "You may go in now," the nurse said. Ron was on his back, his shaven head protruding from the bloated cocoon of the life-support tank. His eyes opened as his father bent over him.

"Dad—I was a damned fool. Knew I was going too fast. . . ."

The senator leaned closer to catch his whisper.

102 "I had to try . . . to get back in time. . . ." He paused and his eyelids flickered. "Limmy told me . . . she went to you. I knew . . . you'd take care . . . my wife."

"Easy, Ron, easy. No need to talk now—"

103 "When Rink told me . . . about the baby . . . I ran out on her. She handed me a contract, all made up. But I couldn't see it, bringing a child into this mess. I thought . . . when I left she'd go in and have it taken care of. Then I heard . . . she didn't. It . . . did something to me. I still had the papers. I registered 'em in Phil. I used your name to get the birth permit. You don't mind . . . ?"

"Ron. . . ."

104 "I wanted to be there. Too late; damned fool. I always was a damn fool, Dad. It'll be different, now. A lot different. Being a father . . . not so easy, eh, Dad? But good. Worth it. Worth everything. . . ." The boy's voice faded.

105 "Better to let him rest now, sir," the nurse whispered.

The senator rose stiffly. At the door, he looked back. Ron seemed to be smiling in his sleep.

106 "Did you say something, sir?" the nurse asked. He looked down at her bright face.

107 "What is there to say?"

Her eyes followed him as he walked away down the bright-lit corridor.

Thinking Questions: *Form*

1. Why is this story told in a completely subjective, third-person narrative? Does the writer want the reader to take a particular side? Or does he want the reader to understand both sides of the central conflict in the story?

2. Give a summary description of the Senator. Include both physical details and a description of his personality, intelligence, and character. Study the story carefully to substantiate your description.

3. What are the social implications of the lawgiver's final decision? Is his desire to define abortion as something other than murder convincing (see paragraphs 4, 40, 50, and 64)? Does his attempt to find his son indicate that, at least at one point in the story, he also wishes to do away with compulsory abortion? If so, does that indicate a flaw, a lack of conviction, or a sign of strength in his character?

4. What is the significance of the opening conversation between the woman and the Senator (see paragraphs 1 through 17)? Is there an inconsistency between what the Senator says in this first scene as he argues with the woman and his later actions and indecision when he is confronted by Ron's pregnant girlfriend? How would you describe the woman who argues with the Senator? Is she any more "human" than he is, despite the fact that she continually argues against the Population Control Act because she thinks it is cold-blooded murder?

5. The events in this narrative are arranged chronologically. Several simultaneous events—Ron's automobile accident and his operation, his girlfriend's death from childbirth, the Senator's interview with Limmy—are told to the reader as they are experienced by the Senator, who is the controlling point of view of the story. Look back over the story and imagine how the events might have been arranged had the story been told from the point of view of another character. Would shifting the point of view have changed the story's message?

Thinking Questions: *Substance*

1. Provide a list of arguments that you believe the Senator would give in support of the Population Control Act. Study the story carefully to find these arguments; look over the Senator's conversations, his brief answers to questions, and the arguments implied by his gestures and actions.

2. Is it significant that the Senator's secretary, Jerry, says, "Big day, eh, Senator, ramrodding the enabling act through like you did." What does that statement tell you about the Senator's personality and character? Compare the Senator's early rigidity and self-assurance with his later wavering from principle in his son's case and to his final words: "What is there to say?" Why has the Senator been silenced?

3. Which of the following statements best approximates the theme of this story, and why? (A theme captures in a brief statement the general or main idea embodied in the story. Every action and every character in the story in one way or another affects a story's theme.)

a. People cannot live by abstract principles alone.

b. Both reason and emotion should have equal control over a person's actions.

c. Abortion is evil.

d. Abortion is justified under special circumstances.

e. Individuals should control their own destinies.

How do different characters relate to one or another aspect of the theme you have selected? What particular scene or group of scenes contributes most directly to your choice of theme?

4. This story takes place in the future. What evidence can you find in the present to justify Laumer's description of future conflicts between an individual's natural desire to have a child whenever he or she wishes and a society's more general desire to preserve itself?

5. Does any character in this story demonstrate the ability to resolve the conflict between the necessity for abstract and absolute laws and the need to satisfy individual instincts? What are the general social implications of your answer to this question?

Writing Exercise II

NARRATION

Most college students have extensive experience working with the educational system, from elementary and high school on into college. Look back over your relations with educational institutions in the past. They can provide you with examples of how rules, policies, and procedures affect individuals. Begin by defining how you have generally responded to the rules, the patterns of behavior requested of you by the educational systems within which you have learned and worked. Have you developed a pattern of response? Are you usually cooperative, even when your own patterns are contradicted by the system? Or are you usually quick to challenge policies or rules you believe are meaningless? *How* do you challenge the system—by personal griping, by following official channels, by writing letters, by open rebellion? Now select a particularly important incident or event from your educational past and use it to illustrate your general reaction to schools and their policies and rules. Be specific; *show* as much as you *tell;* keep your purpose in front of your reader as you also provide a concrete experience to clarify and support that purpose.

WRITING THE NARRATIVE ESSAY

Pure narration should work by suggestion; it should provide specific experiences in support of general ideas. The writer wants to share his or her experience, usually to imply a general idea, attitude, or opinion.

> John walked slowly through the door, swinging his keychain from side to side, one arm held stiffly at his side. His upper lip occasionally twitched.

Narrative descriptions give us a glimpse of a character *in action;* sensations and states of mind are represented by physical action, gesture, and detail. Such observations, of course, become the foundation upon which the reader can build inferences about the subject. John, the reader might infer from the above paragraph, is both nervous and resentful. He tries to seem confident, even a bit arrogant: "swinging his keychain . . . one arm held stiffly at his side." But his seeming confidence is undercut by his twitching upper lip, slow walk, and stiffness. The details show us John in action. *We,* as readers, draw the inferences and compose the impression. Narration, in essence, suggests ideas through concrete actions and observations. Here are some basic dos and don'ts.

1. Let your details, descriptions, and actions *suggest* your meaning; don't break in and tell your readers what to think of your narration. A writer, for example, should not preface a piece of narration—for example, the paragraph on John—with summary: "John was a nervous boy trying to seem calm and confident." Give your readers something to do, but be sure to direct their interpretations by carefully arranging and selecting your material.

2. Use *concrete* words to describe your experience. Don't generalize unless you anchor the generalization in concrete detail.

3. As you prepare to write, be sure to *select* relevant detail. Don't describe everything and don't repeat needlessly. If you have used one detail to establish an emotion, don't use other details to signify the same emotion. Someone, for example, who wishes to establish the sterility of a hospital waiting room might emphasize the hard vinyl seat cushions, the institutional yellow walls, and the rigidly set face of the receptionist. Those three details, specifically described, should establish the idea of sterility. More details of a similar kind would probably become monotonous and pointless.

4. Once you *select* details to establish an idea or purpose, *arrange* them to lead naturally to an emotional climax. *Pace* your writing. Don't include everything; don't include even a few details without thinking of their natural effect on readers. If you are organizing *chronologically,* be

sure you put significant details at the point in your narrative where they will do the most good.

Organizing a narrative essay

There are three general ways to organize a narrated experience. You can organize chronologically, developing your story from beginning to end and moving your story from place to place in a normal time order. If you choose a chronological time sequence, you must be sure to make transitions clearly. Orwell, for example, begins his essay by summarizing his experiences in Burma over a long period of time. Then he shifts naturally to one incident, covering a limited period of time and occurring in a particular place, which he believes represents the longer experience. At that point in his essay, he begins to treat time more specifically; actions and details are presented within a time span that more closely parallels the actual experience. Orwell effectively indicates this shift from summarizing a long period of time to the detailed narration of events in time by the sentence: "One day something happened which in a roundabout way was enlightening" (paragraph 3).

A writer, then, can maintain a strict chronological order, perhaps expanding upon those events in the time sequence that are most relevant to his or her purpose. There is nothing to stop a writer, however, from distorting chronological time to show how an experience was perceived by a particular person. For example, Norman Mailer, in "A Busload of Slogans," jumbles normal time order in one important part of his essay. After telling the story of the bus ride from the Pentagon to the U.S. Post Office in Alexandria, Virginia, in chronological order, Mailer as narrator intrudes in paragraph 9. He remembers something he had learned earlier about Egyptian architecture.

> Then his thoughts began to meander again—down a long broad slow river of thought. He turned a bend—he had it. Delight. He had made the grand connection between Egyptian architecture and the Pentagon.

This connection leads naturally to an explanation of what the connection meant and, finally, in the next paragraph, back to chronological time and the narrator's arrival at the post office.

An expository writer can look back over a personal experience and arrange it by either *objective, chronological* time or by *subjective* time—according to the order of occurrence in the mind of the writer or according to the importance of the events as far as the writer's purpose is concerned. Above all, narratives must be organized *consistently;* once you decide to use either objective or subjective methods of organization, keep to your decision.

These first two methods of organizing a narrative deal explicitly with chronology, with the arrangement of events through time. The third method deals with *point of view.* In fiction, point of view can be extremely complicated. In exposition, however, the writer usually decides on either the first, second, or third person and organizes the essay accordingly.

A first-person narrator (see the Orwell, Reich, and Baldwin essays) addresses the reader as if talking about himself or herself ("I"). The first person creates a more intimate relationship between writer and reader; the writer, like Orwell in "Shooting an Elephant," admits a direct part in the events being narrated and proceeds to interpret and draw conclusions in a very personal manner.

A second-person narrator brings the reader directly into the story ("you"). Again, the second person usually creates a more intimate relationship between reader and writer, with the reader often brought directly into the story as a hypothetical character.

The most common point of view in narration is the third person—*he, she, it, they*, or *one* (see the Mailer and Tuchman essays in this section.) With the third person, a writer usually gains objectivity but sacrifices the closer relationships with the reader that might be possible with the first or second person. The expository third person affords greater control, as exemplified in this brief excerpt from Barbara Tuchman's "Notes from China."

> Perhaps, too, the transfer to collectivism has been made easier because China's life was in some ways collective to begin with. Consider the *kang*, the built-in wall-to-wall bed of north China on which, in the poorer homes, the whole family sleeps. With that in their background, collective adjustment is natural, not to say imperative. (Paragraph 4)

Barbara Tuchman here assumes the objective pose of a writer who knows all the facts (of course, in reality, she is piecing together a past experience from memory and from the personal accounts of observers and other historians). The language is direct and forceful; the reader responds to the facts as facts, without the subjective questioning and introspection of a Baldwin or Mailer (whose third-person "he" is, in fact, himself).

Chronology and point of view are related but not identical. All three points of view will allow a writer to narrate either objectively or subjectively.

Remember these three methods of organizing a narrative essay:

1. *Objective*—events organized according to the normal flow of time. Chronology is the most objective method of telling a story, because chronologically organized events follow time as it is usually perceived by the senses.

2. *Subjective*—events arranged according to their importance, or according to the perception of the writer or narrator. A subjective narrative might, for example, tell later events first because they are more important to the writer's purpose.

3. *Point of view* (first, second or third person)—involves the writer's

choice of *how* to tell the story, using either *I* or *we; you;* or *he, she, it, they,* or *one.*

A final few words on unity in narration. Divide units of time into sentences and paragraphs. If you plan to describe a man, in detail, as he carries out a complicated action, be sure to divide that action into spatial units. Then work your units into paragraphs that move either from general to specific or specific to general. And be sure your reader can follow your narration from one action to another. If you plan to skip over parts of the entire action, then be sure that you include transitions that smooth out the rough jump from one action to another. An extended narration is usually divided naturally into paragraph blocks, each block narrating a significant part of the overall action, each paragraph in the block developing a smaller part of the sequence.

Narrative exposition

In this book, we are primarily interested in narration that is used to provide evidence, support, or clarification in an expository essay. In the narrative essay, the writer compresses his or her experience into little stories that are used to support a thesis. Any informative essay has three general elements: a *subject* (in Orwell's essay the subject is British imperialism); a *thesis* that represents a particular writer's attitude toward that subject (Orwell argues that imperialism can never truly succeed as a form of government because rulers are put into unjustified positions of power); and a foundation in concrete experience in which the writer draws from personal experience, reading, or imagination (Orwell uses the elephant-shooting incident, narrated in detail, to illustrate his thesis). The student of composition who can use his or her personal experience to develop an opinion can then apply writing skills to a large variety of subject areas, without being forced to parrot the ideas of a few quickly read articles or books. Remember these differences between pure narration and exposition as you compose:

An effective expository essay must take readers by the hand and lead them through *both* general ideas and supporting experience, and readers must be able to follow the development from idea to experience.

You can provide natural and clear reading by carefully considering *unity* and *coherence.* Organize your ideas under a simply phrased thesis or main idea; have every word and sentence develop that main idea (unity). And be sure to connect your ideas; use transitions to point out how your experience led to your thesis (coherence). And control arrangement and point of view so that your readers can share your supporting experiences without confusion.

Form and Substance/3

Form:

EXPOSITION

Methods of Development:

A. Definition

B. Comparison and Contrast

C. Classification and Logical Division

D. Cause and Effect

Substance:

A. Men and Women—Together?

SEXUAL IDENTITY IN AMERICA

B. Where Are We Going?

THINKING ON THE FUTURE

C. Living To Learn or Learning To Live:

EDUCATION TODAY AND TOMORROW

D. Fighting for It:

VIOLENCE AND SURVIVAL

Most college writing—in fact, most of the writing that people do in relation to jobs and everyday life—is expository. Exposition *informs;* it is writing in which the writer organizes evidence to help a reader share in an idea. Both descriptive and narrative writing, as we have seen, place emphasis squarely on the *subject* discussed, to show what the subject looks and feels like, how its arrangement as an experience through space and time helps clarify what it is and what the reader should think of it. Description and narration are vital to literature, in which the writer attempts to re-create and share imagined experience. But they can be equally important, in a supportive way, to the development of ideas in expository essays. They often provide, along with statistics, facts, and other forms of evidence, the substance and support for the expository writer's thesis. An architect planning a new library for a small town may, for example, include concrete descriptions of the library's physical appearance to help support the idea that his building plan will add to the aesthetic quality of the town. He may also decide to narrate a typical day in the proposed library to show how the new building would function more efficiently than the old.

Remember these qualities as you distinguish exposition from other kinds of writing:

1. Exposition usually helps a writer show *why, how, when* or *where;* it develops general ideas that the writer then explains to the reader. Exposition, however, is *not* argument, in which a writer attempts to *persuade* his or her readers, often for or against another idea or opinion.

2. An expository writer uses evidence differently from the writers of narration and description. Exposition uses description and narration to support a thesis; it condenses so that the described and narrated experiences relate clearly to the development of a main idea. For example, George Orwell, in "Shooting an Elephant," narrates the elephant-shooting incident in a way that clearly relates to his thesis on imperialism.

3. In contrast with argument, however, exposition often organizes evidence in a less formal or precise way. The writer's relationship with his reader is a bit less formal, with a "take-your-reader-by-the-hand-and-show-him" attitude. Argument creates an opposition and forms evidence to support one side of that opposition. In Part Four, for example, the social and political satirist Art Buchwald writes a mock argument defending and explaining an imaginary group, Fathers for a Moral America. Because he puts such extreme and competitive arguments into the mouths of this group's spokesman, the essay becomes an obvious satire of the more extreme and shallow forms of argument.

4. Exposition has a clearly stated *thesis* that the evidence, organization, and style of the essay are all meant to support. Description and narration, in their pure forms, have no explicit thesis; they may *imply* a thesis by shaping the experience to support a particular attitude, as Studs Terkel does in "Earning One's Bread," when he describes the attitudes of numerous individuals to support the idea that people no longer get pride, satisfaction, or dignity from their work. Still, Terkel never *explicitly* outlines his thesis; he leaves that to the reader.

In sum, exposition presents a thesis less conclusively and competitively than argument, but more explicitly than description or narration. It may take a particular idea and *show* the reader where the idea came from and what particular evidence the writer has gathered to support it. But exposition does not necessarily strive to change the mind of the reader. It informs and shares, while argument divides a subject and attempts to persuade that one idea or position is better than another.

Form:

EXPOSITION

(Definition)

Substance and Theme:

SEXUAL IDENTITY IN AMERICA

American society has always depended on men and women assuming clearly defined and separate roles. Traditionally men have gone *out* to work, to provide for their families, to "make a living." Women have stayed home; they organize the household, keep things in order, and raise the kids. There have, of course, always been many exceptions to these unofficially accepted conventions. Some women have always been aggressive, even in the predominantly male-controlled areas of sports and athletics, but such aggressiveness often resulted in those women being stereotyped as tomboys or "career women," or as not generally fitted to the passive, "feminine" image which our society has emphasized.

What have been the conventionally held definitions of the roles of men and women in our culture? For women, esteem usually has come from three qualities: physical appearance and sexual attractiveness, loyalty and efficiency, and the ability to get along pleasantly with others. Think back to high school. How many women were praised highly, especially by peers, for athletic prowess or for superior academic achievement? Acceptance and praise came more often when the woman succeeded in social areas, in "popularity," in helping to plan proms and dances.

Men, on the other hand, are usually praised for their aggressiveness, whether in athletics or academics. They are supposed to take charge of situations, to dominate and control, to show, above all, courage and determination. Cheerleaders (mostly female), for example, cheer the men who score the touchdowns and hookshots. The male's aggressiveness, at least according to most traditional conceptions, should be complemented by female graciousness, beauty, and efficiency. Such experience with conventional sex roles in high school has conditioned young men and women for later marriages in the conventional pattern, where often the wife cooks dinner, raises children, and encourages the man as he develops a career. We fulfill the sexual expectations of others before adulthood and, as a result, come to expect such patterns of behavior in ourselves and others in later life.

Where have these conventional attitudes and definitions toward men and women come from? Sometimes the lesser physical strength of women causes people to expect a "stay-at-home-and-look-pretty" attitude. At other times, religious beliefs ("woman was created from the rib of a man") control an individual's expectations. And, very often, sexual drives and expectations encourage individuals to use a person of the opposite sex as a means to an end, as a means to physical pleasure, to children, or to domestic tranquility. Rather than expecting a variety of interests, talents, faults, and personality traits in anyone we meet, we often assume that a person of the other sex will display at least some conventional sexual traits and characteristics. The argumentative woman often, for example, surprises the man who expects only acquiescence and charm from women, especially in social situations. The sensitive and courteous man often surprises the woman who expects only aggressiveness and a tendency to dominate.

The results of such sexual role stereotypes often affect our lines much more extensively than these rather simple examples would suggest. Many jobs demand adherence to certain sexual expectations. Many larger social issues are often affected by sexual stereotypes. And, as Lenore Romney points out in her essay in this section, many political issues would be greatly altered if women and men were to respond to political questions as equals, without the disunity that often results when many women demonstrate interest only in the effects politics has on domestic issues (food and clothing prices, for example), while many men reflect interest in only those political issues that directly affect their jobs or careers.

There is nothing inherently wrong, of course, with women who want careers as housewives or secretaries. Nor is there anything necessarily wrong with ambitious, career- or job-oriented men. But very often conventional expectations related to sexual identity can create severe problems for those individuals who, by natural talent and inclination, wish to pursue careers or interests that depart from general sexual expectations: the young girl who, for example, would rather dissect frogs than play with dolls, or, later on, the young woman who wants a career in medicine or law or engineering. Often those in authority do not believe women have the skills and natural abilities to compete in such traditional male professions.

Men, on the other hand, are often discouraged from pursuing careers in day-care or childcare centers, in pre-school and even primary education, as clerical workers or secretaries, usually because at least some people feel such careers are not suited to men—it is women who are supposed to raise, control, and understand the needs of children. Or others might feel that the lower pay and subordinate position of many secretaries make these jobs unsuited to men—who are supposed to demonstrate ambition, leadership, and the will to control and direct, and, in addition, to earn higher pay.

Such stereotyped expectations also have direct effects on marriage. Those individuals who enter marriage both agreeing with the conventional sexual roles may have little trouble. The wife will stay home, cook, sew, clean, shop for food and clothing, and offer encouragement to both her husband and her children as they deal with the outside world. The husband will direct his major energies toward his job while he relaxes with and provides leadership for his family.

If however, two people with unconventional social and professional goals marry, they will need to strive at almost every turn to work out behavior patterns that will allow them to pursue their goals. Suppose both husband and wife wish to have careers. Who will raise the children and clean the house? How will husband and wife divide domestic labors fairly if one mate is actually better prepared by background or social conditioning to cook, sew, or handle a budget? Many of the changes in marriage that are now arising in our society are potential answers to questions like these. Some couples decide not to have children; others decide to put a large portion of their salaries toward housekeepers; still others decide to rent apartments that are easy to maintain instead of buying houses that demand constant maintenance.

The essays in this section develop some of these general concerns in detail. Lenore Romney ran for United States Senate from Michigan in 1970. During that campaign she learned firsthand of the stereotyped thinking many Americans used to evaluate women. Her brief essay becomes an urgent appeal to both men and women to alter these prejudices, to make greater use of the potentials of women in all fields, not just in the home. In the process of making her appeal, Lenore Romney defines many of the external problems women face in our society, much as Betty Friedan defines the internal, psychological problems women face because of the image of themselves which our society gives them.

Betty Friedan worked for women's magazines for several years before she wrote *The Feminine Mystique* in 1963. She used her experience with such magazines to describe what she believed was an effort by mass media and men in management and executive positions to dominate and control the minds of women. Pointing to the lack of women in high-level administrative posts in business and industry, and to the general shortage of women with professional careers, Friedan showed how the image or "mystique" of femininity was often used to keep the woman in her place, subordinate to the men around her.

In "The Problem That Has No Name," which is taken from *The Feminine Mystique,* Friedan defines the problem that she found troubling most women, especially housewives, in the 1950s and early 1960s. Friedan, after describing these problems in detail with numerous examples, also shows why many of these women suffer from "the problem with no name." In essence, she tells us why and how women develop images of themselves that greatly limit their growth as individuals.

Between Romney's and Friedan's essays you will find Kate Millet's brief manifesto for a systematic program of change in sexual politics. Unlike Romney and Friedan, Millet does *not* believe that adjustments in our sexual attitudes will solve the woman's, or even the man's, problems. Instead, she argues, wholesale changes in our entire social and political structure must occur before any meaningful changes in sexual roles will take place.

As these opening three essays suggest, this section begins with considerations of the everyday problems of women as they face sexual discrimination and biased attitudes. As you progress through the section you will find that the problem of sexual identity for both women and men is an inclusive one, with social, political, spiritual, and ethical ramifications of all kinds. Specific examples lead naturally to considerations of more general social problems.

Men, Women—and Politics

LENORE ROMNEY

1 Historian Mary Beard once said, "The dogma of woman's complete historical subjection to men must be rated as one of the most fantastic myths ever created by the human mind."

2 Mary Beard never ran for public office, and her opinion does not apply to the male-dominated world of politics. In my bid to become the first woman senator from the state of Michigan, that so-called myth helped to doom my campaign from the start. And so, the Ninety-Second Congress convened . . . with just one woman—Maine's Margaret Chase Smith—in the United States Senate, a tiny one percent of its total membership.

3 I found in my campaign that many men and women openly resented the idea that a woman would even try to unseat a man. Some bluntly asked me, "You mean you have the nerve to challenge a United States Senator?"

4 I think the rawest example of prejudice came from a farmer who told me, "Ma'am, we don't vote for women or niggers in this county."

5 In factories, I encountered men standing in small groups, laughing, shouting, "Get back in the kitchen. George needs you there. What do you know about politics?"

6 Many wouldn't even listen to my credentials or to my discussion of the issues. Yet for 30 years I have worked at all levels of community endeavor—for the adoption of a new state constitution, for community schools, educational reform, the Council for Human Resources, and with ghetto problems.

7 I was especially discouraged by women themselves saying that women don't know enough to be public officials. Obviously, they were not ready to rally around one who would have represented them in our most important forum.

8 Some women, as well as men, obviously felt a woman would come out second best in the rough give-and-take of politics. Nonsense. We "give and take" with our husbands and children and acquaintances every day and, without being abrasive, come out very well, thank you. We often can do better than men in getting things out of people.

9 At home, both father and mother are needed. In the nation, our collective home, when we place our faith in men and exclude the voice of women, we are shutting out those who, for example, are especially able to communicate with the young.

10 I feel very strongly that women need to be liberated from the belief that they are not pertinent, not relevant. They want equal pay with men, equal jobs, but women are not willing to help one another get elected to deal with the problems of the day. Equal earnings should have been gained back in the Stone Age. Women should not have to be fighting that battle now, and it's too bad they have to. Instead, they should be using their talents in the social and human areas. If they understood their true role, I think they could attain it.

11 It seems so much more important to me for women to communicate effectively. The problems are mounting, but we stay in the background. The few who do step forward are batted down.

12 Who has the gilt-edged credentials to set our children straight? We do. We have the sensitivity, insight, experiences with youngsters that could be invaluable in understanding the emotional and psychological needs of our kids. But first we must understand this, and concentrate our efforts in these areas. For if women and society in general continue to ignore this special feminine understanding in dealing with our human problems and values, we are missing the boat.

13 Unfortunately, the Women's Liberation Movement is not erasing prejudice against women because many members are abrasive and resentful of their own roles in society, and that attitude simply turns people off. Women can be effective by being magnificent figures in their own right rather than small facsimiles of men.

14 Women, for example, could make a unique contribution in the wel-

fare area. Men in government have decided that only impoverished mothers who have been deserted by their husbands may receive welfare checks. This is grossly inadequate. Women of America know that a man cannot be equated with simply a meal ticket. A woman needs her husband in the home; children need their father. Why can't we encourage families to stay together? Why do they have to be driven apart by a Federal program that often forces husbands to desert the home so their wives and children can be eligible for some welfare money?

15 No woman would have written such a law. No woman would see a home destroyed by a dole, a family made rootless, disinherited spiritually and emotionally.

16 American housewives sometimes remind me of Nora in Ibsen's *A Doll's House.* Treated by her husband like a doll and never like a human being, she slammed the door on her family. Like Nora, women are often regarded as ting-a-ling things. Well, I admire ting-a-ling, or sex appeal, as much as anyone, but if that's all a woman has, she will never have real confidence, because there will always be some other gal who will have more ting-a-ling.

17 Lack of confidence is what women suffer from most, and they therefore lack stature, status and any feeling that they can be just as effective as men. Often, they feel their opinions are not valuable. Some are lazy, and others, who have cooked, cleaned and worked all day, are just plain tired. They sit down at night, pick up the newspaper and read only the women's page, bypassing politics, finance, community affairs—the real world.

18 Many women today are college graduates, but after marriage and children, they give up intellectual pursuits. They lose their political acumen and awareness. Too often, the bridge game, clothes and the maid become the main topics of conversation.

19 Compared with her sister overseas, the typical U.S. woman is a poor second, politically. It's silly to ask if women are capable of leading. Look at Golda Meir of Israel.

20 In this country, women are too often placed on an illusory pedestal. What concerned, intelligent woman wants a pedestal when her country is in crisis? To me, that pedestal is used to indicate that women are things to look at and adore but not to converse with, to counsel or deal with.

21 Nowhere in my campaign did I find prejudice stronger than in some male members of the press, who regarded me as nothing more than a stand-in candidate for my husband. Far from being a stand-in for George, I divorced myself from the Administration in that I made my own decisions and discussed the issues as I saw them. But none of this came through to the public.

22 Often, male journalists have had no experience with the type of

woman who knows and cares about public affairs, and instead they see women only as people relegated to the tearooms, the style shows and, yes, the kitchens. When they indicate that women have no business in politics because it's dirty, I take exception. It's the real world, and women have every right—and duty—to be in it.

23 The most gratifying experiences in my campaign were the many direct meetings with our young people, and I will repeat now what I told them then: a revolution against the system is not realistic. It isn't the Government but the people who are in it and who run our institutions, who cause the bottlenecks, who block reform, and delay desegregation. Don't abolish the system: let's change ourselves. Don't our kids realize that regardless of the system, they will have to deal with the Wallaces and the Maddoxes in our country? Not until we can deal with human beings and change their attitudes can we even begin to solve some of our pressing problems. I will continue to work for progress, but I realize only too well that without a forum like the Senate, my task will be more difficult.

24 As for sex discrimination, I say to the men: for goodness' sake, turn the searchlight inward. Are *you* solving our problems adequately? Accept talent wherever you find it, especially if it comes from the experience and humanity of mature women.

Thinking Questions: *Form*

1. Both Betty Friedan (in an essay later in this section) and Lenore Romney define by using examples and descriptions. They work through general descriptions of women's problems, cite more specific illustrations and examples in support of their general definitions, and finally wind up with more particular definitions and proposed solutions. Does Romney add significant insight to what you already knew about how women are kept out of what is usually called "a man's world"? Does she introduce aspects of the problem Friedan ignores?

2. Look at Romney's vocabulary and her sentence and paragraph structure. Where do you think her essay originally appeared? In a newspaper, a scholarly journal, an intellectual magazine like *Atlantic* or *Saturday Review*, or a popular weekly magazine? How can you tell?

3. Put Romney's thesis in your own words. What sentence in her essay comes closest to matching your description of her thesis?

4. Compare Arthur Schlesinger's definition of the American male's problems with Romney's definition of women's problems (Schlesinger's essay also appears later in this section). Is there any causal relationship between the identity problems of men and women as Romney and Schlesinger see them? In fact, one particular section of Schlesinger's essay specifically mentions how men's attitudes toward women might have con-

tributed directly to the "crisis in American masculinity." Consider writing an essay in which you show how men have specifically contributed to women's perceptions of themselves and how women have specifically contributed to men's self-images. You might focus on one or two major attitudes of men and women toward each other and discuss the specific effects of those attitudes.

Thinking Questions: *Substance*

1. Why do you think the farmer whom Romney mentions in paragraph 4 lumped women and "niggers" together in his statement? Why are both groups similar, at least to this farmer? *Are* they similar? In what ways?
2. Why does Romney suppose, in paragraphs 9 and 12, that women are automatically better able to communicate with the young? Why do *you* think a woman might be better able to communicate with the young?
3. Would you consider Lenore Romney a radical feminist? Consider paragraph 13 as you answer.
4. Where does Romney come closest to describing the woman's problem in a way similar to Betty Friedan's in "The Problem That Has No Name"? Do Friedan and Romney share similar attitudes about women, their identities and freedom, their chances for professional careers in contrast to their conventional domestic responsibilities?
5. What do you think of Romney's final admonition to men, concerning politics especially: "Accept talent wherever you find it, especially if it comes from the experience and humanity of mature women"? Is her statement too simple a solution to a complex problem? Will a change in attitude among men assure that women's potential political talents will be used? Do enough women even consider politics? Why or why not? How might more women be encouraged to pursue political careers—through changes in education, in home upbringing, changes in society's attitudes towards family responsibilities?

Sexual Politics: A Manifesto for Revolution

KATE MILLET

1 When one group rules another, the relationship between the two is political. When such an arrangement is carried out over a long period of time it develops an ideology (feudalism, racism, etc.). All historical civilizations are patriarchies: their ideology is male supremacy.

2 Oppressed groups are denied education, economic independence, the power of office, representation, an image of dignity and self-

respect, equality of status, and recognition as human beings. Throughout history women have been consistently denied all of these, and their denial today, while attenuated and partial, is nevertheless consistent. The education allowed them is deliberately designed to be inferior, and they are systematically programmed out of and excluded from the knowledge where power lies today—e.g., in science and technology. They are confined to conditions of economic dependence based on the sale of their sexuality in marriage, or a variety of prostitutions. Work on a basis of economic independence allows them only a subsistence level of life—often not even that. They do not hold office, are represented in no positions of power, and authority is forbidden them. The image of woman fostered by cultural media, high and low, then and now, is a marginal and demeaning existence, and one outside the human condition—which is defined as the prerogative of man, the male.

3 Government is upheld by power, which is supported through consent (social opinion), or imposed by violence. Conditioning to an ideology amounts to the former. But there may be a resort to the latter at any moment when consent is withdrawn—rape, attack, sequestration, beatings, murder. Sexual politics obtains consent through the "socialization" of both sexes to patriarchal policies. They consist of the following:

4 1) the formation of human personality along stereotyped lines of sexual category, based on the needs and values of the master class and dictated by what he would cherish in himself and find convenient in an underclass: aggression, intellectuality, force, and efficiency for the male; passivity, ignorance, docility, "virtue," and ineffectuality for the female.

5 2) the concept of sex role, which assigns domestic service and attendance upon infants to all females and the rest of human interest, achievement and ambition to the male; the charge of leader at all times and places to the male, and the duty of follower, with equal uniformity, to the female.

6 3) the imposition of male rule through institutions: patriarchal religion, the proprietary family, marriage, "The Home," masculine oriented culture, and a pervasive doctrine of male superiority.

7 A Sexual Revolution would bring about the following conditions, desirable upon rational, moral and humanistic grounds:

8 1) the end of sexual repression—freedom of expression and of sexual mores (sexual freedom has been partially attained, but it is now being subverted beyond freedom into exploitative license for patriarchal and reactionary ends).

9 2) Unisex, or the end of separatist character-structure, temperament and behavior, so that each individual may develop an entire —rather than a partial, limited, and conformist—personality.

10 3) re-examination of traits categorized into "masculine" and "feminine," with a total reassessment as to their human usefulness and advisability in both sexes. Thus if "masculine" violence is undesirable, it is so for both sexes, "feminine" dumb-cow passivity likewise. If "masculine" intelligence or efficiency is valuable, it is so for both sexes equally, and the same must be true for "feminine" tenderness or consideration.

11 4) the end of sex role and sex status, the patriarchy and the male supremacist ethic, attitude and ideology—in all areas of endeavor, experience, and behavior.

12 5) the end of the ancient oppression of the young under the patriarchal proprietary family, their chattel status, the attainment of the human rights presently denied them, the professionalization and therefore improvement of their care, and the guarantee that when they enter the world, they are desired, planned for, and provided with equal opportunities.

13 6) Bisex, or the end of enforced perverse heterosexuality, so that the sex act ceases to be arbitrarily polarized into male and female, to the exclusion of sexual expression between members of the same sex.

14 7) the end of sexuality in the forms in which it has existed historically—brutality, violence, capitalism, exploitation, and warfare—that it may cease to be hatred and become love.

15 8) the attainment of the female sex to freedom and full human status after millennia of deprivation and oppression, and of both sexes to a viable humanity.

Thinking Questions: *Form*

1. Write an expository essay in which you define the term *patriarchal society*. How does it work? What is the family and economic structure in a patriarchal society? What are conventional sexual roles in such a society (see paragraph 1)?

2. Point out several terms in paragraph 2 that might require lexical definitions. For example, what *is* an "oppressed group," a "subsistence level of life"? Try giving a general definition for several of these terms and a few examples in support.

3. The "patriarchal policies" and their alternatives listed and defined in paragraphs 4 through 15 provide a general background for many of the issues of contemporary feminism. Take one paragraph in this list, either from the paragraphs defining patriarchal policies (4 through 6) or from paragraphs 7 through 15 which define solutions, and provide examples from our culture to clarify or illustrate.

4. Does Millet provide enough practical illustration for her general assertions on sexism? Choose two or three general assertions, preferably ones that function as topic sentences of paragraphs, and evaluate the support the generality receives in the rest of the paragraph. "Government is upheld by power, which is supported through consent (social opinion), or imposed by violence" is a good example of a topic sentence (paragraph 3) in the form of a general assertion. How well is that assertion clarified and explained in the remainder of paragraph 3 and in the following paragraphs?

Thinking Questions: ***Substance***

1. What gives Kate Millet's essay its authoritative sound? This manifesto clarifies the purposes of the feminist movement, at least as Millet sees them. Can you relate some of Millet's general statements to more specific arguments presented by Betty Friedan and Lenore Romney in other essays in this section? How, for example, does Friedan's description of the relatively meaningless lives of many modern housewives coincide with several of Millet's listed political injustices? How would the "concept of sex role" as our culture defines it lead a woman to develop "the problem that has no name"? (See paragraph 5 in this essay.)

2. Can you cite an example of male supremacy as Millet uses the term in paragraphs 3 through 5?

3. Discuss what you think the family of the future would be like if Millet's manifesto were to be followed. You might want to describe a hypothetical day for a future family of four. How would domestic responsibilities be distributed? How would male and female children be raised so as not to encourage sexual stereotyping? How would husband and wife solve the problems of raising preschool children in a family where both parents work?

The Problem That Has No Name

BETTY FRIEDAN

1 The problem lay buried, unspoken, for many years in the minds of American women. It was a strange stirring, a sense of dissatisfaction, a yearning that women suffered in the middle of the twentieth century in the United States. Each suburban wife struggled with it alone. As she made the beds, shopped for groceries, matched slipcover material, ate peanut butter sandwiches with her children, chauffeured Cub Scouts and Brownies, lay beside her husband at night—she was afraid to ask even of herself the silent question—"Is this all?"

2 For over fifteen years there was no word of this yearning in the millions of words written about women, for women, in all the columns, books and articles by experts telling women their role was to seek fulfillment as wives and mothers. Over and over women heard in voices of tradition and of Freudian sophistication that they could desire no greater destiny than to glory in their own femininity. Experts told them how to catch a man and keep him, how to breastfeed children and handle their toilet training, how to cope with sibling rivalry and adolescent rebellion; how to buy a dishwasher, bake bread, cook gourmet snails, and build a swimming pool with their own hands; how to dress, look, and act more feminine and make marriage more exciting; how to keep their husbands from dying young and their sons from growing into delinquents. They were taught to pity the neurotic, unfeminine, unhappy women who wanted to be poets or physicists or presidents. They learned that truly feminine women do not want careers, higher education, political rights—the independence and the opportunities that the old-fashioned feminists fought for. Some women, in their forties and fifties, still remembered painfully giving up those dreams, but most of the younger women no longer even thought about them. A thousand expert voices applauded their femininity, their adjustment, their new maturity. All they had to do was devote their lives from earliest girlhood to finding a husband and bearing children.

3 By the end of the nineteen-fifties, the average marriage age of women in America dropped to 20, and was still dropping, into the teens. Fourteen million girls were engaged by 17. The proportion of women attending college in comparison with men dropped from 47 percent in 1920 to 35 percent in 1958. A century earlier, women had fought for higher education; now girls went to college to get a husband. By the mid-fifties, 60 percent dropped out of college to marry, or because they were afraid too much education would be a marriage bar. Colleges built dormitories for "married students," but the students were almost always the husbands. A new degree was instituted for the wives—"Ph.T." (Putting Husband Through).

4 Then American girls began getting married in high school. And the women's magazines, deploring the unhappy statistics about these young marriages, urged that courses on marriage. and marriage counselors, be installed in the high schools. Girls started going steady at twelve and thirteen, in junior high. Manufacturers put out brassieres with false bosoms of foam rubber for little girls of ten. And an advertisement for a child's dress, sizes 3–6X, in the *New York Times* in the fall of 1960, said: "She Too Can Join the Man-Trap Set."

5 By the end of the fifties, the United States birthrate was overtaking India's. The birth-control movement, renamed Planned Parent-

hood, was asked to find a method whereby women who had been advised that a third or fourth baby would be born dead or defective might have it anyhow. Statisticians were especially astounded at the fantastic increase in the number of babies among college women. Where once they had two children, now they had four, five, six. Women who had once wanted careers were now making careers out of having babies. So rejoiced *Life* magazine in a 1956 paean to the movement of American women back to the home. . . .

6 Interior decorators were designing kitchens with mosaic murals and original paintings, for kitchens were once again the center of women's lives. Home sewing became a million-dollar industry. Many women no longer left their homes, except to shop, chauffeur their children, or attend a social engagement with their husbands. Girls were growing up in America without ever having jobs outside the home. In the late fifties, a sociological phenomenon was suddenly remarked: a third of American women now worked, but most were no longer young and very few were pursuing careers. They were married women who held part-time jobs, selling or secretarial, to put their husbands through school, their sons through college, or to help pay the mortgage. Or they were widows supporting families. Fewer and fewer women were entering professional work. The shortages in the nursing, social work, and teaching professions caused crises in almost every American city. Concerned over the Soviet Union's lead in the space race, scientists noted that America's greatest source of unused brainpower was women. But girls would not study physics: it was "unfeminine." A girl refused a science fellowship at Johns Hopkins to take a job in a real-estate office. All she wanted, she said, was what every other American girl wanted—to get married, have four children and live in a nice house in a nice suburb.

7 The suburban housewife—she was the dream image of the young American women and the envy, it was said, of women all over the world. The American housewife—freed by science and labor-saving appliances from the drudgery, the dangers of childbirth and the illnesses of her grandmother. She was healthy, beautiful, educated, concerned only about her husband, her children, her home. She had found true feminine fulfillment. As a housewife and mother, she was respected as a full and equal partner to man in his world. She was free to choose automobiles, clothes, appliances, supermarkets; she had everything that women ever dreamed of.

8 In the fifteen years after World War II, this mystique of feminine fulfillment became the cherished and self-perpetuating core of contemporary American culture. Millions of women lived their lives in the image of those pretty pictures of the American suburban housewife, kissing their husbands goodbye in front of the picture window, depositing their stationwagonsful of children at school, and smiling

as they ran the new electric waxer over the spotless kitchen floor. They baked their own bread, sewed their own and their children's clothes, kept their new washing machines and dryers running all day. They changed the sheets on the beds twice a week instead of once, took the rug-hooking class in adult education, and pitied their poor frustrated mothers, who had dreamed of having a career. Their only dream was to be perfect wives and mothers; their highest ambition to have five children and a beautiful house, their only fight to get and keep their husbands. They had no thought for the unfeminine problems of the world outside the home; they wanted the men to make the major decisions. They gloried in their role as women, and wrote proudly on the census blank: "Occupation: housewife."

9 For over fifteen years, the words written for women, and the words women used when they talked to each other, while their husbands sat on the other side of the room and talked shop or politics or septic tanks, were about problems with their children, or how to keep their husbands happy, or improve their children's school, or cook chicken or make slipcovers. Nobody argued whether women were inferior or superior to men; they were simply different. Words like "emancipation" and "career" sounded strange and embarrassing; no one had used them for years. When a Frenchwoman named Simone de Beauvoir wrote a book called *The Second Sex,* an American critic commented that she obviously "didn't know what life was all about," and besides, she was talking about French women. The "woman problem" in America no longer existed.

10 If a woman had a problem in the 1950's and 1960's, she knew that something must be wrong with her marriage, or with herself. Other women were satisfied with their lives, she thought. What kind of a woman was she if she did not feel this mysterious fulfillment waxing the kitchen floor? She was so ashamed to admit her dissatisfaction that she never knew how many other women shared it. If she tried to tell her husband, he didn't understand what she was talking about. She did not really understand it herself. For over fifteen years women in America found it harder to talk about this problem than about sex. Even the psychoanalysts had no name for it. When a woman went to a psychiatrist for help, as many women did, she would say, "I'm so ashamed," or "I must be hopelessly neurotic." "I don't know what's wrong with women today," a suburban psychiatrist said uneasily. "I only know something is wrong because most of my patients happen to be women. And their problem isn't sexual." Most women with this problem did not go to see a psychoanalyst, however. "There's nothing wrong really," they kept telling themselves. "There isn't any problem."

11 But on an April morning in 1959, I heard a mother of four, having coffee with four other mothers in a suburban development fifteen

miles from New York, say in a tone of quiet desperation, "the problem." And the others knew, without words, that she was not talking about a problem with her husband, or her children, or her home. Suddenly they realized they all shared the same problem, the problem that has no name. They began, hesitantly, to talk about it. Later, after they had picked up their children at nursery school and taken them home to nap, two of the women cried, in sheer relief, just to know they were not alone.

12 Gradually I came to realize that the problem that has no name was shared by countless women in America. As a magazine writer I often interviewed women about problems with their children, or their marriages, or their houses, or their communities. But after a while I began to recognize the telltale signs of this other problem. I saw the same signs in suburban ranch houses and split-levels on Long Island and in New Jersey and Westchester County; in colonial houses in a small Massachusetts town; on patios in Memphis; in suburban and city apartments; in living rooms in the Midwest. Sometimes I sensed the problem, not as a reporter, but as a suburban housewife, for during this time I was also bringing up my own three children in Rockland County, New York. I heard echoes of the problem in college dormitories and semi-private maternity wards, at PTA meetings and luncheons of the League of Women Voters, at suburban cocktail parties, in station wagons waiting for trains, and in snatches of conversation overheard at Schrafft's. The groping words I heard from other women, on quiet afternoons when children were at school or on quiet evenings when husbands worked late, I think I understood first as a woman long before I understood their larger social and psychological implications.

13 Just what was this problem that has no name? What were the words women used when they tried to express it? Sometimes a woman would say, "I feel empty somehow . . . incomplete." Or she would say, "I feel as if I don't exist." Sometimes she blotted out the feeling with a tranquilizer. Sometimes she thought the problem was with her husband, or her children, or that what she really needed was to redecorate her house, or move to a better nieghborhood, or have an affair, or another baby. Sometimes, she went to a doctor with symptoms she could hardly describe: "A tired feeling . . . I get so angry with the children it scares me . . . I feel like crying without any reason." (A Cleveland doctor called it "the housewife's syndrome.") A number of women told me about great bleeding blisters that break out on their hands and arms. "I call it the housewife's blight," said a family doctor in Pennsylvania. "I see it so often lately in these young women with four, five and six children who bury themselves in their dishpans. But it isn't caused by detergent and it isn't cured by cortisone."

14 Sometimes a woman would tell me that the feeling gets so strong she runs out of the house and walks through the streets. Or she stays inside her house and cries. Or her children tell her a joke, and she doesn't laugh because she doesn't hear it. I talked to women who had spent years on the analyst's couch, working out their "adjustment to the feminine role," their blocks to "fulfillment as a wife and mother." But the desperate tone in these women's voices, and the look in their eyes, was the same as the tone and the look of other women, who were sure they had no problem, even though they did have a strange feeling of desperation. . . .

15 In 1960, the problem that has no name burst like a boil through the image of the happy American housewife. In the television commercials the pretty housewives still beamed over their foaming dishpans and *Time's* cover story on "The Suburban Wife, an American Phenomenon" protested: "Having too good a time . . . to believe that they should be unhappy." But the actual unhappiness of the American housewife was suddenly being reported—from the *New York Times* and *Newsweek* to *Good Housekeeping* and CBS Television ("The Trapped Housewife"), although almost everybody who talked about it found some superficial reason to dismiss it. It was attributed to incompetent appliance repairmen (*New York Times),* or the distances children must be chauffeured in the suburbs (*Time*), or too much PTA (*Redbook*). Some said it was the old problem—education: more and more women had education, which naturally made them unhappy in their role as housewives. "The road from Freud to Frigidaire, from Sophocles to Spock, has turned out to be a bumpy one," reported the *New York Times* (June 28, 1960). "Many young women—certainly not all—whose education plunged them into a world of ideas feel stifled in their homes. They find their routine lives out of joint with their training. Like shut-ins, they feel left out. In the last year, the problem of the educated housewife has provided the meat of dozens of speeches made by troubled presidents of women's colleges who maintain, in the face of complaints, that sixteen years of academic training is realistic preparation for wifehood and motherhood."

16 There was much sympathy for the educated housewife. ("Like a two-headed schizophrenic . . . once she wrote a paper on the Graveyard poets; now writes notes to the milkman. Once she determined the boiling point of sulphuric acid; now she determines her boiling point with the overdue repairman. . . . The housewife often is reduced to screams and tears. . . . No one, it seems, is appreciative, least of all herself, of the kind of person she becomes in the process of turning from poetess into shrew.")

17 Home economists suggested more realistic preparation for housewives, such as high-school workshops in home appliances. College educators suggested more discussion groups on home management

and the family, to prepare women for the adjustment to domestic life. A spate of articles appeared in the mass magazines offering "Fifty-eight Ways to Make Your Marriage More Exciting." No month went by without a new book by a psychiatrist or sexologist offering technical advice on finding greater fulfillment through sex.

18 A male humorist joked in *Harper's Bazaar* (July, 1960) that the problem could be solved by taking away woman's right to vote. ("In the pre-19th Amendment era, the American woman was placid, sheltered and sure of her role in American society. She left all the political decisions to her husband and he, in turn, left all the family decisions to her. Today a woman has to make both the family *and* the political decisions, and it's too much for her.")

19 A number of educators suggested seriously that women no longer be admitted to the four-year colleges and universities: in the growing college crisis, the education which girls could not use as housewives was more urgently needed than ever by boys to do the work of the atomic age.

20 The problem was also dismissed with drastic solutions no one could take seriously. (A woman writer proposed in *Harper's* that women be drafted for compulsory service as nurses' aides and baby-sitters.) And it was smoothed over with the age-old panaceas: "love is their answer," "the only answer is inner help," "the secret of completeness—children," "a private means of intellectual fulfillment," "to cure this toothache of the spirit—the simple formula of handing one's self and one's will over to God."[1]

21 The problem was dismissed by telling the housewife she doesn't realize how lucky she is—her own boss, no time clock, no junior executive gunning for her job. What if she isn't happy—does she think men are happy in this world? Does she really, secretly, still want to be a man? Doesn't she know yet how lucky she is to be a woman?

22 The problem was also, and finally, dismissed by shrugging that there are no solutions: this is what being a woman means, and what is wrong with American women that they can't accept their role gracefully? As *Newsweek* put it (March 7, 1960):

> She is dissatisfied with a lot that women of other lands can only dream of. Her discontent is deep, pervasive, and impervious to the superficial remedies which are offered at every hand. . . . An army of professional explorers have already charted the major sources of trouble. . . . From the beginning of time, the female cycle has defined and confined woman's role. As Freud was credited with saying: "Anatomy is destiny." Though no group of women has ever pushed these natural restrictions as far as the American wife, it seems that she still cannot accept them with good grace. . . . A young mother with a beautiful family, charm, talent and brains

1. See the Seventy-fifth Anniversary Issue of *Good Housekeeping*, May, 1960, "The Gift of Self," a symposium by Margaret Mead, Jessamyn West, *et al.*

is apt to dismiss her role apologetically. "What do I do?" you hear her say. "Why nothing. I'm just a housewife." A good education, it seems, has given this paragon among women an understanding of the value of everything except her own worth.

23 And so she must accept the fact that "American women's unhappiness is merely the most recently won of women's rights," and adjust and say with the happy housewife found by *Newsweek*: "We ought to salute the wonderful freedom we all have and be proud of our lives today. I have had college and I've worked, but being a housewife is the most rewarding and satisfying role. . . . My mother was never included in my father's business affairs . . . she couldn't get out of the house and away from us children. But I am an equal to my husband; I can go along with him on business trips and to social business affairs."

24 The alternative offered was a choice that few women would contemplate. In the sympathetic words of the *New York Times:* "All admit to being deeply frustrated at times by the lack of privacy, the physical burden, the routine of family life, the confinement of it. However, none would give up her home and family if she had the choice to make again." *Redbook* commented: "Few women would want to thumb their noses at husbands, children and community and go off on their own. Those who do may be talented individuals, but they rarely are successful women."

25 The year American women's discontent boiled over, it was also reported (*Look*) that the more than 21,000,000 American women who are single, widowed, or divorced do not cease even after fifty their frenzied, desperate search for a man. And the search begins early—for seventy percent of all American women now marry before they are twenty-four. A pretty twenty-five-year-old secretary took thirty-five different jobs in six months in the futile hope of finding a husband. Women were moving from one political club to another, taking evening courses in accounting or sailing, learning to play golf or ski, joining a number of churches in succession, going to bars alone, in their ceaseless search for a man.

26 Of the growing thousands of women then getting private psychiatric help in the United States, the married ones were reported dissatisfied with their marriages, the unmarried ones suffering from anxiety and, finally, depression. Strangely, a number of psychiatrists stated that, in their experience, unmarried women patients were happier than married ones. So the door of all those pretty suburban houses opened a crack to permit a glimpse of uncounted thousands of American housewives who suffered alone from a problem that suddenly everyone was talking about, and beginning to take for granted, as one of those unreal problems in American life that can never be solved—like the hydrogen bomb. By 1962 the plight of the trapped American house-

wife had become a national parlor game. Whole issues of magazines, newspaper columns, books learned and frivolous, educational conferences and television panels were devoted to the problem.

27 Even so, most men, and some women, still did not know that this problem was real. But those who had faced it honestly knew that all the superficial remedies, the sympathetic advice, the scolding words and the cheering words were somehow drowning the problem in unreality. A bitter laugh was beginning to be heard from American women. They were admired, envied, pitied, theorized over until they were sick of it, offered drastic solutions or silly choices that no one could take seriously. They got all kinds of advice from the growing armies of marriage and child-guidance counselors, psychotherapists, and armchair psychologists, on how to adjust to their role as housewives. No other road to fulfillment was offered to American women in the middle of the twentieth century. Most adjusted to their role and suffered or ignored the problem that has no name. It can be less painful, for a woman, not to hear the strange, dissatisfied voice stirring within her.

28 It is no longer possible to ignore that voice, to dismiss the desperation of so many American women. This is not what being a woman means, no matter what the experts say. For human suffering there is a reason; perhaps the reason has not been found because the right questions have not been asked, or pressed far enough. I do not accept the answer that there is no problem because American women have luxuries that women in other times and lands never dreamed of; part of the strange newness of the problem is that it cannot be understood in terms of the age-old material problems of man: poverty, sickness, hunger, cold. The women who suffer this problem have a hunger that food cannot fill. It persists in women whose husbands are struggling interns and law clerks, or prosperous doctors and lawyers; in wives of workers and executives who make $5,000 a year or $50,000. It is not caused by lack of material advantages; it may not even be felt by women preoccupied with desperate problems of hunger, poverty or illness. And women who think it will be solved by more money, a bigger house, a second car, moving to a better suburb, often discover it gets worse.

29 It is no longer possible today to blame the problem on loss of femininity: to say that education and independence and equality with men have made American women unfeminine. I have heard so many women try to deny this dissatisfied voice within themselves because it does not fit the pretty picture of femininity the experts have given them. I think, in fact, that this is the first clue to the mystery: the problem cannot be understood in the generally accepted terms by which scientists have studied women, doctors have treated them, counselors have advised them, and writers have written about them.

Women who suffer this problem, in whom this voice is stirring, have lived their whole lives in the pursuit of feminine fulfillment. They are not career women (although career women may have other problems); they are women whose greatest ambition has been marriage and children. For the oldest of these women, these daughters of the American middle class, no other dream was possible. The ones in their forties and fifties who once had other dreams gave them up and threw themselves joyously into life as housewives. For the youngest, the new wives and mothers, this was the only dream. They are the ones who quit high school and college to marry, or marked time in some job in which they had no real interest until they married. These women are very "feminine" in the usual sense, and yet they still suffer the problem.

30 Are the women who finished college, the women who once had dreams beyond housewifery, the ones who suffer the most? According to the experts they are, but listen to these four women:

> My days are all busy, and dull, too. All I ever do is mess around. I get up at eight—I make breakfast, so I do the dishes, have lunch, do some more dishes and some laundry and cleaning in the afternoon. Then it's supper dishes and I get to sit down a few minutes before the children have to be sent to bed. . . . That's all there is to my day. It's just like any other wife's day. Humdrum. The biggest time, I am chasing kids.

> Ye Gods, what do I do with my time? Well, I get up at six. I get my son dressed and then give him breakfast. After that I wash dishes and bathe and feed the baby. Then I get lunch and while the children nap, I sew or mend or iron and do all the other things I can't get done before noon. Then I cook supper for the family and my husband watches TV while I do the dishes. After I get the children to bed, I set my hair and then I go to bed.

> The problem is always being the children's mommy, or the minister's wife and never being myself.

> A film made of any typical morning in my house would look like an old Marx Brothers' comedy. I wash the dishes, rush the older children off to school, dash out in the yard to cultivate the chrysanthemums, run back in to make a phone call about a committee meeting, help the youngest child build a blockhouse, spend fifteen minutes skimming the newspapers so I can be well-informed, then scamper down to the washing machines where my thrice-weekly laundry includes enough clothes to keep a primitive village going for an entire year. By noon I'm ready for a padded cell. Very little of what I've done has been really necessary or important. Outside pressures lash me through the day. Yet I look upon myself as one of the more relaxed housewives in the neighborhood. Many of my friends are even more frantic. In the past sixty years we have come full circle and the American housewife is once again trapped in a squirrel cage. If the cage is now a modern plate-glass-and-broadloom ranch house or a convenient modern apartment, the situation is no less painful than when her grandmother sat over an embroidery hoop in her gilt-and-plush parlor and muttered angrily about women's rights.

31 The first two women never went to college. They live in develop-

ments in Levittown, New Jersey, and Tacoma, Washington, and were interviewed by a team of sociologists studying workingmen's wives.[2] The third, a minister's wife, wrote on the fifteenth reunion questionnaire of her college that she never had any career ambitions, but wishes now she had.[3] The fourth, who has a Ph.D. in anthropology, is today a Nebraska housewife with three children.[4] Their words seem to indicate that housewives of all educational levels suffer the same feeling of desperation.

32 The fact is that no one today is muttering angrily about "women's rights," even though more and more women have gone to college. In a recent study of all the classes that have graduated from Barnard College,[5] a significant minority of earlier graduates blamed their education for making them want "rights," later classes blamed their education for giving them career dreams, but recent graduates blamed the college for making them feel it was not enough simply to be a housewife and mother, they did not want to feel guilty if they did not read books or take part in community activities. But if education is not the cause of the problem, the fact that education somehow festers in these women may be a clue.

33 If the secret of feminine fulfillment is having children, never have so many women, with the freedom to choose, had so many children, in so few years, so willingly. If the answer is love, never have women searched for love with such determination. And yet there is a growing suspicion that the problem may not be sexual, though it must somehow be related to sex. I have heard from many doctors evidence of new sexual problems between man and wife—sexual hunger in wives so great their husbands cannot satisfy it. "We have made woman a sex creature," said a psychiatrist at the Margaret Sanger marriage counseling clinic. "She has no identity except as a wife and mother. She does not know who she is herself. She waits all day for her husband to come home at night to make her feel alive. And now it is the husband who is not interested. It is terrible for the women, to lie there, night after night, waiting for her husband to make her feel alive." Why is there such a market for books and articles offering sexual advice? The kind of sexual orgasm which Kinsey found in

---

2. Lee Rainwater, Richard P. Coleman, and Gerald Handel, *Workingman's Wife,* New York, 1959.

3. Betty Friedan, "If One Generation Can Ever Tell Another," *Smith Alumnae Quarterly,* Northampton, Mass., Winter, 1961. I first became aware of "the problem that has no name" and its possible relationship to what I finally called "the feminine mystique" in 1957, when I prepared an intensive questionnaire and conducted a survey of my own Smith College classmates fifteen years after graduation. This questionnaire was later used by alumnae classes of Radcliffe and other women's colleges with similar results.

4. Jhan and June Robbins, "Why Young Mothers Feel Trapped," *Redbook,* September, 1960.

5. Marian Freda Poverman, "Alumnae on Parade," *Barnard Alumnae Magazine,* July, 1957.

statistical plenitude in the recent generations of American women does not seem to make this problem go away. . . .

34 Can the problem that has no name be somehow related to the domestic routine of the housewife? When a woman tries to put the problem into words, she often merely describes the daily life she leads. What is there in this recital of comfortable domestic detail that could possibly cause such a feeling of desperation? Is she trapped simply by the enormous demands of her role as modern housewife: wife, mistress, mother, nurse, consumer, cook, chauffeur; expert on interior decoration, child care, appliance repair, furniture refinishing, nutrition, and education? Her day is fragmented as she rushes from dishwasher to washing machine to telephone to dryer to station wagon to supermarket, and delivers Johnny to the Little League field, takes Janey to dancing class, gets the lawnmower fixed and meets the 6:45. She can never spend more than 15 minutes on any one thing; she has no time to read books, only magazines; even if she had time, she has lost the power to concentrate. At the end of the day, she is so terribly tired that sometimes her husband has to take over and put the children to bed.

35 This terrible tiredness took so many women to doctors in the 1950's that one decided to investigate it. He found, surprisingly, that his patients suffering from "housewife's fatigue" slept more than an adult needed to sleep—as much as ten hours a day—and that the actual energy they expended on housework did not tax their capacity. The real problem must be something else, he decided—perhaps boredom. Some doctors told their women patients they must get out of the house for a day, treat themselves to a movie in town. Others prescribed tranquilizers. Many suburban housewives were taking tranquilizers like cough drops. "You wake up in the morning, and you feel as if there's no point in going on another day like this. So you take a tranquilizer because it makes you not care so much that it's pointless."

36 It is easy to see the concrete details that trap the suburban housewife, the continual demands on her time. But the chains that bind her in her trap are chains in her own mind and spirit. They are chains made up of mistaken ideas and misinterpreted facts, of incomplete truths and unreal choices. They are not easily seen and not easily shaken off.

37 How can any woman see the whole truth within the bounds of her own life? How can she believe that voice inside herself, when it denies the conventional, accepted truths by which she has been living? And yet the women I have talked to, who are finally listening to that inner voice, seem in some incredible way to be groping through to a truth that has defied the experts.

38 I think the experts in a great many fields have been holding pieces

of that truth under their microscopes for a long time without realizing it. I found pieces of it in certain new research and theoretical developments in psychological, social and biological science whose implications for women seem never to have been examined. I found many clues by talking to suburban doctors, gynecologists, obstetricians, child-guidance clinicians, pediatricians, high-school guidance counselors, college professors, marriage counselors, psychiatrists and ministers—questioning them not on their theories, but on their actual experience in treating American women. I became aware of a growing body of evidence, much of which has not been reported publicly because it does not fit current modes of thought about women—evidence which throws into question the standards of feminine normality, feminine adjustment, feminine fulfillment, and feminine maturity by which most women are still trying to live.

39 I began to see in a strange new light the American return to early marriage and the large families that are causing the population explosion; the recent movement to natural childbirth and breastfeeding; suburban conformity, and the new neuroses, character pathologies and sexual problems being reported by the doctors. I began to see new dimensions to old problems that have long been taken for granted among women: menstrual difficulties, sexual frigidity, promiscuity, pregnancy fears, childbirth depression, the high incidence of emotional breakdown and suicide among women in their twenties and thirties, the menopause crises, the so-called passivity and immaturity of American men, the discrepancy between women's tested intellectual abilities in childhood and their adult achievement, the changing incidence of adult sexual orgasm in American women, and persistent problems in psychotherapy and in women's education.

40 If I am right, the problem that has no name stirring in the minds of so many American women today is not a matter of loss of femininity or too much education, or the demands of domesticity. It is far more important than anyone recognizes. It is the key to these other new and old problems which have been torturing women and their husbands and children, and puzzling their doctors and educators for years. It may well be the key to our future as a nation and a culture. We can no longer ignore that voice within women that says: "I want something more than my husband and my children and my home."

Thinking Questions: ***Form***

1. Define Friedan's "problem that has no name." Develop a general definition; describe some of the kinds of behavior shown by women who suffer from the "problem"; try to develop a more exact definition than

Friedan's "the problem that has no name" as you close your definition.

2. What adjectives would you use to describe Friedan's writing—interesting, forceful, dull, uptight, cynical, picky, any others? Look at her sentences, especially ones like this: "As she made the beds, shopped for groceries, matched slipcover material, ate peanut butter sandwiches with her children, chauffeured Cub Scouts and Brownies, lay beside her husband at night—she was afraid to ask even of herself the silent question—'Is this all?' " Notice how the examples of what housewives do pile atop one another, all pushing toward the clinching question. Each activity is described in a parallel series of clauses, all moving relentlessly toward the ultimate, unanswered question. Sentences such as these create tension; they involve the reader with the mental flow of the writer's ideas. Can you find any other sentences that fulfill such a dual function, accumulating evidence in support of an idea and simultaneously involving the reader in the writer's thought process?

3. Find the sentence you believe comes closest to being the thesis of this essay. Support your choice by showing how the rest of the essay helps develop and define that thesis.

4. Describe the functions of paragraphs 13 and 28 in Friedan's essay. How do they fit into the overall design of the essay? Do they indicate a shift in emphasis; are they the beginnings or ends of a group of paragraphs, all developing a major subidea?

5. Would Friedan argue that the problem she defines in this essay is primarily *psychological, physical,* or both? Provide evidence.

6. Try this experiment. Copy the first sentence of each paragraph in this essay. Do they fall into any pattern, or into a series of groups under different parts of the main idea? Copy the opening sentences into a single paragraph and read it aloud. What does this summary paragraph lack that the entire essay has? Finally, how does Friedan develop most of her main ideas and her central definition—by examples, analysis, comparison, other forms?

Thinking Questions: *Substance*

1. Read this excerpt from The Bible.

> And the Lord God caused a deep sleep to fall upon Adam, and he slept: and he took one of his ribs, and closed up the flesh instead thereof; And the rib, which the Lord God had taken from man, made he a woman, and brought her unto the man. And Adam said, This is now bone of my bones, and flesh of my flesh: she shall be called Woman, because she was taken out of Man.
>
> —Genesis 2:21–23

Do you think that such a description of the creation of woman supports the idea that women should remain subordinate to men? Would the Genesis story of woman's creation support the idea that all women should remain in the home, cooking, sewing, raising children, and shopping—the activities that Friedan believes should *not* be the primary responsibility of women?

2. What do you think Friedan would recommend to resolve the "problem that has no name"? Be specific.

3. Look over the advertisements and tables of contents in several women's magazines—*Redbook, Cosmopolitan, Ladies Home Journal, McCall's, Mademoiselle, Vogue,* or the like. Do these advertisements and general contents encourage a woman to depart from the conventional feminine qualities and functions—sexual attractiveness, domestic expert, child-raiser?

4. Is Friedan describing the problems of only a certain type of woman here? What social class do you believe the women described by Friedan came from? Why does this particular social class seem to encounter "the problem that has no name" more than others?

5. Friedan shows how many young housewives spend most of their lives. What is consistently true about almost all the housewifely activities described in this essay? Do they all exaggerate certain kinds of skills and qualities? Is there much potential for these women to make positive and recognized contributions to society? Do these activities require brains or physical strength?

* * *

MORE ON SEXUAL IDENTITY

In the final paragraph of "The Problem That Has No Name," Betty Friedan tells us that the problem for "American women today is not a matter of loss of femininity or too much education, or the demands of domesticity. It is far more important than anyone recognizes. It is the key to these other new and old problems which have been torturing women and their husbands and children, and puzzling their doctors and educators for years."

Modern women, many argue, have lost a sense of identity; they no longer know who they are. Their traditional function in society provides very little inner satisfaction, since their activities could be performed by anyone willing to put in the time and develop the patience that is necessary to fulfill their domestic duties.

Robert Graves compares the modern woman's condition with her ancient and royal past. Most human societies, he tells us, have evolved through matriarchal forms of government dominated by powerful women who ruled effectively because they were more closely related to the natural cycles of life—to birth, death, the raising of crops, and the cycles of the moon and tides. As human societies moved from an agricultural to a mechanistic and scientific age, Graves argues, power moved away from the woman and her natural forms of rule to men who emphasized logic and the mechanical processes of a scientific age. Graves goes on to argue the natural superiority of *real women,* both over their lesser women companions, past and present, and over the limited competitiveness and power-seeking of most men. Real women are closer to nature, Graves suggests, and can show us how to return to a more natural life-style, far superior to the technological society in which we now live. Simultaneously, he argues for a return to a matriarchal society in which male and female identities are clearly defined by what he might call "natural sexual tendencies": the woman's understanding of natural process, the changing of seasons, the rhythms of day and night, the cycle of growth and decay; the man's more limited understanding of manual labor, production, and work.

Graves's somewhat radical argument for natural female dominance contrasts effectively with Arthur Schlesinger's description of loss of identity among contemporary American males. Schlesinger points out the conventional stereotype of the hero in American literature and film and then shows how this stereotype has influenced collective male identity in America. He concludes by pointing to a general loss of identity among both men and women in modern America, which, he believes, can only be replaced by a new search for identity in the arts and in politics.

Schlesinger also rejects the idea that the "liberation" of women causes this loss of identity: "Masculine supremacy, like white supremacy, was the neurosis of an immature society. It is good for men as well as women that women have been set free." He argues that a much more pervasive and serious problem—a lack of faith and insight into themselves—haunts most men and that they will need to work through the arts, humor and satire, and politics, and along with women, to re-establish their identities. He relates, in other words, the problems of sexual identity to a general search for self in modern culture.

Finally, Joyce Carol Oates weaves a story of a runaway daughter returned, a father consumed with hatred and vengeance, family life at its bleakest. Oates' story reveals many everyday truths about male-female relationships as they are epitomized in this bizarre relationship between father and daughter. Helen's meekness, her desire to please and comfort men, her almost total lack of personal initiative or control, represent the extremes of accepted daughterly behavior in many families: the woman as ornament, created to please and comfort men, whether father, brothers, or lovers.

Helen's father, on the other hand, illustrates, in his compulsion to improve his family's social status, the typical aggressive dominance of the American male carried to a pathological extreme. He wants his daughter to have a better material life than he had previously had or been able to provide. In the process, he destroys himself, his daughter, his entire family.

Real Women

ROBERT GRAVES

1 The most important historical study of all, utterly dwarfing all economic and political ones, is for me the changing relationship between men and women down the centuries—from prehistoric times to the present moral chaos in which both sexes have become equally confused about their roles. . . .

2 A real woman, by my definition, neither despises nor worships men, but is proud not to have been born a man, does everything she can to avoid thinking or acting like one, knows the full extent of her powers, and feels free to reject all arbitrary man-made obligations. She is her own oracle of right and wrong, firmly believing in her five sound senses and intuitive sixth. Once a real woman has been warned by her nose that those apples are tasteless, or assured by her fingertips that this material is shoddy, no salesman in the world can persuade her to the contrary. Nor, once she has met some personage in private, and summed him up with a single keen glance as weak, vain or crooked, will his mounting public reputation convince her otherwise. She takes pleasure in the company of simple, happy, undemanding women; but seldom or never finds a friend worthy of her full confidence. Since she never settles for the second best in love, what most troubles her is the rareness of real men. Wherever she goes, her singularity will arouse strong feelings: adulation, jealousy, resentment, but never pity for her loneliness. Real women are royal women; the words once had the same meaning. Democracy has no welcome for queens.

3 It would be wrong to identify the real woman with the typical wild one who, after a difficult childhood, has left home early to live by her wits at the expense of men. The wild woman is incapable either of friendship for other women, whom she cannot fail to regard as rivals, or of love for a man, her declared enemy. But at least she keeps her eyes open and ridicules the view that women must enthusiastically accept this glorious modern world of plenty bestowed on them by their hard-working menfolk, and that they enjoy being passionately swept off their feet and afterwards treated with amused indulgence. There was never, of course, any truth in the comic-strip legend of a primitive he-man who would grab his woman by the hair, threaten her with a knobbed club if she refused his advances, and haul her off panting ecstatically to his cave. . . .

4 To reach some understanding of real women, one must think back to a primitive age, when men invariably treated women as the holier sex, since they alone perpetuated the race. Women were the sole agriculturists, guardians of springs, fruit trees, and the sacred hearth fire, and lived unaffected by any notions of progress. Tribal queens never thought in terms of historical time, but only of seasons; judged each case on its own merits, not by a legal code, as real women still do; and showed little regard for trade or mechanical invention. Chance discoveries or new techniques in arts and crafts were welcome, so long as these neither upset tribal economy nor enhanced the importance of individuals. It was the queen's task to restrain men from letting their ambition or intellectual curiosity override practical common sense, as it is still the woman's task to ask her husband: "Must you kill yourself making money? Haven't we enough for the next five years at least, even if you stopped working altogether? Surely you don't enjoy your martyrdom?" But even if he cares to listen, social pressures compel him to provide for his family until he drops dead.

5 History begins with the emergence of men from female rule. They had at last discovered that a woman cannot conceive without male assistance—and brooded over the implications of this surprising fact. After long whispered conferences it was agreed that men ought to claim their freedom. They asked, "Why should descent be reckoned in the female line, not the male? Why should a man when he marries go to the woman's home, not contrariwise? Why should a woman, not a man, sow the seed corn? Why should women control the tribe? Surely men are the true creators, sowers of seed, and therefore the holier sex, as well as being physically stronger?" Thus the male habit of reasoning from irrelevant facts, rather than relying on woman's practical wisdom, began the war between the sexes that has been raging ever since. . . .

6 Men consolidated their victory. They reckoned descent in the male line, brought wives to their own homes, invented historical annals, legal codes, weights and measures, standing armies, engineering, logic and philosophy. On the excuse of protecting the weaker sex, they placed woman under male tutelage: henceforward she must serve her father's or husband's domestic needs as though not only spiritually but mentally inferior to him. . . .

7 It seems puzzling that the real women of those days let all this happen to them. The sole reason I can suggest is that they thought far ahead. Since man had a certain undeveloped intellectual capacity, of which it would have been wrong to deny him full use, the real women sat back patiently, prepared to give him a free hand for some hundreds or thousands of years. Only a long series of disastrous experiments could make him realize the error of his headstrong ways.

Eventually he must return to them in willing and chastened dependence.

8 Priests of the new male gods even modified the ancient myth of a sole goddess who had created the world, giving her a male assistant; and in *Genesis*—a comparatively late book—Jehovah creates the world entirely by Himself; and models Eve, the first woman, from man's rib! It is added that this woman's disobedience to God caused man to stumble and sin. In fact, the story is based on a Hebrew pun: the same word means both "rib" and "make to stumble." According to Hesiod's contemporary Greek myth, an inquisitive woman named Pandora opened a divine jar entrusted to her and let loose on mankind all the evils that now plague us. Yet "Eve" was originally a title of the sole creatrix; as was also "Pandora."

9 Financial pressures of men's own making brought about the recent so-called emancipation of women. Grown daughters could no longer stay idling at home, a burden to their parents and to themselves until married off. Industry was booming and, with appropriate moral safeguards, they might fill the widening gaps in manpower. Women, who can now earn and keep their own money, even when wives, and have been granted the franchise—"franchise" originally meant "freedom from being a serf"—need show men no gratitude for this liberality. Their freedom is still limited. They remain citizens of the second degree, auxiliary male personnel barred from all the highest offices; and would never have got where they are so quickly had it not been for two world wars and such loveless male inventions as machine guns, submarines, bombing planes and universal conscription.

10 Strangely enough, it is easier to be a real woman in backwaters of Christianity or Islam or Hinduism, where codes of behavior have not changed for centuries, than in urbanized Europe or America. There she knows what part she must play, and can guard her inborn dignity. Although the husband, as head of the family, makes all decisions, he will never dare overrule even her unspoken protests. Among Majorcan peasants who live beyond the tourist range, no man would ever think of buying or selling so much as a hen without his wife's approval. She is always referred to as *la madonna,* titular guardian of the home.

11 What is home? In ancient days it meant a clan settlement, a camp or kraal, ruled by elders, where men had comrades and women their gossips, and children ran about in packs; and where a happy man-woman relationship could exist in some small corner away from the communal bustle.

12 Among us Westerners, because of man's jealous insistence on marital privacy, *home* has shrunk from settlement to farmhouse, thence to the cottage, thence to the 10-roomed apartment, thence

to three rooms and a kitchenette with the usual labour-saving devices, in a huge residential block full of utter strangers. The housewife has her washing machine, telephone, television, refrigerator, electric cooker, car and door keys, to pay for which a husband must be out working all the week. She cannot regret (because she never knew) the easy companionship of her great-grandmother's day: quilting bees and husking bees, taking the cousins to do a week's washing down at the creek, lending a hand with the shearing and harvest, making jams and pickles, getting up round dances, singing and playing practical jokes. But no real woman can ever accept the present situation.

13 Man's logic has defeated itself. Boredom often drives the married woman back to a job as soon as she can leave her children at a nursery school; or to infidelity; or to an analyst. Home is home for only two days of the week. Which is why some paternally-minded industrialists take advice from professors of sociology and plant their employees all together in a wholesome suburban neighbourhood, where the company's standards of taste and respectability must rule their lives. Husband obeys boss; wife obeys husband, and preserves amicable relations with her fellow company wives, or else. . . . Spouses are thus shackled by a well-paid job to which the husband need no longer commute, by house, garden and swimming pool, by children, by hope of advancement and the prospect of a pension. Any sign of non-compliance is scored against both. No real woman can ever accept this situation either.

14 Attempts to liven things up socially are all too often masked under the dubious name of charity. It is characteristic of a real woman never to support public charities—on the ground that she neither knows the persons to whom her money goes nor has any assurance that it will be properly distributed. She gives only to those whose needs are familiar to her, and then from friendship, not pity. She will not be found at bridge clubs or at cocktail parties. Bridge, which is, after all, a money contest between individual players, cannot be a substitute for the good humour of a communal wash-day; nor can a cocktail party supply the intimate gossip of a quilting bee.

15 Wild women take advantage of this artificial state of affairs by exploiting the dormant dissatisfactions of husbands. One of them told me the other day, "Yes, you may call me a mean, greedy, undependable, lazy, treacherous, spendthrift bitch. That's true enough a good part of the time; but it isn't the whole story. In fact, I've given myself to myself, and to no one else. My beauty is my own, and I take good care of it. If I choose a lover, I grant the lucky fellow no rights over me; and if he has sense, he won't claim any. As for breaking up a home, nobody can do that unless it's already cracked!"

16 A real woman likes beautiful things of her own choosing. She

prefers a handleless cup, a backless chair, a mattress on the floor and a packing-case for the table to good taste conferred on her wholesale by interior decorators. There is an eighteenth-century English song, *Sally in Our Alley:*

> Her father, he sells cabbage nets
>   And through the streets doth cry 'em.
> Her mother, she sells laces long
>   To such as care to buy 'em—
>
> Who'd think such rascals could beget
>   So sweet a girl as Sally?
> She is the darling of my heart
>   And lives in our alley. . . .

The lover was a square: an honest, idealistic London apprentice, intent on becoming a journeyman, a master-craftsman and eventually a rich merchant—perhaps even Lord Mayor:

> When Eastertide comes round again,
>   Oh, then I'll have some money—
> I'll save it up, and box and all
>   I'll give it to my honey. . . .
> And when my seven years' time is o'er
>   Oh, then I'll marry Sally,
> Ay, then we'll wed, and then we'll bed—
>   But not in our alley!

17 Their broken-down, foul-smelling alley was a settlement, a home, the denizens of which were bound together by common poverty, shiftlessness, pugnacity, humour and a hatred of landlords and police. Yet no well-planned housing estate can ever compete with its spirit, which a Sally was always found to keep alive. From 1940 to '43 the German blitz levelled what remained of these alleys, and their sites are now occupied by large all-glass office blocks. The last of the Sallies found herself in a suburban life-box—one of hundreds built to the same design and set down in parallel rows—longing for a return to poverty, vice, dirt and even flying bombs.

18 Marriage, like money, is still with us; and, like money, progressively devalued. The ties between these two male inventions get closer and closer. Originally marriage meant the sale of woman by one man to another; now most women sell themselves, though they may have no intention of delivering the goods listed in the bill of sale. Not only is the wife, on an average, five years younger than her husband, but she lives statistically longer. So money power passes progressively into the hands of women. Also, divorce legislation (forced on guilt-ridden legislators by nagging spouses) grossly favours the wife. A youthful rival figures in most divorce suits, and though she and the wife seldom act collusively, they share an old-fashioned insistence on the honourable state of marriage, which enriches both. Wild women will commit matrimony when things go hard

for them, without the least thought of keeping their obligations. The entranced husbands never know what has hit them, nor do they profit by the experience.

19 The United States, though often described as a matriarchy in all but name, remains patriarchal. Matriarchy, to be effective, needs real women. When women organize themselves intellectually on masculine lines, they merely stimulate the feminization of men, who, for terror of husband-hunting viragoes, are apt to seek refuge in the cul-de-sac of homosexuality.

20 Though men are more conventional than women and fear to infringe the Mosaic law (*Deuteronomy* xxii. 5) which forbids their wearing of women's clothes, women have no scruples about flouting the companion law: "The woman shall not wear that which pertaineth unto a man . . . for all that do so are abomination unto the Lord. . . . Even matrons now unblushingly wear blue jeans zipped in front.

21 The pseudo-patriarchal trend encourages women to respect legality, which they had hitherto found distasteful. A real woman, giving evidence in a court of law, scorns factual truth. Should her sense of equity run counter to the formal demands of justice, she will perjure herself in replies of cool and convincing honesty. When obliged to exercise a vote, she scorns the male axiom that the majority is always right.

22 A few real women survive in the old royal sense among West African queens, who rule with a silver knot-of-wisdom sceptre and claim the moon-goddess Ngame as their remote ancestress. A "knot of wisdom"—known in English as "the true lover's knot"—is the sort that tightens more securely the harder you tug at either end. Symbolically it means, "My command can never be disobeyed!"

23 In civilized society royal women have neither thrones nor territorial queendoms, but the moon inspires them still, and they can wield formidable powers in times of emergency. Yet since they avoid becoming public figures—the personality cult is another male invention—their names pass into history far more seldom than those of notorious wild women. A remarkable exception was Elizabeth I of England, whom her poets addressed as Cynthia—"The Moon"— and whose cynical disparagement of herself as "but a weak woman" concealed an unshaken faith in her royal wisdom. Elizabeth ruled through awe and love, was on playful terms with her ladies-in-waiting, inspired her male subjects to feats of heroism and flights of poetry never known before or since among the English, always said "No" to a doubtful petition and then slept on it.

24 A real woman's main concern is her beauty, which she cultivates for her own pleasure—not to ensnare men. Though she despises fashion as a male financial business, she will not make herself conspicuous by a defiance of conventions. The materials, colours and

cut of her clothes, her hair style and her jewels are all chosen to match a sense of personal uniqueness. She can dress in advance of fashion, yet seem to lead it; and to any irregular features she may have, she lends a lovely ugliness denied to common beauty queens. Perfect detachment from the artificial or second-hand keeps her face unclouded. She has no small talk on current topics, and will suddenly vanish from a party, however grand, as soon as it grows boring.

25 If she plays games, it will be for fun, not competition; and if up against a win-at-all-costs opponent in tennis or golf, she will take care to lose handsomely—as one who competes only against herself. If she drinks, it will be because she likes the taste; and if she smokes, it will be for the same reason, not to steady her nerve.

26 She misses real men—men who would recognize her potentiality and agree that our world, despite its appearance of rational organization, is a wholly haphazard one, clanking on noisily to its fate along a random course once defined as "progress." And that a calamitous collapse must come before a new start can be made—from the point where the sex war was first declared and woman's conservative instinct as the guiding force of humankind repudiated. Because womanhood remains incomplete without a child, most real women marry—preferring simple, affectionate husbands who cannot understand them. This is not a renunciation of real love, since they agree with the thirteenth-century Countess of Narbonne: "Conjugal affection has absolutely nothing in common with love. We say 'absolutely,' and with all consideration, that love cannot exist between husband and wife."

27 Man's biological function is to do; woman's is to be. This difference is not a contrast of mere activity with mere passivity. "To be" is indeed a full-time occupation. A real woman has no leisure in the modern economic sense—leisure as a consumer's relaxed insistence on commercial entertainment—but is always thinking, taking stock of herself, setting a stage on which actors can perform. If she paints or writes, this will be for her own private amusement, not to satisfy ambition; and if forced to earn her livelihood in this way, she repudiates the public personage forced on her by dealers and critics.

28 A real woman is content to dress with a difference, to make her home unmistakably her own, to illuminate any company she enters, to cook by instinct, not by the cookery book. This is her evidence of being, the proof of which lies in her sense of certitude. She is no feminist; feminism, like all "isms," implies an intellectual approach to a subject; and reality can be understood only by transcending the intellect. . . .

29 A real woman somehow avoids suicide, or virtual suicide, or the mental institution; but is always painfully aware of having been born out of her true epoch; considered as either the past, or as the long-

distant future. A sense of humour saves her from defeat. "This is not worthy of me," she will remind herself ten times a day, "but to preserve my inner self I must once more act an alicn part."

None of her women neighbours, idly content with money and what it will buy, feel any need for drastic change in the man-woman relationship; she treats them politely, and has patience. If she ever comes across a real man, the thin thread of human hope that eventually the world will make practical sense again—cannot yet have snapped.

Thinking Questions: *Form*

1. Make a list of the qualities that Graves attributes to *real women.* How do they compare with the qualities displayed by women in the normal roles of American life? Does Graves's definition of the *real woman* leave you with the feeling that any change in our social reactions to sex roles would have to be motivated by her?

2. Tone is the relationship a writer constructs between himself and his readers. How would you define Graves's tone? Does he push his arguments on his readers, leaving them no room to respond or disagree? Or is his tone firm but sensible, without the extreme rhetoric and bombast of a soapbox speaker? Consider this paragraph.

> The most important historical study of all, utterly dwarfing all economic and political ones, is for me the changing relationship between men and women down the centuries—from prehistoric times to the present moral chaos in which both sexes have become equally confused about their roles. . . . (Paragraph 1)

Graves does not mince words here; he comes right out and asserts that he knows what *is* important throughout history—not politics or art, but the shifting roles of men and women. Of course, numerous people might disagree with Graves's assertion. Should he have mentioned his opponent's arguments in this essay? Would the tone have been improved by more attention to opposing arguments? Or would attention to alternatives make Graves's thesis less forceful and effective?

3. Look over Graves's sentences. How would you describe them stylistically? Most are of medium or above-average length, yet they read fluently, without interruptions in sense or rhythm. Why? Where are the main clauses in most of the sentences—at the end, beginning, or middle of the sentence? Are there many subordinate clauses in his sentences or is there a predominance of coordination (two independent clauses connected by a coordinate conjunction)?

4. What does the following parallel structure contribute to Graves's style and tone? Does it make his argument more or less convincing?

> A real woman, by my definition, neither despises nor worships men, but is proud not to have been born a man, does everything she can to avoid thinking or acting like one, knows the full extent of her powers, and feels free to reject all arbitrary man-made obligations. (Paragraph 2)

Here Graves defines the real woman in four parallel verbal constructions, all of which set out her particular reactions to men. Because Graves has enough control over his material to line up his defining points in parallel grammatical structures, do you respect what he says all the more?

5. Graves over and over again uses *balance* to give the reader a clear idea of what the real woman *is* and *is not*. Reread paragraph 29.

> A real woman somehow avoids suicide,/or virtual suicide,/ or the mental institution;/but is always painfully aware of having been born out of her true epoch; considered as either the past, or as the long-distant future. A sense of humor saves her from defeat. "This is not worthy of me," she will remind herself ten times a day,/ "but to preserve my inner self I must once more act an alien part."

The slash marks indicate divisions in balanced presentations of ideas about what the real woman does in a society that does not recognize or value her powers: she avoids despair and suicide (or near suicide)—yet she is always aware of her true identity and role; she considers both the past and the future; she knows she has been forced into a social role that is inferior to her noble heritage, yet she will carry out the demands of that role in order to "preserve . . . [her] inner self." What kind of impression of Graves's character does his verbal balancing act give you?

Thinking Questions: *Substance*

1. What is Graves's point in paragraph 8 about the treatment and definition of women in the Bible? According to him, what have the writers of the Bible done to the previously held attitudes toward women? How does the Bible, especially in Genesis (which Graves points out is a relatively late book), redefine women to depart from the primitive attitude that women were the holier sex because "they alone perpetuated the race" (paragraph 4)?

2. Explain in your own words the comparison Graves makes between a *wild* woman and a *real* woman (see paragraph 3). What is the essential difference between wild women and real women as far as their relations with men are concerned?

3. What might a contemporary feminist, especially one who very much wanted to make her way in the business, industrial, or political worlds, say in response to Graves's contention that the real woman must avoid contact with these worlds, which are, by their natures, the worlds of men? (See paragraphs 24 through 28.)

4. Graves occasionally uses the diction and imagery that an historian might apply to descriptions of war to his descriptions of the changing roles of men and women through history. Paragraphs 3, 5, 6, and 19 give explicit examples of military diction and imagery used to describe these

changes. Do you believe Graves exaggerates the case with such techniques, or does he limit his use of these techniques to appropriate places in the development of his argument?

5. Graves often uses objective description and factual assertion to support his definition of the real woman. As readers, we are supposed to probe the implications of these descriptions ourselves. What are the implications of the following three sentences?

a. A real woman is content to dress with a difference, to make her home unmistakably her own, to illuminate any company she enters, to cook by instinct, not by the cookery book. (Paragraph 28)

b. A real woman's main concern is her beauty, which she cultivates for her own pleasure—not to ensnare men. (Paragraph 24)

c. It is characteristic of a real woman never to support public charities—on the ground that she neither knows the persons to whom her money goes nor has any assurance that it will be properly distributed. (Paragraph 14)

6. Some modern feminists have coined the word *womanizer* to describe the type of man who puts a woman on a pedestal in order to keep her *out* of power. A woman, for example, might be told that she is too gentle and sensitive to overhear the rough talk of construction workers. Do you find Graves vulnerable to this criticism? Does he put women on a different kind of pedestal in a way that will keep them out of government, business, or industry?

The Crisis of American Masculinity

ARTHUR SCHLESINGER, JR.

1 What has happened to the American male? For a long time, he seemed utterly confident in his manhood, sure of his masculine role in society, easy and definite in his sense of sexual identity. The frontiersmen of James Fenimore Cooper, for example, never had any concern about masculinity; they were men, and it did not occur to them to think twice about it. Even well into the 20th century, the heroes of Dreiser, of Fitzgerald, of Hemingway remain men. But one begins to detect a new theme emerging in some of these authors, especially in Hemingway: the theme of the male hero increasingly preoccupied with proving his virility to himself. And by mid-century, the male role had plainly lost its rugged clarity of outline. Today men are more and more conscious of maleness not as a fact but as a problem. The ways by which American men affirm their masculinity

are uncertain and obscure. There are multiplying signs, indeed, that something has gone badly wrong with the American male's conception of himself.

2 On the most superficial level, the roles of male and female are increasingly merged in the American household. The American man is found as never before as a substitute for wife and mother—changing diapers, washing dishes, cooking meals, and performing a whole series of what once were considered female duties. The American woman meanwhile takes over more and more of the big decisions, controlling them indirectly when she cannot do so directly. Outside the home, one sees a similar blurring of function. While men design dresses and brew up cosmetics, women become doctors, lawyers, bank cashiers, and executives. "Women now fill many 'masculine' roles," writes the psychologist Dr. Bruno Bettelheim, "and expect their husbands to assume many of the tasks once reserved for their own sex." Women seem an expanding, aggressive force, seizing new domains like a conquering army, while men, more and more on the defensive, are hardly able to hold their own and gratefully accept assignments from their new rulers. A recent book bears the stark and melancholy title *The Decline of the American Male.*

3 Some of this evidence, it should be quickly said, has been pushed too far. The willingness of a man to help his wife around the house may as well be evidence of confidence in masculinity as the opposite; such a man obviously does not have to cling to masculine symbols in order to keep demonstrating his maleness to himself. But there is more impressive evidence than the helpful husband that this is an age of sexual ambiguity. It appears no accident, for example, that the changing of sex—the Christine Jorgensen phenomenon—so fascinates our newspaper editors and readers; or that homosexuality, that incarnation of sexual ambiguity, should be enjoying a cultural boom new in our history. Such developments surely express a deeper tension about the problem of sexual identity.

4 Consider the theater, that faithful mirror of a society's preoccupations. There have been, of course, popular overt inquiries into sexual ambiguities, like *Compulsion* or *Tea and Sympathy.* But in a sense these plays prove the case too easily. Let us take rather two uncommonly successful plays by the most discussed young playwrights of the United States and Great Britain—Tennessee Williams' *Cat on a Hot Tin Roof* and John Osborne's *Look Back in Anger.* Both deal with the young male in a singular state of confusion and desperation. In *Cat on a Hot Tin Roof,* Brick Pollitt, the professional football player, refuses to sleep with his wife because of guilty memories of his relations with a dead teammate. In *Look Back in Anger,* Jimmy Porter, the embittered young intellectual who can sustain a relationship with his wife only by pretending they are furry animals together,

explodes with hatred of women and finds his moments of happiness roughhousing around the stage with a male pal.

5 Brick Pollitt and Jimmy Porter are all too characteristic modern heroes. They are, in a sense, castrated; one is stymied by fear of homosexuality, the other is an unconscious homosexual. Neither is capable of dealing with the woman in his life: Brick surrenders to a strong woman, Jimmy destroys a weak one. Both reject the normal female desire for full and reciprocal love as an unconscionable demand and an intolerable burden. Now not many American males have been reduced to quite the Pollitt-Porter condition. Still the intentness with which audiences have watched these plays suggests that exposed nerves are being plucked—that the Pollitt-Porter dilemma expresses in vivid and heightened form something that many spectators themselves feel or fear.

6 Or consider the movies. In some ways, the most brilliant and influential American film since the war is *High Noon.* That remarkable movie, which invested the Western with the classic economy of myth, can be viewed in several ways: as an existentialist drama, for example, or as a parable of McCarthyism. It can also be viewed as a mordant comment on the effort of the American woman to emasculate the American man. The sheriff plainly did not suffer from Brick Pollitt's disease. But a large part of the story dealt with the attempt of his girl to persuade him not to use force—to deny him the use of his pistol. The pistol is an obvious masculine symbol, and, in the end, it was the girl herself, in the modern American manner, who used the pistol and killed the villain. (In this connection, one can pause and note why the Gary Coopers, Cary Grants, Clark Gables, and Spencer Tracys continue to play romantic leads opposite girls young enough to be their daughters; it is obviously because so few of the younger male stars can project a convincing sense of masculinity.)

7 Psychoanalysis backs up the theater and the movies in emphasizing the obsession of the American male with his manhood. "Every psychoanalyst knows," writes one of them, "how many emotional difficulties are due to those fears and insecurities of neurotic men who are unconsciously doubting their masculinity." "In our civilization," Dr. Theodor Reik says, "men are afraid that they will not be men enough." Reik adds significantly: "And women are afraid that they might be considered only women." Why is it that women worry, not over whether they can fill the feminine role, but whether filling that role is enough, while men worry whether they can fill the masculine role at all? How to account for this rising tide of male anxiety? What has unmanned the American man?

8 There is currently a fashionable answer to this question. Male anxiety, many observers have declared, is simply the result of female aggression: what has unmanned the American man is the American

woman. The present male confusion and desperation, it is contended, are the inevitable consequence of the threatened feminization of American society. The victory of women is the culmination of a long process of masculine retreat, beginning when Puritanism made men feel guilty about sex and the frontier gave women the added value of scarcity. Fleeing from the reality of femininity, the American man, while denying the American woman juridical equality, transformed her into an ideal of remote and transcendent purity with overriding authority over the family, the home, the school, and culture. This habit of obeisance left the male psychologically disarmed and vulnerable when the goddess stepped off the pedestal and demanded in addition equal economic, political, and legal rights. In the last part of the 19th century, women won their battle for equality. They gained the right of entry into one occupation after another previously reserved for males. Today they hold the key positions of personal power in our society and use this power relentlessly to consolidate their mastery. As mothers, they undermine masculinity through the use of love as a technique of reward and punishment. As teachers, they prepare male children for their role of submission in an increasingly feminine world. As wives, they complete the work of subjugation. Their strategy of conquest is deliberately to emasculate men—to turn them into Brick Pollitts and Jimmy Porters.

9 Or so a standard indictment runs; and no doubt there is something in it. American women have unquestionably gained through the years a place in our society which American men have not been psychologically prepared to accept. Whether because of Puritanism or the frontier, there has been something immature in the traditional American male attitude toward women—a sense of alarm at times amounting to panic. Almost none of the classic American novels, for example, presents the theme of mature and passionate love. Our 19th-century novelists saw women either as unassailable virgins or abandoned temptresses—never simply as women. One looks in vain through *Moby Dick* and *The Adventures of Huckleberry Finn,* through Cooper and Poe and Whitman, for an adult portrayal of relations between men and women. "Where," Leslie Fiedler has asked, "is the American *Madame Bovary, Anna Karenina, Wuthering Heights,* or *Vanity Fair?"*

10 Yet the implication of the argument that the American man has been unmanned by the emancipation of the American woman is that the American man was incapable of growing up. For the 19th-century sense of masculinity was based on the psychological idealization and the legal subjection of women; masculinity so spuriously derived could never—and should never—have endured. The male had to learn to live at some point with the free and equal female. Current attempts to blame "the decline of the American male" on the aggressiveness of

the American female amount to a confession that, under conditions of free competition, the female was bound to win. Simple observation refutes this supposition. In a world of equal rights, some women rise; so too do some men; and no pat generalization is possible about the sexual future of society. Women have gained power in certain ways; in others, they have made little progress. It is safe to predict, for example, that we will have a Roman Catholic, perhaps even a Jew, for President before we have a woman. Those amiable prophets of an impending American matriarchy (all men, by the way) are too pessimistic.

11 Something more fundamental is involved in the unmanning of American men than simply the onward rush of American women. Why is the American man so unsure today about his masculine identity? The basic answer to this is plainly because he is so unsure about his identity in general. Nothing is harder in the whole human condition than to achieve a full sense of identity—than to know who you are, where you are going, and what you mean to live and die for. From the most primitive myths to the most contemporary novels—from Oedipus making the horrified discovery that he had married his mother, to Leopold Bloom and Stephen Dedalus searching their souls in Joyce's Dublin and the haunted characters of Kafka trying to make desperate sense out of an incomprehensible universe —the search for identity has been the most compelling human problem. That search has always been ridden with trouble and terror. And it can be plausibly argued that the conditions of modern life make the quest for identity more difficult than it has ever been before.

12 The pre-democratic world was characteristically a world of status in which people were provided with ready-made identities. But modern Western society—free, equalitarian, democratic—has swept away all the old niches in which people for so many centuries found safe refuge. Only a few people at any time in human history have enjoyed the challenge of "making" themselves; most have fled from the unendurable burden of freedom into the womblike security of the group. The new age of social mobility may be fine for those strong enough to discover and develop their own roles. But for the timid and the frightened, who constitute the majority in any age, the great vacant spaces of equalitarian society can become a nightmare filled with nameless horrors. Thus mass democracy, in the very act of offering the individual new freedom and opportunity, offers new moral authority to the group and thereby sets off a new assault on individual identity. Over a century ago Alexis de Tocqueville, the perceptive Frenchman who ruminated on the contradictions of equality as he toured the United States in the 1830's, pointed to the "tyranny of the majority" as a central problem of democracy. John Stuart Mill, lamenting the decline of individualism in Great Britain, wrote: "That

so few now dare to be eccentric marks the chief danger of the time." How much greater that danger seems a century later!

13 For our own time has aggravated the assault on identity by adding economic and technological pressures to the political and social pressures of the 19th century. Modern science has brought about the growing centralization of the economy. We work and think and live and even dream in larger and larger units. William H. Whyte, Jr., has described the rise of "the organization man," working by day in immense business concerns, sleeping by night in immense suburban developments, deriving his fantasy life from mass-produced entertainments, spending his existence not as an individual but as a member of a group and coming in the end to feel guilty and lost when he deviates from his fellows. Adjustment rather than achievement becomes the social ideal. Men no longer fulfill an inner sense of what they *must* be; indeed, with the cult of the group, that inner sense itself begins to evaporate. Identity consists not of self-realization but of smooth absorption into the group. Nor is this just a matter of passive acquiescence. The group is aggressive, imperialistic, even vengeful, forever developing new weapons with which to overwhelm and crush the recalcitrant individual. Not content with disciplining the conscious mind, the group today is even experimenting with means of violating the subconscious. The subliminal invasion represents the climax of the assault on individual identity.

14 It may seem a long way from the loss of the sense of self to the question of masculinity. But if people do not know *who* they are, it is hardly surprising that they are no longer sure what sex they are. Nigel Dennis' exuberant novel *Cards of Identity* consists of a series of brilliant variations on the quest for identity in contemporary life. It reaches one of its climaxes in the tale of a person who was brought up by enlightened parents to believe that there was no such thing as pure male or female—everyone had elements of both—and who accepted this proposition so rigorously that he (she) could not decide what his (her) own sex was. "In what identity do you intend to face the future?" someone asks. "It seems that nowadays," comes the plaintive reply, "one must choose between being a woman who behaves like a man, and a man who behaves like a woman. In short, I must choose to be one in order to behave like the other." If most of us have not yet quite reached that condition of sexual chaos, yet the loss of a sense of identity is obviously a fundamental step in the decay of masculinity. And the gratification with which some American males contemplate their own decline should not obscure the fact that women, for all their recent legal and economic triumphs, are suffering from a loss of identity too. It is not accidental that the authors of one recent book described modern woman as the "lost sex."

15 If this is true, then the key to the recovery of masculinity does not

lie in any wistful hope of humiliating the aggressive female and restoring the old masculine supremacy. Masculine supremacy, like white supremacy, was the neurosis of an immature society. It is good for men as well as for women that women have been set free. In any case, the process is irreversible; that particular genie can never be put back into the bottle. The key to the recovery of masculinity lies rather in the problem of identity. When a person begins to find out *who* he is, he is likely to find out rather soon what sex he is.

16 For men to become men again, in short, their first task is to recover a sense of individual spontaneity. And to do this a man must visualize himself as an individual apart from the group, whatever it is, which defines his values and commands his loyalty. There is no reason to suppose that the group is always wrong: to oppose the group automatically is nearly as conformist as to surrender to it automatically. But there is every necessity to recognize that the group is one thing and the individual—oneself—is another. One of the most sinister of present-day doctrines is that of *togetherness*. The recovery of identity means, first of all, a new belief in apartness. It means a determination to resist the over-powering conspiracy of blandness, which seeks to conceal all tension and conflict in American life under a blanket of locker-room affability. And the rebirth of spontaneity depends, at bottom, on changes of attitude *within* people—changes which can perhaps be described, without undue solemnity, as moral changes. These changes will no doubt come about in as many ways as there are individuals involved. But there are some general suggestions that can be made about the techniques of liberation. I should like to mention three such techniques: satire, art, and politics.

17 Satire means essentially the belief that nothing is sacred—that there is no person or institution or idea which cannot but benefit from the exposure of comedy. Our nation in the past has reveled in satire; it is, after all, the nation of Abraham Lincoln, of Mark Twain, of Finley Peter Dunne, of H. L. Mencken, of Ring Lardner. Indeed, the whole spirit of democracy is that of satire; as Montaigne succinctly summed up the democratic faith: "Sit he on ever so high a throne, a man still sits on his own bottom." Yet today American society can only be described as a pompous society, at least in its official manifestations. Early in 1958 Mort Sahl, the night-club comedian, made headlines in New York because he dared make a joke about J. Edgar Hoover! It was not an especially good joke, but the fact that he made it at all was an encouraging sign. One begins to feel that the American people can only stand so much reverence—that in the end our native skepticism will break through, sweep aside the stuffed shirts and the stuffed heads and insist that platitudes are platitudinous and the great are made, among other things, to be laughed at. Irony is good for our rulers; and it is even better for our-

selves because it is a means of dissolving the pomposity of society and giving the individual a chance to emerge.

18 If irony is one source of spontaneity, art is another. Very little can so refresh our vision and develop our vision and develop our values as the liberating experience of art. The mass media have cast a spell on us: the popular addiction to prefabricated emotional clichés threatens to erode our capacity for fresh and direct aesthetic experience. Individual identity vanishes in the welter of machine-made reactions. But thoughtful exposure to music, to painting, to poetry, to the beauties of nature, can do much to restore the inwardness, and thereby the identity, of man. There is thus great hope in the immense cultural underground of our age—the paper-bound books, the long-playing records, the drama societies, the art festivals, the new interest in painting and sculpture. All this represents a disdain for existing values and goals, a reaching out for something more exacting and more personal, an intensified questing for identity.

19 And politics in a true sense can be a means of liberation—not the banal politics of rhetoric and self-congratulation, which aims at burying all real issues under a mass of piety and platitude; but the politics of responsibility, which tries to define the real issues and present them to the people for decision. Our national politics have become boring in recent years because our leaders have offered neither candid and clear-cut formulations of the problems nor the facts necessary for intelligent choice. A virile political life will be definite and hard-hitting, respecting debate and dissent, seeking clarity and decision.

20 As the American male develops himself by developing his comic sense, his aesthetic sense, and his moral and political sense, the lineaments of personality will at last begin to emerge. The achievement of identity, the conquest of a sense of self—these will do infinitely more to restore American masculinity than all the hormones in the test tubes of our scientists. "Whoso would be a *man,*" said Emerson, "must be a nonconformist"; and, if it is the present writer who adds the italics, nonetheless one feels that no injustice is done to Emerson's intention. How can masculinity, femininity, or anything else survive in a homogenized society, which seeks steadily and benignly to eradicate all differences between the individuals who compose it? If we want to have *men* again in our theaters and our films and our novels—not to speak of in our classrooms, our business offices, and our homes—we must first have a society which encourages each of its members to have a distinct identity.

Thinking Questions: *Form*

1. Define *identity*, a key word throughout this essay. Schlesinger uses this term to bring together his general discussion of conformity and his specific discussion of a crisis in male identity. See paragraphs 11 through 14 for Schlesinger's discussion of personal identity.

2. In essence, Schlesinger defines in this essay the limits of two general problems: first, he defines the crisis in male identity; second, he devotes a large group of paragraphs to a definition of the more general problem of loss of identity in modern America. Show where these two major definitions occur in the essay and then point out how they are tied together.

3. Single out those paragraphs in this essay where Schlesinger uses lexical or stipulative definitions of key terms. You might begin by going back over the essay and making lists of key terms. (See the formal discussion of definition that closes this section for explanations of *lexical* and *stipulative*.)

4. Notice how Schlesinger ends his essay with solutions to the crisis in masculine identity. Each solution—*satire, art, politics*—requires its own definition. Can you provide specific examples of what men can do within these three areas, as Schlesinger defines them, to solve the problems of male identity? Does, for example, seeing a play such as Osborne's *Look Back in Anger* help men in general to understand their own "masculine" behavior? Or does making fun of one's own male shortcomings, as in satire, help a man to deal with his own inadequacies?

5. Compare the definitions of contrasting sex roles in any two of the essays in this section. What, for example, do you suppose would be Lenore Romney's response to Schlesinger's definition of male and female roles in our culture? How would Betty Friedan respond to Schlesinger's idea that "American women have unquestionably gained through the years a place in our society which American men have not been psychologically prepared to accept"? (See paragraph 9.) The best way to go about developing such comparisons is to single out a general statement in one of the previous essays and compare it with a central idea in Schlesinger's essay.

Thinking Questions: *Substance*

1. Can you point to some signs that "something has gone badly wrong with the American male's conception of himself" (paragraph 1)? Look for signs similar to the ones Schlesinger points out in this essay. Look closely at the males around you. Do they seem to lack the confidence and self-assuredness that Schlesinger says was previously possessed by male heroes in American society? What do your subjects do that signals this lack of confidence?

2. Is there anything wrong with the changes Schlesinger describes in paragraph 2? Does the fact that "men design dresses and brew up cos-

metics [while] women become doctors, lawyers, bank cashiers and executives" necessarily mean that men are losing confidence and control? Could such changes, at least in some instances, represent greater rather than less sexual confidence? Or should certain occupations be limited according to sex? Why?

3. Summarize Schlesinger's argument on the decline of the masculine hero in American films (paragraph 6). Gary Cooper, the hero of *High Noon,* has long been considered a prototype of the individualistic, frontier hero, dependent only on his guns and his courage, a relatively modern example of those frontier heroes who lived without the companionship of women or the security of a larger society, on their own in the wilderness. Yet Schlesinger points out that even Gary Cooper in *High Noon* demonstrates some indecision, in this case because of the interference of his girlfriend, who tries to persuade him not to fight back. Is there something wrong with the heroic image established by actors like Cooper? Or is there something wrong with our modern culture, which consistently threatens that image?

4. Do you agree with Schlesinger's observation that ". . . there has been something immature in the traditional American male attitude toward women—a sense of alarm at times amounting to panic" (paragraph 9)? Can you find specific examples of men who overreact to *any* movement toward liberation by women?

5. Explain why Schlesinger sees the larger society exerting greater psychological pressure to conform on the individual, despite the fact that we live in a political democracy that claims to give *more* freedom and responsibility to the individual (paragraph 13)? Do you agree with Schlesinger when he says that only a few men will be able to take advantage of such potential freedom? Explain why or why not.

6. Arthur Schlesinger wrote this essay in the 1950s, a decade in which many intellectuals and social commentators were pointing out and attacking the dominance of social conformity. Too many people, these commentators said, were dominated by their desire to fit in, to succeed and find happiness and security at the expense of individual needs. How does Schlesinger relate his general criticism of social conformity to his more specific discussion of the crisis in American masculinity? Does this overall criticism of conformity apply in any way to the 1970s?

By the River

JOYCE CAROL OATES

1 Helen thought: "Am I in love again, some new kind of love? Is that why I'm here?"

2 She was sitting in the waiting room of the Yellow Bus Lines station; she knew the big old room with its dirty tile floor and its solitary telephone booth in the corner and its candy machine and cigarette machine and popcorn machine by heart. Everything was familiar, though she had been gone for four months, even the old woman with the dyed red hair who sold tickets and had been selling them there, behind that counter, for as long as Helen could remember. Years ago, before Helen's marriage, she and her girl friends would be driven into town by someone's father and after they tired of walking around town they would stroll over to the bus station to watch the buses unload. They were anxious to see who was getting off, but few of the passengers who got off stayed in Oriskany—they were just passing through, stopping for a rest and a drink, and their faces seemed to say that they didn't think much of the town. Nor did they seem to think much of the girls from the country who stood around in their colorful dresses and smiled shyly at strangers, not knowing any better: they were taught to be kind to people, to smile first, you never knew who it might be. So now Helen was back in Oriskany, but this time she had come in on a bus herself. Had ridden alone, all the way from the city of Derby, all alone, and was waiting for her father to pick her up so she could go back to her old life without any more fuss.

3 It was hot. Flies crawled languidly around; a woman with a small sickly-faced baby had to keep waving them away. The old woman selling tickets looked at Helen as if her eyes were drawn irresistibly that way, as if she knew every nasty rumor and wanted to let Helen know that she knew. Helen's forehead broke out in perspiration and she stood, abruptly, wanting to dislodge that old woman's stare. She went over to the candy machine but did not look at the candy bars; she looked at herself in the mirror. Her own reflection always made her feel better. Whatever went on inside her head—and right now she felt nervous about something—had nothing to do with the way she looked, her smooth gentle skin and the faint freckles on her forehead and nose and the cool, innocent green of her eyes; she was just a girl from the country and anyone in town would know that, even if they didn't know her personally, one of those easy, friendly girls who hummed to themselves and seemed always to be glancing up as if

expecting something pleasant. Her light brown hair curled back lazily toward her ears, cut short now because it was the style; in high school she had worn it long. She watched her eyes in the mirror. No alarm there really. She would be back home in an hour or so. Not her husband's home, of course, but her parents' home. And her face in the mirror was the face she had always seen—twenty-two she was now, and to her that seemed very old, but she looked no different from the way she had looked on her wedding day five years ago.

4 But it was stupid to try to link together those two Helens, she thought. She went back to the row of seats and sat heavily. If the old woman was still watching she did not care. A sailor in a soiled white uniform sat nearby, smoking, watching her but not with too much interest; he had other girls to recall. Helen opened her purse and looked inside at nothing and closed it again. The man she had been living with in the city for four months had told her it was stupid—no, he had not used that word, he said something fancy like "immature"—to confuse herself with the child she had been, married woman as she was now, and a mother, adulterous married woman . . . and the word *adulterous* made her lips turn up in a slow bemused smile, the first flash of incredulous pride one might feel when told at last the disease that is going to be fatal. For there were so many diseases and only one way out of the world, only one death and so many ways to get to it. They were like doors, Helen thought dreamily. You walked down a hallway like those in movies, in huge wealthy homes, crystal chandeliers and marble floors and . . . great sweeping lawns . . . and doors all along those hallways; if you picked the wrong door you had to go through it. She was dreamy, drowsy. When thought became too much for her—when he had pestered her so much about marrying him, divorcing her husband and marrying him, always him! —she had felt so sleepy she could not listen. If she was not interested in a word her mind wouldn't hear it but made it blurred and strange, like words half-heard in dreams or through some thick substance like water. You didn't have to hear a word if you didn't want to.

5 So she had telephoned her father the night before and told him the three-fifteen bus and now it was three-thirty; where was he? Over the telephone he had sounded slow and solemn, it could have been a stranger's voice. Helen had never liked telephones because you could not see smiles or gestures and talking like that made her tired. Listening to her father, she had felt for the first time since she had run away and left them all behind—husband, baby girl, family, in-laws, the minister, the dreary sun-bleached look of the land—that she had perhaps died and only imagined she was running away. Nobody here trusted the city; it was too big. Helen had wanted to go there all her life, not being afraid of anything, and so she had gone, and was coming back; but it was an odd feeling, this dreamy ghostliness, as

if she were really dead and coming back in a form that only looked liked herself . . . She was bored, thinking of this, and crossed her bare legs. The sailor crushed out a cigarette in the dirty tin ashtray and their eyes met. Helen felt a little smile tug at her lips. That was the trouble, she knew men too well. She knew their eyes and their gestures—like the sailor rubbing thoughtfully at his chin, now, as if he hadn't shaved well enough but really liked to feel his own skin. She knew them too well and had never figured out why: her sister, four years older, wasn't like that. But to Helen the same man one hundred times or one hundred men, different men, seemed the same. It was wrong, of course, because she had been taught it and believed what she had been taught; but she could not understand the difference. The sailor watched her but she looked away, half-closing her eyes. She had no time for him. Her father should be here now, he would be here in a few minutes, so there was no time; she would be home in an hour. When she thought of her father the ugly bus station with its odor of tobacco and spilled soft drinks seemed to fade away—she remembered his voice the night before, how gentle and soft she had felt listening to that voice, giving in to the protection he represented. She had endured his rough hands, as a child, because she knew they protected her, and all her life they had protected her. There had always been trouble, sometimes the kind you laughed about later and sometimes not, that was one of the reasons she had married Paul, and before Paul there had been others—just boys who didn't count, who had no jobs and thought mainly about their cars. She had called her father from a roadhouse sixty miles away once, when she was fifteen; she and her best friend Annie had gotten mixed up with some men they had met at a picnic. That had been frightening, Helen thought, but now she could have handled them. She gave everyone too much, that was her trouble. Her father had said that. Even her mother. Lent money to girls at the telephone company where she'd worked; lent her girl friends clothes; would run outside when some man drove up and blew his horn, not bothering to get out and knock at the door the way he should. She liked to make other people happy, what was wrong with that? Was she too lazy to care? Her head had begun to ache.

6 Always her thoughts ran one way, fast and innocent, but her body did other things. It got warm, nervous, it could not relax. Was she afraid of what her father's face would tell her? She pushed that idea away, it was nonsense. If she had to think of something, let it be of that muddy spring day when her family had first moved to this part of the country, into an old farmhouse her father had bought at a "bargain." At that time the road out in front of the house had been no more than a single dirt lane . . . now it was wider, covered with black top that smelled ugly and made your eyesight shimmer and

sweat with confusion in the summer. Yes, that big old house. Nothing about it would have changed. She did not think of her own house, her husband's house, because it mixed her up too much right now. Maybe she would go back and maybe not. She did not think of him—if she wanted to go back she would, he would take her in. When she tried to think of what had brought her back, it was never her husband—so much younger, quicker, happier than the man she had just left—and not the little girl, either, but something to do with her family's house and that misty, warm day seventeen years ago when they had first moved in. So one morning when that man left for work her thoughts had turned back to home and she had sat at the breakfast table for an hour or so, not clearing off the dishes, looking at the coffee left in his cup as if it were a forlorn reminder of him—a man she was even beginning to forget. She knew then that she did not belong there in the city. It wasn't that she had stopped loving this man—she never stopped loving anyone who needed her, and he had needed her more than anyone—it was something else, something she did not understand. Not her husband, not her baby, not even the look of the river way off down the hill, through the trees that got so solemn and intricate with their bare branches in winter. Those things she loved, she hadn't stopped loving them because she had had to love this new man more . . . but something else made her get up and run into the next room and look through the bureau drawers and the closet, as if looking for something. That evening, when he returned, she explained to him that she was going back. He was over forty, she wasn't sure how much, and it had always been his hesitant, apologetic manner that made her love him, the odor of failure about him that mixed with the odor of the drinking he could not stop, even though he had "cut down" now with her help. Why were so many men afraid, why did they think so much? He did something that had to do with keeping books, was that nervous work? He was an attractive man but that wasn't what Helen had seen in him. It was his staring at her when they had first met, and the way he had run his hand through his thinning hair, telling her in that gesture that he wanted her and wanted to be young enough to tell her so. That had been four months ago. The months all rushed to Helen's mind in the memory she had of his keen intelligent baffled eyes, and the tears she had had to see in them when she went out to call her father . . .

7 Now, back in Oriskany, she would think of him no more.

8 A few minutes later her father came. Was that really him? she thought. Her heart beat furiously. If blood drained out of her face she would look mottled and sick, as if she had a rash . . . how she hated that! Though he had seen her at once, though the bus station was nearly empty, her father hesitated until she stood and ran to him.

"Pa," she said, "I'm so glad to see you." It might have been years ago and he was just going to drive back home now, finished with his business in town, and Helen fourteen or fifteen, waiting to go back with him.

9 "I'll get your suitcase," he said. The sailor was reading a magazine, no longer interested. Helen watched her father nervously. What was wrong? He stooped, taking hold of the suitcase handle, but he did not straighten fast enough. Just a heartbeat too slow. Why was that? Helen took a tissue already stained with lipstick and dabbed it on her forehead.

10 On the way home he drove oddly, as if the steering wheel, heated by the sun, were too painful for him to hold. "No more trouble with the car, huh?" Helen said.

11 "It's all right," he said. They were nearly out of town already. Helen saw few people she knew. "Why are you looking around?" her father said. His voice was pleasant and his eyes fastened seriously upon the road, as if he did not dare look elsewhere.

12 "Oh, just looking," Helen said. "How is Davey?"

Waiting for her father to answer—he always took his time—Helen arranged her skirt nervously beneath her. Davey was her sister's baby, could he be sick? She had forgotten to ask about him the night before. "Nothing's wrong with Davey, is there, Pa?" she said.

13 "No, nothing."

"I thought Ma might come, maybe," Helen said.

"No."

"Didn't she want to? Mad at me, huh?"

14 In the past her mother's dissatisfaction with her had always ranged Helen and her father together; Helen could tell by a glance of her father's when this was so. But he did not look away from the road. They were passing the new high school, the consolidated high school Helen had attended for a year. No one had known what "consolidated" meant or was interested in knowing. Helen frowned at the dark brick and there came to her mind, out of nowhere, the word "adulterous," for it too had been a word she had not understood for years. A word out of the Bible. It was like a mosquito bothering her at night, or a stain on her dress—the kind she would have to hide without seeming to, letting her hand fall accidentally over it. For some reason the peculiar smell of the old car, the rattling sun shades above the windshield, the same old khaki blanket they used for a seat cover did not comfort her and let her mind get drowsy, to push that word away.

15 She was not sleepy, but she said she was.

"Yes, honey. Why don't you lay back and try to sleep, then," her father said.

16 He glanced toward her. She felt relieved at once, made simple and

safe. She slid over and leaned her head against her father's shoulder. "Bus ride was long, I hate bus rides," she said. "I used to like them."

"You can sleep till we get home."

"Is Ma mad?"

"No."

18 His shoulder wasn't as comfortable as it should have been. But she closed her eyes, trying to force sleep. She remembered that April day they had come here—their moving to the house that was new to them, a house of their own they would have to share with no one else, but a house it turned out had things wrong with it, secret things, that had made Helen's father furious. She could not remember the city and the house they had lived in there, but she had been old enough to sense the simplicity of the country and the eagerness of her parents, and then the angry perplexity that had followed. The family was big—six children then, before Arthur died at ten—and half an hour after they had moved in the house was crowded and shabby. And she remembered being frightened at something and her father picking her up right in the middle of moving, and not asking her why she cried—her mother had always asked her that, as if there were a reason—but rocked her and comforted her with his rough hands. And she could remember how the house had looked so well: the ballooning curtains in the windows, the first things her mother had put up. The gusty spring air, already too warm, smelling of good earth and the Eden River not too far behind them, and leaves, sunlight, wind; and the sagging porch piled with cartons and bundles and pieces of furniture from the old house. In that old dark house in the city, the grandparents had died—her mother's parents—and Helen did not remember them at all except as her father summoned them back, recalling with hatred his wife's father—some little confused argument they had had years ago, that he should have won. The old man had died and the house had gone to the bank somewhere mysterious, and her father had brought them all out here to the country. A new world, a new life. A farm. And four boys to help, and the promise of such good soil . . .

19 Her father turned the wheel sharply. "Rabbit run acrost," he said. He had this strange air of apology for whatever he did, even if it was something gentle; he hated to kill animals, even weasels and hawks. Helen wanted to cover his right hand with hers, that thickened, dirt-creased hand that could never be made clean. But she said, stirring a little as if he had woken her, "Then why didn't Ma want to come?"

20 They were taking a long, slow curve. Helen knew without looking up which curve this was, between two wheat fields that belonged to one of the old, old families, those prosperous men who drove broken-down pickup trucks and dressed no better than their own hired

hands, but who had money, much money, not just in one bank but in many. "Yes, they're money people," Helen remembered her father saying, years ago. Passing someone's pasture. Those ugly red cows meant nothing to Helen, but they meant something to her father. And so after her father had said that—they had been out for a drive after church—her mother got sharp and impatient and the ride was ruined. That was years ago, Helen's father had been a young man then, with a raw, waiting, untested look, with muscular arms and shoulders that needed only to be directed to their work. "They're money people," he had said, and that had ruined the ride, as if by magic. It had been as if the air itself had changed, the direction of the wind changing and easing to them from the river that was often stagnant in August and September, and not from the green land. With an effort, Helen remembered that she had been thinking about her mother. Why did her mind push her into the past so often these days, she only twenty-two (that was not old, not really) and going to begin a new life? Once she got home and took a bath and washed out the things in the suitcase, and got some rest, and took a walk down by the river as she had as a child, skipping stones across it, and sat around the round kitchen table with the old oil cloth cover to listen to their advice ("You got to grow up, now. You ain't fifteen anymore"—that had been her mother, last time), then she would decide what to do. Make her decision about her husband and the baby and there would be nothing left to think about.

21 "Why didn't Ma come?"

"I didn't want her to," he said.

22 Helen swallowed, without meaning to. His shoulder was thin and hard against the side of her face. Were those same muscles still there, or had they become worn away like the soil that was sucked down into the river every year, stolen from them, so that the farm Helen's father had bought turned out to be a kind of joke on him? Or were they a different kind of muscle, hard and compressed like steel, drawn into themselves from years of resisting violence?

23 "How come?" Helen said.

He did not answer. She shut her eyes tight and distracting, eerie images came to her, stars exploding and shadowy figures like those taking in the first show at eleven in the morning; not because she was in movies—she had gone to the movies all the time in the city, often lonely or had nothing to do but because she liked movies. Five-twenty and he would come up the stairs, grimacing a little with the strange inexplicable pain in his chest: and there Helen would be, back from downtown, dressed up and her hair shining and her face ripe and fresh as a child's, not because she was proud of the look in his eyes but because she knew she could make that pain of his abate for a while. And so why had she left him, when he had needed her more than anyone? "Pa, is something wrong?" she said, as if the recollection of that other man's invisible pain were in some way connected with her father.

24 He reached down vaguely and touched her hand. She was surprised at this. The movie images vanished—those beautiful people she had wanted to believe in, as she had wanted to believe in God and the saints in their movie-world heaven—and she opened her eyes. The sun was bright. It had been too bright all summer. Helen's mind felt sharp and nervous as if pricked by tiny needles, but when she tried to think of what they could be no explanation came to her. She would be home soon, she would be able to rest. Tomorrow she could get in touch with Paul. Things could begin where they had left off—Paul had always loved her so much, and he had always understood her, had known what she was like. "Ma isn't sick, is she?" Helen said suddenly. "No," said her father. He released her fingers to take hold of the steering wheel again. Another curve. Off to the side, if she bothered to look, the river had swung toward them—low at this time of year, covered in places with a fine brown-green layer of scum. She did not bother to look.

25 "We moved out here seventeen years ago," her father said. He cleared his throat: the gesture of a man unaccustomed to speech. "You don't remember that."

26 "Yes, I do," Helen said. "I remember that."

"You don't, you were just a baby."

"Pa, I remember it. I remember you carrying the big rug in the house, you and Eddie. And I started to cry and you picked me up. I was such a big baby, always crying . . . And Ma came out and chased me inside so I wouldn't bother you."

27 "You don't remember that," her father said. He was driving jerkily, pressing down on the gas pedal and then letting it up, as if new thoughts continually struck him. What was wrong with him? Helen had an idea she didn't like: he was older now, he was going to become an old man.

28 If she had been afraid of the dark, upstairs in that big old farmhouse in the room she shared with her sister, all she had had to do was to think of him. He had a way of sitting at the supper table that was so still, so silent, that you knew nothing could budge him. Nothing could frighten him. So, as a child, and even now that she was grown up, it helped her to think of her father's face—those pale surprised green eyes that could be simple or cunning, depending upon the light, and the lines working themselves in deeper every year around his mouth, and the hard angle of his jaw going back to the ear, burned by the sun and then tanned by it, turned into leather, then going pale again in the winter. The sun could not burn its color deep enough into that skin which was almost as fair as Helen's. At Sunday school she and

the other children had been told to think of Christ when they were afraid, but the Christ she saw on the little Bible bookmark cards and calendars was no one to protect you. That was a man who would be your cousin, maybe, some cousin you liked but saw rarely, but he looked so given over to thinking and trusting that he could not be of much help; not like her father. When he and the boys came in from the fields with the sweat drenching their clothes and their faces looking as if they were dissolving with heat, you could still see the solid flesh beneath, the skeleton that hung onto its muscles and would never get old, never die. The boys—her brothers, all older—had liked her well enough, Helen being the baby, and her sister had watched her most of the time, and her mother had liked her too—or did her mother like anyone, having been brought up by German-speaking parents who had had no time to teach her love? But it had always been her father she had run to. She had started knowing men by knowing him. She could read things in his face that taught her about the faces of other men, the slowness or quickness of their thoughts, if they were beginning to be impatient, or were pleased and didn't want to show it yet. Was it for this she had come home?—And the thought surprised her so that she sat up, because she did not understand. Was it for this she had come home? "Pa," she said, "like I told you on the telephone, I don't know why I did it. I don't know why I went. That's all right, isn't it? I mean, I'm sorry for it, isn't that enough? Did you talk to Paul?"

29 "Paul? Why Paul?"

"What?"

"You haven't asked about him until now, so why now?"

"What do you mean? He's my husband, isn't he? Did you talk to him?"

30 "He came over to the house almost every night for two weeks. Three weeks," he said. Helen could not understand the queer chatty tone of his voice. "Then off and on, all the time. No, I didn't tell him you were coming."

31 "But why not?" Helen laughed nervously. "Don't you like him?"

"You know I like him. You know that. But if I told him he'd of gone down to get you, not me."

32 "Not if I said it was you I wanted . . ."

"I didn't want him to know. Your mother doesn't know either."

"What? You mean you didn't tell her?" Helen looked at the side of his face. It was rigid and bloodless behind the tan, as if something inside were shrinking away and leaving just his voice. "You mean you didn't even tell Ma? She doesn't know I'm coming?"

33 "No."

The nervous prickling in her brain returned suddenly. Helen rubbed her forehead.

"Pa," she said gently, "why didn't you tell anybody? You're ashamed of me, huh?"

34 He drove on slowly. They were following the bends of the river, that wide shallow meandering river the boys said wasn't worth fishing in any longer. One of its tributaries branched out suddenly—Mud Creek, it was called, all mud and bullfrogs and dragonflies and weeds—and they drove over it on a rickety wooden bridge that thumped beneath them. "Pa," Helen said carefully, "you said you weren't mad, on the phone. And I wrote you that letter explaining. I wanted to write some more, but you know . . . I don't write much, never even wrote to Annie when she moved away. I never forgot about you or anything, or Ma . . . I thought about the baby, too, and Paul, but Paul could always take care of himself. He's smart. He really is. I was in the store with him one time and he was arguing with some salesmen and got the best of them; he never learned all that from his father. The whole family is smart, though, aren't they?"

35 "The Hendriks? Sure. You don't get money without brains."

"Yes, and they got money too, Paul never had to worry. In a house like his parents' house nothing gets lost or broken. You know? It isn't like it was at ours, when we were all kids. That's part of it—when Paul's father built us our house I was real pleased and real happy, but then something of them came in with it too. Everything is spost to be clean and put in its place, and after you have a baby you get so tired . . . but his mother was always real nice to me. I don't complain about them. I like them all real well."

36 "Money people always act nice," her father said. "Why shouldn't they?"

37 "Oh, Pa!" Helen said, tapping at his arm. "What do you mean by that? You always been nicer than anybody I know, that's the truth. Real nice. A lot of them with those big farms, like Paul's father, and that tractor store they got—they complain a lot. They do. You just don't hear about it. And when that baby got polio, over in the Rapids—that real big farm, you know what I mean?—the McGuires. How do you think they felt? They got troubles just like everybody else."

38 Then her father did a strange thing: here they were seven or eight miles from home, no house near, and he stopped the car. "Want to rest for a minute," he said. Yet he kept staring out the windshield as if he were still driving.

"What's wrong?"

"Sun on the hood of the car . . ."

39 Helen tugged at the collar of her dress, pulled it away from her damp neck. When had the heat ever bothered her father before? She remembered going out to the farthest field with water for him, before he had given up that part of the farm. And he would take the jug from her and lift it to his lips and it would seem to Helen, the sweet

child Helen standing in the dusty corn, that the water flowed into her magnificent father and enlivened him as if it were secret blood of her own she had given him. And his chest would swell, his reddened arms eager with muscle emerging out from his rolled-up sleeves, and his eyes now wiped of sweat and exhaustion. . . . The vision pleased and confused her, for what had it to do with the man now beside her? She stared at him and saw that his nose was queerly white and that there were many tiny red veins about it, hardly more than pen lines; and his hair was thinning and jagged, growing back stiffly from his forehead as if he had brushed it back impatiently with his hand once too often. When Eddie, the oldest boy, moved away now and lost to them, had pushed their father hard in the chest and knocked him back against the supper table, that same amazed white look had come to his face, starting at his nose.

40 "I was thinking if, if we got home now, I could help Ma with supper," Helen said. She touched her father's arm as if to waken him. "It's real hot, she'd like some help."

"She doesn't know you're coming."

"But I . . . I could help anyway." She tried to smile, watching his face for a hint of something: many times in the past he had looked stern but could be made to break into a smile, finally, if she teased him long enough. "But didn't Ma hear you talk on the phone? Wasn't she there?"

41 "She was there."

"Well, but then . . ."

"I told her you just talked. Never said nothing about coming home."

The heat had begun to make Helen dizzy. Her father opened the door on his side. "Let's get out for a minute, go down by the river," he said. Helen slid across and got out. The ground felt uncertain beneath her feet. Her father was walking and saying something and she had to run to catch up with him. He said: "We moved out here seventeen years ago. There were six of us then, but you don't remember. Then the boy died. And you don't remember your mother's parents and their house, that goddam stinking house, and how I did all the work for him in his store. You remember the store down front? The dirty sawdust floor and the old women coming in for sausage, enough to make you want to puke, and pig's feet and brains out of cows or guts or what the hell they were that people ate in that neighborhood. I could puke for all my life and not get clean of it. You just got born then. And we were dirt to your mother's people, just dirt. I was dirt. And when they died somebody else got the house, it was all owned by somebody else, and so we said how it was for the best and we'd come out here and start all over. You don't remember it or know nothing about us."

42 "What's wrong, Pa?" Helen said. She took his arm as they de-

scended the weedy bank. "You talk so funny, did you get something to drink before you came to the bus station? You never said these things before. I thought it wasn't just meat, but a grocery store, like the one in . . ."

43 "And we came out here," he said loudly, interrupting her, "and bought that son of a bitch of a house with the roof half rotted through and the well all shot to hell . . . and those bastards never looked at us, never believed we were real people. The Hendrikses too. They were like all of them. They looked through me in town, do you know that? Like you look through a window. They didn't see me. It was because hillbilly families were in that house, came and went, pulled out in the middle of the night owing everybody money; they all thought we were like that. I said, we were poor but we weren't hillbillies. I said, do I talk like a hillbilly? We come from the city. But nobody gave a damn. You could go up to them and shout in their faces and they wouldn't hear you, not even when they started losing money themselves. I prayed to God during them bad times that they'd all lose what they had, every bastard one of them, that Swede with the fancy cattle most of all! I prayed to God to bring them down to me so they could see me, my children as good as theirs, and me a harder worker than any of them—if you work till you feel like dying you done the best you can do, whatever money you get. I'd of told them that. I wanted to come into their world even if I had to be on the bottom of it, just so long as they gave me a name . . ."

44 "Pa, you been drinking," Helen said softly.

"I had it all fixed, what I'd tell them," he said. They were down by the river bank now. Fishermen had cleared a little area and stuck Y-shaped branches into the dried mud, to rest their poles on. Helen's father prodded one of the little sticks with his foot and then did something Helen had never seen anyone do in her life, not even boys—he brought his foot down on it and smashed it.

45 "You oughtn't of done that," Helen said. "Why'd you do that?"

"And I kept on and on; it was seventeen years. I never talked about it to anyone. Your mother and me never had much to say, you know that. She was like her father.—You remember that first day? It was spring, nice and warm, and the wind came along when we were moving the stuff in and was so different from that smell in the city—my God! It was a whole new world here."

46 "I remember it," Helen said. She was staring out at the shallow muddy river. Across the way birds were sunning themselves stupidly on flat, white rocks covered with dried moss like veils.

"You don't remember nothing!" her father said angrily. "Nothing! You were the only one of them I loved, because you didn't remember. It was all for you. First I did it for me, myself, to show that bastard father of hers that was dead—then those other bastards, those big farms around us—but then for you, for you. You were the baby. I said to God that when you grew up it'd be you in one of them big houses with everything fixed and painted all the time, and new machinery, and driving around in a nice car not this thing we got. I said I would do that for you or die."

47 "That's real nice, Pa," Helen said nervously, "but I never . . . I never knew nothing about it, or . . . I was happy enough any way I was. I liked it at home, I got along with Ma better than anybody did. And I liked Paul too, I didn't marry him just because you told me to. I mean, you never pushed me around. I wanted to marry him all by myself, because he loved me. I was always happy, Pa. If Paul didn't have the store coming to him, and that land and all, I'd have married him anyway—You oughtn't to worked all that hard for me."

48 In spite of the heat she felt suddenly chilled. On either side of them tall grass shrank back from the cleared, patted area, stiff and dried with August heat. These weeds gathered upon themselves in a brittle tumult back where the vines and foliage of trees began, the weeds dead and whitened and the vines a glossy, rich green, as if sucking life out of the water into which they drooped. All along the river bank trees and bushes leaned out and showed a yard or two of dead, whitish brown where the waterline had once been. This river bent so often you could never see far along it. Only a mile or so. Then foliage began, confused and unmoving. What were they doing here, she and her father? A thought came to Helen and frightened her—she was not used to thinking—that they ought not to be here, that this was some other kind of slow, patient world where time didn't care at all for her or her girl's face or her generosity of love, but would push right past her and go on to touch the faces of other people.

49 "Pa, let's go home. Let's go home," she said.

Her father bent and put his hands into the river. He brought them dripping to his face. "That's dirty there, Pa," she said. A mad dry buzzing started up somewhere—hornets or wasps. Helen looked around but saw nothing.

50 "God listened and didn't say yes or no," her father said. He was squatting at the river and now looked back at her, his chin creasing. The back of his shirt was wet. "If I could read him right it was something like this—that I was caught in myself and them money people caught in themselves and God Himself caught in what he was and so couldn't be anything else. Then I never thought about God again."

51 "I think about God," Helen said. "I do. People should think about God, then they wouldn't have wars and things . . ."

52 "No, I never bothered about God again," he said slowly. "If he was up there or not it never had nothing to do with me. A hailstorm that knocked down the wheat, or a drought—what the hell? Whose fault? It wasn't God's no more than mine so I let him out of it. I knew I

was in it all on my own. Then after a while it got better, year by year. We paid off the farm and the new machines. You were in school then, in town. And when we went into the church they said hello to us sometimes, because we outlasted them hillbillies by ten years. And now Mike ain't doing bad on his own place, got a nice car, and me and Bill get enough out of the farm so it ain't too bad, I mean it ain't too bad. But it wasn't money I wanted!"

53 He was staring at her. She saw something in his face that mixed with the buzzing of the hornets and fascinated her so that she could not move, could not even try to tease him into smiling too. "It wasn't never money I wanted," he said.

54 "Pa, why don't we go home?"

"I don't know what it was, exactly," he said, still squatting. His hands touched the ground idly. "I tried to think of it, last night when you called and all night long and driving in to town, today. I tried to think of it."

55 "I guess I'm awful tired from that bus. I . . . I don't feel good," Helen said.

"Why did you live with that man?"

"What? Oh," she said, touching the tip of one of the weeds, "I met him at Paul's cousin's place, where they got that real nice tavern and a dance hall . . ."

56 "Why did you run away with him?"

"I don't know, I told you in the letter. I wrote it to you Pa. He acted so nice and liked me so, he still does, he loves me so much . . . And he was always so sad and tired, he made me think of . . . you, Pa . . . but not really, because he's not strong like you and couldn't ever do work like you. And if he loved me that much I had to go with him."

57 "Then why did you come back?"

"Come back?" Helen tried to smile out across the water. Sluggish, ugly water, this river that disappointed everyone, so familiar to her that she could not really get used to a house without a river or a creek somewhere behind it, flowing along night and day: perhaps that was what she had missed in the city?

58 "I came back because . . . because . . ."

And she shredded the weed in her cold fingers, but no words came to her. She watched them fall. No words came to her, her mind had turned hollow and cold, she had come too far down to this river bank but it was not a mistake any more than the way the river kept moving was a mistake; it just happened.

59 Her father got slowly to his feet and she saw in his hand a knife she had been seeing all her life. Her eyes seized upon it and her mind tried to remember: where had she seen it last, whose was it, her father's or her brother's? He came to her and touched her shoulder as if waking her, and they looked at each other, Helen so terrified by now

that she was no longer afraid but only curious with the mute marble-like curiosity of a child, and her father stern and silent until a rush of hatred transformed his face into a mass of wrinkles, the skin mottled red and white. He did not raise the knife but slammed it into her chest, up to the hilt, so that his whitened fist struck her body and her blood exploded out upon it.

Afterward, he washed the knife in the dirty water and put it away. He squatted and looked out over the river, then his thighs began to ache and he sat on the ground, a few feet from her body. He sat there for hours as if waiting for some idea to come to him. Then the water began to darken, very slowly, and the sky darkened a little while later, as if belonging to another, separate time, the same thing as always, and he had to turn his mind with an effort to the next thing he must do.

Thinking Questions: ***Form***

1. Stories and essays define in different ways. An essay *tells*: it presents a general idea and openly helps a reader to follow the reasoning and experience behind the idea. A story *shows*: the ideas remain in the background, underneath the words, as the writer re-creates human experience in words. To be sure that a reader will interpret a story as the writer wishes, the storyteller uses many storytelling techniques. Consider the form of "By the River" through the following basic questions.

a. From whose *point of view* is the story told? Point of view reflects the storyteller's choice of perspective. Usually, at least in simpler stories, point of view depends upon the character telling the story. Joyce Carol Oates, for example, had the choice of several possible perspectives—that of Helen, of her father, even of Paul, her former husband. Why does Oates decide to tell the story from Helen's point of view? What ideas about characters, especially the sexual roles of the characters, are emphasized by her choice of point of view?

b. What is the *theme* of "By the River"? (*Theme* tells, in capsule form, what a story is about.) "By the River" describes a father's murder of a runaway daughter. Yet the murder itself fills no more than a few sentences. What does the physical action—Helen's return to Oriskany and her subsequent murder—mean on a deeper, psychological level?

c. What images, thoughts, actions, and words are repeated in this story? Why, for example, does Helen constantly see mental images of strength when she sees or thinks of her father? Why does her father constantly talk about his social standing as he drives from the bus station to the river with Helen? Why do physical images such as the knife, the riverbank, the farm, and the old car get so much attention as this story is told?

As you read and consider these questions, remember that this story re-creates a particular human experience in a way that rather obviously comes to have universal meaning, especially in relation to the way men and women interact within the family structure in our society.

Thinking Questions: *Substance*

1. Many of the essays in this section define the "disintegration" of love between men and women in twentieth-century America. The pressures of our competitive, capitalistic society often make two lovers, both of whom might have originally been attracted to each other by physical or emotional passion, into equal partners in a domestic corporation. What about Helen's parents in "By the River"? Look closely at those passages that describe the family's past—their brief stay in the city and subsequent move to a farm—and show how economic and social factors and pressures might have influenced the family.

2. Does Helen ever really think for herself? Why or why not? Who does most or all of her thinking for her? What has she looked for and only partially found in the three men in her life?

3. Define the term *love* as Helen uses it in this story. See paragraph 1, where Helen thinks: "Am I in love again, some new kind of love? Is that why I'm here?" What was Helen's "old" kind of love and how has it changed? *Has* it changed? Helen thinks there is a difference between her present self, as she returns to Oriskany and awaits her father in the bus station, and her old self in high school, before she left for the city. *Is* there really a difference? (See paragraphs 3 and 4.)

4. Why does Helen return to Oriskany and her father? What emotions does she feel upon being reunited with her father (paragraphs 16 through 18)? Do these emotions reflect a basic need in Helen that results from her being a woman? Or do her needs seem to have been put into her by a society that wants to pamper and protect women? Why does Helen constantly think of her father as a protector? "If she had been afraid of the dark, upstairs in that big old farmhouse in the room she shared with her sister, all she had to do was to think of him" (paragraph 28).

5. In her essay, "Men, Women—and Politics," Lenore Romney complains that too many men, especially in politics and other professions, treat women paternalistically, as if they were children who demanded constant attention and were incapable of serious responsibilities. Can you find evidence of such attitudes in "By the River"? What has happened to Helen's character because of the way Helen's father, her husband, and her present lover have treated her?

Writing Exercise III

EXPOSITION

(Definition)

Focus on one aspect of the sexual revolution or crisis and write an essay in which you define the problem clearly. Before you begin, read over the *how, when, why,* and *what* questions that are discussed in the following discussion of definition. Remember to introduce and limit your subject, to clarify your thesis, and to provide clear examples to support your position. Consider these possible topic questions. The key terms in each question are italicized.

1. Should married women *work*?
2. What is a truly dignified and fair *distribution of labor* in marriage?
3. What is *equality* of the sexes?
4. What is *love* in a heterosexual relationship? Can you divide it into types and describe its characteristics?
5. Should jobs ever be defined according to the *sex* of the worker?
6. What is *meaningful work*? Do most women do meaningful work in our society?
7. What is the *role of the father* in most American families?
8. What is *masculinity*?
9. What is *femininity*?
10. What are some alternatives to conventional *sexual roles* in our society?

WRITING THE ESSAY OF DEFINITION

Expository writing informs; it takes an idea, a group of ideas, an object—almost any subject—and tries to show a reader *why, how, when,* or *what.* Expository writing ranges from the relatively simple—how to put a child's toy together or easy directions in a cookbook—to the relatively complex—an explanation of the causes behind the Watergate scandal or a comparison of professional athletics in Europe and America. The readers must, in essence, be taken on a journey through the writer's mind and experience so that when they finish reading they clearly understand the how, when, why, or what of the essay's subject.

Definition appears in almost every expository essay, sometimes as the major strategy of organization, usually as a supporting device. Definition answers the *what* in the how, when, what, why series of expository questions. It sets the limits of an essay's subject and of its parts—its key words and concepts, where the subject overlaps with others, where it contrasts with or complements other subjects.

Most expository essays include a main idea or thesis, a series of supporting gèneral ideas that are related to the thesis, and specific analysis or examples to support and clarify the general ideas. The process of definition can help a writer develop his or her ideas at all three levels: thesis, supporting ideas, and specifics.

Generally the process of definition can be used in three ways:

1. *Lexical defining*. This is the type of defining we find in a dictionary. It can be especially useful when the thesis of an essay includes key terms with several possible definitions or connotations, or when a thesis uses several abstract words that the writer will need to define to help readers follow the essay's reasoning. Usually lexical definitions include a generic term, which places the word being defined into a general class (a robin might, for example, be included in the general class *birds*), and a qualifying term, to add detail to what we know of the word. Additional details usually place the defined word within the general class.

> A robin is a bird (generic term) with a red breast, dark brown wings and head, and a full body.

Of course, the process of lexical definition can sometimes be used as a model for entire paragraphs or essays. Such lexical paragraphs are especially useful in introducing longer essays. Here is an opening paragraph which uses the definition of the robin as a lead-in to an essay on how caretakers in public parks can create healthy environments for all birds.

> A robin is a bird with a red breast, dark brown wings and heat, and a full body. It eats insects, has a quiet, melodious song, and is an efficient flier. A sensitive caretaker who studies the natural characteristics of the robin can easily create a park environment in which this bird will flourish.

In rare cases, a writer can use the lexical process through an entire essay. Someone interested in arguing that government wiretapping should be allowed in cases of national emergency or when serious threats to national security are involved should probably center the entire essay on the definition of *security* and *emergency* as they apply to the general welfare of a country. In most cases, however, lexical definition applies to specific parts of an essay, not to its overall organization. Lexical defining, like all defining, helps the writer set the limits of his or her discussion.

An essayist must remember to focus, to select those key words in the general definition that need more specific defining. Consider this definition:

> *expressway:* a high-speed divided highway for through traffic with access partially or fully controlled and grade separations at important intersections with other roads. *(Webster's Third New International Dictionary)*

Suppose you were writing an essay in which you planned to argue against the proposed routing of a future expressway. You might want to focus on several key terms in this lexical definition—*through traffic, controlled access, grade separation,* for example—and use them to show why the planned expressway would not be efficient. Such an argument would, of course, depend on initially clear definitions of these terms. It would begin with a general definition, work back through specific definitions of key terms, and fill out with examples and illustrations.

2. *Descriptive defining.* Lexical definitions tell what something *is* or *is not.* Once the general limits of a subject are set, however, you may wish to describe by adding detail to what the reader knows of your subject after reading your lexical definition. Descriptive defining provides such detail. If the subject of an essay is a physical object, the writer may wish to add information about size, shape, color, and degree of similarity to or difference from other objects. Notice how the following works from lexical definition to definition by described detail:

> *horse:* a large solid-hoofed herbivorous mammal domesticated by man since a prehistoric period and used as a beast of burden, a draft animal, or for riding, and distinguished from the other existing members of the genus *Equus* and family *Equidae* by the long hair of the mane and tail, the usual presence of a callosity on the inside of the hind leg below the hock and other less constant characters (as the larger size, larger hooves, more arched neck, small neck, small head, short ears). *(Webster's Third New International Dictionary)*

This definition illustrates several characteristics of most effective definitions. It begins with a class definition that includes several descriptive details ("solid-footed herbivorous mammal"), proceeds to distinguish the horse from other members of the general class by pointing out particular details which are not shared by other members, and concludes with a concrete description of the horse.

3. *Stipulative defining.* Many words carry several meanings simultaneously. Also, in some instances, a writer may wish to create a special definition of a commonly used word. Stipulative defining would solve both problems by singling out one particular lexical meaning and applying it throughout an essay or by enabling the writer to work out a personal definition from a variety of definitions.

Betty Friedan's "The Problem That Has No Name," which is included in this section, defines a problem that many women have expressed. The problem occurs for many different women; it manifests itself in a variety of characteristics, in an unexplainable loneliness or nervousness, in boredom, in vague feelings of unimportance. Friedan tells both what the problem is and why it exists. She then combines descriptions with causes to provide a stipulative definition: "But the chains that bind her in her trap are chains in her own mind and spirit. They are chains made up of mistaken ideas and misinterpreted facts, of incomplete truths and unreal choices." Descriptions characterize the problem; the problem itself is defined as a *chain* of inadequate self-concepts that women get from society.

General principles of definition

1. Entire essays should be organized around definition only when the entire subject needs defining. Usually a writer uses definition to develop key terms and ideas and other methods of development—classification, comparison, narration, and description—to develop a thesis more completely.

2. Consider beginning almost every essay by defining the limits of your general subject. What particular aspect of the abortion issue, for example, will *you* discuss—its moral aspects, its effects on attitudes toward children, its effects on poorer women? Then close your introduction by defining a specific thesis: "Abortion laws endanger the lives of many poor women by forcing them to seek out unhealthy and ill-trained abortionists."

Finally, you should define any unfamiliar or complex terms in your thesis before you actually begin developing it. What, for example, *is* abortion? When does a fetus become a human being? All these questions will help you set the limits and terms of your subject and thesis early in your essay.

3. Consider how description can be used to define. Lenore Romney, in "Men, Women—and Politics" (included in this section), defines problems women have when they enter politics. She develops her definition primarily through examples describing how people responded to her own candidacy for public office.

4. Take a conventional definition and rework it so that it more clearly defines the main idea or object of your essay. A writer, for example, knows that most advertisements are persuasive. He or she wants, however, to take the idea that advertisements are persuasive and provide a more specific, complex definition. How are ads persuasive? Are there particular categories of advertising persuasion? Do some advertisements persuade by making prospective buyers want to go along with the crowd, all of whom, for instance, drink a particular beer? Do other advertisements appeal to a person's masculine or feminine ego? Once a general definition is divided into parts, each part can then be stipulatively defined by the writer.

Form:

EXPOSITION

(Comparison and Contrast)

Substance and Theme:

THINKING ON THE FUTURE

Our futures are made by the present; the present is made by the past. In other words, the human vantage point defines what is past, present, and future. Every person looks back over a lifetime of detail and finds some kind of general order. And the collective minds of society find patterns that supposedly explain the present. The writers in this section suggest future patterns by drawing inferences from the past and by examining the present.

Joan Didion begins this section by showing us how her past experiences have led her to a current decision. She reviews scattered experiences during her five or six years in New York, her early expectations and somewhat romantic longings for adventure and romance, her simple love of the city, its buildings, shops, and restaurants. She finally progresses to her later disenchantment with the city and her life in it, to her marriage and her move with her new husband to Los Angeles.

Of course, this minimal summary of Joan Didion's essay is not really what the essay is about. Rather, the essay describes a process of change, a gradual evolution, as one person learns to separate romantic illusion and real value and pleasure, to make distinctions between momentary and illusory pleasures such as eating in a restaurant because it sounds romantic and exciting and actually enjoying a meal with another person. Didion provides us with a model of growth and change in one person. But that growth and change, represented by her move from New York to Los Angeles, are similar to the changes and disenchantments all of us experience as wishes and dreams become realities. New York, the city of adventure and romance for scores of people over scores of years, gradually becomes the city of cockroaches, of trite people in trite places looking for ever more glittering illusions. In essence, large cities embody the hopes and dreams of much of modern civilization, especially in America, where progress often means happiness, and bigness is goodness.

Didion uses her own experience with New York City to represent a general pattern in American culture: we build cities to provide interest and pleasure, but subsequently often find the pleasures and adventures they do provide are momentary and often spiritually destructive.

Melvin Maddocks also gives us one man's view of modern America. The incessant talkers, those people who want to reveal everything because they want to dominate and shock others with their openness, are, Maddocks suggests, part of a new tendency to ignore what some would call "the rights of privacy." Maddocks illustrates his idea with numerous examples of private lives put on open display, ranging from Charlie O. (for Oral), the guy who bends your ear talking of personal problems as you sit next to him on a long-distance plane ride, to the kind of personal revelation we see every day on television talk shows. Joan Didion describes a city of the present and how it affects certain people like herself; Melvin Maddocks illustrates a common type of person and speculates on why these people act as they do, while he also suggests that they change. Both observe the present in ways that suggest future change.

Didion and Maddocks give us individual interpretations of current situations and values. Both suggest future patterns; we can either continue to foster the values of city life and the outgoing, open personality, or we can return to simpler, more traditional values.

Goodbye to All That

JOAN DIDION

How many miles to Babylon?
Three score miles and ten—
Can I get there by candlelight?
Yes, and back again—
If your feet are nimble and light
You can get there by candlelight.

1 It is easy to see the beginnings of things, and harder to see the ends. I can remember now, with a clarity that makes the nerves in the back of my neck constrict, when New York began for me, but I cannot lay my finger upon the moment it ended, can never cut through the ambiguities and second starts and broken resolves to the exact place

on the page where the heroine is no longer as optimistic as she once was. When I first saw New York I was twenty, and it was summertime, and I got off a DC-7 at the old Idlewild temporary terminal in a new dress which had seemed very smart in Sacramento but seemed less smart already, even in the old Idlewild temporary terminal, and the warm air smelled of mildew and some instinct, programmed by all the movies I had ever seen and all the songs I had ever heard sung and all the stories I had ever read about New York, informed me that it would never be quite the same again. In fact it never was. Some time later there was a song on all the jukeboxes on the upper East Side that went "but where is the schoolgirl who used to be me," and if it was late enough at night I used to wonder that. I know now that almost everyone wonders something like that, sooner or later and no matter what he or she is doing, but one of the mixed blessings of being twenty and twenty-one and even twenty-three is the conviction that nothing like this, all evidence to the contrary notwithstanding, has ever happened to anyone before.

2 Of course it might have been some other city, had circumstances been different and the time been different and had I been different, might have been Paris or Chicago or even San Francisco, but because I am talking about myself I am talking here about New York. That first night I opened my window on the bus into town and watched for the skyline, but all I could see were the wastes of Queens and the big signs that said MIDTOWN TUNNEL THIS LANE and then a flood of summer rain (even that seemed remarkable and exotic, for I had come out of the West where there was no summer rain), and for the next three days I sat wrapped in blankets in a hotel room air-conditioned to 35 and tried to get over a bad cold and a high fever. It did not occur to me to call a doctor, because I knew none, and although it did occur to me to call the desk and ask that the air conditioner be turned off, I never called, because I did not know how much to tip whoever might come—was anyone ever so young? I am here to tell you that someone was. All I could do during those three days was talk long-distance to the boy I already knew I would never marry in the spring. I would stay in New York, I told him, just six months, and I could see the Brooklyn Bridge from my window. As it turned out the bridge was the Triborough, and I stayed eight years.

3 In retrospect it seems to me that those days before I knew the names of all the bridges were happier than the ones that came later, but perhaps you will see that as we go along. Part of what I want to tell you is what it is like to be young in New York, how six months can become eight years with the deceptive ease of a film dissolve, for that is how those years appear to me now, in a long sequence of sentimental dissolves and old-fashioned trick shots—the Seagram Building fountains dissolve into snowflakes, I enter a revolving door

at twenty and come out a good deal older, and on a different street. But most particularly I want to explain to you, and in the process perhaps to myself, why I no longer live in New York. It is often said that New York is a city for only the very rich and the very poor. It is less often said that New York is also, at least for those of us who came there from somewhere else, a city for only the very young.

4 I remember once, one cold bright December evening in New York, suggesting to a friend who complained of having been around too long that he come with me to a party where there would be, I assured him with the bright resourcefulness of twenty-three, "new faces." He laughed literally until he choked, and I had to roll down the taxi window and hit him on the back. "New faces," he said finally, "don't tell me about *new faces*." It seemed that the last time he had gone to a party where he had been promised "new faces," there had been fifteen people in the room, and he had already slept with five of the women and owed money to all but two of the men. I laughed with him, but the first snow had just begun to fall and the big Christmas trees glittered yellow and white as far as I could see up Park Avenue and I had a new dress and it would be a long while before I would come to understand the particular moral of the story.

5 It would be a long while because, quite simply, I was in love with New York. I do not mean "love" in any colloquial way. I mean that I was in love with the city, the way you love the first person who ever touches you and never love anyone quite that way again. I remember walking across Sixty-second Street one twilight that first spring, or the second spring, they were all alike for a while. I was late to meet someone but I stopped at Lexington Avenue and bought a peach and stood on the corner eating it and knew that I had come out of the West and reached the mirage. I could taste the peach and feel the soft air blowing from a subway grating on my legs and I could smell lilac and garbage and expensive perfume and I knew that it would cost something sooner or later—because I did not belong there, did not come from there—but when you are twenty-two or twenty-three, you figure that later you will have a high emotional balance, and be able to pay whatever it costs. I still believed in possibilities then, still had the sense, so peculiar to New York, that something extraordinary would happen any minute, any day, any month. I was making only $65 or $70 a week then ("Put yourself in Hattie Carnegie's hands," I was advised without the slightest trace of irony by an editor of the magazine for which I worked), so little money that some weeks I had to charge food at Bloomingdale's gourmet shop in order to eat, a fact which went unmentioned in the letters I wrote to California. I never told my father that I needed money because then he would have sent it, and I would never know if I could do it by myself. At that time making a living seemed a game to me, with arbitrary but

quite inflexible rules. And except on a certain kind of winter evening —six-thirty in the Seventies, say, already dark and bitter with a wind off the river, when I would be walking very fast toward a bus and would look in the bright windows of brownstones and see cooks working in clean kitchens and imagine women lighting candles on the floor above and beautiful children being bathed on the floor above that—except on nights like those, I never felt poor; I had the feeling that if I needed money I could always get it. I could write a syndicated column for teenagers under the name "Debbi Lynn" or I could smuggle gold into India or I could become a $100 call girl, and none of it would matter.

6 Nothing was irrevocable; everything was within reach. Just around every corner lay something curious and interesting, something I had never before seen or done or known about. I could go to a party and meet someone who called himself Mr. Emotional Appeal and ran The Emotional Appeal Institute or Tina Onassis Blandford or a Florida cracker who was then a regular on what he called "the Big C," the Southampton-El Morrocco circuit ("I'm well-connected on the Big C, honey," he would tell me over collard greens on his vast borrowed terrace), or the widow of the celery king of the Harlem market or a piano salesman from Bonne Terre, Missouri, or someone who had already made and lost two fortunes in Midland, Texas. I could make promises to myself and to other people and there would be all the time in the world to keep them. I could stay up all night and make mistakes, and none of it would count.

7 You see I was in a curious position in New York: it never occurred to me that I was living a real life there. In my imagination I was always there for just another few months, just until Christmas or Easter or the first warm day in May. For that reason I was most comfortable in the company of Southerners. They seemed to be in New York as I was, on some indefinitely extended leave from wherever they belonged, disinclined to consider the future, temporary exiles who always knew when the flights left for New Orleans or Memphis or Richmond or, in my case, California. Someone who lives always with a plane schedule in the drawer lives on a slightly different calendar. Christmas, for example, was a difficult season. Other people could take it in stride, going to Stowe or going abroad or going for the day to their mothers' places in Connecticut; those of us who believed that we lived somewhere else would spend it making and canceling airline reservations, waiting for weatherbound flights as if for the last plane out of Lisbon in 1940, and finally comforting one another, those of us who were left, with the oranges and mementos and smoked-oyster stuffings of childhood, gathering close, colonials in a far country.

8 Which is precisely what we were. I am not sure that it is possible for anyone brought up in the East to appreciate entirely what New

York, the idea of New York, means to those of us who came out of the West and the South. To an Eastern child, particularly a child who has always had an uncle on Wall Street and who has spent several hundred Saturdays first at F. A. O. Schwarz and being fitted for shoes at Best's and then waiting under the Biltmore clock and dancing to Lester Lanin, New York is just a city, albeit *the* city, a plausible place for people to live. But to those of us who came from places where no one had heard of Lester Lanin and Grand Central Station was a Saturday radio program, where Wall Street and Fifth Avenue and Madison Avenue were not places at all but abstractions ("Money," and "High Fashion," and "The Hucksters"), New York was no mere city. It was instead an infinitely romantic notion, the mysterious nexus of all love and money and power, the shining and perishable dream itself. To think of "living" there was to reduce the miraculous to the mundane; ones does not "live" at Xanadu.

9 In fact it was difficult in the extreme for me to understand those young women for whom New York was not simply an ephemeral Estoril but a real place, girls who bought toasters and installed new cabinets in their apartments and committed themselves to some reasonable future. I never bought any furniture in New York. For a year or so I lived in other people's apartments; after that I lived in the Nineties in an apartment furnished entirely with things taken from storage by a friend whose wife had moved away. And when I left the apartment in the Nineties (that was when I was leaving everything, when it was all breaking up) I left everything in it, even my winter clothes and the map of Sacramento County I had hung on the bedroom wall to remind me who I was, and I moved into a monastic four-room floor-through on Seventy-fifth Street. "Monastic" is perhaps misleading here, implying some chic severity; until after I was married and my husband moved some furniture in, there was nothing at all in those four rooms except a cheap double mattress and box springs, ordered by telephone the day I decided to move, and two French garden chairs lent me by a friend who imported them. (It strikes me now that the people I knew in New York all had curious and self-defeating sidelines. They imported garden chairs which did not sell very well at Hammacher Schlemmer or they tried to market hair straighteners in Harlem or they ghosted exposés of Murder Incorporated for Sunday supplements. I think that perhaps none of us was very serious, *engagé* only about our most private lives.)

10 All I ever did to that apartment was hang fifty yards of yellow theatrical silk across the bedroom windows, because I had some idea that the gold light would make me feel better, but I did not bother to weight the curtains correctly and all that summer the long panels of transparent golden silk would blow out the windows and get tangled and drenched in the afternoon thunderstorms. That was the year, my

twenty-eighth, when I was discovering that not all of the promises would be kept, that some things are in fact irrevocable and that it had counted after all, every evasion and every procrastination, every mistake, every word, all of it.

11 That is what it was all about, wasn't it? Promises? Now when New York comes back to me it comes in hallucinatory flashes, so clinically detailed that I sometimes wish that memory would effect the distortion with which it is commonly credited. For a lot of the time I was in New York I used a perfume called *Fleurs de Rocaille,* and then *L'Air du Temps,* and now the slightest trace of either can short-circuit my connections for the rest of the day. Nor can I smell Henri Bendel jasmine soap without falling back into the past, or the particular mixture of spices used for boiling crabs. There were barrels of crab boil in a Czech place in the Eighties where I once shopped. Smells, of course, are notorious memory stimuli, but there are other things which affect me the same way. Blue-and-white striped sheets. Vermouth cassis. Some faded nightgowns which were new in 1959 or 1960, and some chiffon scarves I bought about the same time.

12 I suppose that a lot of us who have been young in New York have the same scenes on our home screens. I remember sitting in a lot of apartments with a slight headache about five o'clock in the morning. I had a friend who could not sleep, and he knew a few other people who had the same trouble, and we would watch the sky lighten and have a last drink with no ice and then go home in the early morning light, when the streets were clean and wet (had it rained in the night? we never knew) and the few cruising taxis still had their headlights on and the only color was the red and green of traffic signals. The White Rose bars opened very early in the morning; I recall waiting in one of them to watch an astronaut go into space, waiting so long that at the moment it actually happened I had my eyes not on the television screen but on a cockroach on the tile floor. I liked the bleak branches above Washington Square at dawn, and the monochromatic flatness of Second Avenue, the fire escapes and the grilled storefronts peculiar and empty in their perspective.

13 It is relatively hard to fight at six-thirty or seven in the morning without any sleep, which was perhaps one reason we stayed up all night, and it seemed to be a pleasant time of day. The windows were shuttered in that apartment in the Nineties and I could sleep a few hours and then go to work. I could work then on two or three hours' sleep and a container of coffee from Chock Full O'Nuts. I liked going to work, liked the soothing and satisfactory rhythm of getting out a magazine, liked the orderly progression of four-color closings and two-color closings and black-and-white closings and then The Product, no abstraction but something which looked effortlessly glossy and could be picked up on a newsstand and weighed in the hand. I

liked all the minutiae of proofs and layouts, liked working late on the nights the magazine went to press, sitting and reading *Variety* and waiting for the copy desk to call. From my office I could look across town to the weather signal on the Mutual of New York Building and the lights that alternately spelled out TIME and LIFE above Rockefeller Plaza; that pleased me obscurely, and so did walking uptown in the mauve eight o'clocks of early summer evenings and looking at things, Lowestoft tureens in Fifty-seventh Street windows, people in evening clothes trying to get taxis, the trees just coming into full leaf, the lambent air, all the sweet promises of money and summer.

14 Some years passed, but I still did not lose that sense of wonder about New York. I began to cherish the loneliness of it, the sense that at any given time no one need know where I was or what I was doing. I liked walking, from the East River over to the Hudson and back on brisk days, down around the Village on warm days. A friend would leave me the key to her apartment in the West Village when she was out of town, and sometimes I would just move down there, because by that time the telephone was beginning to bother me (the canker, you see, was already in the rose) and not many people had that number. I remember one day when someone who did have the West Village number came to pick me up for lunch there, and we both had hangovers, and I cut my finger opening him a beer and burst into tears, and we walked to a Spanish restaurant and drank Bloody Marys and *gazpacho* until we felt better. I was not then guilt-ridden about spending afternoons that way, because I still had all the afternoons in the world.

15 And even that late in the game I still liked going to parties, all parties, bad parties, Saturday-afternoon parties given by recently married couples who lived in Stuyvesant Town. West Side parties given by unpublished or failed writers who served cheap red wine and talked about going to Guadalajara, Village parties where all the guests worked for advertising agencies and voted for Reform Democrats, press parties at Sardi's, the worst kinds of parties. You will have perceived by now that I was not one to profit by the experience of others, that it was a very long time indeed before I stopped believing in new faces and began to understand the lesson in that story, which was that it is distinctly possible to stay too long at the Fair.

16 I could not tell you when I began to understand that. All I know is that it was very bad when I was twenty-eight. Everything that was said to me I seemed to have heard before, and I could no longer listen. I could no longer sit in little bars near Grand Central and listen to someone complaining of his wife's inability to cope with the help while he missed another train to Connecticut. I no longer had any interest in hearing about the advances other people had received from their publishers, about plays which were having second-act

trouble in Philadelphia, or about people I would like very much if only I would come out and meet them. I had already met them, always. There were certain parts of the city which I had to avoid. I could not bear upper Madison Avenue on weekday mornings (this was a particularly inconvenient aversion, since I then lived just fifty or sixty feet east of Madison), because I would see women walking Yorkshire terriers and shopping at Gristede's, and some Veblenesque gorge would rise in my throat. I could not go to Times Square in the afternoon, or to the New York Public Library for any reason whatsoever. One day I could not go into a Schrafft's; the next day it would be Bonwit Teller.

17 I hurt the people I cared about, and insulted those I did not. I cut myself off from the one person who was closer to me than any other. I cried until I was not even aware when I was crying and when I was not, cried in elevators and in taxis and in Chinese laundries, and when I went to the doctor he said only that I seemed to be depressed, and should see a "specialist." He wrote down a psychiatrist's name and address for me, but I did not go.

18 Instead I got married, which as it turned out was a very good thing to do but badly timed, since I still could not walk on upper Madison Avenue in the mornings and still could not talk to people and still cried in Chinese laundries. I had never before understood what "despair" meant, and I am not sure that I understand now, but I understood that year. Of course I could not work. I could not even get dinner with any degree of certainty, and I would sit in the apartment on Seventy-fifth Street paralyzed until my hubsand would call from his office and say gently that I did not have to get dinner, that I could meet him at Michael's Pub or at Toots Shor's or at Sardi's East. And then one morning in April (we had been married in January) he called and told me that he wanted to get out of New York for a while, that he would take a six-month leave of absence, that we would go somewhere.

19 It was three years ago that he told me that, and we have lived in Los Angeles since. Many of the people we knew in New York think this a curious aberration, and in fact tell us so. There is no possible, no adequate answer to that, and so we give certain stock answers, the answers everyone gives. I talk about how difficult it would be for us to "afford" to live in New York right now, about how much "space" we need. All I mean is that I was very young in New York, and that at some point the golden rhythm was broken, and I am not that young any more. The last time I was in New York was in a cold January, and everyone was ill and tired. Many of the people I used to know there had moved to Dallas or had gone to Antabuse or had bought a farm in New Hampshire. We stayed ten days, and then we took an afternoon flight back to Los Angeles, and on the way home from the

airport that night I could see the moon on the Pacific and smell jasmine all around and we both knew that there was no longer any point in keeping the apartment we still kept in New York. There were years when I called Los Angeles "the Coast," but they seem a long time ago.

Thinking Questions: *Form*

1. Compare Didion's opening and closing paragraphs. Both describe the sounds, smells, and sights of large cities. Compare the appeals to the senses in both paragraphs: in New York, "the warm air smelled of mildew" and the old songs and movies; eight years later in Los Angeles, "I could see the moon on the Pacific and smell jasmine all around." How does this comparison unify the essay? Does the fact that Didion's senses now find the scents of Los Angeles as pleasing as the remembered scents of New York mean that she has matured and no longer needs to romanticize her environment? Is that why she no longer keeps her apartment in New York?

2. Choose several paragraphs and analyze the alternate comparison structure (see the discussion of this structure in the essay on form at the end of this section). How does Didion accomplish the shifts from her discussion of herself arriving in New York at 21 to her discussions of herself leaving New York at 28?

3. What is the thesis of this essay? And how do the specific comparisons between places (New York and California) and times (Didion at 21 and at 28) contribute to the development of that thesis? Phrase your idea of Didion's thesis as specifically as you can.

4. Look over the diagram of a model essay in the discussion of form at the end of this section. Many writers rearrange the units in this model, but usually the units are there in some overall structure. How well does Didion's essay fit this model? Where does she depart from it? Why does she occasionally depart from it?

Thinking Questions: *Substance*

1. Consider the little poem Didion uses to open her essay. What biblical meaning does Babylon have? Why might it be ironic that the traveler strives to get to Babylon with feet that are "nimble and light" and "by candlelight"?

2. What does Didion mean when she says that New York is a city "only for the very young"? What patterns in her own experiences make this observation true? Why does she find it more difficult to live in New York at 28, when she often found herself crying in elevators and in taxis, than at 21, when she had been enthralled with the smells, sights, and sounds of the city? Was the difference in her or in the city?

3. Now consider Didion's essay in relation to our society's general attitudes toward the city. If you live in a small or medium-sized town, how do the people around you feel about large cities? Do they, for example, believe that people are more sophisticated in large cities because there is more variation in types of people, jobs, ways of life? Are they glad to be away from the city's confusion and tension? Do they make fun of local behavior—in politics, education, civil service, culture—because it cannot compete with those things in cities? Compare these attitudes with those Didion describes in herself in "Goodbye to All That." What do you imagine Joan Didion said about life in Sacramento *before* she went to New York? Do you think she found it exciting or provincial? What does she have to say about life in New York in comparison with life in "the provinces" *after* she has left New York? What causes the shift in attitude? Consider especially the remark her friend makes in the taxi after she has told him that they would meet "new faces" at an upcoming party: "Don't tell me about *new faces*" (paragraph 4). According to Joan Didion, does anyone ever really meet a "new face" in New York? (See paragraph 6, also, where Didion lists the "new faces" she might meet at any one party.)

4. Throughout her essay Didion tells us that she never thought of herself living a "real life" in New York. She lives day by day, always figuring on leaving on the next train or plane. She actually enjoys her loneliness (paragraph 14). Yet this combination of a dream-like existence and lack of roots finally causes her disillusionment. Why?

5. After reading Didion's essay, do you understand why more people have nervous breakdowns and psychological problems in large cities? Define at least a few of the reasons specifically. Finally, do you feel the psychological risks of city living are offset by the cultural advantages? How might these psychological risks be alleviated in the future, especially considering that more and more people seem destined to live in and around cities?

In Praise of Reticence

MELVIN MADDOCKS

1 The DC-9 has climbed to 30,000 ft. You have that serene, floating, god-above-gravity feeling—the small miracle of flying. Your fellow god, the one in the cockpit, is mumbling the usual comforting inaudibles over the P.A. ("Off to the leftmmmmmzzz . . ."). You give the other passengers a quick scan; apparently not a hijacker in sight. A small prayer of thanks might be in order.

2 But then there is a minor throat-clearing on your right. Your seatmate is about to speak. You are about to suffer a disaster that neither man nor computer can guard against: Instant Intimacy. Relentlessly, he tells you all about his business, his childhood, his sex life. Why do the airlines spend their money eliminating the middle seat? Why don't they put up confessional grilles instead?

3 Let's call your seatmate Charlie O. (for Oral). He is not just a minor nuisance, but the personification of a major menace. People today tell complete strangers things they once wouldn't have confessed to a priest, a doctor or a close friend: their cruelest fears; their most shameful inadequacies; their maddest fantasies. We are witnessing something like the death of reticence.

4 Inspect the bestseller list. Charlie O. has it cornered. He is the tattletale from whom we learn *Everything We Always Wanted to Know About Sex*— and a lot we didn't really want to know, thanks all the same. *Charlie O.'s Complaint* is not that he can't help doing it but that he can't help talking about it. In the theater, Charlie O. is the playwright shouting the most four-letter words the loudest. He is also the journalist who will share with 7,000,000 readers a 20-year history of his drinking problem. The short version, or the long one if he can find an editor to pay. Not even his loved ones are safe. He will describe in detail his wife's change of life, his daughter's ordeal with drugs, or his son's battle against not-so-latent homosexuality.

5 Self-disclosure has become an art form—indeed, it threatens to become the only art form. The Charlie O. who shows-and-tells not only earns an automatic reputation for honesty but for talent. Johnny, Merv and Dick fight to get him, and then he tells even more. Hang a mike boom above his big mouth and stand back. Let lesser men insert the bleeps. If he isn't already a celebrity, Instant Intimacy practiced with a closeup camera on a Nielsen audience of 7.2 will make him one. Instantly.

6 You call it exhibitionism? He calls it Moral Courage and Mental Health. *Talking is good.* This is the center and the circumference of Charlie O.'s credo. The more talking, the better.

7 Open your well-dinned ears to the talk show that is life. Charlie O.'s credo has carried the day. The reticent man, even as he mutters "Crashing bore!" in the direction of the nearest Charlie O., is bullied into feeling that he suffers from constipation of the heart ("What are you holding back? Don't you care?"). The old values—talk is cheap, "strong" goes with "silent"—have been reversed. *Articulate and outspoken:* does praise come higher? *He can't communicate:* this is the kiss of death from kindergarten on.

8 Talking It All Out supposedly helps cure everything from bad marriages to war. But your old seatmate Charlie O. is not the pink-cheeked life-giver he pretends to be. He is a monologist whose un-

stinting offer of himself is the purest self-indulgence. One ear is as good as another for him—or even no ear at all. Like Samuel Beckett's Krapp, he might as well be sitting in an empty room droning into a tape recorder. Narcissus with a microphone instead of a mirror.

9 In his life, in his art, Charlie O. wants to be Me. But he has no time to develop a self, he's so busy giving it away. For all his I-witnessing, one is left with remarkable little presence. Charlie O. wears his openness like the ultimate mask. The whine of his voice, the color of his pubic hair—what else is there to remember really? As Psychiatrist Leslie Farber puts it, he has taken the fig leaf off his genitals only to cover up his face.

10 There is a mischief, a self-destructiveness built into garrulity. A little-known law of psychology called the Lombard Effect states that a talker raises the level of his voice in reflex response to an increase in environmental noise (including other voices), but at the cost of intelligibility. The talker puts things less accurately and, furthermore, he is less accurately understood by his equally harassed listeners. The Lombard Effect is a fair metaphor for the distracted life, 1970.

11 The fact that people "can no longer carry on authentic dialogue with one another," philosopher Martin Buber has warned, is "the most acute symptom of the pathology of our time." It is as if in our loneliness, in our anxiety to communicate, we have produced a modern Tower of Babel. Everybody talking at once, but without quite facing one another. Speech, the most social impulse of all, has turned into an act of aggression—against others and finally against ourselves.

12 One of the things talked most shrilly about these days is the need for privacy—for what a friend writing about painter Paul Klee called "creative quiet." Klee's face, he explained, "was that of a man who knows about day and night, sky and sea and air. He did not speak about these things. He had no tongue to tell of them." Our cursed explicitness, our compulsion to tell all, has sacrificed this sense of the ineffable. Perhaps no more severe penalty can be exacted on the gift of speech.

13 What is the alternative? Like Charlie O., the reticent man has his credo. He believes that rests are as much a part of music as the notes, that a man's silences are as much a part of what he means as what he says. The reticent man would not reject the argument: "How do I know what I think until I hear what I say?" But he would add: "How do I know what I *believe* until I hear what I *don't* say?" He would certainly insist that the deepest feelings, as well as the deepest meanings, thrive on understatement—that the ultimate intimacy is shared silence. The reticent man may well be a Romantic at silence, but he tries to be a Classicist at speech. He believes that reticence is the art of knowing what can be said and what cannot be said, and he is prepared to stake civilization on this art.

14 There is a small, very private organization known as Fighters for the Freedom of Silence. They are not necessarily opposed to freedom of speech. In fact, they regard themselves as its truest friends, since they insist through their silence that words are not be to taken lightly. Guidance counselors, bartenders, lay analysts—the career listeners—make the most avid members. The FFFOS have not yet purchased their own airline, on which Trappist flight rules can be enforced. But they do have their own underground soundproof club. Numbed by the unsolicited revelations life daily forces upon them, they retreat there one evening a week to recuperate from fellow man's confessional excesses. Over the door—gold leaf and Old English on fumed oak—reads this inscription: PLEASE SHUT UP.

15 Are you listening—are you for once listening, Charlie O.?

Thinking Questions: *Form*

1. Find the sentence that most closely approximates Maddocks's thesis. How does his comparison between Charley O., the hypothetical representative of contemporary man, and the man of reticence develop that thesis? Is this comparison fair? Is Charley O. an exaggerated version of contemporary man? Do you encounter many compulsive talkers?

2. Compare Maddocks's alternative to "the distracted life, 1970": the small, private organization known as the Fighters for the Freedom of Silence. Which group would you rather belong to and why?

3. Describe Maddocks's personality, the way he presents himself in words. What kind of person is he? How does he dress and speak? How do you think he would act at a party? How does this essay encourage your description of his personality? Describe his sentences, his way of telling little stories, his vocabulary.

4. What about Maddocks's use of the second-person pronoun *you*? Why does he put *you* next to Charley O. in the airplane? Then he shifts to the third-person pronoun *he* to continue his description of Charley O. Do you find the shift in pronouns distracting, awkward, or effective? Why?

5. Describe the method of development in this essay. Notice how the first half provides several related examples of Charley O. in action, while the second half explains what social forces produced Charley O. Do you find this pattern of moving from specific example to general reason in other paragraphs as well?

Thinking Questions: *Substance*

1. This little article argues against complete openness, especially verbal openness. What twentieth-century social trends and changes do you believe have led to Charley O.'s compulsive openness? Are, for example,

people talking more because they actually live *more* private and more isolated lives than people who grew up in rural areas in previous centuries? In other words, might the compulsion to talk be the individual's attempt to overcome or deny an inner sense of loneliness and despair? Look at paragraph 7, in which Maddocks compares some old sayings—"talk is cheap," "strong goes with silent"—with our current tendency to praise the "articulate" person.

2. Is Maddocks necessarily criticizing real communication? Or is he criticizing talk that does *not* communicate, talk that actually results in a monologue: "Narcissus with a microphone instead of a mirror"? Again, can you guess what the psychological reasons for such a compulsion might be?

3. In paragraph 10, Maddocks describes the Lombard Effect. Give your own succinct definition of the Lombard Effect and provide several personal examples of people you know who fit the description. Finally, what does Maddocks mean when he says that "The Lombard Effect is a fair metaphor for the distracted life, 1970"? Why might life in a crowded city, for example, cause a person to become a victim of the Lombard Effect?

4. Compare what Joan Didion says about life in cities with what Maddocks says. Do you find any contradictions? For example, Joan Didion says she found a great deal of privacy, almost too much privacy, in New York. Yet Maddocks describes people who are constantly talking to one another, or at least *at* one another. Might individuals be talking a great deal without communicating? Why?

* * *

Joan Didion and Melvin Maddocks give us examples of individuals confronting new social pressures that have been caused by changes in social structure: Joan Didion confronts the megalopolis, the modern city; Melvin Maddocks confronts new styles of communication with the traditionalist's love of old-fashioned privacy and reticence. In the following essay, however, Warren Bennis looks with the eye of a contemporary university administrator at patterns of change that he would prefer to encourage rather than obstruct. He points out that every large institution includes individuals who will work for and against change; the manager's or leader's task is to promote change without destroying personal trust. Bennis offers us a *group* perspective that contrasts with the personal perspectives of Didion and Maddocks. Although Bennis fully acknowledges the many difficulties that change causes, he concludes by reminding us that many individuals *do* adapt successfully to social change and may even benefit from it.

Didion and Maddocks call for a *return* to previous styles and patterns, a moving away from present conditions in cities and in our general culture back to somewhat simpler values. Bennis suggests wholesale changes in behavior, in *how* we do what we do, without changing *why* we do it. There are, of course, many educators and social commentators who fear the results of change because they are afraid that important values will be sacrificed to technological efficiency.

Everything You Always Wanted to Know About Change (but were afraid to ask)[1]

WARREN BENNIS

1 Change is the metaphysics of our age. There's no need to go into the various shock statistics people cite when they talk about the rate of change in our society, because it's the bread and butter of commencement speeches, of Sunday magazine sections, of all sorts of newspapers, etc. etc. We have books like *Future Shock,* books called the *Tyranny of the Transitory.* I wrote a book myself with Phil Slater a couple of years ago called *The Temporary Society.* The metaphors are all here.

2 What's really fascinating to me is how nothing seems to deter man's almost compulsive desire to unsettle, overthrow or reject the accepted conventions and traditions. *Ecclesiastes,* in the *Old Testament,* glumly observes how man continues to disorder and unsettle his ways. It is a puzzle, because when you look beyond the recent crisis of change in our society and organizations—when you look deep down and see the human tragedies of people and organizations, you realize that's largely what life consists of these days.

3 I remember my first year at the State University of New York at Buffalo, where I and some of my colleagues from East Coast and West Coast colleges had been brought in to take an upstate college into the 20th century with a bang. I talked to a man who had something of a reputation in his field, and who, I felt, was very sad about the changes that were taking place. I noticed how in the course of six or seven months he began to look like a much older man, though

1. This essay is a transcribed version of a speech Warren Bennis gave to an audience interested in how change affects management in large institutions.

he was only in his mid-fifties. He used to walk past my office window almost daily, his shoulders seemed to get more and more stooped as each day went on. Sad affair. He confessed how unhappy he was about the new regime—how angry he felt toward the new president, because the president hadn't consulted him on a number of matters he thought he should have been consulted on. He said: "With the former president, I was in his office every day. I used to do all sorts of things for him. And I used to be called one of his 'commandos.' Now I just feel shoved aside."

4 Most of the book *Future Shock* is a long footnote about what I've just been observing. Yet, I'm puzzled by a whole set of questions. Our organizations and institutions have to change, for all kinds of reasons. But in seeing through the crisis of change to the human and organizational tragedies—like the man with the stooped shoulders—you realize that some people are going to be hurt. It is a dilemma.

5 All of my education and working life has been involved with change. I started off as an undergraduate at Antioch College, an interesting place to me for two reasons. One was its concern with public service and the application of social knowledge to influence society, opinion, and policymakers. The other was that its president at that time, Douglas McGregor, had a great influence on me. He was one of the founding fathers of the Bethel Maine T-group movement, one of the pioneers in group dynamics research and application in this country, one of the first to apply the behavioral sciences to organizational behavior and business. I became interested in small group behavior, which led me to M.I.T. for graduate work, in an interdisciplinary program with an emphasis on social psychology. At that time M.I.T. was the leading intellectual center of group dynamics research in this country, attracting many people in psychoanalytic and social sciences involved in group work.

6 Our study of the small group model led us to some especially interesting insights into understanding how change and innovation occur. Using the small group model, social change is based on a "Truth/Love" model. The assumption behind small group theory is that if we present enough valid data to people and develop a relationship of trust and affection and love, then change can come about. The theory relies on the idea that trust is a historical concept based on repeated interactions. That, if there's enough trust, and enough truth, most changes can take place. This is in contradistinction to a model of change based on dissension, or conflict, or people operating on political, social or economic interest facts.

7 The small group model of change also avoids situations where some people can lose. By and large, the literature in small group theory emphasizes the consensus model, which means that nobody gets too badly hurt.

8 The third aspect of the small group model is that social change tends to take place in an environmental void. Change can come from within, change agents are indigenous to the group, and the group is adaptive to cope with changes from forces within the group.

9 For those who create and manage change, there are many models to choose from. One is the "Truth/Love" model described above, which can also be called the "human relations" model. It relies on three things: participation of the people involved in the change, which is what most of us want; trust in the people who are the basic proponents or advocates or leaders of the change; and, thirdly, clarity about the change. That is, what it's going to be. If those three factors aren't taken into account, tremendous mistakes occur when changes are made.

10 The clearer one is about what the innovation is going to be; all things being equal, the better the chance that the change will be adopted. The more participation of the people to be affected by the change, the better are chances for adoption, and for acceptance rather than limitation. The more trust in the people advocating the change, the more implementation follows.

11 But just to take one problem—clarity. It's very difficult to make innovations really clear. In fact, one of the most interesting things about innovation is that it's really a kind of inkblot. It's a projective screen. And it's seductive as well as projective. People can project their most anxious fantasies about it, but it also seduces interesting people into it, who are usually of two kinds—those who are rebellious and disruptive, and others who are more moderate establishment types.

12 There's some data from research to indicate that the human relations model works. Unfortunately, however, it doesn't work often enough. Clarity, participation, trust—they can't always be brought into the innovation. Sometimes you have to use the *power* model.

13 Despite all the nice things I've said about the human relations model, it is a fact that there has been no really basic radical restructuring of any institution by consensus. The only time restructuring of any institution has ever taken place is when someone in power said it *will* take place. Why? Because people have a terrible time restructuring themselves when they fear that their status, their power, their esteem are going to be lowered.

14 Between these two extremes of the human relations model and the power model there are other, perhaps more subtle, models. At Buffalo, for example, when I set up the new non-disciplinary department of social sciences, I was only able to get away with it partly through power. It was clear that I wanted it very badly, it was clear that this was the honeymoon period of my stay there, and it was clear that I had come to Buffalo in order to set up the new department. It was

also very clear that I had money from Ford. Even with all those forces, the only way I could really get it through the faculty was by setting up the idea of a *temporary system.* And by saying: "What we're going to do is look at this program five years from now. We'll call it a program and not a department, and we'll evaluate it by certain criteria."

15 Part of my ulterior motive was to get the departments as well to evaluate themselves. What I really had in mind was this. "Wouldn't it be marvelous if you made all departments temporary programs?" Instead, what happened is that less than a month later the faculty made this new program a department. They were more than a little concerned with the notion of a program. So they legitimized something, partly for me and partly for their security, long before it should have been legitimized. And now it's permanent.

16 There's a great story about Berkeley, where in the last 10 to 15 years 88 centers were established to function interstitially between the more formal departments. Not one of them has been terminated, with but one exception. That was a one-man center, and the man died.

17 We have an awesome capacity to perpetuate things long after their reason for existence has passed. Which is why I believe in built-in rules of destruction for some situations.

18 My plan at Buffalo didn't work. I got the program, but I lost the principle . . . and I was almost more interested in the principle of temporary systems. You can restructure, but restructuring has to come from above. At Buffalo, we restructured the whole place in such a way that you could remove lots of people from power without confronting that issue of status deprivation, or of people being fired. We removed the anxiety. Or rather, we tended to thwart it. At least, for a while.

19 All groups in general, but professional groups in particular, do not change unless they are forced to, and they are forced to usually by three different means.

20 One thing that forces change is the "Young Turks," which I call cabals. I have a funny distinction, which is arbitrary. I always think about organizations and change in terms of two groups: the cabals and the cliques. The cliques are in power. They have the dough, the resources, they're the establishment. The cabals are usually the younger people who are fighting the cliques. There's a high price to pay in this situation, because it really means revolution. It means that the cabals ultimately take over. Good cliques know how to co-opt cabals. They absorb protest and establish a new equilibrium through a very interesting and important way of politics, which is to co-opt. And when they don't co-opt, they get into very deep trouble. One can almost do a forecast of the growth and adaptability of professional organizations on the basis of how they deal with their younger people coming up. Do they kick them out, or do they try to co-opt them?

21 Talk to young architects, for example. The cabals are gaining a lot of strength, and the changes in society are more or less allied with the cabals. At the same time, our systems of education do not encourage significant change, by and large. One of the big mysteries in my life is how graduate education can be so basically authoritarian and still produce people who grow up to challenge the system. How is it that these young architects, who have been trained by other architects with an older "paradigm" of what architecture is, are challenging their older colleagues to their very core? I think they're getting away with it now because society simply cannot afford to develop another generation of narcissistic architects who want to put up their own beautiful mementos. You now have to think about many people-environment interactions; you have to think about systems. You have to think about the three major deficiencies experienced in all institutions nowadays: purpose, community and power.

22 Another way organizations change is through external events: the forces of society impinging on the organization. Professional groups are particularly immune to change from this source. It is very difficult to get them to redefine their professional competence, because it really seems to be a blow to their narcissism, and what you get is a guarded and defensive response.

23 When I was at Buffalo, I found that my department chairmen would rarely respond to any reality hitting them, except from the narrow viewpoint of their own disciplinary department. This is true of all organizations and institutions. The Army fights the Navy. But it is more severe within professional groupings. I used to kid my department chairman by reminding him of that old story of the Jew, who, when he read the newspaper would ask only one question: "Is it good or bad for the Jews?"

24 Change through external events is usually bad for the "Jews." It's bad for the profession and the organization when it happens.

25 The third way change comes about is more profound. If I had to define what is the most important thing about change in professional and organizational life, I would answer in terms of what might be called the "culture" of a profession, or the "paradigm" of a profession.

26 In a marvelous book called *The Structure of Scientific Revolutions,* Thomas Kuhn wrote about how advances are made in science. His basic concept is that there's something called a "paradigm" in science, something akin to a *Zietgeist,* or a climate of opinion which governs the choices made. Here are his words: "The constellation of values and beliefs shared by the members of a scientific community, that determines the choice, problems which are regarded as significant, and the approaches to be adopted in attempting to solve it."

27 Kuhn's point is that the men who revolutionized science were

always those who changed the paradigm. One of the interesting changes in paradigms today, for example, is in the social sciences: the deep concern with the conscious, introspective phenomenological aspects of personality or the subtle shift away from logical positivism toward intervention research.

28 The professors are saying, "The subjective consciousness is just your feeling, let's talk about objectivity."

29 The students are saying, "I know what I feel." (Or rather, I *know* what I feel.) Their revulsion against the strategy of truth based on symbols that are both verbal and quantitative is very big. There's a real collision of these two paradigms right now, one based on the more accepted canons of science, the other based on subjective feelings.

30 Max Weber, the sociologist, was interested in the same phenomenon. Writing about how scientific change comes about, he said: "At some time the color changes. Men become uncertain about the significance of their viewpoints, which they have used unreflectively. The path becomes lost in the dusk. The life of the great problems of culture has passed on. The science also prepares to change its standpoint and its conceptual apparatus in order to look down from the heights of thought upon the current of events."

31 Paradigms, "domain assumptions"—as Weber called them—they're all talking about the same thing. What is it that governs what a profession does? How does it deal with dissent in that group? What information does it use to change and adapt itself? And how do we in the professions—and in industry—identify, locate and reward people who are *role innovators?* That is, people who don't just change the content of a particular discipline, but change its practice.

32 Role innovators shift the whole paradigm in a practice sense. A Ralph Nader has totally shifted a paradigm of practice about the law. When he was at Harvard Law School, he got but one course that had anything to do with consumers. And that really didn't have much to do with consumers. It was on torts, which was the closest thing to it.

33 Freud, of course, is a great example of a role innovator, as is a Keynes, or Samuelson, or Gropius. What they did was to create a new metaphor of practice in a way that was very compelling, that was not only scientifically valid, but that had a rhetoric and appeal that people found hard to deny.

34 Innovation—new paradigm, a new way of practice, or a role innovation—has to be compelling, because pre-existing theory and practice are never replaced by data disconfirming them. They are only replaced by a new theory or practice, not by studies which show that the old way no longer works.

35 It is not so much the articulation of goals of what a profession *should* be doing that creates a new practice. It's the imagery that

creates the understanding, the compelling moral necessity that the new way is right. You have to ask, "What are the mechanisms?" It was the beautiful writing of Darwin about his travels on the *Beagle,* rather than the content of his writing, that made the difference. Because the evolutionary idea had really been in the air for a while. There were not only parallel mentions of it, but Darwin's uncle had done some of the primary work on it. It was Freud's five cases, it's Erickson's attention to the specimen he chooses, that makes all the difference. It's Kenneth Burke's "representative anecdote."

36 If I were to give off-the-cuff advice to anyone trying to institute change, I would say, "How clear is the metaphor, how is that understood? How much energy are you devoting to it?" Because I think it's more energy than it is courage.

37 Another thing I would ask is, "How well are you policing the people who give birth to what is called the 'Pinocchio' syndrome? That is, people who take your ideas and then convert them, distort them, and create real problems for you?"

38 Innovations are always seductive and bring in interesting people, some of whom do not, in fact, gain you adherents, but instead lose them. I've always thought Branch Rickey was one of the greatest change agents. Before bringing the first Black ball player into the Brooklyn Dodgers he made sure he was impeccable, that he was the best. You can't always do this, but you must try to evaluate the embodiment of innovation in a more vigilant manner than you would when filling more orthodox positions.

39 In innovation, you get a sense of wanting to proselytize. The eagerness to gain adherents often leads to problems about standards. One doesn't want to be old-fashioned about it, but there is a question.

40 There's another thing that worries me about innovation in the present situation. Historically, innovations have occurred during periods of economic abundance and plenty, because then the cruel collisions between two paradigms can be somehow mitigated through running parallel institutions, or through adding and increasing and expanding. It's tough when you're in a situation where you're both clamoring for the same resources. This is why I'm not sanguine right now about almost any innovation.

41 How do you identify and develop role innovators? How do you spot new information in institutions, organizations, professions, etc.?

42 I've discovered that people who are very sensitive to changes of a realistic kind are very often marginal to the institution they're a part of, almost in a geographical sense. They're cut off and not seen as good "company men." They have contacts in other areas, other institutions. Often they're not rewarded, because they're seen as troublemakers, mischievous. Quite often organizations respond to them by reducing their rewards, in turn causing a lowered commitment which

in turn usually leads to more deviant and perhaps, finally, disruptive behavior. It's a sort of vicious cycle. Sometimes these so-called marginal men take on other jobs which realistically makes them less committed to the institution. If an administrator tries to identify those people and make them his own tentacles of change, and bring them together, that's one force for inducing role innovation. I tried to do this at Buffalo, choosing people who were variance sensors yet who were viewed with some respect by their colleagues. Maybe a little bit crazy, or different, but respected. I brought these people together and used them almost as extensions of the things I was interested in.

43 You can also use more formal political rewards for role innovators, by giving them power, money, status. It's that simple. Quite often I also brought in review boards from outside, people carefully selected in part by me, in part by the particular group affected by the innovation. This can be a useful tactic to prevent the innovator from coming into daily conflict with the resistors. It legitimizes and validates whatever changes are taking place.

44 With or without gimmicks like review boards, however, you can simply create a climate which allows accepted conventions to be questioned and challenged. And by God, we'll have to, because this is exactly what's happening with the bright young people coming into these institutions right now. It's a kind of juggernaut situation. If you look at the new and the old culture, along the authoritarian personality scale, along sociological scales, it's very clear what the value differences are. A lot has to do with openness and candor versus the kind of loyalty to accepted conventions, to the kind of secrecy which most institutions seem to use. How do we create a climate of candor and openness, where we embrace error, rather than aim for the safe low-risk goals that get eventual payoffs and rewards? This is especially needed in professional organizations, which are not high-risk institutions. Like the university, in my view one of the most medieval of institutions.

45 What I consider to be the most significant aspect of change is something like this. Organizations, by definition, are social systems where people have norms, values, shared beliefs and paradigms of what's right and what's wrong and what's legitimate and what isn't, of how practice is conducted. One gains status and power on the basis of the agreement, concurrence and conformity with those paradigms. How can you, within a profession, change the paradigms from within, without being seen as too deviant, or too divisively disruptive? How do you learn to evalute information which might be interpreted as antithetical to the particular paradigm which then holds? How do you identify and reward people who continually are dissonant in the organization, who are dissident by continually questioning. Not people who play devil's advocate, for I'm not in favor of establishing

and legitimizing roles called "Devil's Advocate." I know too much of what happens to these people. You begin calling someone the Devil's Advocate. You listen to that person's opposing point of view—all the while feeling very self-righteous and absolving your guilt—and then you continue to do just what you did in the first place. George Ball, the White House dove, serves as a good example. He would be wheeled into Johnson's office, he'd be listened to very politely, and he'd be wheeled out and the whole thing would go on again. I think of it as the "domestication of dissent."

46 So, how do you get role innovation, people who change practice? How do you detect signs, cues, and get the right information ingested into the system? How do you develop an environment that will not squash the role innovators? Because the impulse within any paradigm is to squeeze them out, to make them leave. Their voices are too upsetting, so we ask them to exit. Or, we stop listening.

47 How do you encourage change from within? Or do you have to take a Ralph Nader stance and attack from the outside? Is that the only way institutions can change?

48 When you think about the interdependence of institutions right now, when you think about the turbulence of the environment, and the boundary transactions between and among organizations, the number of technological and other kinds of changes that are forcing themselves on institutions, the question is not how we develop innovation, the question is how do we screen and select the right alternatives. The question is this: Can you develop an organization which sees reality—not becoming faddish, spastic, other-directed and reactive to every trend and whim that takes place—without becoming rigid, guarded and frozen? Can you establish a pro-active, realistic organization? Obviously, if our institutions start adopting everything new, they will merely become trendy, disposable systems, with no inner core or integrity, much like an organizational counterpart to Peer Gynt.

49 Another great concern of mine is this. How do you communicate to people that certain changes *have* to take place, maybe even substantial changes, without creating in them such *deep* resistance based on role irrelevance and incompetence and insensitivities? I'm frankly more worried, from my own experience as consultant and administrator, about the people who really fear change more than disaster. The conservative factor is always there. Where I think change-oriented people make mistakes is in thinking they're going to do away with history. That is the basic problem, because in fact most people interested in change have very ambitious hopes. They have an illusion, an omnipotent fantasy, of the clean slate. I saw it destroyed too many times.

50 Every social system contains the forces for movement and the

forces for conservatism—in the best sense of that word, and that is to conserve the best and to move with some of the things one ought to move with. The point is, there are always conservative and progressive forces within every institution. One or the other of these two sides quite often tries to blot out the other, which is about as successful as blotting out one's ambivalence.

51 If anything, I would call myself a relentless gradualist at this point. Because I've been reading history this year, and I've been very sad about seeing the kind of slowness of really basic changes in our social system. It's not very much. With all the talk about change and temporary society, I'm painfully aware of the famous crack of Crane Brinton, who said that the only thing the French Revolution brought about was the metric system. I should add to that, Napoleon.

52 I'm saddened also by something else. I've had long periods of very deep concern with the fusion of theory and practice, with the hope that rationality was the only way which we could ever reach anything like a civilization And a conviction that the basic "two cultures" problem in the world is not the one that C. P. Snow has revived between scientists and humanists, but between men who had knowledge and no power, and men who had power and no knowledge. I kept hoping, I suppose somewhat romantically, that somehow men who write history and men who make history would have a broadening affinity.

53 One of the things I felt proudest about at Buffalo was developing the new program of applied social sciences—or Policy Sciences—to try to shape and modify and integrate the social sciences so that they can have an impact on systems, on policy, and so on. But this was also something that caused me a good deal of concern, and ambivalence. Quite often I oscillate to feelings of great despair when I realize that, probably, social knowledge is the weakest form of social influence known to man. Then I think of the difficulty of fusing theory and practice, of somehow trying to develop knowledge that really has clout and impact on how people really behave and on policy, and I'm often reminded of that line from an Auden poem, in which a character says something like, "He's lecturing on navigation while the ship is going down."

54 To return to the question of change, and how you implement it. What I'm saying is that there are a variety of ways. Under which conditions you use various models has a great deal to do with the complexity and existential aspect of the group or the organization in question, and its history.

55 It would be foolish to advocate any single model. I have used the power model, the human relations model, the re-structuring model, the temporary systems model. You could also do something which I think is probably best of anything, which is to set up within any unit or sub-unit of the organization a small rotating group of people who

will be called "organization renewal" people, and who will probably use data and other ideas in order to create incremental changes. So, there are lots of ways.

56 What I think most people in institutions really want—and what status, money and power serve as currency for—is affection, acceptance, a belief in their growth, and esteem. I think you can create changes and innovations if you succeed in not losing the affection for the people who, on the face of it, seem to be losing it. I really feel that people stay in organizations, and are satisfied in them, because they're loved and feel competent. And that we use these other things —status, money, power—as fungibles. Is there even a way of shifting some of the tangible resources and still not having that love lost? In many professional organizations it's very difficult. I would never make that statement to my department heads or deans. They would say, "Quit psychologizing, and what's all that love nonsense. We're really interested in the bucks."

57 I don't even want to argue. I've taken an easy way out, which is simply to use the money and status argument and say, "Okay, these are the levers, these are the above-the-surface counters, this is what the meter reads." But in fact it's love and esteem.

58 And so, when you want to make changes, you try to bring along with you those who perhaps have the old way of looking at things, along with the new. You don't make it an Either/Or proposition. Nor do you try to domesticate the resistors. (I've spent too much time in my life with people who cholerically defend obsolete conventions.)

59 What is it that creates within people an identification with the adaptive process? What is it that creates a man who has a high tolerance for ambiguity? What is it that makes people throughout their lives *learning* men and women? I wish I knew. You can see it, and you can feel it, the people who are learning as they go along. But, by God, I wish I knew what the personality aspects were, what the educational components were, what the developmental process is, what the family background was. I don't think we know.

60 But it's clear that some people—and it's not just age—continue to learn and grow throughout their lifetimes.

Thinking Questions: *Form*

1. Consider the following specific comparisons in relation to Warren Bennis's general attitude toward change.

a. In paragraphs 14 and 15, Bennis describes his efforts in constructing an interdisciplinary sociology program at the State University of New York at Buffalo. The description includes a comparison of Bennis's earlier desire to make the program temporary and his later displeasure when it was made permanent. How does this comparison contribute to Bennis's idea that change must become an expected part of anyone's future planning? How can anyone or any institution plan for changes that cannot be foreseen?

b. In paragraphs 20 and 21, Bennis compares two institutional groups: *cabals* or *Young Turks* (young people in an institution who fight the established powers and usually support change) and *cliques* (veterans who hold the power and usually fight change). What does Bennis suggest should be done about this group conflict by those leaders and managers who want to support meaningful change? How might the conflict between the cabals and the cliques be turned into an institutional advantage, according to Bennis?

c. In paragraph 49, Bennis compares his desire, as an administrative leader, to implement and encourage change with his corresponding desire not to threaten those individuals in the institution who wish to avoid change. Does he suggest a way to encourage change without making some individuals feel useless or irrelevant? What does Bennis mean when he says that any leader who wishes to encourage change must remember that he is *not* beginning with a "clean slate"?

All three of these comparisons help Bennis develop his general thesis, each showing contrasting extremes that the moderate administrator uses to his own ends.

2. In paragraph 55, Bennis uses logical division to organize his material. He describes the (1) power, (2) human relations, (3) re-structuring, and (4) temporary systems methods of organizing and implementing change. What particular method does he seem to favor and why? Or does he suggest using any or all of the four methods when the particular situation demands their use? Which method would you prefer and why? Finally, are there other instances of this method of organization in this essay?

3. In paragraph 51, Bennis describes himself as a "relentless gradualist." Define this term fully and explain what it means in relation to sound management. Which of the above methods of implementing change would the "relentless gradualist" prefer?

4. How would you characterize Bennis's voice in this essay? Is he trying to be formal, informal, intimate, or distant with his readers? What do the following sentences tell you about his voice and style? Notice the use of contractions, dashes, parentheses, the predominance of colloquial phrases and simple, cumulative, subject-verb sentence structures, even an occasional sentence fragment.

–I'm saddened also by something else.
–Another great concern of mine is this.
–You listen to that person's opposing point of view–all the while feeling very self-righteous and absolving your guilt–and then you continue to do just what you did in the first place.
–Talk to young architects, for example.

–It's a sort of vicious cycle.

–It's that simple.

–Like the university, in my view one of the most medieval of institutions.

–(I've spent too much time in my life with people who cholerically defend obsolete conventions.)

–I wish I knew.

5. Bennis uses a great variety of strategies to develop his paragraphs. Can you find specific examples of the following five methods of paragraph development? Begin by isolating the main idea or topic sentence of the paragraph, then show how the main idea is developed by one of these methods.

a. simple *illustration by example,* in which a general idea is introduced and examples cited to support the generality.

b. *comparison,* in which a general idea is developed by the comparison of two specific parts of that idea.

c. *classification or logical division,* in which a main idea is developed by division into constituent parts.

d. *definition,* in which a key term or idea is defined, its limits set, examples given, and the reader instructed as to what the term *does* and *does not* mean.

e. *cause and effect,* in which an idea is explained through an analysis of what caused it, or by an enumeration of the effects of a particular cause.

Thinking Questions: *Substance*

1. Throughout his essay Warren Bennis compares the uses of power and of love to implement change. He would prefer to use the small group ideal of truth/love (see paragraph 6) as a model for directing change. But he also recognizes (in paragraph 12) that change often cannot occur without some kind of application of power. By the end of his essay, how does Bennis suggest solving the problem of power versus love?

2. Why does Bennis continually refer to his own administrative experiences? Do they help clarify the general problems that he discusses? Does his description of the failure of his own "temporary systems" model of management (paragraph 15) at Buffalo indicate that he no longer believes in the "temporary systems" approach in general? Show how at least one of his personal experiences relates to his thesis.

3. In your own experiences with groups, is it true that most individuals prefer security over the stress of change, no matter what the results? Or is it more true that most people are too quick to jump on the bandwagon in support of *any* potential change? Give examples. Cite your experience, as Bennis cites his, to support your own ideas.

4. In an essay earlier in this section, Melvin Maddocks criticizes group therapy and analysis because he believes they are one of the reasons people in general no longer respect other people's privacy. Reread paragraphs 6 and 7 in this essay and explain how decisions would be made

in an institution where small group systems were used. Would there be an inevitable tendency for people to invade one another's privacy in a small group system, where *trust, understanding,* and *affection* were continually being emphasized rather than the "hard facts" of the situation?

5. What would you do to relieve the anxiety of the man Bennis describes in paragraph 3? How would you convince him that he was still important and useful? Or, perhaps more importantly, how would you encourage him to contribute to a new system when he does not yet know what he thinks of the system's efficiency and worth?

* * *

Even among scientists themselves, there are fears about a future dominated by technology and "efficiency." In "The Other Road," Rachel Carson argues specifically against the uncontrolled scientific exploitation of nature. We must learn to respect and *live with* our natural environment, learning in the process to see ourselves as part of a very complex ecological system, as much dependent on nature's processes as nature herself depends on our respect for those processes: "The 'control of nature' is a phrase conceived in arrogance, born in the Neanderthal age of biology and philosophy, when it was supposed that nature exists for the convenience of man," Carson argues. We must learn to understand nature as an interdependent system in which every species must exist together, with the hope of fostering balance and control, a give-and-take among all species. Her book *Silent Spring,* in which this essay appeared, was one of the first popular scientific work to raise this question.

Yet Rachel Carson also believes that scientific methods—the objective and systematic analysis of nature as an interdependent system—can help us develop that balance. "The Other Road" specifically examines biologists' recent attempts to develop natural methods of insect control to replace the widespread use of chemical poisons such as DDT. She describes in detail research that has used insect sterilization and the introduction of natural diseases into insect colonies to control the population of harmful insects.

Rachel Carson uses these examples of natural insect control to illustrate in detail how science can help develop a respect for nature rather than continue to encourage a purely exploitative relationship in which people use natural resources and the land without replenishing it. Science, she argues, can help us understand natural systems and, if used wisely, can help us maintain the balance that is necessary to the continued working of complex ecological systems.

But many artists would argue that nature, no matter how efficiently we use scientific methods, can never be reduced to a clearly understood system. Kurt Vonnegut, Jr.'s story "The Euphio Question" illustrates how technology used without forethought can be misused, how machines can provide us with leisure and pleasure while destroying free choice, thought, and all that we traditionally have valued as essentially human. Just as, in Huxley's *Brave New World, soma,* a synthetic, pleasure-producing narcotic, allows the government to control the working and professional classes by providing instant pleasure, Vonnegut's euphio machine provides instant euphoria for all, at a high price in human dignity and freedom. The euphio machine destroys initiative, effort—all the productive pleasures—and replaces them with an innocuous, mindless sensory bath. Such literature raises an essential question: how much control, responsibility, and choice are people willing to sacrifice for lives of ease and pleasure? And, perhaps more importantly, who should make such decisions? Finally, Vonnegut's story also shows us how much we are already controlled by technological devices: television, radio, and all the electronic media. Like the philosopher Herbert Marcuse, Vonnegut asks us what we really want from our leisure time. As machines free us from many of the restraints of work, as eight-hour days are replaced by six-hour days and five-day work weeks by four, what do we want from our "free" time?

The Other Road

RACHEL CARSON

1 We stand now where two roads diverge. But unlike the roads in Robert Frost's familiar poem, they are not equally fair. The road we have long been traveling is deceptively easy, a smooth superhighway on which we progress with great speed, but at its end lies disaster. The other fork of the road—the one "less traveled by"—offers our last, our only chance to reach a destination that assures the preservation of our earth

2 The choice, after all, is ours to make. If, having endured much, we have at last asserted our "right to know," and if, knowing, we have concluded that we are being asked to take senseless and frightening risks, then we should no longer accept the counsel of those who tell us that we must fill our world with poisonous chemicals; we should look about and see what other course is open to us.

3 A truly extraordinary variety of alternatives to the chemical control of insects is available. Some are already in use and have achieved brilliant success. Others are in the stage of laboratory testing. Still

others are little more than ideas in the minds of imaginative scientists, waiting for the opportunity to put them to the test. All have this in common: they are *biological* solutions, based on understanding of the living organisms they seek to control, and of the whole fabric of life to which these organisms belong. Specialists representing various areas of the vast field of biology are contributing—entomologists, pathologists, geneticists, physiologists, biochemists, ecologists—all pouring their knowledge and their creative inspirations into the formation of a new science of biotic controls.

4 "Any science may be likened to a river," says a Johns Hopkins biologist, Professor Carl P. Swanson. "It has its obscure and unpretentious beginning; its quiet stretches as well as its rapids; its periods of drought as well as of fullness. It gathers momentum with the work of many investigators and as it is fed by other streams of thought; it is deepened and broadened by the concepts and generalizations that are gradually evolved."

5 So it is with the science of biological control in its modern sense. In Amercia it had its obscure beginnings a century ago with the first attempts to introduce natural enemies of insects that were proving troublesome to farmers, an effort that sometimes moved slowly or not at all, but now and again gathered speed and momentum under the impetus of an outstanding success. It had its period of drought when workers in applied entomology, dazzled by the spectacular new insecticides of the 1940's, turned their backs on all biological methods and set foot on "the treadmill of chemical control." But the goal of an insect-free world continued to recede. Now at last, as it has become apparent that the heedless and unrestrained use of chemicals is a greater menace to ourselves than to the targets, the river which is the science of biotic control flows again, fed by new streams of thought.

6 Some of the most fascinating of the new methods are those that seek to turn the strength of a species against itself—to use the drive of an insect's life forces to destroy it. The most spectacular of these approaches is the "male sterilization" technique developed by the chief of the United States Department of Agriculture's Entomology Research Branch, Dr. Edward Knipling, and his associates.

7 About a quarter of a century ago Dr Knipling startled his colleagues by proposing a unique method of insect control. If it were possible to sterilize and release large numbers of insects, he theorized, the sterilized males would, under certain conditions, compete with the normal wild males so successfully that, after repeated releases, only infertile eggs would be produced and the population would die out.

8 The proposal was met with bureaucratic inertia and with skepticism from scientists, but the idea persisted in Dr. Knipling's mind. One

major problem remained to be solved before it could be put to the test—a practical method of insect sterilization had to be found. Academically, the fact that insects could be sterilized by exposure to X-ray had been known since 1916, when an entomologist by the name of G. A. Runner reported such sterilization of cigarette beetles. Hermann Muller's pioneering work on the production of mutations by X-ray opened up vast new areas of thought in the late 1920's, and by the middle of the century various workers had reported the sterilization by X-rays or gamma rays of at least a dozen species of insects.

9 But these were laboratory experiments, still a long way from practical application. About 1950, Dr. Knipling launched a serious effort to turn insect sterilization into a weapon that would wipe out a major insect enemy of livestock in the South, the screw-worm fly. The females of this species lay their eggs in any open wound of a warm-blooded animal. The hatching larvae are parasitic, feeding on the flesh of the host. A full-grown steer may succumb to a heavy infestation in 10 days, and livestock losses in the United States have been estimated at $40,000,000 a year. The toll of wildlife is harder to measure, but it must be great. Scarcity of deer in some areas of Texas is attributed to the screw-worm. This is a tropical or subtropical insect, inhabiting South and Central America and Mexico, and in the United States normally restricted to the Southwest. About 1933, however, it was accidentally introduced into Florida, where the climate allowed it to survive over winter and to establish populations. It even pushed into southern Alabama and Georgia, and soon the livestock industry of the southeastern states was faced with annual losses running to $20,000,000.

10 A vast amount of information on the biology of the screw-worm had been accumulated over the years by Agriculture Department scientists in Texas. By 1954, after some preliminary field trials on Florida islands, Dr. Knipling was ready for a full-scale test of his theory. For this, by arrangement with the Dutch Government, he went to the island of Curaçao in the Caribbean, cut off from the mainland by at least 50 miles of sea.

11 Beginning in August 1954, screw-worms reared and sterilized in an Agriculture Department laboratory in Florida were flown to Curaçao and released from airplanes at the rate of about 400 per square mile per week. Almost at once the number of egg masses deposited on experimental goats began to decrease, as did their fertility. Only seven weeks after the releases were started, all eggs were infertile. Soon it was impossible to find a single egg mass, sterile or otherwise. The screw-worm had indeed been eradicated on Curaçao.

12 The resounding success of the Curaçao experiment whetted the appetites of Florida livestock raisers for a similar feat that would relieve them of the scourge of screw-worms. Although the difficulties

here were relatively enormous—an area 300 times as large as the small Caribbean island—in 1957 the United States Department of Agriculture and the State of Florida joined in providing funds for an eradication effort. The project involved the weekly production of about 50 million screw-worms at a specially constructed "fly factory," the use of 20 light airplanes to fly pre-arranged flight patterns, five to six hours daily, each plane carrying a thousand paper cartons, each carton containing 200 to 400 irradiated flies.

13 The cold winter of 1957-58, when freezing temperatures gripped northern Florida, gave an unexpected opportunity to start the program while the screw-worm populations were reduced and confined to a small area. By the time the program was considered complete at the end of 17 months, 3½ billion artificially reared, sterilized flies had been released over Florida and sections of Georgia and Alabama. The last-known animal wound infestation that could be attributed to screw-worms occurred in February 1959. In the next few weeks several adults were taken in traps. Thereafter no trace of the screw-worm could be discovered. Its extinction in the Southeast had been accomplished—a triumphant demonstration of the worth of scientific creativity, aided by thorough basic research, persistence, and determination.

14 Now a quarantine barrier in Mississippi seeks to prevent the re-entrance of the screw-worms from the Southwest, where it is firmly entrenched. Eradication there would be a formidable undertaking, considering the vast areas involved and the probability of re-invasion from Mexico. Nevertheless, the stakes are high and the thinking in the Department seems to be that some sort of program, designed at least to hold the screw-worm populations at very low levels, may soon be attempted in Texas and other infested areas of the Southwest.

15 The brilliant success of the screw-worm campaign has stimulated tremendous interest in applying the same methods to other insects. Not all, of course, are suitable subjects for this technique, much depending on details of the life history, population density, and reactions to radiation.

16 Experiments have been undertaken by the British in the hope that the method could be used against the tsetse fly in Rhodesia. This insect infests about a third of Africa, posing a menace to human health and preventing the keeping of livestock in an area of some 4½ million square miles of wooded grasslands. The habits of the tsetse differ considerably from those of the screw-worm fly, and although it can be sterilized by radiation some technical difficulties remain to be worked out before the method can be applied.

17 The British have already tested a large number of other species for susceptibility to radiation. United States scientists have had some

encouraging early results with the melon fly and the oriental and Mediterranean fruit flies in laboratory tests in Hawaii and field tests on the remote island of Rota. The corn borer and the surgarcane borer are also being tested. There are possibilities, too, that insects of medical importance might be controlled by sterilization. A Chilean scientist has pointed out that malaria-carrying mosquitoes persist in his country in spite of insecticide treatment; the release of sterile males might then provide the final blow needed to eliminate this population.

18 The obvious difficulties of sterilizing by radiation have led to search for an easier method of accomplishing similar results, and there is now a strongly running tide of interest in chemical sterilants.

19 Scientists at the Department of Agriculture laboratory in Orlando, Florida, are now sterilizing the housefly in laboratory experiments and even in some field trials, using chemicals incorporated in suitable foods. In a test on an island in the Florida Keys in 1961, a population of flies was nearly wiped out wthin a period of only five weeks. Repopulation of course followed from nearby islands, but as a pilot project the test was successful. The Department's excitement about the promise of this method is easily understood. In the first place, as we have seen, the housefly has now become virtually uncontrollable by insecticides. A completely new method of control is undoubtedly needed. One of the problems of sterilization by radiation is that this requires not only artificial rearing but the release of sterile males in larger number than are present in the wild population. This could be done with the screw-worm, which is actually not an abundant insect. With the housefly, however, more than doubling the population through releases could be highly objectionable, even though the increase would be only temporary. A chemical sterilant, on the other hand, could be combined with a bait substance and introduced into the natural environment of the fly; insects feeding on it would become sterile and in the course of time the sterile flies would predominate and the insects would breed themselves out of existence.

20 The testing of chemicals for a sterilizing effect is much more difficult than the testing of chemical poisons. It takes 30 days to evaluate one chemical—although, of course, a number of tests can be run concurrently. Yet between April 1958 and December 1961 several hundred chemicals were screened at the Orlando laboratory for a possible sterilizing effect. The Department of Agriculture seems happy to have found among these even a handful of chemicals that show promise.

21 Now other laboratories of the Department are taking up the problem, testing chemicals against stable flies, mosquitoes, boll weevils, and an assortment of fruit flies. All this is presently experimental but in the few years since work began on chemosterilants the project has

grown enormously. In theory it has many attractive features. Dr. Knipling has pointed out that effective chemical insect sterilization "might easily outdo some of the best of known insecticides." Take an imaginary situation in which a population of a million insects is multiplying five times in each generation. An insecticide might kill 90 per cent of each generation, leaving 125,000 insects alive after the third generation. In contrast, a chemical that would produce 90 per cent sterility would leave only 125 insects alive.

22 On the other side of the coin is the fact that some extremely potent chemicals are involved. It is fortunate that at least during these early stages most of the men working with chemosterilants seem mindful of the need to find safe chemicals and safe methods of application. Nonetheless, suggestions are heard here and there that these sterilizing chemicals might be applied as aerial sprays—for example, to coat the foliage chewed by gypsy moth larvae. To attempt any such procedure without thorough advance research on the hazards involved would be the height of irresponsibility. If the potential hazards of the chemosterilants are not constantly borne in mind we could easily find ourselves in even worse trouble than that now created by the insecticides.

23 The sterilants currently being tested fall generally into two groups, both of which are extremely interesting in their mode of action. The first are intimately related to the life processes, or metabolism, of the cell; i.e., they so closely resemble a substance the cell or tissue needs that the organism "mistakes" them for the true metabolite and tries to incorporate them in its normal building processes. But the fit is wrong in some detail and the process comes to a halt. Such chemicals are called antimetabolites.

24 The second group consists of chemicals that act on the chromosomes, probably affecting the gene chemicals and causing the chromosomes to break up. The chemosterilants of this group are alkylating agents, which are extremely reactive chemicals, capable of intense cell destruction, damage to chromosomes, and production of mutations. It is the view of Dr. Peter Alexander of the Chester Beatty Research Institute in London that "any alkylating agent which is effective in sterilizing insects would also be a powerful mutagen and carcinogen." Dr. Alexander feels that any conceivable use of such chemicals in insect control would be "open to the most severe objections." It is to be hoped, therefore, that the present experiments will lead not to actual use of these particular chemicals but to the discovery of others that will be safe and also highly specific in their action on the target insect.

25 Some of the most interesting of the recent work is concerned with still other ways of forging weapons from the insect's own life processes. Insects produce a variety of venoms, attractants, repellants.

What is the chemical nature of these secretions? Could we make use of them as, perhaps, very selective insecticides? Scientists at Cornell University and elsewhere are trying to find answers to some of these questions, studying the defense mechanisms by which many insects protect themselves from attack by predators, working out the chemical structure of insect secretions. Other scientists are working on the so-called "juvenile hormone," a powerful substance which prevents metamorphosis of the larval insect until the proper stage of growth has been reached.

26 Perhaps the most immediately useful result of this exploration of insect secretion is the development of lures, or attractants. Here again, nature has pointed the way. The gypsy moth is an especially intriguing example. The female moth is too heavy-bodied to fly. She lives on or near the ground, fluttering about among low vegetation or creeping up tree trunks. The male, on the contrary, is a strong flier and is attracted even from considerable distances by a scent released by the female from special glands. Entomologists have taken advantage of this fact for a good many years, laboriously preparing this sex attractant from the bodies of the female moths. It was then used in traps set for the males in census operations along the fringe of the insect's range. But this was an extremely expensive procedure. Despite the much publicized infestations in the northeastern states, there were not enough gypsy moths to provide the material, and hand-collected female pupae had to be imported from Europe, sometimes at a cost of half a dollar per tip. It was a tremendous breakthrough, therefore, when, after years of effort, chemists of the Agriculture Department recently succeeded in isolating the attractant. Following upon this discovery was the successful preparation of a closely related synthetic material from a constituent of castor oil; this not only deceives the male moths but is apparently fully as attractive as the natural substance. As little as one microgram (1/1000000 gram) in a trap is an effective lure.

27 All this is of much more than academic interest, for the new and economical "gyplure" might be used not merely in census operations but in control work. Several of the more attractive possibilities are now being tested. In what might be termed an experiment in psychological warfare, the attractant is combined with a granular material and distributed by planes. The aim is to confuse the male moth and alter the normal behavior so that, in the welter of attractive scents, he cannot find the true scent trail leading to the female. This line of attack is being carried even further in experiments aimed at deceiving the male into attempting to mate with a spurious female. In the laboratory, male gypsy moths have attempted copulation with chips of wood, vermiculite, and other small, inanimate objects, so long as they were suitably impregnated with gyplure. Whether such diversion

of the mating instinct into nonproductive channels would actually serve to reduce the population remains to be tested, but it is an interesting possibility.

28 The gypsy moth lure was the first sex attractant to be synthesized, but probably there will soon be others. A number of agricultural insects are being studied for possible attractants that man could imitate. Encouraging results have been obtained with the Hessian fly and the tobacco hornworm.

29 Combinations of attractants and poisons are being tried against several insect species. Government scientists have developed an attractant called methyl-eugenol, which male of the oriental fruit fly and the melon fly find irresistible. This has been combined with a poison in tests in the Bonin Islands 450 miles south of Japan. Small pieces of fiberboard were impregnated with the two chemicals and were distributed by air over the entire island chain to attract and kill the male flies. This program of "male annihilation" was begun in 1960: a year later the Agriculture Department estimated that more than 99 per cent of the population had been eliminated. The method as here applied seems to have marked advantages over the conventional broadcasting of insecticides. The poison, an organic phosphorus chemical, is confined to squares of fiberboard which are unlikely to be eaten by wildlife; its residues, moreover, are quickly dissipated and so are not potential contaminants of soil or water.

30 But not all communication in the insect world is by scents that lure or repel. Sound also may be a warning or an attraction. The constant stream of ultrasonic sound that issues from a bat in flight (serving as a radar system to guide it through darkness) is heard by certain moths, enabling them to avoid capture. The wing sounds of approaching parasitic flies warn the larvae of some sawflies to herd together for protection. On the other hand, the sounds made by certain wood-boring insects enable their parasites to find them, and to the male mosquito the wingbeat of the female is a siren song.

31 What use, if any, can be made of this ability of the insect to detect and react to sound? As yet in the experimental stage, but nonetheless interesting, is the initial success in attracting male mosquitoes to playback recordings of the flight sound of the female. The males were lured to a charged grid and so killed. The repellant effect of bursts of ultrasonic sound is being tested in Canada against corn borer and cutworm moths. Two authorities on animal sound, Professors Hubert and Mable Frings of the University of Hawaii, believe that a field method of influencing the behavior of insects with sound only awaits discovery of the proper key to unlock and apply the vast existing knowledge of insect sound production and reception. Repellant sounds may offer greater possibilities than attractants. The Fringses are known for their discovery that starlings scatter in alarm

before a recording of the distress cry of one of their fellows; perhaps somewhere in this fact is a central truth that may be applied to insects. To practical men of industry the possibilities seem real enough so that at least one major electronic corporation is preparing to set up a laboratory to test them.

32 Sound is also being tested as an agent of direct destruction. Ultrasonic sound will kill all mosquito larvae in a laboratory tank; however, it kills other aquatic organisms as well. In other experiments, blowflies, mealworms, and yellow fever mosquitoes have been killed by airborne ultrasonic sound in a matter of seconds. All such experiments are first steps toward wholly new concepts of insect control which the miracles of electronics may some day make a reality.

33 The new biotic control of insects is not wholly a matter of electronics and gamma radiation and other products of man's inventive mind. Some of its methods have ancient roots, based on the knowledge that, like ourselves, insects are subject to disease. Bacterial infections sweep through their populations like the plagues of old; under the onset of a virus their hordes sicken and die. The occurrence of disease in insects was known before the time of Aristotle; the maladies of the silkworm were celebrated in medieval poetry; and through study of the diseases of this same insect the first understanding of the principles of infectious disease came to Pasteur.

34 Insects are beset not only by viruses and bacteria but also by fungi, protozoa, microscopic worms, and other beings from all that unseen world of minute life that, by and large, befriends mankind. For the microbes include not only disease organisms but those that destroy waste matter, make soils fertile, and enter into countless biological processes like fermentation and nitrification. Why should they not also aid us in the control of insects?

35 One of the first to envision such use of microorganisms was the 19th-century zoologist Elie Metchnikoff. During the concluding decades of the 19th and the first half of the 20th centuries the idea of microbial control was slowly taking form. The first conclusive proof that an insect could be brought under control by introducing a disease into its environment came in the late 1930's with the discovery and use of milky disease for the Japanese beetle, which is caused by the spores of a bacterium belonging to the genus *Bacillus.* This classic example of bacterial control has a long history of use in the eastern part of the United States.

36 High hopes now attend tests of another bacterium of this genus—*Bacillus thuringiensis*—originally discovered in Germany in 1911 in the province of Thuringia, where it was found to cause a fatal septicemia in the larvae of the flour moth. This bacterium actually kills by poisoning rather than by disease. Within its vegetative rods there are formed, along with spores, peculiar crystals composed of a

protein substance highly toxic to certain insects, especially to the larvae of the mothlike lepidopteras. Shortly after eating foliage coated with this toxin the larva suffers paralysis, stops feeding, and soon dies. For practical purposes, the fact that feeding is interrupted promptly is of course an enormous advantage, for crop damage stops almost as soon as the pathogen is applied. Compounds containing spores of *Bacillus thuringiensis* are now being manufactured by several firms in the United States under various trade names. Field tests are being made in several countries: in France and Germany against larvae of the cabbage butterfly, in Yugoslavia against the fall webworm, in the Soviet Union against a tent caterpillar. In Panama, where tests were begun in 1961, this bacterial insecticide may be the answer to one or more of the serious problems confronting banana growers. There the root borer is a serious pest of the banana, so weakening its roots that the trees are easily toppled by wind. Dieldrin has been the only chemical effective against the borer, but it has now set in motion a chain of disaster. The borers are becoming resistant. The chemical has also destroyed some important insect predators and so has caused an increase in the tortricids—small, stout-bodied moths whose larvae scar the surface of the bananas. There is reason to hope the new microbial insecticide will eliminate both the tortricids and the borers and that it will do so without upsetting natural controls.

37 In eastern forests of Canada and the United States bacterial insecticides may be one important answer to the problems of such forest insects as the budworms and the gypsy moth. In 1960 both countries began field tests with a commercial preparation of *Bacillus thuringiensis.* Some of the early results have been encouraging. In Vermont, for example, the end results of bacterial control were as good as those obtained with DDT. The main technical problem now is to find a carrying solution that will stick the bacterial spores to the needles of the evergreens. On crops this is not a problem—even a dust can be used. Bacterial insecticides have already been tried on a wide variety of vegetables, especially in California.

38 Meanwhile, other perhaps less spectacular work is concerned with viruses. Here and there in California fields of young alfalfa are being sprayed with a substance as deadly as any insecticide for the destructive alfalfa caterpillar—a solution containing a virus obtained from the bodies of caterpillars that have died because of infection with this exceedingly virulent disease. The bodies of only five diseased caterpillars provide enough virus to treat an acre of alfalfa. In some Canadian forests a virus that affects pine sawflies has proved so effective in control that it has replaced insecticides.

39 Scientists in Czechoslovakia are experimenting with protozoa against webworms and other insect pests, and in the United States

a protozoan parasite has been found to reduce the egg-laying potential of the corn borer.

40 To some the term microbial insecticide may conjure up pictures of bacterial warfare that would endanger other forms of life. This is not true. In contrast to chemicals, insect pathogens are harmless to all but their intended targets. Dr. Edward Steinhaus, an outstanding authority on insect pathology, has stated emphatically that there is "no authenticated recorded instance of a true insect pathogen having caused an infectious disease in a vertebrate animal either experimentally or in nature." The insect pathogens are so specific that they infect only a small group of insects—sometimes a single species. Biologically they do not belong to the type of organisms that cause disease in higher animals or in plants. Also, as Dr. Steinhaus points out, outbreaks of insect disease in nature always remain confined to insects, affecting neither the host plants nor animals feeding on them.

41 Insects have many natural enemies—not only microbes of many kinds but other insects. The first suggestion that an insect might be controlled by encouraging its enemies is generally credited to Erasmus Darwin about 1800. Probably because it was the first generally practiced method of biological control, this setting of one insect against another is widely but erroneously thought to be the only alternative to chemicals.

42 In the United States the true beginnings of conventional biological control date from 1888 when Albert Koebele, the first of a growing army of entomologist explorers, went to Australia to search for natural enemies of the cottony cushion scale that threatened the California citrus industry with destruction. As we have seen, the mission was crowned with spectacular success, and in the century that followed the world has been combed for natural enemies to control the insects that have come uninvited to our shores. In all, about 100 species of imported predators and parasites have become established. Besides the vedalia beetles brought in by Koebele, other importations have been highly successful. A wasp imported from Japan established complete control of an insect attacking eastern apple orchards. Several natural enemies of the spotted alfalfa aphid, an accidental import from the Middle East, are credited with saving the California alfalfa industry. Parasites and predators of the gypsy moth achieved good control, as did the *Tiphia* wasp against the Japanese beetle. Biological control of scales and mealy bugs is estimated to save California several millions of dollars a year—indeed, one of the leading entomologists of that state, Dr. Paul DeBach, has estimated that for an investment of $4,000,000 in biological control work California has received a return of $100,000,000.

43 Examples of successful biological control of serious pests by importing their natural enemies are to be found in some 40 countries

distributed over much of the world. The advantages of such control over chemicals are obvious: it is relatively inexpensive, it is permanent, it leaves no poisonous residues. Yet biological control has suffered from lack of support. California is virtually alone among the states in having a formal program in biological control, and many states have not even one entomologist who devotes full time to it. Perhaps for want of support biological control through insect enemies has not always been carried out with the scientific thoroughness it requires—exacting studies of its impact on the populations of insect prey have seldom been made, and releases have not always been made with the precision that might spell the difference between success and failure.

44 The predator and the preyed upon exist not alone, but as part of a vast web of life, all of which needs to be taken into account. Perhaps the opportunities for the more conventional types of biological control are greatest in the forests. The farmlands of modern agriculture are highly artificial, unlike anything nature ever conceived. But the forests are a different world, much closer to natural environments. Here, with a minimum of help and a maximum of noninterference from man, nature can have her way, setting up all that wonderful and intricate system of checks and balances that protects the forest from undue damage by insects.

45 In the United States our foresters seem to have thought of biological control chiefly in terms of introducing insect parasites and predators. The Canadians take a broader view, and some of the Europeans have gone farthest of all to develop the science of "forest hygiene" to an amazing extent. Birds, ants, forest spiders, and soil bacteria are as much a part of a forest as the trees, in the view of European foresters, who take care to inoculate a new forest with these protective factors. The encouragement of birds is one of the first steps. In the modern era of intensive forestry the old hollow trees are gone and with them homes for woodpeckers and other tree-nesting birds. This lack is met by nesting boxes, which draw the birds back into the forest. Other boxes are specially designed for owls and for bats, so that these creatures may take over in the dark hours the work of insect hunting performed in daylight by the small birds.

46 But this is only the beginning. Some of the most fascinating control work in European forests employs the forest red ant as an aggressive insect predator—a species which, unfortunately, does not occur in North America. About 25 years ago Professor Karl Gösswald of the University of Würzburg developed a method of cultivating this ant and establishing colonies. Under his direction more than 10,000 colonies of the red ant have been established in about 90 test areas in the German Federal Republic. Dr. Gösswald's method has been adopted in Italy and other countries, where ant farms have been

established to supply colonies for distribution in the forests. In the Apennines, for example, several hundred nests have been set out to protect reforested areas.

47 "Where you can obtain in your forest a combination of birds' and ants' protection together with some bats and owls, the biological equilibrium has already been essentially improved," says Dr. Heinz Ruppertshofen, a forestry officer in Mölln, Germany, who believes that a single introduced predator or parasite is less effective than an array of the "natural companions" of the trees.

48 New ant colonies in the forests at Mölln are protected from woodpeckers by wire netting to reduce the toll. In this way the woodpeckers, which have increased by 400 per cent in 10 years in some of the test areas, do not seriously reduce the ant colonies, and pay handsomely for what they take by picking harmful caterpillars off the trees. Much of the work of caring for the ant colonies (and the birds' nesting boxes as well) is assumed by a youth corps from the local school, children 10 to 14 years old. The costs are exceedingly low; the benefits amount to permanent protection of the forests.

49 Another extremely interesting feature of Dr. Ruppertshofen's work is his use of spiders, in which he appears to be a pioneer. Although there is a large literature on the classification and natural history of spiders, it is scattered and fragmentary and deals not at all with their value as an agent of biological control. Of the 22,000 known kinds of spiders, 760 are native to Germany (and about 2000 to the United States). Twenty-nine families of spiders inhabit German forests.

50 To a forester the most important fact about a spider is the kind of net it builds. The wheel-net spiders are most important, for the webs of some of them are so narrow-meshed that they can catch all flying insects. A large web (up to 16 inches in diameter) of the cross spider bears some 120,000 adhesive nodules on its strands. A single spider may destroy in her life of 18 months an average of 2000 insects. A biologically sound forest has 50 to 150 spiders to the square meter (a little more than a square yard). Where there are fewer, the deficiency may be remedied by collecting and distributing the baglike cocoons containing the eggs. "Three cocoons of the wasp spider [which occurs also in America] yield a thousand spiders, which can catch 200,000 flying insects," says Dr. Ruppertshofen. The tiny and delicate young of the wheel-net spiders that emerge in the spring are especially important, he says, "as they spin in a teamwork a net umbrella above the top shoots of the trees and thus protect the young shoots against the flying insects." As the spiders molt and grow, the net is enlarged.

51 Canadian biologists have pursued rather similar lines of investigation, although with differences dictated by the fact that North Ameri-

can forests are largely natural rather than planted, and that the species available as aids in maintaining a healthy forest are somewhat different. The emphasis in Canada is on small mammals, which are amazingly effective in the control of certain insects, especially those that live within the spongy soil of the forest floor. Among such insects are the sawflies, so-called because the female has a saw-shaped ovipositor with which she slits open the needles of evergreen trees in order to deposit her eggs. The larvae eventually drop to the ground and form cocoons in the peat of tamarack bogs or the duff under spruce or pines. But beneath the forest floor is a world honeycombed with the tunnels and runways of small mammals—whitefooted mice, voles, and shrews of various species. Of all these small burrowers, the voracious shrews find and consume the largest number of sawfly cocoons. They feed by placing a forefoot on the cocoon and biting off the end, showing an extraordinary ability to discriminate between sound and empty cocoons. And for their insatiable appetite the shrews have no rivals. Whereas a vole can consume about 200 cocoons a day, a shrew, depending on the species, may devour up to 800! This may result, according to laboratory tests, in destruction of 75 to 98 per cent of the cocoons present.

52 It is not surprising that the island of Newfoundland, which has no native shrews but is beset with sawflies, so eagerly desired some of these small, efficient mammals that in 1958 the introduction of the masked shrew—the most efficient sawfly predator—was attempted. Canadian officials report in 1962 that the attempt has been successful. The shrews are multiplying and are spreading out over the island, some marked individuals having been recovered as much as ten miles from the point of release.

53 There is, then, a whole battery of armaments available to the forester who is willing to look for permanent solutions that preserve and strengthen the natural relations in the forest. Chemical pest control in the forest is at best a stopgap measure bringing no real solution, at worst killing the fishes in the forest streams, bringing on plagues of insects, and destroying the natural controls and those we may be trying to introduce. By such violent measures, says Dr. Ruppertshofen, "the partnership for life of the forest is entirely being unbalanced, and the catastrophes caused by parasites repeat in shorter and shorter periods . . . We, therefore, have to put an end to these unnatural manipulations brought into the most important and almost last natural living space which has been left for us."

54 Through all these new, imaginative, and creative approaches to the problem of sharing our earth with other creatures there runs a constant theme, the awareness that we are dealing with life—with living populations and all their pressures and counterpressures, their surges and recessions. Only by taking account of such life forces and

by cautiously seeking to guide them into channels favorable to ourselves can we hope to achieve a reasonable accommodation between the insect hordes and ourselves.

55 The current vogue for poisons has failed utterly to take into account these most fundamental considerations. As crude a weapon as the cave man's club, the chemical barrage has been hurled against the fabric of life—a fabric on the one hand delicate and destructible, on the other miraculously tough and resilient, and capable of striking back in unexpected ways. These extraordinary capacities of life have been ignored by the practitioners of chemical control who have brought to their task no "high-minded orientation," no humility before the vast forces with which they tamper.

56 The "control of nature" is a phrase conceived in arrogance, born of the Neanderthal age of biology and philosophy, when it was supposed that nature exists for the convenience of man. The concepts and practices of applied entomology for the most part date from that Stone Age of science. It is our alarming misfortune that so primitive a science has armed itself with the most modern and terrible weapons, and that in turning them against the insects it has also turned them against the earth.

Thinking Questions: ***Form***

1. Divide Carson's essay into sections. How are the paragraphs linked together within the major sections? How do the various sections help develop Carson's general thesis: that we must take the road of natural biological control of insects rather than continue to travel our current road of using chemical insecticides?

2. Define the limits of Carson's introduction, body, and conclusion. Where does each begin and end? How do they support one another? Where are general ideas developed? Where are examples and proofs provided?

3. Devise a plan for a comparative essay of your own. Take a custom or convention in the school you attend. Examine it closely and create your own alternative for the custom. Then plan an essay in which you begin by telling why the custom you have chosen needs changing. Work up examples of how your alternative plan would work in comparison; then apply to your materials the essay model presented in the discussion of form at the end of this section.

4. Analyze the comparative structures of two of the four essays in this section. Show how both essays use either the alternate or block structures. Does each essay give a fair coverage to *both* sides of the comparison? Which essays make specific suggestions for the future in comparison

with what we have now? Which emphasize current problems and merely suggest future changes?

Thinking Questions: *Substance*

1. Does Carson, like many environmentalists, propose that we strive to live with nature, trying as far as possible *not* to alter natural systems? Support your answer by pointing to Carson's comparison between the two roads. What kind of relationship with nature would we have if we were to follow the "other road"?

2. Is Rachel Carson antiscientific because she argues against the widespread use of chemicals to control insects?

3. Most of Carson's essay works from general statements on various methods of natural insect control back through specific discussions of how these methods work and how they are developed. Often she compares the advantages and disadvantages of a method, as in paragraphs 21 and 22. Can you point to other examples of this contrasting method of development? Do you feel that Carson adequately covers *both* the negative and positive possibilities as she discusses her proposed solution?

4. Summarize in a few paragraphs what you believe Carson thinks of science. Does she believe that we have misused science? How? Why? Consider especially her remark, "Only by taking account of such life forces and by cautiously seeking to guide them into channels favorable to ourselves can we hope to achieve a reasonable accommodation between the insect hordes and ourselves" (paragraph 54). How might science be used to foster an "accommodation" rather than a "battle" between ourselves and nature?

The Euphio Question

KURT VONNEGUT, JR.

1 Ladies and gentlemen of the Federal Communications Commission, I appreciate this opportunity to testify on the subject before you.

2 I'm sorry—or maybe "heartsick" is the word—that news has leaked out about it. But now that word is getting around and coming to your official notice, I might as well tell the story straight and pray to God that I can convince you that America doesn't want what we discovered.

3 I won't deny that all three of us—Lew Harrison, the radio announcer, Dr. Fred Bockman, the physicist, and myself, a sociology

professor—found peace of mind. We did. And I won't say it's wrong for people to seek peace of mind. But if somebody thinks he wants peace of mind the way we found it, he'd be well advised to seek coronary thrombosis instead.

4 Lew, Fred, and I found peace of mind by sitting in easy chairs and turning on a gadget the size of a table-model television set. No herbs, no golden rule, no muscle control, no sticking our noses in other people's troubles to forget our own; no hobbies, Taoism, push-ups or contemplation of a lotus. The gadget is, I think, what a lot of people vaguely foresaw as the crowning achievement of civilization: an electronic something-or-other, cheap, easily mass-produced, that can, at the flick of a switch, provide tranquility. I see you have one here.

5 My first brush with synthetic peace of mind was six months ago. It was also then that I got to know Lew Harrison, I'm sorry to say. Lew is chief announcer of our town's only radio station. He makes his living with his loud mouth, and I'd be surprised if it were anyone but he who brought this matter to your attention.

6 Lew has, along with about thirty other shows, a weekly science program. Every week he gets some professor from Wyandotte College and interviews him about his particular field. Well, six months ago Lew worked up a program around a young dreamer and faculty friend of mine, Dr. Fred Bockman. I gave Fred a lift to the radio station, and he invited me to come on in and watch. For the heck of it, I did.

7 Fred Bockman is thirty and looks eighteen. Life has left no marks on him, because he hasn't paid much attention to it. What he pays most of his attention to, and what Lew Harrison wanted to interview him about, is this eight-ton umbrella of his that he listens to the stars with. It's a big radio antenna rigged up on a telescope mount. The way I understand it, instead of looking at the stars through a telescope, he aims this thing out in space and picks up radio signals coming from different heavenly bodies.

8 Of course, there aren't people running radio stations out there. It's just that many of the heavenly bodies pour out a lot of energy and some of it can be picked up in the radio-frequency band. One good thing Fred's rig does is to spot stars hidden from telescopes by big clouds of cosmic dust. Radio signals from them get through the clouds to Fred's antenna.

9 That isn't all the outfit can do, and, in his interview with Fred, Lew Harrison saved the most exciting part until the end of the program. "That's very interesting, Dr. Bockman," Lew said. "Tell me, has your radio telescope turned up anything else about the universe that hasn't been revealed by ordinary light telescopes?"

10 This was the snapper. "Yes, it has," Fred said. "We've found about fifty spots in space, *not hidden by cosmic dust,* that give off powerful radio signals. Yet no heavenly bodies at all seem to be there."

11 "Well!" Lew said in mock surprise. "I should say that *is* something! Ladies and gentlemen, for the first time in radio history, we bring you the noise from Dr. Bockman's mysterious voids." They had strung a line out to Fred's antenna on the campus. Lew waved to the engineer to switch in the signals coming from it. "Ladies and gentlemen, the voice of nothingness!"

12 The noise wasn't much to hear—a wavering hiss, more like a leaking tire than anything else. It was supposed to be on the air for five seconds. When the engineer switched it off, Fred and I were inexplicably grinning like idiots. I felt relaxed and tingling. Lew Harrison looked as though he'd stumbled into the dressing room at the Copacabana. He glanced at the studio clock, appalled. The monotonous hiss had been on the air for five minutes! If the engineer's cuff hadn't accidentally caught on the switch, it might be on yet.

13 Fred laughed nervously, and Lew hunted for his place in the script. "The hiss from nowhere," Lew said. "Dr. Bockman, has anyone proposed a name for these interesting voids?"

14 "No," Fred said. "At the present time they have neither a name nor an explanation."

15 The voids the hiss came from have still to be explained, but I've suggested a name for them that shows signs of sticking: "Bockman's Euphoria." We may not know what the spots are, but we know what they do, so the name's a good one. Euphoria, since it means a sense of buoyancy and well-being, is really the only word that will do.

16 After the broadcast, Fred, Lew, and I were cordial to one another to the point of being maudlin.

17 "I can't remember when a broadcast has been such a pleasure," Lew said. Sincerity is not his forte, yet he meant it.

18 "It's been one of the most memorable experiences of my life," Fred said, looking puzzled. "Extraordinarily pleasant."

19 We were all embarrassed by the emotion we felt, and parted company in bafflement and haste. I hurried home for a drink, only to walk into the middle of another unsettling experience.

20 The house was quiet, and I made two trips through it before discovering that I was not alone. My wife, Susan, a good and lovable woman who prides herself on feeding her family well and on time, was lying on the couch, staring dreamily at the ceiling. "Honey," I said tentatively, "I'm home. It's suppertime."

21 "Fred Bockman was on the radio today," she said in a faraway voice.

22 "I know. I was with him in the studio."

23 "He was out of this world," she sighed. "Simply out of this world. That noise from space—when he turned that on, everything just seemed to drop away from me. I've been lying here, just trying to get over it."

24 "Uh-huh," I said, biting my lip. "Well, guess I'd better round up Eddie." Eddie is my ten-year-old son, and captain of an apparently invincible neighborhood baseball team.

25 "Save your strength, Pop," said a small voice from the shadows.

"You home? What's the matter? Game called off on account of atomic attack?"

26 "Nope. We finished eight innings."

27 "Beating 'em so bad they didn't want to go on, eh?"

28 "Oh, they were doing pretty good. Score was tied, and they had two men on and two outs." He talked as though he were recounting a dream. "And then," he said, his eyes widening, "everybody kind of lost interest, just wandered off. I came home and found the old lady curled up here, so I lay down on the floor."

29 "Why?" I asked incredulously.

30 "Pop," Eddie said thoughtfully, "I'm damned if I know."

31 "Eddie!" his mother said.

32 "Mom," Eddie said. "I'm damned if *you* know either."

33 I was damned if anybody could explain it, but I had a nagging hunch. I dialed Fred Bockman's number. "Fred, am I getting you up from dinner?"

34 "I wish you were," Fred said. "Not a scrap to eat in the house, and I let Marion have the car today so she could do the marketing. Now she's trying to find a grocery open."

35 "Couldn't get the car started, eh?"

36 "Sure she got the car started," said Fred. "She even got to the market. Then she felt so good she walked right out of the place again." Fred sounded depressed. "I guess it's a woman's privilege to change her mind, but it's the lying that hurts."

37 "Marion lied? I don't believe it."

38 "She tried to tell me everybody wandered out of the market with her—clerks and all."

39 "Fred," I said, "I've got news for you. Can I drive out right after supper?"

40 When I arrived at Fred Bockman's farm, he was staring dumbfounded, at the evening paper.

41 "The whole town went nuts!" Fred said. "For no reason at all, all the cars pulled up to the curb like there was a hook and ladder going by. Says here people shut up in the middle of sentences and stayed that way for five minutes. Hundreds wandered around in the cold in their shirt-sleeves, grinning like toothpaste ads." He rattled the paper. "This *is* what you wanted to talk to me about?"

42 I nodded. "It all happened when that noise was being broadcast, and I thought maybe—"

43 "The odds are about one in a million that there's any maybe about it," said Fred. "The time checks to the second."

44 "But most people weren't listening to the program."

45 "They didn't have to listen, if my theory's right. We took those faint signals from space, amplified them about a thousand times, and rebroadcast them. Anybody within reach of the transmitter would get a good dose of the stepped-up radiations, whether he wanted to or not." He shrugged. "Apparently that's like walking past a field of burning marijuana."

46 "How come you never felt the effect at work?"

47 "Because I never amplified and rebroadcast the signals. The radio station's transmitter is what really put the sock into them."

48 "So what're you going to do next?"

49 Fred looked surprised. "Do? What is there to do but report it in some suitable journal?"

50 Without a preliminary knock, the front door burst open and Lew Harrison, florid and panting, swept into the room and removed his great polo coat with a bullfighterlike flourish. "You're cutting him in on it, too?" he demanded, pointing at me.

51 Fred blinked at him. "In on what?"

52 "The millions," Lew said. "The billions."

53 "Wonderful," Fred said. "What are you talking about?"

54 "The noise from the stars!" Lew said. "They love it, it drives 'em nuts. Didja see the papers?" He sobered for an instant. "It *was* the noise that did it, wasn't it, Doc?"

55 "We think so," Fred said. He looked worried. "How, exactly, do you propose we get our hands on these millions or billions?"

56 "Real estate!" Lew said raptly. " 'Lew,' I said to myself, 'Lew, how can you cash in on this gimmick if you can't get a monopoly on the universe? And, Lew,' I asked myself 'how can you sell the stuff when anybody can get it free while you're broadcasting it?' "

57 "Maybe it's the kind of thing that shouldn't be cashed in on," I suggested. "I mean, we don't know a great deal about—"

58 "Is happiness bad?" Lew interrupted.

59 "No," I admitted.

60 "Okay, and what we'd do with this stuff from the stars is make people happy. Now I suppose you're going to tell me that's bad?"

61 "People ought to be happy," Fred said.

62 "Okay, okay," Lew said loftily. "That's what we're going to do for the people. And the way the people can show their gratitude is in real estate." He looked out the window. "Good—a barn. We can start right there. We set up a transmitter in the barn, run a line out to your antenna, Doc, and we've got a real-estate development."

63 "Sorry," Fred said. "I don't follow you. This place wouldn't do for a development. The roads are poor, no bus service or shopping center, the view is lousy and the ground is full of rocks."

64 Lew nudged Fred several times with his elbow. "Doc, Doc, Doc—

sure it's got drawbacks, but with that transmitter in the barn, you can give them the most precious thing in all creation—happiness."

65 "Euphoria Heights," I said.

66 "That's great!" said Lew. "I'd get the prospects, Doc, and you'd sit up there in the barn with your hand on the switch. Once a prospect set foot on Euphoria Heights, and you shot the happiness to him, there's nothing he wouldn't pay for a lot."

67 "Every house a home, as long as the power doesn't fail," I said.

68 "Then," Lew said, his eyes shining, "when we sell all the lots here, we move the transmitter and start another development. Maybe we'd get a fleet of transmitters going." He snapped his fingers. "Sure! Mount 'em on wheels."

69 "I somehow don't think the police would think highly of us," Fred said.

70 "Okay, so when they come to investigate, you throw the old switch and give *them* a jolt of happiness." He shrugged. "Hell, I might even get bighearted and let them have a corner lot."

71 "No," Fred said quietly. "If I ever joined a church, I couldn't face the minister."

72 "So we give *him* a jolt," Lew said brightly.

73 "No," Fred said. "Sorry."

74 "Okay," Lew said, rising and pacing the floor. "I was prepared for that. I've got an alternative, and this one's strictly legitimate. We'll make a little amplifier with a transmitter and an aerial on it. Shouldn't cost over fifty bucks to make, so we'd price it in the range of the common man—five hundred bucks, say. We make arrangements with the phone company to pipe signals from your antenna right into the homes of people with these sets. The sets take the signal from the phone line, amplify it, and broadcast it through the houses to make everybody in them happy. See? Instead of turning on the radio or television, everybody's going to want to turn on the happiness. No casts, no stage sets, no expensive cameras—no nothing but that hiss."

75 "We could call it the euphoriaphone," I suggested, "or 'euphio' for short."

76 "That's great, that's great!" Lew said. "What do you say, Doc?"

77 "I don't know." Fred looked worried. "This sort of thing is out of my line."

78 "We all have to recognize our limitations, Doc," Lew said expansively. "I'll handle the business end, and you handle the technical end." He made a motion as though to put on his coat. "Or maybe you don't want to be a millionaire?"

79 "Oh, yes, yes indeed I do," Fred said quickly. "Yes indeed."

80 "All righty," Lew said, dusting his palms, "the first thing we've gotta do is build one of the sets and test her."

81 This part of it *was* down Fred's alley, and I could see the problem interested him. "It's really a pretty simple gadget," he said. "I suppose we could throw one together and run a test out here next week."

82 The first test of the euphoriaphone, or euphio, took place in Fred Bockman's living room on a Saturday afternoon, five days after Fred's and Lew's sensational radio broadcast.

83 There were six guinea pigs—Lew, Fred and his wife Marion, myself, my wife Susan, and my son Eddie. The Bockman's had arranged chairs in a circle around a card table, on which rested a gray steel box.

84 Protruding from the box was a long buggy whip aerial that scraped the ceiling. While Fred fussed with the box, the rest of us made nervous small talk over sandwiches and beer. Eddie, of course, wasn't drinking beer, though he was badly in need of a sedative. He was annoyed at having been brought out to the farm instead of to a ball game, and was threatening to take it out on the Bockmans' Early American furnishings. He was playing a spirited game of flies and grounders with himself near the French doors, using a dead tennis ball and a poker.

"Eddie," Susan said for the tenth time, "please stop."

85 "It's under control, under control," Eddie said disdainfully, playing the ball off four walls and catching it with one hand.

86 Marion, who vents her maternal instincts on her immaculate furnishings, couldn't hide her distress at Eddie's turning the place into a gymnasium. Lew, in his way, was trying to calm her. "Let him wreck the dump," Lew said. "You'll be moving into a palace one of these days."

87 "It's ready," Fred said softly.

88 We looked at him with queasy bravery. Fred plugged two jacks from the phone line into the gray box. This was the direct line to his antenna on the campus, and clockwork would keep the antenna fixed on one of the mysterious voids in the sky—the most potent of Bockman's Euphoria. He plugged a cord from the box into an electrical outlet in the baseboard, and rested his hand on a switch. "Ready?"

89 "Don't, Fred!" I said. I was scared stiff.

90 "Turn it on, turn it on," Lew said. "We wouldn't have the telephone today if Bell hadn't had the guts to call somebody up."

91 "I'll stand right here by the switch, ready to flick her off if something goes sour," Fred said reassuringly. There was a click, a hum, and the euphio was on.

92 A deep, unanimous sigh filled the room. The poker slipped from Eddie's hands. He moved across the room in a stately sort of waltz, knelt by his mother, and laid his head in her lap. Fred drifted away from his post, humming, his eyes half closed.

93 Lew Harrison was the first to speak, continuing his conversation

with Marion. "But who cares for material wealth?" he asked earnestly. He turned to Susan for confirmation.

94 "Uh-uh," said Susan, shaking her head dreamily. She put her arms around Lew, and kissed him for about five minutes.

95 "Say," I said, patting Susan on the back, "you kids get along swell, don't you? Isn't that nice, Fred?"

96 "Eddie," Marion said solicitously, "I think there's a real baseball in the hall closet. A *hard* ball. Wouldn't that be more fun than that old tennis ball?" Eddie didn't stir.

97 Fred was still prowling around the room, smiling, his eyes now closed all the way. His heel caught in a lamp cord, and he went sprawling on the hearth, his head in the ashes. "Hi-ho, everybody," he said, his eyes still closed. "Bunged my head on an andiron." He stayed there, giggling occasionally.

98 "The doorbell's been ringing for a while," Susan said. "I don't suppose it means anything."

99 "Come in, come in," I shouted. This somehow struck everyone as terribly funny. We all laughed uproariously, including Fred, whose guffaws blew up little gray clouds from the ashpit.

100 A small, very serious old man in white had let himself in, and was now standing in the vestibule, looking at us with alarm. "Milkman," he said uncertainly. He held out a slip of paper to Marion. "I can't read the last line in your note," he said. "What's that say about cottage cheese, cheese, cheese, cheese, cheese . . ." His voice trailed off as he settled, tailor-fashion, to the floor beside Marion. After he'd been silent for perhaps three quarters of an hour, a look of concern crossed his face. "Well," he said apathetically, "I can only stay for a minute. My truck's parked out on the shoulder, kind of blocking things." He started to stand. Lew gave the volume knob on the euphio a twist. The milkman wilted to the floor.

101 "Aaaaaaaaaah," said everybody.

102 "Good day to be indoors," the milkman said. "Radio says we'll catch the tail end of the Atlantic hurricane."

103 "Let 'er come," I said. "I've got my car parked under a big, dead tree." It seemed to make sense. Nobody took exception to it. I lapsed back into a warm fog of silence and thought of nothing whatsoever. These lapses seemed to last for a matter of seconds before they were interrupted by conversation of newcomers. Looking back, I see now that the lapses were rarely less than six hours.

104 I was snapped out of one, I recall, by a repetition of the doorbell's ringing. "I said come in," I mumbled.

105 "And I did," the milkman mumbled.

106 The door swung open, and a state trooper glared in at us. "Who the hell's got his milk truck out there blocking the road?" he demanded. He spotted the milkman. "Aha! Don't you know somebody

could get killed, coming around a blind curve into that thing?" He yawned, and his ferocious expression gave way to an affectionate smile. "It's so damn' unlikely," he said, "I don't know why I ever brought it up." He sat down by Eddie. "Hey, kid—like guns?" He took his revolver from its holster. "Look—just like Hoppy's."

107 Eddie took the gun, aimed it at Marion's bottle collection and fired. A large blue bottle popped to dust and the window behind the collection splintered. Cold air roared in through the opening.

108 "He'll make a cop yet," Marion chortled.

109 "God, I'm happy," I said, feeling a little like crying. "I got the swellest little kid and the swellest bunch of friends and the swellest old wife in the world." I heard the gun go off twice more, and then dropped into heavenly oblivion.

110 Again the doorbell roused me. "How many times do I have to tell you—for Heaven's sake, come in," I said, without opening my eyes.

111 "I *did,*" the milkman said.

112 I heard the tramping of many feet, but had no curiosity about them. A little later, I noticed that I was having difficulty breathing. Investigation revealed that I had slipped to the floor, and that several Boy Scouts had bivouacked on my chest and abdomen.

113 "You want something?" I asked the tenderfoot whose hot, measured breathing was in my face.

114 "Beaver Patrol wanted old newspapers, but forget it," he said. "We'd just have to carry 'em somewhere."

115 "And do your parents know where you are?"

116 "Oh, sure. They got worried and came after us." He jerked his thumb at several couples lined up against the baseboard, smiling into the teeth of the wind and rain lashing in at them through the broken window.

117 "Mom, I'm kinda hungry," Eddie said.

118 "Oh, Eddie—you're not going to make your mother cook just when we're having such a wonderful time," Susan said.

119 Lew Harrison gave the euphio's volume knob another twist. "There, kid, how's that?"

120 "Aaaaaaaaaah," said everybody.

121 When awareness intruded on oblivion again, I felt around for the Beaver Patrol, and found them missing. I opened my eyes to see that they and Eddie and the milkman and Lew and the trooper were standing by a picture window, cheering. The wind outside was roaring and slashing savagely and driving raindrops through the broken window as though they'd been fired from air rifles. I shook Susan gently, and together we went to the window to see what might be so entertaining.

122 "She's going, she's going, she's going," the milkman cried ecstatically.

123 Susan and I arrived just in time to join in the cheering as a big elm crashed down on our sedan.

124 "Kee-*runch!*" said Susan, and I laughed until my stomach hurt.

125 "Get Fred," Lew said urgently. "He's gonna miss seeing the barn go!"

126 "H'mm?" Fred said from the fireplace.

127 "Aw, Fred, you missed it," Marion said.

128 "Now we're really gonna see something," Eddie yelled. "The power line's going to get it this time. Look at that poplar lean!"

129 The poplar leaned closer, closer, closer to the power line; and then a gust brought it down in a hail of sparks and a tangle of wires. The lights in the house went off.

130 Now there was only the sound of the wind. "How come nobody cheered?" Lew said faintly. "The euphio—it's off!"

131 A horrible groan came from the fireplace. "God, I think I've got a concussion."

132 Marion knelt by her husband and wailed. "Darling, my poor darling—what happened to you?"

133 I looked at the woman I had my arms around—a dreadful, dirty old hag, with red eyes sunk deep in her head, and hair like Medusa's. "Ugh," I said, and turned away in disgust.

134 "Honey," wept the witch, "it's me—Susan."

Moans filled the air, and pitiful cries for food and water. Suddenly the room had become terribly cold. Only a moment before I had imagined I was in the tropics.

135 "Who's got my damn' pistol?" the trooper said bleakly.

136 A Western Union boy I hadn't noticed before was sitting in a corner, miserably leafing through a pile of telegrams and making clucking noises.

137 I shuddered. "I'll bet it's Sunday morning," I said. "We've been here twelve hours!" It was Monday morning.

138 The Western Union boy was thunderstruck. "Sunday morning? I walked in here on a Sunday night." He stared around the room. "Looks like them newsreels of Buchenwald, don't it?"

139 The chief of the Beaver Patrol, with the incredible stamina of the young, was the hero of the day. He fell in his men in two ranks, haranguing them like an old Army top-kick. While the rest of us lay draped around the room, whimpering about hunger, cold, and thirst, the patrol started the furnace again, brought blankets, applied compresses to Fred's head and countless barked shins, blocked off the broken window, and made buckets of cocoa and coffee.

140 Within two hours of the time that the power and the euphio went off, the house was warm and we had eaten. The serious respiratory cases—the parents who had sat near the broken window for twenty-four hours—had been pumped full of penicillin and hauled off to the

hospital. The milkman, the Western Union boy, and the trooper had refused treatment and gone home. The Beaver Patrol had saluted smartly and left. Outside, repairmen were working on the power line. Only the original group remained—Lew, Fred, and Marion, Susan and myself, and Eddie. Fred, it turned out, had some pretty important-looking contusions and abrasions, but no concussion.

141 Susan had fallen asleep right after eating. Now she stirred. "What happened?"

142 "Happiness," I told her. "Incomparable, continuous happiness—happiness by the kilowatt."

143 Lew Harrison, who looked like an anarchist with his red eyes and fierce black beard, had been writing furiously in one corner of the room. "That's good—happiness by the kilowatt," he said. "Buy your happiness the way you buy light."

144 "Contract happiness the way you contract influenza," Fred said. He sneezed.

145 Lew ignored him. "It's a campaign, see? The first ad is for the long-hairs: 'The price of one book, which may be a disappointment, will buy you sixty hours of euphio. Euphio never disappoints.' Then we'd hit the middle class with the next one—"

146 "In the groin?" Fred said.

147 "What's the matter with you people?" Lew said. "You act as though the experiment had failed."

148 "Pneumonia and malnutrition are what we'd *hoped* for?" Marion said.

149 "We had a cross section of America in this room, and we made every last person happy," Lew said. "Not for just an hour, not for just a day, but for two days without a break." He arose reverently from his chair. "So what we do to keep it from killing the euphio fans is to have the thing turned on and off with clockwork, see? The owner sets it so it'll go on just as he comes home from work, then it'll go off again while he eats supper; then it goes on after supper, off again when it's bedtime; on again after breakfast, off when it's time to go to work, then on again for the wife and kids."

150 He ran his hands through his hair and rolled his eyes. "And the selling points—my God, the selling points! No expensive toys for the kids. For the price of a trip to the movies, people can buy thirty hours of euphio. For the price of a fifth of whisky, they can buy sixty hours of euphio!"

151 "Or a big family bottle of potassium cyanide," Fred said.

152 "Don't you see it?" Lew said incredulously. "It'll bring families together again, save the American home. No more fights over what TV or radio program to listen to. Euphio pleases one and all—we proved that. And there is no such thing as a dull euphio program."

153 A knock on the door interrupted him. A repairman stuck his head

in to announce that the power would be on again in about two minutes.

154 "Look, Lew," Fred said, "this little monster could kill civilization in less time than it took to burn down Rome. We're not going into the mind-numbing business, and that's that."

155 "You're kidding!" Lew said, aghast. He turned to Marion. "Don't you want your husband to make a million?"

156 "Not by operating an electronic opium den," Marion said coldly.

157 Lew slapped his forehead. "It's what the public wants. This is like Louis Pasteur refusing to pasteurize milk."

158 "It'll be good to have the electricity again," Marion said, changing the subject. "Lights, hot-water heater, the pump, the—oh, Lord!"

159 The lights came on the instant she said it, but Fred and I were already in mid-air, descending on the gray box. We crashed down on it together. The card table buckled, and the plug was jerked from the wall socket. The euphio's tubes glowed red for a moment, then died.

160 Expressionlessly, Fred took a screwdriver from his pocket and removed the top of the box.

161 "Would you enjoy doing battle with progress?" he said, offering me the poker Eddie had dropped.

162 In a frenzy, I stabbed and smashed at the euphio's glass and wire vitals. With my left hand, and with Fred's help, I kept Lew from throwing himself between the poker and the works.

163 "I thought you were on my side," Lew said.

164 "If you breathe one word about euphio to anyone," I said, "what I just did to euphio I will gladly do to you."

165 And there, ladies and gentlemen of the Federal Communications Commission, I thought the matter had ended. It deserved to end there. Now, through the medium of Lew Harrison's big mouth, word has leaked out. He has petitioned you for permission to start commercial exploitation of euphio. He and his backers have built a radio-telescope of their own.

166 Let me say again that all of Lew's claims are true. Euphio will do everything he says it will. The happiness it gives is perfect and unflagging in the face of incredible adversity. Near tragedies, such as the first experiment, can no doubt be avoided with clockwork to turn the sets on and off. I see that this set on the table before you is, in fact, equipped with clockwork.

167 The question is not whether euphio works. It does. The question is, rather, whether or not America is to enter a new and distressing phase of history where men no longer pursue happiness but buy it. This is no time for oblivion to become a national craze. The only benefit we could get from euphio would be if we could somehow lay down a peace-of-mind barrage on our enemies while protecting our own people from it.

168 In closing, I'd like to point out that Lew Harrison, the would-be czar of euphio, is an unscrupulous person, unworthy of public trust. It wouldn't surprise me, for instance, if he had set the clockwork on this sample euphio set so that its radiations would addle your judgments when you are trying to make a decision. In fact, it seems to be whirring suspiciously at this very moment and I'm so happy I could cry. I've got the swellest litle kid and the swellest bunch of friends and the swellest old wife in the world. And good old Lew Harrison is the salt of the earth, believe me. I sure wish him a lot of good luck with his new enterprise.

Thinking Questions: *Form*

1. Compare two of the central characters in "The Euphio Question." How are they similar or different? How are their values similar or different?

2. Use your imagination. Take a fairly common electronic device and create a new machine—with greater powers—based on the present machine. Perhaps a tape recorder that can record what a person thinks? Or you might invent a television that "sees" both ways. What effects would your future machine have on people you know? Exactly how would it be different from and similar to the machine you started with?

3. Is there anything wrong with Lew Harrison's reasoning when he says "Is happiness bad?" (paragraph 58). Is the kind of happiness we find at the end of "The Euphio Question" the right kind? If not, why not? What is the *right kind* of happiness? Compare the happiness produced by the euphio machine with what you might call "real" or "proper" happiness.

Thinking Questions: *Substance*

1. Do you find what happens in "The Euphio Question" credible, once you accept the fact that the euphio machine exists? Would people you know respond to the euphio machine in ways that would be similar to the way the characters in Vonnegut's stories respond? Would they, for example, try to make money off the machine the way Lew Harrison, the radio announcer, does in the story?

2. What is *good* about the euphio machine? What is *bad* about the machine? Would you rather have complete, mindless pleasure, or would you rather have some control over your future, even at the expense of pain or suffering?

3. Would you call the euphio machine a scientific triumph or a scientific tragedy? Should science and technology strive to do *everything* for people?

4. Can you see any similarities between television and the euphio machine, especially in their effects on those who use them?

5. People in the twentieth century, often because machines and science have taken over much of their work, have greater amounts of leisure time than people of previous centuries. Do you think discoveries like the euphio machine would provide a useful way to spend leisure time? Why or why not?

* * *

SUMMARY QUESTIONS: THE FUTURE

The essays in this section leave us with these central questions as we consider the future:

1. What function and place should cities have in our future? Should people continue to think of them as places of romance and escape? Or should they recognize the city as a place, as Joan Didion suggests, for the very rich and the very poor, while the middle classes move to the suburbs? Or are there other ways to view the cities?

2. Are cities *unnatural?* Or can they be made environmentally functional, even beautiful and more natural?

3. How should human behavior be changed in the future? Can you pick one or two currently fashionable characteristics of behavior, as Melvin Maddocks does, and use them to suggest how people might change for the better in the future? What specific changes in behavior would create a better social atmosphere? Warren Bennis suggests ways in which individuals can change social structures without creating institutional upheaval. Would his suggestions work on a larger social level?

4. Is it possible for individuals to change social customs and trends? Both Joan Didion and Melvin Maddocks go over past experiences in order to suggest changes in the future. How useful are such attempts? Do they take into consideration the deeper social causes of certain patterns of behavior? Have psychiatry and psychology, for example, by encouraging individuals to probe for the motivations behind other people's and their own behavior, helped cause the lack of privacy that Maddocks points out? Has job specialization encouraged people to speak out about their private experiences? Have many people been driven to cities for economic reasons, or to the suburbs around the cities because they are dependent on suburban conveniences?

5. Will science and technology control us or will we learn to control them to better our environment? Rachel Carson argues that science and technology, properly used, can help us understand each other and nature

better. Kurt Vonnegut implies, however, that misuse of science and technology is almost inevitable, given the characteristics of human nature.

6. Should people continually try to dominate their environment? Or should they use science and the arts to understand and live naturally with their environment? How can scientists balance their drive toward discovery with an appreciation of nature's mysteries which they may never fully comprehend?

Writing Exercise IV

EXPOSITION

(Comparison and Contrast)

Project yourself into the future. Begin by analyzing what you are like now, your likes or dislikes, your particular talents or weaknesses, projects you have enjoyed and completed successfully. Then imagine yourself into a specific situation in the year 2000 and write an essay in which you compare yourself in the future with yourself now. How will you have changed in personality, in skills? How will your environment have changed?

Do some brainstorming with others before you begin. Imagine the future *in detail.* If, for example, you are doing a certain job, describe the purpose and activities of the job specifically. How does the job fit into the overall social picture? What do you wear on the job? In what type of environment do you work? After you have taken some notes, plan your comparative essay in paragraph blocks in which you introduce a thesis explaining the differences between you now and then. Then decide on an alternate or a block structure for your essay, moving from present to future and back. As you edit, check your transitions and your overall essay for *coherence.* Refer to the inverted triangle structure explained in the following essay on form, and notice how paragraphs can be blocked off and interrelated within that structure.

WRITING THE COMPARATIVE ESSAY

Comparison controls much of our thinking and writing, even when we are not conscious of it. Look at the comparisons in this paragraph:

> It is easy to see the beginnings of things, and harder to see the ends. I can remember now, with a clarity that makes the nerves in the back of my neck constrict, when New York began for me, but I cannot lay my finger upon the moment it ended, can never cut through the ambiguities and second starts and broken resolves to the exact place on the page where the heroine is no longer as optimistic as she once was. When I first saw New York I was twenty, and it was summertime, and I got off a DC-7 at the old Idlewild temporary terminal in a new dress which had seemed very smart in Sacramento but seemed less smart already, even in the old Idlewild temporary terminal, and the warm air smelled of mildew and some instinct, programmed by all the movies I had ever seen and all the songs I had ever heard sung and all the stories I had ever read about New York, informed me that it would never be quite the same again. In fact it never was. Some time later there was a song on all the jukeboxes on the upper East Side that went "but where is the schoolgirl who used to be me," and if it was late enough at night I used to wonder that. I know now that almost everyone wonders something like that, sooner or later and no matter what he or she is doing, but one of the mixed blessings of being twenty and twenty-one and even twenty-three is the conviction that nothing like this, all evidence to the contrary notwithstanding, has ever happened to anyone before. (Paragraph 1, Joan Didion's "Goodbye to All That")

In this paragraph, Didion introduces the comparison that will become the focus of her entire essay: the contrast between the beginning and the end of her eight-year stay in New York City. Most of us recall the smells and sensations of a place from our past; these sensations often come to remind us of whole experiences, of periods in our lives in which we dreamed different dreams and held different values. Didion tells us about the physical sensations that were important to her in those early days in New York—the warm air smelling of mildew, the memories of popular songs—and she uses these details and sensations as points of comparison with her later attitude. Joan Didion at twenty-one, breathless and romantic and in love with the mystique of New York, becomes twenty-eight-year-old Joan Didion, tired and cynical, already feeling as if she has seen all that there is to see, even in New York.

The opening paragraph of "Goodbye to All That" shows how most comparisons work. The writer takes a general purpose—Didion, for example, wants to explain *why* she became disillusioned with New York, why her romance with the city faded—and uses the contrasting points of the comparison to develop that purpose. The opening paragraph in a comparative essay should establish the points of comparison *in detail*—as Didion does when she reminds us of how she felt on arriving in New

York and how she later began to change her feelings—and it should relate to the writer's purpose in making the comparison in the first place.

The following visual diagram provides a clear idea of how the parts—Introduction, Body, and Conclusion—of a comparative essay ought to function. Experienced writers, of course, rework and rearrange this basic model, but most comparative essays use the units and principles in this diagram in some form or another.

ESSAY MODEL

Introduction: Either one paragraph or a block of related paragraphs	**Lead-in sentences:** To narrow the subject **Thesis statement:** Should clearly define the purpose of the comparison
Body: Either several related paragraphs that develop different points of comparison, or several related groups of paragraphs on each point of comparison	First paragraph or paragraph grouping—related to *one* point in comparison Second paragraph or grouping— *second* point in comparison Third paragraph—*third* point Fourth paragraph—*fourth* point Fifth paragraph—*fifth* point Sixth paragraph—*sixth* point
Conclusion: Either one paragraph or a block of related paragraphs	**Thesis statement:** Usually a clincher sentence that reminds the reader of how each point of the comparison relates to or develops the essay's thesis

Lead-out paragraphs:
Move the reader back to the general subject

Introductory paragraphs

The opening sentences in your essay should introduce the general subject and begin to point the way to your thesis. In a conventional essay, the thesis usually appears at the end of this opening paragraph or group of paragraphs. Notice how Joan Didion describes her general subject—when New York began and ended for her and why her attitude changed toward the city—in her opening sentences. Then she gradually works toward her thesis: that people have to live through their dreams before they know what is good and bad in those dreams and that is what happens to many people who move to New York from other areas of the country. From general remarks and comparisons she works to a specific thesis.

Body paragraphs

In any essay, the main parts of a thesis are divided into separate paragraphs or paragraph groupings. The writer leads the reader from the thesis, which usually appears at the end of the introduction, to separate ideas within that thesis. Each unit in the body of the essay should be clearly related to the thesis.

In comparative essays, you can usually use either of two general organizing patterns to unify your body paragraphs:

Alternate comparison treats one side of a comparison in one paragraph and then moves to a consideration of the other side in the following paragraph. Once the alternate structure is established, you can use it throughout the essay to keep your readers with you. If you plan an essay around alternate comparison, you should outline the three or four major points on each side of the comparison before you begin writing. Then, as you move from one contrasting point to another, you will have the entire plan before you.

Block comparison simply explains all the ideas related to one side of the comparison in the first half of an essay and all the ideas related to the other side of the comparison in the second half. Alternate structure allows the writer to break the comparison down into small units and to compare those units with one another. Block structure encourages larger groupings of contrasting ideas, with a bit less attention to comparisons between one small part of a subject and another.

There are several basic principles to remember in using these two kinds of organization.

1. Alternate comparisons are better fitted to complex subjects. Simple comparisons—for example, the advantages and disadvantages of rotary lawnmowers—can easily be dealt with in a simple block structure, in which the writer can point out clear and simple advantages in one part of the essay and equally clear disadvantages in the second. A comparison of two very different states of mind, as in Joan Didion's "Goodbye to All

That," almost demands alternate comparison, because each contrasting part of the overall comparison demands its own support and evidence before the writer can move on to the next part. Notice how Didion continually shifts from discussions of how she felt and acted when she arrived in New York to how she felt and acted as she began to consider leaving New York.

2. Be sure to point out both similarities and differences as you compare. All the essays in this section strive to point out what the writers believe are major differences between the two sides of their comparison. Yet each writer is careful to consider similarities as well.

3. Comparison in essays usually needs to be combined with other organizing strategies. If you were writing an essay on "The Euphio Question," for example, in which you compared Vonnegut's vision of the future with another science fiction writer's vision, you might also need to organize your comparison around several science fiction classifications—for instance, comparisons of characterization, of attitudes toward technology, and of setting or background in each story.

Melvin Maddocks, in his essay "In Praise of Reticence," compares the traditional gentleman with modern man. He further organizes his comparison by dividing his essay into considerations of various places where we might be apt to meet an example of modern man—on airplanes, in television talk shows, in books revealing the private lives of their authors.

Paragraph grouping

In college you will write a good many medium and longer length essays. Such essays call for some knowledge of paragraph blocking, and for the ability to take a thesis, subdivide it into subordinate, second-level ideas, and finally, organize blocks or units of paragraphs around those subideas. In a comparison essay, you can begin the blocking process by bringing together paragraphs under each side of your comparison. Rachel Carson in "The Other Road," for example, begins her essay by comparing "two roads"—the road of poisonous chemical control of insects, which she believes we now mistakenly follow, and the road of biological solutions to insect problems, which she suggests we follow from now on. Once she has introduced the general comparison, she offers numerous examples of the second road, each example developed in groups or units of related paragraphs.

Joan Didion organizes her paragraph blocks around time sequences. Each paragraph grouping describes a specific stage in her life in New York and is then related periodically back to the general comparison between her arrival and her departure from New York. The more complex the thesis of your essay, the more paragraph groupings you will probably use. And the more paragraph groups you use, the more attention you will need to give to relating paragraph blocks to one another.

Remember, paragraph groups are like paragraphs themselves: they must relate general ideas to particular experiences, facts, reasons, or examples. Some writers work from the specific to the general, others from the general to the specific. Whatever plan you choose, remember to work generalities and specifics together to support *both* sides of your comparison.

Final words on comparison

Comparative essays bring together two objects, ideas, or subjects to reveal a thesis. Essentially, there are three general ways to develop an extended comparison. All these methods of developing extended comparisons are closely related to methods of developing more specific comparisons—analogies, figures of speech, metaphors, and similes. You may wish to review these specific methods in the discussion of form (description) in Part One.

1. Compare a *known* to an *unknown*. Kurt Vonnegut, in "The Euphio Question," uses our knowledge of existing conditions to build a future situation. We know what machines are accomplishing now; therefore, it is not that difficult to imagine, with Vonnegut's help, a machine capable of producing the effects of the euphio machine.

2. Compare two objects or ideas that are *similar* in one important way but *different* in many others. Warren Bennis, for example, points out similarities among many individuals as they confront the possibilities of change within the institutions in which they work. Some promote change at any cost because they have very little to lose—the "cabals," or "Young Turks." Others resist change at any cost because they already hold power —the "cliques." The individuals in these groups are often very different from one another in every way *except* in their attitudes toward change within the institution. Bennis uses that similarity to develop his own thesis on effective leadership in relation to promoting change.

3. *Contrast* two examples from the same general class. Junior colleges and four-year colleges are often grouped together when educators consider college students and their needs. Often students in both types of schools are of similar ages; they attend schools of similar physical construction; they take comparable courses and programs and often share common textbooks. Yet the students from two-year and four-year schools are *different* in some equally important ways: they may come from different economic and educational backgrounds; one group may be less well-read, and many may hold part-time and full-time jobs as they attend school. A writer who wishes to argue that a two-year college student should undertake a different program than the four-year student may want to base his argument on these important and often neglected differences between the two types. A writer, in other words, must decide in advance whether to emphasize similarities or differences.

Form:

EXPOSITION

(Classification and Logical Division)

Substance and Theme:

EDUCATION TODAY AND TOMORROW

"Where should emphasis be placed in the educational process?" Some of the writers in this section, especially Jonathan Kozol and Paul Goodman, argue that the learners, the "students," should decide what they want and need to learn. They criticize American education because, as Goodman suggests, it puts a learner in a situation in which educational professionals specify and evaluate the personal goals of others. To make matters worse, Goodman reminds us, most professional educators accept the idea that the individual should be trained for a job and that the educational system should structure itself around the productive needs of society rather than around the personal needs of students. Although many "free" schools alter the content of specific courses, they usually continue the idea of a *curriculum*—an abstract collection of activities selected by the professional educator to fit the student into some ideal definition of the "educated person." Jonathan Kozol, in fact, denounces the radical free school and progressive educational movements because they do not question the basic assumptions of our production-oriented educational system.

Paul Goodman, also an educational radical, provides, in his "Memorandum to the Office of Education," a few concrete suggestions, all of which are built on the kind of radical theory espoused by Kozol. In essence, Goodman advocates an educational apprentice system in which students would work, according to their own present interests, on community projects, with local businessmen and tradesmen, with community agencies such as Model Cities or Head Start, with radio, television, and newspaper staffs. Goodman supports *education by doing;* abstract principles and theories would be developed by students as they worked. Such a system, Goodman argues, would create immediate interest, give students practical choices as they went about developing career skills, and, perhaps most importantly, make learning *practical.*

In contrast to Goodman's proposed apprentice system, Mary Frances Greene and Orletta Ryan describe an educational system in which the home and school environments inevitably and tragically clash. As a result, the ghetto students described in their essay are almost totally unable to understand *why* they should learn what the school teaches. This rift between school subject matter and the student's neighborhood and home environment works against learning.

Memorandum to the Office of Education

PAUL GOODMAN

Premises:

1 1. For many bright "under-achievers" it is not the curriculum and methods that are at fault, but their lack of interest in lessons and scholastic environment altogether. They need real products to show, not examinations that have been passed.

> Among the underprivileged this shows up as dropout of the obviously gifted. In the middle class, it tends to show up as emphasis on "social life" and performance far below ability.

2 2. The problem is what educational environment suits these bright youngsters, that is real field work. There are certain enterprises that can give a well-rounded intellectual apprenticeship: *e.g.* radio stations, newspapers, little theaters, photographic agencies, architecture and engineering offices.

> For these to be educational environments, the professionals in charge must see to it that the youth works on the several aspects of the enterprise: technical, artistic, manual, social, humanistic.

3 Our society has a critical need for independent cultural media to countervail the present mass media of communications and bureaucratic offices of design. But, though necessary, such small independents seem to find it impossible to survive economically, and must in

some way be subsidized. In general, the chief costs in these enterprises, that spell the difference between survival and failure, are for staff.

E.g. to run a Pacifica radio station with professional staff plus volunteers costs $38 an hour. Of the total cost of the Living Theater (New York City) about half was staff salary, twenty staff at Equity minimum of $40 a week.

4 There is continual demand for new construction of high schools to meet the overcrowding; and the Federal government is asked to share in the expense.

E.g. Chicago has just asked for twenty new high schools (at about $6,000,000 each) to accommodate forty thousand who do not have seats. Besides this capital cost, the operating expense in an urban high school is about $1,000 a year per student.

Proposal:

5 Instead of putting all the new capital and operating money into new schools, I propose supporting or underwriting existing or new non-scholastic educational environments for bright underachieving youth. *E.g.* community radio stations, local newspapers, little theaters, design offices.

6 These would provide real social needs now not economically feasible, instead of passed (or failed) examinations by those who are not suited for the academic environment.

7 I am thinking of enterprises run by about six professionals and twenty to twenty-five apprentices of ages sixteen to twenty. The apprenticeship is to serve as an *alternative* to the last two years of high school (and perhaps first year of college).

8 Apprentices to be paid $20 a week, in lieu of the $1,000 a year for schooling. Enterprises to be further helped out of the capital costs saved from new school construction.

Remarks:

9 What is needed for such a program is an earnest search around the country for existing small independent enterprises that warrant supporting, *e.g.* country papers that could provide a more valuable service than they do (they are mainly Social Notes) if they had the staff.

10 Halleck Hoffman, the president of Pacifica radio federation, has expressed eagerness to provide or suggest professionals.

11 The program could be, in one way, regarded as a means of upgrading the present Job Training Corps program, providing educational opportunity for intellectually superior youth (and being a means of desegregation).

12 A preferable way of looking at the program is as aid to small businesses—giving the seed-money as part of an educational function.

13 Finally, after two or three years, many such apprentices will want to continue in college. I do not think it would be difficult to arrange for their admission.

Thinking Questions: *Form*

1. Goodman logically classifies both the premises behind his alternative educational system and the specific aspects of that system. Do you feel that his classification of premises leads naturally to his classification of suggested alterations? Show, for example, how premise number 2 (paragraph 2), which discusses the need for field work, leads to one or two of the points in Goodman's list of proposals.

2. Goodman limits his memorandum to a certain type of student. Define that type and explain why these proposals would suit these students rather than others.

3. This memorandum divides itself into specific premises and proposals; there is no directly stated purpose or thesis. Compose a single-sentence thesis for the entire memorandum, one that defines the general drift of both the premises and the proposals.

Thinking Questions: *Substance*

1. Many of Paul Goodman's ideas have been used as the basis for some recently developed "free schools." What would Goodman's proposed school be "free" of? Be specific. What particular activities in the traditional curriculum would students in Goodman's school avoid? How would the learning atmosphere change?

2. What is the difference between the existing vocational curriculum, where students often do field work in local automobile shops and hospitals, and Goodman's proposed curriculum? Does Goodman ever directly discuss this difference? If so, where? If not, why not?

3. In paragraph 2, Goodman says that work in "radio stations, newspapers, little theaters, photographic agencies, architecture and engineering offices" can provide "a well-rounded intellectual apprenticeship." What is "a well-rounded intellectual apprenticeship"? And how does the traditional high school or college curriculum attempt to provide it? After you have answered these questions, select *one* of Goodman's sample "enterprises" and show how it might be "well-rounded" intellectually. How might, for example, a student working and learning at a radio station combine technical, scientific, and artistic training?

Free School as a Term Meaning Too Many Different Things: What Other People Mean: What I Mean: What I Do Not Mean

JONATHAN KOZOL

1 The term *Free School* is used very often, in a cheerful but unthinking way, to mean entirely different kinds of things and to define the dreams and yearnings of entirely disparate and even antagonistic individuals and groups. It is honest, then, to say, right from the start, that I am speaking mainly of one type of Free School and that many of the ventures which go under the name of Free School will not be likely to find much of their own experience reflected here.

2 At one end of the spectrum, there is the large, public-school-connected, neighborhood-created and politically controversial operation best exemplified perhaps by I.S. 201, in its initial phase, or later by Ocean Hill–Brownsville in New York. Somewhat smaller, but still involving some of the same factors, and still tied in with the public education apparatus, is the Morgan School in Washington, D.C. At the opposite extreme is a rather familiar type of relatively isolated, politically non-controversial and generally all-white rural Free School. This kind of school is often tied in with a commune or with what is described as an "intentional community," attracts people frequently who, if not rich themselves, have parents who are wealthy, and is often associated with a certain kind of media-promoted counter-culture.

3 Neither of the two descriptions just preceding would apply directly to the kind of Free School I have tended to be most intensively involved with, though certainly I have been a great deal closer to the first than to the second. There is also a considerable difference in the way I feel about the two. The large, political and public-school-associated ventures like Ocean Hill–Brownsville are, in my opinion, brave, significant and in many ways heroic struggles for survival on the part of those who constitute the most despised and brutalized and properly embittered victims of North American racism and class-exploitation. While these are not the kinds of schools that I am writing about here, they seem to me to be of vast importance and I look upon the people who are active in them with immense respect.

4 The other end of the spectrum does not seem to me to be especially courageous or heroic. In certain ways, it appears to me to be a dan-

gerous and disheartening phenomenon. I know, of course, that very persuasive arguments can be presented for the idea of escaping from the turmoil and the human desperation of the cities, and for finding a place of physical isolation in the mountains of Vermont or in the hills of Southern California. Like many people here in Boston and New York, I have often felt the urge to run away, especially when I see a picture or read something in a magazine about these pastoral and isolated Free Schools in their gentle and attractive settings of hillside, farmland and warm country-meadow. When I am the most weary, the inclination to escape is almost overwhelming.

5 Despite this inclination, which I feel so often, I believe we have an obligation to stay here and fight these battles and work out these problems in the cities where there is the greatest need and where, moreover, we cannot so easily be led into a mood of falsified euphoria. If a man should feel, as many people do, that whites should not be working in black neighborhoods, then there are plenty of poor-white neighborhoods in major cities, or neighborhoods of the marginal lower-middle-class along the edges of the major cities, in which we might establish roots and settle down to try to build our Free Schools and to develop those communities of struggle which so frequently grow up around them. I know it is very appealing and, for people who are weary from a long, long period of fruitless struggle and rebellion, it is almost irresistible to get away from everything. I don't believe, however, that we should give in to this yearning, even if it is very appealing and even if we are very, very weary. In any case, I am addressing this book primarily to those who do not plan to run away.

6 There is one point about the exodus to the woods and hills which is, to me, particularly disturbing. Some of the most conscientious and reflective of the people in the country Free Schools will seek to justify their manner of escape by pointing out that they, and their young children with them, have in a sense "retired" from the North American system as a whole, and especially from its agencies of devastation, power and oppression. Though earnestly presented, this argument does not seem honest. Whether they like it or not, or whether they wish to speak of it or not, the beautiful children of the rich and powerful within this nation are going to be condemned to wield that power also. This power, which will be theirs if they are cognizant of it and even if they aren't, will be the power to affect the lives of millions of poor men and women in this nation, to do so often in the gravest ways, often indeed to grant or to deny life to these people. It will be the power, as well, to influence the lives of several hundred million people who are now subject to North American domination in far-distant lands. Even in the idealistic ritual of formal abdication of that power, as for example, by going out into the isolated hills of Western Massachusetts or into the mountains of Vermont to start a Free School, they will still

be profiting from the consequences of that power and from the direct profits and extractions of a structure of oppression.

7 Free Schools, then, cannot with sanity, with candor or with truth, endeavor to exist within a moral vacuum. However far the journey and however many turnpike tolls we pay, however high the spruce or pine that grow around the sunny meadows in which we live and dream and seek to educate our children, it is still one nation. It is not one thing in Lebanon, New Hampshire, one thing in the heart of Harlem. No more is it one thing in Roxbury or Watts, one thing in Williamsburg or Sausalito, California. The passive, tranquil and protected lives white people lead depend on strongly armed police, well-demarcated ghettos. While children starve and others walk the city streets in fear on Monday afternoon, the privileged young people in the Free Schools of Vermont shuttle their handlooms back and forth and speak of love and of "organic processes." They do "their thing." Their thing is sun and good food and fresh water and good doctors and delightful, old and battered eighteenth-century houses, and a box of baby turtles; somebody else's thing may be starvation, broken glass, unheated rooms and rats inside the bed with newborn children. The beautiful children do not *wish* cold rooms or broken glass, starvation, rats or fear for anybody; nor will they stake their lives, or put their bodies on the line, or interrupt one hour of the sunlit morning, or sacrifice one moment of the golden afternoon, to take a hand in altering the unjust terms of a society in which these things are possible.

8 I know that I will antagonize many people by the tenor of these statements; yet I believe them deeply and cannot keep faith with the people I respect, and who show loyalty to me, if I put forward a piece of writing of this kind and do not say these things. In my belief, an isolated upper-class rural Free School for the children of the white and rich within a land like the United States and in a time of torment such as 1972, is a great deal too much like a sandbox for the children of the SS Guards at Auschwitz. If today in our history books, or in our common conversation, we were to hear of a network of exquisite, idealistic little country-schools operated with a large degree of personal freedom, but within the bounds of ideological isolation, in the beautiful sloping woodlands outside of Munich and Berlin in 1939 or 1940, and if we were to read or to be told that those who ran these schools were operating by all innovative methods and enlightened notions and that they had above their desks or on their walls large poster-photographs of people like Maria Montessori and Tolstoi and Gandhi, and that they somehow kept beyond the notice of the Nazi government and of the military and of the police and SS Guards, but kept right on somehow throughout the war with no experience of rage or need for intervention in the lives of those defined by the German press and media as less than human, but kept right on with

waterplay and innovative games while smoke rose over Dachau . . . I think that we would look upon those people now as some very fine and terrifying breed of alienated human beings.

9 It is not a handsome or a comfortable parallel; yet, in my judgment it is not entirely different from the situation of a number of the country communes and the rural Free Schools that we now see in some sections of this nation. At best, in my belief, these schools are obviating pain and etherizing evil; at worst, they constitute a registered escape-valve for political rebellion. Least conscionable is when the people who are laboring and living in these schools describe themselves as revolutionaries. If this is revolution, then the men who have elected Richard Nixon do not have a lot to fear. They would do well in fact to subsidize these schools and to covertly channel resources to their benefactors and supporters, for they are an ideal drain on activism and the perfect way to sidetrack ethical men from dangerous behavior.

Thinking Questions: ***Form***

1. In this brief essay Jonathan Kozol defines two categories of "free" schools. One type exists in large cities and is run by the people of a particular community within the city. The other is represented by the suburban or rural free school in which students escape from what the administrators of these schools believe is an immoral society. Why does Kozol favor the city "free" school? From the sketchy information in this essay, can you explain how an urban free school would operate? Who would decide curriculum? Would the community running the school allow the city school board to set educational standards?

2. Write an essay in which you classify several types of schools that you have either attended, visited, heard or read about. After you have described the characteristics of each school, tell why you favor one over the others.

3. Explain the metaphor that Kozol uses in paragraph 8 to explain why he reacts negatively to "upper-class rural Free Schools." How are these schools "like a sandbox for the children of the SS Guards at Auschwitz"? Why does Kozol argue that such schools support the status quo while they actually claim to oppose it?

4. Clarify the assumptions behind Kozol's analysis of free schools. Do you believe the following statements accurately describe the essay's assumptions? (Assumptions are foundation blocks, basic beliefs on which a writer builds his or her arguments. Often they are implied or taken for granted, rather than specifically expressed.)

– Our capitalistic society must be radically changed, even destroyed.

– Education must prepare students to make changes, to rectify injustices, and *not* to accept the status quo merely because it is more comfortable to do so.

– Schools should emphasize personal growth over material or social growth.

Show how one or all of these statements are supported by Kozol's arguments.

Thinking Questions: *Substance*

1. What do you feel Jonathan Kozol would think of Paul Goodman's suggestions for educational apprenticeships for bright students? How are these writers' proposals similar and different? Would Goodman's suggestions (that students work in community-based enterprises, for example, to earn academic credit) help the poor and disadvantaged in cities? How?
2. Why is Kozol against rural free schools for the rich? Does his negative attitude have something to do with his belief, which is implied rather than directly stated in this essay, that education should encourage *confrontation* rather than *escape, dispute* rather than *easy agreement?* Explain the italicized terms in the previous sentence, especially as they apply to this essay and to education in general.
3. Consider your own educational background. Does it encourage confrontation and dispute or escape and agreement? Have your relationships with teachers and administrators encouraged dispute or open disagreement with the status quo or with authority? Be specific.
4. These first two essays both argue against traditional education. What arguments can you think of to support the traditional educational system—the idea of a set curriculum that all students must take, the traditional authority of teachers and administrators, the ideas that learning should take place in a school with classrooms and that education should train students to be cooperative citizens?

What It's Like to Go to School

MARY FRANCES GREENE and ORLETTA RYAN

Religion

1 Richard's church sends him to a summer camp sponsored by middle-class Negro members of a small community in Michigan. Asked what they'd think of the writing on a third- to fourth-floor stair wall, he says, "Oh, those people wouldn't even know one of those words on the wall. They are church people!"

2 Curtis brings in a cross at lunch hour he says he found somewhere.

3 *Vernon.* That's a Catholic cross.

4 *Curtis.* It is not!

5 *Vernon.* It is so, they a body on it, it's Catholic.

6 (Others are ducking at Curtis's chest to see the cross, and imitate vomiting at the sight.)

7 *Richard.* Well, you got to have a cross in my church too! A big cross is at that door.

8 *Josie* (calls out). You get communion in that church, boy?

9 *Harold.* We do! We gets crackers and cherry pop!

10 *Ruby.* You been *confirmed* in that church?

Richard. I been everything. I been saved. If I gets bumped in the ass by a cab, that cab driver just got to take one look at this card. (Shows card; card gives prescription, ending ". . . and must respect and speak well to members of our race (colored).") We got a lot of baptism too, but not like on 116th Street. I know they got complete diversion there. You got to wear a white gown to the floor for that.

11 *Josie* (hanging on to Leanore's chair in excitement). *I'm gonna get me that diversion,* my sisters had it. They look so beau-ti-ful in their gowns! The reverend hold you head so you don'ts drownd.

12 —In my church in the South, when the singing gets glorious, everyone faints!

13 —Oh, that's *Pentecostal* Church. Christian reform don't do that kinda thing.

14 *Vernon.* In my church everyone gets communion, but you gots to be eleven.

15 *Ruby.* When you eats the crackers, that's eatin up Baby Jesus.

16 *Vernon.* If you go to church every week, my preacher will send you to camp for two weeks. You gotta bring four T shirts and swimming trunks.

17 *Richard.* Well, I am a *Christian.* The Catholics prays to the idol Mary. But it ain't wrong to be a Catholic, if it's okay for you. My preacher says I'm going to have salvation, and he musta *read my mind* cause that's just what I got in minds for myself. I go to Sunday School twice a week, and I learn about Adam and Eve—Adam and Eve was stark naked; and the second worst sin. But I forgets what that is. And that's why I gets to go to Michigan in the summer, with the light-skinned Negro people—they never lock doors in Michigan and no one steals nothing.

18 *Ruby.* That's nothing. I'm Baptist and we goes to Atlantic City, but I never heard of Michigan. We goes with lightskin people and we sing beautiful hymns that makes everyone smile.

Addicts

19 A drizzling day. Richard arrives half an hour late to school. During the night, addicts had stumbled onto a pile of broken plate glass on his street, then into his building to sleep. His father, the superintendent, had found the hall so full of blood at early dawn he'd gone to the police station about getting the addicts out.

20 *Richard.* The lieutenant told him, "Dial my private number. I'll send every man in the place out."

21 *Monty.* They gets blood on the floor because they misses their bein, too.

22 *Richard.* They sleep on garbage buckets in the basement. My father tries to get 'em out with his Derringer; but sometimes they get so high they can't get off the piles.

23 *Reggie.* But they can't help theirself. It's their life. They don't want to hurt no one, just theirselfs.

24 *Monty.* You has to be careful with that needle, and be sure you go in your bein, and carry a baby's nipple over the tube or you hurt someone.

25 *Reggie.* They feel they in the snow—walking in tennis shoes in the snow. They feel like they in another world. I don't mind if I was an addict—they *warm* in winter.

26 *Richard.* The reverend at our church, he tried for years to he'p them, but he say he about ready to quit. They do be so greedy, the reverend had four chickens for Christmas for the poor, and the addicts come and eat them all.

27 *Ruby.* Children must stay away from them, they kisses you in a funny way, they wants to expose you. They splits open some candy and fill it with gray powder. They wants you to get funny with them.

28 *Monty.* An addict always brings his equipment with him. Cover his needle with a *baby's nipple,* and he need a big black belt for his arm so he can set that needle right in his bein.

29 *Richard.* They cut when they sees the cops. The cops swing up they billies; they poke to the addicts' chin.

30 *Virgil.* Oh, there was an addic', and I was *so* scared. I had my mother's twenty dollars; I was going down to the store. He came up behind me and put a knife on me and say, "Don't turn aroun', *don't breathe."* Sometimes I'm nutty, and I run away! And I was lucky. You gets it right *there.* (Shows on his back.)

31 Addiction is higher than anything in any book, Mrs. Weiss says. Relatives of school aides may be hooked; parents may be. "In junior high, children go on the needle. Children with their heads down in cafeteria, falling asleep in class. I know of a fifteen-year-old in Jeffer-

son, sister of one of our kids, whose mother is on the needle and got the girl hooked—so she'd keep quiet."

32 Every doorway in the morning—men with brown paper bags and bottles. Addicts high, standing, leaning, staring. Not drinking. Fifteen in a block on the way to school. Signs in front of every building: "No Loitering, Order of Police." Three addicts are stripped naked at noon on a side street. The police horse off a square around them. Children watch on the way back from lunch as the cops go up each rectum with rubber gloves. ("They private places, they might hi' it.")

33 Eight bent over a burning ashcan, a block down from school, warming gray hands. All night. Someone tips alcohol on the can; blue flame licks up for a moment.

34 A young addict puts his head in a cab:

35 *Addict.* Gimme a dime, that's a' I wan', a dime. . . . Okay, then gi' a cigarette.

36 *Driver.* Buddy, I just don't have it.

37 *Addict.* Then fuck off.

38 *Monty.* They keeps moving, and stay together so the cops don't see. They take lights from the hallways; that's why they always so dark. It is *expensive!* A bag of reefers, that cost a buck! And they shares them in the hall.

39 *Josie.* You on'y needs blue pills now. The doctor sell them to you for a quarter.—In my block, Brother and Little John are addic'. Little John he's nineteen, he pretty and very light. Has processed hair.

40 *Reggie.* A lady addic' in our block. I don't know how she have her life. She's an addic'; and she's a lady. There's *nothin* will stop an addic' that needs a fix. They'll cut a head off and mess around with the body. They *gots to do somethin* . . . they won't stop at nothin. But when they attacks you, you gotta fight back. *You gotta do somethin.* I'm gonna pick up detective work when I grow up. You get a Derringer. I'd have my Derringer here, right under my arm. I'd say, "Excuse me, you need a cigarette?" to the addic', and reach up and grab down my Derringer!

41 *Richard.* I go to my grandmother's building, she live on the top floor. I like that roof of hers, there's pigeons flyin, but addicts up there too! It's scary! I take my Pepsi bottle and break the top off. Then I'm safe.

42 *Vernon.* I always carry my broken bottle when I go out to someone's building. But they's no addicts in my building.

43 *Reggie.* You jivin? 122 is full of addicts.

44 *Vernon.* Well, they *don't touch my grandmother.* No addict in our block'd touch my grandmother. They calls her Maw.

45 *Richard.* Hey, Mrs. Weiss, that a real diamond or glass?

46 *Mrs. Weiss.* Hmmph . . . it is quite real.

47 *Richard.* You shouldn't wear that, some addict take and get it off you.

48 *Mrs. Weiss.* He'd have to take my arm off to get that, Richard.

49 *Richard.* Well that's just what he's gonna do. He's gonna take off your arm if he needs that fix.

50 *Noah.* My father was addic', but he went down to Florida, got hisself cured. No addic' can work, no addic' ever been known to work, except maybe when he were a small child.

51 *Reggie.* You has to put on coconut butter to cover up the marks cause you can' go round with those hole in you' arm, everyone'll know you.

52 *Malcolm.* But you can't just *start* addict. First sniffin glue; you 'bout nine. Later you goes on reefers on the roof with older kids. My brother smokes reefers but he won't let me come up, he say he'll cut my ass.

53 —About ten hangs out on *my* block. My super keep them moving in our hall. We live on the first floor, my mom got a police lock on our door. But it's *scary.* They call in soft through the keyhole when my mom be out.

54 —*My* mother don't answer that door at night. She says Who's there? but don't open it. And she keeps that can of lye by the door.

55 —My mother too!

56 *Malcolm.* Lye! But you suppose' to use that for the stuffed pipes.

57 —No, you got to keep that lye. But people do anything with it. A lady in my block, she threw lye in a man's face. He owed her nine dollars, and she needed that. He said, "You better not throw that, there's kids around here." But she didn't even hear that, she was too crazy for her money. Threw it at him and he starts to scream, "My eyes, my eyes!" And the ambulance come, and a lot of people was there. They took him away, I don't know where. But I know when he comes out of that hospital, he's gonna shot her.

Leanore

58 She spends a morning cleaning her desk whenever my back's turned. Her head goes all the way into the desk with Kleenex; many trips up to the wastebasket with things she's throwing out, into the cabinet to get paste while I'm out in the hall chasing Curtis. She pastes a picture inside her desk top to give it a home atmosphere. "Please get your head out of there, Leanore. Will you, please?" Comes out banging it so hard, it sends shivers through William,

Roger, and Monty. "Pardon meee?" Opens her book angrily.

59 *Harold* (reading). Is . . . th-th-is—

60 *Leanore* (reads at double speed). Eagle befriends this baby bear. Now Eagle has *two* pets. Is *this* the baby bear? *Mama Bear's baby bear?* (Tears her math paper into one thousand pieces and throws the confetti over her shoulder.)

61 "I'm going to the washroom," she calls, and walks out. Returns in half an hour.

62 "No lunch, Leanore, until you finish the math paper."

63 "You're not keeping me from any lunch—my mother'd love to hear about that. You want a paper? Here, I'll give you a paper." (Tosses blank paper on desk.)

64 "Well, your mother hasn't answered any of three notes; I should see your mother. Straighten up this afternoon, or I go home with you."

65 She laughs: "Lady, you better not visit my mother! My mother doesn't want to be bothered."

66 All afternoon she has the boys on pins and needles. At two o'clock, drops on all fours like a graceful panther, glides halfway up the aisle, stops, calls up something through the rows in a velvety, strange language, so wild the children are shocked.

67 *Josie.* Shame! I never thought I'd hear a child talk to a teacher like that! Don't you have no mind in your brain, Leanore? Girl, get up.

68 *Vernon.* Listen girl, you think you're at home now? No wonder my mother don't want you in our house.

69 At three o'clock, as the children were lining up and William passed her desk, she snatched his folder of corrected papers and tore it in half. "All right, get your coat, here we go," I said to her, and dismissed the other children. She slipped outside the door and stood laughing. "You wouldn't dare."

70 "We'll see."

71 "I'm not going anywhere with you. Fifty times you've said, 'I'll visit your mother,' but I'm on to you."

72 She dashed away and down the stairs, laughing. I locked the room and in a few moments was following her out of the building. The air was sharp and cold, but boys played with bottles along the curbs or sat eating penny candy—one eating, two looking on. Leanore had appeared ahead, and trailed and shadowed me, always keeping about half a block ahead. She'd cross from one side of the street, cross back, calling insults, running. She didn't think I'd keep going. We reached her block. Adults talked in groups in the store fronts, and at the candy store on her corner, people of different ages stood in coats looking out.

73 I asked a woman, "Do you know where 153 is? I can't find the number." "No." People stood in the next building hallway—some-

thing going on inside. A little boy said, "I'm her brother; her mother's out." (She has no brother.)

74 At this point I heard my name suddenly called out—Leanore's voice! She appeared from somewhere in the dark. "Miss Burke, I'm here. Over here!" And she ducked around the fender of a Buick and into a building entrance.

75 The kid who'd said he was her brother sprinted in after Leanore, announcing me: "Leanore, you teacher's comin!" Then dashed back out and onto the street to tell others. I walked up three flights with Leanore hightailing it ahead of me.

76 When I knocked a few times, the door opened a crack. "Are you Leanore Hazle's mother?" A woman in plastic curlers peered out: "Yeah, what'd she do?"

77 It was freezing in the hall. "I'd like to talk to you about Leanore, about her behavior at school." The crack did not get any wider, and from within Leanore's voice screamed, "It's gonna be a lie!" "I wrote you a note," I continued, and with this the door opened. "Listen, miss, the reason I didn't come, I had to go to court. I been very sick. You wanta come in?"

78 The apartment was spotlessly clean, though dark. Plastic drapes, flowered linoleum, 27-inch television that Mrs. Hazle went to turn down. Big end tables with kewpie dolls and crowds of furniture. Beyond, a bedroom with doubledecker bunks, Leanore stretching out on one and peeking around the door to see what would happen.

79 Mrs. Hazle fixed a few doilies, pulled shades even, and went out to turn down something bubbling in the kitchen. She re-entered with a baby that she set about diapering, with an appearance of listening while I said, "I've been meaning to come and talk to you about Leanore. She is a nice-looking child who comes to school beautifully groomed, she has a quick mind, shows leadership qualities. However—" The mother was not really listening. I turned to the trouble side: hooky playing, no classwork, language, tormenting of children, leaves seat or room when she pleases, drops small change all over the room—*"Stealing?"* the mother cut in sharply. "Oh, not exactly, it's more that—" "Well, boy, she better not be *stealing,* I'll tell you that much. That'd be just about the next thing I'd hear about that girl. Can't keep her cooped up here, but can't let her go down on that street any more; the neighbors want me to keep her in," said Mrs. Hazle, delivering the last words with a gaze toward the bedroom that hinted at the long antisocial years of Leanore. Leanore was now calling from the bedroom, "Oh, Mama, don't believe this woman, she's a liar herself! Tried to take my lunch money, said it was Iris's, it was mine! She steals money, that's the kind of woman you're talking to, Mama!"

80 "Leanore answers me back, swears—" ("Dirty lie! This woman lies!")

"—chews gum constantly, obeys no rules, starts fights all day." The longer the list grew, the less I felt that Mrs. Hazle and I took the same view of the list. It sounded like nothing but a list. Particularly when she now stood up, placed the baby on the floor, and walked to a cabinet just inside the kitchen door. She did call, "Go on, go on, I'm diggin you," back over her shoulder.

81 "I thought if the three of us could talk this over, we could discover a way to correct some of these things. She often leaves the building. I was about to report her truant two different times this semester—" ("Lie! Lie! Mama, don't listen, the only time I leave the room is when I have to get something, like if I have to borrow something in another room, Mama. This woman's been saying she's gonna come up here for three weeks and never came, so you can't believe her! If I do my homework she says it's wrong, that's why I don't do it!")

82 "Miss Bowser took her as a favor to me for four days and tells me that last year Leanore's behavior was so antisocial she was about to be expelled—" ("Mrs. Bowser's a big, fat black cow!") "—So that's what I've come to tell you, that this is possible again. I've warned Leanore that I might see you, and she always says you can't be bothered." The mother now came out of the kitchen carrying a strap with a buckle.

83 "I can't be bothered?" She walked into the bedroom. "You told this woman I can't be bothered?" Sounds of strapping began. "Oh, I'll tell you something! You've just about had what you're gonna get out of my life, baby! I'm not going to no court for no kid again!" (Strapping. Cries of "Mama!")

84 "There's no point in beating her, Mrs. Hazle. We must try to find out what is making her unhappy," I said, going to the door, but inside the strap arm was now working mechanically over Leanore who clung to the bed. The voice droned along with the arm, "Oh yes! I've got a couple of things going for myself now, no one's gonna ruin it! Oh no, no more trouble outa you, girl!" (Strap, strap!) "I've got me this new baby, life looks okay for a little while right now," (strap, strap) "and nothin's gonna go wrong again. No teacher's ever coming here again, no trouble, no judges; I've had it from you! This woman don't want you swearing, chewing gum in your mouth, fighting, and that's what she don't want." (Strap, strap.) "—Shut your mouth —and when you go to that school do that, shut your mouth." (Strap. Pause.) "—Another thing baby. No guy wants you if you don't have the diploma; they'll sweet-talk you, but they don't want you." (Strap, strap, strap! Nothing could now be heard in the room but the strap going in a burst of new energy, the cries, and the drone.)

85 "Mrs. Hazle—please!" But just as I spoke, not in answer to my voice but because of some loss of interest on her own part, the strap fell to her side. Staring at Leanore, she wound up, "And when Sidney

comes Sunday, he can take you, lock, stock, and barrel, baby. I've got my own scene going; you ain't ruining it again. You can just go up the Hudson this time where they know how to handle kids like you. Where they take those radiator brushes. Remember? Louise there, and she is a forgotten child. No one gonna go to see her; Martin ain't; Ravelle ain't. I got me this baby. You and me are two different parties from now on. I spent a lotta time on you; now I lost interest in you, baby."

86 At this point an older sister walked in with, "Listen, Mama, I heard about some more things Leanore's been doing," and the mother got in a few more licks, saying, "Yes, Sidney can take you and your stuff in the bag Sunday. Sidney always tellin' me y'got bad blood, but it ain't my bad blood; it's his. And when Farrel comes Tuesday, he can take you, too," she added to the other daughter without looking around or ceasing to strap Leanore. "That bus goes from Forty-second Street right up the Hudson to that school" (strap) "and there's plenty of room."

87 Here I said goodbye and walked out. The strap stopped, but sobbing still came through the door. I stood in the corridor for a moment. No other sound. Then water began running in the kitchen.

88 Leanore was very quiet in class the next day but at noon brushed past my desk to snicker and drop a few words stranger than anything in the visit had been: "I never thought you'd come there."

The Children's World

89 Richard comes in late one morning with a fine German shepherd puppy. He says, "I'm afraid about having him at home; the rats might get him."

90 *Monty.* You gotta put him up on the kitchen table. If you leave him alone, put a leash on him. Formica top table; they slips on the legs.

91 *Richard.* They jump pretty high, though. I hate leaving him alone. I don't know what to do.

92 —A rat bit my baby sister on the finger. My father's done everything: he sets traps, he beats them, but they tunnel through those walls.

93 —You got to kill them with orange poison. Traps dangerous, babies get their hands or feet in them. You puts the orange poison on the bread, they swells up and strangles.

94 —You gots to put the food away. My mother say our neighbor must like rats. She leave all that food around. Leave a dish of corn and rice on the table, they play in it like nothing wrong.

95 —You leave food, that's just wasting money. Jump up on the table and eat through a forty-cent loaf of bread, right to the other end. Cost you a great expense, not puttin things away. Don't put your bread in a plastic breadbox; they go right through it. Get yourself a tin breadbox.

96 *Jason.* Rats left feet marks across my birthday cake; it had blue flowers on it. My mother has to throw it out.

97 —My aunt put a roast in the oven and the next day open that oven, and a rat popped right out at her. She screamed and screamed! She ran out of the room. Man, was that rat big!

98 —My mother don't leave one single food for rats; but even if she don't leave no food around, she still puts that orange powder around, up high so the baby don't get in it.

99 —No, you puts lye down, very thick aroun' the borders and thick on the floor, and the rat's stomach gets burnt up from that lye. A rat died from that lye. He this long and this fat! (Holding up hands a foot apart.)

100 —They eat right through wood and plaster, not tin. They's tunnels all through your walls. You need tin—if you can't get flat tin, stick tin can in there, beat 'em flat, till you get tin.

101 —My mother always plugging up that hole, but she don't know how to hammer it right. Sometimes at that hole I just waits until they comes out. My big brother, he got combat boots, he steps on 'em; if they little, I can kill them with the broom.

102 —The only good thing is, they don't like to come out in the daytime. They're more for the night. Love garbage, hate light. My mother leaves the hall light on. Never cut lights out when there's rats.

103 *Reggie.* I dare you to come in my basement, honey. Those dead and alive rats will keep you moving. I always carry a stick or a broken soda bottle. Hide that stick up my arm. Sometimes, in an emergency, I have to go down get the garbage buckets. I'm too scared to even think about it now.

> Your house is so classy,
> You got rats as big as Lassie.
>
> I went to your house for a piece of cheese.
> A rat jumped up and said, "Heggies, please."

104 *Vernon.* They comes out from behind the refrigerator when you puts the lights on, when you come in from the show. But don't scare me. I sleep in a top bunk.
(Others laugh: "That won't help anything; they climb right up some nights if they want to.")

105 *Josie.* I don't want to hear about rats no more—I'm gettin scared!

106 —They likes the night. Don't come out in day too much. If all the rats came out around up here, they'd be pushing people off the sidewalk, but they don't. They stay in till it's night.

107 *Vernon.* Rats when they born they red, but when they gets old they long and *gray,* man. My father when he see a baby rat bein born, he say they keep comin and comin.

108 —Our landlord should live in my house just one day, just one day! But it's no good to bother him, he live out on Long Island and he don't like people to call him up there much.

109 —You can sue the landlord if the rats eat the baby; otherwise you can't.

110 *Virgil.* No point in calling the super; half the time he's drunk. He's a bum, my father said.

111 —Our super's drunk most of the time, so he don't be sending up the steam. He singing spirituals on Sunday and sends his little kids down to the basement to fix the furnace and big flames leaps out.

112 —It's bad when he don't send up that steam. My two little sisters has asthma. My mother have to keep the oven on all day.

113 *Reggie.* Boy, my father ain't that bad, gets drunk but never more than once a month. If he gets drunk he send me down to send up the steam. But always he send up the steam.

114 —Our super never once makes hot water.

115 —Yeah, us either.

116 —Those rats look at you! You better not curse them or look back. Don't never curse a rat right to him cause he'll take your clothes—go right into your closet and eat up everything.

117 —They give you blood poisoning, and their teeth has more germs than to kill an army.

118 —I'm afraid to go to sleep, they's rats. I'm afraid of the dark, and my room's way down the hall.

119 —Not me. My cat comes in my bed and saves me.

120 —You gets yourself a cat. If your cat kills a rat, put it in a newspaper and throw it out back, for the old mean cats to eat. No home cat is gonna truck with no dead thrown-out rat. Before you throw them out, you picks them up with the pliers because he's got every kind of germs on his teeth. And his tail's got germs too. You look out that back window sometime, it make you sick, there's so many cats eating old dead rats.

121 —Best way to do, always try to break their backs. If you gots combat boots that weigh more you can step on them. That breaks their backs too.

122 —If you're lucky they come out from the pipe and go right in the bathtub. My mother and me, once we saw eight of them. You hit them with the broom handle and the other person keeps filling the tub

with scalding water, and you drown them. The other person keep on hitting with that broom.

123 —We're gonna move to Brooklyn to a new project where there's no rats.

124 —My aunt's movin' to Long Island so no rats can get at her baby. There's gonna be hardly any cars on the street. And everyone have their own garden.

125 —I'm movin' south where there's no rats, just snakes.

126 *Richard.* In Michigan, they got very friendly white rats. They never heard of nothing else.

127 —Rats and cockroaches go together. In my basement you don't see just rats and cats; you see billions of roaches, too.

128 *Josie.* Roaches are all right, they washes themselves in sand. But my mother won't let my brother play with them. You can get rid of roaches. But a fly's no good: a fly sits in a dog's mess and then rub its back and front feets together and sit on your food. A roach would never sit on your food.

129 *Noah.* That's not true! Don't *never* eat grapes or nothing's been in your desk overnight. We had grapes, every cockroach in the neighborhood come sat over those grapes.—I walk into a lady's house and steps on some roaches. She say, "Don't do that. Let my people go."

130 *Curtis.* Wouldn't you get mad if a rat touched your daughter's head? Wouldn't you kill every one you saw? We're gonna move to the project in Brooklyn. I don't know how, though. My mother's gotta get herself an operation. I guess my uncle's gonna help.

131 *Richard.* In Michigan, if you talk about rats, they think you from the outer limits. They country hicks. When first they seen my skin, they call me nigger baby; never seen something like me before. They call like this: "Nig-ger baby! Nig-ger ba-by!" (He demonstrates, skipping in front of desks.) I was ashamed, but they didn't know.

132 Later Richard speaks of his dog again. The children advise him: "If he be that little, I keep that dog in bed with me. Then you can feel his heart on your heart."

Teaching. No Effort. No Attention

133 Harold is the first finished and has three wrong. *Teacher*: "When you've corrected these, you may read a library book." *Harold:* "I finished it, so why do I have to correct it?"

134 He corrects, with tears in his eyes, jabbing the pencil. Breaks the pencil. Then an argument over what to read: "Get a book from the library table." "I read all of 'em." "You read them or you looked at

the pictures? . . . Please go get one. . . . Try the story of the lost sailor." "I read it."

135 Josie's head is down. I've seen her fall asleep in the sun on a bench outside. Utter exhaustion.

136 Reggie finishes and wants to talk about his new boots.

137 *Teacher:* "No, the third problem's wrong—do you see? You added; you didn't multiply. Reggie, please look at the paper. The third problem. Look at what the paper says: three eights are twenty-four; four sixes are twenty-four; two twelves are—?" Repeat. He clamps his lips shut, digs his boot heel in the floor. The button in his head has turned off. He wants to be left alone. Can't watch the numbers. "Please watch my tens frame." Suddenly he clenches his teeth, grabs the paper, stomps back to his desk.

138 Mrs. Weiss and I stand at the classroom door. "I don't know where to start or finish. That's what I didn't expect. Two weeks ago, five children could do long and short vowels. Now, none of the five know all the vowels. And math. That's the best thing they do. Now I find out they can't do it—today, I say, 'Three twos are six, *five* twos (they expect "four") are—?' Silence."

139 *Mrs. Weiss:* "I've gone through it year after year. You think you're batting a thousand—then it blows up on you. They've forgotten everything. No one of them is ever with the school scene."

140 "Mrs. Weiss, what are they doing? Look at them. What is Reggie doing right now? What is Malcolm doing? Look how they're sitting. Doing nothing because I've stepped out of the door—is that it?"

141 Not even any noise in the room. Most children have stopped work and sit with vacant stares. Malcolm is looking out the window, his mouth open slack. He is looking on a blank courtyard. There is nothing out there. Reggie is hunched in his seat, angry tears in his eyes. He wanted to talk about the after-shave lotion he was wearing; I had told him to open his reader. He is ruined for the day.

142 "I thought Virgil was really ticking. He can read. Last week he knew homonyms. When there's a correlation he sees it, shouts it out. Today, I asked him to correct a Rexographed sheet. 'No, I'm not gonna.' '*Virgil.* What is it?' Something is always eating them. No one can correct anything. They take it as a personal insult—they've given me the sheet; what do I want from them now? Won't try, can't bear to fail."

143 *Mrs. Weiss:* "It's always the children with problems who can't read. For most of these children, life is a burden that they want to put down. They are really very sad children. And the school doesn't work for them. The curriculum has to be overhauled. They hate school; they really do.

144 "And what comes next for your babies? Sick Jefferson. Jefferson is

the terminal date. Kids give each other fixes and have sex in the washrooms, at Jefferson. You know that in the spring there aren't so many wars and rumbles around here any more; the thing is cool it, go on the needle. I know your kids say, 'I ain't goin to Jefferson, that's a *bad* school'; but actually they will—for a while. Then most of them will drop out."

Thinking Questions: ***Form***

1. Why do Greene and Ryan divide their essay into the subdivisions "Religion," "Addicts," "Leanore," "The Children's World," and "Teaching. No Effort. No Attention"? How do these classifications help define, limit, and explain the subject and purpose of the essay? Devise a thesis sentence for the essay and show how these classifications would help support it.

2. Although Greene and Ryan use several specific classifications, most of the material in this essay can be divided between *home* and *school.* Why is the contrast between the home and school environments of these children important?

3. Again, as in earlier sections of this book, we have an essay that describes and narrates, tells several little stories in detail, to support a thesis. The thesis is not explicitly stated. What sentence or sentences come closest to clarifying Greene and Ryan's purpose in writing? Can you put their thesis on the education of ghetto children into your own words?

4. There is a definite cause-and-effect logic behind this essay. Certain classroom problems are caused by certain discrepancies and conflicts between home and school. How, for example, does Leanore's home environment cause her problems in school? What particular effect is caused in the classroom by the younger children's problems with rats at home? Why are the children generally happier when they tell stories about their home life than when they are discussing English or arithmetic?

Thinking Questions: ***Substance***

1. How might these students' classroom experiences be improved? Should they be encouraged to tell more stories about home, to discuss new boots and drug addicts as well as mathematics and English? Is it possible to apply basic skills in reading, writing, and mathematics to the students' lives at home? Or should they simply be disciplined and taught these skills "by the hickory stick"?

2. Could any of Goodman's proposals be used to solve the problems described in this essay? Could some of these students learn to read and write, for example, by working part of each day on a local newspaper?

3. What do you think of the idea that the students' parents, rather than being set against their children by the school as Leanore and her

mother are, might work with students and teachers in the schools to solve local problems—making the problems of rats and addicts, for example, a part of the school curriculum? Parents might serve as teacher's aides, or they might be asked to join with teachers and administrators in devising a practical curriculum. Do you think Jonathan Kozol would support such an idea?

* * *

While Jonathan Kozol and Paul Goodman ask for changes in our attitudes toward students and their learning environment, R. Buckminster Fuller asks that we use educational technology to change the *methods* of education while we maintain traditional subject matter. Every educational system, he argues, helps students to respect what has gone before, what previous thinkers and learners have struggled to produce. Education, Fuller says, should do the same in the future, but it should also use these insights into the past to establish more freedom for the best thinkers, by using technology to free great teachers from the drudgeries of lecturing and of teaching basic skills. He describes an educational future in which many of the external practices will be different from the present; the underlying principles of education, however, will remain similar.

Fuller asks explicit questions about future methods of education; he then provides an explicit illustration of future educational programs in answer to these questions. Education, he says, will be more of a group process. It will bring together the individual mind of a topnotch researcher or thinker and, with the aid of technology—television, motion pictures, and tapes, for example—and disciplines such as psychology and speech, education will disseminate large numbers of concepts and information in dramatic fashion. We will come to know a true "education for the masses."

Fuller speaks positively of the future and of its potential. Machines were made to help people live easier and more pleasant lives, he believes, and we can continue to progress with the aid of machines as long as we continue to use them to free ourselves for other, more important, challenges: for complex thinking, the solving of social problems, and more creative use of leisure.

In essence, Fuller believes that people can *control* technology to ensure that it provides a better life. In education, machines and technology should provide more education for more people; they should also free topflight thinkers to pursue their ideas without the drudgery of lecture notes, lectures, and manual teaching.

Technology and Education

R. BUCKMINSTER FULLER

1 The big question is how are we, as educators, going to handle the enormous increase in the new life. How do we make available to these new students what we have been able to discover fairly accurately about the universe and the way it is operating? How are we going to be able to get to them the true net value won blindly through the long tradition of ignorant dedications and hard-won lessons of all the unknown mothers and all the other invisible heroic people who have given hopefully to the new life, such as, for instance, the fabulous heritage of men's stoic capacity to carry on despite immense hardships?

2 The new life needs to be inspired with the realization that it has all kinds of new advantages that have been gained through great dedications of unknown, unsung heroes of intellectual exploration and great intuitively faithful integrities of men groping in the dark. Unless the new life is highly appreciative of those who have gone before, it won't be able to take effective advantage of its heritage. It will not be as regenerated and inspired as it might be if it appreciated the comprehensive love invested in that heritage.

3 The old political way of looking at things is such that the political machine says we first must get a "school house" for our constituents, and it must look like Harvard University, or it must be Georgian and a whole big pile of it. "We see that the rich kids went to school in automobiles; so let's get beautiful buses for our kids." "Harvard and Yale have long had football; our school is going to have football." There is nothing boys used to have that they are not going to "get" from their politicians, who, above all, know best how to exploit the inferiority complex which they understand so well as handed down from the ages and ages of 99 per cent have-not-ness of mankind. There is a sort of class inferiority amelioration battle that goes on with the politicos in seeking the favor of their constituents to get into or back into office, and little if any attention is paid to the real educational problems at hand.

4 In thinking about these problems, I have thought a lot about what I have learned that may be useful as proven by experiments in my own self-discipline. I have met some powerful thinkers. I met Dr. Einstein. I wrote three chapters in a book about Dr. Einstein, and my publishers said that they wouldn't publish it because I wasn't on the list of people who understood Einstein. I asked them to send the typescript

to Einstein, and they did. He then said he approved of it—that I had interpreted him properly—and so the chapters did get published. When Einstein approved of my typescript he asked me to come and meet him and talk about my book. I am quite confident that I can say with authority that Einstein, when he wanted to study, didn't sit in the middle of a school room. That is probably the poorest place he could have gone to study. When an individual is really thinking, he is tremendously isolated. He may manage to isolate himself in Grand Central Station, but it is *despite* the environment rather than because of it. The place to study is not in a school room.

5 Parents quite clearly love their children; that is a safe general observation. We don't say parents send their children to school to get rid of them. The fact is, however, that it is very convenient for mothers, in order to be able to clean the house for the family, to have the children out of the way for a little while. The little red school house was not entirely motivated by educational ambitions.

6 There is also a general baby-sitting function which is called school. While the children are being "baby sat," they might as well be given something to read. We find that they get along pretty well with the game of "reading"; so we give them more to read, and we add writing and arithmetic. Very seriously, much of what goes on in our schools is strictly related to social experiences, and that is fine—that's good for the kids. But I would say we are going to add much more in the very near future by taking advantage of the children's ability to show us what they need.

7 I have taken photographs of my grandchildren looking at television. Without consideration of the "value," the actual concentration of a child on the message which is coming to him is fabulous. They really "latch on." Given the chance to get accurate, logical, and lucid information at the time when they want and need to get it, they will go after it and inhabit it in a most effective manner. I am quite certain that we are soon going to begin to do the following: At our universities we will take the men who are the faculty leaders in research or in teaching. We are not going to ask them to give the same lectures over and over each year from their curriculum cards, finding themselves confronted with another roomful of people and asking themselves, "What was it I said last year?" This is a routine which deadens the faculty member. We are going to select, instead, the people who are authorities on various subjects—the men who are most respected by other men within their respective departments and fields. They will give their basic lecture course just once to a group of human beings, including both the experts in their own subject and bright children and adults without special training in their field. This lecture will be recorded as Southern Illinois University did my last lecture series of fifty-two hours in October 1960. They will make moving picture

footage of the lecture as well as hi-fi tape recording. Then the professor and his faculty associates will listen to this recording time and again.

8 "What you say is very good," his associates may comment, "but we have heard you say it a little better at other times." The professor then dubs in a better statement. Thus begins complete reworking of the tape, cleaned up, and cleaned up some more, as in the moving picture cutting, and new illustrative "footage" will be added on. The whole of a university department will work on improving the message and conceptioning of a picture for many months, sometimes for years. The graduate students who want to be present in the university and who also qualify to be with the men who have great powers and intellectual capability together with the faculty may spend a year getting a documentary ready. They will not even depend upon the diction of the original lecturer, because the diction of that person may be very inadequate to his really fundamental conceptioning and information, which should be superb. His knowledge may be very great, but he may be a poor lecturer because of poor speaking habits or false teeth. Another voice will take over the task of getting his exact words across. Others will gradually process the tape and moving picture footage, using communications specialists, psychologists, etc.

9 For instance, I am quite certain that some day we will take a subject such as Einstein's Theory of Relativity, and with the "Einstein" of the subject and his colleagues working on it for a year, we will finally get it reduced down to what is "net" in the subject and enthusiastically approved by the "Einstein" who gave the original lecture. What is *net* will become communicated so well that any child can turn on a documentary device, a TV, and get the Einstein lucidity of thinking and get it quickly and firmly. I am quite sure that we are going to get research and development laboratories of education where the faculty will become producers of extraordinary moving-picture documentaries. That is going to be the big, new educational trend.

Thinking Questions: *Form*

1. Compare the function of Fuller's college of the future with the "babysitting" function of the schools he describes in his early paragraphs. What will be the functions of education in those film classes Fuller describes—to transfer knowledge, to show great thought developing? Is that the function of classes in your educational environment?

2. Fuller carefully points out both similarities and differences between the present and the future in education. What are they?

3. Point to several minor comparisons in Fuller's essay. For example, Fuller compares Einstein, who, he argues, never did his serious thinking in a classroom, with ordinary students, who often pay closer attention to television than they do to classroom lectures or discussions. How does this secondary comparison relate to Fuller's major comparison? Show how other minor or secondary comparisons function as well.

4. Is this essay unified? What do the first two paragraphs have to do with the rest of the essay? If there is a connection, does Fuller make it clear enough? (Unity exists when every sentence in an essay clearly relates to the essay's general purpose or thesis.)

5. Fuller divides his descriptions of the future in education into two areas: what teachers and researchers will do in the future and what students will do in the future. Teachers will become filmmakers, learning to present what they know through films rather than through books and lectures. Students will get the knowledge they need more efficiently by watching educational films than they had in the past by listening to lectures or reading books. Both teachers and students, then, would be free to pursue private thought and research. Would the absence of personal interaction between teacher and student harm this new system?

Thinking Questions: *Substance*

1. Do you see potential disadvantages in the future educational system that Fuller describes? Explain those possibilities specifically. For example, in his opening paragraphs, Fuller argues that we must change the way we educate and learn without altering our respect for the discipline and effort involved in great thought. Later in his essay Fuller describes mass education based on mass media and technology, specifically documentary films. Will students trained through films and other mass media maintain their respect for "the fabulous heritage of man's stoic capacity to carry on despite immense hardships"? Especially if they have not found it necessary to undergo those hardships in their own learning?

2. People often think according to the conventions through which they have learned to think. In paragraph 3, Fuller describes situations and structures—the conventional "schoolroom" and athletic programs, for example—that he believes are maintained merely because people are used to them. Can you point to conventions in your educational environment that seem to serve no real purpose or that might be better replaced by more imaginative structures?

3. Many people believe that conventions, even those without a completely useful purpose, should be maintained in order to retain a sense of purpose and tradition. Consider an educational convention such as the lecture or the small-class discussion, both of which Fuller suggests should be abolished to make education more efficient. What traditional advantages might be sacrificed if these conventions *were* abolished?

4. Is there more to teaching than Fuller acknowledges when he says, "We are not going to ask them [college teachers] to give the same lectures over and over each year from their curriculum cards. . ."? Will his film-tape substitute for the live teacher dehumanize teaching? Why or

why not? (See paragraph 8, where Fuller describes how classes will be taught in the future.)

5. Might Fuller's description of technology used to facilitate education apply more effectively to the dissemination of information than to the communication of complex concepts, human values, and attitudes? Perhaps the ideal educational system would combine the new modes of educational communication described by Fuller with opportunities for group discussions and classroom dialectic?

☼ ☼ ☼

Of course, the best traditional educators have always had their own answers to the question, "Where should the emphasis in education be placed?" Craig Eisendrath and Thomas J. Cottle argue that the traditional educational system can be adapted to meet the necessarily changing needs of students and society. They point out that the traditional educational structure often put too much emphasis on subject matter and gave very scant attention to the question of *how* students learn.

After close observation and study of recent unrest and discontent in universities and colleges across the nation, they propose that higher education in America become more experience-oriented, offering students the immediate opportunity to apply abstract knowledge. They also recommend greater student participation in university governance, and they encourage more emphasis on faculty performance in the classroom. Paul Goodman's suggestion that students be given more opportunity to learn by doing must, Eisendrath and Cottle argue, be supplemented by strong and pointed faculty control over the process of learning. In other words, as students gain a greater voice in the classroom, faculty must not retreat; rather they must assert ever greater influence to assure that subjective student expression is eventually combined with the objective, scholarly, and intellectual habits of their teachers.

University Discontent and Reform

CRAIG R. EISENDRATH and THOMAS J. COTTLE

1 Listen to the language of faculty discontent: "I come back from class emotionally drained. Not tired. Spent like an actor who's constantly afraid of losing his audience. You know the feeling? It's not good. I've had to put on such an act to make them interested. I'm

not teaching but performing. Even when I carry them along, I come home feeling something's wrong."

2 "I can't get my kids to read fifty pages. I'm lucky if half of them read ten."

3 "The faculty in my department tried T-grouping because we felt something was wrong. So we went out to this place in the country, a beautiful ivy-covered house, and we talked around two clocks—a whole weekend, about our problems in relating to the kids, our defensiveness, our projections of adolescent anxieties. Some of the junior people came back saying they thought it had been really useful. And yet it rather left a bad taste in my mouth. . . . I mean, is that what my main job is, relating to my students?"

Sources of Academic Discontent

4 The conversations go on. And year after year, it is evident that a good many of the most gifted academics devise ways to divest themselves of small, then larger portions of their teaching. Sometimes they seek reduced course loads; sometimes they withdraw from teaching altogether in institutes and research sinecures. Here, they claim, they can "do their work." Such men and women are not necessarily inarticulate nor temperamentally incapable or unwilling to share their ideas, but still they find teaching unsatisfying, and there comes a time when they seek to avoid it.

5 In so doing, some draw censure from their colleagues, particularly their younger ones, who may accuse them of shirking responsibilities, indeed the most essential responsibilities, or of retreating into an ivory tower promising a complacent end to involvement with students. Such academics, the younger ones might also allege, seem unwilling to adjust the university to today's realities which is why they lose the students' interest. Academic course work should meet the immediate concerns of students, like the draft, Viet Nam, welfare laws and pollution. The "now generation" has become more than a metaphor, and students, the younger academicians argue, are tuned to a sense of social and personal immediacy and the content of contemporary issues to such an extent that it is little wonder they remain uninterested in traditional subjects, or, for that matter, in contemporary course content if taught in a traditional manner. For quite a few young persons, relevance is the keynote. When their generation is getting shot in Viet Nam or politically repressed in America, it is absurd, the younger faculty say, to expect students to be interested in Aristotle, or Yeats, or American Progressivism. Such academic subjects might better be forfeited while the class moves asymptotically toward "life."

6 Against this movement, the traditionalist defends himself as best

he can. He speaks of the timeless relevance of the classics, of the scarcity of quality in the thin layer of the contemporaneous, of the need for intellectual roots and classic grounding. But often he is rather quickly silenced. The university remains a buyer's market, and if he is to attract and retain his customers, he feels he will have to make his product more appealing. So he may drop Thucydides from his reading list and add Malcolm X or Jerry Rubin and quietly hope for the best.

7 Yet even with their courses redirected toward relevance, some faculty members still seem shaken by the limitations of many of their students' interests. For what some students want to talk about is often not Viet Nam or urban blight, but themselves, or perhaps the "educational process" as they are implicated in it. They want to use class time to speak about their feelings of aggressiveness toward teachers or administrators or "the system"; or about why they cannot study; or how they relate to other students or their parents; or what sorts of opportunities exist in their future; or about contemporary life styles. Such discussions provide what students might call "meaningful encounters"; they are immersions into a collective emotional involvement that resembles, among other things, the family dinner table conversations of a few years ago. Naturally, a good number of faculty members enjoy being a part of these discussions and members of this expressive communion. Some even count themselves as professional observers of the young, but many, who do not, value the meetings all the same since the discussions offer outlets for their natural sympathies and their desires for understanding. Indeed, some teachers, perhaps through the process of role playing, which some are only too willing to perform, feel themselves to be nineteen again instead of twenty-nine or thirty-nine or ageless academic careerists. So, while there may be a melancholy quality to these interludes or "bull sessions," as students sometimes call them, there is also a sense of psychic rejuvenation and, by projection, a reconciliation with one's age.

8 Erik Erikson once said that adolescents would rather talk about themselves than make love. Perhaps there is something timeless about this observation. Certainly, one aspect of the prolongation of adolescence, which for many is represented in America by the four or more years spent in college, is a moratorium on objectivity or an ambivalence about dealing with the world in terms of objective or self-sufficient entities. Despite the cool and toughness affected by some, a chrysalis of romantic solipsism still surrounds many young people. Within this chrysalis they appear more concerned with their own feelings and projections than with other people or the "system." They seem to be "sitting it out" for a while before emerging into a rather depersonalized world demanding the kind of autonomy which,

inevitably, depends on objective control, a world which, for good or bad, places constraints on personal expression and idosyncratic style.

9 Of course adolescents like to speak about themselves; they are like most of us. However, what remains novel about adolescents' behavior in the twenty years since the publication of Erikson's *Childhood and Society*[1] is the way in which students have succeeded in transporting much of their formerly private or late night roommate talks into the classroom and procured a legitimate sanction for this activity. Some faculty members and students are opposed to this change, but, by many students' own standards, the transformation of classroom content has not succeeded nearly enough.

10 Still, beyond the classroom, the university, according to these students, remains virtually unchanged. It is, in their contemporary protest, an unfeeling, impersonal place, a dehumanizing campsite erected between a computerized administration and an indifferent faculty given to a sodden routine of lectures, examination booklets and term papers. Thus, while students are attempting to project their own feelings and personal problems into the content of the classroom, they are protesting the dehumanization of the university. But what they are protesting psychologically is what the university is doing to them—sealing them up in a suspended state of adolescence, thwarting their development into adults. At some schools, the reaction of faculty to student protests is either to ask less of students or, more usually, to resist student demands and dig in their heels in defense of the traditional system.

The Message of Progressive Education

11 As repressed materials presumably were both the cause of illness and one source of creativity, their release became a prime object of psychotherapy and of many of the progressive schools to which the intellectual classes chose to send their children. Quite likely, the progressive school movement, begun by Francis W. Parker and John Dewey but critically altered by the popular acceptance of psychoanalysis, augured the commencement of the "let it all hang out" generation. At these progressive schools, suppression, repression, constraints and restraints became unequivocally bad words. Involved teachers permitted the children to throw clay, cry and have temper tantrums without fear of harsh evaluation or punishment. Teachers asked children what they wanted to do on a particular morning rather than follow any of the schedules tradition had always provided. Meanwhile, gifted psychologists stayed on duty to test and protect

1. New York: W. W. Norton, 1950.

the psyches of their very young pupils, and worried about motivating rather than compelling them. If only the children wanted to do *something,* whatever it was, the teachers and counselors could feel relief.[2]

12 Children were not only encouraged to express themselves, they were told that they could and should do it in school. In the classroom, therefore, they were allowed to "act out," as they called it then, aggress, be loving, sexy, playful, angry, indeed, be anything they wished, just as long as whatever they possessed inside would not be "stifled." Life and the classroom were to become synonymously the scene for the bringing forth of whatever inner urgings the child experienced. All of this bothered many parents, teachers, and social critics of the day. Can we, they questioned, encourage the expression of feelings, good and bad, hateful and loving, destructive and healing, and still control children, or at least trust in their ability to control themselves? Even today, many of us wonder whether, if the time comes, children can be stopped. We see in the student demonstrations, for example, in the acts of violence, sexual license, loud music and sloppy clothes, the opening acts of the apocalypse. We see children, now bursting out with fantasies and feelings, flooding our public land, our personal privacy, our sense of decency and propriety to the extent that they will drown us along with their own kind in a sea of frenzied and bizarre craziness. We fear that eventually they will bring down the social structure of our country, as they might tear down the sets of a great drama.

13 Ironically, young people often reveal a more realistic view of their own weakness. They are amazed and not little amused at the fright they are able to engender in adults. But even less fearful adults are often dismayed by youth's seeming unconcern for the sense of privacy in others, and by young people's violation of limits and rules which most cultures have maintained as a way of grading and differentiating experience. These particular adults, while acknowledging the immense gains in self expression and creativity made possible by progressive education, feel that the young have forgotten the uses of restraint. It is restraint, they would remind us, that prevents us from committing violence or insulting or shocking our neighbors, and widens our range of expression so that the strength of our words and gestures are not debauched in our own minds and in those of others by overuse. Restraint, they argue, provides a power through

---

2. This anxiety over motivation arose in part because teachers had failed to master the technique of giving their students clues for eliciting interest in some subject or activity and help in structuring the activity into a constructive educational experience. With this failure of technique, teachers were reduced to the options of letting children do what they wanted, or telling them what to do, with the children developing a growing sense of their own power in fighting authority. As a result, the potentiality of the open classroom for creative learning was subverted.

the simplicity of means or concentration in one field rather than a loose and possibly trivial involvement in many.

14 The apparent lessening of restraints, or what one student has recently called the "tyranny of openness," can be a personal tryanny for students themselves. The expression of "feelings in their immediacy," to use Croce's phrase, has always been antithetical to art if it is unsustained by deeper, less frenzied structures. Moreover, the entertainment of mood and whim, if unchecked, tends to thwart the realization of long-range purposes, whether economic, educational or political. The license of immediacy, therefore, both liberates and frustrates. "Let it all hang out" has unfortunately been read as "let it all hang out now," and this directive has severe consequences for the will and for the sustaining of purpose, although it has sometimes meant an important gain in freedom and spontaneity.

15 In assessing progressive education, a similar ambiguity continues to hang over the question of motivation. At their best, progressive schools made learning a free response of the student to the emotional and intellectual appeal of the materials before him. Progressive schools attempted to take this response and guide it into clarity of thought and fullness of expression. This was in contrast to the traditional schools which more often than not relied on the authority of the teacher and on disciplined learning routines being implanted in the student. The progressive institutions recognized that the student's interest and self generated activity were the best vehicles for learning. They emphasized learning through action and social involvement, and cut through the layers of passive pedantic formulae in order to deal directly with the real mental operations underlying traditional disciplines. They also experimented with classes without walls, independent study, and ad hoc arrangements of various kinds. Most significantly, they emphasized freedom and the experience of the autonomous child as the basis of learning.

16 But the followers of Parker and Dewey often lacked the insight of their masters, and progressive education too frequently degenerated to a distorted caricature of the sort of experience Dewey had articulated in *Democracy and Education.* At its worst, progressive schooling tended to dismiss subject matter as having legitimate appeal of its own, and subverted the intellectual landscape into a mere scene on which the child might act out his feelings and fantasies. It also reduced the role of the teacher to that of an anxious den mother who, not unlike the parents we have been describing, was afraid both to express emotions and to give to the class explicit intellectual directions. While it was proper that the teacher should carry some of the burden for motivating students, the result was often that the student did not respond with motivation himself but merely shared his teacher's anxiety.

17 Progressive schools mirrored the family in one additional way, as they tried to convince the student that he was free to do as he wished and that he was following his own inclinations. At the same time, however, these schools covertly pushed their students harder and harder to earn class standing and lofty Scholastic Aptitude Test scores in order to gain the proportionately diminishing number of places at the "better" colleges and universities. In this way, the schools reflected the rarely stated but intense career ambitions of the parents and magnified the ambiguity and confusion of the students. There was, in other words, a hidden agenda which in fact tended to go against the grain of freedom, expression and self generated exploration.

18 In pushing students quite hard, progressive education might have lost faith in itself and in its belief that students could motivate themselves. Indeed, through ignorance and anxiety, they often lost faith in their own basic pedagogic principles. The ideals and techniques of progressive education remain to guide all attempts at educational reform from elementary school, for which they were originally intended, to college, where these ideals and techniques only slowly came to exercise an important influence. Nevertheless, while progressive education has undoubtedly benefited the entire educational system, including higher education, it has also left the system with problems which colleges and universities wrestle with today.

The Place of Experience in Learning

19 For the most part, universities represent neither the extremes of exclusive great books classicism or vocational education. But the middle ground they strike has not been sufficiently appealing to great numbers of students and university faculty members. The new university, for the most part, will be built with the personal resources available, namely students, faculty and administrators, but it will have to begin its reconstruction by taking into account the life styles and dispositions associated with these groups.

20 Here we are making an assumption that we believe undergirds our entire discussion: experience is the basic reference for teaching and learning; the traditional content of education—concepts, facts, scholarly exposition or argument—should ultimately refer to experience. This is not to derogate from the enormous importance of the classics and the traditional disciplines which universities have undertaken as their special charge to instill in their students; it is, however, to conceive of them differently than universities traditionally have done. The classics, for example, have been studied as self-contained conceptual expositions without reference to the ground of human experience from which they were written. How much richer is the poem, "Bright

Star, Would I Were Steadfast as Thou Art," for a knowledge of the dying Keats and some experience with the tragedy of unfulfilled love. Keats writes out of his life and time, and out of the human condition. The price of forgetting this, and treating his expressions as self-enclosed, is a violation of the meaning of language which robs it of reality and use. This sense of reality comes from what Whitehead called the "environment of the proposition"; use comes from applying what one has read to the world of one's experience. Without that double reference learning becomes sterile and ultimately unsatisfying, particularly to this generation of students which remains so keyed to the value of direct experience.

21 Accordingly, the value of abstractions lies in their ultimate reference to the real experiential world. This assumption recognizes the expansion of experience that conceptual abstraction has made possible, the ease of expression, the control in thought and action, and reference to large areas of unreplicable experience. But it must be recognized, too, that in many fields, conceptual abstraction is purchased at a great price, namely, the detachment from direct involvement with the objects of reference.[3]

22 Consider, for example, the difference in learning between reading about the sociology of black power and knowing people in the movement or being a participant and observer in the movement. In the latter case, direct experience yields a wealth of impressions, situational involvements and perspectives which the reading of a book simply cannot provide.

23 Finally, continual reference to experience is the surest way to avoid the delusions associated with "pure thought." It is often only by recourse to experience that we realize those factors we previously have overlooked.

24 John Dewey's point that we learn by doing applies equally to processes involving motor skills as to thought. We best learn how to fix something by attempting the repair as we learn how to use ideas by thinking.

25 Still, the university has often refused to recognize the value of the students' experience, and in addition has failed to make clear the limitations of abstract or conceptual knowledge. Instead, it often continues to place exclusive value on conceptual knowledge as that knowledge has been codified by the professional communities, living and dead, which correspond to the university departments. As it is transmitted in courses, this is the knowledge to be credited.

---

3. Parts of mathematics, music and non-objective art reveal possibilities of order and composition not experientially realizable, at least not through *direct* reference to real objects. Nevertheless, the feeling that these are human expressions and the corresponding search for reference to the experiential world, are part of the process of appreciating them.

Said extremely, experience which is not curricular or which cannot bear the Aristotelian imprimatur of being "sociological" or "psychological" or "biological" is not legitimated if not openly disparaged.

26 The results of this philosophy of knowledge are disastrous. Not only does the view equate all learning with book learning and course learning, but by denigrating a student's experience outside of class, it lowers his level of attention and expectancy, and thereby diminishes what ultimately is learned. It makes possible, however, the appalling thought that education stops outside of college because classes are where one exclusively learns. To be sure, no academic would maintain this fiction in its pure form, but in subtle ways many professors manage to transmit their disparagement of those student experiences which do not fall under their jurisdiction.

27 There is another reason, too, for the derogation by professors of student experience. Quite a few professors proceed with their work guided by the assumption that in the things that really count, students are, in Lord Chesterfield's phrase, "inexperienced adults," or mere children whose experience is qualitatively less significant than that of adults. Behind the phrase "inexperienced adult" lurks the belief that the teleological payload of childhood and adolescence is adult life, and accordingly, what precedes it has value only as it contributes to the final product. Experience, in this eighteenth century view, is experience, and however insignificant an "inexperienced" person may be, he may at least feel that he is learning. But when the very quality of his experience is questioned, the result is to take away his dignity and self-esteem and render him childish, not in the sense of being naive and adventuresome, but listless, dull and inept, the very adjectives, as Stanley Elkins and Joel Kovel[4] have pointed out, which a racist society has attributed to southern blacks.

28 There is still another point of view one may take toward experience and inexperience. It argues that any experience has value in itself, and that each period of life possesses its peculiar self interest and quality that render a unique dignity to life in all its moments. First articulated by Rousseau, this conception of experience is at the heart of progressive education. As it is felt by the student, this particular conception of experience releases him from the stigma of second class citizenship and places on his activities a pride which stimulates and ennobles. Not unlike the Black Revolution, which urges that blackness or black experience be seen as beautiful, this new conception beautifies by assuming that beauty exists just as it accomplishes by assuming accomplishment.

---

4. Stanley M. Elkins, *Slavery: A Problem in American Institutional and Intellectual Life.* (2nd Edition). Chicago: University of Chicago Press, 1968; Joel Kovel, *White Racism: A Psychohistory.* New York: Pantheon, 1970.

29 At the university, the basic assumptions of twentieth century psychology and progressive education have been reinforced by the influx of Black and working class students on campus and what has now emerged as a stress on the *experience* of these people. Indeed, the very use of the word, experience, its legitimation and exploration in books, movies and television has reawakened in the richer white students, historically the exclusive tenants of higher education, the desire to transport their own experiences into classroom discussions and assignments.

30 Yet, at the same time that students have emphasized experience and perhaps excessively repudiated the purely intellectual and esoteric aspects of higher education, many middle class white students have come to believe that only the black or lower class experience is real and worthwhile. Indeed, many of these students now feel self-conscious about their purely intellectual capacities, what they disparagingly call their "smarts," and their handsome social backgrounds. Part of this feeling may be due to a modicum of guilt, and a corresponding inversion of self abnegation due to the advantages they realize they have enjoyed, and their association, however unwilled, with a system that has been responsible for race prejudice and poverty. Some of the sense of inferiority or inadequacy may also stem from what they take as the greater excitement and challenge of what they imagine to be the more physical experiences of the poor and the blacks. Manual labor, violence, uninhibited sex, emotional expression and warm relationships are among the experiences they attribute to these newcomers to higher education, the very experiences which may have been denied to them. Blacks say they have something called "soul." Whites feel that they themselves do not have it, and hence they envy black students for having it and what they feel is closely allied to it, namely a facility of expression which appears to be a vehicle for feelings unlike their own stilted, artificial and overintellectualized language.

31 But white students also allege, in a well meaning but unintentionally condescending tone, that it is precisely the lack of intellectual development in black or working class communities which allows the expression of soul to be so direct. Simultaneously, they depreciate their own experience and resent the newcomers to higher education for making them do this, although their resentment is rarely revealed openly. Quite possibly they feel "shown up" by the newcomers because their professors have failed to endow their own experience with any importance, and, further, failed to identify history or literature or philosophy as experience or as the distillates of experience. It may be that too much academic material is presented to students as abstract intellectual fare whose justification must be sought in some Aristotelean bit of snobbery. Ellison, Cleaver and Brown,

therefore, are made into experience; *Hamlet* and *Lord Jim* are not.

32 While a university must encourage students to value their own experience, the university will be wise which counsels students not to preoccupy themselves with it. The objective detachment necessary for clear thought is best learned in dealing with materials not based directly on one's own experience. In this sense, the hardest mote to see is in one's own eye. It is from faculty that students can receive a sense of freedom to express themselves as well as the push toward objectivity they will need to understand objective material and their own lives as well.

33 Student need for faculty presence and guidance is quite real in other ways. While students want to hear the sounds of their own voices, and try out their opinions and passions on contemporaries, they need as well to speak in the presence of legitimate and interested authority, men and women older than themselves who may just "know" more, and whose evaluation and encouragement are required, partly as a residue of family life. Then too, students still believe that professors have something to give them intellectually which they cannot get themselves, or get as well.

34 Learning from older, more knowledgeable people, and having these people witness and sanction their growth remain major reasons for students going to college. It is precisely this need, moreover, for contact with older persons which causes the idea of a facultyless university to prove unsatisfactory for so many young persons. Among those for whom career and achievement remain prominent ideals, a school without professors seems illicit, if not misguided; childish, if not unreal.

35 Many students find themselves eager to discover or construct environments in which they might express the needs and feelings that tend to dominate their lives on campus. Yet these very same people admit to the dependencies, loneliness and lack of a secure autonomy that in part motivate these urges, and which appear to them to block their ability to pursue regular course work. Although there well may be a high degree of indulgence in the search for relevance and a seeking for dependency and even a type of psychodynamic procrastination, students themselves recognize that their personal needs must eventually be resolved if they are to "get on" with life and its work.

36 At the same time it must be maintained that the central business of the university is the training of the mind, and that faculty, by tending to this work, will perform their greatest service. In the context of the classroom, and in the types of relationships between faculty and students we have described, faculty can help students strike their peculiar balance between valuing experience without wallowing in narcissism, and realizing the experience of autonomy and the support of authority.

37 In psychological terms, the college experience is predicated on a temporary though intense struggle for personal intellectual engagement whereby the student can pass from his adolescent tensions between dependence and independence to a mature autonomy and understanding of the utility and limitations of objective thought. There is much teachers can do to aid this process. The social, psychological and cognitive skills required make teaching as difficult an art as any in our society. But it is not a work which can be performed by the faculty alone operating within the microcosm of the classroom or the office. It requires a systematic restructuring of the university, such as is now being undertaken in part at a number of schools. Thus, we must talk not only of a change of address between students and faculty, but of a change of curriculum and program.

38 At many American colleges and universities planning for such changes is difficult because there is often no one with sufficient authority to provide leadership. The typical university president is involved primarily with external affairs like fund raising, and hence has little time for academic issues. In his absence there may be no one with sufficient authority to overcome the inertia, the interdepartmental rivalries or downright opposition from faculty to anything like comprehensive changes, particularly those that would take courses away from their departmental control, which would put teachers in the same room with other teachers, which might seek an alteration in teachers' style of presentation or relation with students.

39 Another difficulty is that planning costs money. Faculty must be released from their regular teaching duties if they are to do an adequate job, consultants may have to be brought in; faculty members may have to travel to other institutions to learn about educational innovation at first hand. Finally, workshops and training sessions may be required. Given the set of priorities which govern the donation and use of college funds, it may be difficult to find money for planning. Trustees would rather donate money for brick and mortar, which, like the Egyptian pyramids, will bear their names for eternity, than contribute funds for anything as ephemeral as planning. And too often, college administrations support this predisposition.[5]

---

5. Recently we visited a small private college which had applied to the Federal Government for a modest sum to plan a revision of its curriculum, a sum which it claimed the college was unable to raise itself. We sat in on classes and observed students bored to desperation by rote lectures and uninspired material. We learned that faculty salaries were low and that the average teaching load at the school was high, fifteen hours a week and sometimes more. The college president took us for a tour of the plant .There was a new gymnasium, a new science building, and a new two million dollar dormitory. "Look," the president said to us with a wave of his hand, "what we are doing for our students!"

40 Even when leadership, money and time are available, even when a president or energetic provost, dean or department chairman has rallied his people behind him or at least seems willing to go along with new proposals, there will be other difficulties to overcome. The first has to do with the subtle byplay between institutions and people. All revolutionaries and reformers have had to face the fact that when the revolution is over, when the new system is finally installed, one is left with the same sort of men as before. The maddening bureaucracy which served the Czar has been replaced by a maddening Soviet bureaucracy ostensibly serving the people. Always the hope exists that by putting people into different relations asking different tasks of them, they will change. In the case of education, similarly, we assume that new systems will enable teachers to perform better in class and relate more effectively with students. By allowing teachers to be creative, by relieving them of certain burdens, we believe we can enhance their capabilities. But there is always the danger that this will not happen and that teachers will revert back to their old methods and styles of relations. Thus, team teaching, which when intelligently employed can result in cross-disciplinary interchange, often degenerates into a sterile series of mini-lectures by members of the "team." Under the protective cover of a new name, the lecture system has returned.

41 One obvious answer to this problem is to prepare teachers for the kinds of reform that are likely to occur. Such faculty training can include faculty and student workshops, instruction in new techniques and the use of media, exposure to gifted consultants, and travel to other schools.[6] But faculty are notoriously difficult to retrain primarily because college teaching entails no training to begin with, whereas elementary and secondary school teachers are required to practice teach under the guidance of a master teacher, and to take courses in instructional technique; college teachers receive no help at all in carrying out what will be for most of them their major professional activity. For many faculty members, training would seem an imposition, a questioning of their competence, a diminution of their autonomy in the classroom, and, perhaps, an infringement of their academic freedom. Thus, there will always be considerable resistance to faculty training, particularly by those who may be set in their ways and who, insulated by tenure, may be fairly immune from pressure. And this is but one obstacle to effective educational planning.

42 A second major obstacle is that there are no completely adequate models to follow. Every institution has the job of planning for itself.

---

6. Just such a faculty retraining program over a number of years is being planned by Austin College in Sherman, Texas, under a grant jointly funded by the National Endowment for the Humanities and the National Science Foundation.

Other institutions which have put through major reforms can offer some suggestion, but each institution must face the fact of its own uniqueness and devise a plan specially suited to itself, to its basic academic goals, its particular population and physical plant, and to its relation to its surrounding community, governing boards and sources of finance and tradition. The variety of colleges and universities around the country is astounding. There are community colleges, four year colleges and universities with graduate departments, research centers and institutes; there are all white schools, black schools, Chicano schools, schools with every variety of racial mixture; there are rich, well established and endowed schools and schools barely surviving from month to month; there are innovative, fast paced schools and slow, traditional schools; there are open admissions schools and schools more difficult to enter than the gates of heaven; there are eastern schools and northern schools and western schools and southern schools, all with their peculiar characteristics; and there are schools whose students come from suburban, progressive communities, and schools whose students are just off the farm and as poor and traditional as can be imagined. The range of variety and the recognition of their uniqueness by their faculties and students are among the most winning qualities of American higher education. But they are also qualities which make educational planning difficult. Thus, when someone comes onto a campus from the "outside" glibly suggesting reform, he is often met with statements that may indeed be defensive, but which reflect as well that special understanding of local conditions without which any plan for educational reform cannot succeed.

43 Reform is exportable, however, if it is presented as a set of alternative options and in somewhat generalized form, or, less theoretically, as case studies. For what is clear as one goes about the country looking at colleges is that there is a growing interest in academic reform and a body of common doctrine despite the differences among schools. The reforms being undertaken are still too scattered for one to talk about a wave of reform, much less an academic revolution, but there are signs that this may indeed happen.

44 Educational reform requires a subtle form of cooperation between the administration, faculty and students. The variety of schools would suggest no common rule for this cooperation. But, in general, pressure for reform traditionally comes from students as their discontent and demands are interpreted by faculty. Yet, because the community of teachers is, despite the departmental structure, essentially atomized, the administration must often establish the format in which reform may take place. In large measure, it must set up the workshops and symposia, effect the release of faculty time, encourage the constitution of committees, establish the summer sessions,

as well as secure the funds in which reform can take place. But administrations usually will be wise to confine their efforts to establishing the climate and to making the administrative arrangements. They generally should rely on the faculty and the students for the substance of the reform, as a reform for which the students and faculty themselves feel responsible is more likely to be soundly based and, ultimately, to succeed.

45 More and more colleges and universities are not only taking the views of students into account, but are giving students a permanent advisory voice or role in the decision making process. At Antioch College, the central governing body is an Administrative Council of five faculty members and three students. Two of the faculty members are elected solely by the faculty; the other five members by the entire campus, and thus, principally by students. The president and dean complete the Council's membership. For thirty years this body has acted as a kind of executive committee for the entire college on central budgetary, policy and personnel matters. In addition, Antioch students hold a number of managerial jobs, including that of Community Manager of the community government which finances publications, conferences, student-initiated educational experiences and concerts.[7]

46 The bestowal of power to students can be performed grudgingly in the face of pressure or revolt. But it can also reflect the desire of faculty and administrators to give students a democratic sense of responsibility for the affairs of the academic community. Recognizing that for too long students have been stultified into adolescence by being considered wards of the university, many administrators have learned that an opportunity to exercise responsibility is essential for the growth of students. In those schools in which faculty and students alike desire to remake the university to meet the needs of its constituents, such measures are also a recognition that faculty and administrators cannot do the job alone.

47 Remaking a university or any other institution represents a political act. What the youth movement can bring to this process, namely, a sense for close, informal relations, spontaneity and openness to experience, a rejection of formal distinctions and bureaucratic rigidities, an address to human experience, a refusal to countenance cruelty and injustice, and a willingness to carry out the implications of this refusal into institutional change, must become part of the new university else it will be only half made up. But these gifts must be

7. At Western College in Oxford, Ohio, the Academic Council, which deals with such academic matters as the hiring of faculty and curriculum content, has one student for every four professors and administrators. The Community Council, which is concerned with living arrangements in the community and so-called parietal laws, is composed of students with professors and administrators in reverse ratio.

incorporated with a faculty's knowledge and skills, their sense of history and tradition, an address to objectivity, and finally, a dedication to students' learning and growth. This merger can produce an institution which in itself is a political statement of how people can mutually enhance their lives.

48 In the end, there can be no perfect college or university and no single route for education to follow. Because of a very real need for educational pluralism and an explicit range of possibilities and resources with which to build, it is improper to argue that one and only one solution exists, that free schools must supplant contemporary programs, or that contemporary institutions must now be made over in the model of the nineteenth century university. Many arrangements may prove effective, provided they fit the capacities and interests of the students and faculty who comprise the particular university community. It is now the task of all parties at the university, students, faculty and administration, to create anew their institution, in order to bring out the best that each has. At many schools quite a few people are willing to give it a try.

Thinking Questions: ***Form***

1. Consider the four major divisions of this essay: sources of academic discontent, progressive education, the place of experience in learning, and university reform. How does one division lead to another? What is the logical pattern behind the subdivisions of the entire essay?

2. What major methods of support are used in each section of this essay? Where do the authors rely primarily on illustrations from personal experience to substantiate their opinions? Where do they most often cite reading, research, and authority? Where do they most often rely on the internal logic of their argument?

3. In paragraph 10, Eisendrath and Cottle characterize the students' attitudes toward the university. "Thus, while students are attempting to project their own feelings and personal problems into the content of the classroom, they are protesting the dehumanization of the university." This sentence provides an excellent example of the essay's tone. How would you describe that tone—objective and scientific or subjective and opinionated? Do Eisendrath and Cottle take sides with the students in this section of the essay? In the entire essay? Or do they usually adopt the point of view of the side they are discussing at the moment? What about the structure of the above sentence gives it the sound of moderation?

4. In paragraphs 11 through 18, Eisendrath and Cottle illustrate the effects of the progressive movement on higher education. What paradox do the authors point to in the progressive movement itself, and how does

that paradox represent the ambiguous situation in which most American college and high school students were placed in the last half of this century? (A paradox is an apparent contradiction that, when closely analyzed, proves to be logical. For example, an individual might consistently support both sides of an argument if his or her personal situation created an understanding of the values of both.)

5. Look over the five major parts of this essay (paragraphs 1 through 10; 11 through 18; 19 through 36; 37 through 46; and 47-48). Define Eisendrath and Cottle's thesis for each of the first four sections; then show how each of the sub-theses combine into the general thesis in the final two paragraphs.

Thinking Questions: *Substance*

1. Eisendrath and Cottle, like Paul Goodman, argue for more attention to experiential learning. According to them, what function should the teacher have in relation to the student's practical learning? Does Goodman provide particular examples of experiential learning that Eisendrath and Cottle would find worthwhile? What particular educational problems would practical experience help solve?

2. What were the strengths and weaknesses of the progressive education movement, according to Eisendrath and Cottle? How did these strengths and weaknesses contribute to the academic discontent that colleges are experiencing now?

3. Why do Eisendrath and Cottle close their essay by saying "there can be no perfect college or university and no single route for education to follow"? Why is it important that innovators on every college campus remember the truism embodied in that sentence? If the perfect college cannot be created, what particular combination of qualities would these authors suggest for the best possible college curriculum?

4. What particular concerns keep faculty members from contributing to educational innovations in universities and colleges? What particular qualities often make students eager to force change in educational curriculum? Can you think of changes in college or university structures that would reverse or alter this situation?

5. Eisendrath and Cottle did their research for this essay in the late 1960s and early 1970s. They found numerous expressions of discontent among both faculty and students. Many critics of higher education today say that the activity of the late sixties and early seventies has subsided and been replaced by passivity, by hard-working, vocationally-directed students who do not question the system under which they learn. Do you agree with this observation? Or do you believe contemporary students merely express their dissatisfactions in different ways?

* * *

A FINAL NOTE

All this deliberation about how people learn and what education ought to do for society brings us to a central issue: Do people need schools and professional teachers? Might learning best go on *outside* schools, away from academic hallways and carefully designed "courses" of study? Probably more to the point, how can schools provide learning that has a clear relationship to what students do outside of school, including work and leisure?

Sammy, the hero of John Updike's story "A & P," provides us the opportunity to evaluate and analyze education outside the classroom. In the process, the story emphasizes the fact that all learning must somehow be integrated with the decisions we make everyday. In essence, we test what we learn as we make choices. All the details that precede Sammy's decision to quit his job at the A & P coalesce to create his decisive act. This practical example of education should help you answer some of the questions the previous essays have raised.

A & P

JOHN UPDIKE

1 In walks these three girls in nothing but bathing suits. I'm in the third checkout slot, with my back to the door, so I don't see them until they're over by the bread. The one that caught my eye first was the one in the plaid green two-piece. She was a chunky kid, with a good tan and a sweet broad soft-looking can with those two crescents of white just under it, where the sun never seems to hit, at the top of the backs of her legs. I stood there with my hand on a box of HiHo crackers trying to remember if I rang it up or not. I ring it up again and the customer starts giving me hell. She's one of these cash-register-watchers, a witch about fifty with rouge on her cheekbones and no eyebrows, and I know it made her day to trip me up. She'd been watching cash registers for fifty years and probably never seen a mistake before.

2 By the time I got her feathers smoothed and her goodies into a bag —she gives me a little snort in passing, if she'd been born at the right time they would have burned her over in Salem—by the time I get her

on her way the girls had circled around the bread and were coming back, without a pushcart, back my way along the counters, in the aisle between the checkouts and the Special bins. They didn't even have shoes on. There was this chunky one, with the two-piece—it was bright green and the seams on the bra were still sharp and her belly was still pretty pale so I guessed she just got it (the suit)—there was this one, with one of those chubby berry-faces, the lips all bunched together under her nose, this one, and a tall one, with black hair that hadn't quite frizzed right, and one of those sunburns right across under the eyes, and a chin that was too long—you know, the kind of girl other girls think is very "striking" and "attractive" but never quite makes it, as they very well know, which is why they like her so much—and then the third one, that wasn't quite so tall. She was the queen. She kind of led them, the other two peeking around and making their shoulders round. She didn't look around, not this queen, she just walked straight on slowly, on these long white prima-donna legs. She came down a little hard on her heels, as if she didn't walk in her bare feet that much, putting down her heels and then letting the weight move along to her toes as if she was testing the floor with every step, putting a little deliberate extra action into it. You never know for sure how girls' minds work (do you really think it's a mind in there or just a little buzz like a bee in a glass jar?) but you got the idea she had talked the other two into coming in here with her, and now she was showing them how to do it, walk slow and hold yourself straight.

3 She had on a kind of dirty-pink—beige maybe, I don't know—bathing suit with a little nubble all over it and, what got me, the straps were down. They were off her shoulders looped loose around the cool tops of her arms, and I guess as a result the suit had slipped a little on her, so all around the top of the cloth there was this shining rim. If it hadn't been there you wouldn't have known there could have been anything whiter than those shoulders. With the straps pushed off, there was nothing between the top of the suit and the top of her head except just *her,* this clean bare plane of the top of her chest down from the shoulder bones like a dented sheet of metal tilted in the light. I mean, it was more than pretty.

4 She had sort of oaky hair that the sun and salt had bleached, done up in a bun that was unravelling, and a kind of prim face. Walking into the A & P with your straps down, I suppose it's the only kind of face you *can* have. She held her head so high her neck, coming up out of those white shoulders, looked kind of stretched, but I didn't mind. The longer her neck was, the more of her there was.

5 She must have felt in the corner of her eye me and over my shoulder Stokesie in the second slot watching, but she didn't tip. Not this queen. She kept her eyes moving across the racks, and stopped, and

turned so slow it made my stomach rub the inside of my apron, and buzzed to the other two, who kind of huddled against her for relief, and then they all three of them went up the cat-and-dog-food-breakfast-cereal-macaroni-rice-raisins-seasonings-spreads-spaghetti-soft-drinks-crackers-and-cookies aisle. From the third slot I look straight up this aisle to the meat counter, and I watched them all the way. The fat one with the tan sort of fumbled with the cookies, but on second thought she put the package back. The sheep pushing their carts down the aisle—the girls were walking against the usual traffic (not that we have one-way signs or anything)—were pretty hilarious. You could see them, when Queenie's white shoulder dawned on them, kind of jerk, or hop, or hiccup, but their eyes snapped back to their own baskets and on they pushed. I bet you could set off dynamite in an A & P and the people would by and large keep reaching and checking oatmeal off their lists and muttering "Let me see, there was a third thing, began with A, asparagus, no, ah, yes, applesauce!" or whatever it is they do mutter. But there was no doubt, this jiggled them. A few houseslaves in pin curlers even looked around after pushing their carts past to make sure what they had seen was correct.

6 You know, it's one thing to have a girl in a bathing suit down on the beach, where what with the glare nobody can look at each other much anyway, and another thing in the cool of the A & P, under the fluorescent lights, against all those stacked packages, with her feet paddling along naked over our checkerboard green-and-cream rubber-tile floor.

7 "Oh Daddy," Stokesie said beside me. "I feel so faint."

8 "Darling," I said. "Hold me tight." Stokesie's married, with two babies chalked up on her fuselage already, but as far as I can tell that's the only difference. He's twenty-two, and I was nineteen this April.

9 "Is it done?" he asks, the responsible married man finding his voice. I forgot to say he thinks he's going to be manager some sunny day, maybe in 1990 when it's called the Great Alexandrov and Petrooshki Tea Company or something.

10 What he meant was, our town is five miles from a beach, with a big summer colony out on the Point, but we're right in the middle of town, and the women generally put on a shirt or shorts or something before they get out of the car into the street. And anyway these are usually women with six children and varicose veins mapping their legs and nobody, including them, could care less. As I say, we're right in the middle of town, and if you stand at our front doors you can see two banks and the Congregational church and the newspaper store and three real-estate offices and about twenty-seven old freeloaders tearing up Central Street because the sewer broke again. It's not as if we're on the Cape; we're north of Boston and there's people in this town haven't seen the ocean for twenty years.

11 The girls had reached the meat counter and were asking McMahon something. He pointed, they pointed, and they shuffled out of sight behind a pyramid of Diet Delight peaches. All that was left for us to see was old McMahon patting his mouth and looking after them sizing up their joints. Poor kids, I began to feel sorry for them, they couldn't help it.

12 Now here comes the sad part of the story, at least my family says it's sad, but I don't think it's so sad myself. The store's pretty empty, it being Thursday afternoon, so there was nothing much to do except lean on the register and wait for the girls to show up again. The whole store was like a pinball machine and I didn't know which tunnel they'd come out of. After a while they come around out of the far aisle, around the light bulbs, records at discount of the Caribbean Six or Tony Martin Sings or some such gunk you wonder they waste the wax on, sixpacks of candy bars, and plastic toys done up in cellophane that fall apart when a kid looks at them anyway. Around they come, Queenie still leading the way, and holding a little gray jar in her hand. Slots Three through Seven are unmanned and I could see her wondering between Stokes and me, but Stokesie with his usual luck draws an old party in baggy gray pants who stumbles up with four giant cans of pineapple juice (what do these bums *do* with all that pineapple juice? I've often asked myself) so the girls come to me. Queenie puts down the jar and I take it into my fingers icy cold. Kingfish Fancy Herring Snacks in Pure Sour Cream: 49¢. Now her hands are empty, not a ring or a bracelet, bare as God made them, and I wonder where the money's coming from. Still with that prim look she lifts a folded dollar bill out of the hollow at the center of her nubbled pink top. The jar went heavy in my hand. Really, I thought that was so cute.

13 Then everybody's luck begins to run out. Lengel comes in from haggling with a truck full of cabbages on the lot and is about to scuttle into that door marked MANAGER behind which he hides all day when the girls touch his eye. Lengel's pretty dreary, teaches Sunday school and the rest, but he doesn't miss that much. He comes over and says, "Girls, this isn't the beach."

14 Queenie blushes, though maybe it's just a brush of sunburn I was noticing for the first time, now that she was so close. "My mother asked me to pick up a jar of herring snacks." Her voice kind of startled me, the way voices do when you see the people first, coming out so flat and dumb yet kind of tony, too, the way it ticked over "pick-up" and "snacks." All of a sudden I slid right down her voice into her living room. Her father and the other men were standing around in ice-cream coats and bow ties and the women were in sandals picking up herring snacks on toothpicks off a big glass plate and they were all holding drinks the color of water with olives and sprigs of mint in them. When my parents have somebody over they get lemonade and if it's a real

racy affair Schlitz in tall glasses with "They'll Do It Every Time" cartoons stencilled on.

15 "That's all right," Lengel said. "But this isn't the beach." His repeating this struck me as funny, as if It had just occurred to him, and he had been thinking all these years the A & P was a great big dune and he was the head lifeguard. He didn't like my smiling—as I say he doesn't miss much—but he concentrates on giving the girls that sad Sunday-school-superintendent stare.

16 Queenie's blush is no sunburn now, and the plump one in plaid, that I liked better from the back—a really sweet can—pipes up, "We weren't doing any shopping. We just came in for the one thing."

17 "That makes no difference," Lengel tells her, and I could see from the way his eyes went that he hadn't noticed she was wearing a two-piece before. "We want you decently dressed when you come in here."

18 "We *are* decent," Queenie says suddenly, her lower lip pushing, getting sore now that she remembers her place, a place from which the crowd that runs the A & P must look pretty crummy. Fancy Herring Snacks flashed in her very blue eyes.

19 "Girls, I don't want to argue with you. After this come in here with your shoulders covered. It's our policy." He turns his back. That's policy for you. Policy is what the kingpins want. What the others want is juvenile delinquency.

20 All this while, the customers had been showing up with their carts but, you know, sheep, seeing a scene, they had all bunched up on Stokesie, who shook open a paper bag as gently as peeling a peach, not wanting to miss a word. I could feel in the silence everybody getting nervous, most of all Lengel, who asks me, "Sammy, have you rung up their purchase?"

21 I thought and said "No" but it wasn't about that I was thinking. I go through the punches, 4, 9, GROC, TOT—it's more complicated than you think, and after you do it often enough, it begins to make a little song, that you hear words to, in my case "Hello (*bing*) there, you (*gung*) hap-py *pee*-pul (*splat*)!"—the *splat* being the drawer flying out. I uncrease the bill, tenderly as you may imagine, it just having come from between the two smoothest scoops of vanilla I had ever known were there, and pass a half and a penny into her narrow pink palm, and nestle the herrings in a bag and twist its neck and hand it over, all the time thinking.

22 The girls, and who'd blame them, are in a hurry to get out, so I say "I quit" to Lengel quick enough for them to hear, hoping they'll stop and watch me, their unsuspected hero. They keep right on going, into the electric eye; the door flies open and they flicker across the lot to their car, Queenie and Plaid and Big Tall Goony-Goony (not that as raw material she was so bad), leaving me with Lengel and a kink in his eyebrow.

23 "Did you say something, Sammy?"

"I said I quit."

"I thought you did."

"You didn't have to embarrass them."

"It was they who were embarrassing us."

24 I started to say something that come out "Fiddle-de-doo." It's a saying of my grandmother's, and I know she would have been pleased.

25 "I don't think you know what you're saying," Lengel said.

26 "I know you don't," I said. "But I do." I pull the bow at the back of my apron and start shrugging it off my shoulders. A couple customers that had been heading for my slot begin to knock against each other, like scared pigs in a chute.

27 Lengel sighs and begins to look very patient and old and gray. He's been a friend of my parents for years. "Sammy, you don't want to do this to your Mom and Dad," he tells me. It's true, I don't. But it seems to me that once you begin a gesture it's fatal not to go through with it. I fold the apron, "Sammy" stitched in red on the pocket, and put it on the counter, and drop the bow tie on top of it. The bow tie is theirs, if you've ever wondered. "You'll feel this for the rest of your life," Lengel says, and I know that's true, too, but remembering how he made that pretty girl blush makes me so scrunchy inside I punch the No Sale tab and the machine whirs "pee-pul" and the drawer splats out. One advantage to this scene taking place in summer, I can follow this up with a clean exit, there's no fumbling around getting your coat and galoshes, I just saunter into the electric eye in my white shirt that my mother ironed the night before, and the door heaves itself open, and outside the sunshine is skating around on the asphalt.

28 I look around for my girls, but they're gone, of course. There wasn't anybody but some young married screaming with her children about some candy they didn't get by the door of a powder-blue Falcon station wagon. Looking back in the big windows, over the bags of peat moss and aluminum lawn furniture stacked on the pavement, I could see Lengel in my place in the slot, checking the sheep through. His face was dark gray and his back stiff, as if he'd just had an injection of iron, and my stomach kind of fell as I felt how hard the world was going to be to me hereafter.

Thinking Questions: *Form*

1. Write a brief essay in which you give a general analysis of Sammy's character. Before you begin writing, compose three or four statements describing one major element of his character. Use these statements as the

organizing sentence for each part of your essay, and refer to one or two examples from the story to support each statement.

2. Story writers show rather than tell. They let what a person does or say define his character. After you have read Updike's story carefully, pick out three incidents that you believe clearly establish Sammy's character. After you have analyzed these incidents, put your interpretation of Sammy's character into a simple sentence.

3. This entire story is written from Sammy's point of view. We have very little explicit factual information about him. Look closely at the way Sammy talks and thinks in the story, the way he uses slang and addresses his readers, and try to infer some biographical facts about Sammy. How old is he? How do you think he dresses? How much formal schooling has he had? Is he rich, poor, or in-between? Is or was he a good student? Is he intelligent? What specific examples of Sammy's thought or speech create your "facts"?

4. Why does Updike tell Sammy's story from his point of view? How might the story's meaning have been changed if it had been told from Lengel's point of view?

5. Do you think what happens to Sammy is tragic or comic, serious or inconsequential?

Thinking Questions: *Substance*

1. Why does Sammy say that he looks "around for *my* girls" in the final paragraph (28) of the story? In what sense are the three girls "his"? Is his defense of them useless because they know nothing of what he has done—not even that he quit his job?

2. Look back over paragraph 1 and tell what Sammy thought of his job even before the incident with Lengel and Queenie. What words or phrases give away his attitude toward his job?

3. What *has* Sammy learned? Why did he say that he knew, after he had quit his job and was walking through the A & P parking lot, "how hard the world was going to be to me hereafter"? What do Lengel's "dark gray" face and "stiff" back have to do with Sammy's final recognition? Do you admire or criticize Sammy's decision?

4. Do you think that any of Sammy's formal school training contributed to his decision to quit? *Should* the content of formal education have anything to do with personal decisions such as this one?

5. Might this story be called "sexist"? Why? What images of women are presented? Are they stereotyped or from a particularly male point of view? What do Sammy's nicknames for the three girls—"Queenie, Plaid, and Big Tail Goony-Goony" (paragraph 22)—reveal about his attitudes toward women? Does Sammy's education in the story seem to include a change in attitude toward women?

Writing Exercise V

EXPOSITION

(Classification and Logical Division)

Write an essay in which you define and describe at least three different types of education. Your definitions should all relate to some key educational goals. Once you have spelled out your general goals, begin to describe three alternate ways of achieving those goals. Mix your personal observations of formal and informal education with information from your reading and research. You might, for example, want to define your types by describing three classrooms or schools you have previously attended or observed. Whatever you choose to describe, remember that you should carefully relate specific educational experience to the general types you have defined.

WRITING THE ESSAY OF CLASSIFICATION AND LOGICAL DIVISION

Classification is usually one of the first skills acquired by human societies as they develop sophistication. The primitive may first notice individual trees without distinguishing among them at all. After considerable experience with numerous individual trees, he or she may also notice that, though every particular tree is different from every other, they are similar in many ways as well. From these similarities, the primitive *abstracts*, or generalizes, to create the idea *tree*, which may include the stripped-down image of trunk, branches, and leaves distributed to produce a general, tree-like appearance.

At the point of abstraction or generalization, classification and logical division usually begin. The man or woman who has first noticed many different trees and then generalized to form the idea *tree* may begin to classify trees according to their different shapes, by the form of their leaves or textures of bark, by their length or the breadth of their trunks. From the abstraction *tree*, in other words, the primitive begins to form categories of trees. Whenever sophisticated or highly educated people begin to examine a new area of knowledge, they usually follow one form or another of this basic organizing pattern. They examine bits of data piece by piece; they form a general definition or description that successfully explains the similarities among all the particulars included in a category; and they examine all the data to define other possible categories or types.

Classification can be used to organize the elements of numerous writings. If you, for example, were asked to classify the essays in this section, you might begin to define general categorizing principles and then proceed to explain how particular essays fit the categories. Some essays argue that education should encourage change. Others point out that educational systems must serve the society that supports them. Still others argue that students rather than teachers should control what goes into a school's curriculum. And others believe that the concept of curriculum ought to be entirely abolished. All these similarities and differences can provide bases for subdivision and classification.

There are various methods of organizing a classifying essay. Most writers use some combination of these guidelines.

1. Early in a classifying essay you should define your general subject. If you plan to write about *small towns* you might begin by providing a general definition of a small town. What characteristics do all small towns share? How does a small town differ from a *large city* or a *village?*

2. Before you actually begin to classify, you should tell how you arrived at your definitions of the class. Have you lived in or visited several small towns? Have you read several books on small towns? Is your method of classification limited by any important lack of evidence, experience, or observation? Perhaps you are generalizing after living in only two small towns?

3. As you actually begin to classify, remember to use your *principle of classification* consistently. If, in formulating step 1 in this process, you decide to classify small towns according to their varying abilities to provide jobs for a large variety of people, be sure that you do not, as you form one category, suddenly begin to discuss the libraries of small towns. Every characteristic you discuss should relate to your basic principle of classification.

4. As you classify, be sure you divide into enough categories to include at least the majority of examples within the general class. If you divide small towns into three classes and your reader can easily think of a fourth or fifth class, your essay will seem inadequate and incomplete.

5. Remember that ideas and large institutions are usually more difficult to classify than concrete objects or simple processes. You will need, for example, to spend more time in defining the principles behind your classes if you are classifying the major parts of a university than if you are classifying the parts of a commercial bakery or the main parts of an automobile engine.

6. When you classify, you are examining a large number of items or ideas from a particular type or perspective. If you develop a system

within which novelists in America are divided into *women* writers, *old* writers, *passionate* writers, and *experimental* writers, you will have crossed categories. Old writers may also be women writers, the class of experimental writers may include examples of all the other three categories. Such classifications serve no useful purpose; in fact, they often make readers more rather than less confused. Stick to one principle of classification at a time; if you wish to classify from several different perspectives, go through all your examples from one perspective, conclude with a generalization, and then proceed to classify the same examples from a different perspective.

7. Be aware of *overclassification.* Do not bend and twist every example so that it fits your general definitions of classes. Be complete; cover enough examples to satisfy your reader; but do not create too many classes and do not pretend, as you write, to have classified everything. Fashion models might be divided into categories such as *slick, sensuous, charming,* and *wild.* But you might stretch things a bit too far by including *long-hairs, fat-lips, underwear-types,* and *mink-coat types*—unless you want your readers to laugh with you.

All the rhetorical methods of organization discussed in this section on exposition—comparison, definition, classification, and cause and effect—often must be used in combination. To explain why a particular example fits into a specific category, for example, you might *compare* it with an example from another category. Or, to show how one type of small town is different from another, you may want to apply logical or *cause-and-effect* analysis to the town's governing structure. You do, however, want to select *one* method of organization for your entire essay. Then you can use another method to develop specific paragraphs or groups of paragraphs without sacrificing overall unity.

Finally, remember that some of the best essays are produced by writers who create new classes. Suppose you have considered the conventional classes of students: bookworms, lovers, athletes, achievers, social-strivers, whatever. You are struck by an entire group of students who do not fit conventional categories but are worth examining as a new type. Your entire essay, then, might define the characteristics of this new type and show how and why it exists. Such essays need plenty of concrete detail and careful distinguishing of examples.

Consider writing an essay in which you do either of these two things:

1. Examine some examples of class stereotypes. What are, for example, the most common stereotypes of doctors? Show how those stereotypes evolved. Or, better yet, show how they might be inaccurate and describe some new types.

2. Examine a group of people who have not yet been typed. For example, you might have heard a good deal about the average suburban family. What, however, might the average teacher's family be like? Give plenty of examples and form your generalities carefully.

Form:

EXPOSITION

(Cause and Effect)

Substance:

VIOLENCE AND SURVIVAL

> But mostly he wanted to spit rage. He believes that he has been cheated. The Dodgers released him while he was injured. He fought back with litigation. "You can't beat them bastards," he says. (Roger Kahn on Carl Furillo in *The Boys of Summer*)

Carl Furillo played baseball for the old Brooklyn Dodgers. He played very well. In fact, some think he was the best rightfielder ever. Yet he ended his baseball career sullen and enraged, feeling that baseball, the *business* of major league baseball, had used and discarded him cruelly.

Many of us, at one time or another, feel Furillo's rage. Statistics on violent crime rise each year, telling us that many Americans, unlike Carl Furillo who used legal means to avenge what he felt were unjustified acts against him, resort to violence in response to personal injuries, frustrations, and anguish.

We will not be able to cover fully the complex phenomena of violence in as brief a section as this. But we can isolate several key perspectives on violence and use the essays in this section to define causes and effects, to apply particular perspectives to specific discussions of violent behavior.

Perspectives on violence

Generally three perspectives on violence are implied in the essays in this section: the *cosmic* or natural, the personal or *psychological,* and the *social.*

Virginia Woolf takes a universal perspective. Her general discussion of how death and life work in a cycle throughout nature is based on a very specific and careful observation of a dying moth. On a mild, sunny September morning, when crops have begun to yield to harvesting, she watches a moth struggle against death. The moth's struggle and his inevitable submission help the writer to see the constant battle between life and death in all nature; Woolf's observations of the dying moth coincide with the passing of a day and with the growing stillness in all nature as summer turns to fall and preparations for winter begin.

Woolf's cosmic, almost godlike, perspective leaves her spent, resigned, ready to acquiesce to the natural rhythms of life and death, struggle and resignation, getting and giving, which are everywhere apparent in nature. She is subdued, but she understands. Such understanding and acceptance can perhaps help us get along and live with frustration, anger, and tension, whether these tensions come from within ourselves, are created by others, or evolve from the natural give-and-take required in living.

In modern society, however, many of us are not able to take the cosmic or natural view of violence. For many, violence becomes a deeply personal concern; we do not see it as part of an overall natural process, or as something to be controlled in everyone's life. Instead, as isolated individuals, we contend alone with the violence in our own and others' behavior.

We live in a crowded, busy society in which few people are ever encouraged to look beyond immediate concerns. Our work, our travel to and from work, our domestic lives, present immediate struggles and interactions that seldom lead us to consider larger points of view. The man caught in a traffic jam and late for an important business appointment vents his anger on the person in the next car; that person, annoyed by the sound of our businessman's horn, takes her frustration out by cutting off a pedestrian who is trying to cross the street. These everyday activities give us little time for the kind of cosmic reflection we find in Virginia Woolf's "Death of a Moth."

Roger Kahn and Bruno Bettelheim, in contrast with Woolf, provide us with personal perspectives on violence. Carl Furillo's fears and resentments evolve from a variety of background circumstances: his feeling that he was an outcast among a group of very articulate ballplayers, his resentment of ballplayers who received more attention than he did, his ethnic, small-town Pennsylvania childhood which often made him feel out of place in New York. Furillo's violence is seldom and rather harmlessly expressed, but it is there—more as a seething discontent than as an outright physical display. If we understand the frustration and turmoil of Carl Furillo, we understand the repressed violence of a great many Americans who, like Furillo, feel overpowered and powerless in the face of large institutions and machine-like regulations.

Both Carl Furillo and Joey, Bruno Bettelheim's "mechanical boy," are victimized by similar social forces. Joey wants to become a machine to avoid being a burden, a responsibility to others. His mother had always seemed bothered by Joey's human needs. He was able to please her only when he functioned as a trouble-free, well-oiled machine. Soon Joey actually *becomes* a machine—in his own mind, fed by a tangle of imaginary wires and tubes, totally dependent on his mechanical lifelines for survival.

Joey inflicts violence upon himself to satisfy the demands of a mechanized and impersonal society; Furillo silently rages because of the impersonal violence others have inflicted on him.

Despite these superficial differences, however, both Joey and Carl Furillo are fighting a similar enemy: they struggle against what they perceive are impersonal forces in their society. Their struggles create frustrations that result in two very different violent reactions—one psychological and directed inward, the other physical and directed toward others.

The Death of the Moth

VIRGINIA WOOLF

1 Moths that fly by day are not properly to be called moths; they do not excite that pleasant sense of dark autumn nights and ivy-blossom which the commonest yellow-underwing asleep in the shadow of the curtain never fails to rouse in us. They are hybrid creatures, neither gay like butterflies nor sombre like their own species. Nevertheless the present specimen, with his narrow hay-coloured wings, fringed with a tassel of the same colour, seemed to be content with life. It was a pleasant morning, mid-September, mild, benignant, yet with a keener breath than that of the summer months. The plough was already scoring the field opposite the window, and where the share had been, the earth was pressed flat and gleamed with moisture. Such vigour came rolling in from the fields and the down beyond that it was difficult to keep the eyes strictly turned upon the book. The rooks too were keeping one of their annual festivities; soaring round the tree tops until it looked as if a vast net with thousands of black knots in it had been cast up into the air; which, after a few moments sank slowly down upon the trees until every twig seemed to have a knot at the end of it. Then, suddenly, the net would be thrown into the air again in a wider circle this time, with the utmost clamour and vociferation, as though to be thrown into the air and settle slowly down upon the tree tops were a tremendously exciting experience.

2 The same energy which inspired the rooks, the ploughmen, the horses, and even, it seemed, the lean bare-backed downs, sent the moth fluttering from side to side of his square of the window-pane.

One could not help watching him. One was, indeed, conscious of a queer feeling of pity for him. The possibilities of pleasure seemed that morning so enormous and so various that to have only a moth's part in life, and a day moth's at that, appeared a hard fate, and his zest in enjoying his meagre opportunities to the full, pathetic. He flew vigorously to one corner of his compartment, and, after waiting there a second, flew across to the other. What remained for him but to fly to a third corner and then to a fourth? That was all he could do in spite of the size of the downs, the width of the sky, the far-off smoke of houses, and the romantic voice, now and then, of a steamer out at sea. What he could do he did. Watching him, it seemed as if a fibre, very thin but pure, of the enormous energy of the world had been thrust into his frail and diminutive body. As often as he crossed the pane, I could fancy that a thread of vital light became visible. He was little or nothing but life.

3 Yet, because he was so small, and so simple a form of the energy that was rolling in at the open window and driving its way through so many narrow and intricate corridors in my own brain and in those of other human beings, there was something marvellous as well as pathetic about him. It was as if someone had taken a tiny bead of pure life and decking it as lightly as possible with down and feathers, had set it dancing and zigzagging to show us the true nature of life. Thus displayed one could not get over the strangeness of it. One is apt to forget all about life, seeing it humped and bossed and garnished and cumbered so that it has to move with the greatest circumspection and dignity. Again, the thought of all that life might have been had he been born in any other shape caused one to view his simple activities with a kind of pity.

4 After a time, tired by his dancing apparently, he settled on the window ledge in the sun, and, the queer spectacle being at an end, I forgot about him. Then, looking up, my eye was caught by him. He was trying to resume his dancing, but seemed either so stiff or so awkward that he could only flutter to the bottom of the window-pane; and when he tried to fly across it he failed. Being intent on other matters I watched these futile attempts for a time without thinking, unconsciously waiting for him to resume his flight, as one waits for a machine, that has stopped momentarily, to start again without considering the reason of its failure. After perhaps a seventh attempt he slipped from the wooden ledge and fell, fluttering his wings, on to his back on the window sill. The helplessness of his attitude roused me. It flashed upon me that he was in difficulties; he could no longer raise himself; his legs struggled vainly. But, as I stretched out a pencil, meaning to help him to right himself, it came over me that the failure and awkwardness were the approach of death. I laid the pencil down again.

5 The legs agitated themselves once more. I looked as if for the enemy against which he struggled. I looked out of doors. What had happened there? Presumably it was midday, and work in the fields had stopped. Stillness and quiet had replaced the previous animation. The birds had taken themselves off to feed in the brooks. The horses stood still. Yet the power was there all the same, massed outside indifferent, impersonal, not attending to anything in particular. Somehow it was opposed to the little hay-coloured moth. It was useless to try to do anything. One could only watch the extraordinary efforts made by those tiny legs against an oncoming doom which could, had it chosen, have submerged an entire city, not merely a city, but masses of human beings; nothing, I knew, had any chance against death. Nevertheless after a pause of exhaustion the legs fluttered again. It was superb this last protest, and so frantic that he succeeded at last in righting himself. One's sympathies, of course, were all on the side of life. Also, when there was nobody to care or to know, this gigantic effort on the part of an insignificant little moth, against a power of such magnitude, to retain what no one else valued or desired to keep, moved one strangely. Again, somehow, one saw life, a pure bead. I lifted the pencil again, useless though I knew it to be. But even as I did so, the unmistakable tokens of death showed themselves. The body relaxed, and instantly grew stiff. The struggle was over. The insignificant little creature now knew death. As I looked at the dead moth, this minute wayside triumph of so great a force over so mean an antagonist filled me with wonder. Just as life had been strange a few minutes before, so death was now as strange. The moth having righted himself now lay most decently and uncomplainingly composed. O yes, he seemed to say, death is stronger than I am.

Thinking Questions: *Form*

1. This is not a strict cause-and-effect essay. Yet we feel throughout an underlying tone of search and inquiry. Why is this moth dying? Why is his death fascinating? How does the moth's death relate to the passing of time, the changes in nature? Write a thesis statement for this essay, one that Woolf might have used had she been writing argument rather than exposition. Then show how this thesis is supported by Woolf's concrete description of the moth's death. Can the underlying *causes* of death and violence in nature be found in Woolf's essay?

2. This essay presents an ideal example of a complex *tone*. Tone is the writer's method of addressing his or her readers. Some writers have a clear, simple argument in mind; they are often pushy in tone, using emo-

tionally charged words, emphatic sentence forms, all the methods of tone that they use to *persuade* readers. Woolf's tone, on the other hand, is not pushy—she wants to *share* a very personal, seemingly insignificant, experience with her readers. To her the moth's struggles were important; she persuades her readers to see this importance by retelling and sharing the experience, not by presenting and arguing a thesis. Woolf's tone, as a result, must be appropriate to her desire to persuade by sharing an experience. Define her tone, pointing to specifics in the essay to support your definition. How does she address you, the reader? How would you describe the tone of her long, often rambling, yet carefully written, sentences? Then tell why you think Woolf's tone is or is not appropriate to her intention.

3. Pick two sentences that you believe are representative of Woolf's style of writing. Analyze them, pointing out how they work and why she chose to write the sentence as she did. Remember that every sentence has a general idea behind it that might have been expressed in a number of ways. Take, for example, the final sentence of the essay:

> O yes, he seemed to say, death is stronger than I am.

Consider these possible variations, all expressing a similar idea:

> He seemed to say that death was stronger than he was.
>
> Death was surely stronger than he was!
>
> Stronger than he was, death had triumphed.

These variations are created by changes in both words and sentence structure. Why did Woolf decide on her version, given the purpose and method of the essay? Would any or all of the variations change the essay's meaning? Its tone? Why and how?

Thinking Questions: *Substance*

1. Why is Virginia Woolf both attracted and repulsed by the death struggles of the moth? Does she find any value or truth embodied in the story of the moth's death? Can you put that truth in your own words?

2. Notice how, in her first paragraph and at intervals throughout the essay (see the opening of paragraph 5), Woolf carefully describes the weather, season, and time of day: "It was a pleasant morning, mid-September, mild, benignant. . . . Presumably it was midday, and work in the fields had stopped. Stillness and quiet had replaced the previous animation." Do you find any parallels between the description of the moth's death and the descriptions of nature? Does the everyday cycle of morning, noon, evening, and night and the resulting changes in people and animals during those times relate to what happens to the moth? Is there also a purposeful contrast between the moth's struggle and the descriptions of nature?

3. This essay is not specifically about violence, but violence does play an integral part in what happens to the moth. What is the source of that violence? Is there a cause behind the moth's death? Explain that cause, if it exists, as clearly as you can.

4. Do you find the moth's struggle pathetic or heroic? Why? Certainly the moth seems an insignificant part of the total scene; even the rooks that continually soar around the treetops seem far more important and elegant. Yet Woolf focuses her essay on the moth? Why?

5. In the introduction to this section, we mentioned three different perspectives on violence: the cosmic, the social, and the personal or psychological. Woolf's essay takes the cosmic approach. How does this perspective relate to her personal attitude toward violence? Do you ever apply this perspective on violence in your everyday life?

The Hard Hat Who Sued Baseball

ROGER KAHN

> *Disability directly resulting from injury . . . shall not impair the right of the Player to receive his full salary for the period of such disability or for the season in which the injury was sustained.*
>
> *Clause in the Official Player's Contract, cited in the original* Baseball Encyclopedia

1 The wine has soured. There are not going to be any more hurrahs for Carl Furillo, and those that he remembers, if he truly remembers any, are walled from him by harsher, newer memories. His career ended in anger, lawsuits, frustration. He speaks of one prominent baseball official as "that prick." Another is "a lying bastard." One of his lawyers "ended up buddies with the guy I paid him five thousand bucks to sue."

2 When I found Carl Furillo, he was a laborer, installing Otis Elevator doors in one tower of the World Trade Center, rising bright, massive, inhuman, at the foot of Manhattan Island. We sat in a basement shack, beneath incalculable tons of metal and cement, and talked across ham sandwiches at lunch. Furillo seemed to enjoy being interviewed. He wanted to hear about some of his teammates, Carl Erskine and Preacher Roe. But mostly he wanted to spit rage. He believes that he has been cheated. The Dodgers released him while he was injured. He fought back with litigation. "You can't beat them bastards," he says. "I won. I got my money. Then all of a sudden I was blacklisted. Nobody wanted me to coach, to pinch-hit, not even in the minors. You seen me. Could I play ball?"

3 Carl Anthony Furillo was pure ball player. In his prime he stood six feet tall and weighed 190 pounds and there was a fluidity to his frame you seldom see, among such sinews. His black hair was thick, and tightly curled. His face was strong and smooth. He had the look of a

young indomitable centurion. I can image Reese running a Chevrolet dealership and Andy Pafko coaching high school football and Duke Snider operating a dude ranch in Nevada. But I cannot imagine Carl Furillo in his prime as anything other than a ball player. Right field in Brooklyn was his destiny.

4 He was a solitary, private man, but not unhappy. He had stopped school at the eighth grade, and on a team of facile, verbal athletes, he felt self-conscious. He thought that he and his wife, a Pennsylvania Dutch girl named Fern, were treated as outsiders. His locker stood diagonally across from the tumult of Reese, Robinson and Snider. "Where I dress," he said, "is where I am. They don't want me in the middle of things."

5 "Does that bother you?"

"Nah. I ain't got the mouth for that crap"—he said, nodding at the others—"if you know what I mean."

6 He played with dedication and he played in pain and he was awesome in his strength and singleness. People came early just to watch Furillo unlimber his arm. The throws whined homeward, hurtled off a bounce and exploded against Roy Campanella's glove—pom, pom, pom, pom—knee-high fast balls thrown from three hundred feet. Throws climaxed his most remarkable plays. With a man on first, someone stroked a hard, climbing line drive. It was going to hit the wall, then carom at one of five angles. Furillo glanced up and ran to a spot. The drive cracked into cement and bounced into his hands. He whirled and loosed a throw. The base runner had to stop at third. The batter had to settle for a single. The crowd gasped at the throw, and then Dodger fans, appreciating how Furillo had read the right-field wall, began to clap, not wildly but rather with respect. Throughout the grandstands men said to one another, "He's a master."

7 Off the field, Furillo sized up people slowly, then made intuitive, unshakable decisions. He hated Leo Durocher. He disliked Jackie Robinson. He respected Campanella. He admired Dick Young. For reasons I never knew, he accepted me. He spoke with honesty rather than discretion and trusted you to keep him out of trouble. Once in a while, when something he said fired controversy, he stood by his remark. "Maybe I shouldn'ta said it, but I did." He was a man of uncomplicated virtues.

8 He was proud of the way he had learned to hit good righthanded pitching and of the way he played the wall, but his deepest pride was in his arm. After Willie Mays followed a remarkable catch by whirling and throwing out Billy Cox at home, Furillo said, "I'd like to see him do that again."

9 "Well," I said, "he did it once."

"I'd like to see him do it again, know what I mean?" Furillo said.

"He can't throw with you," I said, and Furillo nodded.

10 He seemed enduring as granite in Ebbets Field. It shocked me to see him playing in Los Angeles. Without the old wall, he had lost his native backdrop. He ranged an Antony without the Capitoline, a gladiator in a cardboard coliseum.

11 I had not kept close track of Furillo when *Newsweek* magazine dispatched me in 1959 to Los Angeles, where the Dodgers and White Sox thrashed through a World Series. In a crowded press row, I found myself beside the Hollywood columnist for the *Herald Tribune,* who had been ordered to cover the Dodger clubhouse and complained periodically, "I don't know what I'm doing here. I haven't seen any baseball since I was thirteen, and I never liked it."

12 Furillo was no longer starting, but that day he pinch-hit a single with the bases loaded. The ball scooted up the middle, hopping narrowly over the shortstop's glove. It was not an old-time Furillo hit, but it won the game. (And the Dodgers went on and won the Series.) Some ninety thousand people cheered, and I told the columnist, "If you think that's something, you should have seen the homer Furillo hit off Allie Reynolds."

13 The columnist frowned. Near dusk I saw him alone in the press row, crumpled yellow paper scattered about his typewriter. He seemed near tears. "I can't write *anything,*" he said. "I don't know these people, so I thought I'd write down quotes and look at their backs and get the numbers and check the program later and see who it was who'd said what. But"—terror touched his face—"they take off their *clothes* in the dressing room. They weren't wearing shirts. Who is the black-haired, handsome guy who talks in short sentences?"

14 That is how I came to write three sports stories for an infirm *Herald Tribune* under the by-line of a gossip columnist. It was fun trying my hand again and the columnist provided obbligatos of Hollywood chatter, plus door-to-door transportation in the Mercedes-Benz he said had been given to him by Lauren Bacall. But among the shine of walnut dashboards, the glitter of pool parties, I thought, what a hard way for stolid Carl to finish: pinch-hitting in a strange town and being interviewed by people who were surprised to discover that a baseball was stitched with red yarn.

15 That next spring the Dodgers fired Furillo. Newspapers told a fragmented story of lawsuits, and Furillo faded. Episodic publicity greeted his reappearance as part owner of a delicatessen in Queens, but then he sold his interest and no one seemed to know where he had moved. Several ball clubs offered me addresses, but Furillo no longer lived at any. The telephone company had no record of him in New York City. Someone said he had gone south. Someone said he was living out west. Someone else was certain he had remained in Queens, under another name. I looked for months and mailed half a

dozen letters, but I had all but given up when the telephone rang at 9:30 of a Friday morning and a large voice boomed my name.

16 "Who's this?"

"Carl Furillo."

"Where in the world are you?"

"Downtown. The family's back where I come from, but I'm working in the city during the week."

17 "Nobody knows that."

"You want to be bothered a hundred times a week? But I got your letters and I been thinking and it's okay. But look, when you come down, do me one favor. Put it down right. I ain't greedy. I ain't nuts. I only wanted what I had coming. I read my fucking contract so many times I got that part memorized by heart." Then he recited the lines that precede this chapter.

18 By the time Furillo called, winter had come. One tower of the World Trade Center had been topped and sheathed. It stood 1,350 feet, the tallest building on earth, an aluminum hulk against the sky. The other tower still showed girders. Wind was slamming across the Hudson, blowing bits of debris from unfinished floors. Four thousand men had been working for two years, and the sprawling site had acquired the scarred desolation that comes with construction or with aerial bombardment. The sun gleamed chilly silver. It was 11 degrees and getting colder.

19 A broad stairway led below grade to a cement floor that was wet and patched with ice. Enough daylight entered the vast basement so that wall signs were clear. *"To hell with Goodell." "Vote Buckley." "Vote Conservative."* This was hard-hat country.

20 "Otis is over there," someone said, pointing toward a clutch of unpainted wood cabins. "Furillo? The ball player? He dresses in that one."

21 Inside, a workman standing under a bare bulb said Furillo would be down in a minute. "See that paper bag on that bench? You *know* he's gonna be here. That's his lunch."

22 The workman's name was Chester; Chester Yanoodi. "Carl stays with me out on the island," Chester said. "He's moved his family back to Pennsylvania. He's in good shape. Real good." Chester was a compact man, with leathery skin and eyeglasses. "I've played some ball myself. On the Grumman Aircraft softball team. I could hit a few."

23 Furillo entered. "Ho," he called for "hello." Then "Cold mother out there, huh?" He wore baggy brown pants and layers of clothing. His hair was still black, but he looked heavier. He peeled off a windbreaker and walked in front of an electric heater, beating his arms and blowing on his hands. "Ho," he said again. Then, "Hey, what do you think of the building? It's something, huh? I'm still learning about

elevator doors, but I'm not bad. Do I look fatter? I go around 220. Preacher called me one time, and when I told him, he said he was ready to wrestle. Him, that skinny guy, Preacher weighs 223. How do you like that?"

24 According to a spokesman for the Port of New York Authority, each tower of the World Trade Center requires a thousand elevator doors. "What do you do, Carl," I said, "when all the doors are in and the job is through?"

25 "Then I'm through."

"Meaning?"

"Back to Pennsylvania. Hunt. Fish. You remember my boy, Butch? He's gonna be a trooper. We'll be all right where we came from. I like to hunt and fish."

26 "And clam," Chester Yanoodi said. "He's a helluva clam-digger."

27 "I'm bitter about baseball," Furillo said.

"He could break some necks," Yanoodi said.

"Lousy bastards," Furillo said.

28 He sat on a bench and opened a sandwich and offered me half. Chester handed me a Thermos cup full of coffee. Three other workmen ate silently along the opposite wall, under another naked bulb. Furillo was one of them in the work clothes, but an interview reminded them that he was set apart, too. They knew it. They sat respectful. Furillo began to tell what had happened.

29 He never won the batting championship again after 1953, but he had six more good years. In 1955 he hit 26 homers and batted .314. In 1958, when the Dodgers sank to seventh at Los Angeles, he was still the solid man, with a .290 average and 18 homers. By then he was fighting pain. Under the beating of fifteen thousand innings and five thousands sprints to first base, his legs began to cramp. He had to miss days and later weeks. Professionalism and toughness drove him, but in 1959, the year of the World Series ground single, he played in the outfield only twenty-five times.

30 During the first week of the following season, Furillo was running out a ground ball, hurrying across first base, when his left foot found a soft spot on the floor of the Los Angeles Coliseum. Something tore in the calf. Pain crippled him.

31 Buzzy Bavasi wanted change. The Dodgers of 1959 were ribbed by Brooklyn veterans. Nineteen-sixty was a time to turn over personnel. A team must change constantly if it is to win. The calf injury convinced Bavasi that Furillo's glories were history. He summoned Furillo to his office at the Statler Hilton Hotel and asked, "What do you think of Frank Howard, Carl?"

32 "I don't think he hits the curve good."

33 "But he has promise."

"You don't hit the curve, you don't belong here."

"How's your leg?"

"Coming along, but slow."

"That Howard's gonna be something," Bavasi said.

34 Bavasi was bearing a message down Byzantine ways. He was suggesting that Frank Howard had arrived, and that Furillo, like Carl Erskine, should make way gracefully to the judgment of years. Retire. Then, perhaps, the Dodgers would find him a job.

35 Fighting for his career and the last days of his youth, Furillo beat off that conclusion. Three days later, as the Dodgers prepared to fly to San Francisco, an official telephoned and said, "Carl, don't bother to pack." Furillo decided that Bavasi was giving him more time to rest his leg. But after the series Bavasi himself called and said, "I'm sorry to have to inform you that you've been given an unconditional release."

36 Furillo cursed and hung up. Then he studied his contract. He drove through thirty-two arid paragraphs until he found the clause he wanted. He was hurt, unable to play, and the Dodgers had released him. It didn't matter how slick Bavasi was or how much money O'Malley had. They *couldn't* release him when he was hurt. He took out a pencil and began to calculate.

37 His salary for 1960 was to be $33,000. He had drawn $12,000. That meant the Dodgers were welshing on $21,000. "You know, Fern," he said, "I think I'm gonna do something. I got an idea."

38 Within an hour reporters came unannounced to the house he rented in Long Beach. A Dodger official had tipped them to the story. "What do you think about being released?" one sportswriter said.

39 "I don't like it."

"Are you hurt bad?"

"I can't play, and that means they can't release me." Furillo explained the official contract succinctly.

40 "What are you going to do?"

"You asked me so I got to tell you. I'm gonna talk to two guys I know."

"What two guys?"

"You asked me so I got to tell you. Two guys who're lawyers."

41 Furillo had not intended to reveal his scheme, but he felt that principle forced him to speak. When a man is released, he had to face reporters, and when he faces reporters, he has to answer what he is asked. He was surprised the next day to see his name and projected lawsuit in headlines.

42 Bavasi's secretary called and asked him to stop in again. "Soon as I take care of something," Furillo said.

43 He found Bavasi enraged. "Of all the dumb dago things to do. I was going to find a spot for you. Now I can't. You've made trouble for you and me and everybody. What a rock."

44 "Hey, Buzz," Furillo said. "I got a message for you. It's from the clubhouse man."

"What's that?"

45 "In my pocket here." Furillo reached into his jacket and withdrew a subpoena.

46 Bavasi maintains that he "would really have looked after the guy, but not at $33,000." He speaks of sending Furillo to Spokane and developing him into a coach. O'Malley shakes his head and says a man has to learn to accept things as they are. Both feel Furillo broke a code. In the extralegal world of baseball, a dissatisfied player may protest to the Commissioner, who is supposed to look upon club owners and their chattels without partiality, but is hired and fired by the owners. Turning to the courts is considered nihilistic. No one in baseball, or in the law, knows just when a judge will decide that the official player's contract is itself invalid. The people who run baseball regard anyone exposing them to such risk as indecent. "I'm not sure what would have happened with Furillo," Bavasi said, "but there were options." Hiring lawyers foreclosed every option but one. There would be battle.

47 While the legal proceedings dragged, one of Walter O'Malley's representatives asked if Carl would settle for a job as counselor in the Dodgertown Camp for Boys at Vero Beach. Furillo moved toward court and the following spring wrote letters to eighteen major league teams. He would pinch-hit or play; he had plenty left. Nobody hired him. "It's gotta be because I'm hurt," he said. "That damn injury is still messing me up." He wanted to sue for two years, instead of one.

48 In May of 1961, a year after the injury, Furillo met with Ford Frick, the Commissioner, and Paul Porter, Frick's attorney. According to Furillo, he collected the $21,000 due for 1960, and collected nothing for 1961.

49 If one thinks of blacklist in terms of the old McCarthyism when the three television networks in concert refused to employ writers or actors with a so-called radical past, then Carl Furillo was not blacklisted. As far as anyone can learn, the owners of the eighteen major league clubs operating in 1961 did *not* collectively refuse to hire him. What they did was react in a patterned way. Here was one more old star who wanted to pinch-hit and coach. He could have qualified marginally, but once he sued, people in baseball's conformist ambiance decided he was a "Bolshevik." Hiring him at thirty-nine was not worth the potential trouble. Walter O'Malley was no Borgia, plotting to bar Furillo from the game. Only Furillo's decision to hire lawyers was at play. The existential result was identical.

50 Furillo returned to Reading, investigated several businesses and liked none. In 1963 he resettled in Queens. Then he bought a half interest in a small delicatessen and restaurant on Thirty-second Ave-

nue under the shadow of a Consolidated Edison gas tank. At Furillo and Totto's cheeses hung from the ceiling. Neighborhood people bought prosciutto and Italian sausage. Children loitered and in the afternoon you could hear Furillo's voice booming. "Hey, kid. The candy's for buying not for touching." Late at night, in the restaurant, you could order hero sandwiches prepared by Furillo himself.

51 The trouble, said Fern, was the hours. Carl had to get up early and he had to work late. "You hardly see the family any more," Fern said.

"I got to make a living."

52 After seven years, Furillo sold his share in the store and moved his family back to Stony Creek Mills, on the north side of Reading, where he was born. Then he took his job with Otis. He wanted to think several years ahead. He would work hard until he was fifty, spending only weekends with the family. But then, with the money he made in construction and with his pension, he would be set. There would be nothing but time for hunting and fishing, for Fern and the boys. That was how, he explained, he had come to be wearing a yellow hard hat and these rough clothes in this barren workingman's shack.

53 "You've missed some damn nice years," I said.

"They really screwed him," pronounced Chester Yanoodi.

54 "Aah," Furillo said. "It ain't been bad."

55 He reached back in memory beyond the bitter time. He could always play ball, he said. He could throw, and his brother Nick encouraged him to play and, hell, he said, when he got through with grade school what were the jobs? Picking in an apple orchard for $5 a week. Helping in a woolen mill for $15. But the family kept him close, and it wasn't till he was eighteen and his mother died that he could go off to be a professional. He spent a year at Pocomoke City on the Eastern Shore of Maryland and hit .315. A season after, he played at Reading under Fresco Thompson, who watched him throw, gasped and encouraged him to pitch. "The experiment," Fresco said, "ended within three games. He could certainly throw, but who knew where? He broke four ribs and two writsts before we decided as an act of public safety to make him spend all his time in the outfield."

56 He came to Brooklyn in 1946, the vanguard of Branch Rickey's youth movement, and moved into center field between Dixie Walker and Pete Reiser. Once he spoke to Reiser about a radio program he enjoyed. "Hey," Reiser shouted. "This guy thinks 'The Dorothy and Dick Show' is 'The Dorothy Dix Show.' What a rock. Hiya, Rock." With Furillo's hard body and deliberate ways, ball players thought the cruel nickname fit. Furillo felt like an outsider because in many ways he was made to feel that way.

57 "I started having trouble with Durocher the year after that," he said in the Otis shack. "A guy's no good, he's no good. He didn't want to

play me against righthanders, and Mike Gaven asked how I liked being platooned. He asked. I had to tell. I didn't like it. He wrote the story. Durocher said, 'Hey, kid. You trying to run my team?' Why didn't he get on Gaven?"

58 "It's a good thing for Durocher Carl can't get his hands on him today," Chester said.

59 "Forget it," Furillo said.

60 In 1949 Durocher was managing the Giants, but before one game in Brooklyn he poked his head into the Dodger clubhouse. Furillo was sitting on a black equipment trunk. "Hey," Durocher shouted. "We had you skipping rope with the lefthander last night. Tonight we got the righthander. You'll be ducking."

"Go fuck yourself," Furillo said.

61 A minute later Herman Franks looked in. "In your ear," he cried. "Tonight we get you, dago."

62 Chester broke into the story. *"Dago?* They called *you* 'dago' to your face?"

63 "All the time," Furillo said. Then, kindly to the old Grumman softball player, "Things are different in the big leagues."

64 That night the righthander, Sheldon Jones, hit Furillo with a pitch. The next afternoon, Jones visited the hospital where Furillo was recovering from a concussion. "I'm sorry, Carl," Jones said. "It was a curve."

65 "First fucking curve that never bent," Furillo said.

"I just threw what Durocher told me to," Jones said.

66 "I know," Furillo said. "I ain't blaming you." He promised himself to get even. It was that 1949 promise that flared at the Polo Grounds when Furillo charged to tackle Durocher and the entire Giant ball club in 1953.

67 "Six times I got hit in the head," Furillo said. "Maybe I ducked slow, but they was always gunning for me. So I had a right to gun for the guy that started it. Right?"

68 "You gunned 'em yourself," I said. "How many did you throw out from right field?"

69 "They all the time write eight. They count seven I caught rounding the bag. I threw behind them. There's only one guy I really threw out. A pitcher. Mel Queen. He hit a liner at me. I grabbed it on a hop and my throw beat him. Write the truth. I threw out *one* guy."

"About the right-field wall," I said.

"I knew you'd ask that." His dark face lit.

"Well, how did you get to play it like that?"

70 "I worked, that's fucking how. I'd be out early and study it. Preacher and Billy Cox hit fungoes for me. Now as the ball goes out you sight it, like you were sighting down a gun barrel. Except you got to imagine where it's going. Is it gonna hit above the cement?

Then you run like hell toward the wall, because it's gonna drop dead. Is it gonna hit the cement? Then run like hell to the infield. It's gonna come shooting out. Now you're gonna ask me about where the scoreboard came out and the angles were crazy. I worked. I worked every angle in the fucking wall. I'd take that sight line and know just where it would go. I wasn't afraid to work."

71 "Do you still play ball?" I said.

"He don't even play catch," said Chester.

"Arm still hurt?"

72 "It ain't that. The Mets were after me when I had the store. Play in old-timers' games. I figured, why? I got the store and I got to work at it, but once the Yankees was having one and Fern said, 'Go ahead. See the guys you played with.' I went. I put on spikes. I'd been off 'em ten years. I rocked. I thought I was gonna fall over. I couldn't walk on spikes. I made it to the outfield. Someone hit a little fly. I ain't caught a fly in ten years. Son of a bitch, the ball looked as though it was six miles up. I said to myself, 'See the old guys if you want to, but for Christ's sakes, don't do this no more. Don't ever put on spikes again.' "

73 The three young workers across the shack sat wide-eyed. "You got to watch out for yourself," Furillo told them. "There was this guy on the team, Carl Erskine, and he was such a nice guy that when they ordered him to throw at a hitter, he'd throw ten feet over the man's head. And he had arm trouble and he quit young and they put out stories that they were really looking after him. He was through in 1959, the year before I got hurt. I said to him, 'Hey, is that right? The ball club treated you fair?' He didn't want no trouble, but I'll never forget what he told me. He said, 'Carl. Take care of Carl.' "

74 Furillo puffed air and offered me more coffee. "If I really wanted to hit 'em," he said, "I'd have another suit. Two back operations. The bad leg had me walking funny and I had to have two operations for a ruptured disc. That come on account of the injury, but I figure, fuck it, I got to take care of myself and I can do it." The young hard hats nodded vigorously.

75 "Hey," Furillo said, "what is it with the colored today? They got to get welfare? It's tough, but was it easy for the Italians? Five dollars a week in the apple orchard, was that easy? Why should the colored have it easier than anybody?"

More nods.

76 "It isn't the same," I said. "You were playing ball and Robinson couldn't."

"He wasn't the only guy got thrown at."

"Ah, you're talking like a hard hat."

77 "That's what I fucking am. But when this building gets through, it's in the barrel. I put the lid on this city, New York, where I had some

good times, and Los Angeles, where I should never have gone, and back with Fern up around Reading and hunt and fish and take my pension. I'll be fifty. Hey, I like a lot of colored. Campy and Joe Black, he was a nice guy. I don't think they ought to have it easy, that's all."

78 He does talk like a hard hat and he was a baseball Bolshevik. He fits no label. He is too human, too large, too variable, too much the independent. In one voice he talks against welfare, like a Buckley, and in another voice, which is the same, he talks about ball players' rights and defies a system, like Bartolomeo Vanzetti.

79 "Hey," he shouted. "Who got a hammer? I need a hammer. Having trouble with a door." He turned. "I got plenty tricks to learn," he said. Someone found him the hammer and he began zipping into his winter clothes, gruff, cheerful and defiant of pity.

80 "Come 'round in spring," Furillo said, slamming a yellow hard hat on his head. "In spring we'll sit outside and you and me can take a little sun."

Thinking Questions: *Form*

1. What particular combination of intellectual, psychological, and physical traits cause Carl Furillo's problems? Might he have been a successful hero in an earlier time? Why?

2. Some critics might argue that ballplayers like Carl Furillo should know enough, have enough foresight, to plan for careers *after* their playing days are finished. Carl Furillo waited until he was in his forties to do so. Why? What encouraged him to live in the present and not think of the future?

3. Play psychologist: Do a careful written analysis of Carl Furillo's character. List and explain his primary character traits. Then write a summary in which you show how those traits led to particular effects or results. Why, for example, did Furillo form quick opinions about other people (see paragraph 7) and refuse to change them over the years?

4. Roger Kahn gives us a good example of psychological or personal violence. Do you think this kind of violence is more or less prevalent than other forms of violence? Why? Is it always less dangerous or damaging than more explicit forms of physical violence? What forces in our society seem to encourage the psychological violence represented in this essay by Carl Furillo's seething resentment and frustration?

Thinking Questions: *Substance*

1. Why *was* Carl Furillo fired by the Los Angeles Dodgers? Was his firing justified because he no longer contributed enough to the team? Did the Dodgers owe Furillo anything for his past contributions?

2. Consider this statement (paragraph 31) by Roger Kahn, which de-

scribes how the Dodger administration in 1959 felt about many of the older Dodger players: "Buzzy Bavasi [the Dodger vice president] wanted change. The Dodgers of 1959 were ribbed by Brooklyn veterans. Nineteen-sixty was a time to turn over personnel. A team must change constantly if it is to win. The calf injury convinced Bavasi that Furillo's glories were history." This attitude led to Carl Furillo's rage. Why?

3. Contrast Carl Furillo's "violence" with that of Joey, the mechanical boy, in the next essay. How are their expressions of violence different? How are they similar? What causes violent behavior in both their cases?

4. In paragraph 46, Kahn tells how Walter O'Malley, the Dodger owner, feels that "a man has to learn to accept things as they are." Furillo does not. To keep itself in operation, the system denies him individual rights. Can you see this pattern in other areas of American culture?

5. Early in this essay Roger Kahn describes Furillo as a "man of uncomplicated virtues." By the essay's end we come to feel that simple, uncomplicated virtues, however admirable, do not prepare a man to face a system as complex as modern major league baseball or, for that matter, any large bureaucracy. Do you agree with Kahn's assessment of Furillo, with his combination of respect for Furillo's power, strength, and honesty and his criticism of Furillo's lack of complexity? Might an executive in a large corporation, nearing retirement age, feel the same rage and frustration as Furillo does?

Joey: A "Mechanical Boy"

BRUNO BETTELHEIM

1 Joey, when we began our work with him, was a mechanical boy. He functioned as if by remote control, run by machines of his own powerfully creative fantasy. Not only did he himself believe that he was a machine but, more remarkably, he created this impression in others. Even while he performed actions that are intrinsically human, they never appeared to be other than machine-started and executed. On the other hand, when the machine was not working we had to concentrate on recollecting his presence, for he seemed not to exist. A human body that functions as if it were a machine and a machine that duplicates human functions are equally fascinating and frightening. Perhaps they are so uncanny because they remind us that the human body can operate without a human spirit, that body can exist without soul. And Joey was a child who had been robbed of his humanity.

2 Not every child who possesses a fantasy world is possessed by it. Normal children may retreat into realms of imaginary glory or magic powers, but they are easily recalled from these excursions. Disturbed children are not always able to make the return trip; they remain withdrawn, prisoners of the inner world of delusion and fantasy. In many ways Joey presented a classic example of this state of infantile autism.

3 At the Sonia Shankman Orthogenic School of the University of Chicago it is our function to provide a therapeutic environment in which such children may start life over again. I have previously described the rehabilitation of another of our patients. . . . This time I shall concentrate upon the illness, rather than the treatment. In any age, when the individual has escaped into a delusional world, he has usually fashioned it from bits and pieces of the world at hand. Joey, in his time and world, chose the machine and froze himself in its image. His story has a general relevance to the understanding of emotional development in a machine age.

4 Joey's delusion is not uncommon among schizophrenic children today. He wanted to be rid of his unbearable humanity, to become completely automatic. He so nearly succeeded in attaining his goal that he could almost convince others, as well as himself, of his mechanical character. The descriptions of autistic children in the literature take for their point of departure and comparison the normal or abnormal human being. To do justice to Joey I would have to compare him simultaneously to a most inept infant and a highly complex piece of machinery. Often we had to force ourselves by a conscious act of will to realize that Joey was a child. Again and again his acting-out of his delusions froze our own ability to respond as human beings.

5 During Joey's first weeks with us we would watch absorbedly as this once fragile-looking and imperious nine-year-old went about his mechanical existence. Entering the dining room, for example, he would string an imaginary wire from his "energy source"—an imaginary electric outlet—to the table. There he "insulated" himself with paper napkins and finally plugged himself in. Only then could Joey eat, for he firmly believed that the "current" ran his ingestive apparatus. So skillful was the pantomime that one had to look twice to be sure there was neither wire nor outlet nor plug. Children and members of our staff spontaneously avoided stepping on the "wires" for fear of interrupting what seemed the source of his very life.

6 For long periods of time, when his "machinery" was idle, he would sit so quietly that he would disappear from the focus of the most conscientious observation. Yet in the next moment he might be "working" and the center of our captivated attention. Many times a day he would turn himself on and shift noisily through a sequence of higher

and higher gears until he "exploded," screaming "Crash, crash!" and hurling items from his ever present apparatus—radio tubes, light bulbs, even motors or, lacking these, any handy breakable object. (Joey had an astonishing knack for snatching bulbs and tubes unobserved.) As soon as the object thrown had shattered, he would cease his screaming and wild jumping and retire to mute, motionless nonexistence.

7 Our maids, inured to difficult children, were exceptionally attentive to Joey; they were apparently moved by his extreme infantile fragility, so strangely coupled with megalomaniacal superiority. Occasionally some of the apparatus he fixed to his bed to "live him" during his sleep would fall down in disarray. This machinery he contrived from masking tape, cardboard, wire and other paraphernalia. Usually the maids would pick up such things and leave them on a table for the children to find, or disregard them entirely. But Joey's machine they carefully restored: "Joey must have the carburetor so he can breathe." Similarly they were on the alert to pick up and preserve the motors that ran him during the day and the exhaust pipes through which he exhaled.

8 How had Joey become a human machine? From intensive interviews with his parents we learned that the process had begun even before birth. Schizophrenia often results from parental rejection, sometimes combined ambivalently with love. Joey, on the other hand, had been completely ignored.

9 "I never knew I was pregnant," his mother said, meaning that she had already excluded Joey from her consciousness. His birth, she said, "did not make any difference." Joey's father, a rootless draftee in the wartime civilian army, was equally unready for parenthood. So, of course, are many young couples. Fortunately most such parents lose their indifference upon the baby's birth. But not Joey's parents. "I did not want to see or nurse him," his mother declared. "I had no feeling of actual dislike—I simply didn't want to take care of him." For the first three months of his life Joey "cried most of the time." A colicky baby, he was kept on a rigid four-hour feeding schedule, was not touched unless necessary and was never cuddled or played with. The mother, preoccupied with herself, usually left Joey alone in the crib or playpen during the day. The father discharged his frustrations by punishing Joey when the child cried at night.

10 Soon the father left for overseas duty, and the mother took Joey, now a year and a half old, to live with her at her parents' home. On his arrival the grandparents noticed that ominous changes had occurred in the child. Strong and healthy at birth, he had become frail and irritable; a responsive baby, he had become remote and inaccessible. When he began to master speech, he talked only to himself. At an early date he became preoccupied with machinery, includ-

ing an old electric fan which he could take apart and put together again with surprising deftness.

11 Joey's mother impressed us with a fey quality that expressed her insecurity, her detachment from the world and her low physical vitality. We were struck especially by her total indifference as she talked about Joey. This seemed much more remarkable than the actual mistakes she made in handling him. Certainly he was left to cry for hours when hungry, because she fed him on a rigid schedule; he was toilet-trained with great rigidity so that he would give no trouble. These things happen to many children. But Joey's existence never registered with his mother. In her recollections he was fused at one moment with one event or person; at another, with something or somebody else. When she told us about his birth and infancy, it was as if she were talking about some vague acquaintance, and soon her thoughts would wander off to another person or to herself.

12 When Joey was not yet four, his nursery school suggested that he enter a special school for disturbed children. At the new school his autism was immediately recognized. During his three years there he experienced a slow improvement. Unfortunately a subsequent two years in a parochial school destroyed this progress. He began to develop compulsive defenses, which he called his "preventions." He could not drink, for example, except through elaborate piping systems built of straws. Liquids had to be "pumped" into him, in his fantasy, or he could not suck. Eventually his behavior became so upsetting that he could not be kept in the parochial school. At home things did not improve. Three months before entering the Orthogenic School he made a serious attempt at suicide.

13 To us Joey's pathological behavior seemed the external expression of an overwhelming effort to remain almost nonexistent as a person. For weeks Joey's only reply when addressed was "Bam." Unless he thus neutralized whatever we said, there would be an explosion, for Joey plainly wished to close off every form of contact not mediated by machinery. Even when he was bathed he rocked back and forth with mute, engine-like regularity, flooding the bathroom. If he stopped rocking, he did this like a machine too; suddenly he went completely rigid. Only once, after months of being lifted from his bath and carried to bed, did a small expression of puzzled pleasure appear on his face as he said very softly: "They even carry you to your bed here."

14 For a long time after he began to talk he would never refer to anyone by name, but only as "that person" or "the little person" or "the big person." He was unable to designate by its true name anything to which he attached feelings. Nor could he name his anxieties except through neologisms or word contaminations. For a long time he spoke about "master paintings" and "a master painting room"

(*i.e.,* masturbating and masturbating room). One of his machines, the "criticizer," prevented him from "saying words which have unpleasant feelings." Yet he gave personal names to the tubes and motors in his collection of machinery. Moreover, these dead things had feelings; the tubes bled when hurt and sometimes got sick. He consistently maintained this reversal between animate and inanimate objects.

15 In Joey's machine world everything, on pain of instant destruction, obeyed inhibitory laws much more stringent than those of physics. When we came to know him better, it was plain that in his moments of silent withdrawal, with his machine switched off, Joey was absorbed in pondering the compulsive laws of his private universe. His preoccupation with machinery made it difficult to establish even practical contacts with him. If he wanted to do something with a counselor, such as play with a toy that had caught his vague attention, he could not do so: "I'd like this very much, but first I have to turn off the machine." But by the time he had fulfilled all the requirements of his preventions, he had lost interest. When a toy was offered to him, he could not touch it because his motors and his tubes did not leave him a hand free. Even certain colors were dangerous and had to be strictly avoided in toys and clothing, because "some colors turn off the current, and I can't touch them because I can't live without the current."

16 Joey was convinced that machines were better than people. Once when he bumped into one of the pipes on our jungle gym he kicked it so violently that his teacher had to restrain him to keep him from injuring himself. When she explained that the pipe was much harder than his foot, Joey replied: "That proves it. Machines are better than the body. They don't break; they're much harder and stronger." If he lost or forgot something, it merely proved that his brain ought to be thrown away and replaced by machinery. If he spilled something, his arm should be broken and twisted off because it did not work properly. When his head or arm failed to work as it should, he tried to punish it by hitting it. Even Joey's feelings were mechanical. Much later in his therapy, when he had formed a timid attachment to another child and had been rebuffed, Joey cried: "He broke my feelings."

17 Gradually we began to understand what had seemed to be contradictory in Joey's behavior—why he held on to the motors and tubes, then suddenly destroyed them in a fury, then set out immediately and urgently to equip himself with new and larger tubes. Joey had created these machines to run his body and mind because it was too painful to be human. But again and again he became dissatisfied with their failure to meet his need and rebellious at the way they frustrated his will. In a recurrent frenzy he "exploded" his light bulbs and tubes, and for a moment became a human being—for one

crowning instant he came alive. But as soon as he had asserted his dominance through the self-created explosion, he felt his life ebbing away. To keep on existing he had immediately to restore his machines and replenish the electricity that supplied his life energy.

18 What deep-seated fears and needs underlay Joey's delusional system? We were long in finding out, for Joey's preventions effectively concealed the secret of his autistic behavior. In the meantime we dealt with his peripheral problems one by one.

19 During his first year with us Joey's most trying problem was toilet behavior. This surprised us, for Joey's personality was not "anal" in the Freudian sense; his original personality damage had antedated the period of his toilet-training. Rigid and early toilet-training, however, had certainly contributed to his anxieties. It was our effort to help Joey with this problem that led to his first recognition of us as human beings.

20 Going to the toilet, like everything else in Joey's life, was surrounded by elaborate preventions. We had to accompany him; he had to take off all his clothes; he could only squat, not sit, on the toilet seat; he had to touch the wall with one hand, in which he also clutched frantically the vacuum tubes that powered his elimination. He was terrified lest his whole body be sucked down.

21 To counteract this fear we gave him a metal wastebasket in lieu of a toilet. Eventually, when eliminating into the wastebasket, he no longer needed to take off all his colthes, nor to hold on to the wall. He still needed the tubes and motors which, he believed, moved his bowels for him. But here again the all-important machinery was itself a source of new terrors. In Joey's world the gadgets had to move their bowels, too. He was terribly concerned that they should, but since they were so much more powerful than men, he was also terrified that if his tubes moved their bowels, their feces would fill all of space and leave him no room to live. He was thus always caught in some fearful contradiction.

22 Our readiness to accept his toilet habits, which obviously entailed some hardships for his counselors, gave Joey the confidence to express his obsessions in drawings. Drawing these fantasies was a first step toward letting us in, however distantly, to what concerned him most deeply. It was the first step in a year-long process of externalizing his anal preoccupations. As a result he began seeing feces everywhere; the whole world became to him a mire of excrement. At the same time he began to eliminate freely wherever he happened to be. But with this release from his infantile imprisonment in compulsive rules, the toilet and the whole process of elimination became less dangerous. Thus far it had been beyond Joey's comprehension that anybody could possibly move his bowels without mechanical aid. Now Joey took a further step forward; defecation be-

came the first physiological process he could perform without the help of vacuum tubes. It must not be thought that he was proud of this ability. Taking pride in an achievement presupposes that one accomplishes it of one's own free will. He still did not feel himself an autonomous person who could do things on his own. To Joey defecation still seemed enslaved to some incomprehensible but utterly binding cosmic law, perhaps the law his parents had imposed on him when he was being toilet-trained.

23 It was not simply that his parents had subjected him to rigid, early training. Many children are so trained. But in most cases the parents have a deep emotional investment in the child's performance. The child's response in turn makes training an occasion for interaction between them and for the building of genuine relationships. Joey's parents had no emotional investment in him. His obedience gave them no satisfaction and won him no affection or approval. As a toilet-trained child he saved his mother labor, just as household machines saved her labor. As a machine he was not loved for his performance, nor could he love himself.

24 So it had been with all other aspects of Joey's existence with his parents. Their reactions to his eating or noneating, sleeping or wakening, urinating or defecating, being dressed or undressed, washed or bathed did not flow from any unitary interest in him, deeply embedded in their personalities. By treating him mechanically his parents made him a machine. The various functions of life—even the parts of his body—bore no integrating relationship to one another or to any sense of self that was acknowledged and confirmed by others. Though he had acquired mastery over some functions, such as toilet-training and speech, he had acquired them separately and kept them isolated from each other. Toilet-training had thus not gained him a pleasant feeling of body mastery; speech had not led to communication of thought or feeling. On the contrary, each achievement only steered him away from self-mastery and integration. Toilet-training had enslaved him. Speech left him talking in neologisms that obstructed his and our ability to relate to each other. In Joey's development the normal process of growth had been made to run backward. Whatever he had learned put him not at the end of his infantile development toward integration but, on the contrary, farther behind than he was at its very beginning. Had we understood this sooner, his first years with us would have been less baffling.

25 It is unlikely that Joey's calamity could befall a child in any time and culture but our own. He suffered no physical deprivation; he starved for human contact. Just to be taken care of is not enough for relating. It is a necessary but not a sufficient condition. At the extreme where utter scarcity reigns, the forming of relationships is certainly hampered. But our society of mechanized plenty often

makes for equal difficulties in a child's learning to relate. Where parents can provide the simple creature-comforts for their children only at the cost of significant effort, it is likely that they will feel pleasure in being able to provide for them; it is this, the parents' pleasure, that gives children a sense of personal worth and sets the process of relating in motion. But if comfort is so readily available that the parents feel no particular pleasure in winning it for their children, then the children cannot develop the feeling of being worthwhile around the satisfaction of their basic needs. Of course parents and children can and do develop relationships around other situations. But matters are then no longer so simple and direct. The child must be on the receiving end of care and concern given with pleasure and without the exaction of return if he is to feel loved and worthy of respect and consideration. This feeling gives him the ability to trust; he can entrust his well-being to persons to whom he is so important. Out of such trust the child learns to form close and stable relationships.

26 For Joey relationship with his parents was empty of pleasure in comfort-giving as in all other situations. His was an extreme instance of a plight that sends many schizophrenic children to our clinics and hospitals. Many months passed before he could relate to us; his despair that anybody could like him made contact impossible.

27 When Joey could finally trust us enough to let himself become more infantile, he began to play at being a papoose. There was a corresponding change in his fantasies. He drew endless pictures of himself as an electrical papoose. Totally enclosed, suspended in empty space, he is run by unknown, unseen powers through wireless electricity. . . .

28 As we eventually came to understand, the heart of Joey's delusional system was the artificial, mechanical womb he had created and into which he had locked himself. In his papoose fantasies lay the wish to be entirely reborn in a womb. His new experiences in the school suggested that life, after all, might be worth living. Now he was searching for a way to be reborn in a better way. Since machines were better than men, what was more natural than to try rebirth through them? This was the deeper meaning of his electrical papoose.

29 As Joey made progress, his pictures of himself became more dominant in his drawings. Though still machine-operated, he has grown in self-importance. . . . Another great step forward is represented in . . . [another picture]. Now he has acquired hands that do something, and he has had the courage to make a picture of the machine that runs him. Later still the papoose became a person, rather than a robot encased in glass.

30 Eventually Joey began to create an imaginary family at the school: the "Carr" family. Why the Carr family? In the car he was enclosed as he had been in his papoose, but at least the car was not

stationary; it could move. More important, in a car one was not only driven but also could drive. The Carr family was Joey's way of exploring the possibility of leaving the school, of living with a good family in a safe, protecting car. . . .

31 Joey at last broke through his prison. In this brief account it has not been possible to trace the painfully slow process of his first true relations with other human beings. Suffice it to say that he ceased to be a mechanical boy and became a human child. This newborn child was, however, nearly 12 years old. To recover the lost time is a tremendous task. That work has occupied Joey and us ever since. Sometimes he sets to it with a will; at other times the difficulty of real life makes him regret that he ever came out of his shell. But he has never wanted to return to his mechanical life.

32 One last detail and this fragment of Joey's story has been told. When Joey was 12, he made a float for our Memorial Day parade. It carried the slogan: "Feelings are more important than anything under the sun." Feelings, Joey had learned, are what make for humanity; their absence, for a mechanical existence. With this knowledge Joey entered the human condition.

Thinking Questions: *Form*

1. Sometimes, especially in an essay such as Bettelheim's, which implies rather than directly states its general thesis, it is useful to work out a logical equation for the entire essay. What do you think of these related equations as definitions of Bettelheim's general purpose?

GENERAL EQUATION

Major premise: Feelings must be recognized and supported if human beings are to develop fully.

Minor premise: The size and impersonality of modern American society often does *not* allow or encourage people to take other people's feelings into consideration.

Conclusion: Many individuals do not develop into full thinking and feeling human beings in modern America.

SPECIFIC EQUATION

Major premise: Joey required recognition and emotional response from his parents.

Minor premise: Joey had been treated as an object by his parents; his feelings had been ignored.

Conclusion: Joey tried to become an object or machine in order to deny his own feelings and to deny his emotional need for his parents.

These equations, of course, explain only some of the reasoning in the essay. Try to come up with other equations that explain other parts of the essay.

2. Much of Bettelheim's essay is based upon a central analogy: that Joey's condition and behavior is a greatly exaggerated form of the conditions and behavior of many individuals in our society. Does the analogy work? How is Joey's condition special? Do these special conditions destroy the extended analogy?

3. Bettelheim very carefully organizes his material. His introduction (paragraphs 1 through 3) gives a general description of Joey's case and suggests its implications. The body of his essay begins with paragraph 4 and is divided into four major sections:

a. Paragraphs 4 through 15 describe Joey's behavior and its outside causes—primarily his parents' treatment of him.

b. Paragraphs 16 and 17 summarize the effects of these outside causes on Joey's condition.

c. Paragraphs 18 through 23 describe the internal or psychological causes for Joey's condition.

d. Paragraphs 24 through 26 summarize the outward effects of the internal or psychological causes on Joey's behavior.

The essay concludes, in paragraphs 27 through 32, with a narrative description of Joey's most recent treatment, with emphasis on his partially successful rehabilitation. Why does Bettelheim use this particular arrangement of his material? Does it put his thesis in a stronger light? Might it create more sympathy with his subject? Does this particular arrangement allow Bettelheim to combine more effectively his ideas and his physical descriptions of Joey's case?

Thinking Questions: *Substance*

1. Point out the differences between Joey's reactions to what he perceives as psychological violence by his mother and Carl Furillo's response to his employers. Which type of violent response is most damaging to the individual or to society?

2. Explain succinctly what caused Joey's condition. How many causes does Bettelheim give? Why does Bettelheim argue (see paragraph 3) that "His [Joey's] story has a general relevance to the understanding of emotional development in a machine age"? How does Joey's mother's behavior fit into the overall pattern of cause and effect in Joey's case study?

3. What psychological reasons lie behind Joey's decision to become a machine? Why would a machine-like existence seem attractive to a boy like Joey? Why are most "normal" people like Carl Furillo frustrated and often enraged when they are treated as machines by employers, the government, or teachers?

4. Can you think of occasions where adults might feel completely "ignored," not by parents as Joey was ignored, but by parental substitutes in later life—employers, corporations, governmental agencies, and

politicians? Does Carl Furillo's situation as he nears retirement age provide one example of an individual ignored by a system?

5. In paragraph 25, Bettelheim begins his conclusion by saying, "It is unlikely that Joey's calamity could befall a child in any time and culture but our own." Joey had suffered no severe physical hardships: his parents had properly fed and clothed him; they had never physically mistreated him. Yet, Bettelheim suggests, merely being taken care of is not enough; people must feel that others believe they are of some importance, worth some human effort beyond the necessities of life. Obviously such statements apply to adults as well as children. Why do you think Bettelheim suggests that psychological alienation such as Joey's seems more of a problem in our society than it has ever been before?

* * *

VIOLENCE AS A SOCIAL PHENOMENA

The first three essays in this section provide us with firsthand observations of cosmic and personal violence. Woolf shows us violence in nature by describing the life (and death) struggle of a particular moth, while Roger Kahn and Bruno Bettelheim give us insights into deeply personal, psychological forms of violence. In these opening essays, an individual moth and individual persons are pitted against larger forces in nature and society.

The following two essays concentrate on violence expressed on a larger scale, by the society itself. Tom Wolfe, a journalist whose articles are based on personal research and on-the-spot observation of developing social fads and patterns of behavior, here analyzes the contemporary phenomenon he calls "porno-violence." Wolfe, in a style all his own, examines the potential causes of porno-violence, partially ridiculing the phenomenon, partially analyzing its deeper causes.

Robert Jay Lifton, a psychologist who has studied the effects of mass social violence like the atomic bombing of Hiroshima and the massacre at My Lai, begins by giving us a firsthand experience of the institutionalized violence of war. Lifton emphasizes the effects war has on individuals; he attempts to show that contemporary people have gradually become so accustomed to institutionalized technological violence that they ultimately grow insensitive to individual forms of violence. Both Wolfe and Lifton, then, base their arguments on the violent effects produced by general social conditions.

Military "atrocities," Lifton suggests, are caused by a variety of social phenomena. All these contributing phenomena, however, grow out of feelings of mass frustration—like those of Joey in Bettelheim's essay and Carl Furillo in Kahn's reminiscences about the old Brooklyn Dodgers—where individuals believe and act as if they have no control over what happens to them. Sometimes the enemy is a large institution, such as major league baseball; often it is an adult world that seems to want children (and adults as well) to behave like machines; sometimes, as Robert Jay Lifton indicates, the enemy or adversary is institutionalized warfare which, in encouraging people to treat other human beings as objects, creates mass feelings of guilt, anxiety, and personal frustration.

All these essays provide us with repeated central questions: How can we learn to live in a violent world, with both natural and human forms of violence? When is violence justified? Is violence justified when individual dignity is lost in the face of impersonal or unjust social forces? Is violence justified when larger societies decide that a social cause demands war? Is violence inevitable and, if so, how should our impulses to violence be controlled? And, as Tom Wolfe's article on porno-violence suggests, is our society promoting the use of mass media as a means of sublimating individual anger and tendencies toward violence?

Porno-Violence

TOM WOLFE

1 "*Keeps His Mom-in-law in Chains,* meet *Kills Son and Feeds Corpse to Pigs*. Pleased to meet you. *Teenager Twists Off Corpse's Head . . . To Get Gold Teeth,* meet *Strangles Girl Friend, then Chops Her to Pieces*. Likewise, I'm sure. *Nurse's Aide Sees Fingers Chopped Off in Meat Grinder,* meet. . . ."

2 In ten years of journalism I have covered more conventions than I care to remember. Podiatrists, theosophists, Professional Budget Finance dentists, oyster farmers, mathematicians, truckers, dry cleaners, stamp collectors, Esperantists, nudists and newspaper editors—I have seen them all, together, in vast assemblies, sloughing through the wall-to-wall of a thousand hotel lobbies (the nudists excepted) in their shimmering grey-metal suits and Nicey Short Collar white shirts with white Plasti-Coat name cards on their chests, and I have sat through their speeches and seminars (the nudists included) and attentively endured ear baths such as you wouldn't believe. And yet some of the truly instructive conventions of our times

I seem to have missed altogether. One, for example, I only heard about from one of the many anonymous men who have labored in . . . a curious field. This was a convention of the stringers for *The National Enquirer.*

3 *The Enquirer* is a weekly newspaper that is probably known by sight to millions more than know it by name. In fact, no one who ever came face-to-face with *The Enquirer* on a newsstand in its wildest days is likely to have forgotten the sight: a tabloid with great inky shocks of type all over the front page saying something on the order of *Gouges Out Wife's Eyes to Make Her Ugly, Dad Hurls Hot Grease in Daughter's Face, Wife Commits Suicide After 2 Years of Poisoning Fails to Kill Husband. . . .*

4 The stories themselves were supplied largely by stringers, i.e., correspondents, from all over the country, the world, for that matter, mostly copy editors and reporters on local newspapers. Every so often they would come upon a story, usually via the police beat, that was so grotesque the local sheet would discard it or run it in a highly glossed form rather than offend or perplex its readers. The stringers would preserve them for *The Enquirer,* which always rewarded them well and respectfully.

5 In fact, one year *The Enquirer* convened and feted them at a hotel in Manhattan. It was a success in every way. The only awkward moment was at the outset when the stringers all pulled in. None of them knew each other. Their hosts got around the problem by introducing them by the stories they had supplied. The introductions, I am told, went like this:

6 "Harry, I want you to meet Frank here. Frank did that story, you remember that story, *Midget Murderer Throws Girl Off Cliff After She Refuses To Dance With Him.*"

7 "Pleased to meet you. That was some story."

8 "And Harry did the one about *I Spent Three Days Trapped at Bottom of Forty-foot-deep Mine Shaft and Was Saved by a Swarm of Flies.*"

"Likewise, I'm sure."

9 And *Midget Murderer Throws Girl Off Cliff* shakes hands with *I Spent Three Days Trapped at Bottom of Forty-foot-deep Mine Shaft,* and *Buries Her Baby Alive* shakes hands with *Boy, Twelve, Strangles Two-year-old Girl,* and *Kills Son and Feeds Corpse to Pigs* shakes hands with *He Strangles Old Woman and Smears Corpse with Syrup, Ketchup and Oatmeal* . . . and. . . .

10 . . . There was a great deal of esprit about the whole thing. These men were, in fact, the avant-garde of a new genre that since then has become institutionalized throughout the nation without anyone knowing its proper name. I speak of the new pornography, the pornography of violence.

11 Pornography comes from the Greek word *porne,* meaning harlot, and pornography is literally the depiction of the acts of harlots. In the new pornography, the theme is not sex. The new pornography depicts practitioners acting out another, murkier drive: people staving teeth in, ripping guts open, blowing brains out and getting even with all those bastards. . . .

12 The success of *The Enquirer* prompted many imitators to enter the field, *Midnight, The Star Chronicle, The National Insider, Inside News, The National Close-up, The National Tattler, The National Examiner.* A truly competitive free press evolved, and soon a reader could go to the newspaper of his choice for *Kill the Retarded! (Won't You Join My Movement?)* and *Unfaithful Wife? Burn Her Bed!, Harem Master's Mistress Chops Him with Machete, Babe Bites Off Boy's Tongue,* and *Cuts Buddy's Face to Pieces for Stealing His Business and Fiancée.*

13 And yet the last time I surveyed the Violence press, I noticed a curious thing. These pioneering journals seem to have pulled back. They seem to be regressing to what is by now the Redi-Mix staple of literate Americans, plain old lust-o-lech sex. *Ecstasy and Me (By Hedy Lamarr),* says *The National Enquirer. I Run A Sex Art Gallery,* says *The National Insider.* What has happened, I think, is something that has happened to avant-gardes in many fields, from William Morris and the Craftsmen to the Bauhaus group. Namely, their discoveries have been preempted by the Establishment and so thoroughly dissolved into the mainstream they no longer look original.

14 Robert Harrison, the former publisher of *Confidential,* and later publisher of the aforementioned *Inside News,* was perhaps the first person to see it coming. I was interviewing Harrison early in January of 1964 for a story in *Esquire* about six weeks after the assassination of President Kennedy, and we were in a cab in the West Fifties in Manhattan, at a stoplight, by a newsstand, and Harrison suddenly pointed at the newsstand and said, "Look at that. They're doing the same thing *The Enquirer* does."

15 There on the stand was a row of slick-paper, magazine-size publications, known in the trade as one-shots, with titles like *Four Days That Shook the World, Death of a President, An American Tragedy* or just *John Fitzgerald Kennedy* (1921-1963). "You want to know why people buy those things?" said Harrison. "People buy those things to see a man get his head blown off."

16 And, of course, he was right. Only now the publishers were in many cases the pillars of the American press. Invariably, these "special coverages" of the assassination bore introductions piously commemorating the fallen President, exhorting the American people to strength and unity in a time of crisis, urging greater vigilance and safeguards for the new President, and even raising the nice meta-

physical question of collective guilt in "an age of violence."

17 In the three and a half years since then, of course, there has been an incessant replay, with every recoverable clinical detail, of those less than five seconds in which a man got his head blown off. And throughout this deluge of words, pictures and film frames, I have been intrigued with one thing. The point of view, the vantage point, is almost never that of the victim, riding in the Presidential Lincoln Continental. What you get is . . . the view from Oswald's rifle. You can step right up here and look point-blank right through the very hairline cross in Lee Harvey Oswald's Optics Ordinance four-power Japanese telescopic sight and watch, frame by frame by frame by frame by frame, as that man there's head comes apart. Just a little History there before your very eyes.

18 The television networks have schooled us in the view from Oswald's rifle and made it seem a normal pastime. The TV viewpoint is nearly always that of the man who is going to strike. The last time I watched *Gunsmoke,* which was not known as a very violent Western in TV terms, the action went like this: The Wellington agents and the stagecoach driver pull guns on the badlands gang leader's daughter and Kitty, the heart-of-gold saloonkeeper, and kidnap them. Then the badlands gang shoots two Wellington agents. Then they tie up five more and talk about shooting them. Then they desist because they might not be able to get a hotel room in the next town if the word got around. Then one badlands gang gunslinger attempts to rape Kitty while the gang leader's younger daughter looks on. Then Kitty resists, so he slugs her one in the jaw. Then the gang leader slugs him. Then the gang leader slugs Kitty. Then Kitty throws hot stew in a gang member's face and hits him over the back of the head with a revolver. Then he knocks her down with a rock. Then the gang sticks up a bank. Here comes the sheriff, Matt Dillon. He shoots a gang member and breaks it up. Then the gang leader shoots the guy who was guarding his daughter and the woman. Then the sheriff shoots the gang leader. The final exploding bullets signal The End.

19 It is not the accumulated slayings and bone-crushings that make this porno-violence, however. What makes it porno-violence is that in almost every case the camera angle, therefore the viewer, is with the gun, the fist, the rock. The pornography of violence has no point of view in the old sense that novels do. You do not live the action through the hero's eyes. You live with the aggressor, whoever he may be. One moment you are the hero. The next, you are the villain. No matter whose side you may be on consciously, you are in fact with the muscle, and it is you who disintegrate all comers, villains, lawmen, women, anybody. On the rare occasions in which the gun is emptied into the camera—i.e., into your face—the effect is so

startling that the pornography of violence all but loses its fantasy charm. There are not nearly so many masochists as sadists among those little devils whispering into your ears.

20 In fact, sex—"sadomasochism"—is only a part of the pornography of violence. Violence is much more wrapped up, simply, with status. Violence is the simple, ultimate solution for problems of status competition, just as gambling is the simple, ultimate solution for economic competition. The old pornography was the fantasy of easy sexual delights in a world where sex was kept unavailable. The new pornography is the fantasy of easy triumph in a world where status competition has become so complicated and frustrating.

21 Already the old pornography is losing its kick because of overexposure. In the late Thirties, Nathaniel West published his last and best-regarded novel, *The Day of the Locust,* and it was a terrible flop commercially, and his publisher said if he ever published another book about Hollywood it would "have to be *My Thirty-nine Ways of Making Love by Hedy Lamarr." Ecstasy and Me* is not quite that . . . but maybe it is. I stopped counting. I know her account begins: "The men in my life have ranged from a classic case history of impotence, to a whip-brandishing sadist who enjoyed sex only after he tied my arms behind me with the sash of his robe. There was another man who took his pleasure with a girl in my own bed, while he thought I was asleep in it."

22 Yawns all around. The sin itself is wearing out. Pornography cannot exist without certified taboo to violate. And today Lust, like the rest of the Seven Deadly Sins—Pride, Sloth, Envy, Greed, Anger, and Gluttony—is becoming a rather minor vice. The Seven Deadly Sins, after all, are only sins against the self. Theologically, the idea of Lust—well, the idea is that if you seduce some poor girl from Akron, it is not a sin because you are ruining her, but because you are wasting your time and your energies and damaging your own spirit. This goes back to the old work ethic, when the idea was to keep every able-bodied man's shoulder to the wheel. In an age of riches for all, the ethic becomes more nearly: Let him do anything he pleases, as long as he doesn't get in my way. And if he does get in my way, or even if he doesn't . . . well . . . we have *new* fantasies for that. *Put hair on the walls.*

23 *Hair on the Walls* is the invisible subtitle of Truman Capote's book, *In Cold Blood*. The book is neither a who-done-it nor a will-they-be-caught, since the answers to both questions are known from the outset. It does ask why-did-they-do-it, but the answer is soon as clear as it is going to be. Instead, the book's suspense is based largely on a totally new idea in detective stories: the promise of gory details, and the withholding of them until the end. Early in the game one of the two murderers, Dick, starts promising to put "plenty of

hair on them-those walls" with a shotgun. So read on, gentle readers, and on and on; you are led up to the moment before the crime on page 60—yet the specifics, what happened, the gory details, are kept out of sight, in grisly dangle, until page 244.

24 But Dick and Perry, Capote's killers, are only a couple of lower-class bums. With James Bond the new pornography has already reached dead center, the bureaucratic middle class. The appeal of Bond has been explained as the appeal of the lone man who can solve enormously complicated, even world problems through his own bravery and initiative. But Bond is not a lone man at all, of course. He is not the Lone Ranger. He is much easier to identify than that. He is a salaried functionary in a bureaucracy. He is a sport, but a believable one; not a millionaire, but a bureaucrat on expense account. He is not even a high-level bureaucrat. He is an operative. This point is carefully and repeatedly made by having his superiors dress him down for violations of standard operating procedure. Bond, like the Lone Ranger, solves problems with guns and fists. When it is over, however, the Lone Ranger leaves a silver bullet. Bond, like the rest of us, fills out a report in triplicate.

25 Marshall McLuhan says we are in a period in which it will become harder and harder to stimulate lust through words and pictures—i.e., the old pornography. In an age of electronic circuitry, he says, people crave tactile, all-involving experiences. The same thing may very well happen to the new pornography of violence. Even such able craftsmen as Truman Capote, Ian Fleming, NBC and CBS may not suffice. Fortunately, there are historical models to rescue us from this frustration. In the latter days of the Roman Empire, the Emperor Commodus became jealous of the celebrity of the great gladiators. He took to the arena himself, with his sword, and began dispatching suitably screened cripples and hobbled fighters. Audience participation became so popular that soon various *illuminati* of the Commodus set, various boys and girls of the year, were out there, suited up, gaily cutting a sequence of dwarves and feebles down to short ribs. Ah, swinging generations, what new delights await?

Thinking Questions: *Form*

1. Notice how Wolfe begins his essay with a paragraph of narration. How does the information in this paragraph function in relation to the rest of the essay? Why is the background Wolfe provides in this paragraph important to his later analysis of *The National Enquirer* and papers like it? Also, does this paragraph help establish Wolfe's credentials in the minds of his readers?

2. Why does Wolfe repeatedly mention the titles of articles in *The National Enquirer*? Are they used effectively as support for his thesis on porno-violence? In fact, does Wolfe need to go any deeper into his analysis of *The National Enquirer* to prove his thesis?

3. Can you point out several instances in which Wolfe defines key terms in his thesis? By the time you finish reading his essay, do you feel familiar with all the important concepts and terms in his essay?

4. Tom Wolfe is one of the major originators of the "New Journalism," a kind of journalism in which the writer attempts to re-create, often through fictional techniques such as dialogue and narrative, the drama and concrete reality of the newsmaking moment. Notice how Wolfe uses the dialogue among the stringers at a hypothetical convention to establish a sense of actually being there—on the scene—for his readers. Do you find that Wolfe's use of fictional techniques distorts the truth and objectivity of his writing? What about Tom Wolfe's voice; compare its diction and structure with Robert Jay Lifton's in the next essay.

5. Wolfe repeatedly uses examples from contemporary culture—movies, television shows, slick popular magazines, a popular book by movie actress Hedy Lamarr—to illustrate his thesis about porno-violence. Do you find these examples convincing? Or do you feel that Wolfe is facile in his relating these numerous violent effects to a single cause: contemporary people's desire to experience violence vicariously because they are frustrated in their own social striving? *Was* the nation's interest in reading about the Kennedy assassination really caused by a desire to help Lee Harvey Oswald pull the trigger, to feel or share in that moment of violent power?

Thinking Questions: *Substance*

1. Since the assassination of John F. Kennedy and the subsequent Warren Commission report which placed the entire blame on Lee Harvey Oswald, many investigators have continued to study the case with the idea that a conspiracy was responsible for the murder. Although the original investigators were probably sincere in their efforts, do you feel that a compulsion to share in a violent crime, as Tom Wolfe suggests, might be luring many "interested" readers into the subject? Might Wolfe's thesis still apply to the case, in other words?

2. What is the point of Tom Wolfe's analysis of James Bond (paragraph 24) as a violent hero? How does Wolfe's point about Bond relate to his central thesis on porno-violence?

3. What is the major difference between James Bond and the Lone Ranger, both fairly typical fictional heroes? Are we supposed to identify with Bond as an agent for moral good as we did in watching the Lone Ranger help individuals in distress? Or are we merely, as Wolfe points out, supposed to identify with Bond's tendency to use violence to fight his adversaries, whether his intentions are morally justified or not? In other words, do we watch James Bond, for instance, or Clint Eastwood in the "Dirty Harry" movies, in order to share in their violent acts, *not* to see them do in the bad guys?

4. Compare the overt forms of violence described and explained by Tom Wolfe with the more implicit and personal observations of violence in the essays by Virginia Woolf, Roger Kahn, and Bruno Bettelheim. How are these general forms of violence similar and different? Would you consider one form of violence obscene and unnatural and the other form human and understandable? Why? Are the effects and causes of one form of violence different from the effects and causes of the other?

5. In his final paragraph, Tom Wolfe concludes with, "Ah, swinging generations, what new delights await?" Apply Wolfe's ironic final comment to some aspect of American culture during the past five years—to movies, magazines (both popular and sensational), politics, television detective or police shows, whatever you feel you know well enough to analyze in the light of Wolfe's thesis on porno-violence. What "new delights" do you find? Or has the mass interest in porno-violence diminished? If so, why?

Beyond Atrocity

ROBERT J. LIFTON

> *The landscape doesn't change much. For days and days you see just about nothing. It's unfamiliar—always unfamiliar. Even when you go back to the same place, it's unfamiliar. And it makes you feel as though, well, there's nothing left in the world but this. . . . You have the illusion of going great distances and traveling, like hundreds of miles . . . and you end up in the same place because you're only a couple of miles away. . . . But you feel like it's not all real. It couldn't possibly be. We couldn't still be in this country. We've been walking for days. You're in Vietnam and they're using real bullets. . . . Here in Vietnam they're actually shooting people for no reason. Any other time you think. It's such an extreme. Here you can go ahead and shoot them for nothing. As a matter of fact it's even . . . smiled upon, you know. Good for you. Everything is backwards. That's part of the kind of unreality of the thing. To the "grunt" [infantryman] this isn't backwards. He doesn't understand. . . . But something [at Mylai 4] was missing. Something you thought was real that would accompany this. It wasn't there. . . . There was something missing in the whole business that made it seem like it really wasn't happening. . . .*
>
> —American GI's recollections of Mylai.

1 When asked to speak on recent occasions, I have announced my title as "On Living in Atrocity." To be sure, neither I nor anyone else lives there all or even most of the time. But at this moment, in early 1971, an American investigator of atrocity finds himself dealing with something that has become, for his countrymen in general, a terrible subterranean image that can be neither fully faced nor wished away. There is virtue in bringing that image to the surface.

2 In one sense, no matter what happens in the external world, personal atrocity, for everyone, begins at birth. It can also be said that some of us have a special nose for atrocity. Yet I can remember very well, during the early stirrings of the academic peace movement taking place around Harvard University during the mid- and late 1950s—about two hundred years ago, it now seems—how hard it was for us to *feel* what might happen at the other end of a nuclear weapon. Whatever one's nose for atrocities, there are difficulties surrounding the imaginative act of coming to grips with them.

3 After six months of living and working in Hiroshima, studying the human effects of the first atomic bomb, I found that these difficulties were partly overcome and partly exacerbated. On the one hand, I learned all too well to feel what happened at the other end of an atomic bomb. But on the other hand, I became impressed with the increasing gap we face between our technological capacity for perpetrating atrocities and our imaginative ability to confront their full actuality. Yet the attempt to narrow that gap can be enlightening, even liberating. For me, Hiroshima was a profoundly "radicalizing" experience—not in any strict ideological sense but in terms of fundamental issues of living and dying, of how one lives, of how one may die.

4 Whatever the contributing wartime pressures, Hiroshima looms as a paradigm of technological atrocity. Each of the major psychological themes discernible in Hiroshima survivors—death immersion, psychic numbing, residual guilt—has direct relationship to the atrocity's hideously cool and vast technological character. The specific technology of the bomb converted the brief moment of exposure into a lifelong encounter with death—through the sequence of the survivor's early immersion in massive and grotesque death and dying, his experiencing or witnessing bizarre and frequently fatal acute radiation effects during the following weeks and months, his knowledge of the increased incidence over the years of various forms (always fatal) of leukemia and cancer, and finally his acquisition of a death-tainted group identity, an "identity of the dead" or shared sense of feeling emotionally bound both to those killed by the bomb and to the continuing worldwide specter of nuclear genocide.

5 The experience of psychic numbing, or emotional desensitization—what some survivors called "paralysis of the mind"—was a necessary defense against feeling what they clearly knew to be happening. But when one looks further into the matter he discovers that those who made and planned the use of that first nuclear weapon—and those who today make its successors and plan their use—require their own form of psychic numbing. They too cannot afford to feel what they cognitively know would happen.

6 Victims and victimizers also shared a sense of guilt, expressed

partly in a conspiracy of silence, a prolonged absence of any systematic attempt to learn about the combined physical and psychic assaults of the bomb on human beings. Survivors felt guilty about remaining alive while others died, and also experienced an amorphous sense of having been part of, having imbibed, the overall evil of the atrocity. The perpetrators of Hiroshima (and those in various ways associated with them)—American scientists, military and political leaders, and ordinary people—felt their own forms of guilt, though, ironically, in less tangible ways than the victims. Yet one cannot but wonder to what extent Hiroshima produced in Americans (and others) a guilt-associated sense that if we could do this we could do anything, and that anyone could do anything to us—in other words, an anticipatory sense of unlimited atrocity.

7 If these are lessons of Hiroshima, one has to learn them personally. My own immersion in massive death during investigations in that city, though much more privileged and infinitely less brutal, will nonetheless be as permanent as that of Hiroshima survivors themselves. As in their case, it has profoundly changed my relationship to my own death as well as to all collective forms of death that stalk us. I had a similarly personal lesson regarding psychic numbing. During my first few interviews in Hiroshima I felt overwhelmed by the grotesque horrors described to me, but within the short space of a week or so this feeling gave way to a much more comfortable sense of myself as a psychological investigator, still deeply troubled by what he heard but undeterred from his investigative commitment. This kind of partial, task-oriented numbing now strikes me as inevitable and, in this situation, useful—yet at the same time potentially malignant in its implications.

8 By "becoming" a Hiroshima survivor (as anyone who opens himself to the experience must), while at the same time remaining an American, I shared something of both victims' and victimizers' sense of guilt. This kind of guilt by identification has its pitfalls, but I believe it to be one of the few genuine psychological avenues to confrontation of atrocity. For these three psychological themes are hardly confined to Hiroshima: Death immersion, psychic numbing, and guilt are a psychic trinity found in all atrocity.

9 Hiroshima also taught me the value and appropriateness of what I would call the apocalyptic imagination. The term offends our notions of steadiness and balance. But the technological dimensions of contemporary atrocity seem to me to require that we attune our imaginations to processes that are apocalyptic in the full dictionary meaning of the word—processes that are "wildly unrestrained" and "ultimately decisive," that involve "forecasting or predicting the ultimate destiny of the world in the shape of future events" and "foreboding imminent disaster or final doom."

10 In the past this kind of imagination has been viewed as no more than the "world-ending" delusion of the psychotic patient. But for the people of Hiroshima the "end of the world"—or something very close to it—became part of the actuality of their experience. Thus one survivor recalled: "My body seemed all black; everything seemed dark, dark all over . . . then I thought, 'The world is ending.' " And another: "The feeling I had was that everyone was dead. . . . I thought this was the end of Hiroshima—of Japan—of humankind." Those witnessing Nazi mass murder—the greatest of all man's atrocities to date—called forth similar images, though they could usually perceive that the annihilating process was in some way selective (affecting mainly Jews or anti-Nazis or other specific groups). As Hiroshima took me to Auschwitz and Treblinka, however, I was struck mostly by the similarities and parallels in the overall psychology of atrocity.

11 Yet similar end-of-the-world impressions have been recorded in connection with "God-made" atrocities, as in the case of survivors' accounts of the plagues of the Middle Ages:

> How will posterity believe that there has been a time when without the lightings of heaven or the fires of earth, without wars or other visible slaughter, not this or that part of the earth, but well-nigh the whole globe, has remained without inhabitants. . . . We should think we were dreaming if we did not with our eyes, when we walk abroad, see the city in mourning with funerals, and returning to our home, find it empty, and thus know that what we lament is real.

12 The plagues were God-made not only in the sense of being a mysterious and deadly form of illness outside of man's initiation or control but also because they could be comprehended as part of a God-centered cosmology. To be sure, scenes like the above strained people's belief in an ordered universe and a just God, but their cosmology contained enough devils, enough flexibility, and enough depth of imprint to provide, if not a full "explanation" of holocaust, at least a continued psychic framework within which to go on living. In contrast, Hiroshima and Auschwitz were carried out by men upon men, and at a time when old cosmologies had already lost much of their hold and could provide little explanatory power. Survivors were left with an overwhelming sense of dislocation and absurdity: Like the GI quoted earlier in relationship to Mylai, something for them was "missing"—namely, meaning, or a sense of reality. With Hiroshima and Auschwitz now part of man's historical experience, it is perilously naïve to insist that our imaginative relationship to world-destruction can remain unchanged—that we can continue to make a simple-minded distinction between psychotic proclivity for, and "normal" avoidance of, that image.

13 Yet, whatever the force of external events, there is a subjective, imaginative component to the perceived "end of the world." Hiro-

shima survivors had to call forth early inner images of separation and helplessness, of stasis and annihilation, images available from everyone's infancy and childhood, but with greater force to some than to others. There is, therefore, a danger, not just for Hiroshima survivors but for all of us, of being trapped in such images, bound by a psychic sense of doom to the point of being immobilized and totally unable or unwilling to participate in essential day-by-day struggles to counter atrocity and prevent the collective annihilation imagined.

14 Psychological wisdom, then, seems to lie in neither wallowing in, nor numbing ourselves to, our imaginings of apocalypse. A simple example of the constructive use of the apocalytic imagination is recorded by Eugene Rabinowitch, from the beginning an articulate leader in scientists' anti-atomic bomb movements. Rabinowitch describes how, when walking down the streets of Chicago during the summer of 1945, he looked up at the city's great buildings and suddenly imagined a holocaust in which skyscrapers crumbled. He then vowed to redouble his efforts to prevent that kind of event from happening by means of the scientists' petition he and others were drawing up to head off the dropping of an atomic bomb, without warning, on a populated area. The effort, of course, failed, but this kind of apocalytic imagination—on the part of Rabinowitch, Leo Szilard, and Bertrand Russell, among others—has made it possible for at least a small minority of men and women to name and face the true conditions of our existence. (Bertrand Russell had earlier exhibited the dangers of the apocalyptic imagination when he advocated that we threaten to drop atomic bombs on Russia in order to compel it to agree to a system of international control of nuclear weapons.) For we live in the shadow of the ultimate atrocity, of the potentially terminal revolution—and if that term is itself a contradition, the same contradiction is the central fact of our relationship to death and life.

15 We perpetrate and experience the American atrocity at Mylai in the context of these apocalyptic absurdities and dislocations. The GI's quoted description suggests not only that atrocity can be a dreamlike affair (in this sense, resembling the quoted passage about the plague) but that it is committed by men living outside of ordinary human connection, outside of both society and history. Mylai was acted out by men who had lost their bearings, men wandering about in both a military and psychic no man's land. The atrocity itself can be seen as a grotesquely paradoxical effort to put straight this crooked landscape, to find order and significance in disorder and absurdity. There is at the same time an impulse to carry existing absurdity and disorder to their logical extremes as if both to transcend and demonstrate that aberrant existential state.

16 Atrocities are committed by desperate men—in the case of Mylai, men victimized by the absolute contradictions of the war they were

asked to fight, by the murderous illusions of their country's policy. Atrocity, then, is a perverse quest for meaning, the end result of a spurious sense of mission, the product of false witness.

17 To say that American military involvement in Vietnam is itself a crime is also to say that it is an atrocity-producing situation. Or to put the matter another way, Mylai illuminates, as nothing else has, the essential nature of America's war in Vietnam. The elements of this atrocity-producing situation include an advanced industrial nation engaged in a counter-insurgency action, in an underdeveloped area, against guerrillas who merge with the people—precisely the elements that Jean-Paul Sartre has described as inevitably genocidal. In the starkness of its murders and the extreme dehumanization experienced by victimizers and imposed on victims, Mylai reveals to us how far America has gone along the path of deadly illusion.

18 Associated with this deadly illusion are three psychological patterns as painful to the sensitized American critic of the war as they are self-evident. The first is the principle of atrocity building upon atrocity, because of the need to deny the atrocity-producing situation. In this sense, Mylai itself was a product of earlier, smaller Mylais; and it was followed not by an ending of the war but by the American extension of the war into Laos and Cambodia.

19 The second principle involves the system of non-responsibility. One searches in vain for a man or group of men who will come forward to take the blame or even identify a human source or responsibility for what took place—from those who fired the bullets at Mylai (who must bear some responsibility, but were essentially pawns and victims of the atrocity-producing situation, and are now being made scapegoats as well); to the junior-grade officers who gave orders to do the firing and apparently did some of it themselves; to the senior-grade officers who seemed to have ordered the operation; to the highest military and civilian planners in Vietnam, the Pentagon, and the White House who created such things as a *"permanent free-fire zone"* (which, according to Richard Hammer, means "in essence . . . that any Americans operating within it had, basically, a license to kill and any Vietnamese living within it had a license to be killed"), planners who made even more basic decisions about continuing and even extending the war; to the amorphous conglomerate of the American people who, presumably, chose, or at least now tolerate, the aforementioned as their representatives. The atrocity-producing situation, at least in this case, depends upon what Masao Maruyama has called a "system of non-responsibility." Situation and system alike are characterized by a technology and a technicized bureaucracy not checked by sentient human minds.

20 The third and perhaps most terrible pattern is the psychology of nothing happening. General Westmoreland gives way to General

Abrams, President Johnson to President Nixon, a visibly angry student generation to one silent with rage—and the war, the atrocity-producing situation, continues to grind out its thousands of recorded and unrecorded atrocities. To be more accurate, something does happen: The subliminal American perception of atrocity edges toward consciousness, making it more difficult but, unfortunately, not impossible to defend and maintain the atrocity-producing situation. The widespread feeling of being stuck in atrocity contributes, in ways we can now hardly grasp, to a national sense of degradation and a related attraction to violence, for nothing is more conducive to collective rage and totalism than a sense of being bound to a situation perceived to be both suffocating and evil.

21 Atrocity in general, and Mylai in particular, brings its perpetrators—even a whole nation—into the realm of existential evil. That state is exemplified by what another GI described to me as a working definition of the enemy in Vietnam: "If it's dead, it's VC—because it's dead. If it's dead, it *had* to be VC. And of course, a corpse couldn't defend itself anyhow." When at some future moment, ethically sensitive historians get around to telling the story of the Vietnam War—assuming that there will be ethically sensitive (or, for that matter, any) historians around—I have no doubt that they will select the phenomenon of the "body count" as the perfect symbol of America's descent into evil. What better represents the numbing, brutalizing illusion (most of the bodies, after all, turn out to be those of civilians), grotesque competition (companies and individuals vie for the highest body counts), and equally grotesque technicizing (progress lies in the *count*) characteristic of the overall American crime of the war in Vietnam.

22 Mylai is rather unusual in one respect. It combines two kinds of atrocity: technological overkill (of unarmed peasants by Americans using automatic weapons) and a more personal, face-to-face gunning-down of victims at point-blank range. This combination lends the incident particular psychic force, however Americans may try to fend off awareness of its implications. A participating GI could characterize Mylai as "just like a Nazi-type thing" (as recorded in Seymour Hersh's book *My Lai 4*), a characterization made by few if any pilots or crewmen participating in the more technologically distanced killings of larger numbers of Vietnamese civilians from the air.

23 The sense of being associated with existential evil is new to Americans. This is so partly because such perceptions have been suppressed in other atrocity-producing situations, but also because of the humane elements of American tradition that contribute to a national self-image of opposing, through use of force if necessary, just this kind of "Nazi-type thing." The full effects of the war in Vietnam

upon this self-image are at this point unclear. The returns from Mylai are not yet in. Perhaps they never are for atrocity. But I for one worry about a society that seems to absorb, with some questioning but without fundamental self-examination, first Hiroshima and now Mylai.

24 For there is always a cost. Atrocities have a way of coming home. The killings by National Guardsmen of Kent State students protesting the extension of the war into Cambodia reflect the use of violence in defense of illusion and denial of evil—and the killings of blacks at Augusta, Georgia, and of black students at Jackson State in Mississippi reflect more indirectly that atmosphere. Indeed there is a real danger that the impulse to preserve illusion and deny evil could carry America beyond Vietnam and Cambodia into some form of world-destroying nuclear confrontation. In this sense, as well as in its relationship to existential evil, Mylai symbolized a shaking of the American foundations—a bitterly mocking perversion of what was left of the American dream. Like Hiroshima and Auschwitz, Mylai is a revolutionary event: Its total inversion of moral standards raises fundamental questions about the institutions and national practices of the nation responsible for it.

25 The problem facing Americans now is: What do we do with our atrocities? Do we simply try our best to absorb them by a kind of half-admission that denies their implications and prevents genuine confrontation? That is the classical method of governments for dealing with documented atrocities, and it is clearly the method now being used by the U.S. government and military in holding trials of individuals. Those who did the shooting and those who covered up the event are being labeled aberrant and negligent, so that the larger truth of the atrocity-producing situation can be avoided. The award of a Pulitzer Prize to Seymour Hersh for his journalistic feat in uncovering the story of Mylai and telling it in detail would seem to be a step in the direction of that larger truth. Yet one cannot but fear that such an award—as in the case of the National Book Award I received for my work on Hiroshima—can serve as a form of conscience-salving token recognition in place of confrontation. Surely more must be faced throughout American society, more must be articulated and given form by leaders and ordinary people, if this atrocity is to contribute to a national process of illumination instead of further degradation.

26 I am struck by how little my own profession has had to say about the matter—about the way in which aberrant *situations* can produce collective disturbance and mass murder. The psychiatry and psychohistory I would like to envisage for the future would put such matters at its center. It would also encourage combining ethical involvement with professional skills in ways that could simultaneously shed light upon such crimes of war and contribute to the transformation

our country so desperately requires. In dealing with our dislocations, we need to replace the false witness of atrocity with the genuine witness of new and liberating forms and directions. The task, then, is to confront atrocity in order to move beyond it.

Thinking Questions: *Form*

1. Robert Jay Lifton poses the central question of his essay in paragraph 25: "The problem facing Americans now is: What do we do with our atrocities? Do we simply try our best to absorb them by a kind of half-admission that denies their implications and prevents genuine confrontation?" Organize a debate around a clear, precise answer to that question. In other words, make your answer to Lifton's question the resolution in your debate. Then probe the essay for the reasoning behind your support or opposition to the resolution. Remember that debaters are judged on both the accuracy and the emotional force of their positions.

2. Use Lifton's essay to work up a single paragraph that precisely defines *atrocity*. Use brief quotations from the essay, but make the definition an original compilation of the main points of the essay.

3. Analyze the overall form of Lifton's essay. In the process, list specific rhetorical devices that are used in the essay and point out their functions in developing the general purpose of the essay. Consider specific devices such as rhetorical questions, the anecdotal opening, uses of analogy and extended comparison, and the citation of authorities on the writer's subject, as well as the use of more general rhetorical devices such as comparison, definition, classification, and illustration by example.

Thinking Questions: *Substance*

1. What significance is attached to the American GI's description of his existence in Vietnam, which Lifton uses as the headnote of this essay? Consider closely his remark: "Something you thought was real that would accompany this. It wasn't there." What effects would result from this GI's feeling that he was existing in a fantasy world? Why would such a feeling make the cruelties of war seem easier to bear? Many television viewers, for example, became so accustomed to the violence of war in news reports that they began to accept the reported violence as just another fact of everyday living. Once television makes cruelty routine, people usually condone more violence in their own and other people's behavior. The war, as a result, makes the people in it and connected to it less human, less compassionate.

2. Throughout this section we have attempted to understand the relationships between individual feelings of frustration, confusion, and anger and the social conditions that cause those personal difficulties. Look back over the individual cases of different kinds of violence discussed in these essays. Can you find any common patterns? Are there

common causes for the violent behavior expressed in the case of Joey, the mechanical boy; in Roger Kahn's essay on Carl Furillo; or in Robert Jay Lifton's example of a Vietnam GI's response to My Lai? Are there some common violent effects?

3. What are the differences among all these cases? Do some of these differences in behavior point out the varying effects of different social contexts? For example, does a GI in a war zone find himself in a *totally* different environment than a ballplayer finishing up a major league career? Are some of the specific physical differences in these two social situations undercut by some important overall similarities?

4. Why does Lifton argue that however "common" atrocities eventually become, it will remain difficult for individuals who are not directly involved to imagine those atrocities (see paragraph 3)?

5. What place does technology play in modern man's "emotional desensitization," as Lifton calls it (paragraph 5)? How does technology help modern man to ignore the physical horrors of war?

6. What is the point of Lifton's comparison of "God-made" atrocities like the plagues of the Middle Ages (paragraph 11) and modern atrocities? Why were most people at least able to remain sane during the devastations of the plagues? What enabled them to keep a "sense of reality," while people today seem unable to retain that same sense in the face of man-made devastations?

7. Lifton suggests that people who lack a clear sense of reality will create illusions to guide their lives. In paragraphs 18 through 20, Lifton defines three types of illusionary responses common in a society in which individuals wish to explain away what is actually happening right in front of their eyes. Review these illusions and explain how they cause individuals to develop a higher tolerance for violence.

* * *

PSYCHOLOGICAL AND PHYSICAL VIOLENCE

In the past, humankind has worried more about the physical effects of violence. Wars resulted in the deaths of many people; lack of food caused starvation; lack of material and spiritual well-being fostered violent social upheavals, revolts, and revolutions.

In modern societies, however, we are confronted with extreme degrees of physical and psychological violence. If, for example, large groups of people exist at a basic subsistence level, psychologists tell us, they will suffer psychological as well as physical impairments to learning because of improper diets and poor learning environments. Robert Jay Lifton describes a vicious circle in which groups of people do technological violence to others; they then experience guilt because of the violence they have done, which they then cover up and express in newer and sometimes more devastating forms of violence

All three perspectives on violence—cosmic, personal, and social—apply in Flannery O'Connor's story "A Good Man Is Hard to Find." The Misfit and his group are physically violent—they terrorize, maim, and kill at random. Yet even the story's central characters illustrate constant but less destructive violent outbursts: June Star's cutting tongue, Bailey and the mother's insensitive reactions to both the grandmother and children. Perhaps most importantly, the grandmother, who on the surface seems the kindest, most civilized character in the story, actually *causes* all the violence. A good man is indeed hard to find, and The Misfit's final remarks—"She would of been a good woman . . . if it had been somebody there to shoot her every minute of her life. . . . It's no real pleasure in life."—seem to capture the author's intent.

Perhaps nature, as a cosmic perspective on violence might suggest, demands violence from human beings. Perhaps people themselves are essentially evil, as the personal and social perspectives presented in these essays might suggest, and, as a result, demand violence from one another. And perhaps, as The Misfit suggests, they are good only when there is somebody there to shoot them every minute of their lives.

A Good Man Is Hard to Find

FLANNERY O'CONNOR

1 The grandmother didn't want to go to Florida. She wanted to visit some of her connections in east Tennessee and she was seizing at every chance to change Bailey's mind. Bailey was the son she lived with, her only boy. He was sitting on the edge of his chair at the table, bent over the orange sports section of the *Journal.* "Now look here, Bailey," she said, "see here, read this," and she stood with one hand on her thin hip and the other rattling the newspaper at his bald head. "Here this fellow that calls himself The Misfit is aloose from the Federal Pen and headed toward Florida and you read here what it says he did to these people. Just you read it. I wouldn't take my children in any direction with a criminal like that aloose in it. I couldn't answer to my conscience if I did."

2 Bailey didn't look up from his reading so she wheeled around then and faced the children's mother, a young woman in slacks, whose face was as broad and innocent as a cabbage and was tied around with a green head-kerchief that had two points on the top like rabbit's ears. She was sitting on the sofa, feeding the baby his apricots out of a jar. "The children have been to Florida before," the old lady

said. "You all ought to take them somewhere else for a change so they would see different parts of the world and be broad. They never have been to east Tennessee."

3 The children's mother didn't seem to hear her but the eight-year-old boy, John Wesley, a stocky child with glasses, said, "If you don't want to go to Florida, why dontcha stay at home?" He and the little girl, June Star, were reading the funny papers on the floor.

4 "She wouldn't stay at home to be queen for a day," June Star said without raising her yellow head.

5 "Yes and what would you do if this fellow, The Misfit, caught you?" the grandmother asked.

6 "I'd smack his face," John Wesley said.

"She wouldn't stay at home for a million bucks," June Star said. "Afraid she'd miss something. She has to go everywhere we go."

7 "All right, Miss," the grandmother said. "Just remember that the next time you want me to curl your hair."

June Star said her hair was naturally curly.

8 The next morning the grandmother was the first one in the car, ready to go. She had her big black valise that looked like the head of a hippopotamus in one corner, and underneath it she was hiding a basket with Pitty Sing, the cat, in it. She didn't intend for the cat to be left alone in the house for three days because he would miss her too much and she was afraid he might brush against one of the gas burners and accidentally asphyxiate himself. Her son, Bailey, didn't like to arrive at a motel with a cat.

9 She sat in the middle of the back seat with John Wesley and June Star on either side of her. Bailey and the children's mother and the baby sat in front and they left Atlanta at eight forty-five with the mileage on the car at 55890. The grandmother wrote this down because she thought it would be interesting to say how many miles they had been when they got back. It took them twenty minutes to reach the outskirts of the city.

10 The old lady settled herself comfortably, removing her white cotton gloves and putting them up with her purse on the shelf in front of the back window. The children's mother still had on slacks and still had her head tied up in a green kerchief, but the grandmother had on a navy blue straw sailor hat with a bunch of white violets on the brim and a navy blue dress with a small white dot in the print. Her collars and cuffs were white organdy trimmed with lace and at her neckline she had pinned a purple spray of cloth violets containing a sachet. In case of an accident, anyone seeing her dead on the highway would know at once that she was a lady.

11 She said she thought it was going to be a good day for driving, neither too hot nor too cold, and she cautioned Bailey that the speed limit was fifty-five miles an hour and that the patrolmen hid them-

selves behind billboards and small clumps of trees and sped out after you before you had a chance to slow down. She pointed out interesting details of the scenery: Stone Mountain; the blue granite that in some places came up to both sides of the highway; the brilliant red clay banks slightly streaked with purple; and the various crops that made rows of green lace-work on the ground. The trees were full of silver-white sunlight and the meanest of them sparkled. The children were reading comic magazines and their mother had gone back to sleep.

12 "Let's go through Georgia fast so we won't have to look at it much," John Wesley said.

13 "If I were a little boy," said the grandmother, "I wouldn't talk about my native state that way. Tennessee has the mountains and Georgia has the hills."

14 "Tennessee is just a hillbilly dumping ground," John Wesley said, "and Georgia is a lousy state too."

15 "You said it," June Star said.

"In my time," said the grandmother, folding her thin veined fingers, "children were more respectful of their native states and their parents and everything else. People did right then. Oh look at the cute little pickaninny!" she said and pointed to a Negro child standing in the door of a shack. "Wouldn't that make a picture, now?" she asked and they all turned and looked at the little Negro out of the back window. He waved.

16 "He didn't have any britches on," June Star said.

"He probably didn't have any," the grandmother explained. "Little niggers in the country don't have things like we do. If I could paint, I'd paint that picture," she said.

17 The children exchanged comic books.

The grandmother offered to hold the baby and the children's mother passed him over the front seat to her. She set him on her knee and bounced him and told him about the things they were passing. She rolled her eyes and screwed up her mouth and stuck her leathery thin face into his smooth bland one. Occasionally he gave her a far-away smile. They passed a large cotton field with five or six graves fenced in the middle of it, like a small island. "Look at the graveyard!" the grandmother said, pointing it out. "That was the old family burying ground. That belonged to the plantation."

18 "Where's the plantation?" John Wesley asked.

"Gone With the Wind," said the grandmother. "Ha. Ha."

When the children finished all the comic books they had brought, they opened the lunch and ate it. The grandmother ate a peanut butter sandwich and an olive and would not let the children throw the box and the paper napkins out the window. When there was nothing else to do they played a game by choosing a cloud and making the other two guess what shape it suggested. John Wesley took one the shape of a cow and June Star guessed a cow and John Wesley said, no, an automobile, and June Star said he didn't play fair, and they began to slap each other over the grandmother.

19 The grandmother said she would tell them a story if they would keep quiet. When she told a story, she rolled her eyes and waved her head and was very dramatic. She said once when she was a maiden lady she had been courted by a Mr. Edgar Atkins Teagarden from Jasper, Georgia. She said he was a very good-looking man and a gentleman and that he brought her a watermelon every Saturday afternoon with his initials cut in it, E. A. T. Well, one Saturday, she said, Mr. Teagarden brought the watermelon and there was nobody at home and he left it on the front porch and returned in his buggy to Jasper, but she never got the watermelon, she said, because a nigger boy ate in when he saw the initials, E. A. T.! This story tickled John Wesley's funny bone and he giggled and giggled but June Star didn't think it was any good. She said she wouldn't marry a man that just brought her a watermelon on Saturday. The grandmother said she would have done well to marry Mr. Teagarden because he was a gentleman and had bought Coca-Cola stock when it first came out and that he had died only a few years ago, a very wealthy man.

20 They stopped at The Tower for barbecued sandwiches. The Tower was a part stucco and part wood filling station and dance hall set in a clearing outside of Timothy. A fat man named Red Sammy Butts ran it and there were signs stuck here and there on the building and for miles up and down the highway saying, TRY RED SAMMY'S FAMOUS BARBECUE. NONE LIKE FAMOUS RED SAMMY'S! RED SAM! THE FAT BOY WITH THE HAPPY LAUGH! A VETERAN! RED SAMMY'S YOUR MAN!

21 Red Sammy was lying on the bare ground outside The Tower with his head under a truck while a gray monkey about a foot high, chained to a small chinaberry tree, chattered nearby. The monkey sprang back into the tree and got on the highest limb as soon as he saw the children jump out of the car and run toward him.

22 Inside, The Tower was a long dark room with a counter at one end and tables at the other and dancing space in the middle. They all sat down at a board table next to the nickelodeon and Red Sam's wife, a tall burnt-brown woman with hair and eyes lighter than her skin, came and took their order. The children's mother put a dime in the machine and played "The Tennessee Waltz," and the grandmother said that tune always made her want to dance. She asked Bailey if he would like to dance but he only glared at her. He didn't have a naturally sunny disposition like she did and trips made him nervous. The grandmother's brown eyes were very bright. She swayed her head from side to side and pretended she was dancing in her chair.

June Star said play something she could tap to so the children's mother put in another dime and played a fast number and June Star stepped out onto the dance floor and did her tap routine.

23 "Ain't she cute?" Red Sam's wife said, leaning over the counter. "Would you like to come be my little girl?"

24 "No I certainly wouldn't," June Star said. "I wouldn't live in a broken-down place like this for a million bucks!" and she ran back to the table.

25 "Ain't she cute?" the woman repeated, stretching her mouth politely.

"Arn't you ashamed?" hissed the grandmother.

Red Sam came in and told his wife to quit lounging on the counter and hurry up with these people's order. His khaki trousers reached just to his hip bones and his stomach hung over them like a sack of meal swaying under his shirt. He came over and sat down at a table nearby and let out a combination sigh and yodel. "You can't win," he said. "You can't win," and he wiped his sweating red face off with a gray handkerchief. "These days you don't know who to trust," he said. "Ain't that the truth?"

26 "People are certainly not nice like they used to be," said the grandmother.

27 "Two fellers come in here last week," Red Sammy said, "driving a Chrysler. It was a old beat-up car but it was a good one and these boys looked all right to me. Said they worked at the mill and you know I let them fellers charge the gas they bought? Now why did I do that?"

28 "Because you're a good man!" the grandmother said at once.

"Yes'm, I suppose so," Red Sam said as if he were struck with this answer.

29 His wife brought the orders, carrying the five plates all at once without a tray, two in each hand and one balanced on her arm. "It isn't a soul in this green world of God's that you can trust," she said. "And I don't count nobody out of that, not nobody," she repeated, looking at Red Sammy.

30 "Did you read about that criminal, The Misfit, that's escaped?" asked the grandmother.

31 "I wouldn't be a bit surprised if he didn't attack this place right here," said the woman. "If he hears about it being here, I wouldn't be none surprised to see him. If he hears it's two cent in the cash register, I wouldn't be a tall surprised if he . . ."

"That'll do," Red Sam said. "Go bring these people their Co'-Colas," and the woman went off to get the rest of the order.

32 "A good man is hard to find," Red Sammy said. "Everything is getting terrible. I remember the day you could go off and leave your screen door unlatched. Not no more."

33 He and the grandmother discussed better times. The old lady said that in her opinion Europe was entirely to blame for the way things were now. She said the way Europe acted you would think we were made of money and Red Sam said it was no use talking about it, she was exactly right. The children ran outside into the white sunlight and looked at the monkey in the lacy chinaberry tree. He was busy catching fleas on himself and biting each one carefully between his teeth as if it were a delicacy.

34 They drove off again into the hot afternoon. The grandmother took cat naps and woke up every few minutes with her own snoring. Outside of Toombsboro she woke up and recalled an old plantation that she had visited in this neighborhood once when she was a young lady. She said the house had six white columns across the front and that there was an avenue of oaks leading up to it and two little wooden trellis arbors on either side in front where you sat down with your suitor after a stroll in the garden. She recalled exactly which road to turn off to get to it. She knew that Bailey would not be willing to lose any time looking at an old house, but the more she talked about it, the more she wanted to see it once again and find out if the little twin arbors were still standing. "There was a secret panel in this house," she said craftily, not telling the truth but wishing that she were, "and the story went that all the family silver was hidden in it when Sherman came through but it was never found . . ."

35 "Hey!" John Wesley said. "Let's go see it! We'll find it! We'll poke all the woodwork and find it! Who lives there? Where do you turn off at? Hey Pop, can't we turn off there?"

36 "We never have seen a house with a secret panel!" June Star shrieked. "Let's go to the house with the secret panel! Hey Pop, can't we go see the house with the secret panel!"

37 "It's not far from here, I know," the grandmother said. "It wouldn't take over twenty minutes."

38 Bailey was looking straight ahead. His jaw was as rigid as a horseshoe. "No," he said.

39 The children began to yell and scream that they wanted to see the house with the secret panel. John Wesley kicked the back of the front seat and June Star hung over her mother's shoulder and whined desperately into her ear that they never had any fun even on their vacation, that they could never do what THEY wanted to do. The baby began to scream and John Wesley kicked the back of the seat so hard that his father could feel the blows in his kidney.

40 "All right!" he shouted and drew the car to a stop at the side of the road. "Will you all shut up? Will you all just shut up for one second? If you don't shut up, we won't go anywhere."

41 "It would be very educational for them," the grandmother murmured.

42 "All right," Bailey said, "but get this: this is the only time we're going to stop for anything like this. This is the one and only time."

43 "The dirt road that you have to turn down is about a mile back," the grandmother directed. "I marked it when we passed."

44 "A dirt road," Bailey groaned.

After they had turned around and were headed toward the dirt road, the grandmother recalled other points about the house, the beautiful glass over the front doorway and the candle-lamp in the hall. John Wesley said that the secret panel was probably in the fireplace.

45 "You can't go inside this house," Bailey said. "You don't know who lives there."

46 "While you all talk to the people in front, I'll run around behind and get in a window," John Wesley suggested.

47 "We'll all stay in the car," his mother said.

They turned onto the dirt road and the car raced roughly along in a swirl of pink dust. The grandmother recalled the times when there were no paved roads and thirty miles was a day's journey. The dirt road was hilly and there were sudden washes in it and sharp curves on dangerous embankments. All at once they would be on a hill, looking down over the blue tops of trees for miles around, then the next minute, they would be in a red depression with the dust-coated trees looking down on them.

48 "This place had better turn up in a minute," Bailey said, "or I'm going to turn around."

49 The road looked as if no one had traveled on it in months.

"It's not much farther," the grandmother said and just as she said it, a horrible thought came to her. The thought was so embarrassing that she turned red in the face and her eyes dilated and her feet jumped up, upsetting her valise in the corner. The instant the valise moved, the newspaper top she had over the basket under it rose with a snarl and Pitty Sing, the cat, sprang onto Bailey's shoulder.

50 The children were thrown to the floor and their mother, clutching the baby, was thrown out the door onto the ground; the old lady was thrown into the front seat. The car turned over once and landed right-side-up in a gulch off the side of the road. Bailey remained in the driver's seat with the cat—gray-striped with a broad white face and an orange nose—clinging to his neck like a caterpillar.

51 As soon as the children saw they could move their arms and legs, they scrambled out of the car, shouting, "We've had an ACCIDENT!" The grandmother was curled up under the dashboard, hoping she was injured so that Bailey's wrath would not come down on her all at once. The horrible thought she had had before the accident was that the house she had remembered so vividly was not in Georgia but in Tennessee.

52 Bailey removed the cat from his neck with both hands and flung it out the window against the side of a pine tree. Then he got out of the car and started looking for the children's mother. She was sitting against the side of the red gutted ditch, holding the screaming baby, but she only had a cut down her face and a broken shoulder. "We've had an ACCIDENT!" the children screamed in a frenzy of delight.

53 "But nobody's killed," June Star said with disappointment as the grandmother limped out of the car, her hat still pinned to her head but the broken front brim standing up at a jaunty angle and the violet spray hanging off the side. They all sat down in the ditch, except the children, to recover from the shock. They were all shaking.

54 "Maybe a car will come along," said the children's mother hoarsely.

"I believe I have injured an organ," said the grandmother, pressing her side, but no one answered her. Bailey's teeth were clattering. He had on a yellow sport shirt with bright blue parrots designed in it and his face was as yellow as the shirt. The grandmother decided that she would not mention that the house was in Tennessee.

55 The road was about ten feet above and they could see only the tops of the trees on the other side of it. Behind the ditch they were sitting in there were more woods, tall and dark and deep. In a few minutes they saw a car some distance away on top of a hill, coming slowly as if the occupants were watching them. The grandmother stood up and waved both arms dramatically to attract their attention. The car continued to come on slowly, disappeared around a bend and appeared again, moving even slower, on top of the hill they had gone over. It was a big black battered hearse-like automobile. There were three men in it.

56 It came to a stop just over them and for some minutes, the driver looked down with a steady expressionless gaze to where they were sitting, and didn't speak. Then he turned his head and muttered something to the other two and they got out. One was a fat boy in black trousers and a red sweat shirt with a silver stallion embossed on the front of it. He moved around on the right side of them and stood staring, his mouth partly open in a kind of loose grin. The other had on khaki pants and a blue striped coat and a gray hat pulled down very low, hiding most of his face. He came around slowly on the left side. Neither spoke.

57 The driver got out of the car and stood by the side of it, looking down at them. He was an older man than the other two. His hair was just beginning to gray and he wore silver-rimmed spectacles that gave him a scholarly look. He had a long creased face and didn't have on any shirt or undershirt. He had on blue jeans that were too tight for him and was holding a black hat and a gun. The two boys also had guns.

"We've had an ACCIDENT!" the children screamed.

58 The grandmother had the peculiar feeling that the bespectacled man was someone she knew. His face was as familiar to her as if she had known him all her life but she could not recall who he was. He moved away from the car and began to come down the embankment, placing his feet carefully so that he wouldn't slip. He had on tan and white shoes and no socks, and his ankles were red and thin. "Good afternoon," he said. "I see you all had you a little spill."

59 "We turned over twice!" said the grandmother.

"Once," he corrected. "We seen it happen. Try their car and see will it run, Hiram," he said quietly to the boy with the gray hat.

60 "What you got that gun for?" John Wesley asked. "Whatcha gonna do with that gun?"

61 "Lady," the man said to the children's mother, "would you mind calling them children to sit down by you? Children make me nervous. I want all you all to sit down right together there where you're at."

62 "What are you telling US what to do for?" June Star asked.

Behind them the line of woods gaped like a dark open mouth. "Come here," said their mother.

63 "Look here now," Bailey began suddenly, "we're in a predicament! We're in . . ."

64 The grandmother shrieked. She scrambled to her feet and stood staring. "You're The Misfit!" she said. "I recognized you at once!"

65 "Yes'm," the man said, smiling slightly as if he were pleased in spite of himself to be known, "but it would have been better for all of you, lady, if you hadn't of reckernized me."

66 Bailey turned his head sharply and said something to his mother that shocked even the children. The old lady began to cry and The Misfit reddened.

67 "Lady," he said, "don't you get upset. Sometimes a man says things he don't mean. I don't reckon he meant to talk to you thataway."

68 "You wouldn't shoot a lady, would you?" the grandmother said and removed a clean handkerchief from her cuff and began to slap at her eyes with it.

69 The Misfit pointed the toe of his shoe into the ground and made a little hole and then covered it up again. "I would hate to have to," he said.

70 "Listen," the grandmother almost screamed, "I know you're a good man. You don't look a bit like you have common blood. I know you must come from nice people!"

71 "Yes mam," he said, "finest people in the world." When he smiled he showed a row of strong white teeth. "God never made a finer woman than my mother and my daddy's heart was pure gold," he said. The boy with the red sweat shirt had come around behind them and was standing with his gun at his hip. The Misfit squatted down on the ground. "Watch them children, Bobby Lee," he said. "You know they

make me nervous." He looked at the six of them huddled together in front of him and he seemed to be embarrassed as if he couldn't think of anything to say. "Ain't a cloud in the sky," he remarked, looking up at it. "Don't see no sun but don't see no cloud neither."

72 "Yes, it's a beautiful day," said the grandmother. "Listen," she said, "you shouldn't call yourself The Misfit because I know you're a good man at heart. I can just look at you and tell."

73 "Hush!" Bailey yelled. "Hush! Everybody shut up and let me handle this!" He was squatting in the position of a runner about to sprint forward but he didn't move.

74 "I pre-chate that, lady," The Misfit said and drew a little circle in the ground with the butt of his gun.

75 "It'll take a half a hour to fix this here car," Hiram called, looking over the raised hood of it.

76 "Well, first you and Bobby Lee get him and that little boy to step over yonder with you," The Misfit said, pointing to Bailey and John Wesley. "The boys want to ast you something," he said to Bailey. "Would you mind stepping back in them woods there with them?"

77 "Listen," Bailey began, "we're in a terrible predicament! Nobody realizes what this is," and his voice cracked. His eyes were as blue and intense as the parrots in his shirt and he remained perfectly still.

78 The grandmother reached up to adjust her hat brim as if she were going to the woods with him but it came off in her hand. She stood staring at it and after a second she let it fall on the ground. Hiram pulled Bailey up by the arm as if he were assisting an old man. John Wesley caught hold of his father's hand and Bobby Lee followed. They went off toward the woods and just as they reached the dark edge, Bailey turned and supporting himself against a gray naked pine trunk, he shouted, "I'll be back in a minute, Mamma, wait on me!"

79 "Come back this instant!" his mother shrilled but they all disappeared into the woods.

80 "Bailey Boy!" the grandmother called in a tragic voice but she found she was looking at The Misfit squatting on the ground in front of her. "I just know you're a good man," she said desperately. "You're not a bit common!"

81 "Nome, I ain't a good man," The Misfit said after a second as if he had considered her statement carefully, "but I ain't the worst in the world neither. My daddy said I was a different breed of dog from my brothers and sisters. 'You know,' Daddy said, 'it's some that can live their whole life out without asking about it and it's others has to know why it is, and this boy is one of the latters. He's going to be into everything!' " He put on his black hat and looked up suddenly and then away deep into the woods as if he were embarrassed again. "I'm sorry I don't have on a shirt before you ladies," he said, hunching his shoulders slightly. "We buried our clothes that we had on when

we escaped and we're just making do until we can get better. We borrowed these from some folks we met," he explained.

82 "That's perfectly all right," the grandmother said. "Maybe Bailey has an extra shirt in his suitcase."

83 "I'll look and see terrectly," The Misfit said.

"Where are they taking him?" the children's mother screamed.

"Daddy was a card himself," The Misfit said. "You couldn't put anything over on him. He never got in trouble with the Authorities though. Just had the knack of handling them."

84 "You could be honest too if you'd only try," said the grandmother. "Think how wonderful it would be to settle down and live a comfortable life and not have to think about somebody chasing you all the time."

85 The Misfit kept scratching in the ground with the butt of his gun as if he were thinking about it. "Yes'm, somebody is always after you," he murmured.

86 The grandmother noticed how thin his shoulder blades were just behind his hat because she was standing up looking down on him. "Do you ever pray?" she asked.

87 He shook his head. All she saw was the black hat wiggle between his shoulder blades. "Nome," he said.

88 There was a pistol shot from the woods, followed closely by another. Then silence. The old lady's head jerked around. She could hear the wind move through the tree tops like a long satisfied insuck of breath. "Bailey Boy!" she called.

89 "I was a gospel singer for a while," The Misfit said. "I been most everything. Been in the arm service, both land and sea, at home and abroad, been twict married, been an undertaker, been with the railroads, plowed Mother Earth, been in a tornado, seen a man burnt alive oncet," and he looked up at the children's mother and the little girl who were sitting close together, their faces white and their eyes glassy; "I even seen a woman flogged," he said.

90 "Pray, pray," the grandmother began, "pray, pray . . ."

"I never was a bad boy that I remember of," The Misfit said in an almost dreamy voice, "but somewheres along the line I done something wrong and got sent to the penitentiary. I was buried alive," and he looked up and held her attention to him by a steady stare.

91 "That's when you should have started to pray," she said. "What did you do to get sent to the penitentiary that first time?"

92 "Turn to the right, it was a wall," The Misfit said, looking up again at the cloudless sky. "Turn to the left, it was a wall. Look up it was a ceiling, look down it was a floor. I forget what I done, lady. I set there and set there, trying to remember what it was I done and I ain't recalled it to this day. Oncet in a while, I would think it was coming to me, but it never come."

93 "Maybe they put you in by mistake," the old lady said vaguely.

"Nome," he said. "It wasn't no mistake. They had the papers on me."

94 "You must have stolen something," she said.

The Misfit sneered slightly. "Nobody had nothing I wanted," he said. "It was a head-doctor at the penitentiary said what I had done was kill my daddy but I known that for a lie. My daddy died in nineteen ought nineteen of the epidemic flu and I never had a thing to do with it. He was buried in the Mount Hopewell Baptist churchyard and you can go there and see for yourself."

95 "If you would pray," the old lady said, "Jesus would help you."

"That's right," The Misfit said.

"Well then, why don't you pray?" she asked trembling with delight suddenly.

96 "I don't want no hep," he said. "I'm doing all right by myself."

Bobby Lee and Hiram came ambling back from the woods. Bobby Lee was dragging a yellow shirt with bright blue parrots in it.

97 "Thow me that shirt, Bobby Lee," The Misfit said. The shirt came flying at him and landed on his shoulder and he put it on. The grandmother couldn't name what the shirt reminded her of. "No, lady," The Misfit said while he was buttoning it up, "I found out the crime don't matter. You can do one thing or you can do another, kill a man or take a tire off his car, because sooner or later you're going to forget what it was you done and just be punished for it."

98 The children's mother had begun to make heaving noises as if she couldn't get her breath. "Lady," he asked, "would you and that little girl like to step off yonder with Bobby Lee and Hiram and join your husband?"

99 "Yes, thank you," the mother said faintly. Her left arm dangled helplessly and she was holding the baby, who had gone to sleep, in the other. "Hep that lady up, Hiram," The Misfit said as she struggled to climb out of the ditch, "and Bobby Lee, you hold onto that little girl's hand."

100 "I don't want to hold hands with him," June Star said. "He reminds me of a pig."

101 The fat boy blushed and laughed and caught her by the arm and pulled her off into the woods after Hiram and her mother.

102 Alone with The Misfit, the grandmother found that she had lost her voice. There was not a cloud in the sky nor any sun. There was nothing around her but woods. She wanted to tell him that he must pray. She opened and closed her mouth several times before anything came out. Finally she found herself saying, "Jesus. Jesus," meaning, Jesus will help you, but the way she was saying it, it sounded as if she might be cursing.

103 "Yes'm," The Misfit said as if he agreed. "Jesus thown everything

off balance. It was the same case with Him as with me except He hadn't committed any crime and they could prove I had committed one because they had the papers on me. Of course," he said, "they never shown me my papers. That's why I sign myself now. I said long ago, you get you a signature and sign everything you do and keep a copy of it. Then you'll know what you done and you can hold up the crime to the punishment and see do they match and in the end you'll have something to prove you ain't been treated right. I call myself The Misfit," he said, "because I can't make what all I done wrong fit what all I gone through in punishment."

104 There was a piercing scream from the woods, followed closely by a pistol report. "Does it seem right to you, lady, that one is punished a heap and another ain't punished at all?"

105 "Jesus!" the old lady cried. "You've got good blood! I know you wouldn't shoot a lady! I know you come from nice people! Pray! Jesus, you ought not to shoot a lady. I'll give you all the money I've got!"

106 "Lady," The Misfit said, looking beyond her into the woods, "there never was a body that give the undertaker a tip."

107 There were two more pistol reports and the grandmother raised her head like a parched old turkey hen crying for water and called, "Bailey Boy, Bailey Boy!" as if her heart would break.

108 "Jesus was the only One that ever raised the dead," The Misfit continued, "and He shouldn't have done it. He thown everything off balance. If He did what He said, then it's nothing for you to do but thow away everything and follow Him, and if He didn't, then it's nothing for you to do but enjoy the few minutes you got left the best way you can—by killing somebody or burning down his house or doing some other meanness to him. No pleasure but meanness," he said and his voice had become almost a snarl.

109 "Maybe He didn't raise the dead," the old lady mumbled, not knowing what she was saying and feeling so dizzy that she sank down in the ditch with her legs twisted under her.

110 "I wasn't there so I can't say He didn't," The Misfit said. "I wisht I had of been there," he said, hitting the ground with his fist. "It ain't right I wasn't there because if I had of been there I would of known. Listen lady," he said in a high voice, "if I had of been there I would of known and I wouldn't be like I am now." His voice seemed about to crack and the grandmother's head cleared for an instant. She saw the man's face twisted close to her own as if he were going to cry and she murmured, "Why you're one of my babies. You're one of my own children!" She reached out and touched him on the shoulder. The Misfit sprang back as if a snake had bitten him and shot her three times through the chest. Then he put his gun down on the ground and took off his glasses and began to clean them.

111 Hiram and Bobby Lee returned from the woods and stood over the ditch, looking down at the grandmother who half sat and half lay in a puddle of blood wlth her legs crossed under her like a child's and her face smiling up at the cloudless sky.

112 Without his glasses, The Misfit's eyes were red-rimmed and pale and defenseless-looking. "Take her off and throw her where you thown the others," he said, picking up the cat that was rubbing itself against his leg.

113 "She was a talker, wasn't she?" Bobby Lee said, sliding down the ditch with a yodel.

114 "She would of been a good woman," The Misfit said, "if it had been somebody there to shoot her every minute of her life."

115 "Some fun!" Bobby Lee said.

"Shut up, Bobby Lee," The Misfit said. "It's no real pleasure in life."

Thinking Questions: *Form*

1. Are there logical causes for the violence in this story? Or does the violence just happen—by coincidence and chance? For example, consider the dialogue of June Star and John Wesley, the children in the story. Does their dialogue suggest a tendency toward violence? If it does, where did those tendencies come from? Are any of these tendencies shared by the larger American society? Where might you see these values communicated everyday?

2. What function does the family's stop at Red Sammy's The Tower restaurant serve in the story? Does it highlight any particular psychological qualities in the characters? Are these qualities later seen as some justification for the family's death by violence?

3. Review the family and social background of The Misfit. What causes his violent behavior? Many readers believe that The Misfit functions as an anti-Christ in this story. How is he like and unlike your image of Christ? Why does The Misfit tell the grandmother, shortly before shooting her, that "Jesus was the only One that ever raised the dead"? What do The Misfit's ideas about Christ have to do with his feeling that the best one can do is "enjoy the few minutes you got left . . . by killing somebody or burning down his house or doing some other meanness to him. No pleasure but meanness"?

4. Compare this story with a family situation comedy on television. How are the family relationships different? Which version of American family life is more accurate?

5. Write a case study or analysis of one of the story's major characters. Before you begin, plan your strategy. Will you begin with a summary of the character and then move, example by example, through details

from the story to give the reader a clear idea of what went into your summary? Or will you begin by showing the effects produced by an earlier action of your character and then work back to what caused those effects? Be careful to *link* effects with causes in your writing; do not expect the reader to fill in background reasoning and information.

Thinking Questions: *Substance*

1. At the beginning of this section, we discussed three perspectives on violence: the cosmic, the personal or psychological, and the social. Choose one of these perspectives and apply it to Flannery O'Connor's story. Can you, for example, apply the personal perspective to the grandmother in the story and come up with an explanation of why, although she *seems* the kindest character in the story, she *causes* much of the violence that occurs?

2. After reading this story, do you believe Flannery O'Connor believes that people are inherently good or inherently evil? Or has humankind somewhere gone wrong and corrupted an essentially good nature? Remember, examine the story carefully for supporting evidence to your answer. What evidence of good, for example, can you find in any of these characters?

3. Consider the place of nature in this story. How would you define O'Connor's descriptions of the Georgia countryside? How do those descriptions relate to her treatment of character? Does the human violence in the story seem paralleled by violence in nature?

Writing Exercise VI

EXPOSITION

(Cause and Effect)

The essays and story in this section ought to provide fertile material for an argument on the causes and effects of violence. Begin by developing a clear resolution or argumentative thesis on violence. Consider each of the readings in this section carefully as you form your thesis. You might, for example, argue that one particular social condition has contributed directly to a certain form of violence in our society. Or you might develop a more general thesis on the entire problem, much as Robert Jay Lifton does in his definition of the causes of atrocities. Be sure that your argument is carefully worded and limited to a single, precise statement.

After forming a thesis, plan your offensive. What particular evidence will you use? Isolate specific passages from the essays in this section for quotation and paraphrase. Get the facts of your argument securely in mind. Work out the inferences you will draw from those facts and be sure that you will be able to illustrate those inferences to your readers.

Remember that a large part of any argument depends on the writer's ability to understand, include, and refute the arguments of the opposing side. If, for example, you decide to argue that technology has increased people's capacity for violence, be sure that you give full consideration to the major counter-arguments. Many technologists and scientists would say that technology has helped us develop better food production and that, because of these increases in production, many violent revolutions and social upheavals have been avoided.

You may also want to read the following essay on cause-and-effect essays. Arguments depend on appeals to the emotion and reason of your readers. Most rational appeals depend on the writer's use of logic, the ability to combine causes and effects in logical sequences. The following essay should help you sharpen your ability to analyze and write logically.

If you need help in developing a thesis, consider these possible topics. (Each topic could, of course, also be stated in the negative.) All of them are covered somewhere in the essays in this section:

1. Modern technology has increased our tendency toward violence.

2. Emotions such as frustration and anger are bound to increase in a mass society, where individuals are often manipulated by social forces they neither understand nor control. These emotions will eventually lead to some form of violence—directed either inward toward the self or outward toward others.

3. People are inherently violent and must be physically controlled by their governments.

4. People are essentially good and must be given the greatest amount of potential freedom by their government.

5. Violence is not justified in *any* social context.

6. Violence is justified only in defense of personal rights.

7. Violence is justified only when a society will be noticeably improved by violent behavior.

8. Athletics and other forms of organized competition and violence serve a useful social function: they help people work off frustrations, anger, and violent tendencies.

9. Athletics and other forms of organized competition and violence are socially disruptive because they increase people's appetite for violence.

10. No one can tell when violence is *generally* justified or unjustified. We can only proceed with analyses of individual cases.

WRITING THE CAUSE-AND-EFFECT ESSAY

Why and *what* are key words in any cause-and-effect essay. *Why* did something happen? *What* will happen now because of what already exists?

Most cause-and-effect essays follow two general patterns. An essay that emphasizes *causes* usually begins with a description of a social situation—for example, Robert Jay Lifton in "Beyond Atrocity" begins by describing scenes from the My Lai massacre in Vietnam and the aftermath of the bombing of Hiroshima and then proceeds to move backward to an analysis of why My Lai and Hiroshima occurred. That is, he begins by describing effects and proceeds by postulating general causes. Modern technology, psychological numbing, and mass rationalization of what actually happened are ultimately presented as the major causes of modern atrocities.

An essay that emphasizes *effects* rather than causes usually moves *forward.* A sociologist who wishes to demonstrate how an unstable home environment can affect a child's classroom performance might begin an essay by describing an argument between parents at the breakfast table and then show how that argument interrupts the child's train of thought in school. The child's daydreaming, her thinking back on the morning argument between her parents, is the *effect.* A cause-oriented essay would emphasize the breakfast-table argument; an effect-oriented essay would emphasize its *consequences.*

As you plan and write cause-and effect essays, be sure to avoid these common errors.

1. *Do not assume a single cause when there are many.* Perhaps our schoolchild has been disturbed as much by a violent television program that she watched the previous night as she was by her parents' argument.

2. *Do not assume that two events occurring simultaneously or one after the other are necessarily related.* A man who feels guilty about throwing litter from his car window might erroneously assume that an accident he is involved in moments later was caused by his littering. You should analyze carefully to get beyond superficial appearances.

3. *Be sure to distinguish between remote and immediate causes.* An effective cause-and-effect essay gets right to the point. Do not involve yourself in wide-ranging background discussion in an essay in which you wish to point out the immediate causes of traffic tie-ups downtown.

4. *Remember that some causes have actually produced the opposite of what most people expected.* Did prohibition really cut down alcohol consumption? Did civil rights laws improve racial relations? Has the busing of schoolchildren really promoted integration? Whatever the purpose of your essay, be sure to question your definition of causes. Do not take what *seems to be true* for granted.

5. *Do not argue that contradictory effects resulted from a similar cause.* If you really do wish to point out a paradox, make your intentions clear to the reader. A politician looking for votes might, for example, tell potential voters that he will cut the state budget while greatly expanding the state's allocations to education. The voters deserve a full explanation of such a seemingly contradictory promise; the mere fact of the politician's election would not assure that both these effects would occur.

Planning a cause-and-effect essay

Most analytical essays use either an inductive or a deductive pattern. An inductive essay begins with particular instances and examples, analyzes them closely, and then winds up with a generalization that applies to other similar situations. A deductive essay works something like a mathematical equation or formula. The writer begins with a statement of a general principle or group of assumptions. He or she then applies the principle or assumption to the specific subject of the essay and concludes by showing how it either explains or is supported by the particular subject.

Both Virginia Woolf and Roger Kahn write inductive essays: they observe and analyze particular experiences and move suggestively toward general statements on different kinds of violence. Inductive essays are most appropriate when a writer wants the readers to *discover* as they read. Roger Kahn, for example, takes us on a narrative excursion through

Carl Furillo's baseball career, highlighting important facts and descriptions, relating Furillo's feelings as he went through particular experiences. Kahn manipulates his material in a way that leads the reader to share Furillo's frustration and anger and ultimately to agree with him in his fight against organized baseball. In fact, the entire essay leads up to the following paragraph, which summarizes Furillo's character and captures the gist of his battle with the Brooklyn Dodgers:

> He does talk like a hard hat and he was a baseball Bolshevik. He fits no label. He is too human, too large, too variable, too much the independent. In one voice he talks against welfare, like a Buckley, and in another voice, which is the same, he talks about ball players' rights and defies a system. . . .

Deductive essays, on the other hand, are usually not suggestive; in such essays, the writer explicitly develops a thesis, applies it to the subject and finishes by demonstrating how this particular subject substantiates the thesis. The writer who wants to provide a clear, direct argument, to summarize a general position and provide supporting ideas as efficiently as possible, usually uses a deductive pattern of organization.

Remember that you can use inductive and deductive patterns to analyze your material before you write and also that you can use either pattern to organize your writing itself. Do whatever develops naturally. If you have a clear idea or thesis you want to apply to particular materials, plan your essay deductively. If you want to evolve a thesis from a careful analysis of selected examples, plan your essay inductively.

Whatever technique of analysis you use to plan your essay, you can alter the plan as you write to meet the needs of a particular audience. Readers who wish to analyze and discover on their own usually prefer inductive writing. Writer and reader go through examples, evolve generalizations, and work toward a conclusion together. Readers who want forceful and explicit summaries of a writer's position—with a few selected examples and analysis—usually prefer deductive writing, where a thesis appears early and the results of analysis are cited and summarized throughout the essay.

Form and Substance/4

Form:

ARGUMENT AND PERSUASION

Substance:

What Should We Believe?
How Should We Live?

MORALITY IN AMERICA

/4 *Substance and Theme:*

MORALITY IN AMERICA

A person's way of life is often controlled or directed by his or her environment. Yet we all, to a greater or lesser degree, act *as if* our lives, especially our social lives, were entirely within our control. Most of us live by some kind of moral or ethical code, or at least we base our actions on personally chosen groups of principles. Those who most of all wish to be liked by others try to develop an open, pleasant personality, the ability to get along with others, the ability to keep and satisfy a large group of friends.

Others, who believe strongly that people should live by principle—no matter what the social conditions—might value most highly the ability to live *consistently,* to behave day-in and day-out according to certain absolute rules. Without these rules, and the behavior that follows from them, society might disintegrate. When personal principles clash, these people believe social customs and laws must intervene and impose order.

Consider a situation described earlier in this book, in an essay by Charles Reich. Several British seamen are shipwrecked. After the catastrophe, they find themselves on a small lifeboat faced with limited provisions of food and water. They survive quite a while by rationing their food, yet it soon becomes clear that they will run out of food, that, unless something drastic is done, they will all starve. They draw lots, and two of the men proceed to carve up and eat the third—with his initial agreement. Both men survive because of their human meal. Is their cannibalism justified by circumstances? Or is cannibalism below human dignity, no matter what the circumstances? Would human beings, faced with such circumstances, be better off choosing death? The shipwrecked men have chosen as a group to live by a standard that places physical survival above all. When they return to England after their rescue, however, a judge decides that their cannibalism trespasses against British custom and law. They are punished for their action, despite the fact that it was undertaken in a democratic fashion and under different circumstances than most British citizens would ever face.

Not all moral choices, thank goodness, are as bizarre or extreme as this. Yet all of us, in our everyday lives, face situations that demand just such difficult choice-making, although the consequences of our acts may not be as severe as those of the shipwrecked survivors. We have seen numerous examples of conflicts between private and public conscience throughout this book.

This final section presents a group of essays that treat, in both serious and humorous form, the difficulties involved for those who try to live consistently in a world where complex, contradictory demands are continually made by their circumstances and environment. Many popular and professional sociologists and psychologists tell us that many Americans are indeed driven to near-frenzy by the contrasting values in our culture. Traditional values are questioned; new values are ridiculed and found superficial. The industrialist, for example, argues that industry has made America what it is and that it must not be subject to the controls demanded by environmentalists. Environmentalists, however, remind us that our country's natural resources must be preserved, that a country without natural beauty and resources cannot survive on the mechanisms of industry alone. There is truth in the claims of both sides. How, then, should we proceed?

Examples like these suggest that moral issues, especially in a society and world as large and as complex as ours, raise no easy questions and accept no easy answers. People must face every decision with the seriousness and logic of statesmen. Yet they must also recognize their own limitations in the face of terribly complex issues and be able to live with the idea that people must go on living no matter what problems they face. Levity and humor become necessary ingredients in any moral recipe. The essays in this section reflect both serious and humorous reactions to the answers individuals have developed to the questions "What should we believe?" and "How should we live?"

In the late 1960s many young Americans, because of the fighting of what they thought was an unjustified war and because of numerous examples of racial prejudice and cruelty, both questioned and fought against the established government and the American way of life. Cecelia Holland attacks the tendencies toward oversimplification and closed-mindedness among those young people who were associated with popular protest. Her serious criticisms are pointed at both anti-Vietnam war critics and civil rights demonstrators, as well as hippies. Holland wrote the essay for a popular magazine in 1968—in the midst of heated controversy over, as she calls it, "the American Way of Life." Notice that she does not really criticize the issues or positions the young people were supporting; rather, she bitterly points out how these issues were either clouded or made into catch terms by the young people who supported them. The war, Holland suggests, became an excuse that idealistic young people used to put all the blame on those older than themselves. The real conformists in 1968 were the students and young people themselves who refused to accept any thinking contrary to their own proclaimed beliefs.

Certainly Holland's criticism did not apply to all young people. But her harsh criticism of her peers does point out an essential danger in any form of idealistic or reform thinking. Once a moral position catches on, becomes kinky and "in," the people who support that position can become as dogmatic and as simple-minded as those they argued against. Many of the late sixties drop-outs, for example, ran off to join communes where they could be with people who thought like themselves. Many found, however, that a life-style they thought would be ideal became intolerable because no one was encouraged to express or live out counter-beliefs. Any form of oversimplification or dogmatism, no matter how morally right or wrong the ideas being espoused, makes life less worth living, less rich and varied, less *free*. Those, in other words, who oppose what is established must be careful not to create customs more absolute than those they replace.

In the next essay, Jim Murray focuses on one of the most controversial figures of authority in our culture: Woody Hayes, football coach at Ohio State University. Hayes has been called a General Patton in football coach's clothing. A firm believer in military discipline and Spartan living,

Hayes has put Ohio State at or near the top of collegiate football rankings every year. Murray tells us, however, that Coach Hayes merely does what he believes will motivate his players; he suggests through satire that Woody might well become less authoritarian in an age when players respond more favorably to liberal, understanding coaches. In essence, Murray shows us that a man who seems to live by one moral code actually lives by another. The seeming "man of discipline" is really a "man of expediency."

I Don't Trust Anyone Under Thirty

CECELIA HOLLAND

1 Militant, committed, articulate and radical, the generation under thirty claims to be the hope of the world. Our parents believe it. They contrast the purity of our motives and the energy of our commitments with their own corrupted morality and corroded traditions and decide that everything we say *must* be right. "Don't let the kids down," says an advertisement for Gene McCarthy. Not since the Children's Crusade in the early 13th century has an older generation entrusted so much of its salvation to the young. Not since the Renaissance have we wielded so much influence over our elders. (Did Cesare Borgia trust anybody over thirty?)

2 Much of the work in the civil-rights crusade is done by people under thirty years of age. Almost all the protesters of the Vietnam war (and the great majority of those fighting in it) are under thirty. There are very few hippies over thirty, and the hippie movement stands out as the single most visible protest against the syndrome commonly called the American Way of Life. My generation is the most idealistic, the most dynamic and the most liberal in history; just ask us, we'll tell you. We're strong on freedom and long on love, and there are enough of us around to change the very definitions of the words to make these statements fact.

3 Are we strong on freedom? It would be hard to find a young person outside the South who isn't all for the Negro revolution. The freedom to protest the Vietnam war—to protest anything (except the protesters)—is as hallowed as the bones of a saint. Yet to hold a conservative viewpoint, however honestly, can only be a sign of cowardice. Anybody over thirty will ask first what your opinion is on the war. Anybody under thirty will automatically assume you're against it; if you aren't, you're a heretic.

4 Freedom and free speech should mean that anyone can hold any opinion he wants on the Negro or the war in Vietnam, as long as he doesn't try to enforce his views on anybody else. But our generation's conception of freedom goes more like this: "Do your own thing and all will be well, as long as your own thing is certified pure by the rest of us."

5 But what if your own thing doesn't happen to conform to that of the hip world, the militant students, the nonstudents or any other faction? There are, after all, people in this world who manage to live entirely within the existing social structure, and who do so by choice. There are people who find it possible to go through life neither rebelling nor conforming. Are they all hypocrites? To the under-thirty group, nonalignment is as abhorrent as slavish devotion to the *status quo.*

6 Let's face it, my generation is *not* strong on freedom. Basically, we simply want to do what we like, without being bothered by anything silly like antique conventions and laws. But why the devil can't we just say so and let it go at that? Why do we dress our preferences in the vestments of a quasi-religion?

7 Part of the reason, I suspect, is that we're still bound by at least one antique convention: doing things for the right reasons, the socially acceptable motives. We have a party line, certain things and opinions that must be professed under certain conditions. Deviation labels one unfit. Anybody who's ever ventured into the wilderness of conversation with more than one hip or militant student or political fanatic or fellow-traveler knows that there is a striking similarity, not only in the lines of argument taken on almost all subjects but in the words and slogans used, not only within each faction but across partisan lines. Doctrine has hardened into dogma. (I am a fellow-traveler with the "straights," which means that sometimes I'm self-consciously hip; and making the transition from one vernacular to the other is difficult enough to suggest that the differences are not merely linguistic. Hip-think doesn't require logic or clarity, which makes it easier, of course, to sound profound.)

8 The drug issue is a good example of our dogmatism. If you don't smoke or pop pills, you're narrow-minded, tradition-bound and a chicken. Your reasons for denying the Nirvana of drugs make no difference. There are people for whom "grass," "acid," "speed" and their relatives hold no interest, just as there are people who dislike roast beef. Usually they manage to commune with the infinite quite well without an interpreter. Yet these people are as square to the drug-user as the housewife who won't wear short skirts because the neighbors might talk.

9 What does love mean to the Love Generation? It can mean purging oneself of hatred and prejudice and welcoming everyone else as a

brother, and it can mean preaching the gospel while pushing Methedrine. It can mean the L.A. Diggers, a group of well-off, sympathetic people who give runaway kids a place to stop and catch their breath, and it can mean the "rank sweat of an enseamèd bed." There's something of calf-love in all our uses of the word, and something else that's just a little weird. The widely published off-campus living arrangements of college students like Barnard's Linda Leclair is another indication, with *Playboy* magazine and Ingmar Bergman, that sex is rapidly becoming a spectator sport. Why is it we can't love without announcing it to the world in infinite detail?

10 Love, as the song-makers know, is a private thing, and those who proclaim it in public tend to slip a little in the practice. Whatever the Columbia students were thinking about when they threw rocks, mailboxes and desks at the cops during their recent fit of self-expression, it wasn't love. If it was, it lost a lot in the translation.

11 Actually, when you cut out the preaching and look at the action, we're all sharpshooters—in the old sense—and our major target is that famous bogeyman, the world we never made. We think our parents made it—the hypocrisy, the prejudice, the materialism, the hatred, the uncertainty—and we know we have the answers for improving it. It takes the wisdom that comes with some age to realize that if the solution looks simple you probably don't understand the problem. And it takes the kind of minds we haven't got to realize that what you say means less than what you do.

12 The hip world isn't the whole of our generation, but it's a good microcosm. Its values and flaws characterize us all. The hippie drops out of society. But luckily for him, society sticks around, because the hippie is a parasite. The straight world supports him. Without this country's prosperity, there could be no hippies. They'd have nobody to bum from, nobody to give them easy jobs to tide them over the winter. There would be no leisure time in which to practice being hip, and no straight public to be titillated and fleeced. The hip world is neither self-supporting nor self-perpetuating, and it's hypocritical to claim that it is.

13 This kind of hypocrisy creeps into almost all our debunking of the Bad World. The institutions that create the atmosphere conducive to protest are inextricably bound up with the institutions we protest against. If it weren't for the Establishment, what would we fight against? And if we couldn't fight, who knows but—horrors—we might become Establishment ourselves? History is full of rebellious crusades that demolished the *status quo* and wound up becoming the *status quo* themselves.

14 To protect ourselves, we try to cover the deck with protests—prove our unimpeachable nobility by knocking everything in sight as ignoble. How well do we listen to what we say?

15 Materialism in this country has taken the odd turn of becoming a form of idealism: things put aside for tomorrow. Our parents live for tomorrow, in a thingy kind of way. They dream of the bright world ahead, a utopia which we find rather pathetic because we quit believing in utopias a long time ago. We live for today. We grab what we can get, now. Tomorrow never comes anyway. And when it does, it's just like today. Actually we aren't even particularly cynical about it, just sad.

16 The deadly corollary to this kind of thinking is that what you have to work for isn't worth having. (A woman's magazine recently declared that the emphasis is on "roles, not goals," a decent square translation of "do your own thing.") We think knowledge that must be learned isn't valuable; only intuitive, revealed knowledge is worth while. The college "grind" is a pitiable figure. It's so much easier to fake your way through. College isn't a place where you learn; it's an object to be revolutionized. You don't find knowledge, it comes to you, complete with bright colors and dogs barking flowers.

17 If we work, we do just enough to survive. A job exists to keep one fed—we accept employment as a token reason for accepting a living. We're a generation of grasshoppers.

18 We love Marshall McLuhan because he makes it impossible, and therefore unnecessary, to think logically. Our passion for J. R. R. Tolkien is, I think, due not to the clear-cut moral position he espouses but to the blatantly mythological character of his books; they aren't about the real world, which makes them safe to handle. ("We can dig the morality, but we don't have to do anything about it, because we aren't mythological people," says my sister, who is seventeen.) The fads borrowed from Oriental and Indian cultures are deliberate archaisms. We long for the safe, still, dead worlds in which all values are only reflections of eternity. We don't like change, and we doubt we can cope with it, so we pretend it doesn't exist. Reality has become elusive, painful, a blind god that isn't dead but probably isn't human either, so we prefer ambiguity.

19 If we're grasshoppers, what about the ants? "Of course they're straight—they're parents." Nobody over thirty can possibly have access to the Truth. Actually, we don't dislike our parents so much as we resent them—their money-fever, their ability to muddle (and meddle in) almost everything and, above all, their timidity. J. Alfred Prufrocks, the batch of them. It's the lack of authority they display that revolts us, and their readiness to be fooled. If our parents were a bolder, tougher generation, we would be a meeker, sweeter pack of grasshoppers.

20 The harshness of our indictment of our parents stems from our essential innocence, and our innocence stems from ignorance. We're the best-educated generation around, judging by the number of

years we spend in schools, but we really don't know much. Colleges insist on graduating students who can't write an intelligible English sentence, who don't speak three words of a foreign language, who have read neither Marx nor Keynes nor Freud nor Joyce, and who never will. It isn't necessarily the colleges' fault: The books and the professors are there, but we've lost the ability to take advantage of them. Nevertheless, we feel ourselves entitled to hold an opinion on everything, whether we know anything about it or not. And we've discovered that the less we know about something, the easier it is to hold a strong opinion about it.

21 The Berkeley sit-in in defense of free speech was followed by the protest against the presence of a Navy recruiting booth on campus; many of the same students (and non-students) took part in both. Isn't this in some small, tiny way inconsistent? This may be an unfair parallel, but this kind of behavior reminds me of the U.S.S.R., where Benjamin Spock is considered a hero because he defies the United States Government; and where Soviet writers who publish anything in opposition to the Party are tried and punished as traitors.

22 Heaven preserve us from our own children.

(1968)

Thinking Questions: *Form*

1. Holland writes a clear, tough, straightforward argument. What obvious organizational and unifying devices does she use to keep her argument pointed and clear? Consider, for example, the rhetorical questions that keep Holland's thesis before the reader; analyze the way she uses classification and division in organizing related parts of her discussion to make the reader's task less difficult.

2. Holland's attitude toward her subject is obviously negative. How would you describe her speaking voice and tone? Is she distant and objective with her readers? Does she want to create an impression that is rational and reserved? More importantly, considering the nature of her arguments and the time in which she was writing, why do you think she chose to develop the tone she did? Did she have more or less chance of being listened to by general readers?

3. This argument is deductively organized—it mores from thesis through carefully selected and organized pieces of evidence. Do you think, however, that Holland initially arrived at her thesis through a set group of experiments all set up to prove an initial hypothesis about young people? Or do you suppose that Holland's argument developed inductively, with pieces of experience accumulated, analyzed, and reworked until the thesis became clear?

4. To your mind, is there enough fact in Holland's essay? How well does the author use what facts she does include? Do they pile up to make a convincing argument?

Thinking Questions: ***Substance***

1. Tell in a single simple sentence exactly what Cecelia Holland says was wrong with young people in 1968. Find one sentence in the essay that accurately reflects Holland's thesis; then put her thesis in your own words.

2. In paragraph 7, Holland coins the term "hip-think," which she says requires the use of popular words and slogans, but never logic or clarity. Have you ever overheard a conversation in which two people use a meaningless language of their own in order to befuddle a third party? Why was the game being played? Who won and why? What issues were being discussed, if any? Be as specific as you can in your description of hip-think. You might want to work together with a group of classmates to create a hypothetical hip-think dialogue on some contemporary issue like ecology or consumer rights.

3. Do you feel, after reading Holland's essay thoroughly, that she practices what she preaches? In paragraph 8, for example, Holland severely criticizes many young people's attitudes toward the drug issue: "If you don't smoke or pop pills, you're narrow-minded, tradition-bound and chicken." Yet some critics might find Holland's criticism of young people just as dogmatic and narrow as the arguments of those she is criticizing. What might be Holland's defense of her own argumentative tactics?

4. As you look around, do you find Holland's charges relevant to today's young people? Why or why not? Are there no more important issues or problems? Have students and their goals changed? What social conditions have caused the changes in behavior you perceive?

5. What is the point behind Holland's tricky title? What popular saying does it alter and why? Why might the title attract the reader's attention?

New Leaf for Woody

JIM MURRAY

1 LOS ANGELES: The first look you get at Woody Hayes, you're surprised he's not wearing a bearskin loincloth and carrying a club with spikes sticking out of it.

2 You want to say, "Hey, Woody, how're things back in the cave?"

Or, "OK, Woody, where'd you park the dinosaur?" Or, "Hey, Woody, did you hear the latest? They discovered fire over in the valley the other day."

3 Woody is the Piltdown Man of Football.[1] When no one's looking, he rambles across the hills on all fours, it is claimed. He didn't walk erect till he was 24 years old. Ohio State University found him in a tar pit. He writes in drawings. He escaped from a paleontology museum. He's the Creature from One Million B.C. If he ever sees Raquel Welch he'll grab her by the hair and take her home and cook her.

4 Woody's image is hard-won. He's a football coach in the jet era, but his football tactics were right out of Princeton-Rutgers, 1869. They don't really have to inflate the football for Woody's teams. In fact, they don't even need one. Woody's attack is just a kind of complicated flying wedge.

5 Woody always kept his teams as secret as if they were wanted for murder when they came to the Rose Bowl. The Dalton Gang was never more furtive. You would have thought they were representing San Quentin instead of Ohio State. They were just numbers, not people. The frustrated press had to make do with caricatures of Woody Hayes. After all, you couldn't justify 10 days in California writing stories about palm trees.

6 But that, as they say, was prologue . . .

7 The other day, Wayne Woodrow Hayes, a citizen of the 20th century, who was born in 1913, not the Pleistocene Age, on St. Valentine's Day, not in some indeterminate period between glaciers, showed up for an interview. Historians of the future will not speculate if he really existed or was mythical like the All-American team.

8 Hayes came into a room at the Huntington-Sheraton Hotel in store-boughten clothes with his hair cut and the first thing he announced was that he had given the team the day off. The press couldn't have been more shocked if Brezhnev announced he was emptying his prisons. Woody's teams don't get days off. They're either tackling somebody or they're sleeping.

9 Nearly 20 years ago, Hayes was the first Rose Bowl coach to take his team up to a monastery on the night before the game, the first group of people in history to spend New Year's Eve in cells without getting their heads shaved first. Woody didn't want his team listening to a lot of guys in paper hats blowing horns at midnight.

10 "I wanted to get away from the noise in the hotel," explained Woody. It's possible Woody has since taken a closer look at the

1. Piltdown man was supposedly discovered, or authenticated, in 1915 from a skull found near Piltdown Common in Sussex, England. Later, in 1953, the "discovery" was proved a forgery; the skull was of a modern, not an ancient man. The Piltdown man proves an excellent comparison for Woody Hayes because Murray closes his article with the idea that Hayes, too, is a forgery—not a real "caveman."

clientele and decided the most noise any of them would make at midnight would be snoring.

11 There is another consideration which might have brought coach Hayes into the 20th century. Football coaches are the most resilient of characters. They show up in black suits and gloomy faces—IF IT WORKS. They'll show up in buckskin fringes and Doc Severinsen outfits with long hair and love beads and funny handshakes—if THAT works.

12 The evidence that the prehistoric approach was wearing out was devastating: on his last two appearances, with full, bloody-nosed practices and the New Year's Eve in a musty abbey, Woody was 0-and-2. Stanford won, 27-17, and USC, 42-17.

13 Woody's no different from any other coach. He'd let the boys spend New Year's Eve in the Copacabana or on a yacht for 42 points. "We were the ones who pioneered getting away from the celebrating," explained Woody, ignoring the suggestion that what REALLY happened was that he found out the monastery was noisier than the Huntington lobby. "Football players are not geared to religious retreats, one to a room, rows of silence. They are extremely social people, gregarious animals. They get jittery alone where they can't watch TV and move around and talk. We were the first to go up there and we're the first to quit."

14 The rumor that some of the players squawked that, if they wanted to spend New Year's Eve in a monastery or a nunnery they would have joined the Franciscans first, was squelched.

15 But, then, Woody showed convincingly and shockingly how mod he had become. He trooped four of his first-string players into the room!

16 Now, the longtime Rose Bowl press and longtime Woody-watchers couldn't have been more thunderstruck to see William of Orange doing the Cha-cha-cha.

17 They looked with jaws agape at Pete Cusick, Neal Colzie, Tim Fox and the starting quarterback, Cornelius Greene. It was the first time any of them on the Coast had seen an Ohio State player without a number on his back and a muzzle on his face. It was the first time they had heard them talk.

18 They didn't look at all as if they had been promised amnesty for testifying.

Thinking Questions: *Form*

1. Consider the voice of this essay, especially sentences such as "Woody is the Piltdown Man of Football" or "He's a football coach in the jet era, but his football tactics were right out of Princeton-Rutgers, 1869." Murray constantly uses figurative language and extended, catchy comparisons. His subject, Woody Hayes and the Ohio State football team, is compared to a variety of bizarre subjects—the Dalton gang, cavemen, religious fanatics—in order to clarify the essential and surprising change Murray has observed in Hayes's attitudes toward his players. Does Murray's voice give you any indication of his attitude?

2. Read between the lines and put into one sentence what you believe Jim Murray is saying about Woody Hayes, about *all* football coaches. Then go back through the essay and show where your idea of Murray's thesis is supported in the essay.

3. Does Murray's exaggeration distort the facts of the situation? Or is it clear that he exaggerates merely to make his point more effective and his essay more entertaining to read?

4. Describe the sentence and paragraph structure in this article. How can you tell from sentences and paragraphs that this article was written for a newspaper? Why do newspapers encourage this kind of writing? What are the advantages or disadvantages of Murray's style—of all newspaper style?

Thinking Questions: *Substance*

1. In paragraph 11 of "I Don't Trust Anyone Over Thirty," Cecelia Holland criticizes young people for not realizing that "it takes the kind of minds we [young people] haven't got to realize that what you say means less than what you do." Yet Jim Murray implies the opposite in his satiric column on Woody Hayes (see paragraph 11). Football coaches, he suggests, are better off doing what is popular with their players than doing what they believe, in principle, is right. In arguments or games where only winning counts, Cecelia Holland's worries about the consistency, logic, and integrity of her peers' arguments seem out of place. Are they? Might Holland include Woody Hayes in her criticism of bad thinking? Or can we resolve the question merely by saying that different situations demand different kinds of morality?

2. Is Woody Hayes, as Jim Murray describes him, a hypocrite or a clever and successful man who knows how to stay on top? If you were one of his players, would you admire or ridicule his shift in coaching style and his changing attitudes toward his players?

3. Can you figure out Jim Murray's attitude toward Woody Hayes? Is he criticizing Hayes's changes in behavior at the Rose Bowl? What particular paragraphs support your answer?

* * *

Both Cecelia Holland and Jim Murray criticize the morals of people and leaders they find around them—one seriously and analytically, the other satirically and humorously. John Fitzgerald Kennedy, in contrast, takes advantage of a ceremonious and serious context—a presidential inauguration ceremony seen by millions of people—to deliver a highly serious plea for cooperation. Kennedy outlines a moderate plan—not too soft on our enemies, yet also ready to extend a helping hand—and uses numerous formal and rhetorical devices to get people's support. Oddly enough, Kennedy's speech in 1961 probably created much of the youthful idealism that Cecelia Holland later criticized in 1968. His overtures about a New Frontier led directly to the Peace Corps and Vista (both voluntary public service organizations), which later produced many of the individuals active in the social movements of the late sixties.

Art Buchwald, a nationally syndicated political satirist, takes a satiric poke at moral hypocrisy, here seen in the form of a group of middle-aged men who supposedly are banded together to fight smut and pornography. Many people organize groups to hold the line against what they think are threats to traditional values. The "middle American" has often been stereotyped as a sexual prude. Yet, paradoxically enough, our country produces a vast amount of pornography in films, books, and magazines, much of it probably viewed by middle-class Americans.

Buchwald focuses on this paradox in his satire, "Fathers for Moral America." As we read about the "Fathers for Moral America" we discover that these men seem to enjoy the films they claim to hate and, in fact, use the group's identity and espoused purpose to cover up and create an excuse for their own viewing of pornographic films.

Buchwald, then, suggests yet another difficulty in arriving at and defending moral and ethical positions in contemporary America. When popular causes become so numerous that many people have difficulty separating one from another, the causes themselves lose much of their impact. In fact, they often become the "in" thing to do for many people who really have no concern with the problem the cause is supposed to solve. The causes, themselves, meanwhile, become objects of ridicule to those people who meet and listen to such trendy and simple-minded revolutionaries.

Buchwald, then, is not merely criticizing up-tight middle-class Americans; he criticizes a general social context in which everyone has a Cause—whether ecology, the poor, civil rights, equal housing, equal education, or peace—but very few really understand the complex social problems behind their Cause. Art Buchwald and Cecelia Holland, although their specific subjects and their approaches are very different, both point out the dangers of oversimplifying, popularizing and, in the process, destroying moral principles.

Inaugural Address

JOHN FITZGERALD KENNEDY

Vice President Johnson, Mr. Speaker, Mr. Chief Justice, President Eisenhower, Vice President Nixon, President Truman, reverend clergy, fellow citizens:

1 We observe today not a victory of party but a celebration of freedom—symbolizing an end as well as a beginning—signifying renewal as well as change. For I have sworn before you and Almighty God the same solemn oath our forebears prescribed nearly a century and three quarters ago.

2 The world is very different now. For man holds in his mortal hands the power to abolish all forms of human poverty and all forms of human life. And yet the same revolutionary beliefs for which our forebears fought are still at issue around the globe—the belief that the rights of man come not from the generosity of the state but from the hand of God.

3 We dare not forget today that we are the heirs of that first revolution. Let the word go forth from this time and place, to friend and foe alike, that the torch has been passed to a new generation of Americans—born in this century, tempered by war, disciplined by a hard and bitter peace, proud of our ancient heritage—and unwilling to witness or permit the slow undoing of those human rights to which this Nation has always been committed, and to which we are committed today at home and around the world.

4 Let every nation know, whether it wishes us well or ill, that we shall pay any price, bear any burden, meet any hardship, support any friend, oppose any foe to assure the survival and the success of liberty.

5 This much we pledge—and more.

6 To those old allies whose cultural and spiritual origins we share, we pledge the loyalty of faithful friends. United, there is little we cannot do in a host of cooperative ventures. Divided, there is little we can do—for we dare not meet a powerful challenge at odds and split asunder.

7 To those new states whom we welcome to the ranks of the free, we pledge our word that one form of colonial control shall not have passed away merely to be replaced by a far more iron tyranny. We shall not always expect to find them supporting our view. But we shall always hope to find them strongly supporting their own freedom —and to remember that, in the past, those who foolishly sought power by riding the back of the tiger ended up inside.

8 To those peoples in the huts and villages of half the globe struggling to break the bonds of mass misery, we pledge our best efforts to help them help themselves, for whatever period is required—not because the Communists may be doing it, not because we seek their votes, but because it is right. If a free society cannot help the many who are poor, it cannot save the few who are rich.

9 To our sister republics south of our border, we offer a special pledge—to convert our good words into good deeds—in a new alliance for progress—to assist free men and free governments in casting off the chains of poverty. But this peaceful revolution of hope cannot become the prey of hostile powers. Let all our neighbors know that we shall join with them to oppose aggression or subversion anywhere in the Americas. And let every other power know that this hemisphere intends to remain the master of its own house.

10 To that world assembly of sovereign states, the United Nations, our last best hope in an age where the instruments of war have far outpaced the instruments of peace, we renew our pledge of support—to prevent it from becoming merely a forum for invective—to strengthen its shield of the new and the weak—and to enlarge the area in which its writ may run.

11 Finally, to those nations who would make themselves our adversary, we offer not a pledge but a request: that both sides begin anew the quest for peace, before the dark powers of destruction unleashed by science engulf all humanity in planned or accidental self-destruction.

12 We dare not tempt them with weakness. For only when our arms are sufficient beyond doubt can we be certain beyond doubt that they will never be employed.

13 But neither can two great and powerful groups of nations take comfort from our present course—both sides overburdened by the cost of modern weapons, both rightly alarmed by the steady spread of the deadly atom, yet both racing to alter that uncertain balance of terror that stays the hand of mankind's final war.

14 So let us begin anew—remembering on both sides that civility is not a sign of weakness, and sincerity is always subject to proof. Let us never negotiate out of fear. But let us never fear to negotiate.

15 Let both sides explore what problems unite us instead of belaboring those problems which divide us.

16 Let both sides, for the first time, formulate serious and precise

proposals for the inspection and control of arms—and bring the absolute power to destroy other nations under the absolute control of all nations.

17 Let both sides seek to invoke the wonders of science instead of its terrors. Together let us explore the stars, conquer the deserts, eradicate disease, tap the ocean depths, and encourage the arts and commerce.

18 Let both sides unite to heed in all corners of the earth the command of Isaiah—to "undo the heavy burdens . . . [and] let the oppressed go free."

19 And if a beachhead of cooperation may push back the jungle of suspicion, let both sides join in creating a new endeavor, not a new balance of power, but a new world of law, where the strong are just and the weak secure and the peace preserved.

20 All this will not be finished in the first one hundred days. Nor will it be finished in the first one thousand days, nor in the life of this Administration, nor even perhaps in our lifetime on this planet. But let us begin.

21 In your hands, my fellow citizens, more than mine, will rest the final success or failure of our course. Since this country was founded, each generation of Americans has been summoned to give testimony to its national loyalty. The graves of young Americans who answered the call to service surround the globe.

22 Now the trumpet summons us again—not as a call to bear arms, though arms we need—not as a call to battle, though embattled we are—but a call to bear the burden of a long twilight struggle, year in and year out, "rejoicing in hope, patient in tribulation"— a struggle against the common enemies of man: tyranny, poverty, disease, and war itself.

23 Can we forge against these enemies a grand and global alliance, North and South, East and West, that can assure a more fruitful life for all mankind? Will you join in that historic effort?

24 In the long history of the world, only a few generations have been granted the role of defending freedom in its hour of maximum danger. I do not shrink from responsibility—I welcome it. I do not believe that any of us would exchange places with any other people or any other generation. The energy, the faith, the devotion which we bring to this endeavor will light our country and all who serve it—and the glow from that fire can truly light the world.

25 And so, my fellow Americans: ask not what your country can do for you—ask what you can do for your country.

26 My fellow citizens of the world: ask not what America will do for you, but what together we can do for the freedom of man.

27 Finally, whether you are citizens of America or citizens of the world, ask of us here the same high standards of strength and sacri-

fice which we ask of you. With a good conscience our only sure reward, with history the final judge of our deeds, let us go forth to lead the land we love, asking His blessing and His help, but knowing that here on earth God's work must truly be our own.

Thinking Questions: *Form*

1. Classical rhetoricians said that every speech should make three successful appeals—a *logical* appeal to the minds and rational faculties of an audience, an *emotional* appeal to the feelings and senses of an audience, an *ethical* appeal to the audience's moral beliefs and feelings. Can you find instances of all three appeals in John Kennedy's address? Consider, for example, sentences such as those below. What particular appeals or appeal are they emphasizing?

   a. Finally, whether you are citizens of America or citizens of the world, ask of us here the same high standards of strength and sacrifice which we ask of you. (Paragraph 27)

   b. In the long history of the world, only a few generations have been granted the role of defending freedom in its hour of maximum danger. (Paragraph 24)

   c. All this will not be finished in the first one hundred days. (Paragraph 20)

   d. But neither can two great and powerful groups of nations take comfort from our present course—both sides overburdened by the cost of modern weapons, both rightly alarmed by the steady spread of the deadly atom, yet both racing to alter that uncertain balance of terror that stays the hand of mankind's final war. (Paragraph 13)

   e. To those old allies whose cultural and spiritual origins we share, we pledge the loyalty of faithful friends. (Paragraph 6)

2. The *New Yorker* magazine published a laudatory response to Kennedy's speech in which they said that Kennedy had emphasized emotional appeal over all others (see *New Yorker*, Feb. 4, 1961, pp. 23-24). Do you agree? If you do, why do you think Kennedy would make his Inaugural Address primarily emotional in appeal? If you do not agree with the editors of the *New Yorker*, what appeals do you think *are* emphasized in the speech?

3. John Kennedy uses a ceremonious, grand style to fit a ceremonious, grand situation. What *makes* his style grand? He does *not* use many big or learned words; he *does* use a number of short sentences; his reasoning is *never* exaggeratedly complex or ornate. You might want to read the rhetorical essay at the end of this section for definitions and examples of some of the techniques a writer might use to create a grand style. In any case, consider the use of *figurative language*—Kennedy's metaphors include a torch, a beachhead, jungles, a trumpet, a tiger, a twilight, chains—and *personification*—giving inanimate objects or ideas a human quality, as

in "yet both racing to alter that uncertain balance of terror *that stays the hand of mankind's final war.*"

4. Compare Kennedy's sentences with Jim Murray's. How are they different—in length, in word order, in parallelism and balance, in the way they build up emotional and logical appeals by linking generalities, opinions, and facts?

5. Speakers at ceremonious occasions always face the problem of extremes: they can become too general and clichéd because they do not want to offend anyone, or they can chance losing an audience by using very specific and elaborate arguments and appeals which normal listeners cannot possibly follow. Does Kennedy keep an effective balance between the complex and the inane, the esoteric and the clichéd? Does he ever sound like a trite and bragging politician? Are any of his metaphors tired and conventional (consider "the chains of poverty" in paragraph 9)?

Thinking Questions: *Substance*

1. Kennedy, both directly and indirectly, bases his speech on several important values. Make a list of these values and show how each section of the speech depends on their acceptance.

2. Throughout this address Kennedy establishes an opposition between power and benevolence, between the ability to inflict harm and the ability to offer help: "For man holds in his mortal hands the power to abolish all forms of human poverty and all forms of human life" (paragraph 2). How does Kennedy want people to work out this opposition during his administration? How, for example, does he suggest that force and generosity might be applied equally in our relations with foreign countries?

3. Does this speech call for change? If so, what specific kinds of change? Does, for example, Kennedy wish to alter the shared cultural and spiritual origins of America (see paragraphs 3 and 6)? Does he want to change beliefs and assumptions, or does he want people to change the ways they live out and support those beliefs and assumptions?

4. One of the most prominent criticisms of the Vietnam War was that America was trying and failing to help another, smaller country help itself (see paragraph 8). These critics argued that larger and more powerful countries had no right to interfere in the governing of smaller countries, even if they felt that other larger countries had interfered in the first place. As you read over Kennedy's entire speech, would you agree that the kind of thinking displayed in this Inaugural Address might have led to our involvement in Vietnam? Do you think the address justifies our intervention in the affairs of other small nations, when and if we feel their rights and dignity are being threatened by other nations?

5. Look closely at the final five or six paragraphs of this speech (paragraphs 23 through 27). These brief, balanced statements are Kennedy's attempt to move people to action. What particular kinds of actions, as you look back over the speech, would be necessary to achieve the ends that are mentioned earlier?

Fathers for Moral America

ART BUCHWALD

1 There has been a great deal written about an organization called Mothers for Moral America. The Mothers organization had planned to put a "moral decay" film on television which showed the worst aspect of American life, from topless bathing suits to pornographic literature. At the last minute the film was withdrawn.

2 Another organization has just been started, called Fathers for Moral America, which is also concerned with moral decay in the United States.

3 When I visited its headquarters the other day, a spokesman for the organization told me, "The mothers have done so much to point out the decadent aspects of the United States that we felt the fathers should help out, too."

4 "What do you do?"

"We have a screening room in the back where we show dirty movies every two hours. We want to alert the fathers of America to the terrible degeneration that is going on in the United States. The response has been heartwarming. Ever since we started the screenings, there hasn't been an empty seat in the house."

5 "What has been the reaction?"

"The majority of them leave shocked that things like this could be happening in this country, and many come back a second time because they can't believe it."

6 "What else do you do?"

"At luncheon every day we hold a fashion show at which we display the latest topless bathing suits which have been put on the market.

7 "We want the fathers to know just exactly how far this nation has slipped, and, believe me, once they see the models in the topless bathing suits, they never forget it."

8 "It must be terrible to see," I said.

"I've seen men so horrified they have refused to eat their lunch."

9 "What else have you done to show the deterioration in American morals?"

"We have a reading room over there where we display the latest collection of salacious books and magazines. Any indignant father can go in there and see the type of literature that is being peddled around the country."

10 "The room seems very crowded," I said.

"It is one of the most popular exhibits. Many fathers have requested permission to take the books home, but we're afraid we'd have trouble getting them back. Some of the stuff would make your hair stand on end."

11 I walked into the reading room and noticed many of the fathers' hair standing up straight.

12 My guide took me out into the hall. "This is our souvenir counter where we sell photographs and slides of the different burlesque queens. We've been urging fathers to show them at home and at smokers to illustrate what we're up against. We also sell twist records and French postcards as part of our educational program."

13 "It seems to be doing well," I commented.

"You would be surprised how many alarmed fathers have offered to help in this great crusade."

14 My guide took me upstairs. "This is our telephone center. We have father volunteers who tell anyone who calls in what to watch for on television or at their local theatres, and what books to read. This is one of the best ways of getting our story over to the American people."

15 "I'm emotionally impressed with your great work," I said. "When does the next movie go on?"

Thinking Questions: *Form*

1. Point out occasions where Buchwald uses platitudes and clichés to ridicule the fathers. Nothing sounds so ridiculous as a supposedly high moral sentiment or ideal in a situation where the reader knows that the person offering the sentiment really believes or feels the opposite of what he or she says. And nothing is more monotonous and dull than a person who uses a saying that has been repeated a thousand times to make what he or she believes is an important point.

2. Try creating your own satire by having a character use the highly serious and ceremonious language of John Kennedy's Inaugural Address in a context that obviously does *not* call for such language.

3. Apply Buchwald's parody to American society in general. Put his implied thesis into your own words. Is his thesis applicable, in some degree or another, to a variety of causes espoused by a variety of people? Could you write a similar satire of one of these other groups, picking one character to represent the entire group and having that character reveal inconsistencies in the cause in the same ways that Buchwald's representative "father" reveals his group's hypocrisy?

4. Where do you find satire by exaggeration in this article? Does the exaggeration work, or do you feel that Buchwald's exaggerations are too absurd to make a serious criticism?

Thinking Questions: ***Substance***

1. Just what does Art Buchwald ridicule in his satire of the Fathers for Moral America? What particular inconsistencies and hypocrisies do the fathers display? Why do people often cover up what they really want to do with serious-sounding moral pronouncements like "We want to alert the fathers of America to the terrible degeneration that is going on in the United States"?

2. Can you think of other reactionary groups that have espoused causes like that of the Fathers of Moral America? Point out the inconsistency in their "causes."

3. Do you think that hypocritically supported moral causes such as these actually weaken the collective morality of an entire nation? Is there such a phenomena as "collective morality"? Do you believe Buchwald describes an exaggerated parallel to Woody Hayes's "expediency" as Jim Murray describes it in "New Leaf for Woody"? Might a football coach who abruptly changes his code seem almost as hypocritical to some people as an "outraged" father who stays to watch a pornographic film a second time?

4. Compare Cecelia Holland's explicit criticism of the under-thirty generation with Art Buchwald's satire of over-thirty fathers. Is Holland's specific criticism of young people—that they, too, are conforming to an oversimplified code when they say that everyone in the Establishment is corrupt—similar to or different from Buchwald's implied criticism of the Fathers for Moral America? What are the moral assumptions underlying both criticisms?

* * *

MORE ON MORALITY IN AMERICA

In the following four essays, we hear distinctly different voices addressing specific moral wrongs in contemporary America. William Buckley, editor of the conservative *National Review* and a widely-read national political columnist, attacks what he believes are the extremes of popular music in "How I Came to Rock." Buckley satirizes, in a sophisticated and erudite tone, the simplistic hero worship and "noise" he finds associated with rock music, whether he is speaking with promoters, performers, or fans. Throughout his essay, Buckley suggests that rock music is symptomatic of a much more widespread chaos and confusion in the fields of art and music, indeed, in our entire culture.

George Jackson and Martin Luther King, two black writers espousing social causes, give us very serious and forceful appeals to moral righteousness. George Jackson spent more than ten years in California prisons for a crime he committed in adolescence. In prison, both because of individuals like Angela Davis and other leaders in the black revolutionary movements and because of his own intense and widespread reading in political theory and radical literature, Jackson came to believe that he and other black and poor prisoners had been victimized by a system that kept wealth and education for the few while it excluded the masses from wealth and social mobility. Jackson speaks as a disciplined, militaristic leader of fellow black prisoners, engaging in hunger strikes and, occasionally, in outright physical force to achieve what he believed he and his companions deserved. In his letter to Angela Davis, Jackson speaks of continuing his struggle even after his release from prison. He was killed by guards in a prison uprising in 1971, relatively shortly after this letter was written.

Notice how Jackson's harsh tone matches his disciplined life-style. He speaks as a tough, assured revolutionary, yet mixes his hard-nosed assertions with sensitive and romantic asides to his lover. What kind of general image does this letter create? Would Jackson prove a difficult person to get along with? Why?

Compare Martin Luther King's more moderate and reasoned tone with Jackson's. Remember the differences in their audiences: both men are in prison, but King sends his letter to a group of white clergymen who have opposed his recent participation in a nonviolent demonstration and sit-in in support of integration in the Birmingham, Alabama, schools. King, always an advocate of nonviolent civil disobedience in support of black civil rights, combines moral pleading—"You deplore the demonstrations taking place in Birmingham. But your statement, I am sorry to say, fails to express a similar concern for the conditions that brought about the demonstrations" (paragraph 5)—and moral outrage and direct assertion—"Things are different now. So often the contemporary church is a weak, ineffectual voice with an uncertain sound" (paragraph 41). His strategy is to raise moral consciousness and then to incite nonviolent moral action; George Jackson's strategy is to state moral wrongs and to shore up for eventual moral battle.

Both Jackson and King, like the other essayists in this section, speak out against what they believe are injustices in established custom or belief. They speak in seriousness, in the tones of men committed to social change. As you read, ask yourself whether the criticisms that Cecelia Holland, Art Buchwald, and William Buckley level against contemporary social trends and causes could be justifiably used against George Jackson and Martin Luther King. Do Jackson and King seem deeply committed, or are they, too, merely striving to support a popular cause *because* it is popular? Base your answers on the writings in this section, *not* on what you know of these writers from other sources.

William Faulkner, in his speech accepting the Nobel Prize for literature, returns us to the tone of a highly serious public ceremony—similar to that of Kennedy's Inaugural Address. But Faulkner writes differently than Jackson and King in another important way. His address tells us that serious writers, especially serious writers of fiction, should never allow immediate social causes to dominate their writings. The novelist's job is to get at the truth through re-creating, in all its complexity, what he perceives through his senses and imagination.

This section began by raising questions about the substance and integrity of those who espouse popular causes. But as we read on, we discover that the *how* and *why* of morality usually depends on the individuals who ask the questions. How a person sounds when he or she writes, how thoroughly they examine the problems before them, and how carefully they address a specific audience—these questions of technique and know-how are often our best gauges of a writer's deeper moral integrity. We believe in those writers who know themselves, their subjects, and their audiences well. We tend to agree with those who probe deeply and give us the results of their probing in clear and committed prose.

How I Came to Rock

WILLIAM F. BUCKLEY, JR.

August 24, 1968

1 I speak for those who have had difficulty cultivating a convincing admiration for the popular culture of the rockers, foremost among them, of course, the Beatles.

2 Those who were not born into the movement can usually remember their first experience with it. Mine is vivid. I first remember engaging rock on learning years ago that a Mr. Alan Freed (1) was very famous; (2) was generally credited with launching the new musical form; and (3) had bought the house a couple of dwellings down from my own in the country; whence (4) he was broadcasting three hours daily as a network disc jockey.

3 He and his wife came calling one day. It was late on a summer afternoon, and I had been up the night before, and my mind wandered as he talked about this and whatever. My watchful wife managed,

unnoticed, to nudge me. I jerked back into consciousness and, fumbling for something apposite to say, ventured with, "Tell me, Mr. Freed, do you know Elvis Presley?" This elicited from my wife a shaft of social despair such as to make me feel that I had just asked Mr. Gilbert whether he had ever heard of Mr. Sullivan. Alan Freed, upon recovering, explained to me that he had *discovered* Elvis. I couldn't think what was appropriate to say under the circumstances, but, having to say something, I asked, "Is he nice?" "Is he nice!" Freed responded, clearly indicating that I had moved from ignorance into idiocy. "Why, do you know, he makes *ten times* as much as I make, and *he* calls *me sir!"*—he slapped me on the knee, so that I might share with him the full force of the paradoxes of life. I had, by that time, come to and was now a working member of the band. I knew—I have a sense, baby, for that kind of thing, only just warm me up—I know where to go from there, and all those bits and pieces of information I had run across in years of traversing the newspapers and magazines since first the phenomenon had occurred focused into the question which was totally to redeem my previous ineptitudes: "But will the rock and roll movement last?" My guest was made a happy man. He answered that question as lustily as the evangelist being asked whether God exists. Will it last! Why, he said, I must have appeared on one million panel discussions where they asked me just that question, and I told them all, I told them, rock and roll is here not just for a month or two, not like Davy Crockett and hoola hoops, it's here *forever*. What was my opinion? he asked dutifully. I don't know, I said, I've never heard it. He told me numbly that the next day he was giving a party, down the road at his house, celebrating an anniversary, and Fats Domino and his orchestra were going to play, and would I like to hear some real rock. Indeed I would, I said; and we strolled over, my wife and I, not at the hour of seven, as suggested, but at ten, knowing the likely length of the preliminaries; but when we got there, we found Fats and his entire group, fully clothed, in the swimming pool, their instruments somehow unavailing. But Mr. Freed, still shaken by my question of the night before, was clearly concerned that I should not arrive at the impression that here was a sign of the deliquescence of the art: "Don't you forget it," he said—only a few months before being indicted for provoking to riot by musical orgy, and a very few years before his sad, unrhythmical death—"Rock is here to stay." He was, of course, right.

4 And he had persuaded me to make a serious effort. I spent an evening—a very short evening—listening to one part of my son's collection. I found the noise quite scandalous. I remember a critic, writing for *National Review* after seeing Mr. Presley writhe his way through one of Ed Sullivan's shows, remarking that an extrapolation from the demure bumps and grinds of Frank Sinatra, on to the

orgiastic b's and g's of Elvis Presley, suggested that future entertainers would have to wrestle with live octopuses in order to entertain a mass American audience. The Beatles don't in fact do this, I observed at the end of that brain-rattling evening, but how one wishes they did, and how this listener wishes the octopus would win. I proceeded to write a most unfortunate judgment. "Let me say as evidence of my final measure of devotion to the truth," said I in a newspaper column, "the Beatles are not merely awful, I would consider it sacrilegious to say anything less than that they are God-awful. They are so unbelievably horrible, so appallingly unmusical, so dogmatically insensitive to the magic of the art, that they qualify as the crowned heads of antimusic."

5 The response was, to say the least, emphatic. I received more than 500 letters denouncing—not my musical judgment, or my stodginess, or my Philistinism—but my infidelity. To manifest truth and beauty, I picked out one letter to reply to, because I found it so wonderfully direct, and eloquent. "Dear Mr. Buckley," the young lady wrote from San Francisco, "you are a ratty, lousy, stinky, crummy idiot. P.S. You are too crummy to be called a person." After an exchange of four or five progressively amiable letters, I came upon the final effusiveness of the human spirit. It was Christmastime, and my new girlfriend sent me, by registered mail, a square inch of white cloth. She explained that it was exactly 50 percent of her entire holdings in life, since she had sold or mortgaged everything in order to participate at a public auction the week before. She had been able to bid for only two square inches of the sheet on which Ringo Starr had slept while at the St. Francis Hotel. Thus did the Lord melt the heart of the pharaoh.

6 I mean, how can one prevail against them? The answer is: One cannot. And even if they are hard to listen to, there is an exuberance there that is quite unmatched anywhere else in the world. Imagine a group calling itself the Peanut Butter Conspiracy! You figure it can't ever be beaten, and the next day you run into the Strawberry Alarm Clock. And then you see the peace feelers. Truman Capote in *Playboy,* telling us that the young popular musicians are the most creative people around. Ditto, of course, such youth watchers as Jack Newfield. *Time* magazine, relenting, puts the Beatles on the cover. Suddenly one day, riding in the back of the car, you look up, startled. That was *music* you just heard, blaring out of the radio. It's gone now, but not long after, you hear it again. And soon, like the ordeal of Gilbert Pinfold, it is coming in regularly, from everywhere. And you realize, finally, that, indeed, rock is here to stay.

Thinking Questions: *Form*

1. Like Art Buchwald, William Buckley uses numerous examples of rhetorical irony, as in the following sentences describing a series of letters written by a young admirer of the Beatles: "To manifest truth and beauty, I picked out one letter to reply to, because I found it so wonderfully direct, and eloquent. 'Dear Mr. Buckley,' the young lady wrote from San Francisco, 'you are a ratty, lousy, stinky, crummy idiot. P.S. You are too crummy to be called a person'" (see paragraph 5). Obviously Buckley finds the letter neither "eloquent" nor an example of "truth and beauty." Find other examples where Buckley uses a word or phrase in a context where the reader knows the writer means the opposite of what he says. Do you enjoy reading Buckley because of his irony, or do you find his attempts at irony and wit exaggerated and representative of a man in love with himself rather than with the truth?

2. Consider the irony of Buckley's title. *Has* Buckley really come to appreciate and enjoy rock music himself? To whom do you believe Buckley has written his essay? Does he really want to change anyone's opinions about rock music, or is he writing primarily for those who already agree with him and merely wish to enjoy his clever ridicule of his subject?

3. Analyze Buckley's description of Alan Freed (paragraphs 2 and 3). What character traits and bits of concrete description does Buckley emphasize? How do these traits and details contribute to his overall ridicule of Alan Freed and all that he represents?

4. Do you find any logical leaps or breakdown in the reasoning pattern of Buckley's essay? Buckley shifts, for example, from a criticism of rock music itself to a criticism of rock fans and the performers whom they adore. Do these shifts bother you, or do you feel that Buckley is justified because he did not intend to write a rational argument in the first place?

Thinking Questions: *Substance*

1. Notice the similarities in theme and form in Buchwald's and Buckley's essays. Both writers ridicule by setting up simple-minded characters whom the writer then interviews to establish the lack of quality in the causes or movements these characters represent. Both Buckley and Buchwald choose to satirize popular movements that they believe represent the deterioration of thought in our culture. What are some of the *differences* between the two writers' techniques and ideas?

2. Does Buckley ever give satisfying and convincing reasons for his dislike of rock music? Does he ever attempt to appeal to his reader's ability to analyze the reasons behind his opinions?

3. Can you come up with substantive arguments against Buckley's attitude toward rock music? *Is* it "noisy"? Does rock music ever approach serious music in quality? Are there gradations of talent in rock music, just as there are in serious music? Might there be good reason *not* to

evaluate musical quality in popular music, but rather to find and analyze why the music *is* popular?

4. Does William Buckley really want to give his subject and its proponent, Alan Freed, a fair trial? Why or why not? Who or what *is* the subject of this essay—William F. Buckley, Jr., or Alan Freed?

A Letter to Angela Davis

GEORGE JACKSON

George Jackson spent over ten years in Soledad Prison in southern California for assault and armed robbery. During that time he began to discuss and read Karl Marx, Che Guevara, and many black socialists and gradually adapted his personal frustration and anger into a code of beliefs fitted to a broader social context. Angela Davis, then a member of the American Communist Party and a California college teacher, helped Jackson in his legal defense while she also assisted him in his reading and self-education. Jackson spent much of his prison time in solitary confinement; his quiet resentment of the entire prison system kept him from parole. He was ultimately killed in a gun battle between guards and prisoners at Soledad in 1971. This letter expresses Jackson's growing feeling of black pride and his education in socialism. It also reflects his moral outrage at bigotry, the social repression of blacks, and the suppression of the poor—forces that led him to develop a strict revolutionary's code of behavior. His last years were spent in rigorous physical and mental discipline, exercising in his cell to keep fit, voraciously reading revolutionary literature to keep mentally prepared, and generally getting ready for what he hoped would be an imminent social upheaval.

May 29, 1970

Dearest Angela,

1 I'm thinking about you. I've done nothing else all day. This photograph that I have of you is not adequate. Do you recall what Eldridge said regarding pictures for the cell?[1] Give Frances several color enlargements for me. This is the cruelest aspect of the prison experience. You can never understand how much I hate them for this, no one could, I haven't been able to gauge it myself.

2 Over this ten years I've never left my cell in the morning looking for trouble, never once have I initiated any violence. In each case

1. Eldridge Cleaver, author of *Soul on Ice*, was, like George Jackson, a prisoner who became involved in the black movement during the 1960s. He is still a symbol of the repressed black man in America and continues to write and work for social change.

where it was alleged, it was defense/attack response to some aggression, verbal or physical. Perhaps a psychiatrist, a Western psychiatrist that is, could make a case against me for anticipating attacks. But I wasn't born this way. Perhaps this same psychiatrist would diagnose from the overreactions that I am not a very nice person. But again I refer you to the fact that I was born innocent and trusting. The instinct to survive and all that springs from it developed in me as it is today out of necessity.

3 I am not a very nice person, I confess. I don't believe in such things as free speech when it's used to rob and defame me. I don't believe in mercy or forgiveness or restraint. I've gone to great lengths to learn every dirty trick devised and have improvised some new ones of my own. I don't play fair, don't fight fair. As I think of this present situation, the things that happen all day, the case they've saddled me with, in retrospection of the aggregate injury—all now drawn against the background of this picture you've given me—no one will profit from this, sister. No one will ever again profit from our pain. This is the last treadmill I'll rún. They created this situation. All that flows from it is their responsibility. They've created in me one irate, resentful nigger—and it's building—to what climax? The nation's undertakers have grown wealthy on black examples, but I want you to believe in me, Angela. I'm going to make a very poor example, no one will profit from my immolation. When that day comes they'll have to bury ten thousand of their own with full military honors. They'll have earned it.

4 Do you sense how drunk this photograph has made me?

5 You've got it all, African woman. I'm very pleased, if you don't ask me for my left arm, my right eye, both eyes, I'll be very disappointed. You're the most powerful stimulus I could have.

6 From now on when you have books for me to read in preparing my motions and jury selection questions, send them through John Thorne, people's lawyer, he is less pressed. And I do want Lenin, Marx, Mao, Che, Giap, Uncle Ho, Nkrumah, and any Black Marxists. Mama has a list. Tell Robert to provide money for them, and always look for the pocket editions, all right? My father—you'll have to try to understand him. He'll be with me in the last days in spite of whatever he says and thinks now. I've told him that I love you, and I told him that if he respects me at all, and wants me to spare his neck at Armageddon, he must be kind to you.

7 I got a letter from him this evening wherein he called the pigs by their very accurate moniker—pigs—he'll be all right. I see your influence already. But back to the books. With each load of heavy stuff throw in a reference book dealing with pure fact, figures, statistics, graphs for my further education. Also books on the personnel and structure of today's political, military, and economic front. I am doing

some serious theory work for you concerning the case, dedicated to Huey and Angela.[2] If you understand what I want, let me know. Sister, it's been like being held incommunicado these last ten years. No one understood what I was attempting to do and to say. We belong among the righteous of the world. We are the most powerful. We are in the best position to do the people's work. To win will involve taking a chance, crawling on the belly, naming, numbering, infiltrating, giving up meaningless small comforts, readjusting some values. My life means absolutely nothing without positive control over the factors that determine its quality. If you understand, rush to send all that I've asked for. A load should come in each day. I've read it all, once anyway, but I need it now . . . and time has become very important. I want you to believe in me. I love you like a man, like a brother, and like a father. Every time I've opened my mouth, assumed my battle stance, I was trying in effect to say I love you, African—African woman. My protest has been a small one, something much more effective is hidden in my mind—believe in me, Angela. This is one nigger who's got some sense and is not afraid to use it. If my enemies, your enemies, prove stronger, at least I want them to know that they made one righteous African man extremely angry. And that they've strained the patience of a righteous and loving people to the utmost.

8 I've stopped several times in this writing to exercise, to eat, and it has grown late. I want to get this off tonight. I must know as soon as you get this and the others. Are you sure about your mail? I can imagine that the CIA is reading all your mail before you get it and deciding what you should and shouldn't have. Big Brother. He is rather transparent. I don't care about him. I have his number. I know he's a punk, he can't stop me.

9 Should we make a lovers' vow? It's silly, with all my tomorrows accounted for, but you can humor me.

10 Power to the People!

George

---

2. Huey Newton was a leader in the Black Power movement in the late 1960s. He was arrested, tried, and eventually acquitted for the murder of a white Oakland policeman. He continues to work in the black movement today.

Thinking Questions: *Form*

1. George Jackson strives to achieve a very difficult and complex tone. On the one hand, he vents his hatred against the ruling establishment in a hard, tough, even violent, voice; he promises retribution to those among his readers who are on the "other side." On the other hand, however, he takes on a lover's voice when he addresses Angela Davis, making valiant promises, directly proclaiming his love and allegiance. Do you find this two-sided tone successful? Are you convinced of both the power and the sensitivity of the writer?

2. Is Jackson's letter written in the plain, middle, or grand style? Look closely at his diction and sentence structure as you answer. Where does Jackson's letter sound a bit like John Kennedy's Inaugural Address, although the subject is much different? Where does the letter sound more like Cecelia Holland's tough, argumentative essay on young people? Which style predominates and why?

3. Is the appeal in Jackson's letter predominantly emotional, ethical, or rational? Does Jackson most wish his reader to think, feel, or believe in him? What in the language and form of the letter suggests your answer?

4. Jackson uses very little figurative language (see John Kennedy's address as an obvious contrast). Why does Jackson avoid metaphors and extended comparisons? Why might he think that such devices would lessen the power and forcefulness of his writing, at least in the situation in which *he* writes?

5. Does paragraph 9—"Should we make a lover's vow? It's silly, with all my tomorrows accounted for, but you can humor me"—help Jackson's ethical appeal in this letter? Does he seem more human, less the hard-nosed revolutionary machine, after that paragraph?

Thinking Questions: *Substance*

1. Notice how love and hatred mix in this letter. Toward whom does Jackson direct his hatred and why? Do you feel, even from such a short letter, that Jackson's hatred is justified? *Was* he born "innocent and trusting"? Toward whom does he direct his love and why?

2. Consider Jackson's statement that "This is the last treadmill I'll run. They created this situation. All that flows from it is their responsibility. They've created in me one irate, resentful nigger—and it's building—to what climax?" (paragraph 3). Who are "they"? Has Jackson mentioned any explicit examples of the cruelty of prison officials earlier in the letter? Do you believe Jackson could be justified in saying that he "is not a very nice person" because of the pressures put on him by his society?

3. Do you believe it would be just to ridicule George Jackson's cause in a manner similar to the way Art Buchwald ridicules the hypocritical Fathers for Moral America? What differences are there between the two? Consider their situations, backgrounds, race, and any other factors that might affect your response to them. Then also consider how they present

their views. Who sounds more convincing and why? Who probes more deeply into the problem he is discussing?

4. Would Cecelia Holland include George Jackson in her criticism of young people? Remember Holland's main criticism is of the *thinking patterns*, the tendency to oversimplify and conform to set patterns of thought, not the *ages* of young people in the late sixties. Would she find Jackson's reasoning just as oversimplified and narrow as the young people she criticizes in her essay?

5. What do you suppose George Jackson would have said about John Kennedy's Inaugural Address, its powerful and formal language, its pleas for a cooperative venture to save the poor at home and abroad, its plea for strength *and* gentleness?

Letter from Birmingham Jail

MARTIN LUTHER KING, JR.

Dr. Martin Luther King, Jr., led many nonviolent civil rights protests in the 1950s and 1960s as head of the Southern Christian Leadership Council. He was a powerful and grand speaker whose eloquence contributed greatly to the growth of the civil rights movement in those decades.

In this letter, written in 1963 in a Birmingham jail, King explains to a group of white clergymen why he believed it necessary to use nonviolent disruption to make people give more attention to the plight of blacks in Birmingham and throughout the South. Many of King's immediate goals were achieved shortly after the demonstration and writing of this letter, although many black leaders believe that the deeper prejudices and bigotry of Americans are yet to be abolished. Martin Luther King was assassinated in 1968 by James Earl Ray, a white sniper, in a Memphis motel. He continues to be referred to as a central motivating figure in nonviolent, civil rights protest movements, especially within the Christian church.

April 16, 1963

My Dear Fellow Clergymen:

1 While confined here in the Birmingham city jail. I came across your recent statement calling my present activities "unwise and untimely." Seldom do I pause to answer criticism of my work and ideas. If I sought to answer all the criticisms that cross my desk, my secretaries would have little time for anything other than such correspondence in the course of the day, and I would have no time for constructive work. But since I feel that you are men of genuine good

will and that your criticisms are sincerely set forth, I want to try to answer your statement in what I hope will be patient and reasonable terms.

2 I think I should indicate why I am here in Birmingham, since you have been influenced by the view which argues against "outsiders coming in." I have the honor of serving as president of the Southern Christian Leadership Conference, an organization operating in every southern state, with headquarters in Atlanta, Georgia. We have some eighty-five affiliated organizations across the South, and one of them is the Alabama Christian Movement for Human Rights. Frequently we share staff, educational and financial resources with our affiliates. Several months ago the affiliate here in Birmingham asked us to be on call to engage in a nonviolent direct-action program if such were deemed necessary. We readily consented, and when the hour came we lived up to our promise. So I, along with several members of my staff, am here because I was invited here. I am here because I have organizational ties here.

3 But more basically, I am in Birmingham because injustice is here. Just as the prophets of the eighth century B.C. left their villages and carried their "thus saith the Lord" far beyond the boundaries of their home towns, and just as the Apostle Paul left his village of Tarsus and carried the gospel of Jesus Christ to the far corners of the Greco-Roman world, so am I compelled to carry the gospel of freedom beyond my own home town. Like Paul, I must constantly respond to the Macedonian call for aid.

4 Moreover, I am cognizant of the interrelatedness of all communities and states. I cannot sit idly by in Atlanta and not be concerned about what happens in Birmingham. Injustice anywhere is a threat to justice everywhere. We are caught in an inescapable network of mutuality, tied in a single garment of destiny. Whatever affects one directly, affects all indirectly. Never again can we afford to live with the narrow, provincial "outside agitator" idea. Anyone who lives inside the United States can never be considered an outsider anywhere within its bounds.

5 You deplore the demonstrations taking place in Birmingham. But your statement, I am sorry to say, fails to express a similar concern for the conditions that brought about the demonstrations. I am sure that none of you would want to rest content with the superficial kind of social analysis that deals merely with effects and does not grapple with underlying causes. It is unfortunate that demonstrations are taking place in Birmingham, but it is even more unfortunate that the city's white power structure left the Negro community with no alternative.

6 In any nonviolent campaign there are four basic steps: collection of the facts to determine whether injustices exist; negotiation; self-

purification; and direct action. We have gone through all these steps in Birmingham. There can be no gainsaying the fact that racial injustice engulfs this community. Birmingham is probably the most thoroughly segregated city in the United States. Its ugly record of brutaliy is widely known. Negroes have experienced grossly unjust treatment in the courts. There have been more unsolved bombings of Negro homes and churches in Birmingham than in any other city in the nation. These are the hard, brutal facts of the case. On the basis of these conditions, Negro leaders sought to negotiate with the city fathers. But the latter consistently refused to engage in good-faith negotiation.

7 Then, last September, came the opportunity to talk with leaders of Birmingham's economic community. In the course of the negotiations, certain promises were made by the merchants—for example, to remove the stores' humiliating racial signs. On the basis of these promises, the Reverend Fred Shuttlesworth and the leaders of the Alabama Christian Movement for Human Rights agreed to a moratorium on all demonstrations. As the weeks and months went by, we realized that we were the victims of a broken promise. A few signs, briefly removed, returned; the others remained.

8 As in so many past experiences, our hopes had been blasted, and the shadow of deep disappointment settled upon us. We had no alternative except to prepare for direct action, whereby we would present our very bodies as a means of laying our case before the conscience of the local and the national community. Mindful of the difficulties involved, we decided to undertake a process of self-purification. We began a series of workshops on nonviolence, and we repeatedly asked ourselves: "Are you able to accept blows without retaliating?" "Are you able to endure the ordeal of jail?" We decided to schedule our direct-action program for the Easter season, realizing that except for Christmas, this is the main shopping period of the year. Knowing that a strong economic-withdrawal program would be the by-product of direct action, we felt that this would be the best time to bring pressure to bear on the merchants for the needed change.

9 Then it occurred to us that Birmingham's mayoralty election was coming up in March, and we speedily decided to postpone action until after election day. When we discovered that the Commissioner of Public Safety, Eugene "Bull" Connor, had piled up enough votes to be in the run-off, we decided again to postpone action until the day after the run-off so that the demonstrations could not be used to cloud the issues. Like many others, we waited to see Mr. Connor defeated, and to this end we endured postponement after postponement. Having aided in this community need, we felt that our direct-action program could be delayed no longer.

10 You may well ask: "Why direct action? Why sit-ins, marches and so forth? Isn't negotiation a better path?" You are quite right in calling for negotiation. Indeed, this is the very purpose of direct action. Nonviolent direct action seeks to create such a crisis and foster such a tension that a community which has constantly refused to negotiate is forced to confront the issue. It seeks so to dramatize the issue that it can no longer be ignored. My citing the creation of tension as part of the work of the nonviolent-resister may sound rather shocking. But I must confess that I am not afraid of the word "tension." I have earnestly opposed violent tension, but there is a type of constructive, nonviolent tension which is necessary for growth. Just as Socrates felt that it was necessary to create a tension in the mind so that individuals could rise from the bondage of myths and half-truths to the unfettered realm of creative analysis and objective appraisal, so must we see the need for nonviolent gadflies to create the kind of tension in society that will help men rise from the dark depths of prejudice and racism to the majestic heights of understanding and brotherhood.

11 The purpose of our direct-action program is to create a situation so crisis-packed that it will inevitably open the door to negotiation. I therefore concur with you in your call for negotiation. Too long has our beloved Southland been bogged down in a tragic effort to live in monologue rather than dialogue.

12 One of the basic points in your statement is that the action that I and my associates have taken in Birmingham is untimely. Some have asked: "Why didn't you give the new city administration time to act?" The only answer that I can give to this query is that the new Birmingham administration must be prodded about as much as the outgoing one, before it will act. We are sadly mistaken if we feel that the election of Albert Boutwell as mayor will bring the millennium to Birmingham. While Mr. Boutwell is a much more gentle person than Mr. Connor, they are both segregationists, dedicated to maintenance of the status quo. I have hope that Mr. Boutwell will be reasonable enough to see the futility of massive resistance to desegregation. But he will not see this without pressure from devotees of civil rights. My friends, I must say to you that we have not made a single gain in civil rights without determined legal and nonviolent pressure. Lamentably, it is an historical fact that privileged groups seldom give up their privileges voluntarily. Individuals may see the moral light and voluntarily give up their unjust posture; but, as Reinhold Niebuhr has reminded us, groups tend to be more immoral than individuals.

13 We know through painful experience that freedom is never voluntarily given by the oppressor; it must be demanded by the oppressed. Frankly, I have yet to engage in a direct-action campaign that was

"well timed" in the view of those who have not suffered unduly from the disease of segregation. For years now I have heard the word "Wait!" It rings in the ear of every Negro with piercing familiarity. This "Wait" has almost always meant "Never." We must come to see, with one of our distinguished jurists, that "justice too long delayed is justice denied."

14 We have waited for more than 340 years for our constitutional and God-given rights. The nations of Asia and Africa are moving with jet-like speed toward gaining political independence, but we still creep at horse-and-buggy pace toward gaining a cup of coffee at a lunch counter. Perhaps it is easy for those who have never felt the stinging darts of segregation to say, "Wait." But when you have seen vicious mobs lynch your mothers and fathers at will and drown your sisters and brothers at whim; when you have seen hate-filled policemen curse, kick and even kill your black brothers and sisters; when you see the vast majority of your twenty million Negro brothers smothering in an airtight cage of poverty in the midst of an affluent society; when you suddenly find your tongue twisted and your speech stammering as you seek to explain to your six-year-old daughter why she can't go to the public amusement park that has just been advertised on television, and see tears welling up in her eyes when she is told that Funtown is closed to colored children, and see ominous clouds of inferiority beginning to form in her little mental sky, and see her beginning to distort her personality by developing an unconscious bitterness toward white people; when you have to concoct an answer for a five-year-old son who is asking: "Daddy, why do white people treat colored people so mean?"; when you take a cross-country drive and find it necessary to sleep night after night in the uncomfortable corners of your automobile because no motel will accept you; when you are humiliated day in and day out by nagging signs reading "white" and "colored"; when your first name becomes "nigger," your middle name becomes "boy" (however old you are) and your last name becomes "John," and your wife and mother are never given the respected title "Mrs."; when you are harried by day and haunted by night by the fact that you are a Negro, living constantly at tiptoe stance, never quite knowing what to expect next, and are plagued with inner fears and outer resentments; when you are forever fighting a degenerating sense of "nobodiness"—then you will understand why we find it difficult to wait. There comes a time when the cup of endurance runs over, and men are no longer willing to be plunged into the abyss of despair. I hope, sirs, you can understand our legitimate and unavoidable impatience.

15 You express a great deal of anxiety over our willingness to break laws. This is certainly a legitimate concern. Since we so diligently urge people to obey the Supreme Court's decision of 1954 outlawing

segregation in the public schools, at first glance it may seem rather paradoxical for us consciously to break laws. One may well ask: "How can you advocate breaking some laws and obeying others?" The answer lies in the fact that there are two types of laws: just and unjust. I would be the first to advocate obeying just laws. One has not only a legal but a moral responsibility to obey just laws. Conversely, one has a moral responsibility to disobey unjust laws. I would agree with St. Augustine that "an unjust law is no law at all."

16 Now, what is the difference between the two? How does one determine whether a law is just or unjust? A just law is a man-made code that squares with the moral law or the law of God. An unjust law is a code that is out of harmony with the moral law. To put it in the terms of St. Thomas Aquinas: An unjust law is a human law that is not rooted in eternal law and natural law. Any law that uplifts human personality is just. Any law that degrades human personality is unjust. All segregation statutes are unjust because segregation distorts the soul and damages the personality. It gives the segregator a false sense of superiority and the segregated a false sense of inferiority. Segregation, to use the terminology of the Jewish philosopher Martin Buber, substitutes an "I—it" relationship for an "I—thou" relationship and ends up relegating persons to the status of things. Hence segregation is not only politically, economically and sociologically unsound, it is morally wrong and sinful. Paul Tillich has said that sin is separation. Is not segregation an existential expression of man's tragic separation, his awful estrangement, his terrible sinfulness? Thus it is that I can urge men to obey the 1954 decision of the Supreme Court, for it is morally right; and I can urge them to disobey segregation ordinances, for they are morally wrong.

17 Let us consider a more concrete example of just and unjust laws. An unjust law is a code that a numerical or power majority group compels a minority group to obey but does not make binding on itself. This is *difference* made legal. By the same token, a just law is a code that a majority compels a minority to follow and that it is willing to follow itself. This is *sameness* made legal.

18 Let me give another explanation. A law is unjust if it is inflicted on a minority that, as a result of being denied the right to vote, had no part in enacting or devising the law. Who can say that the legislature of Alabama which set up that state's segregation laws was democratically elected? Throughout Alabama all sorts of devious methods are used to prevent Negroes from becoming registered voters, and there are some counties in which, even though Negroes constitute a majority of the population, not a single Negro is registered. Can any law enacted under such circumstances be considered democratically structured?

19 Sometimes a law is just on its face and unjust in its application.

For instance, I have been arrested on a charge of parading without a permit. Now, there is nothing wrong in having an ordinance which requires a permit for a parade. But such an ordinance becomes unjust when it is used to maintain segregation and to deny citizens the First-Amendment privilege of peaceful assembly and protest.

20 I hope you are able to see the distinction I am trying to point out. In no sense do I advocate evading or defying the law, as would the rabid segregationist. That would lead to anarchy. One who breaks an unjust law must be so openly, lovingly, and with a willingness to accept the penalty. I submit that an individual who breaks a law that conscience tells him is unjust, and who willingly accepts the penalty of imprisonment in order to arouse the conscience of the community over its injustice, is in reality expressing the highest respect for law.

21 Of course, there is nothing new about this kind of civil disobedience. It was evidenced sublimely in the refusal of Shadrach, Meshach and Abednego to obey the laws of Nebuchadnezzar, on the ground that a higher moral law was at stake. It was practiced superbly by the early Christians, who were willing to face hungry lions and the excruciating pain of chopping blocks rather than submit to certain unjust laws of the Roman Empire. To a degree, academic freedom is a reality today because Socrates practiced civil disobedience. In our own nation, the Boston Tea Party represented a massive act of civil disobedience.

22 We should never forget that everything Adolf Hitler did in Germany was "legal" and everything the Hungarian freedom fighters did in Hungary was "illegal." It was "illegal" to aid and comfort a Jew in Hitler's Germany. Even so, I am sure that, had I lived in Germany at the time, I would have aided and comforted my Jewish brothers. If today I lived in a Communist country where certain principles dear to the Christian faith are suppressed, I would openly advocate disobeying that country's antireligious laws.

23 I must make two honest confessions to you, my Christian and Jewish brothers. First, I must confess that over the past few years I have been gravely disappointed with the white moderate. I have almost reached the regrettable conclusion that the Negro's great stumbling block in his stride toward freedom is not the White Citizen's Counciler or the Ku Klux Klanner, but the white moderate, who is more devoted to "order" than to justice; who prefers a negative peace which is the absence of tension to a positive peace which is the presence of justice; who constantly says: "I agree with you in the goal you seek, but I cannot agree with your methods of direct action"; who paternalistically believes he can set the timetable for another man's freedom; who lives by a mythical concept of time and who constantly advises the Negro to wait for a "more convenient

season." Shallow understanding from people of good will is more frustrating than absolute misunderstanding from people of ill will. Lukewarm acceptance is much more bewildering than outright rejection.

24 I had hoped that the white moderate would understand that law and order exist for the purpose of establishing justice and that when they fail in this purpose they become the dangerously structured dams that block the flow of social progress. I had hoped that the white moderate would understand that the present tension in the South is a necessary phase of the transition from an obnoxious negative peace, in which the Negro passively accepted his unjust plight, to a substantive and positive peace, in which all men will respect the dignity and worth of human personality. Actually, we who engage in nonviolent direct action are not the creators of tension. We merely bring to the surface the hidden tension that is already alive. We bring it out in the open, where it can be seen and dealt with. Like a boil that can never be cured so long as it is covered up but must be opened with all its ugliness to the natural medicines of air and light, injustice must be exposed, with all the tension its exposure creates, to the light of human conscience and the air of national opinion before it can be cured.

25 In your statement you assert that our actions, even though peaceful, must be condemned because they precipitate violence. But is this a logical assertion? Isn't this like condemning a robbed man because his possession of money precipitated the evil act of robbery? Isn't this like condemning Socrates because his unswerving commitment to truth and his philosophical inquiries precipitated the act by the misguided populace in which they made him drink hemlock? Isn't this like condemning Jesus because his unique God-consciousness and never-ceasing devotion to God's will precipitated the evil act of crucifixion? We must come to see that, as the federal courts have consistently affirmed, it is wrong to urge an individual to cease his efforts to gain his basic constitutional rights because the quest may precipitate violence. Society must protect the robbed and punish the robber.

26 I had also hoped that the white moderate would reject the myth concerning time in relation to the struggle for freedom. I have just received a letter from a white brother in Texas. He writes: "All Christians know that the colored people will receive equal rights eventually, but it is possible that you are in too great a religious hurry. It has taken Christianity almost two thousand years to accomplish what it has. The teachings of Christ take time to come to earth." Such an attitude stems from a tragic misconception of time, from the strangely irrational notion that there is something in the very flow of time that will inevitably cure all ills. Actually, time itself

is neutral; it can be used either destructively or constructively. More and more I feel that the people of ill will have used time much more effectively than have the people of good will. We will have to repent in this generation not merely for the hateful words and actions of the bad people but for the appalling silence of the good people. Human progress never rolls in on wheels of inevitability; it comes through the tireless efforts of men willing to be co-workers with God, and without this hard work, time itself becomes an ally of the forces of social stagnation. We must use time creatively, in the knowledge that the time is always ripe to do right. Now is the time to make real the promise of democracy and transform our pending national elegy into a creative psalm of brotherhood. Now is the time to lift our national policy from the quicksand of racial injustice to the solid rock of human dignity.

27 You speak of our activity in Birmingham as extreme. At first I was rather disappointed that fellow clergymen would see my nonviolent efforts as those of an extremist. I began thinking about the fact that I stand in the middle of two opposing forces in the Negro community. One is a force of complacency, made up in part of Negroes who, as a result of long years of oppression, are so drained of self-respect and a sense of "somebodiness" that they have adjusted to segregation; and in part of a few middleclass Negroes who, because of a degree of academic and economic security and because in some ways they profit by segregation, have become insensitive to the problems of the masses. The other force is one of bitterness and hatred, and it comes perilously close to advocating violence. It is expressed in the various black nationalist groups that are springing up across the nation, the largest and best-known being Elijah Muhammad's Muslim movement. Nourished by the Negro's frustration over the continued existence of racial discrimination, this movement is made up of people who have lost faith in America, who have absolutely repudiated Christianity, and who have concluded that the white man is an incorrigible "devil."

28 I have tried to stand between these two forces, saying that we need emulate neither the "do-nothingism" of the complacent nor the hatred and despair of the black nationalist. For there is the more excellent way of love and nonviolent protest. I am grateful to God that, through the influence of the Negro church, the way of nonviolence became an integral part of our struggle.

29 If this philosophy had not emerged, by now many streets of the South would, I am convinced, be flowing with blood. And I am further convinced that if our white brothers dismiss as "rabble-rousers" and "outside agitators" those of us who employ nonviolent direct action, and if they refuse to support our nonviolent efforts, millions of Negroes will, out of frustration and despair, seek solace and security

in black-nationalist ideologies—a development that would inevitably lead to a frightening racial nightmare.

30 Oppressed people cannot remain oppressed forever. The yearning for freedom eventually manifests itself, and that is what has happened to the American Negro. Something within has reminded him of his birthright of freedom, and something without has reminded him that it can be gained. Consciously or unconsciously, he has been caught up by the *Zeitgeist,* and with his black brothers of Africa and his brown and yellow brothers of Asia, South America and the Caribbean, the United States Negro is moving with a sense of great urgency toward the promised land of racial justice. If one recognizes this vital urge that has engulfed the Negro community, one should readily understand why public demonstrations are taking place. The Negro has many pent-up resentments and latent frustrations, and he must release them. So let him march; let him make prayer pilgrimages to the city hall; let him go on freedom rides—and try to understand why he must do so. If his repressed emotions are not released in nonviolent ways, they will seek expression through violence; this is not a threat but a fact of history. So I have not said to my people: "Get rid of your discontent." Rather, I have tried to say that this normal and healthy discontent can be channeled into the creative outlet of nonviolent direct action. And now this approach is being termed extremist.

31 But though I was initially disappointed at being categorized as an extremist, as I continued to think about the matter I gradually gained a measure of satisfaction from the label. Was not Jesus an extremist for love: "Love your enemies, bless them that curse you, do good to them that hate you, and pray for them which despitefully use you, and persecute you." Was not Amos an extremist for justice: "Let justice roll down like waters and righteousness like an ever-flowing stream." Was not Paul an extremist for the Christian gospel: "I bear in my body the marks of the Lord Jesus." Was not Martin Luther an extremist: "Here I stand; I cannot do otherwise, so help me God." And John Bunyan: "I will stay in jail to the end of my days before I make a butchery of my conscience." And Abraham Lincoln: "This nation cannot survive half slave and half free." And Thomas Jefferson: "We hold these truths to be self-evident, that all men are created equal . . ." So the question is not whether we will be extremists, but what kind of extremists we will be. Will we be extremists for hate or for love? Will we be extremists for the preservation of injustice or for the extension of justice? In that dramatic scene on Calvary's hill three men were crucified. We must never forget that all three were crucified for the same crime—the crime of extremism. Two were extremists for immorality, and thus fell below their environment. The other, Jesus Christ, was an extremist for love, truth and

goodness, and thereby rose above his environment. Perhaps the South, the nation and the world are in dire need of creative extremists.

32 I had hoped that the white moderate would see this need. Perhaps I was too optimistic; perhaps I expected too much. I suppose I should have realized that few members of the oppressor race can understand the deep groans and passionate yearnings of the oppressed race, and still fewer have the vision to see that injustice must be rooted out by strong, persistent and determined action. I am thankful, however, that some of our white brothers in the South have grasped the meaning of this social revolution and committed themselves to it. They are still all too few in quantity, but they are big in quality. Some—such as Ralph McGill, Lillian Smith, Harry Golden, James McBride Dabbs, Ann Braden and Sarah Patton Boyle—have written about our struggle in eloquent and prophetic terms. Others have marched with us down nameless streets of the South. They have languished in filthy, roach-infested jails, suffering the abuse and brutality of policemen who view them as "dirty nigger-lovers." Unlike so many of their moderate brothers and sisters, they have recognized the urgency of the moment and sensed the need for powerful "action" antidotes to combat the disease of segregation.

33 Let me take note of my other major disappointment. I have been so greatly disappointed with the white church and its leadership. Of course, there are some notable exceptions. I am not unmindful of the fact that each of you has taken some significant stands on this issue. I commend you, Reverend Stallings, for your Christian stand on this past Sunday, in welcoming Negroes to your worship service on a nonsegregated basis. I commend the Catholic leaders of this state for integrating Spring Hill College several years ago.

34 But despite these notable exceptions, I must honestly reiterate that I have been disappointed with the church. I do not say this as one of those negative critics who can always find something wrong with the church. I say this as a minister of the gospel, who loves the church; who was nurtured in its bosom; who has been sustained by its spiritual blessings and who will remain true to it as long as the cord of life shall lengthen.

35 When I was suddenly catapulted into the leadership of the bus protest in Montgomery, Alabama, a few years ago, I felt we would be supported by the white church. I felt that the white ministers, priests and rabbis of the South would be among our strongest allies. Instead, some have been outright opponents, refusing to understand the freedom movement and misrepresenting its leaders; all too many others have been more cautious than courageous and have remained silent behind the anesthetizing security of stained-glass windows.

36 In spite of my shattered dreams, I came to Birmingham with the hope that the white religious leadership of this community would see

the justice of our cause and, with deep moral concern, would serve as the channel through which our just grievances could reach the power structure. I had hoped that each of you would understand. But again I have been disappointed.

37 I have heard numerous southern religious leaders admonish their worshipers to comply with a desegregation decision because it is the law, but I have longed to hear white ministers declare: "Follow this decree because integration is morally right and because the Negro is your brother." In the midst of blatant injustices inflicted upon the Negro, I have watched white churchmen stand on the sideline and mouth pious irrelevancies and sanctimonious trivialities. In the midst of a mighty struggle to rid our nation of racial and economic injustice, I have heard many ministers say: "Those are social issues, with which the gospel has no real concern." And I have watched many churches commit themselves to a completely other-worldly religion which makes a strange, un-Biblical distinction between body and soul, between the sacred and the secular.

38 I have traveled the length and breadth of Alabama, Mississippi and all the other southern states. On sweltering summer days and crisp autumn mornings I have looked at the South's beautiful churches with their lofty spires pointing heavenward. I have beheld the impressive outlines of her massive religious-education buildings. Over and over I have found myself asking: "What kind of people worship here? Who is their God? Where were their voices when the lips of Governor Barnett dripped with words of interposition and nullification? Where were they when Governor Wallace gave a clarion call for defiance and hatred? Where were their voices of support when bruised and weary Negro men and women decided to rise from the dark dungeons of complacency to the bright hills of creative protest?"

39 Yes, these questions are still in my mind. In deep disappointment I have wept over the laxity of the church. But be assured that my tears have been tears of love. There can be no deep disappointment where there is not deep love. Yes, I love the church. How could I do otherwise? I am in the rather unique position of being the son, the grandson and the great-grandson of preachers. Yes, I see the church as the body of Christ. But, oh! How we have blemished and scarred that body through social neglect and through fear of being nonconformists.

40 There was a time when the church was very powerful—in the time when the early Christians rejoiced at being deemed worthy to suffer for what they believed. In those days the church was not merely a thermometer that recorded the ideas and principles of popular opinion; it was a thermostat that transformed the mores of society. Whenever the early Christians entered a town, the people in power became disturbed and immediately sought to convict the Christians for being

"disturbers of the peace" and "outside agitators." But the Christians pressed on, in the conviction that they were "a colony of heaven," called to obey God rather than man. Small in number, they were big in commitment. They were too God-intoxicated to be "astronomically intimidated." By their effort and example they brought an end to such ancient evils as infanticide and gladiatorial contests.

41 Things are different now. So often the contemporary church is a weak, ineffectual voice with an uncertain sound. So often it is an archdefender of the status quo. Far from being disturbed by the presence of the church, the power structure of the average community is consoled by the church's silent—and often even vocal—sanction of things as they are.

42 But the judgment of God is upon the church as never before. If today's church does not recapture the sacrificial spirit of the early church, it will lose its authenticity, forfeit the loyalty of millions, and be dismissed as an irrelevant social club with no meaning for the twentieth century. Every day I meet young people whose disappointment with the church has turned into outright disgust.

43 Perhaps I have once again been too optimistic. Is organized religion too inextricably bound to the status quo to save our nation and the world? Perhaps I must turn my faith to the inner spiritual church, the church within the church, as the true *ekklesia* and the hope of the world. But again I am thankful to God that some noble souls from the ranks of organized religion have broken loose from the paralyzing chains of conformity and joined us as active partners in the struggle for freedom. They have left their secure congregations and walked the streets of Albany, Georgia, with us. They have gone down the highways of the South on tortuous rides for freedom. Yes, they have gone to jail with us. Some have been dismissed from their churches, have lost the support of their bishops and fellow ministers. But they have acted in the faith that right defeated is stronger than evil triumphant. Their witness has been the spiritual salt that has preserved the true meaning of the gospel in these troubled times. They have carved a tunnel of hope through the dark mountain of disappointment.

44 I hope the church as a whole will meet the challenge of this decisive hour. But even if the church does not come to the aid of justice, I have no despair about the future. I have no fear about the outcome of our struggle in Birmingham, even if our motives are at present misunderstood. We will reach the goal of freedom in Birmingham and all over the nation, because the goal of America is freedom. Abused and scorned though we may be, our destiny is tied up with America's destiny. Before the pilgrims landed at Plymouth, we were here. Before the pen of Jefferson etched the majestic words of the Declaration of Independence across the pages of history, we were here.

For more than two centuries our forebears labored in this country without wages; they made cotton king; they built the homes of their masters while suffering gross injustice and shameful humiliation—and yet out of a bottomless vitality they continued to thrive and develop. If the inexpressible cruelties of slavery could not stop us, the opposition we now face will surely fail. We will win our freedom because the sacred heritage of our nation and the eternal will of God are embodied in our echoing demands.

45 Before closing I feel impelled to mention one other point in your statement that has troubled me profoundly. You warmly commended the Birmingham police force for keeping "order" and "preventing violence." I doubt that you would have so warmly commended the police force if you had seen its dogs sinking their teeth into unarmed, nonviolent Negroes. I doubt that you would so quickly commend the policemen if you were to observe their ugly and inhumane treatment of Negroes here in the city jail; if you were to watch them push and curse old Negro women and young Negro girls; if you were to see them slap and kick old Negro men and young boys; if you were to observe them, as they did on two occasions, refuse to give us food because we wanted to sing our grace together. I cannot join you in your praise of the Birmingham police department.

46 It is true that the police have exercised a degree of discipline in handling the demonstrators. In this sense they have conducted themselves rather "nonviolently" in public. But for what purpose? To preserve the evil system of segregation. Over the past few years I have consistently preached that nonviolence demands that the means we use must be as pure as the ends we seek. I have tried to make clear that it is wrong to use immoral means to attain moral ends. But now I must affirm that it is just as wrong, or perhaps even more so, to use moral means to preserve immoral ends. Perhaps Mr. Connor and his policemen have been rather nonviolent in public, as was Chief Pritchett in Albany, Georgia, but they have used the moral means of nonviolence to maintain the immoral end of racial injustice. As T. S. Eliot has said: "The last temptation is the greatest treason: To do the right deed for the wrong reason."

47 I wish you had commended the Negro sit-inners and demonstrators of Birmingham for their sublime courage, their willingness to suffer and their amazing discipline in the midst of great provocation. One day the South will recognize its real heroes. They will be the James Merediths, with the noble sense of purpose that enables them to face jeering and hostile mobs, and with the agonizing loneliness that characterizes the life of the pioneer. They will be old, oppressed, battered Negro women, symbolized in a seventy-two-year-old woman in Montgomery, Alabama, who rose up with a sense of dignity and with her people decided not to ride segregated buses, and who responded

with ungrammatical profundity to one who inquired about her weariness: "My feets is tired, but my soul is at rest." They will be the young high school and college students, the young ministers of the gospel and a host of their elders, courageously and nonviolently sitting in at lunch counters and willingly going to jail for conscience' sake. One day the South will know that when these disinherited children of God sat down at lunch counters, they were in reality standing up for what is best in the American dream and for the most sacred values in our Judaeo-Christian heritage, thereby bringing our nation back to those great wells of democracy which were dug deep by the founding fathers in their formulation of the Constitution and the Declaration of Independence.

48 Never before have I written so long a letter. I'm afraid it is much too long to take your precious time. I can assure you that it would have been much shorter if I had been writing from a comfortable desk, but what else can one do when he is alone in a narrow jail cell, other than write long letters, think long thoughts and pray long prayers?

49 If I have said anything in this letter that overstates the truth and indicates an unreasonable impatience, I beg you to forgive me. If I have said anything that understates the truth and indicates my having a patience that allows me to settle for anything less than brotherhood, I beg God to forgive me.

50 I hope this letter finds you strong in the faith. I also hope that circumstances will soon make it possible for me to meet each of you, not as an integrationist or a civil rights leader but as a fellow clergyman and a Christian brother. Let us all hope that the dark clouds of racial prejudice will soon pass away and the deep fog of misunderstanding will be lifted from our fear-drenched communities, and in some not too distant tomorrow the radiant stars of love and brotherhood will shine over our great nation with all their scintillating beauty.

Yours for the cause of Peace and Brotherhood,

Martin Luther King, Jr.

Thinking Questions: *Form*

1. Consider Martin Luther King's persona in this letter. Do you agree with the following appraisal of King's character?

> Martin Luther King sincerely believes in what he says and in the causes that he supports. He has studied history, both general American history and the history of his people, and he thinks hard about the influence of the past on what he says about the present and future. Dr. King is capable of dreaming, without losing his sense of morality and his moral and physical strength. His character blends discipline and understanding.

What specific elements in King's letter offer either support for or opposition to this description? Do you feel that King's letter demonstrates this kind of tone throughout?

2. What specific language devices lend force and toughness to King's letter? Consider his sentence patterns, his use of imperatives and rhetorical questions, and his vocabulary.

3. Compare the sentence structures in one of Martin Luther King's paragraphs (paragraph 47 provides a good sample for comparison) with the sentences in John F. Kennedy's Inaugural Address. Do you find balance, antithesis, parallelism, and subordination in King's essay as well? Why might both writers want to create a similar tone, considering their subjects and their audiences? King speaks to a group of white ministers; Kennedy speaks to an entire population. King talks about racial bigotry and prejudice and the remedies he foresees for it; Kennedy talks about the state of the nation, its ideals and projected behavior; King talks about the oppressed and the oppressors and the actions that must be taken to change our social construct.

4. "Letter from Birmingham Jail" is a long and carefully reasoned piece. Can you put King's general argument in the form of an outline and relate each section of the essay to each point in the outline? The first five paragraphs, for example, provide a general answer to the question raised by King's fellow clergymen. These paragraphs define the central question and offer three general answers to it. Then, in paragraph 5, King turns the argument around and chides his fellow clergymen for *their* inaction, implying that *they* are part of the reason that he felt it necessary to come to Birmingham. Continue to reread the essay in this way, relating particular paragraphs to one another under general ideas and arguments.

5. Somewhere in his letter, King uses all the general methods of organization covered in this book. Can you point to several related paragraphs that follow a chronological, narrative order? Can you find individual paragraphs that divide a part of the general subject into subdivisions, using classification and logical division? Where can you find examples of cause-and-effect reasoning, comparison, or concrete description?

6. King often cites authority to convince his readers that he is right. He refers to the Bible (paragraphs 3, 21, and 31), to American and modern history (paragraphs 22 and 31), to well-known and respected philoso-

phers and "great men" (see paragraphs 15, 16, 21, 22, and 31). What do all these citations of authority contribute to the letter? Why do they make it more persuasive, especially when we consider the letter's subject, message, and audience?

7. Where does King develop a primarily ethical appeal—an appeal to the morality of his audience, an attempt to convince his readers of his own strong character and integrity?

8. Many rhetoricians argue that every good essay should include elements of the grand, the middle, and the plain style. What style dominates in this essay? Where can you find evidence, however, of the other styles? What elements of language combine to create all three styles?

9. Read aloud paragraph 14 of this letter. Notice how the long series of parallel *when*-clauses help unite all the evidence King uses to support his main idea. Such repetition and parallel phrasing help the reader to follow the reasoning in the paragraph, while they also create a cumulative and powerful emphasis on the suffering Negroes have experienced in the past. What other rhetorical devices help make this paragraph persuasive both emotionally and rationally?

10. King makes extensive use of figurative language in his letter; see paragraphs 25, 26, 38, and 50 for excellent specific examples. Select one example of figurative language—for example, "Human progress never *rolls in on wheels of inevitability*," a metaphor in paragraph 26—and analyze its function. How does it forward the logical development of ideas in the letter? How does it contribute to the emotional appeal of the letter?

Thinking Questions: *Substance*

1. Would you consider Martin Luther King a "moral extremist"? Or is he a moderate man, in morality as well as in other terms? Is he, for example, less extreme than George Jackson? Does he escape the criticism that Cecelia Holland applied to many young people in the late sixties—that they oversimplified the truth in the process of trying to persuade others that they were right? Does King give enough attention to opposing arguments?

2. Why does King consistently use a serious tone? What aspects of the situation in which he writes call for a direct, serious, and reflective tone—with no irony or humor?

3. Many people would agree with King's moral arguments. Why, then, were not people more actively supporting the principles King espouses in this letter? Do you believe that King's letter would motivate many of those people who agree with him but do nothing about it?

4. Imagine yourself in Birmingham in 1963. Do you believe Martin Luther King was right to lead a demonstration and protest that, at least temporarily, obstructed the free movement of many bystanders and pedestrians who might have had very little explicit effect on Negro rights? Suppose you had been driving to the post office to pick up an important letter and had been held up by King's demonstration for civil rights. What would have been your response? What *should* have been your response, now that you have read his letter?

Speech of Acceptance Upon the Award of the Nobel Prize for Literature

WILLIAM FAULKNER

1 I feel that this award was not made to me as a man, but to my work—a life's work in all the agony and sweat of the human spirit, not for glory and least of all for profit, but to create out of the materials of the human spirit something which did not exist before. So this award is only mine in trust. It will not be difficult to find a dedication for the money part of it commensurate with the purpose and significance of its origin. But I would like to do the same with the acclaim too, by using this moment as a pinnacle from which I might be listened to by the young men and women already dedicated to the same anguish and travail, among whom is already that one who will some day stand here where I am standing.

2 Our tragedy today is a general and universal physical fear so long sustained by now that we can even bear it. There are no longer problems of the spirit. There is only the question: When will I be blown up? Because of this, the young man or woman writing today has forgotten the problems of the human heart in conflict with itself which alone can make good writing because only that is worth writing about, worth the agony and the sweat.

3 He must learn them again. He must teach himself that the basest of all things is to be afraid; and, teaching himself that, forget it forever, leaving no room in his workshop for anything but the old verities and truths of the heart, the old universal truths lacking which any story is ephemeral and doomed—love and honor and pity and pride and compassion and sacrifice. Until he does so, he labors under a curse. He writes not of love but of lust, of defeats in which nobody loses anything of value, of victories without hope and, worst of all, without pity or compassion. His griefs grieve on no universal bones, leaving no scars. He writes not of the heart but of the glands.

4 Until he relearns these things, he will write as though he stood among and watched the end of man. I decline to accept the end of man. It is easy enough to say that man is immortal simply because he will endure; that when the last ding-dong of doom has clanged and faded from the last worthless rock hanging tideless in the last red and dying evening, that even then there will still be one more sound: that of his puny inexhaustible voice, still talking. I refuse to accept this. I believe that man will not merely endure: he will prevail. He is

immortal, not because he alone among creatures has an inexhaustible voice, but because he has a soul, a spirit capable of compassion and sacrifice and endurance. The poet's, the writer's, duty is to write about these things. It is his privilege to help man endure by lifting his heart, by reminding him of the courage and honor and hope and pride and compassion and pity and sacrifice which have been the glory of his past. The poet's voice need not merely be the record of man, it can be one of the props, the pillars to help him endure and prevail.

Thinking Questions: *Form*

1. Compare and contrast the voices of Faulkner, Cecelia Holland, and John F. Kennedy, all of whom appear in this section. What causes the differences in their written personalities? Look at language *and* content as you answer. Does the situation within which each one writes explain the differences in their voices? Does Cecelia Holland's audience in the *Saturday Evening Post,* for example, require a different voice than Kennedy's and Faulkner's more formal audiences? How do subject and occasion affect their writing styles?

2. Would you describe Faulkner's style in this speech as plain, middle, or grand? Give some specific evidence to support your answers.

3. Why does Faulkner switch from first-person (paragraphs 1 and 2) to third-person address (paragraphs 3 and 4)? How does this switch in point of view follow along with the logic of his message?

4. Why do you think Faulkner provides less specific evidence for his argument than Martin Luther King, Jr., does in his letter? Is Faulkner's address less convincing because of its brevity or lack of detail? What would Faulkner have sacrificed if he had delivered a longer, more carefully reasoned appeal? Would William Faulkner's reputation as a writer and the fact that he had already been awarded the Nobel Prize have anything to do with the brevity and generality of his address? Would a speaker with a lesser reputation need to say more to defend and illustrate his points?

Thinking Questions: *Substance*

1. William Faulkner addresses a scholarly, literary audience in a formal situation. What does Faulkner ask this audience to look for in literature? Can you give your own examples of what Faulkner might mean by "problems of the human heart in conflict with itself" (paragraph 2)? Does this mean that writers should write about what people *really* think and feel, rather than what they *say* they think or feel? How does a writer find those deeper emotions? Would such a search for deeper emotional and spiritual meaning hinder or help a writer in making money?

2. Why, according to Faulkner, do many modern writers seem to avoid the deeper emotional and spiritual problems of existence? What causes the "fear" that Faulkner argues keeps many modern writers from dealing with issues of the heart?

3. How many of the stories or books you have read in the past few years do you feel have dealt with "the old universal truths," which Faulkner lists as "love and honor and pity and pride and compassion and sacrifice" (paragraph 3)? Can you explain why these books, in contrast with others, captured these universal emotions?

4. What does Faulkner mean when he says that writers who do not write of the heart will write from the "glands" (paragraph 3)? Explain how these two metaphors—glands and heart—apply to Faulkner's argument for writing that deals with universal truths and deeper emotions. Also explain the function of the "prop and pillar" metaphor that Faulkner uses to close his message. How does literature serve as a pillar for society rather than as a record?

* * *

THURBER ON MORALITY

James Thurber, probably the foremost twentieth-century American humorist, writes a story that shows how our everyday behavior—the way we work, talk, even the way we eat and sit at a desk—is often dictated by hidden or semiconscious ideas about how life should be lived. These hidden ideas are usually not clearly enough formulated to be called Moral Principles, but they guide what we do in just as powerful—often in *more* powerful—ways than our formal religious and philosophical beliefs.

Mr. Martin, the man of efficiency, order, and respectability, considers murder totally justified when he is confronted by the blustering, meddling, and boisterous Mrs. Ulgine Barrows. "The Catbird Seat," coming after we have read the more formal pronouncements on morality in many of the essays in this section, should remind us that people are often motivated by set, established personality traits rather than by clearly held moral principles. In fact, personalities often dictate what people do; beliefs merely dictate what people *say* they will do. Examine the actions of Mr. Martin and Mrs. Barrows according to the different views of life they represent. Consider their actions as manifestations of personalities formed long ago and set in the concrete of everyday habit.

The Catbird Seat

JAMES THURBER

1 Mr. Martin bought the pack of Camels on Monday night in the most crowded cigar store on Broadway. It was theater time and seven or eight men were buying cigarettes. The clerk didn't even glance at Mr. Martin, who put the pack in his overcoat pocket and went out. If any of the staff at F & S had seen him buy the cigarettes, they would have been astonished, for it was generally known that Mr. Martin did not smoke, and never had. No one saw him.

2 It was just a week to the day since Mr. Martin had decided to rub out Mrs. Ulgine Barrows. The term "rub out" pleased him because it suggested nothing more than the correction of an error—in this case an error of Mr. Fitweiler. Mr. Martin had spent each night of the past week working out his plan and examining it. As he walked home now he went over it again. For the hundredth time he resented the element of imprecision, the margin of guesswork that entered into the business. The project as he had worked it out was casual and bold, the risks were considerable. Something might go wrong anywhere along the line. And therein lay the cunning of his scheme. No one would ever see in it the cautious, painstaking hand of Erwin Martin, head of the filing department at F & S, of whom Mr. Fitweiler had once said, "Man is fallible but Martin isn't." No one would see his hand, that is, unless it were caught in the act.

3 Sitting in his apartment, drinking a glass of milk, Mr. Martin reviewed his case against Mrs. Ulgine Barrows, as he had every night for seven nights. He began at the beginning. Her quacking voice and braying laugh had first profaned the halls of F & S on March 7, 1941 (Mr. Martin had a head for dates). Old Roberts, the personnel chief, had introduced her as the newly appointed special adviser to the president of the firm, Mr. Fitweiler. The woman had appalled Mr. Martin instantly, but he hadn't shown it. He had given her his dry hand, a look of studious concentration, and a faint smile. "Well," she had said, looking at the papers on his desk, "are you lifting the oxcart out of the ditch?" As Mr. Martin recalled that moment, over his milk, he squirmed slightly. He must keep his mind on her crimes as a special adviser, not on her peccadillos as a personality. This he found difficult to do, in spite of entering an objection and sustaining it. The faults of the woman as a woman kept chattering on in his mind like an unruly witness. She had, for almost two years now,

baited him. In the halls, in the elevator, even in his own office, into which she romped now and then like a circus horse, she was constantly shouting these silly questions at him. "Are you lifting the oxcart out of the ditch? Are you tearing up the pea patch? Are you hollering down the rain barrel? Are you scraping around the bottom of the pickle barrel? Are you sitting in the catbird seat?"

4 It was Joey Hart, one of Mr. Martin's two assistants, who had explained what the gibberish meant. "She must be a Dodger fan," he had said. "Red Barber announces the Dodger games over the radio and he uses those expressions—picked 'em up down South." Joey had gone on to explain one or two. "Tearing up the pea patch" meant going on a rampage; "sitting in the catbird seat" meant sitting pretty, like a batter with three balls and no strikes on him. Mr. Martin dismissed all this with an effort. It had been annoying, it had driven him near to distraction, but he was too solid a man to be moved to murder by anything so childish. It was fortunate, he reflected as he passed on to the important charges against Mrs. Barrows, that he had stood up under it so well. He had maintained always an outward appearance of polite tolerance. "Why, I even believe you like the woman," Miss Paird, his other assistant, had once said to him. He had simply smiled.

5 A gavel rapped in Mr. Martin's mind and the case proper was resumed. Mrs. Ulgine Barrows stood charged with willful, blatant, and persistent attempts to destroy the efficiency and system of F & S. It was competent, material, and relevant to review her advent and rise to power. Mr. Martin had got the story from Miss Paird, who seemed always able to find things out. According to her, Mrs. Barrows had met Mr. Fitweiler at a party, where she had rescued him from the embraces of a powerfully built drunken man who had mistaken the president of F & S for a famous retired Middle Western football coach. She had led him to a sofa and somehow worked upon him a monstrous magic. The aging gentleman had jumped to the conclusion there and then that this was a woman of singular attainments, equipped to bring out the best in him and in the firm. A week later he had introduced her into F & S as his special adviser. On that day confusion got its foot in the door. After Miss Tyson, Mr. Brundage, and Mr. Bartlett had been fired and Mr. Munson had taken his hat and stalked out, mailing in his resignation later, old Roberts had been emboldened to speak to Mr. Fitweiler. He mentioned that Mr. Munson's department had been "a little disrupted" and hadn't they perhaps better resume the old system there? Mr. Fitweiler had said certainly not. He had the greatest faith in Mrs. Barrows' ideas. "They require a little seasoning, a little seasoning, is all," he had added. Mr. Roberts had given it up. Mr. Martin reviewed in detail all the changes wrought by Mrs. Barrows. She had begun chipping at the cornices

of the firm's edifice and now she was swinging at the foundation stones with a pickaxe.

6 Mr. Martin came now, in his summing up, to the afternoon of Monday, November 2, 1942—just one week ago. On that day, at 3 p.m., Mrs. Barrows had bounced into his office. "Boo!" she had yelled. "Are you scraping around the bottom of the pickle barrel?" Mr. Martin had looked at her from under his green eyeshade, saying nothing. She had begun to wander about the office, taking it in with her great, popping eyes. "Do you really need *all* these filing cabinets?" she had demanded suddenly. Mr. Martin's heart had jumped. "Each of these files," he had said, keeping his voice even, "plays an indispensable part in the system of F & S." She had brayed at him, "Well, don't tear up the pea patch!" and gone to the door. From there she had bawled, "But you sure have got a lot of fine scrap in here!" Mr. Martin could no longer doubt that the finger was on his beloved department. Her pickaxe was on the upswing, poised for the first blow. It had not come yet; he had received no blue memo from the enchanted Mr. Fitweiler bearing nonsensical instructions deriving from the obscene woman. But there was no doubt in Mr. Martin's mind that one would be forthcoming. He must act quickly. Already a precious week had gone by. Mr. Martin stood up in his living room, still holding his milk glass. "Gentlemen of the jury," he said to himself, "I demand the death penalty for this horrible person."

7 The next day Mr. Martin followed his routine, as usual. He polished his glasses more often and once sharpened an already sharp pencil, but not even Miss Paird noticed. Only once did he catch sight of his victim; she swept past him in the hall with a patronizing "Hi!" At five-thirty he walked home, as usual, and had a glass of milk, as usual. He had never drunk anything stronger in his life—unless you could count ginger ale. The late Sam Schlosser, the S of F & S, had praised Mr. Martin at a staff meeting several years before for his temperate habits. "Our most efficient worker neither drinks nor smokes," he had said. "The results speak for themselves." Mr. Fitweiler had sat by, nodding approval.

8 Mr. Martin was still thinking about that red-letter day as he walked over to the Schrafft's on Fifth Avenue near Forty-sixth Street. He got there, as he always did, at eight o'clock. He finished his dinner and the financial page of the *Sun* at a quarter to nine, as he always did. It was his custom after dinner to take a walk. This time he walked down Fifth Avenue at a casual pace. His gloved hands felt moist and warm, his forehead cold. He transferred the Camels from his overcoat to a jacket pocket. He wondered, as he did so, if they did not represent an unnecessary note of strain. Mrs. Barrows smoked only Luckies. It was his idea to puff a few puffs on a Camel (after the rubbing-out), stub it out in the ashtray holding her lipstick-stained

Luckies, and thus drag a small red herring across the trail. Perhaps it was not a good idea. It would take time. He might even choke, too loudly.

9 Mr. Martin had never seen the house on West Twelfth Street where Mrs. Barrows lived, but he had a clear enough picture of it. Fortunately, she had bragged to everybody about her ducky first-floor apartment in the perfectly darling three-story red-brick. There would be no doorman or other attendants; just the tenants of the second and third floors. As he walked along, Mr. Martin realized that he would get there before nine-thirty. He had considered walking north on Fifth Avenue from Schrafft's to a point from which it would take him until ten o'clock to reach the house. At that hour people were less likely to be coming in or going out. But the procedure would have made an awkward loop in the straight thread of his casualness, and he had abandoned it. It was impossible to figure when people would be entering or leaving the house, anyway. There was a great risk at any hour. If he ran into anybody, he would simply have to place the rubbing-out of Ulgine Barrows in the inactive file forever. The same thing would hold true if there were someone in her apartment. In that case he would just say that he had been passing by, recognized her charming house and thought to drop in.

10 It was eighteen minutes after nine when Mr. Martin turned into Twelfth Street. A man passed him, and a man and a woman, talking. There was no one within fifty paces when he came to the house, halfway down the block. He was up the steps and in the small vestibule in no time, pressing the bell under the card that said "Mrs. Ulgine Barrows." When the clicking in the lock started, he jumped forward against the door. He got inside fast, closing the door behind him. A bulb in a lantern hung from the hall ceiling on a chain seemed to give a monstrously bright light. There was nobody on the stair, which went up ahead of him along the left wall. A door opened down the hall in the wall on the right. He went toward it swiftly, on tiptoe.

11 "Well, for God's sake, look who's here!" bawled Mrs. Barrows, and her braying laugh rang out like the report of a shotgun. He rushed past her like a football tackle, bumping her. "Hey, quit shoving!" she said, closing the door behind them. They were in her living room, which seemed to Mr. Martin to be lighted by a hundred lamps. "What's after you?" she said. "You're as jumpy as a goat." He found he was unable to speak. His heart was wheezing in his throat. "I—yes," he finally brought out. She was jabbering and laughing as she started to help him off with his coat. "No, no," he said. "I'll put it here." He took it off and put it on a chair near the door. "Your hat and gloves, too," she said. "You're in a lady's house." He put his hat on top of the coat. Mrs. Barrows seemed larger than he had thought. He kept his gloves on. "I was passing by," he said. "I recognized—is

there anyone here?" She laughed louder than ever. "No," she said, "we're all alone. You're as white as a sheet, you funny man. Whatever *has* come over you? I'll mix you a toddy." She started toward a door across the room. "Scotch-and-soda be all right? But say, you don't drink, do you?" She turned and gave him her amused look. Mr. Martin pulled himself together. "Scotch-and-soda will be all right," he heard himself say. He could hear her laughing in the kitchen.

12 Mr. Martin looked quickly around the living room for the weapon. He had counted on finding one there. There were andirons and a poker and something in a corner that looked like an Indian club. None of them would do. It couldn't be that way. He began to pace around. He came to a desk. On it lay a metal paper knife with an ornate handle. Would it be sharp enough? He reached for it and knocked over a small brass jar. Stamps spilled out of it and it fell to the floor with a clatter. "Hey," Mrs. Barrows yelled from the kitchen, "are you tearing up the pea patch?" Mr. Martin gave a strange laugh. Picking up the knife, he tried its point against his left wrist. It was blunt. It wouldn't do.

13 When Mrs. Barrows reappeared, carrying two highballs, Mr. Martin, standing there with his gloves on, became acutely conscious of the fantasy he had wrought. Cigarettes in his pocket, a drink prepared for him—it was all too grossly improbable. It was more than that; it was impossible. Somewhere in the back of his mind a vague idea stirred, sprouted. "For heaven's sake, take off those gloves," said Mrs. Barrows. "I always wear them in the house," said Mr. Martin. The idea began to bloom, strange and wonderful. She put the glasses on a coffee table in front of a sofa and sat on the sofa. "Come over here, you odd little man," she said. Mr. Martin went over and sat beside her. It was difficult getting a cigarette out of the pack of Camels, but he managed it. She held a match for him, laughing. "Well," she said, handing him his drink, "this is perfectly marvelous. You with a drink and a cigarette."

14 Mr. Martin puffed, not too awkwardly, and took a gulp of the highball. "I drink and smoke all the time," he said. He clinked his glass against hers. "Here's nuts to that old windbag, Fitweiler," he said, and gulped again. The stuff tasted awful, but he made no grimace. "Really, Mr. Martin," she said, her voice and posture changing, "you are insulting our employer." Mrs. Barrows was now all special adviser to the president. "I am preparing a bomb," said Mr. Martin, "which will blow the old goat higher than hell." He had only had a little of the drink, which was not strong. It couldn't be that. "Do you take dope or something?" Mrs. Barrows asked coldly. "Heroin," said Mr. Martin. "I'll be coked to the gills when I bump that old buzzard off." "Mr. Martin!" she shouted, getting to her feet. "That will be all of that. You must go at once." Mr. Martin took another swallow of

his drink. He tapped his cigarette out in the ashtray and put the pack of Camels on the coffee table. Then he got up. She stood glaring at him. He walked over and put on his hat and coat. "Not a word about this," he said, and laid an index finger against his lips. All Mrs. Barrows could bring out was "Really!" Mr. Martin put his hand on the doorknob. "I'm sitting in the catbird seat," he said. He stuck his tongue out at her and left. Nobody saw him go.

15 Mr. Martin got to his apartment, walking, well before eleven. No one saw him go in. He had two glasses of milk after brushing his teeth, and he felt elated. It wasn't tipsiness, because he hadn't been tipsy. Anyway, the walk had worn off all effects of the whisky. He got in bed and read a magazine for a while. He was asleep before midnight.

16 Mr. Martin got to the office at eight-thirty the next morning, as usual. At a quarter to nine, Ulgine Barrows, who had never before arrived at work before ten, swept into his office. "I'm reporting to Mr. Fitweiler now!" she shouted. "If he turns you over to the police, it's no more than you deserve!" Mr. Martin gave her a look of shocked surprise. "I beg your pardon?" he said. Mrs. Barrows snorted and bounced out of the room, leaving Miss Paird and Joey Hart staring after her. "What's the mater with that old devil now?" asked Miss Paird. "I have no idea," said Mr. Martin, resuming his work. The other two looked at him and then at each other. Miss Paird got up and went out. She walked slowly past the closed door of Mr. Fitweiler's office. Mrs. Barrows was yelling inside, but she was not braying. Miss Paird could not hear what the woman was saying. She went back to her desk.

17 Forty-five minutes later, Mrs. Barrows left the president's office and went into her own, shutting the door. It wasn't until half an hour later that Mr. Fitweiler sent for Mr. Martin. The head of the filing department, neat, quiet, attentive, stood in front of the old man's desk. Mr. Fitweiler was pale and nervous. He took his glasses off and twiddled them. He made a small, bruffing sound in his throat. "Martin," he said, "you have been with us more than twenty years." "Twenty-two, sir," said Mr. Martin. "In that time," pursued the president, "your work and your—uh—manner have been exemplary." "I trust so, sir," said Mr. Martin. "I have understood, Martin," said Mr. Fitweiler, "that you have never taken a drink or smoked." "That is correct, sir," said Mr. Martin. "Ah, yes." Mr. Fitweiler polished his glasses. "You may describe what you did after leaving the office yesterday, Martin," he said. Mr. Martin allowed less than a second for his bewildered pause. "Certainly, sir," he said. "I walked home. Then I went to Schrafft's for dinner. Afterward I walked home again. I went to bed early, sir, and read a magazine for a while. I was asleep before eleven." "Ah, yes," said Mr. Fitweiler again. He was silent for a moment, searching for the proper words to say to the head

of the filing department. "Mrs. Barrows," he said finally, "Mrs. Barrows has worked hard, Martin, very hard. It grieves me to report that she suffered a severe breakdown. It has taken the form of a persecution complex accompanied by distressing hallucinations." "I am very sorry, sir," said Mr. Martin. "Mrs. Barrows is under the delusion," continued Mr. Fitweiler, "that you visited her last evening and behaved yourself in an—uh—unseemly manner." He raised his hand to silence Mr. Martin's little pained outcry. "It is the nature of these psychological diseases," Mr. Fitweiler said, "to fix upon the least likely and most innocent party as the—uh—source of persecution. These matters are not for the lay mind to grasp, Martin. I've just had my psychiatrist, Dr. Fitch, on the phone. He would not, of course, commit himself, but he made enough generalizations to substantiate my suspicions. I suggested to Mrs. Barrows when she had completed her—uh—story to me this morning, that she visit Dr. Fitch, for I suspected a condition at once. She flew, I regret to say, into a rage, and demanded—uh—requested that I call you on the carpet. You may not know, Martin, but Mrs. Barrows had planned a reorganization of your department—subject to my approval, of course, subject to my approval. This brought you, rather than anyone else, to her mind—but again that is a phenomenon for Dr. Fitch and not for us. So, Martin, I am afraid Mrs. Barrows' usefulness here is at an end." "I am dreadfully sorry, sir," said Mr. Martin.

18 It was at this point that the door to the office blew open with the suddenness of a gas-main explosion and Mrs. Barrows catapulted through it. "Is the little rat denying it?" she screamed. "He can't get away with that!" Mr. Martin got up and moved discreetly to a point beside Mr. Fitweiler's chair. "You drank and smoked at my apartment," she bawled at Mr. Martin, "and you know it! You called Mr. Fitweiler an old windbag and said you were going to blow him up when you got coked to the gills on your heroin!" She stopped yelling to catch her breath and a new glint came into her popping eyes. "If you weren't such a drab, ordinary little man," she said, "I'd think you'd planned it all. Sticking your tongue out, saying you were sitting in the catbird seat, because you thought no one would believe me when I told it! My God, it's really too perfect!" She brayed loudly and hysterically, and the fury was on her again. She glared at Mr. Fitweiler. "Can't you see how he has tricked us, you old fool? Can't you see his little game?" But Mr. Fitweiler had been surreptitiously pressing all the buttons under the top of his desk and employees of F & S began pouring into the room. "Stockton," said Mr. Fitweiler, "you and Fishbein will take Mrs. Barrows to her home. Mrs. Powell, you will go with them." Stockton, who had played a little football in high school, blocked Mrs. Barrows as she made for Mr. Martin. It took him and Fishbein together to force her out of the door into the hall,

crowded with stenographers and office boys. She was still screaming imprecations at Mr. Martin, tangled and contradictory imprecations. The hubbub finally died out down the corridor.

19 "I regret that this has happened," said Mr. Fitweiler. "I shall ask you to dismiss it from your mind, Martin." "Yes, sir," said Mr. Martin, anticipating his chief's "That will be all" by moving to the door. "I will dismiss it." He went out and shut the door, and his step was light and quick in the hall. When he entered his department he had slowed down to his customary gait, and he walked quietly across the room to the W20 file, wearing a look of studious concentration.

Thinking Questions: *Form*

1. Find examples of dramatic irony in the story and show how it contributes to the story's satiric purpose (see the discussion of *dramatic irony* in the essay on form at the end of this section). Take, for example, paragraph 12, in which Mrs. Barrows yells from her kitchen, "Are you tearing up the pea patch?" and Mr. Martin gives "a strange laugh." At this point, we and Mr. Martin know more than Mrs. Barrows: we know of Mr. Martin's planned murder, of his distaste for Mrs. Martin's clichés and loud sayings; and we know, as well, that Mr. Martin is in fact planning to "tear up the pea patch." Mrs. Barrows's question is dramatically ironic because we judge what she does from a broader, more philosophical, perspective than she can herself.

2. What physical facts does Thurber use to establish Mr. Martin's character? For example, he drinks milk, eats at Schrafft's *every night* at eight; he carefully polishes his glasses, sharpens his pencils, and never smokes or drinks. How do these facts combine to shape our image of Mr. Martin's character? What other concrete details contribute to your overall image of Mr. Martin?

3. All the events, actions, and dialogue of this story are given to us from Mr. Martin's point of view. In fact, we work back through Mr. Martin's memory for information about the past in the story; then we follow him as he visits Mrs. Barrows's apartment, plans his strategy, and follows through with his plan the next day. How might the story and our impression of its characters and themes have changed if it had been relayed to us by an objective narrator or storyteller, or by Mrs. Barrows?

4. Why does Mrs. Barrows underestimate Mr. Martin? What does she think of him; how does her impression affect her response to him at the end of the story?

Thinking Questions: *Substance*

1. What motivates Mr. Martin? What particular gestures, actions, appearances, and speech habits of Mrs. Ulgine Barrows prod Mr. Martin's

actions? Are Mr. Martin and Mrs. Barrows consistent characters? Are they always acting "in character"?

2. Describe the code behind Mr. Martin's entire way of life. Which one of these words best defines him—efficient, moral, consistent, loud, prudish, logical, sentimental, secure?

3. Does James Thurber *like* Mr. Martin? Can you tell? Does the fact that Martin "does in" Mrs. Barrows mean that he is a better person? What does his "victory" depend on?

4. Why does Thurber have Mr. Martin go through the facts of his "case" against Mrs. Barrows as if she were on trial? What effect does that have on you as a reader (see paragraphs 3 through 6)?

5. What idea "began to bloom, strange and wonderful" in paragraph 13? Why does Mr. Martin become calmer as the idea grows? Does the new idea seem much more fitted to Mr. Martin's character than his earlier idea of murdering Mrs. Barrows?

6. What moral principle evolves from this story? Does this principle seem at all parallel to the moral principles espoused by Martin Luther King, William Faulkner, or John Kennedy?

Writing Exercise VII

ARGUMENT AND PERSUASION

Imagine yourself in one of the following three writing situations:

1. You have been asked to write an editorial for your local newspaper on the importance of students' knowing how to write well, no matter what career they decide to enter. Begin the planning of your essay by interviewing teachers in several different departments in your university or college. Ask these teachers whether they believe individuals who enter their fields will need to know how to write. Will, for example, law students need writing skills? Doctors? Prospective mathematics teachers? Future businessmen or chemists? What kind of writing will they need to learn, if any?

After you have examined and thought out your evidence, plan a satirical approach to your editorial. You might, for example, begin with an example of a badly trained administrator who tries to write a memo to his staff and fails miserably to communicate his message. In other words, *show* your readers what will happen if they cannot write, and let them draw their own conclusions. Use exaggeration, understatement, irony—all the devices of satire covered in this section and in the following essay on the forms of argument and persuasion.

2. Choose someone you dislike but must work or study with every day. Look back over paragraphs 3 to 6 in James Thurber's "The Catbird Seat," in which Thurber has Mr. Martin put Mrs. Ulgine Barrows through a mock trial. Write your own mock trial of the person whom you dislike. Combine satire and serious criticism. Use both logical arguments against and satiric exaggerations of the personality of your subject. Keep to courtroom formality in your style.

3. Consider all the commercials you have seen on television; select the worst one, or the one that annoys you the most, and write either a satirical or a straightforward attack on it. Fasten on the specifics of the commercial to make your attack plausible and realistic. Consider the emotional, rational, and ethical appeals of your satire or argument. You are to imagine writing your essay for a general group of people who have indicated an interest in improving the quality of television.

WRITING THE ARGUMENTATIVE OR PERSUASIVE ESSAY

Every persuasive writer has a particular slant on a subject; he or she wishes to persuade readers to agree with or act from that perspective or slant, and, of course, every writer uses language in a particular way, creates a particular voice as he or she writes. A persuasive writer, then, must consider three elements: the argument in relation to the subject; the argument in relation to the personality his or her words create in writing (*voice* and *style*); the argument in relation to the emotional and intellectual needs of the readers. All three perspectives, of course, work together; this essay should help you use these related perspectives as you plan, write, and rewrite a persuasive essay.

Your argument and your subject

Most persuasive writers begin by planning their strategies for presenting their *subjects*. In most explicitly persuasive writing situations, the subject begins with an idea or opinion. Someone interested in the argument for or against municipal fluoridation of water, for example, might begin to organize a persuasive essay by sharpening up the facts and opinions on a subject.

> Water fluoridation saves taxpayers money because it eliminates the need for dental repair work. We should fluoridate our water.

The first sentence introduces the subject—water fluoridation—and provides a reason for the writer's thesis, which appears in the second sentence. How might a writer build a sound argumentative essay from this base?

Fact, Opinion, and Convention. We can answer the previous question by explaining the differences among statements of *fact,* assertions of *opinion,* and statements of *convention.* If our writer has really checked other cities, we can assume that the initial sentence—"Water fluoridation saves taxpayers money because it eliminates the need for dental repair work"—is a statement of fact. Of course, a writer who wants to present a subject as convincingly as possible would tell the reader the *source* of such facts—where surveys of fluoridated water systems had been taken, what the results were in as exact terms as possible, what factors made the surveyed city either like or unlike the city under consideration.

As you read, you want to be wary of unsupported or unverified "facts"—maybe the writer, for example, is basing his or her claims of improved dental health on one very small sample when other more important surveys have given no substantial proof that users of fluoridated water have improved dental health.

Many writers, in other words, mistake opinions for facts. Facts need *verification* and *explanation;* opinions need *support* and *substantiation,* usually with logical or emotional illustrations.

In most persuasive writings, the *thesis* is the writer's main opinion on the subject; it tells the readers what they should believe by the time they have read the entire essay.

Think back to the writer's thesis on fluoridated water systems: *We should fluoridate our water.* This sentence should become the opinion that guides the writer throughout the essay. It directs the selection of supporting facts and explanations, helps the writer decide how to arrange his or her materials in an emphatic and convincing order, suggests just how the writer ought to blend emotional and rational appeals.

If you cannot tell statements of fact from assertions of opinion, you will not realize when your sentences and ideas need development. You will expect complete belief from your readers when they are expecting more support, explanation, or proof. A reader ought to ask, "Can you *show* rather than *tell* me why I should agree with your opinion?" As you reread a rough draft, ask yourself this question repeatedly, for in editing you must become your own reader, demanding evidence and facts, illustrations, and reasons for every important opinion you offer. As you write, you look over your own shoulder, telling yourself just what a reader would need to know to believe your assertions. You become your own reader.

Some statements, however, do not need much explanation or supporting evidence, although they do not qualify as facts. The following is a statement of *convention:* "Any municipally supported system should provide tangible benefits to a majority of a city's citizenry." In an essay for or against fluoridation of a municipal water system, this statement, although it does not strictly qualify as a verified fact, could be left as is. The sentence describes a general political and moral truth—at least in a democratic state—and most readers, even those opposed to fluoridation, could be expected to agree with it. A persuasive writer should recognize the difference between an opinion that needs support and a conventional statement. Never bore a reader by defending the obvious or by ignoring the main point.

Keep these guidelines in mind as you work with the basic materials of a persuasive essay.

1. Distinguish statements of opinion from those of fact and convention.

2. Decide on your most important opinion, which is usually worded in general form, and list more specific supporting opinions under it.

3. Decide on methods or strategies of development for each opinion—by examples, by concrete descriptions, or by step-by-step illustrations (these strategies and methods are, of course, the focus of attention in each of the earlier sections of this book).

Remember these simplified definitions of fact, opinion, and convention.

Fact: something you believe your readers will accept as true without a great deal of supporting material. If you say that 32,893 people live in a particular neighborhood in Detroit, or that handguns are most often used in armed robberies, you can expect your readers to accept your statement as fact, as long as you cite a reputable source for your information.

Opinion: a belief held with confidence, but not substantiated by positive knowledge or proof. A careful writer evaluates his or her opinions to decide the amount of support they will need. Which of the following statements is an opinion? "Johnny Bench is the best catcher in baseball." "Johnny Bench is a catcher for the Cincinnati Reds?"

Convention: a statement with which a writer can assume most readers will agree. Customs, established practices, and general moral principles might all be used in statements of convention—*One man should not kill another, Stealing is against the law,* and *The Golden Rule* would all qualify. Remember, however, that too many conventional statements make for uninspiring reading. Remember, as well, that many effectively persuasive essays take what most people would believe are statements of convention and disprove or qualify them. In some cases, for example, killing might be justified, or stealing might be within the law.

Your argument and your persona: Appeals to voice and style

Once you have planned and drafted an argument, you will need to consider how you sound as you present your case. No one listens to a pushy, pig-headed arguer; most readers grow suspicious of an emotional plea, no matter how eloquent, that makes no attempt to provide supporting rational explanations or substantiating evidence. And, above all, few readers enjoy reading an argument that is stiff or pedantic when it should contain some humor or, at least, some sign that the writer is a human being. Yet most readers do not want a writer's sense of humor to get in the way of the message.

Here are a few essential definitions:

Voice: the sound of you, your personality on paper. On paper, however, the words you choose and the sentences you write create your personality, just as the ideas and the facts and illustrations you use to support them create your message.

Style: We distinguish writers' styles by their words, by how they make sentences, by their sense of humor or lack of one, by what they choose to write about, and by how they choose to treat their readers. Cecelia Holland, in "I Don't Trust Anyone Under Thirty," develops an attack on the radical youth movement in the late 1960s. Her thesis is a simple one: "Young radicals, for all their pious attacking of establishment conformity, are themselves bound by social conformity, by the desire to do things for the right reasons." Holland's essay is persuasive because her logical reasoning is combined with a tough, direct *style;* we enjoy her *manner* as well as her *method* of arguing. In sum, style depends upon the way the writer *chooses* to present his or her argument.

Persona: the mask a writer wears as he or she presents an argument. The term comes from Greek theater, where members of the audience identified the personalities of characters by the masks they wore. This term helps us understand that every time we pick up a pen we, in essence, create a new identity on paper. A writer can *control* that identity; he or she can make choices in voice and style that will create an effective persona for any situation.

Consider voice, style, and persona in these excerpts from essays (all included in this section) by William Buckley, John Kennedy, and William Faulkner. Notice how each writer uses these elements to meet the needs of his readers, his subject, and his purpose.

> I speak for those who have had difficulty cultivating a convincing admiration for the popular culture of the rockers, foremost among them, of course, the Beatles.
>
> Those who were not born into the movement can usually remember their first experience with it. Mine is vivid. I first remember engaging rock on learning years ago that a Mr. Alan Freed (1) was very famous; (2) was generally credited with launching the new musical form; and (3) had bought the house a couple of dwellings down from my own in the country; whence (4) he was broadcasting three hours daily as a network disc jockey.

We observe today not a victory of party but a celebration of freedom—symbolizing an end as well as a beginning—signifying renewal as well as change. For I have sworn before you and Almighty God the same solemn oath our forebears prescribed nearly a century and three quarters ago.

The world is very different now. For man holds in his mortal hands the power to abolish all forms of human poverty and all forms of human life. And yet the same revolutionary beliefs for which our forebears fought are still at issue around the globe—the belief that the rights of man come not from the generosity of the state but from the hand of God.

I feel that this award was not made to me as a man, but to my work—a life's work in all the agony and sweat of the human spirit, not for glory and least of all for profit, but to create out of the materials of the human spirit something which did not exist before. So this award is only mine in trust. It will not be difficult to find a dedication for the money part of it commensurate with the purpose and significance of its origin. But I would like to do the same with the acclaim too, by using this moment as a pinnacle from which I might be listened to by the young men and women already dedicated to the same anguish and travail, among whom is already that one who will some day stand here where I am standing.

No one writes in a vacuum. All three of these writers have particular subjects and audiences in mind. All three use language to create particular voices, to project particular personas into the situations in which they are writing.

William Buckley, for example, uses the informal voice of a witty and ironic man. His sentences are naturally formed, with the usual subject/verb/object order; Buckley's vocabulary, however, is relatively sophisticated—*whence, dwellings* (for the more common *houses*), *foremost, engaging* (rather than the more common verb, *being introduced to*)—or, at least, just sophisticated enough to let his readers know that this writer, although he is writing about rock-and-roll, is not a complete swinger himself. In fact, he is someone who worries a good deal about the language he uses, about choosing one word over another, about putting a sentence carefully so that it says just what he hopes it will say.

What additional evidence of Buckley's voice—his personality on paper—do we find? His sentences are simply constructed, but they are also nicely varied in length. In fact, the second paragraph includes an opening sentence of medium length, a second sentence of three emphatic words, and a final sentence which is the longest in the two opening paragraphs.

The contrast between William Buckley's style (his choice of words and sentence structures) and his subject (Alan Freed and the latest rock-and-roll craze) helps him create a sophisticated, mocking voice. We hear the urbane man gently mocking the latest fad in popular music; although, of course, we know that he will often claim to like what he describes when he very obviously really believes the opposite. In essence, Buckley can say the opposite of what he really means and be sure, because of his careful creation of an ironic voice, that we as readers will know that he speaks with tongue in cheek.

Both John Kennedy and William Faulkner, in contrast, speak to us seriously and straightforwardly, as we are accustomed to expect at public occasions such as inaugurations and the awarding of Nobel Prizes. Both Kennedy and Faulkner rely on two rhetorical devices which are commonly used to create the formal voice of the public speaker.

Antithesis: the technique of setting contrasting ideas side by side to emphasize both problem and solution: ". . . *not a victory of party, but a celebration of freedom* symbolizing *an end* as well as a *beginning*—signifying *renewal* as well as *change*." This technique of pairing contrasting ideas in parallel grammatical structures occurs throughout Kennedy's address; it is used consistently to clarify the theme of the entire address—that basic divisions can be reconciled by the spirit of unification and strength. After a particularly heated political campaign and election, we can understand why John Kennedy's emphasis on reconciliation was appropriate and effective.

Parallelism: Both Kennedy and Faulkner emphasize the reconciliation of opposites by using parallel grammatical structures within sentences. Most of the clauses in their sentences are connected by coordinate conjunctions (*and, but, yet,* or *nor*) which emphasize the parallel ideas and grammatical structures in each clause. Look closely at the parallelism in Faulkner's opening sentence.

parallelism I feel this award *was not made to me as a man / but to my work*—a life's work in all the agony and sweat of the human spirit,

parallelism *not for glory / and least of all for profit, but to create out of the materials of the human spirit something which did not exist before.*

After the initial appearance of the main subject and verb (*I feel . . .*), Faulkner introduces two extended relative clauses, both of which contain antithesis within themselves: the award belongs to his work, not to him personally. Then, after the dash, which indicates a shift in the direction of thought, Faulkner qualifies his work as representing "the agony and sweat of the human spirit." After qualifying the kind of work he has done, Faulkner returns to his use of parallelism and antithesis: the work was done "not for glory and least of all for profit" (parallel prepositional phrases introduced by *not* and *least of all* and linked by the coordinate conjunction *and*); the entire sentence is then rounded off by a summarizing statement that is the second half of a final antithesis: "but to create out of the materials of the human spirit something which did not exist before." Notice how the use of *to create* brings us back to Faulkner's *work,* his art, and all that he believes it stands for.

This sentence illustrates the general value of antithesis and parallelism as rhetorical devices. Both devices create the polished sound, the rhythm and balance, of an accomplished public speaker. But, perhaps most importantly, they also focus and emphasize the central ideas of the sentence. By putting his main idea into an antithetical structure, Faulkner clarifies his thesis (that the Nobel Prize represents the suffering and agony of a universal, creative spirit) by contrasting it with what the prize does *not* represent (a personal triumph, representative of a personal profit). And the parallel phrasing (*not to me as a man / but to my work . . . not for glory and least of all for profit. . . .*) helps keep the contrast in ideas firmly in the listener's or reader's mind.

Both Faulkner's and Kennedy's speeches provide excellent examples of sound coming to the aid of sense. The voices of these pieces are controlled in order to create in their audiences the impression of sober, serious-minded men speaking on important issues; yet the rhetorical devices these writers use clarify their messages as well as their personalities.

Relaxed and Controlled Sentences. As our close reading of particular sentences by Faulkner and Kennedy indicates, both of these writers want their sentences to take readers or listeners by the hand and lead them carefully to an emphatic point. As we read, it is as if we feel the controlling hand of the writer on our shoulder.

Other writers in different situations, however, want to make readers feel more relaxed; they would rather the readers get the information they need without a directing and controlling hand. Look over these sentences from Cecelia Holland's "I Don't Trust Anyone Under Thirty."

> Are we strong on freedom? It would be hard to find a young person outside the South who isn't all for the Negro revolution. The freedom to protest the Vietnam war—to protest anything (except the protesters)—is as hallowed as the bones of a saint. Yet to hold a conservative viewpoint, however honestly, can only be a sign of cowardice.

Certainly Holland develops a logical idea in these sentences, but her logic comes to us in more direct, more relaxed sentences, mostly written in normal syntactical order, with one clause or phrase *adding* to the meaning of a previous clause. Even when Holland wishes to interrupt one thought with another, she does not resort to coordinate or subordinate clauses, nor does she use antithesis or parallelism. She depends, instead, on dashes and parentheses—more natural and relaxed indicators of a shift in direction or thought. Because of her reliance on normal speech patterns, on relatively simple diction, and on natural rhythms and pauses, Holland's prose creates the voice of an everyday, concerned citizen, speaking to us informally on a controversial issue. As readers, we relax, listen; we flow with her argument. In contrast, we must, to read Kennedy and Faulkner effectively, become poised readers, riding with the ebbs and flows of their rhythmic, controlled prose, noticing always how the sentences are formed to clarify and emphasize ideas.

Your argument and your audience: Appeals to emotion, reason, and moral character

A writer's voice and his or her appeal to an audience are intricately related. An irate citizen almost naturally appeals primarily to the emotions of the audience, unless he or she carefully considers voice and decides to control anger by using facts and logical reasoning. Whatever the writer's situation, he or she must leaven emotion with reason and consider carefully what general impression the voice chosen will make on an audience. Above all, a writer must be able to *choose* to reject some emotional appeals as irresponsible, to blend fact with emotion, to use language in a way that presents a balanced personality.

Consider Cecelia Holland's essay, "I Don't Trust Anyone Under Thirty." Her voice presents an effective blend of emotional and logical appeal.

Paragraphs 1 through 6 clarify both the emotional and moral appeals in Holland's essay. Her use of sharp rhetorical questions, the general forcefulness of her language and style, her clever use of the colloquialisms and speech patterns of the young people she supposedly opposes all lead us, as we read, to share her emotional and moral indignation. Phrases such as "let's face it," her use of talky contractions all through these paragraphs, her use of the colloquial "strong on" and "long on" in the sentence "We're strong on freedom and long on love. . . ." all combine to put us in the frame of mind necessary to make her argument effective.

Beginning with paragraph 7, however, Holland begins to provide the essential ideas and reasons behind her thesis. Why do her young peers conform? "Part of the reason . . . is that we're still bound by at least one antique convention: doing things for the right reasons, the socially acceptable motives" (paragraph 7). In each succeeding paragraph, the reasons behind this thesis are clarified and examined in more depth. Specific examples of her peers' reactions to contemporary issues are given to support Holland's reasoning; for example, in paragraph 8, the young people's reasoning on the drug issue is shown to be narrow and closed-minded, reasoning in which anyone who opposes the popular way of thinking is automatically assumed to be wrong. The rest of Holland's essay continues to propose logical reasons in support of her contention that young people in her generation oversimplify their responses to social issues because they are conforming to accepted modes of thought. The emotional and moral appeals of her early paragraphs are blended, as the essay progresses, with careful enumeration of the logical reasons behind her opinions.

In an essay later in this section on persuasion, Martin Luther King blends emotional, rational, and moral appeals just as effectively as Holland, despite the obvious differences in their language and style. King begins his letter to Birmingham clergymen by establishing the humane, rational, tolerant qualities of his own character. In a situation in which King's opponents would be quick to emphasize any moral faults as they were implied in his own words and actions, he must successfully create the image of a rational, fair-minded, morally concerned individual. Yet he must not, in doing so, appear eager to give in to his opponent's demands.

> While confined here in the Birmingham city jail, I came across your recent statement calling my present activities "unwise and untimely." Seldom do I pause to answer criticism of my work and ideas. If I sought to answer all the criticisms that cross my desk, my secretaries would have little time for anything other than such correspondence in the course of the day, and I would have no time for constructive work. But since I feel that you are men of genuine good will and that your criticisms are sincerely set forth, I want to try to answer your statement in what I hope will be patient and reasonable terms. (Paragraph 1)

Here we find the voice of an eminently reasonable man, recognizing the sincere concern of those he will argue against, realizing and admitting that he may fail in his attempt to convince ("I want to try . . ."). In a social context where his readers were apt to charge him with being "too radical" in his demands, King must carefully develop the image of a sincere, morally righteous man. His plea that we understand his difficult situation is one method of assuring that his readers respect his character.

Later in his letter, when King believes his audience is convinced of his morally justified intentions, he launches into logical analyses of contemporary racial problems.

> Let me give another explanation. A law is unjust if it is inflicted on a minority that, as a result of being denied the right to vote, had no part in enacting or devising the law. Who can say that the legislature of Alabama which set up that state's segregation laws was democratically elected? Throughout Alabama all sorts of devious methods are used to prevent Negroes from becoming registered voters, and there are some counties in which, even though Negroes constitute a majority of the population, not a single Negro is registered. Can any law enacted under such circumstances be considered democratically structured? (Paragraph 18)

Here King shows us why the supposedly "democratically legislated" segregation laws do not really reflect the will of all potential voters in Alabama and thus should not be obeyed. He adds logical reasoning to his already established moral appeal; the voice of the man willing to negotiate and explain his cause is blended with the debater's or lawyer's appeal to facts logically strung together in support of an opinion.

King, of course, also appeals to his reader's emotions. Once we come to believe that we are reading a sincere, respectable writer, and once we feel the intellectual impact of the writer's facts and reasoning, we want and need to have our emotions involved; we want, in essence, to share in the fear, anger, suffering, and anguish of the people for whom King is speaking. Simultaneously, we need to share King's sense of elevated purpose, his dream of what might come to be. Notice how King accomplishes both kinds of emotional sharing in the final paragraph of his letter. The "deep fog of racial prejudice" will be replaced by the "radiant stars of love and brotherhood."

> I hope this letter finds you strong in the faith. I also hope that circumstances will soon make it possible for me to meet each of you, not as an integrationist or a civil rights leader but as a fellow clergyman and a Christian brother. Let us all hope that the dark clouds of racial prejudice will soon pass away and the deep fog of misunderstanding will be lifted from our fear-drenched communities, and in some not too distant tomorrow the radiant stars of love and brotherhood will shine over our great nation with all their scintillating beauty.

The paragraph begins by reasserting King's moral character, his intention to reunite rather than divide, his desire to befriend rather than further antagonize his readers. The third and final sentence of the paragraph shifts to a directly emotional appeal, intended to elevate the entire argument, to bring the readers to a point at which they will transcend smaller differences in order to approach a higher unity.

Several language devices help create this appeal. The imperative "Let us . . ." calls readers together, much as a political leader might call together his followers. Figurative language—"dark clouds of racial prejudice . . . deep fog of misunderstanding . . . fear-drenched communities . . . radiant stars of love and brotherhood"—then brings the reader from considerations of the immediate situation to a higher, more spiritual level of consideration. This final sentence also illustrates parallelism. The relative clause following "Let us hope . . ." is divided into two equal syntactical structures: *the dark clouds of racial prejudice,* which serves as the first half of the subject of the clause, is paired with *the deep fog of misunderstanding,* the second part of the clause's subject; *will soon pass away,* the first part of a compound predicate, is matched later in the clause by *will be lifted from,* the second half of the clause's compound predicate. This type of syntactical parallelism gives King's voice a momentous and elevating sound. Read the sentence aloud a few times and imagine how it would sound in front of a large audience.

A sound and convincing argument usually blends the appeals to emotion, reason, and character. The following rhetorical devices will help strengthen these appeals in your persuasive writing.

Rhetorical Techniques and the Appeal to Emotions. Rhetoric is the art of persuasion; it is the area of study describing the means a writer can use to develop reader identification. In any persuasive situation, the writer hopes to convince readers to see things as he or she sees them—to share a perspective or point of view on a subject. Here is a list of rhetorical techniques that most writers, including those represented in this section, use to arouse the *emotions* of their audience.

1. *Concrete description and narration.* Perhaps the most powerful method of arousing an audience's emotions is *to re-create a scene in words.* Use as much concrete and figurative language as you can to make your readers feel that they are part of the experience you describe (see Parts One and Two to review narrative and descriptive writing skills). Most readers need concrete experience to support the reasoning behind an argument; when you use words to create a scene that appeals to readers' senses, you are providing opportunities for them to share in the experience that led up to the reasoning. In most argumentative contexts you will need to condense your narration and description into brief capsules of the original experience, without sacrificing the emotional impact you wish to achieve.

In paragraph 14 of "Letter from Birmingham Jail," Martin Luther King strings together a convincing series of brief narrative and descriptive examples of white people's oppression of blacks.

> Perhaps it is easy for those who have never felt the stinging darts of segregation to say, "Wait." But when you have seen vicious mobs lynch your mothers and fathers at will and drown your sisters and brothers at whim; when you have seen hate-filled policemen curse, kick and even kill your black brothers and sisters . . . when you suddenly find your tongue twisted and your speech stammering as you seek to explain to your six-year old daughter why she can't go to the public amusement park that has just been advertised on television, and see tears welling up in her eyes when she is told that Funtown is closed to colored children, and see ominous clouds of inferiority beginning to form in her little mental sky, and see her beginning to distort her personality by developing an unconscious bitterness toward white people. . . .

King begins this excerpt with a generalization: "Perhaps it is easy for those who have never felt the stinging darts of segregation to say, 'Wait.'" Then his briefly narrated examples of concrete situations in which blacks are repeatedly oppressed help to explain why blacks themselves cannot "wait." Readers, whether black or white, are thrust inside the skin of black people by these narrative examples. The implied question, "Would *you* wait?" carries the emotional message to the reader. King's use of concrete description and narration help make his readers *receptive;* his logical arguments then provide the clinching appeal.

2. *Emotionally charged words.* This rhetorical device can be used to arouse the emotions of an audience in almost any persuasive context. In general, use of emotionally charged diction depends on three audience considerations.

a. When you wish to share the experience behind an argument or thesis, be sure to include *concrete words* that will appeal to the senses of your readers. A reader who shares in an experience that leads up to an opinion already knows something about *why* a writer supports that opinion.

b. Every reader associates certain attitudes and connotations with particular words. The effective writer takes these secondary aspects of meaning into consideration as he or she writes. A *pejorative* word signifies or brings out a negative emotional and intellectual reaction in a reader; an *honorific* word signifies or brings out a positive emotional and intellectual reaction. Consider the use of pejorative and honorific terms in this brief excerpt from Edmund Burke's *Reflections on the Revolution in France, 1790,* a work in which Burke attempted to arouse his readers' emotions against the revolutionary mobs that had seized Marie Antoinette and imprisoned her. The queen and her children, of course, were eventually beheaded. (I have italicized the pejorative and honorific diction.)

> It is now sixteen or seventeen years since I saw the queen of France, then the dauphiness, at Versailles; and surely never *lighted* on this *orb,* which she hardly seemed to touch, a more *delightful* vision. I saw her just above the *horizon, decorating* and *cheering* the *elevated sphere* she just began to move in—*glittering* like the *morning-star,* full of *life,* and *splendor,* and *joy.* Oh! what a revolution! and what a heart must I have, to contemplate without emotion that *elevation* and that *fall!* Little did I dream when she added titles of *veneration* to those of *enthusiastic, distant, respectful love,* that she should ever be obliged to carry the sharp antidote against *disgrace* concealed in that bosom; little did I dream that I should have lived to see such *disasters fallen* upon her in a nation of *gallant* men, in a nation of men of *honour* and of *cavaliers.* I thought ten thousand swords must have leaped from their scabbards to avenge even a look that threatened her with insult.—But the age of chivalry is gone.—That of *sophisters, economists,* and *calculators,* has succeeded; and the *glory* of Europe is extinguished forever. Never, never more, shall we behold that *generous loyalty* to rank and sex, that *proud submission,* that *dignified obedience,* that *subordination* of the heart, which kept alive, even in servitude itself, the spirit of an *exalted freedom.* The *unbought grace* of life, the *cheap defence* of nations, the *nurse* of *manly sentiment* and *heroic enterprise* is gone! It is gone, that *sensibility* of *principle,* that *chastity* of *honour,* which felt a *stain* like a *wound,* which inspired *courage* whilst it *mitigated ferocity,* which *ennobled* whatever it touched, and under which *vice* itself lost half its *evil,* by losing all its *grossness.*

Notice how Burke uses honorific terms to describe the queen and his reactions to her, especially as he begins his description in the opening lines of the passage. Then, as we read on, we see honorific and pejorative terms linked together in contrasting pairs—in the final sentence of the passage, honorific terms such as *grace of life, cheap defence of nations, nurse of manly sentiment, heroic enterprise, courage,* and *ennobled* contrast with pejorative terms such as *stain like a wound, ferocity, vice, evil,* and *grossness.* The reader, subsequently, develops emotional responses similar to Burke's, looking favorably on the young and beautiful queen and unfavorably on the revolutionary "mobs."

Denotation refers to the exact, dictionary definitions of words. A writer intending accuracy—someone, for example, who wants to write a cogent and clear laboratory report or description—usually puts emphasis on denotation. A persuasive writer, however, always makes some use of connotation, emphasizing the emotions that readers often associate with a word.

In fact, no writer can completely control all connotative meaning, since some readers will associate very personal emotions with particular words. But we can, as writers, control connotational meaning in our use of many currently popular words. Take, for example, the news reporter who, in reporting a political meeting, describes one state senator as a "*pol*" and another as a *statesman.* Denotatively, both words accurately describe the function of the senator. "*Pol,*" however, would bring to most readers' minds the negative emotions associated with smoky backroom meetings, where political leaders make deals that may or may not reflect concern for the people. *Statesman,* on the other hand, brings to mind the virtues of political honesty, integrity, and general good will. Often, in the pose of objective reporting, news writers will take sides by exploiting word connotations they know will arouse the emotions of their readers.

Well-intentioned writers fit their choices of diction to the necessities created by the situations in which they are writing. Emotionally charged words should, of course, be used to *support* logically developed arguments, not to *prevent* a reader from applying reason to a subject. If the state senators mentioned above really are, after close analysis, what the reporter suggests that they are, then connotation has been used effectively and well. If, however, the reporter is merely manipulating the readers through word connotation in ways that have very little to do with the essential characters of the senators, then we feel tricked, manipulated, and cheated; our opinions and beliefs about the politicians are based on the writer's rhetoric, not on a consistent interpretation of their characters.

3. *Direct appeals to particular emotions.* Aristotle, in the second book of his *Rhetoric,* defined numerous human emotions in paired opposites such as *anger* and *meekness, love* and *hatred,* and *shame* and *shamelessness,* and described three ways that writers could appeal to each emotion and its opposite. A writer, Aristotle suggests, should ask these questions when considering appealing to the emotions of his or her readers.

a. *What is the nature of the emotion itself?* What do people *do* when they are hating? From what does hatred develop? How can hatred be described in the abstract?

b. *What is the object of an emotion?* To or at whom is an emotional response such as hatred directed?

c. *What causes an emotion?* Why do people hate other people? Is the cause in the one who hates or in the object, or in both?

Aristotle gives us a common-sense basis for emotional appeals. He tells us to ask ourselves what emotions we wish to evoke from a reader; he then tells us to develop a complete understanding of how a person influenced by a particular emotion usually behaves and why; finally, he tells us to appeal to emotions only when they can be used to support what has already been rationally developed.

Rhetorical Techniques and the Appeal to Character. We have mentioned, in our previous discussions of the essays by Cecelia Holland, Martin Luther King, and William Buckley, the following particular methods of creating a good impression with your readers.

1. Make it clear as you argue or persuade that you do know your opponent's arguments, even as you attack them.
2. You may, like Cecelia Holland, want to be tough, direct, and forceful, but be sure that your verbal free-swinging is backed up with facts, reasons, and examples.
3. When you use emotional appeals, avoid cheap shots. Readers admire sharp critics who really know their material and their opponents; they merely laugh at and ridicule someone who tries to sound like a tough critic but does not know the facts.
4. Every time you write, imagine your audience; clarify the situation within which you are writing. What do your readers already know; what do they need to know and why? A writer who considers what his or her readers need to know simultaneously creates a positive moral impression.

The doubting game and the believing game[1]

Philosophers, rhetoricians, and psychologists throughout recent history have supplemented and built upon Aristotle's analysis of the emotions. Recent thinkers and experts in theories of writing have tended to place much more emphasis on the *sharing* of emotional states than on the manipulation of a reader's emotions.

1. I take this phrase from the final section of Peter Elbow's *Writing Without Teachers* (Oxford University Press, 1973), pp. 147-191. This little essay does a sound and readable job of discussing the new and old rhetorics as, in essence, they develop from contrasting human intentions and states of mind.

A rhetorician, Kenneth Burke, and a psychologist, Carl Rogers, have strongly influenced this tendency toward *sharing* rather than debating or competing. Burke, in *A Rhetoric of Motives* and in *The Philosophy of Literary Form,* uses the word *identification* to signify this sharing between reader and writer.

In William Buckley's "How I Came to Rock," for example, the writer tells a story in order to develop an opinion; we know from the article's title that Buckley is being ironic, and as we read on we realize that Alan Freed's absurd behavior and simplistic statements are being repeated by Buckley as objects of ridicule. In essence, many modern writers, even when they are writing persuasively, are more interested in showing their readers why they hold an opinion, rather than simply telling them what to think.

A writer who wishes to share, to have readers *identify,* must *re-create* in writing the process through which an emotion was developed. Rather than stacking up reasons against what he or she opposes, the writer creates an essay in which ideas opposed and agreed with work together; he or she creates an essay in which the readers go through, as they read, the same thinking processes, the same doubts, confusions and ultimate understandings, the same original *experiences* as the writer.

Imagine William Buckley's article as straight exposition. His first paragraph would introduce the general subject—the latest rock-and-roll craze—and close with Buckley's thesis: the popular interest in rock-and-roll demonstrates the superficiality and lack of quality in contemporary American culture. The paragraphs following the introduction would then provide the reasons behind Buckley's attack on rock-and-roll and the larger culture's admiration of it.

In contrast, "How I Came to Rock," as the title suggests, focuses on the personal experience that created and shaped the idea in the mind of the writer. The reader, rather than getting the writer's experience cut up and reshaped to fit a thesis, receives the experience as if it were occurring firsthand, with a brief plot, dialogue, and setting to put the reader inside the skin of the writer.

Some writing situations, of course, demand straight exposition or argument. The history teacher expects facts in support of a thesis when you are writing a history examination. The City Council expects facts and a concluding interpretation as it listens to a citizen group's report on the feasibility of bussing school children.

In many persuasive writing situations, however, the writer will want to involve his or her readers; the best way to accomplish "involvement" and identification is often through the sharing of experiences as they contributed to the writer's opinions. Strictly competitive reasoning often makes readers into doubters, always looking for the loopholes in a writer's logic. Writing that combines logical reasoning and appealing description and narration can help make believers out of doubting readers.

Carl Rogers suggests other ways to make doubting opponents into believing readers, while still holding to the principles of sound argument.[2] The key to successful interpersonal communication, Rogers suggests, is the writer's ability to get readers to share his or her point of view or perspective on the subject. To see an experience or a collection of data from another's point of view means that you try to feel how experiences have affected the other person's senses, how certain ideas have been associated with other ideas in another person's mind.

Of course, the writer who truly attempts to take on the points of view of those he or she opposes, must, like the readers, be ready to alter a thesis in the light of new information. Remember these points.

1. You can improve the emotional appeal of an argument and help open the minds of your readers by including the process through which you have arrived at your thesis. Consider describing or narrating, at a few points in your writing, the process or experience that led to your thesis.

2. The most effective arguments combine the doubting and sharing games; they provide descriptions and evidence along with the rational arguments a reader needs to share in and agree with a thesis.

3. If you are writing on a controversial issue, remember to give a full presentation of opposing arguments.

Then describe the *process* through which you came to oppose these arguments. In many writing situations, the best way to get readers to come around to your point of view is to describe *their* points of view thoroughly. Then they know that you have attempted to understand them and will be more apt to give you the same consideration.

Arguing indirectly: Irony and satire

When you are faced with the task of writing on a subject that has been argued back and forth so often that you feel you can add nothing new to the controversy, try indirect argument. Irony can put a fresh look on a tired subject. Notice the opening sentence of Art Buchwald's "Fathers for Moral America": "There has been a great deal written about an organization called Mothers for Moral America." Right away we feel that a conventional subject—the existence of numerous groups whose main purpose is to defend against moral corruption—is going to be handled in an original way. This writer knows about all the writing on moral issues; he will, we expect, be wary of merely repeating what others have said. Buchwald then makes up his own group, Fathers for Moral America, and creates a mock interview with the group's spokesman. As we listen in on

---

2. Carl R. Rogers, "Communication: Its Blocking and Facilitation," from a paper delivered at Northwestern University's Centennnial Conference on Communications, October 11, 1951, and reprinted in part in Maxine Hairston's *A Contemporary Rhetoric* (Boston: Houghton Mifflin Company, 1974), pp. 207-211.

the interview, we learn that the fathers are actually more interested in seeing dirty movies than they are in defending against the corruption these movies cause. Buchwald's little piece shows how a thesis can be developed and supported through irony without the writer ever explicitly stating his true purpose.

Consider the possibilities for irony in the following topics:

"Corruption in Government"

a. An ironic writer might develop a thesis on political corruption by writing a short sketch of a successful politician who had to take political bribes in order to finance his campaigns.

b. An ironic writer might make a tongue-in-cheek suggestion that certain corrupt practices be made lawful since most politicians are using them anyhow.

c. An ironic writer might produce a tongue-in-cheek defense of a convicted Watergate conspirator.

"Women in Athletics"

a. An ironic writer might describe a girl showing up the boys in Little League baseball, while simultaneously developing a mock-argument against allowing little girls to participate in Little League.

b. An ironic writer might begin with a definition of women as the fragile sex and then proceed to describe numerous women who do physically *and* intellectually challenging jobs. The reader would be left to see the absurd contradiction between thesis and evidence.

c. An ironic writer might counter the idea that women who work cannot have families by describing a woman who has obviously been successful as housewife *and* career woman. The thesis of the essay would then obviously contrast with the evidence described.

"Fundamentals versus New Ideas in Education"

a. An ironic writer might compose an extended dialogue between spokesmen for the new versus the old in education, emphasizing the clichés and conventional logic on both sides in order to ridicule their extreme arguments.

b. An ironic writer might develop an exaggeratedly bizarre image of a future classroom in order to point out the absurdity of current classroom innovations.

c. An ironic writer might provide an exaggerated description of the "ideal" future teacher in order to ridicule tendencies among many current teachers.

The Techniques of Irony. Generally, ironic writers emphasize several related techniques. They usually develop a satiric persona who speaks for them in the context of their essay. Art Buchwald, for example, creates the voice and persona of a relatively simpleminded, unsophisticated, factual journalist.

> There has been a great deal written about an organization called Mothers for Moral America. The Mothers organization had planned to put a "moral decay" film on television which showed the worst aspect of American life, from topless bathing suits to pornographic literature. At the last minute the film was withdrawn.

We find no sign of high critical intelligence here, no fancy words or complex ideas, just an everyday guy speaking on an everyday subject to everyday people. But as we read on we realize that somebody behind this simple-minded persona is saying much more than appears on the surface. The point of the interview with the spokesman for Fathers for Moral America is satiric; we know from the context that Art Buchwald is different from his persona, that he would ridicule the obviously hypocritical actions and words of the man interviewed.

> "We have a reading room over there where we display the latest collection of salacious books and magazines. Any indignant father can go in there and see the type of literature that is being peddled around the country."

"And read it for his own pleasure," we and Buchwald might add.

In "Fathers for Moral America," Art Buchwald creates a context in which the reader takes what is implied to be the opposite of what is actually said. Actions and statements are so blatantly hypocritical that we know something is fishy.

Buchwald also effectively uses understatement. He never directly points out the absurd hypocrisy in the fathers' statements. Rather they come to us as purely factual statements. Understated irony usually increases the reader's awareness of incongruity and absurdity precisely because it leaves the final judgment, the conclusion, to the reader.

Other writers use *exaggeration,* where particular weaknesses or defects are magnified. James Thurber, for example, takes a fairly common character type—the quiet, highly efficient organization man (Mr. Martin)—and exaggerates his every trait until he becomes a point of satire. He treats Mrs. Ulgine Barrows, the loud-mouthed, over-friendly and gregarious type, to similar exaggeration. As a result, the central conflict in "The Catbird Seat" exists between two extreme characters and the values they represent.

Above all, a writer must work hard to establish a consistent ironic relationship with readers. Know what the implied thesis of your essay is *before* you begin. Then carefully decide whether you will use exaggeration or understatement to develop your point. And remember to work by indirection, staying consistently within your ironic persona.

Rhetorical Index

Author and Title Index